D1067669

THE CAMBRIDGE HISTORY OF WAR

Volume IV of *The Cambridge History of War* offers a definitive new account of war in the most destructive period in human history. Opening with the massive conflicts that erupted in the mid nineteenth century in the United States, Asia, and Europe, leading historians trace the global evolution of warfare through "the age of mass," "the age of machine," and "the age of management." They explore how industrialization and nationalism fostered vast armies whilst the emergence of mobile warfare and improved communications systems made possible the "total warfare" of the two world wars. With military conflict regionalized after 1945, they show how guerrilla and asymmetrical warfare highlighted the limits of the machine and mass as well as the importance of the media in winning "hearts and minds." This is a comprehensive guide to every facet of modern war from strategy and operations to its social, cultural, technological, and political contexts and legacies.

ROGER CHICKERING is Professor Emeritus of History at Georgetown University, Washington, DC. He has published widely in German and European history, particularly on war and German society.

DENNIS SHOWALTER is Professor of History at Colorado College, where he specializes in comparative military history.

HANS VAN DE VEN is Professor of Modern Chinese History at Cambridge University. He has written extensively on warfare in modern Chinese history and especially on China during World War II.

THE CAMBRIDGE HISTORY OF WAR

★

VOLUME IV

War and the Modern World

★

Edited by

ROGER CHICKERING

DENNIS SHOWALTER

and

HANS VAN DE VEN

CAMBRIDGE UNIVERSITY PRESS
Cambridge, New York, Melbourne, Madrid, Cape Town,
Singapore, São Paulo, Delhi, Mexico City

Cambridge University Press
The Edinburgh Building, Cambridge CB2 8RU, UK

Published in the United States of America by Cambridge University Press, New York

Information on this title: www.cambridge.org/9780521875776

First published 2012

Printed and bound in the United Kingdom by the MPG Books Group

A catalogue record for this publication is available from the British Library

ISBN 978-0-521-87577-6 Hardback

Contents

List of illustrations viii
List of maps x
Notes on contributors xi

Introduction to volume IV *1*

PART I
THE INDUSTRIALIZATION OF WARFARE, 1850–1914

Introduction to Part I *9*
HANS VAN DE VEN

1 · A hinge in time: the wars of the mid nineteenth century *16*
HANS VAN DE VEN

2 · War, technology, and industrial change, 1850–1914 *45*
GEOFFREY WAWRO

3 · War and imperial expansion *69*
BRUCE VANDERVORT

4 · The non-western world responds to imperialism, 1850–1914 *94*
JOHN P. DUNN

5 · War, society, and culture, 1850–1914: the rise of militarism *119*
ROGER CHICKERING

6 · War-making and restraint by law: the formative years, 1864–1914 *142*
JEAN H. QUATAERT

7 · The arms race: qualitative and quantitative aspects *163*
ANTULIO J. ECHEVARRIA II

PART II
THE ERA OF TOTAL WAR, 1914–1945

Introduction to Part II *183*
ROGER CHICKERING

8 · World War I *192*
MICHAEL S. NEIBERG

9 · Military captivity in two world wars: legal frameworks and camp regimes *214*
IRIS RACHAMIMOV

10 · Military occupations, 1914–1945 *236*
SOPHIE DE SCHAEPDRIJVER

11 · Home fronts: the mobilization of resources for total war *257*
PIERRE PURSEIGLE

12 · The search for peace in the interwar period *285*
CAROLE FINK

13 · Commemorating war, 1914–1945 *310*
JAY WINTER

14 · Military doctrine and planning in the interwar era *327*
EUGENIA C. KIESLING

15 · The military and the revolutionary state *352*
ROGER R. REESE

16 · World War II *378*
GERHARD L. WEINBERG

PART III
POST-TOTAL WARFARE, 1945–2005

Introduction to Part III
DENNIS SHOWALTER *413*

17 · Military occupations, 1945–1955 *428*
DENNIS SHOWALTER

18 · The wars after the war, 1945–1954 *452*
ODD ARNE WESTAD

19 · Weapons technology in the two nuclear ages *472*
C. DALE WALTON

20 · Conventional war, 1945–1990 *493*
WILLIAMSON MURRAY

21 · Wars of decolonization, 1945–1975 *515*
ANTHONY CLAYTON

22 · War and memory since 1945 *542*
RANA MITTER

23 · The era of American hegemony, 1989–2005 *566*
MARK MOYAR

Select bibliography *589*
Index *625*

Illustrations

1. Heavy guns at Sebastopol © Imperial War Museum (IWM) *page* 22
2. Prussian army encampment during the Siege of Metz, Bundesarchiv, Bild 146-1970-053-03 41
3. Maxim machine gun used during the Boer War at Mafeking © Van Hoepen/Hulton Archive/Getty Images 56
4. German Navy at Kiel © Mary Evans Picture Agency 59
5. Scottish Highland Regiment of the British Army © Paul Popper/Popperfoto/Getty Images 83
6. Senegalese soldiers in the French army © Branger/Roger Viollet/Getty Images 89
7. Japanese soldiers before the attack on Fakumen (China) during the Russo-Japanese War © Underwood & Underwood/Corbis 116
8. School classroom, London © Mary Evans Picture Agency 123
9. Enlistment at Royal Army Service Corps HQ © General Photographic Agency/Hulton Archive/Getty Images 124
10. Kaiser Parade, 1905, Bundesarchiv, Bild 136-C1139/ photo: Oscar Tellgmann 128
11. The Geneva Convention © Fabrice Coffrini/AFP/Getty Images 144
12. Bomb dropped by hand from a German plane (1915) © Hulton-Deutsch Collection/CORBIS 179
13. British artillery officers at rest behind the lines on homemade furniture © Universal Images Group/Getty Images 197
14. Russian battlefield, 1915. © Hulton Archive/Getty Images 201
15. Tank in West Flanders © IWM 209
16. Defeated Russian soldiers marching to internment © Mary Evans Picture Agency 226
17. German POWs listen to a speech by Vice-Chancellor Franz Bluecher © Bettmann/CORBIS 234

18. Poster used by German occupying forces in France. Poster Collection, Poster FR 1055, Hoover Institution Archives. 244
19. Portrait of Marius Jonker Roelants 245
20. Deportation of Jews from Warsaw © Imagno/Hulton Archive/Getty Images 255
21. Women workers in British munitions factory © IWM 263
22. Shipyard in Britain © IWM 272
23. Celebrations at the first assembly of the League of Nations in Geneva © UNOG Library, League of Nations Archives 290
24. Permanent Court of International Justice, The Hague © UNOG Library, League of Nations Archives 297
25. Vladslo monument, Belgium © DACS, 2012. Photo: akg-images/Bildarchiv Monheim 313
26. Cenotaph, London, Armistice Day, 1920 © IWM 314
27. Communist soldiers in Shanghai © Bettmann/CORBIS 353
28. Popular Front Army parade in Spain © Bettmann/CORBIS 370
29. Refugees on their way to a UNHCR camp © Jack Wilkes/Time & Life Pictures/Getty Images 429
30. GI and Japanese policemen direct traffic in Tokyo © John Florea/Time & Life Pictures/Getty Images 433
31. Nurses delouse a German refugee at a UNICEF camp © Hulton-Deutsch Collection/CORBIS 436
32. UN forces cross the 38th Parallel after withdrawal from Pyongyang © Time & Life Pictures/Getty Images 458
33. Sacking of the Communist Youth Organization Headquarters in Jakarta © Carol Goldstein/Hulton Archive/Getty Images 467
34. "Little Boy" – the first atomic bomb being loaded onto the *Enola Gay* © PhotoQuest/Archive Photos/Getty Images 474
35. Displaying an ICBM at a Coney Island amusement park © Hulton Archive/Archive Photos/Getty Images 477
36. Ho Chi Minh © AFP/Getty Images 522
37. Questioning of Mau Mau leader © Bert Hardy/Picture Post/Getty Images 537
38. The Nanjing Massacre Memorial – the Ship of Peace © China Photos/Getty Images News/Getty Images. 551
39. Srebrenica memorial © Maxime Gyselinck/Demotix/Corbis 563

Maps

1.	Taiping Rebellion, 1850–1864	*page* 17
2.	Crimean War, 1853–1856	21
3.	American Civil War, 1861–1865	27
4.	Franco-Prussian War, 1870–1871	50
5.	Growth of western empires after 1850	70
6.	Meiji Japan and the Japanese empire	105
7.	German offensives, 1914	195
8.	Ludendorff offensives, 1918	210
9.	Allied counteroffensives, 1918	212
10.	Axis advances, 1939–1941	384
11.	German offensive, May–June 1940	385
12.	Operation Barbarossa, 1941	387
13.	Defeat of Germany, 1944–1945	405
14.	Defeat of Japan, 1943–1945	408
15.	The early Cold War	464
16.	Decolonization in Asia and Africa	516
17.	Collapse of the Soviet Union, 1990–1991	568
18.	Yugoslav wars, 1991–1995	577
19.	Operation Desert Storm, 1991	578

Notes on contributors

Roger Chickering was Professor of History in the BMW Center for German and European Studies at Georgetown University. His publications include *Imperial Germany and the Great War* (2nd edn. 2004) and *The Great War and Urban Life in Germany* (2007).

Anthony Clayton was a senior lecturer at the Royal Military Academy Sandhurst from 1965 to 1993 and Associate Lecturer in Conflict Studies, University of Surrey, Guildford, from 1993 to 2008. His publications include *Counter-Insurgency in Kenya 1952–60* (1984) and *The Wars of French Decolonisation* (1994).

Sophie De Schaepdrijver is Associate Professor of History at Pennsylvania State University. Her previous publications include *La Belgique et la Première Guerre Mondiale* (2004) and *We Who Are So Cosmopolitan: The War Diary of Constance Graeffe, 1914–1915* (2008).

John P. Dunn is Associate Professor of History at Valdosta State University. His publications include articles in *War and History*, *The Journal of Military History*, *Naval History*, *The Journal of the Middle East and Africa*, and *Khedive Ismail's Army* (2005).

Antulio J. Echevarria II is the Director of Research at the United States Army War College. He is the author of *Clausewitz and Contemporary War* (2007); *Imagining Future War* (2007); *After Clausewitz: German Military Thinkers before the Great War* (2001).

Carole Fink is Humanities Distinguished Professor Emerita in the Department of History at Ohio State University. She is the author of *Defending the Rights of Others: The Great Powers, the Jews, and International Minority Protection, 1878–1938* (2004); *Marc Bloch: A Life in History* (1989); and *The Genoa Conference: European Diplomacy, 1921–1922* (1984).

Eugenia C. Kiesling is Professor of History at the United States Military Academy, West Point. She is the author of *Arming against Hitler: France and the Limits of Military Planning* (1996).

Rana Mitter is Professor of the History and Politics of Modern China at Oxford University. His books include *The Manchurian Myth: Nationalism, Resistance and Collaboration in Modern China* (2000); *A Bitter Revolution: China's Struggle with the Modern World* (2004, winner Times Higher Young Academic Author of the Year); *Modern China:*

A Very Short Introduction (2008); and (edited with Sheila Miyoshi Jager) *Ruptured Histories: War, Memory and the Post-Cold War in Asia* (2007).

MARK MOYAR is a research fellow at the US Marine Corps University. His publications include *Phoenix and the Birds of Prey: The CIA's Secret Campaign to Destroy the Viet Cong* (1999); *Triumph Forsaken: The Vietnam War, 1954–1965* (2006); and *A Question of Command: Counterinsurgency from the Civil War to Iraq* (2009).

WILLIAMSON MURRAY is currently Professor Emeritus of History at Ohio State University. He has also served as the Harold Johnson Professor of Military History at the United States Army War College. Professor Murray is the author and editor of a number of major works, the most recent of which is *A War to Be Won: Fighting the Second World War* (2000).

MICHAEL S. NEIBERG is Professor of History at the United States Army War College. He is the author of numerous works on World War I including *Fighting the Great War: A Global History* (2005) and *Dance of the Furies: Europe and the Outbreak of War in 1914* (2011).

PIERRE PURSEIGLE is Senior Lecturer in Modern History at the University of Birmingham and President of the International Society for First World War Studies. He is the author of *Mobilisation, sacrifice, et citoyenneté: Angleterre – France, 1914–1918* (forthcoming).

JEAN H. QUATAERT is Professor of History and Women's Studies at Binghamton University, SUNY. Her most recent publications include *The Gendering of Human Rights in the International Systems of Law in the Twentieth Century* (2006) and *Advocating Dignity: Human Rights Mobilizations in Global Politics* (2009).

IRIS RACHAMIMOV is Director of the Cummings Center for Russian and East European Studies at Tel Aviv University. Her publications include *POWs and the Great War: Captivity on the Eastern Front* (2002), which was awarded the Fraenkel Prize for Contemporary History for a first major work, and the article "The Disruptive Comforts of Drag," which was published in the April 2006 issue of the *American Historical Review*.

ROGER R. REESE is Professor of History at Texas A&M University, where he has taught courses on European, Russian, and Soviet history since 1990. He has authored numerous articles and four books on the Red Army, most recently *Why Stalin's Soldiers Fought* (2011).

DENNIS SHOWALTER is Professor of History at Colorado College and Past President of the Society for Military History. His publications include *The Wars of Frederick the Great* (1995); *Patton and Rommel: Men of War in the Twentieth Century* (2006); and *Hitler's Panzers* (2009).

BRUCE VANDERVORT teaches modern European and African history at the Virginia Military Institute. He is also the editor of *The Journal of Military History* and the author *of Wars of Imperial Conquest in Africa, 1830–1914* (1998) and *Indian Wars of Mexico, Canada and the United States, 1812–1900* (2006). He is currently at work on a history of the Italian invasion of Libya in 1911–12.

Hans van de Ven is Professor of Modern Chinese History at Cambridge University. His main publications are *From Friend to Comrade: The Founding of the Chinese Communist Party, 1920–1927* (1991) and *War and Nationalism in China, 1925–1945* (2003). He has also edited *Warfare in Chinese History* (2000), *New Perspectives on the Chinese Communist Party* (1994), and *The Battle for China* (2010).

C. Dale Walton is Lecturer in International Relations and Strategic Studies at the University of Reading. His publications include *Geopolitics and the Great Powers in the Twenty-First Century* (2007); *The Myth of Inevitable US Defeat in Vietnam* (2002); and (as a co-author) *Understanding Modern Warfare* (2008).

Geoffrey Wawro is Professor of Military History and Director of the Military History Center at the University of North Texas. He is the author of *The Austro-Prussian War* (1996); *Warfare and Society in Europe, 1792–1914* (2000); *The Franco-Prussian War* (2003); and *Quicksand: America's Pursuit of Power in the Middle East* (2010).

Gerhard L. Weinberg is retired William Rand Kenan, Jr., Professor from the University of North Carolina at Chapel Hill, having previously taught at the universities of Chicago, Kentucky, and Michigan. He is the author of numerous books including *A World at Arms: A Global History of World War II* (2nd edn. 2005); *Hitler's Foreign Policy 1933–1939: The Road to World War II* (2010); and *Visions of Victory: The Hopes of Eight World War II Leaders* (2005).

Odd Arne Westad is Professor of International History at the London School of Economics and Political Science (LSE). He served as co-editor of the *Cambridge History of the Cold War* (2010). Among his books are *The Global Cold War* (2005), which won the Bancroft Prize, and *Decisive Encounters: The Chinese Civil War, 1946–1950* (2003). His most recent book is a history of China's international affairs since 1750, which will be published in 2012.

Jay Winter is Charles J. Stille Professor of History at Yale University. His publications include *Sites of Memory, Sites of Mourning: The Great War in European Cultural History* (1995) and *Remembering War: The Great War between History and Memory in the Twentieth Century* (2006).

Introduction to volume IV

The period covered in this volume, from about 1850 until the dawn of the twenty-first century, was the most belligerent in human history. More people were involved in the preparation and prosecution of warfare, and more men, women, and children fell victim to military violence than in all previous eras put together. The period since 1850 is the era of modern war. It can be considered under three headings, as the age of mass, the age of machines, and the age of management.

The age of mass is the principal subject of Part I of this volume. The dramatic growth of military capacity involved creating and sustaining not only the largest armies in history, but also the most complex and demanding societies. Size and complexity were products of the Industrial Revolution. Developments in farm technology and steam transportation created a global agricultural revolution, which enabled large-scale transfers of young men to barracks and battlefields. Weapons and uniforms became items of mass production. Telephones, telegraphs, and typewriters made increased control possible, keeping mass armies from becoming armed hordes.

This last achievement reflected the advance of administrative skills. The late nineteenth century was an age of bureaucratization – of expanding, standardizing, and enforcing policy. To borrow Charles Tilly's phrase, bureaucratization transformed both states and armed forces from wasps to locomotives, focusing and extending their structural capacity to sustain war without imploding.

The third necessary element of mass war was soldiers – of a particular kind. Industrialization and bureaucratization enhanced the risk and sacrifice of combat, as they diminished the prospect of direct material or moral reward. These developments created the need for willing participants – a requirement that was fulfilled by nationalism, reciprocity, and a new kind of moral reward. Nationalism fostered group identification and rationalized participation. Reciprocity reflected the growing ability of governments to requite military service with social services, such as schools, post offices, public utilities, pensions, and education. Even conscription could seem like a fair exchange, particularly when service confirmed the formal and informal adult status of males, both as citizens and men.

The wars of the mid nineteenth century – the Crimea, the American Civil War, the wars of Italian and German unification – were what one might call chrysalis conflicts. They juxtaposed muzzle-loading small arms, cavalry charges, and amputation without anesthesia to railroads and telegraphs, breech-loading cannon, and antiseptic surgery. In each of these wars, tradition made place for technology, albeit not always smoothly. In each case as well, war became grimmer and dirtier. "Hard war," which aimed at crushing civilian will to resist, was christened by the Union general W. T. Sherman and adopted with zeal by German armies in 1870–71. Although the Battle of the Nations in Leipzig in 1813 retained the blood palm with some hundred thousand casualties in three days, Gettysburg, where thirty thousand fell casualty in the same time-span, and Gravelotte–St.Privat, with over thirty thousand casualties in twenty-four hours, were hecatombs by any standards, grim harbingers of events to come.

For over forty years after German unification, Europe avoided general war. This long peace was due less to a conscious retreat from the abyss than to the shrinking of the continent's intellectual and psychological dimensions. Industrialized transportation and communications made states increasingly aware of each other's military advances and correspondingly conscious of their own shortcomings. The result was that the armed forces of the great powers – although not smaller states like Denmark, Holland, and Switzerland – became increasingly symmetrical; they engaged in arms races that failed to alter the status quo but exponentially increased the consequences of a breakdown.

Europe was not the only region that shrank as the century progressed. A portent of mass war was the increasing ability of states to project, sustain, and utilize power externally for purposes of conquest. The newly created colonies of Africa and Asia were governed in a variety of ways, but they were ultimately ruled by force. This situation involved a paradox. Europe still lacked the power to wage mass war everywhere. The result was an imperial project that remained incomplete, offering enough advantages to generate indigenous elites as mediators.

World War I of 1914–18 proved to be a "Grand Illusion." The initial encounters alone produced casualty lists unmatched in any other stage of the conflict. For four years the combatants vied with each other in seeking quick fixes and ways around the stalemate, particularly on the western front. Gas, tanks, and submarines, Gallipoli and eleven battles of the Isonzo bore witness to the combatants' ingenuity, as well as to their frustration. The Somme, Verdun, Passchendaele, the German offensives of 1918 affirmed the fall-back position of using mass war to swing bigger hammers.

Not until the summer of 1918 did the British Expeditionary Force implement the combined-arms, semi-mobile battle, which synergized mass and management, shock and technology, and was held together by a still rudimentary but adequate communications system. This harbinger of the future, and its French and American variations, were enough to finish a German army exhausted by its own earlier victories.

Military success was not sufficient, however, to still the forces that had been liberated by the guns of August 1914. Years of military occupation, the disappearance of historic state systems, and the effects of general military service had dissolved certainties. These had been replaced in Europe, the Middle East, and throughout the colonial world by aspirations and ambitions that defied compromise. The European mystique had been shaken to its foundations by the consequences of total war.

At the same time, efforts to establish alternatives to conflict after World War I, whether by principles or institutions, proved ephemeral. The League of Nations neither generated trust nor inspired fear. For all the rhetoric that another great war meant the end of civilization, military leaders remained skeptical and put their trust in devising better ways of conflict. Initially the dominant approach was to refine mass war. The French brought the concept of managed battle to an art form. In Germany Erich Ludendorff called for permanent, total national mobilization – the virtual conflation of peace and war. The new Soviet Union added state and international mobilization through revolutionary ideology.

At the same time, however, refinements in technology offered a new spectrum of force-multipliers, as the military age of the machine dawned in the 1920s. The basics lay in the internal-combustion engine and the radio. Germany is usually credited with initiating technology-focused war. In fact, innovations introduced under the Weimar Republic and its National Socialist successor were parts of a general process. There were other heavy players – Italy to the limits of its capacity, the Soviet Union to the detriment of its economy, Great Britain as far as its imperial commitments allowed. And with an army based on a comprehensive mixture of "gasoline and manure," France was in principle no less successful than Germany.

The challenge lay in application. And here the initial German successes of 1939–41 continue to obscure the limitations of high-tech war. Machines exponentially expanded war's destructive capacity, diminishing the already limited role of foot-soldiers. But individually machines were limited, too. They were most effective in mass, as operations such as the combined bomber offensive against Germany and the Soviet counterattack on the eastern front in 1943–45 revealed. One might even suggest a positive synergy between machines and morality. The Axis predators sank ever deeper into infamy. Among their enemies, concern for decent, lawful conduct survived, if tenuously, on the margins of conflict. The victors' visions of the future differed significantly. None, however, was, in the words of George Orwell, of "a boot stamping on a human face – forever."

This fact shaped the third age of modern war, the age of management. Since 1945, war has taken protean forms. Of strategy's three elements – ends, means, and will – the last has taken center stage. The Cold War was based on ideological principles, but it was pragmatic in practice, as much propaganda contest as military conflict. It involved an increasingly symmetrical matching of force between the superpowers, but it evolved into mutual feints and challenges not merely at a sub-nuclear, but a sub-violent level. While it was always a threat, armed engagement was never implemented, at least not directly between the two main contenders. Incidents were mutually processed as isolated phenomena. Mid-level conventional wars, such as those in Korea, between India and Pakistan, Muslims and Israelis, Iran and Iraq, were characterized by radical rhetoric but limited execution without the will to develop the means for a fight to the finish.

Insurgencies have been more complex; and they have illustrated the limits of machine war. Mao Zedong's victory over the Chinese Nationalists, like North Vietnam's triumph in the South, represented a total victory, although the issue of Formosa or Taiwan has yet to be resolved and North Vietnam's manipulation of the United States was also a magnificent exercise in management. The national liberation struggles that dominated the 1950s and 1960s were based in the first instance on a negative imperative: the colonial powers were to "go away." The wars were managed to this limited end, however absolute the methods.

Asymmetric war, the most recent manifestation of military conflict, grew out of insurgency. Its purpose has been to exploit systematically and comprehensively over a long term the vulnerabilities of an irreversibly stronger adversary. Its aims have been more susceptible to interpretation in absolute terms. Its conduct has seemed to be transdimensional, insofar as the antagonists in it have been able to feel each other, but not decisively. Yet asymmetric war, too, has involved mutual managerial approaches. Each participant has been uncertain about how far, and in what ways, the other can be pushed without generating an extreme response. Sparring-matches rather than death-grapples have been the usual response, as management on both sides has sought limitation.

In less than three-quarters of a century, war-making has proceeded in an arc, first toward total war, then toward something much more tentative. Perhaps this retreat represents an approach to the abyss and pulling back. Or perhaps Clio has a sense of irony.

PART I

*

THE INDUSTRIALIZATION OF WARFARE, 1850–1914

Introduction to Part I

HANS VAN DE VEN

"If this war breaks out, then its duration and its end will be unforeseeable. Woe to him who sets Europe alight" – Helmuth von Moltke (1890)

Part I of this volume on the modern period in the *Cambridge History of War* opens with the massive conflicts that erupted in the United States, China, and Europe in the middle of the nineteenth century, including the American Civil War, the Taiping Rebellion in China, the Indian Rebellion, and the wars of German unification. They did not form part of a single world war, nor even of a generalized global crisis. They shared some common origins, including population growth, the spread of new ideologies such as nationalism, and a deepening agricultural crisis, and suggest that to speak of a long nineteenth century is myopic. They did form a rupture, which speeded up four key processes, namely industrialization, the disintegration of traditional empires outside Europe, nationalism, and the rise of the bureaucratic nation-state in Europe and Japan that enabled the total war of World War I.[1]

During this period, newly confident European elites believed that they were forging a path toward "Civilization," which would be marked by more inclusive polities, rapid technological and scientific change, a public realm in which people argued rationally and behaved respectfully, and efficient bureaucracies that worked for the common good. The march toward progress promised the end of corruption, unfair privilege, disease, poverty, disorder, and superstition, as well as the barbarous warfare of the past. In reality, the institutions, societies, and cultures that were created in pursuit of this illusion provided the mechanisms, loyalties, and institutions that made total war possible, even if they were not designed for this purpose.

1 For an excellent overview, see Christopher Bayly, *The Birth of the Modern World, 1780–1914* (Oxford, 2004), especially Parts II and III.

The mid-century wars, as Hans van de Ven explains Chapter 1, signaled the moment when industrialization began to affect warfare. Germany, France, and other European countries, including Russia, had begun to catch up with Britain. This was in part the story of new types of weapons, such as the rifle, the machine gun, high-explosive shells, and breech-loading artillery. European armies, too, became mobile because of the railroad and steamships, while the telegraph improved communication and coordination. The pace of change accelerated enormously. Before the mid nineteenth century, weapons had changed little for a century and a half. New production techniques that relied on interchangeable parts, the assembly line, and managerial planning enabled European states to reequip large standing armies with new weapons within years.

As Geoffrey Wawro argues in his chapter, industrialization triggered "the obsessive, competitive way in which each of the Great Powers had built vast armies, fleets, and infrastructures that all but ensured their mutual destruction." Wawro emphasizes that military leaders were unsettled by the primacy of *matériel* in warfare and continued to seek a place for the human factor – the genius of a Napoleon, the daring act, and troop morale. At least one reason why trench warfare became so murderous was that military leaderships held fast to the idea that the human will could overcome the walls of steel thrown up by modern artillery. In his chapter on the arms race among Germany, France, Britain, Russia, Japan, and the United States, Antulio Echeverria II stresses that each aimed not just to out-produce the others and gain a decisive advantage in mass, but also to develop new breakthrough weapons to achieve a decisive qualitative edge: "each party was endeavoring to create a similar situation to that of 1866 [in the Austro-Prussian War], when one enemy entered the arena with the needle-gun and the other armed with only a muzzle loader." The arms race was deeply political; it was used domestically, as a tool by militaries to gain higher budget shares and to maintain the prestige of the armed forces, as well as diplomatically, to achieve changes in international relations without having to fire a shot. The German naval build-up in the late nineteenth century was a gamble undertaken by Admiral Tirpitz to compel Britain to relocate parts of its navy to the North Sea and so enable Germany to acquire colonies.

The "rise of the west and the collapse of the rest" was the second main development during this period. European empires in 1800 claimed considerable territory, but their authority was superficial and restricted to coastal areas. Most parts of Asia, especially east Asia, were hardly affected. A century later, the British were in firm control of India, the French had established French Indochina, and the Dutch had suppressed stubborn resistance to their rule in the Dutch East Indies. The Qing, which had doubled its size in the eighteenth century, tottered on the edge and succumbed to revolution in 1911. While China escaped colonization or partition, treaty ports, gunboats, extraterritoriality, and European spheres of influence made it a semi-colony.

While Europe's rise had many causes, in analyzing its military superiority, Bruce Vandervort argues that Europe's military advantage was not just in the superiority of its weapons but also in the greater mobility of its armed forces, their discipline, and their ability to recruit supposedly martial races from their colonies. Their opponents were internally fragmented and demonstrated "a proclivity to fight pitched battles." Vandervort makes the important point that Europeans fought total wars in their colonies before they did in Europe. Racialism and civilizational hubris made the demonization of opponents easier there. Because assaulting cities made no sense, colonial warfare aimed at the destruction of armies, livestock, and food. Distinctions between warriors and civilians, too, were rarely clear. The Indian Rebellion generated irrational fears about the "revenge of the native," which were later sustained by the Boxer Rebellion in China in 1900. Such fears brutalized European armies.

In response to the arrival of the Europeans, non-European societies embarked on self-strengthening movements, which failed except for one minor and one major case, those of Ethiopia and Japan; this too was important to Europe's rise. Mehmet Ali made a promising start, but Egypt had become "a veiled colony" by the 1880s. The Chinese Self-Strengthening Movement held out the promise of success until the Japanese destroyed the Chinese fleet and its armies in 1895; the European powers and Japan carved out spheres of influence across China over the next few years. The Young Turks were unable to prevent the dissolution of the Ottoman Empire during World War I. The problem was that the transformation of an empire into a nation-state required a profound refashioning of loyalties, state structures, and governing ideologies. Empires had always tolerated limited commitments to the center and thrived on fragmentation. Such empires required few, other than a small warrior class, to be prepared to make the ultimate sacrifice or to pay large amounts of tax. Subjects were, after all, only subjects. Yet, that transition was necessary for a society to form a modern mass army, which was hugely expensive, depended on the willingness of its population to accept universal military service and to die for their country, and could not have operated without a capable bureaucracy.

John Dunn demonstrates that the Japanese state succeeded where others failed, despite intense internal resistance. It developed a centralized political structure, a social system, and a national narrative capable of generating intense loyalties to the nation-state. That effort required the destruction of the samurai class, instituting universal recruitment, a rapid industrialization program, and fiscal centralization. Japan's success depended on the fact that it was a relatively easy to defend homogeneous island nation. A nation-myth could easily be constructed around the sacred figure of the emperor. Britain's victories over the Qing from the 1840s provided an object lesson of the risks of refusing to open up and modernize. Japan too profited from the fact that the competition between European empires in Asia focused on China and Southeast Asia with their vast populations and hence potentially huge markets. Tellingly, Japan too acquired its own colonies in Taiwan and Korea. The nation-states that emerged in the late nineteenth century required colonial possessions. To see them as opposites is a development of the late twentieth century, itself born from war.

This was not only because colonies enhanced national prestige and served as an indicator of a nation's vitality. They provided practical advantages, in terms of access to material and human resources drawn from their empires. One reason the Allies won in World War I was because they could mobilize more extensive colonial resources and dominate the world's shipping lanes. In the trenches of World War I, British and French soldiers were fed with meat from Argentina, New Zealand, China, and Australia. Some two hundred thousand Chinese coolies cleaned up the trenches or served in munitions factories. Indian Army soldiers served on the western front, at Gallipoli, in Mesopotamia, and in Palestine. The French were aided by *tirailleurs* from Africa and Indochina.

The rise of strong nationalisms in Europe, the third process, was as crucial as it was, at least initially, surprising. In 1848 populations had turned on their rulers in Europe; during the subsequent two decades they became patriots, supporting their countries, right or wrong. The Italian Risorgimento and the unification of Germany were the most notable expressions of nationalism's power, but elsewhere, too, nationalism strengthened. Once Germany demonstrated during the Franco-Prussian War that armies recruited on the basis of military service could be trusted and made to fight enthusiastically for the state, other states quickly followed suit, also placing their trust in the loyalty of their populations as they fashioned large standing armies. Earlier in the century, European monarchs had preferred to rely on largely mercenary forces, whose ranks, unlike their aristocratic officers, were drawn from outsiders, including foreigners.

Roger Chickering describes the growth of militarism, which accompanied the strengthening of nationalism. The relationship between the state and the armed forces changed fundamentally, he argues, because of the "three pillars" of the late-nineteenth-century state: universal conscription, compulsory primary education, and male suffrage. These institutions helped bind together state and society and gave males a set of common experiences as the military assumed the role of regulating the passage from boyhood to manhood: the army made a man out of the boy. The militarism of the age inculcated manly values, such as toughness, loyalty, discipline, and will. It also instilled a sharp awareness of friend and foe and the belief that the country's survival was always endangered from within and without. Militarism was on display not just in the armed forces and schools, but also in public life, in parades, marches, songs, naval days, and other military spectacles, while children (and men) played with toy soldiers. As Chickering notes, the claims of nationalism bumped into rival religious, regional, and ethnic loyalties: militarism was a vehicle for states to veil or suppress other loyalties; it provided "social control in an age of rapid transformation."

The fourth major development of this era was the great increase in bureaucratic capacity and the deepening of the reach of the state. European states became much better at raising money through taxation and borrowing in increasingly efficient financial markets. There is no better indication of the growing strength of European nation-states than the fact that while their armies became far larger and armaments far more expensive, the proportion of military expenditures in national budgets declined by more than 50 percent over the course of the nineteenth century. Even in the run-up to World War I, when all parties were rushing to strengthen their forces, military budgets claimed only several percentage points of their countries' gross domestic products.[2] State-strengthening was not only a matter of increasing extractive capacity. Bureaucracies became skilled in accumulating information, maintaining accurate registers, and producing statistics, thus strengthening their ability to keep track of human and material resources and to mobilize them for the state's narrowly focused purpose. The Prussian victory over France in 1870 depended on the skills of its general staff to ensure that Prussian soldiers, including reservists, entrained with provisions and equipment at designated stations on pre-allocated trains and that they were transported to the right spot at the front in accordance with pre-arranged timetables. The state's bureaucracies became more widely respected because recruitment was increasingly

2 Niall Ferguson, *The Pity of War: Explaining World War I* (New York, 1999), 109–10.

based on merit rather than patronage, because they emphasized competence, expertise, and rational planning, and because they were supposed to serve the entire population.

None of these developments made the carnage of total war inevitable. Warnings had been given, as the quotation at the head of this introduction by Helmuth von Moltke indicated. Others, too, believed that technological advances, industrialization, bureaucratization, and the consolidation of nation-states might end in Armageddon. Friedrich Engels warned in 1887 that "the only war for Prussia-Germany to fight will be a world war, a world war, moreover, of an extent and violence hitherto unimagined. Eight to ten million soldiers will be at each other's throats and strip Europe barer than a swarm of locusts."[3] Ivan Bloch, a Polish banker and analyst of modern warfare, distributed a pamphlet at The Hague Peace Conference in which he warned that the next war could result in "the break-up of the whole social organization."[4] Alfred von Schlieffen's pre-emptive strike into Belgium and France, with which World War I began, was "a desperate gamble" to prevent a horrendous war of attrition and "an old general's dream to prevent a nightmare."[5]

Such premonitions propelled both states and civic actors to try to prevent the outbreak of war, or at least to contain its damage and isolate civilian populations from its harm. Jean Quataert shows how after the Crimean War, when the first war reporters informed home populations about battlefield horrors through the emergent mass media, the Red Cross attempted to humanize war through transnational institutions and civic mobilization. The Geneva Convention of 1864 gave legal protection to individuals on the battlefield, such as wounded soldiers, medical personnel, and prisoners of war. In the Hague Conventions of 1899 and 1907, states agreed to measures that outlawed certain types of weapons, decreed that military action target only the forces of the enemy, and proscribed "excess suffering." Both developments had beneficial results. Yet, the humanization of warfare also made war more acceptable to the publics whose active support had become essential to war-making.

3 Friedrich Engels, "Introduction to Sigismund Borkheim's Pamphlet, *In Memory of the German Blood-and-Thunder Patriots*, 1806–1807," in Karl Marx and Friedrich Engels, *Collected Works* (London, 1975), vol. XXVI, p. 451.

4 Ivan Bloch, *Is War Now Impossible*, quoted in Ferguson, *Pity of War*, 9.

5 Stig Förster, "Dreams and Nightmares: German Military Leadership and the Images of Future Warfare," in Manfred F. Boemeke, Roger Chickering, and Stig Förster, eds., *Anticipating Total War: The German and American Experiences, 1871–1914* (Cambridge, 1999), 361.

In the late nineteenth century, European states built the institutions that enabled them to wage hugely destructive warfare. It remains astonishing that a minor incident, such as the murder of Franz Ferdinand, could trigger a major catastrophe. Even hindsight makes it difficult to see why decision-makers of the time believed that going to war was their best option. Some observers have put the blame on politicians for their folly and on generals for persisting in ways of fighting that could only destroy lives.[6] Mobilization by railroad timetable, the idea that once one state ordered the entrainment of its men others had to follow or face certain extinction, is another important explanation.[7] Military and political leaders became used to taking huge risks, adopting the mindset of gamblers. There was also the belief that war, and the threat of war, was a legitimate tool of politics. Important, too, were the decay of the Congress of Europe and the entrenchment of absolutist attitudes about state sovereignty.[8] The place of war had changed. It was no longer the specialized but routine activity of a circumscribed group, but something that while extraordinary was also all-embracing.[9] It was seen as awful and dreaded, but also a rare opportunity at fulfilling a collective mission, even at redemption. Limited wars were difficult in this context. Nonetheless, war was not inevitable and it is wrong to see the four key developments identified here as inevitably and inexorably leading to the total war of World War I. After all, total war was improvised during World War I, as Purseigle makes clear, as the institutions were engineered to sustain it. As so often, war proved easier to begin than to conclude, had unintended consequences, and produced a new reality, in this case that of total war.

6 A. J. P. Taylor, *History of the First World War* (Harmondsworth, 1966).
7 A. J. P. Taylor, *War by Timetable: How the First World War Began* (London, 1969).
8 Robert Brinkley, *Realism and Nationalism, 1852–1871* (New York, 1935).
9 David Bell, *The First Total War: Napoleon's Europe and the Birth of Warfare as We Know It* (Boston and New York, 2007), 5–13.

I

A hinge in time: the wars of the mid nineteenth century

HANS VAN DE VEN

A series of military cataclysms rocked the world in the middle decades of the nineteenth century. The Taiping Rebellion of 1850–64 in China was the most devastating, laying waste to provinces along the middle and lower stretches of the Yangzi River and causing some 20–30 million deaths. During the 1861–65 American Civil War, some five hundred thousand men lost their lives and a similar number died from wounds and diseases. The 1853–56 Crimean War led to the deaths of more than a hundred thousand British and French soldiers and a far higher number of Russian ones. The casualty figures of the Indian Rebellion of 1857–58 were small by comparison, but they nonetheless had important consequences, as London took direct control of India, racialist prejudices became entrenched, and empire became a subject of intense and broad public concern. In Europe's core, wars were few and short but also deadly. The Franco-Prussian War of 1870–71 caused 150,000 to 200,000 deaths.

These conflicts were not part of a world war, nor did they arise from a general world crisis. There were connections between them nonetheless, including in personnel. General Charles Gordon saw action in the Crimea and led a British expedition to China, before finally being killed in Khartoum in 1885. General George McClellan, who briefly served as the Union's commander-in-chief during the American Civil War, observed the Crimean War in person, drawing lessons from it that later informed the North's initial approach to the war. The wars impacted on each other. The Crimean War and the Indian Rebellion left the British short of troops in China. Chinese officials interpreted the temporary inability of the British to back up their demands and threats with force as a sign of persistent weakness. The Crimean War also stoked British fears of Russian expansionism in East Asia. Once the Crimean War had ended and the Indian Rebellion was mostly suppressed, concerns about Russian designs in Asia formed one reason for the British to strengthen the Royal Navy's China Station and seek to extend their influence northward from Canton. Common causes underlying these upheavals included population growth, dislocations

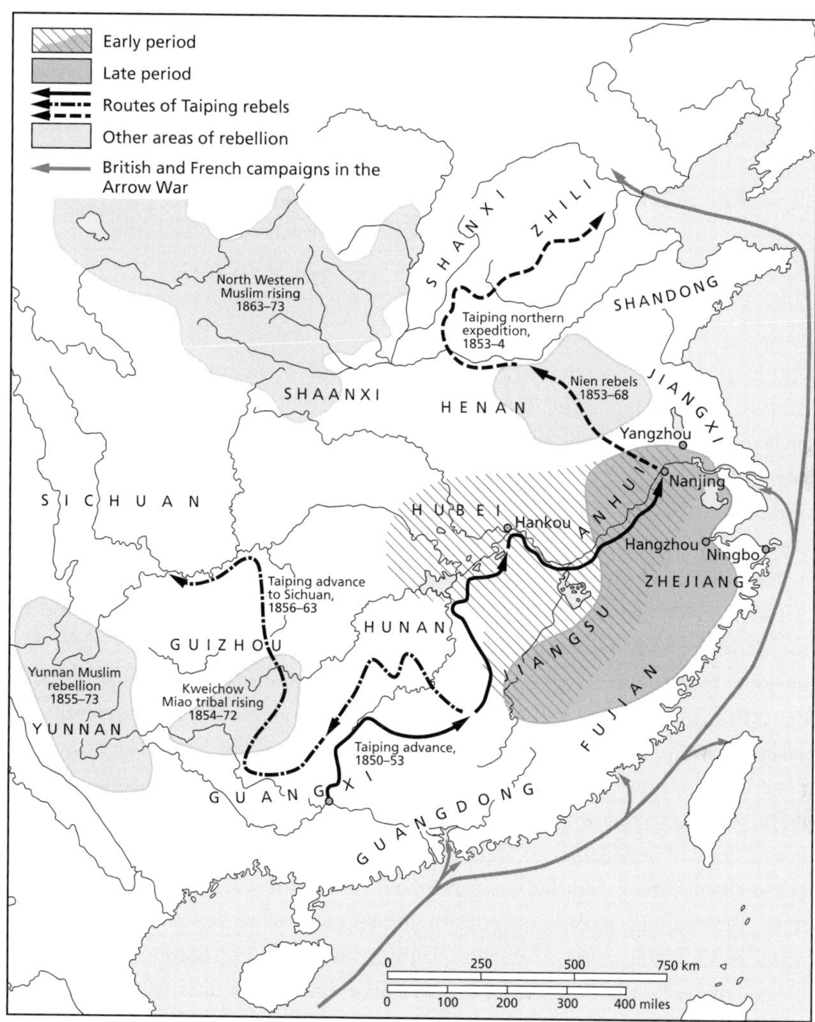

MAP 1. Taiping Rebellion, 1850–1864

caused by the uneven impact of industrialization, the spread of epidemic diseases such as cholera, and disruptions resulting from Britain's free trade policy, often enforced at gun point. Nonetheless, because the world was as yet little connected, most historians have rightly written about these wars as distinct events and concentrated on analyzing their implications for the societies in which they took place. In analyzing the warfare of this period, this chapter follows this approach, discussing each conflict separately.

Still, the mid-century cataclysms formed a hinge in time, with a "before" and an "after" in at least three areas. First, significant changes occurred in armaments, military organization, and tactics. If the Crimean War was a Cabinet war with armies drawn from the poor and led by nobilities, by the time of the Franco-Prussian War soldiers were armed with modern rifles and powerful cannon; they were transported by railroad, and the telegraph enabled close contact between battlefield commanders and military and political leaders in the rear. During the Crimean War, British troops in red jackets still formed up in lines of two or three men to fire volleys from close range at the Russians. By the end of these decades, the battlefield had flattened, as soldiers took to the ground or dug in and spread out. Increased firepower advantaged the defensive, and single battles rarely proved decisive. In 1850 navies were still largely made up of sailing vessels; by the end of the period they had been transformed by the steam engine, the screw propeller, and the use of iron for armor. The effect of rapid technological change on the conduct of war is thus one consistent focus of this chapter.

Not only technological change revolutionized warfare. During these two decades, European states began to nationalize, industrialize, and bureaucratize their armies, while their societies gained in cohesiveness and political leadership became both more complex and important to victory. In many European countries, the army became a key institution of the nation, both symbolically and practically, as the largest state-wide organization. Universal military service linked most strata of the population to the most violent arm of the state. Armies were used less to safeguard the regime, as they still had been during the revolutions of 1848, than to fight for the nation. Soldiers became "our boys": home fronts developed that were informed and concerned about troops at the front. Bureaucracy became important, as armies came to depend on centralized ministries for their arms, uniforms, training, and provisions, and as bureaucratic coordination became necessary to recruit, train, house, and transport them. Armies also adopted, and sometimes pioneered, bureaucratic managerial practices that stressed competence, training, merit, efficiency, and achievement. The exercise of command was no longer seen as the product of intuition or genius, but as a result of training and experience. Military academies sprang up to teach promising cadets in leadership skills, surveying, history, mathematics, engineering, and logistics. This theme, of the move toward a nation-in-arms in Europe, with competence replacing privilege and armies enjoying broad legitimacy, forms a second thread running through this chapter.

The wars of these two decades threw up in sharp relief the difference in military capability between "the West and the Rest." In Europe these decades ended what Christopher Bayly has called the "period of flux and hiatus" between the Napoleonic wars and the mid-century cataclysms, when weak regimes in Europe sought to stuff the genies of revolution, democracy, and nationalism back into their bottles.[1] Resistance to colonization, as the French discovered in Algeria, could be fierce. In 1833, Chinese officials peremptorily refused to meet or even communicate with Lord Napier, who had been sent to China to extend trade beyond Canton. He left empty-handed, without having met his counterparts, and died from fever in Macao after two British frigates had been destroyed. In India, some ruling houses remained independent, especially in the south, while in areas that were controlled by the East India Company great families remained socially and politically influential.

By the end of this period, the world lay open to the aggressive imperialisms of newly confident European states. As with all crime, opportunity, motive, and means conspired to make this outcome possible. Opportunity resulted from the shocks these conflicts inflicted on established, if already fragile, structures of governance and legitimacy in what we now call East Asia, South Asia, and the Middle East. The means were the much stronger armies and navies that had come about, backed by the more centralized and cohesive states that had taken root in Europe. The motive was partly economic, as industrialization led to a quest for markets and primary resources, and efficient financial markets released capital in search of investment opportunities. Geopolitics was also important, as social Darwinism led to an anarchic live-or-die view of international relations. Culturally, many Europeans saw empire as a matter of national pride and as necessary to fulfill a civilizing duty. The third theme running through this chapter therefore is the weakening of non-European states, especially in Asia, and the move toward what has been called the new imperialism, which after 1880 culminated in the partition of Africa.

The Crimean War was the last of the cabinet wars. It was fought by small armies led by aristocrats for limited goals derived from European power politics. Napoleonic models of warfare, as interpreted by Antoine-Henri Jomini in his *Précis de l'art de la guerre*, dominated military thinking about how to conduct a military campaign. The *Précis* had been published in 1826 and was widely read in Europe and the United States, more so than the writings of Carl von Clausewitz, whose 1832 *Vom Kriege* came to overshadow Jomini only after the Franco-Prussian War.[2] Jomini argued that from his study of Napoleonic warfare he had derived scientific principles for successful

1 Christopher Bayly, *The Birth of the Modern World: 1780–1914* (Oxford, 2004), 125.
2 Hew Strachan, *European Armies and the Conduct of War* (London, 2004), 60–75, 98.

combat. He stressed the importance of siting a strong base of operations, maintaining lines of communication between the front and this base, and maneuver to get at the breaking points in the enemy's formation. The Crimean War began as a limited war, led by commanders whose actions were shaped by Jominian doctrines, but new arms, the decline of hand-to-hand combat, new naval ship designs, and the emergence of the home front provided hints of the future.

Dubbed by Friedrich Engels "a colossal comedy of errors,"[3] the Crimean War arose out of a religious dispute about who – France or Russia – was the protector of Christians and Christian sacred sites in Ottoman lands. Napoleon III, seeking to strengthen his reputation after his *coup d'état* of 1851, had compelled the Ottoman Sultan Abdulmecid I to accept a treaty that assigned this right to France and the Roman Catholic Church, rather than to Russia as in the past. The more fundamental issues were the fate of the tottering Ottoman Empire and the role of Russia in Europe. If Russia aimed at a division of the Ottomon Empire, which would enhance its position in Eastern Europe, the British aimed to forestall this breakup in order to prevent Russian domination of the Balkans and access to the Mediterranean.

The opening battles of the Crimean War illustrated the hold of Napoleonic warfare. From September 13, 1854, French and British forces led by Marshal Jacques St. Arnaud and Lord Raglan made an unopposed landing on the Crimean peninsula some 35 miles from Sebastopol, where a major Russian naval base was located. They put on shore 60,000 troops, 1,000 cavalry, and 132 guns. Their aim was to break through Russian lines and then to take Sebastopol. At the Battle of the Alma River, the Allies confronted General Prince Aleksandr Menshikov, who deployed 33,000 infantry, 3,200 cavalry, and 120 guns. On the day on which battle was given – September 20 – British soldiers cooked breakfast and drank coffee, after which they marched to the front for a day of fighting in closed formation, coordinated by officers on horseback. Still dressed in red coats, they were formed into a two-mile-long line of two men deep. They advanced with regimental colors flying and bugles sounding.[4] The battle was decided in favor of the Allies in the traditional way – by bayonets in a melee.

During the Crimean War, old nobilities continued to dominate. In the case of the British, their commanders were also old in years: Raglan had served under the

3 Alex Troubetzkoy, *The Crimean War* (London, 2006), xv.

4 Ian Fletcher and Natalia Ischenko, *The Crimean War: A Clash of Empires* (Staplehurst, 2004), 84.

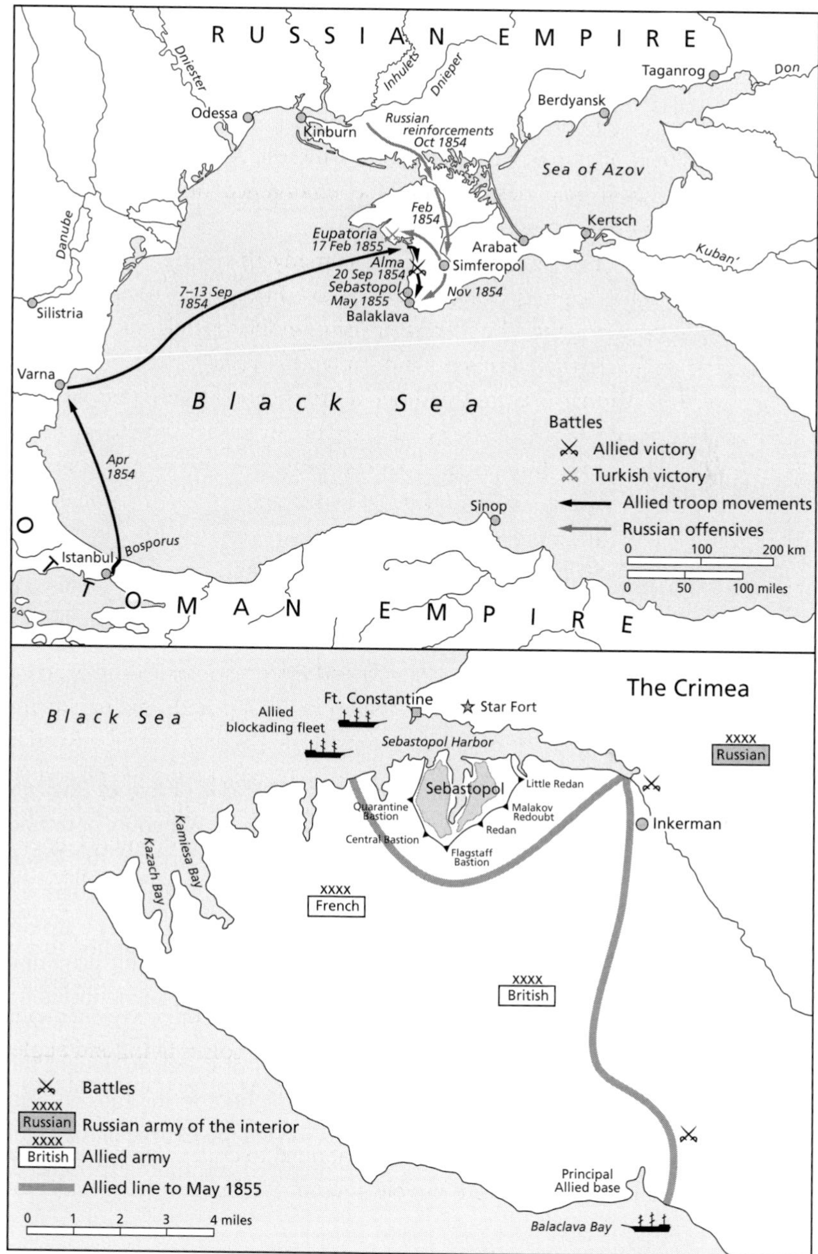

MAP 2. Crimean War, 1853–1856

1. Heavy guns at Sebastopol

Duke of Wellington during the Napoleonic wars. Four out of five of Raglan's divisional commanders had fought in the Peninsular War, at Waterloo, or during the British-American War of 1812. Sir John Burgoyne, in charge of the Royal Engineers, was seventy-two and had first seen service in 1800.[5] The Duke himself still counted as a sage and was widely consulted, including about strategy against Qing China during the Taiping Rebellion. The purchase system for acquiring commissions remained in place, defended by leading statesmen, including Palmerston, as "desirable to connect the higher classes of Society with the army."[6] These commissions were expensive. The Earl of Cardigan bought the lieutenant-colonelship in the 11th Light Dragoons for his son for £40,000.[7] An extreme version of the hide-bound aristocrat, this son led the Charge of the Light Brigade. The French commanders were better prepared and more experienced,

5 Fletcher and Ischenko, *Crimean War*, 25–27.
6 Troubetzkoy, *Crimean War*, 24.
7 Ibid.

having fought during the French conquest of Algeria, but they too were largely drawn from the nobility. The same was true of the Russians.

The Charge of the Light Brigade at the Battle of Balaclava exposed the shortcomings of old habits. Menshikov had sent his second in command, General Pavel Liprandi, into two valleys near Balaclava with the aim of disrupting the major British supply base at the port and then attacking the Allied besiegers at Sebastopol from the rear. A Russian cavalry column of twenty-five hundred men drove down the road toward the port. They were repulsed by "The Thin Red Line" of two rows of infantry soldiers – the only defense that protected the British base. While the British Heavy Brigade drove back a second Russian cavalry column, the Light Brigade led by Cardigan charged into a valley surrounded by Russian forces.[8] A Russian observer wrote that the British "presented the height of perfection and were riding at a trot as if on manoeuvres."[9] The futile charge ended with 298 casualties and 497 horses lost. The querulous Cardigan, who had spent lavishly to make his unit appear thoroughly aristocratic, refused to draw his sword after a Russian lancer had wounded him in his thigh; instead he went off for a champagne dinner on his luxury steam yacht, the *Dryad*, earning himself the nickname "The Noble Yachtsman."[10]

While fun could be made of such examples, major changes were underway. The British military had been equipped with rifles shooting Minié bullets. These replaced the smooth-bore muskets that had been the standard infrantry weapon since the early seventeenth century and whose effective range had been a mere 60–70 meters. The much larger range and better accuracy of the rifle made assaults with bayonets difficult to achieve, rarely decisive, and very costly, as was discovered during the Battle of Inkerman on November 5. Effective musket fire depended on maintaining tight discipline, because of the difficulty and time required to reload, and compact formations. The Minié rifle, and later breech-loaders, were much simpler to handle and could be reloaded rapidly. Formations could, and had, to spread out.

When the British and French reached Sebastopol, they discovered that enhanced firepower, if combined with a new method of fortification, advantaged the defensive. The chief engineer of the Russians was Lieutenant Major

8 Vague orders, lack of reconnaissance, and personal animosities among Lord Raglan, Lord Lucan, and his brother-in-law, Lord Cardigan, too played a role. Fletcher and Ischenko, *Crimean War*, 178–83.

9 Ibid., 182.

10 Cecil Woodham-Smith, *The Reason Why: The Story of the Fatal Charge of the Light Brigade* (London, 1953), 262; Troubetzkoy, *Crimean War*, 261.

Eduourd Totleben. In designing the defenses of Sebastopol, he improvised fortifications that were as effective as they were simple. He sank the Russian fleet in Sebastopol Harbor to prevent British and French naval vessels from entering the port, and he transferred their cannon to the city. He then ringed the city with a low but thick earthen wall, just high enough to protect Russian soldiers and cannon. Any attack had to overcome a series of obstacles that he constructed in the upward sloping ground. Pits were filled with rocks that flung upwards after gunpowder under them was detonated; attackers then had to cross an abattis of tangled trees and sharp stakes; they had then to traverse a large expanse of flat terrain while being shot at by Russian soldiers behind the rampart and in manholes in front of it. If the attackers managed these obstacles, they faced a trench seven feet deep and a stockade.[11]

One advantage of this style of fortification was that it was easy to repair. What the British and French destroyed by day, the Russians repaired by night. Totleben extended his system of fortification to outlying redoubts, including the Redan, the Flagstaff Bastion, and the Malakoff. He dug trenches around them, from which Russian soldiers killed huge numbers of French and British soldiers as they charged these strong points. The Crimean War, then, exemplified what soon became a common theme of warfare in Europe and the United States: the defenders dug in.

The Crimean War became a slugfest. Especially during the first winter the British suffered grievously, as they had not counted on having to spend the winter at Sebastopol. The consequences were brought home after a storm in November 1854 destroyed tents, kitchens, and hospitals and ravaged supply lines. Exposed to the harsh winter without proper clothing and malnourished, a great number fell ill or died of typhus, cholera, and dysentery. Medical services were frightful, with the main hospitals more than 500 kilometers away in Turkey and so filthy that infections killed those saved on the operation table.

These disasters spurred the British to action. Prime Minister Palmerston established a Land Transport Corps and a Sea Transport Corps to ensure that sufficient supplies reached British forces. A Sanitary Commission cleaned up hospitals. A chief of staff was sent to the front to reinvigorate staff work and ensure that decisions in London were obeyed in the Crimea. A railroad was built from Balaclava to Sebastopol to ferry food, ammunition, and weapons, including hundreds of cannon, to the siege lines. Steam supply ships brought in the required *matériel* from Britain. By the end of the war, the Allies could bombard Sebastopol with some five hundred cannon for days on end. The

11 Troubetzkoy, *Crimean War*, 274–75.

commission system too came under criticism. Training and battlefield performance, rather than status, came to determine promotion.

The home front began to emerge as a significant factor. Dispatches from the Crimea by W. H. Russell of *The Times* of London, the first professional war correspondent, made the British public aware of the horrors of the fighting and the dismal conditions of the troops. Battlefield reporting helped make the war an object of patriotic passion with the reputation of Britain at stake. Florence Nightingale was moved to pioneer battlefield medical care. Britain's new wealth, industrial capacity, and the efficiency of its financial markets enabled the country to respond rapidly to the shortcomings in its armed forces, which the first battles of the Crimea had exposed.

The Russians lost the Crimean War because they had to supply their troops over an impossibly long supply line which ran largely overland. The Allies began to gain the upper hand when, on May 24, 1855, they took Kerch on the eastern side of the Crimea, cutting the Russian supply route over the Don River and the Azov Sea. Yet, hard fighting lay ahead. Following five attempts to carry the city, the Allies were able to take the Malakoff and the Redan only in early September with an attack that deployed sixty thousand soldiers, while they maintained an intense barrage on Sebastopol. With these two forts lost, the Russians decided that further combat was futile and withdrew from the city.

A peace treaty was signed on March 30, 1856. It closed the Black Sea to all warships, and Russia lost the territory it had been given at the mouth of the Danube. Russian influence in the Balkans was greatly reduced, as it was in European politics more generally, while the Ottoman Empire survived.

Besides its consequences for the conduct of war, one important development that came out of the Crimean War was a revolution in naval design. As with hand-held guns, naval architecture had changed little during the eighteenth and early nineteenth centuries. The Crimean War demonstrated that wooden sailing ships had become outmoded. During the Battle of Sinope on November 30, 1853 in the Black Sea, the Russian navy sailed into Sinope, anchored alongside the Turkish fleet, and destroyed it using Paixhans guns, which fired explosive shells on a flat trajectory. In April 1854, coastal batteries near Odessa set wooden Allied warships on fire, while the Sebastopol forts destroyed another five in October. Conversely, in 1855, five French armor-plated floating batteries towed by tugs fired three thousand rounds into Sebastopol with devastating effect. Small gunboats carrying two to four heavy guns also proved their worth.[12] Able to move against wind and

12 Jeremy Black, *Western Warfare 1775–1882* (Bloomington, 2001), 72–74.

current and lying low in the water, they were more maneuverable and less vulnerable. A few heavy cannon mounted on deck could fire in all directions and suppress coastal fortifications from a distance. Naval battles never again saw two navies draw alongside to fire broadsides at each other from close range. Steam transports proved equally important, allowing the French and British to solve their supply problems.

Once the Crimean War had confirmed the obsolescence of wooden sailing ships, change became rapid. In 1859 the French launched *La Gloire*, the first ocean-going ironclad warship. *The Warrior*, made of iron, capable of 14 knots, and armed with 7-inch Armstrong breech-loading rifled guns, was the Royal Navy's answer. Thus began a naval arms race that heated up toward the end of the century, as naval power came to be seen as a determinant of great-power status. Small gunboats, able to penetrate deep into inland territories along rivers, became a key instrument of colonial conquest, as well as potent symbols of western power. Britain's policy in China was to station them in each Treaty Port, where they heartened settler communities and served as everyday reminders of Britain's destructive capacity. It was as if Britain had put a small nuclear device in every port.[13]

Both the Union and the Confederacy began the American Civil War believing that it would be of short duration, that only limited numbers of soldiers would have to be mobilized, and that it would be concluded by a decisive battle.[14] Instead, it developed into a war of attrition, as battle after battle demonstrated that in the sparsely populated vastness of the United States there was no Jominian "centre of gravity." Abraham Lincoln's 1863 Emancipation Proclamation made the Union's aims ideological, as opposed to territorial, and hence more total and punitive. Only the destruction of the enemy, or the enemy's surrender, could end the war. The American Civil War also foreshadowed the total war of the twentieth century in that the Union brought the war home to the population of the South. As General William Sherman remarked, "we are not only fighting hostile armies, but a hostile people, and we must make old and young, rich and poor, feel the hard hand of war."[15] The American Civil War showed that civilian and military objectives

13 Paul M. Kennedy, *The Rise and Fall of British Naval Mastery* (London, 1976), 175–207; Gerald S. Graham, *The China Station: War and Diplomacy, 1830–1860* (Oxford, 1978); Daniel Headrick, *Tools of Empire: Technology and European Imperialism in the Nineteenth Century* (New York, 1981), 43–57.

14 James McPherson, *Battle Cry of Freedom: The Civil War Era* (New York, 1988) remains justly celebrated. For a short overview, see Larry Addington, *The Patterns of War since the Eighteenth Century* (Bloomington, 1994), 68–97.

15 Brian Bond, *The Pursuit of Victory from Napoleon to Saddam Hussein* (Oxford, 1998), 67.

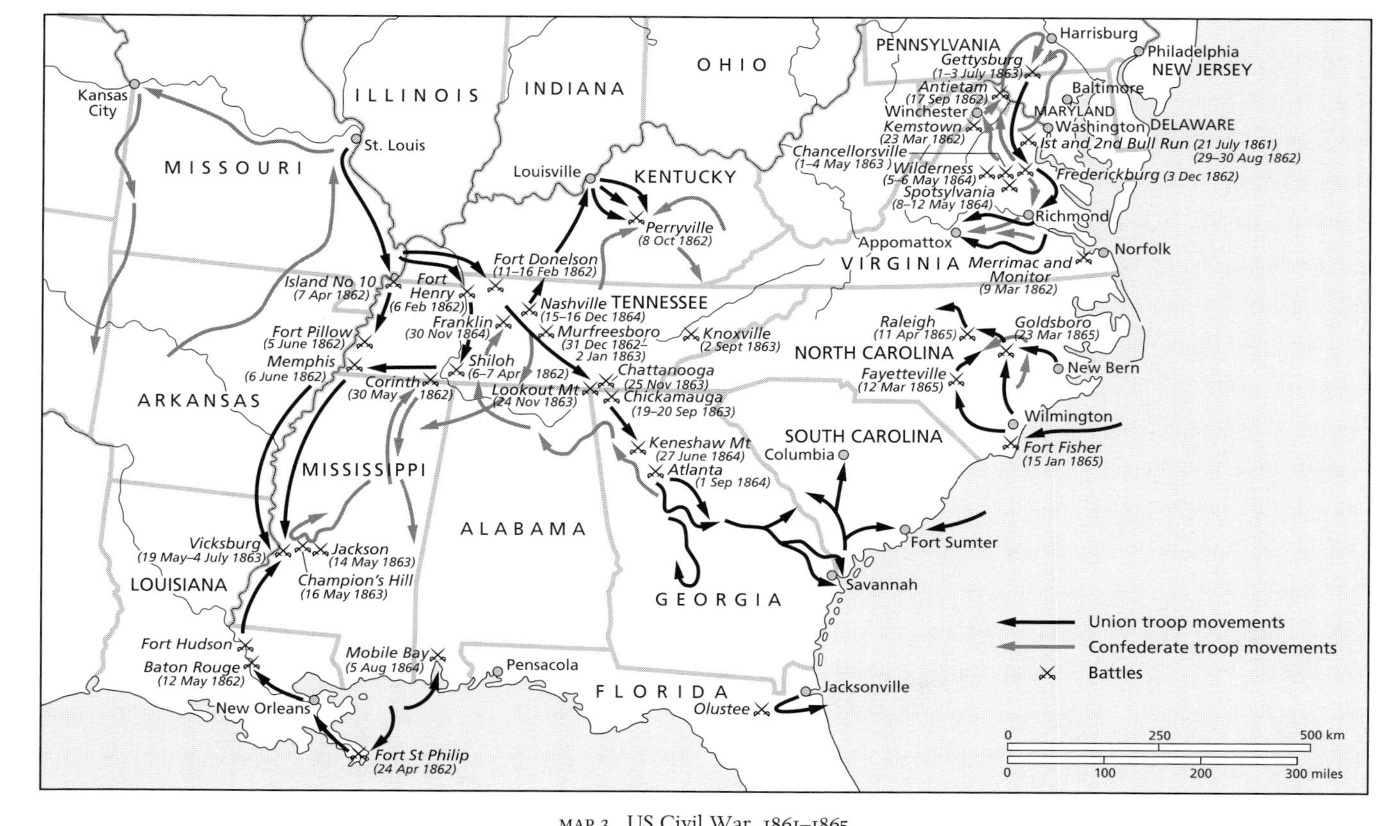

MAP 3. US Civil War, 1861–1865

had to be carefully coordinated so as to keep publics committed to the fight.[16] Adroit political leadership became an important ingredient for victory in modern war.

The American Civil War broke out when long-simmering tensions about slavery and state rights were rendered explosive by the formation of new states and the incorporation of new territories in the west, including Texas, New Mexico, and California following the 1846–48 war with Mexico; the rapid growth of the Northern population as a result of immigration, which made the South fear a loss of influence in Washington; and the election of Abraham Lincoln to the presidency without a single Southern electoral vote. War broke out on April 12, 1861, when Southern Confederate forces under General P. Beauregard took Fort Sumter in South Carolina.

At the outbreak of war, the Union trusted that the majority of the Southern population, as opposed to slave owners, could be won over. The South hoped that a quick but decisive victory on the battlefield would lead to negotiations and recognition of southern independence. Under President Jefferson Davis, the Confederacy adopted a defensive strategy: it needed only to avoid defeat in order to break the Union's will to fight. The Union's first war plan, Anaconda, called for embargoing the coast to end Southern cotton exports to Europe, seizing control of the Mississippi to cut the Confederacy into two, and taking the Confederate capital at Richmond in Virginia, which, the North believed, would end the war.

General George McClellan's Peninsula campaign in the spring of 1862 was an effort to force a quick decision. After earlier attempts to invade northern Virginia by moving straight south from Washington ended in ignominious defeat, McClellan decided to embark 120,000 troops to bypass Confederate forces and land at Fort Monroe in southeast Virginia. While he had done sterling work in building up the Army of the Potomac, he was a cautious battlefield commander. As he crawled up the Virginia Peninsula, Confederate forces, including General Robert E. Lee's Army of Northern Virginia, reinforced their lines and pushed McClellan back. Fearing an attack on Washington, Lincoln called the Army of the Potomac back to the Union capital. The Battle of Antietam of September 17, 1862 and the Battle of Fredericksburg of December 11–15, 1862 were further attempts to bring the war to an end quickly. Despite enormous loss of men, they failed to do so.

The Union had a significantly larger population, an immensely more productive industrial base and, because of its better-developed rail net,

16 Ibid., 67–68.

superior communication links. As the civil war turned into a war of attrition, the Union mobilized these advantages effectively. The 1861 Morrill Tariff Act raised Customs dues to 47 percent to protect Northern industries. In the same year, an income tax was introduced, while Salmon P. Chase reformed the banking system, imposing capital requirements on banks. The Legal Tender Act enabled Washington to issue currency by fiat. Immigration was made more attractive, while the 1862 Homestead Act brought new agricultural land under cultivation. Mechanization accelerated, including in agriculture, where the thresher and the reaper increased productivity. Government purchases stimulated the output of industry and agriculture. Coal production more than doubled to 12 million tons, wool nearly trebled, and wheat production grew by 50 percent. Already by 1862, the North could produce two hundred thousand rifles annually.[17] New industrial production methods, such as using machine-driven lathes to produce standardized, interchangeable parts, increased productivity. The Federal Government even introduced a primitive draft to compel states to deliver the required numbers of men. The North's greater industrial and financial capacity was fundamental to its victory, as was Lincoln's adroit political and military leadership.

Besides mobilizing its industrial and agricultural resources, the Union abandoned its focus on Richmond, shifted the war west, and targeted the Southern population. Its forces had achieved better successes in the west even in the early stages of the war. A turning point was General Ulysses S. Grant's successful siege of the city of Vicksburg on the Mississippi River. Leading the Army of Tennessee, Grant cut loose from his base, jettisoning a Jominian axiom, crossed the Mississippi, beat back a force that tried to attack his rear, and invested the city. Trenches were dug, mines laid, tunnels dug, and batteries erected. Gunboats shelled Vicksburg from the Mississippi. Vicksburg fell to the Union on July 4, 1863, and the Mississippi was in the Union's hands.

Grant became general-in-chief in early 1864. He ordered new attacks on Lee's Army of Northern Virginia and Richmond, in part to encourage the Union's public opinion, which was focused on the war here, but his main effort was in the west, where he demanded constant harassment of the Confederacy's logistical lines and supply bases. General William Sherman followed a scorched-earth policy to crush the population's will to fight. He invaded Georgia, taking Atlanta in September 1864, where he burned all government and military buildings, and

17 T. Harry Williams, "The American Civil War," in J. P. T. Bury, ed., *The New Cambridge Modern History*, Vol. X: *The Zenith of European Power* (Cambridge, 1960), 642ff.

a few others, to the ground. He then took off on his famous march to the sea, capturing Savannah on December 21 and leaving a sea of Chimneyvilles in his wake. He did the same as he moved north through South Carolina. "War is cruelty, and you cannot refine it," he said.[18]

In the eastern theater, Robert E. Lee proved a tenacious opponent to the end. From the spring of 1864, Grant used his superiority in numbers and *matériel* to push Lee's Army of Northern Virginia further south toward Richmond. Lee entrenched around Richmond and Petersburg, a city just south of the capital on the Appomattox River and linked to Richmond by rail. Lee beat back Grant's assaults repeatedly, but he was unable to replenish his mounting losses. In March 1865, he had no option but to abandon Richmond and Petersburg. He agreed to surrender on April 9 after finding his forces surrounded. This was the fatal blow; over the next few months the Confederate armies still in the field also gave up the fight.

The United States emerged from its civil war in control of the whole continent between Mexico and Canada. It faced no serious foreign threat and henceforth tolerated no European meddling in American affairs. France, with the support of Britain and Spain, had attempted to exploit America's misery by invading Mexico and setting up a Mexican monarchy with a Habsburg on the throne. After the civil war, the United States intervened by instituting a naval blockade, massing troops along the Rio Grande, and supporting Mexican republican forces. The French had to abort their adventure.

Unlike European states, the United States did not join the new imperialism that emerged out of the mid-century wars, at least not until the end of the century. The United States demobilized its armed forces. Tired of war and ideologically opposed to the large standing armies characteristic of European states, the USA turned inward, focusing on the challenges of rehabilitating the South, bringing the regions of the newly acquired states in the west under cultivation, and building transcontinental railroads.

If, from a European perspective, the American Civil War looked different, the Taiping Rebellion shared several features with the war in the United States. It too was a civil war over constitutional issues and was fought as a war of attrition in a vast country. However, Lincoln had enhanced the legitimacy and moral authority of the presidency, fostered a sense of US patriotism, and worked out a way to contain the centrifugal and centripetal forces inevitable in a country as large as the United States. In contrast, in the Qing a group of powerful regional leaders emerged during the Taiping Rebellion. They, rather

18 Bond, *Pursuit of Victory*, 67.

than Beijing, held the initiative in setting policy, although they, in turn, could do little without Beijing's approval. The rebellion and the humiliating foreign demands the Qing had to accept during the Arrow War damaged the prestige of the emperor. The Qing lacked the legitimacy, political authority, and broad social support to make necessary reforms.

The Qing's loss of grip had been rapid. Founded by the Manchu Aisin Gioro clan in 1644, it was one of the most expansionist dynasties in Chinese history. It brought vast new territories, including Xinjiang (Chinese Eastern Turkestan), Mongolia, and Tibet under its control, almost doubling China's landmass. While the eighteenth century was known as China's Prosperous Age, by the early nineteenth century the Qing was buffeted by several storms: financial shortages caused by the halt to silver imports from South America; a high-profile corruption scandal involving the emperor's favorite; rebellion in peripheral areas; and rapid population growth.

The outbreak of the Taiping Rebellion in 1850 put the survival of the dynasty in doubt. It took place in a military context radically different from the one in Europe or the United States. Most Chinese dynasties had aimed at demilitarizing the interior and avoided reliance on martial races or classes. While this policy ensured long periods of peace, it also meant that if an armed challenger were able to break into China's heartland, it found little opposition, as the Taiping Rebellion demonstrated. The Qing had focused on land-based threats, especially on the western periphery of the empire; it had not developed navies that could secure its borders and patrol its rivers. The Taiping sailed unopposed down the Yangzi River in thousands of junks (Chinese vessels). Chinese fortifications consisted of vertical walls of ramped earth with a single layer of masonry. Such walls protected towns and cities, in which government offices, arsenals, granaries, and silver stores were housed.

The leader of the Taiping Rebellion was Hong Xiuquan.[19] Born near Canton in a minority Hakka household, Hong turned against the Qing after failing in the civil-service examination system, thus finding the most important path to glory in pre-modern China closed to him. Possibly as a result of a nervous breakdown after a fourth failed attempt to pass the examination, Hong concluded from dreams he had had that he was the Second Son of Jesus Christ and that God had instructed him to slay China's demons, which he identified as the Manchus.

19 Jonathan Spence, *God's Chinese Son: The Taiping Heavenly Kingdom of Hong Xiuquan* (New York, 1996) is a readable and well-informed biography. Franz Michael, *The Taiping Rebellion: History and Documents* (Seattle, 1971) remains indispensable.

Hounded out of Guangdong, he built a following of believers in the violent valleys of Guangxi Province. This area housed populations with useful military skills: miners expert in the use of gunpowder; ex-pirates driven inland from the south China and Cochin coasts by the British in the name of protecting free trade; managers of pawnshops who were capable of handling money; coolies thrown out of work by the decline of Canton as China's main harbor; and smiths capable of forging swords, halberds, spears, and knives. Christianity provided a common belief system, which was used by Hong as a new authorizing regime.

In 1850, Taiping followers gathered on Thistle Mountain in Guangxi Province after local elites had begun to hunt their leaders. Their numbers swelled, as feuding between locals and recent arrivals caused many to turn to the Taiping for protection. Forced by shortages to leave the area, they formed an army. Unable to feed their followers and pursued by Qing forces, in September 1851 the Taiping crossed the mountains of northern Guangxi and on the twenty-fifth they took Yong'an, a wealthy but lightly defended walled town in the south of Hunan Province. They seized food, clothing, money, and weapons, rested and regrouped, and absorbed many new followers.[20] The escape from Guangxi and the capture of Yong'an enabled the Taiping to use waterways to thrust into China's core regions.

As the Chinese saying goes, they did so with the force of splitting bamboo. In November 1852, a surprise assault delivered Yuezhou on the Yangzi River into their hands. Moving down the Yangzi on captured junks, they took Wuhan, the central Chinese metropolis, a month later. After some discussion about whether to strike north toward Beijing, they decided to follow the Yangzi east in order to avoid Qing armies that shielded the approaches to Beijing. In March 1853, the Taiping were in possession of Nanjing, which they made their capital after slaughtering the Manchu garrison. They also destroyed its magnificent Porcelain Pagoda.

The Qing nevertheless overcame the challenge of the Taiping, and other simultaneous rebellions in the north, but only barely. They had to decentralize power, give up the Manchu monopoly on armed force, empower Han local elites, and even turn to foreign assistance. A Confucian revival movement had spread through the central China provinces in the decades before the outbreak of the rebellion. Its leaders reinvented Confucianism as a puritan but pragmatic ideology, which required active engagement with the problems of the age. These reformers took the lead in countering the Taiping in central

20 Spence, *God's Chinese Son*, 139.

China. They mobilized local elites to recruit militia, levied taxes to finance them, and organized local society. The armies drawn from these militias were outside the Qing's regular military system and therefore a potential challenge to it. They fought the Taiping many years for control of provinces in central China. As rice-basket areas that straddled the main communication routes, they were strategically important. The turning point came only in 1861, when Zeng Guofan seized the city of Anqing in Anhui Province, 250 kilometers west of Nanjing on the Yangzi River, after a year-long siege.

The Taiping were at times their own worst enemy. Their iconoclasm and promises of land redistribution made enemies of the local elites. They introduced the solar calendar, proscribed footbinding and concubinage, banned opium smoking and alcohol consumption, and sacked Confucian temples, schools, libraries, and ancestral shrines. A spectacular outbreak of infighting among the leadership cost the Taiping dearly. In 1856, Hong turned on Yang Xiuqing, the Taiping's commander-in-chief, who, as a kind of prime minister, had worked to dampen the harshness of Hong's rule and forge an accommodation with Confucianism. After suffering repeated humiliation from Yang, Hong ordered one of his other commanders, Wei Changhui, to abort a campaign in Jiangxi Province and come to Nanjing. Here he massacred Yang and thousands of his followers. Deeply angered, General Shi Dakai, a capable and popular Taiping commander, marched to Nanjing with a hundred thousand troops to demand Wei's head. Hong delivered it, but Shi then abandoned the Taiping and left for Sichuan Province. While Hong, increasingly paranoid, turned to kinsmen to staff the upper ranks of his regime, Taiping fortunes revived after 1858 as the Arrow War took its toll on the Qing and a new cohort of capable and adventurous generals restored Taiping military morale.

The Taiping Rebellion shattered the reputation of the Qing's elite regular forces, the Banners, as well as its auxiliary force, the Green Standard, which had functioned like a gendarmerie. These forces had been unable to prevent the Taiping from marching into China's heartland, although they were not irrelevant. Qing forces under the Mongol General Senggelinqin defeated the northern expedition that the Taiping launched in May 1853. While the Taiping marched just south of Beijing, Senggelinqin defeated them during the harsh northern winter, for which the Taiping were not prepared. Banner armies also maintained two large field forces to the north and east of Nanjing, to prevent the Taiping from reaching the coast. But when Taiping fortunes revived after 1858, these forces were defeated. By then the Banners and the Green Standard were widely criticized, among others by the Confucian elites who led the regional armies in central China, for being ineffectual, undisciplined, and corrupt.

At the beginning of the rebellion, Britain and France had adopted a policy of neutrality. Frustrated by the Qing's failure to meet its obligations under the 1842 Treaty of Nanjing and no longer occupied elsewhere, the two countries even went to war with the Qing in 1858 – the Arrow War – seeking better trade conditions, the opening of more ports, and the right of their diplomats to reside in Beijing. After a humiliating defeat in 1859, when a British force was defeated at Tianjin, the British sent an armada of 41 warships, 143 troop ships, and a force of 10,000 men to Beijing in 1860, accompanied by 60 French naval vessels and 6,500 troops. They smashed their way into Beijing and burned the Summer Palace, forcing the Xianfeng Emperor to flee the city. A treaty, negotiated earlier, was ratified, opening the Yangzi River to foreign trade, increasing the number of Treaty Ports, and permitting foreigners to travel throughout China to trade and evangelize.

After these events, the British and the French changed their policy and began to support the Qing in its war against the Taiping. Reports about Taiping ruthlessness had diminished earlier enthusiasm for the movement's Christianity. Western missionaries felt insulted when the second son of God lectured them in Nanjing. The Taiping too had begun to campaign in coastal areas, and thus directly threatened foreign interests. Having what they wanted from the Qing, Britain, France, and the United States supported it much as they did the Ottoman Empire. They helped impose an embargo on the smuggling of arms to the Taiping and forbade their citizens from joining them as mercenaries. A project was begun to deliver to China a steam navy to secure the Yangzi River and the coast, although this project proved stillborn. They agreed to the formation of a mixed Chinese and foreign army in the lower Yangzi region. It was armed with Prussian and British cannon and rifles, while its gunboats proved their worth in the waterlogged terrain of the area. The Taiping were never able to take Shanghai, while the Ever Victorious Army assisted in the recovery of Ningbo (whose Manchu garrison had committed mass suicide after a British attack during the Arrow War) and Suzhou.

By relying on regional forces such as that of Zeng Guofan, by using regular forces to keep the Taiping out of north China, and by keeping the Taiping out of coastal China partly by relying on a foreign force, the Qing gradually hemmed them in at Nanjing. By the summer of 1864, Zeng Guoquan, the brother of Zeng Guofan, had encircled Nanjing and began a leisurely siege. The Taiping were gradually starved to death. When Zeng entered the city, it was flattened to erase all vestiges of a movement that had nearly brought down the dynasty.

Unlike the American Civil War, the Taiping Rebellion undermined the central government's authority. Powerful regional leaders involved themselves in commercial, political, diplomatic, and financial affairs. They supported, or at least tolerated, the dynasty, but the Qing could neither afford to alienate them nor allow them to grow too strong. They, rather than the Qing, led a vigorous self-strengthening movement, but whenever their projects made them too powerful, the Qing curtailed them, hampering not just the industrialization of the country but also the construction of a modern army. The Qing had great trouble developing an adequate revenue stream, relying on duties levied on foreign trade rather than on taxes on landholding, as in the past, which changed its relationship with its subjects. An added problem was racial identity. The Qing became increasingly regarded as an alien Manchu dynasty. The Arrow War had shown that the Qing could not resist a foreign attack even on its capital. Having to recognize foreigners as equals dented its claims to universal kingship. This humiliation and its military defeats damaged its reputation with its neighbors, including Japan, which later sought to take over its position in Asia.

Occurring just after the fall of Sebastopol and the British adoption of a more forward policy toward China, the Indian Rebellion came as a great shock to the British. Although in the end it was suppressed with ease, initially there were fears that Britain might be driven from India. The rebellion had lasting consequences. As the nation-state in Europe became more bureaucratic and oriented toward competence and efficiency, so did the administration of empire. London took over the running of the Raj from the East India Company. The Indian Civil Service became a bureaucracy staffed by officers who were forbidden to engage in commercial pursuits. These officials saw themselves as serving a general public good. At times they acted in opposition to private commercial interests as well as to evangelizing missionaries, regarding the rapaciousness of businessmen and the insensitivity of missionaries to Indian religious traditions as causes of the rebellion. This bureaucratization of empire occurred elsewhere too. In China, Treaty Ports were managed by the consular service and the Maritime Customs Service, which was under Chinese sovereignty but staffed at its higher levels by British subjects.

The rebellion also helped make the Raj a concern of the larger British public.[21] The Indian Rebellion led to lurid tales in the British mass media.

21 Niall Ferguson, *Empire: How Britain Made the Modern World* (London, 2001), 150.

Incandescent evangelicals saw the uprising not as evidence that the Christianization of India was foolhardy, but as a sign that they had to work even harder. *The Times* clamoured for vengeance as reports of atrocities proliferated, and Queen Victoria developed a commitment to the British Empire which earlier she had lacked. In this light, colonial rule was not an act of violation and spoliation, but a noble, if sometimes unpleasant, duty. "You cannot have omelettes without breaking eggs; you cannot destroy the practices of barbarism, of slavery, of superstition . . . without the use of force," stated Joseph Chamberlain.[22]

There also emerged a sharp separation between the colonizer and the colonized. If in the first half of the nineteenth century, interracial marriages had been common, they became rare at least among those who regarded themselves as part of respectable society. This development was tied up with the entrenchment of racialist attitudes, but it also stemmed from the belief that the rebellion had resulted from an ever present possibility of native revenge. This conviction surfaced during subsequent outbreaks of violence, for instance during the Boxer Rebellion in China.

The rebellion began in 1857 when sepoys – soldiers in the Indian Army who were drawn from Indian warrior castes – turned on their British commanding officers. The spark that ignited the violence was a rumor that paper cartridges for new muzzle-loading Enfield rifles had been greased with pork or cow fat. Both Muslims and Hindus would be defiled, as the end of these cartridges had to be bitten off before the gunpowder could be poured into the barrel.

The cartridge issue was a symbol of deeper grievances. Sepoys were frustrated by the lack of promotion opportunities, poor housing, uncomfortable uniforms, and declining status. The distance between them and their British officers had begun to widen during the preceding decades. Beyond the Indian Army, the overbearing behavior of evangelical missionaries and modernizing East India Company officials, who were impatient with Indian traditions and politics, had sown widespread resentment. Using the "doctrine of lapse," which held that the territory of a ruler could be taken over by the East India Company if he had no direct heir, the British had seized much new territory.[23] These areas included the vast state of Awadh, an epicenter of the rebellion, which had been incorporated only a year before. Reallocation of land to peasant farmers had disgruntled large landholders, while British economic penetration had harmed Indian merchants and artisans. Once the

22 Quoted in ibid., 221.

23 Saul David, *The Indian Mutiny: 1857* (London, 2003), 19–33.

rebellion broke out, it took hold quickly among the many groups with grievances in Indian society, especially in the north.

The rebellion began at Meerut near Delhi on May 9, when soldiers turned on their British officers after they had jailed some eighty men of the Bengal Light Infantry for refusing to use the cartridges. After breaking the jail open, the rebels left Meerut for Delhi, which was lightly defended but did have a big arsenal. Delhi too housed Bahadur Shah Zafar, the last Mogul king, who lived in the Red Fort. The city was quickly conquered, after which Bahadur, the nature of whose involvement remains in dispute, was prevailed upon to lend his authority to the uprising and to be proclaimed Emperor of India.[24] While the rebellion was never a true national uprising against the British – a large number of Indian soldiers fought on the British side and much of the southern part of the continent was not involved – Bahadur nonetheless gave the Indian Rebellion a powerful rallying point.

In Awadh, the Siege of Lucknow began on May 30. As soon as he heard news of the Meerut uprising, Henry Lawrence, the chief commissioner of Awadh, moved all British into the sixty-acre Residency Compound. Lawrence was in a weak position with only a thousand British soldiers in dispersed locations around Lucknow to defend against twenty times that number. He had trenches dug around the compound in an octagonal shape, and moved the arsenal and local cannon into its confines.

Events at Kanpur, the capital of Awadh and home of one of the largest British communities in India, became etched in the British colonial mind. General Wheeler, the commanding officer of the Kanpur Division, had been in India since 1805. He was fluent in the vernacular, married to a high-caste Indian woman, and had good relations in Indian society, including with Nana Sahib, the adopted heir of the disposed Baji Rao II. Wheeler had made few preparations for hostilities, trusting in the respect he enjoyed among his men and in his connections with Nana Sahib. As unrest spread, he entrenched two barracks in the military compound and moved British women and children there while calling for reinforcements.

Following several weeks of tension, the Kanpur Indian troops mutinied and began a siege of Wheeler's compound. Negotiations between Nana Sahib and Wheeler led after three weeks to an offer of safe passage. Either on purpose or as the result of confusion, many evacuees were killed as they boarded the boats that were to take them away.[25] Two hundred British women survivors

24 Ibid., 78–94.
25 Ibid., 52–55.

were later murdered in the Bibighar, the Ladies' Home, when a British relief force approached the city. Gory reports in the British press unleashed calls for revenge, which were satiated in a reign of terror.

While the British were initially overstretched – additional uprisings took place at Benares, Allahabad, Jhansi, Gwalior, and other places – they recovered quickly. Delhi was back in British hands by September 1857, after reinforcements and artillery had been brought in. The British were weakest at Lucknow, but here too they held out. On September 25, a first relief force fought through the Indian siege lines to the Residency Compound, followed by a second in November. By late autumn 1857, it was clear that the British would not be driven from India. With the fall of Gwalior on June 20, 1858 and the signing of a peace treaty in July, the rebellion came to an end.

By 1870, the mid-century wars had shown that industrialization, the strengthening of the nation-state, and patriotism were changing warfare. Yet, with many Jominian axioms proved wrong, how best to fight wars in the new age was less clear, especially because combat had become more costly in both men and treasure. The 1870–71 Franco-Prussian War had a huge impact, because the lesson many chose to draw was that a quick victory on the battlefield remained possible. The model of the modern Prussian army, recruited from the entire population, linked by railway to the home front, guided by a general staff, and following a battlefield doctrine of using the advantages of the defensive for offensive purposes, became the new norm, widely imitated in Europe and elsewhere.[26]

Prussia had stayed out of the military conflicts of the mid nineteenth century until the late 1860s. Its ignominious defeat by Napoleon in the 1806 Battle of Jena and its vulnerable position as a middle-ranking country with a small population surrounded by larger and stronger states ensured that military reformers, who were determined to overcome entrenched interests, could implement their plans. First under Gerhard von Scharnhorst and then under Helmuth von Moltke, the Prussian military was thoroughly reformed. Neither military conservatism nor rural romanticism nor aristocratic privilege was allowed to stand in the way of military efficiency.

An outstanding capacity for planning, the ability to mobilize large numbers of reservists quickly, the effective use of railways, and the adoption of new weapons, such as Krupp steel cannon and the Dreyse needle gun, laid the

26 David Ralston, *Importing the European Army: The Introduction of Military Techniques and Institutions into the Extra-European World, 1600–1914* (Chicago and London, 1990).

groundwork for Prussia's stunning victories. Prussia's general staff, which had been formally established in 1814 by Scharnhorst, developed from a small unit in the War Ministry into a key institution that reported to the king. It concerned itself with gathering intelligence, studying strategy and tactics, and planning operations. Its officers were selected on the basis of merit and intelligence rather than patronage. Besides detailed operational planning and threat assessments, the general staff promoted expertise and professionalism more generally, for instance in map-making and terrain surveying, thus marking a break with military traditions that had privileged intuition, genius, improvisation, and élan.[27] The staff corps formed a single nervous system of officers who thought and acted alike throughout the army. A culture of reflection was stimulated by staff rides, maneuvers, and war gaming, as well as in debate and discussion in periodicals that were read in military circles.[28]

Prussia's recruitment system was essential to its success. With the strength of the army dependent to a degree on how many men could be put into the field with a rifle in their hands, and with the country's population smaller than its potential enemies', Prussia implemented universal military service. The period of active service, to which all Prussian men were liable, was three years, after which recruits served in the first reserve for five years and then entered the second reserve.[29] This arrangement gave Prussia an affordable standing army that could be rapidly enlarged for combat. In this way Prussia institutionalized the *levée en masse*, except that its forces were well trained and socialized into the state.

Moltke adopted an "offensive defensive" operational doctrine. Prussian forces aimed to concentrate rapidly at the front. They then assumed a defensive stance, making using of battlefield cover and entrenchment, as well as the much greater firepower available to them, to pin down the enemy. They deployed artillery at the front rather than at the rear, as had been standard during Napoleonic times. Their armies then conducted flanking movements to attack the enemy from the rear or the side. Prussian forces spurned frontal assaults and sieges; breaking the will of the enemy to fight was the aim.[30]

The Prussian victory at Sedan on September 1, 1870 was one of the most stunning of all time. It followed earlier successes, first against Denmark in 1864, when Prussian military successes led to Denmark's cession of Schleswig and Holstein to Prussia, and the 1866 war with Austria, which loosened the

27 Dennis Showalter, *The Wars of German Unification* (London, 2004), 23.
28 Ibid., 22–27.
29 Ibid., 75–87.
30 Ibid., 209.

latter's grip on south German states. The Prussian victory over France, however, made the world take note. Backed by the northern German states, as well as Baden, Bavaria, and Württemberg, Prussia went to war to unify Germany. War broke out on July 19, 1870. Napoleon III took personal command of the more than two hundred thousand soldiers in the Army of the Rhine, setting up his headquarters in the garrison city of Metz. Putting his faith in French élan and improvisation, he opted for a rapid march into the Bavarian Palatinate, in the hope that he would be joined by Austria and south German states hostile to Prussian expansionism.

The Prussians completed their concentration of three armies with three hundred thousand men more quickly and further forward than the French had believed possible. The battle of Gravelotte, not far from Metz, on August 18 proved a turning point. The French armies had by then begun to suffer the consequences of a poor logistical and supply system. Moltke threw 180,000 men and more than 700 cannon into the battle. Initially the French held their ground, in part because in the chassepot they had the better infantry weapon. However, the Krupp steel breech-loading artillery gradually established control over the battlefield. By the end of the day the battle turned in favor of the Prussians.

Having lost heart, the French retreated the next day to Metz, where the Prussians encircled them. Napoleon, fighting for the survival of his reign, formed a new army to attack the Prussians and relieve Metz. However, Moltke left the First and Second German Armies at Metz, and detached three corps from them to form the Army of the Meuse. These forces together with the Third German Army caught Napoleon in a pincer grip. Following a first engagement, Napoleon retreated to Sedan, where Moltke encircled him on September 1. After several desperate attempts to break out and with the Krupp guns keeping up a murderous barrage, Napoleon III surrendered on September 2 after losing seventeen thousand men.

Bismarck's political leadership was instrumental in securing durable political results. For Moltke, the army had to serve the interest of the state, and he was willing to subordinate himself to Bismarck, albeit grudgingly. After Sedan, the Prussians did not pursue the French armies that remained in the field but marched on Paris. A new government there had called all of France to arms, hoping for a repeat of the success of the *levée en masse* during the revolutionary wars. On Bismarck's orders, Prussian guns bombarded the city, unnerving the new government. Unsure of the support of the city's population or the loyalty of the armies in the rest of France, the French government chose to come to terms with the Prussians, in order to gain

2. Prussian army encampment during the Siege of Metz

international recognition and improve its legitimacy at home. The great gain for Prussia was the acceptance by the other German states of a unified Germany under the Prussian king. Wilhelm was crowned German emperor in Paris. The only territorial concession that Bismarck demanded from France was Alsace-Lorraine. Like the American Civil War, the Franco-Prussian War underscored the importance of effective political leadership.

The Franco-Prussian War had profound consequences. The loose German Confederation dominated by Austria was replaced by a unified Germany under Prussian leadership. Austria lost its position in northern Italy, where a reinvigorated Italian nationalism culminated in unification under King Victor Emmanuel II. The French lost their preeminent position in Europe and Napoleon III was deposed. The war ended the Congress of Europe, which had formed after the Napoleonic wars and preserved European peace through diplomacy. This was a fateful development.

One hoary belief among military historians has been that the middle decades of the nineteenth century set into motion processes that culminated in the total warfare of the twentieth century. The rifle, steel artillery, the armored naval vessel, trench warfare, and the mass national army admittedly made their appearance in these years. Especially in Europe and the USA, states gained greater authority and social cohesion, making mass mobilization socially and politically feasible. Technologically, a step change occurred not just in weaponry but also communication. The telegraph, the railroad, and the steamship slashed transport times and costs, and they enabled states in Europe and North America to deploy resources and manpower from areas around the globe and concentrate them at real or perceived points of danger, as happened during the Indian Rebellion and the Arrow War. The undermining of the Congress of Europe, the hardening of nationalisms, and the rise of Social Darwinism limited possibilities for collective responsibility and compromise in resolving international conflict.[31] Prussia's unification of Germany suggested that war could pay, while Bismarck's success suggested the shrewd poker player, who used armies and nations as his cards. One gamble, however, could spell disaster for all.

Confronted with the challenge of finding the origins of the wars that inflicted so much damage in Europe in the twentieth century, it is understandable that military historians turned their eyes toward these developments, often assigning them an aura of inevitability. Yet there were counter-currents. As Akira Iriye has pointed out, the mid-century wars also fuelled the "internationalist imagination."[32] The Red Cross, the world's first non-governmental organization (NGO), was established in response to press reports about the terrible conditions of soldiers on the Crimean front and the horrendous wounds they suffered in battle. Following the Arrow War in China, the British did not simply seize territory, as they had done a century earlier in India, but insisted on negotiating binding international treaties with the Qing, to help China, as they saw it, become a modern state, a part of an international community that behaved in accordance with approved standards. International law became established as a separate field of study. International conferences reached agreements on common standards for measurements and weights, weather reporting, mapping, and buoyage.

With a broader perspective, attuned to global connections and ramifications, recent scholarship has emphasized not the trajectory to total war in Europe, but the effects of the mid-century upheavals elsewhere.[33] The Manchu hierarchy did not recover from the Taiping Rebellion and increasingly became seen as an alien ruling group that had enfeebled China. In India, the old ruling families were pensioned off, given grand British titles, such as

31 Robert Binkley, *Realism and Nationalism, 1852–1871* (New York, 1935).
32 Akire Iriye, *Cultural Internationalism and World Order* (Baltimore, 1997).
33 Bayly, *Birth of the Modern World*, 148–55.

"Choicest Son of the British Government," while their public roles were reduced to ceremonial functions. The Ottoman Empire, already seen as the "sick man of Europe," was kept in place. But the founding of the Ottoman Bank in 1856 to pay for debts incurred during the Crimean War further limited its independence, as the bank depended not on domestic revenue but on foreign, especially British and French lending. The bank soon took control of the Ottoman state budget. Centrifugal forces were strengthened in both the Qing and Ottoman empires. In both internal challengers emerged, especially in peripheral areas that challenged the dominance of the center, while both also lost areas to foreign occupation.

Some of the mid-century shocks reverberated around the world, including the end to monopolies and privilege dependent on status.[34] In the United States, the Southern plantation aristocracy, which had been based on slavery, lost power. In the Ottoman Empire, Christian populations were empowered, as they could rely on foreign backing and exploit their exemption from local taxation. In China, Han elites became more powerful, while the position of the Manchus declined. Many Manchus became indebted to wealthy Han. In India and China, the East India Company and the Cohong monopolies were disbanded, while the old British trading houses in Canton, which had relied on family capital, were replaced by gentlemanly capitalists operating across China. High-value commodities, such as opium and tea, became less important in the trade of countries, while the "muck and truck" trade in a variety of primary and secondary products took off. Around the world, port cities emerged as vibrant meeting points for people from different classes and ethnicities. Shanghai, Beirut, Alexandria, Trieste, Penang, Capetown, and San Francisco were cases in point.

The military success of the west gave rise to self-strengthening movements in many areas, including Japan, China, Egypt, Turkey, and Ethiopia, which sought to import the European army,[35] build an industrial base for it, and reform their political structures to create cohesive nations. Only the Ethiopians and especially the Japanese were successful, in the latter case with disastrous consequences for its neighbors and ultimately Japan itself. Elsewhere, these movements were hampered by low tariffs imposed by Britain under the dogma of free trade and the privileges enjoyed by foreigners in Treaty Ports. Another problem, particularly in China, was that self-strengthening movements were spearheaded by regional leaders. They were often capable

34 Ibid., 151–69.
35 Ralston, *Importing the European Army.*

and energetic, but their successes challenged the center. The Qing played these regional leaders off against one another and undermined them when they threatened to grow too powerful. Simple mismanagement, shortages of capital, and the high cost of borrowing were additional problems.[36] The lack of social cohesion, political legitimacy, and strong governance doomed most self-strengthening movements, triggering responses that added to the accumulating instabilities of the world at the turn of the century.

36 There is no general history of self-strengthening movements. But see Ralston, *Importing the European Army*; Khaled Fami, *All the Pasha's Men: Mehmed Ali, His Army, and the Making of Modern Egypt* (Cambridge, 1997); Marius Jansen, "The Meiji Restoration," in Jansen, ed., *The Cambridge History of Japan*, Vol. V: *The Nineteenth Century* (New York, 1989), 308–66; Kuo Ting-yee, "Self-Strengthening: The Pursuit of Western Technology," in John Fairbank, ed, *The Cambridge History of China*, Vol. X: *Late Ch'ing*, Part I (Cambridge, 1978), 491–542.

2

War, technology, and industrial change, 1850–1914

GEOFFREY WAWRO

F. Scott Fitzgerald's Dick Diver, a self-appointed historian, captured the great changes in warfare before 1914. A "beautiful lovely safe world blew itself up with a great gust of high explosive love," Diver tells a party of American tourists, who were poking around the old trenches on the Somme. By "love," he meant the obsessive, competitive way in which the great powers had built vast armies, fleets, infrastructure, and arsenals that ensured their mutual destruction in a conflict that Friedrich Engels had predicted (in 1887) would "telescope all of the devastation of the Thirty Years War into three or four years" and gnaw Europe bare "in a way that a swarm of locusts never could."[1] Aware of the awful risks, European militaries plunged ahead in a general lust for armaments and military organization.

Napoleon Bonaparte had launched warfare into the modern age, and Helmuth von Moltke drove it into the industrial age. Napoleon and his revolutionary colleagues had discovered the merits of general staff work, march tables, army divisions, *ordre mixte* (alternating shock and fire tactics), and mobile field artillery. Every major army had adopted those Napoleonic "lessons" by the mid nineteenth century, and most assumed that, in so doing, they had done enough. Moltke was not so complacent. Named chief of the Prussian general staff in 1857, he gaped at Prussia's vulnerabilities. Prussia was a flat, sandy kingdom with growing industries, and surprising quantities of coal, but no natural frontiers. The Rhineland territories that Prussia had acquired in 1815 bordered France but were divided from Brandenburg-Prussia by hostile or unhelpful states like Hanover and Hesse. The Austrian Empire overshadowed (and coveted) Prussian Silesia. Russia flanked Prussia's eastern heartland from its outposts in Poland and the Baltic. Whereas some of Moltke's colleagues recommended a pacific foreign policy and continued subordination to Austria and Russia, Moltke, supported by Prussian Minister-President Otto von Bismarck, carried out a

1 H. P. Willmott, *When Men Lost Faith in Reason: Reflections on War and Society in the Twentieth Century* (Westport, CT, 2002), 46–47.

military-technological revolution designed not only to solidify Prussia's defenses, but also to give Prussia the weapons to beat any great power in Europe.

Whereas Russia, Austria, and France were still planning to mobilize and deploy slowly behind a screen of cavalry and frontier fortresses before marching into battle, Moltke rethought the entire question. Prussia, he reasoned, could win only if it mobilized and deployed faster, carried the war into enemy territory, and forced a rapid defeat and armistice on its opponent. To fashion this capability, Moltke decommissioned fortresses and directed the savings into railways and telegraphs. Most European railways were private concerns, but Moltke created a railway bureau in the general staff and made plans to bring the German companies under Prussian army control if war came. Battalions, squadrons, and batteries were assigned specific trains, and arrangements were made for civilian rolling stock to transport horses, field guns, and soldiers. Moltke, an imposing, bookish man, whose only line experience had been in command of a battalion, used the telegraph to direct armies. This practice created tensions. Field generals resented Moltke's "meddling" from behind the lines (even from Berlin), but support from King Wilhelm I gave him the authority to wrestle the most obstreperous officers into line.

Prussia could win only if it could match or exceed the manpower of its rivals. Moltke vastly expanded the Prussian army by general conscription. Other armies relied on limited conscription with the right of substitution (which wealthy peasants and educated bourgeois exploited), voluntary enlistments – "serving for the soup," as they said in France – or press gangs. Moltke conscripted every able-bodied twenty-year-old Prussian male, a practice that yielded a bigger and, thanks to the state's public school system, a more intelligent army than Prussia's rivals could raise. This manpower, trained for three years, was then released into the active reserves for five years and into the *Landwehr* (national guard) for five more. These institutions gave Prussia an expandable army, which could be stretched on short notice from its peacetime strength of 300,000 to 1.2 million in wartime. These numbers were revolutionary. In 1870 France confronted the Prussians with 400,000 long-term veterans, who seemed more than adequate against Prussia's 300,000 regulars, but were utterly inadequate against Prussia's total mobilized strength of over a million. When a French general boasted about the long experience of France's "old grumblers" (*grognards*), a Prussian general retorted: "You may win in the morning, but by the evening we will have conquered you with our reserves."[2]

2 Geoffrey Wawro, *The Franco-Prussian War: The German Conquest of France in 1870–71* (Cambridge, 2003), 41–42.

Prussia also created permanent corps districts. These provided a home base for the constituent regiments of each of Prussia's seventeen army corps, which could be prepared here for fast mobilization. This system contrasted with a generally chaotic state of affairs elsewhere in Europe, where army units were scattered geographically to prevent revolts or secessionism – Bretons to Algeria, Neapolitans to Milan, Croats to Vienna. The French army under Napoleon III prided itself on its *non-endivisionnement* (non-divisioning), which the French considered an essential ingredient in imbuing provincial lads with a sense of French national greatness, as it rotated them back and forth across the hexagon.[3] Such "extraterritorial" armies had domestic-political uses as a substitute for police forces that were small or nonexistent, but they entailed complex mobilizations (units had to be found, returned to their garrisons, and equipped for battle) and slow deployments. Scattered battalions had to be convened into regiments, then fitted into brigades, divisions, and corps, and finally marched to the point of attack.

The Prussians were also early to adopt advanced military technology. To facilitate mobilization and logistics, they made full use of railroads and telegraphs. In battle, they were the first European army to adopt the breech-loading rifle, as well as the breech-loading, rifled Krupp cannon.[4] Noisy debates swirled around both of these procurement decisions. The American experience with the breech-loading rifle had been inconclusive during the civil war. Lever-action and repeating rifles had generated impressive rates of fire, but they had often led to the squandering of ammunition, as excited troops fired too fast and inaccurately. Robert E. Lee argued in favor of muzzle-loaders, which made it easier for officers to direct volley fire. Undeterred, Moltke insisted that Prussian troops be trained to conserve their ammunition and fire only at effective ranges. He spent heavily in peacetime on target practice (budgeting more than rival armies) and trained conscripts about what to expect in the heat of combat.[5]

Moltke's reforms saved several steps and stole marches on Prussia's adversaries. His battalions entrained immediately for the front. He merged

3 Ibid., 48.

4 Dennis E. Showalter, *Railroads and Rifles: Soldiers, Technology and the Unification of Germany* (Hamden, CT, 1975), 38–46.

5 Hew Strachan, *European Armies and the Conduct of War* (London, 1983), 112. Jay Luvaas, *The Military Legacy of the Civil War: The European Inheritance* (Chicago, 1959), 42, 173; Geoffrey Wawro, *The Austro-Prusssian War: Austria's War with Prussia and Italy in 1866* (Cambridge and New York, 1996), 13–25; Geoffrey Wawro, "An 'Army of Pigs': The Technical, Social and Political Bases of Austrian Shock Tactics, 1859–1866," *Journal of Military History* 59 (1995): 407–34.

mobilization and deployment, as troops filed onto trains in their home districts and deployed to the frontiers, where corps and armies were ready for combat. Faster, forward-leaning deployments led to an overhaul of operations. Moltke's signal innovation was to attack operationally and defend tactically. In other words, he exploited the superior speed of Prussia's armies to invade enemy territory, and then briefly staked out defensive positions, which maximized the impact of Prussia's rifles and field artillery. Slow-moving adversaries arrived late on foot and blundered into Prussian positions. Gutted by aimed defensive fire, they fell back, only to be destroyed by the enveloping wings of Moltke's counterattacking forces.

In the Austro-Prussian War of 1866, Moltke deployed four armies, sent three of them into the Austrian province of Bohemia, and the fourth to crush a largely Bavarian "federal army," which had been raised to block Prussia's attempt to consolidate the thirty-six-state German Confederation. In this campaign, Moltke took tremendous risks. His armies were individually too weak to resist the massed Austrian army, and they passed into Austria through steep, forested mountain passes, which magnified the isolation and vulnerability of the Prussian units. Moving quickly to narrow the gaps among his scattered armies, Moltke was forced to trim supplies in favor of combat units and ammunition, so his armies often went hungry and slept in the open, which sapped morale and increased the "sick ratio." Moltke's "West Army" in Germany was smaller than the combined forces it faced, but here, as in Bohemia, Moltke rightly calculated that his enemies would move too slowly to combine against him. In 1866, the Prussians routed the Austrians at Königgrätz and beat the German contingents too. Moltke famously said that "no plan of battle survives the first collison with the main enemy body," and these campaigns were no exception.[6] But even when Prussian arrangements faltered and Moltke's armies found themselves hard-pressed, they fought their way out of danger using quick-firing rifles and swarming tactics. The Austrians deployed in battalion columns, which were flanked and shredded by Prussian units that could fire four times as quickly as the Austrians (or Bavarians).

The military revolution engineered by Moltke in 1866 was sensational. Every army in the world took notice, and most tried to imitate it. The war between France and the German states four years later was closely studied

6 Gunther E. Rothenberg, "Moltke, Schlieffen and the Doctrine of Strategic Envelopment," in Peter Paret, ed., *Makers of Modern Strategy: From Machiavelli to the Nuclear Age* (Princeton, 1986), 299–300.

down to 1914 precisely because it matched Europe's two great armies at a time when both were implementing the Prussian military revolution. France scrambled to retool and reorganize after 1866. The army had rested on its laurels since 1859, when it defeated Austria in Italy with the same organization and tactics that the Austrians thereupon adopted from the French and employed so disastrously against Prussia in 1866.

Revered for its military prowess since the eighteenth century, France failed to grasp and implement the Prussian reforms. French military culture resisted the Prussian changes. Moltke was a Clausewitzian in his assumption that "fog and friction" constituted the environment of war and that army leadership, organization, and tactics must always be nimble and inspired. Although he never spoke of *Auftragstaktik* – mission tactics – they represented his principle. Officers were expected to sniff out opportunity, "march to the guns," fight ferociously, and keep attacking under all circumstances to keep closing on a less dynamic enemy.

The planners who shaped French procurement and tactics after 1866 misunderstood the reasons for Prussia's success. French commanders assumed that with the best breech-loading rifle in Europe – the chassepot, which was superior to Prussia's Dreyse "needle rifle" – they could remain on the defensive and force the Prussians to attack. The chassepot had an effective range of 1,000 yards, the Dreyse 400. French planners took for granted that they could defeat the Prussians at long range. They assumed that they could frustrate Moltke's ideas of attack and tactical defense by refusing infantry attacks in the Austrian style. Furthermore, they assumed that their men enlisted for long service would perform better than Prussia's conscripts ("lawyers and oculists," as one French general snorted).[7] The French made no allowance for the Prussian army's tactical dynamism. While the French refused to move out of excellent positions (as at Spicheren and Froeschwiller) or seemingly excellent positions (as at Sedan), the Prussians exploited their own superior numbers to outflank or obliterate them with artillery. The "lessons learned" by the French in 1866 did not include flexibility. French officers were forbidden to leave the safety of their positions to attack. Each French brigade was equipped with a thousand shovels and axes, so troops could scoop out rifle pits and chop up *abatis*. So the Prussians retained the initiative, and Moltke, who had regarded war with France as inevitable after 1866, was prepared to seize it. "The secret of our success is in our legs," he

7 Michael Howard, *The Franco-Prussian War: The German Invasion of France, 1870–1871* (London, 1961), 29.

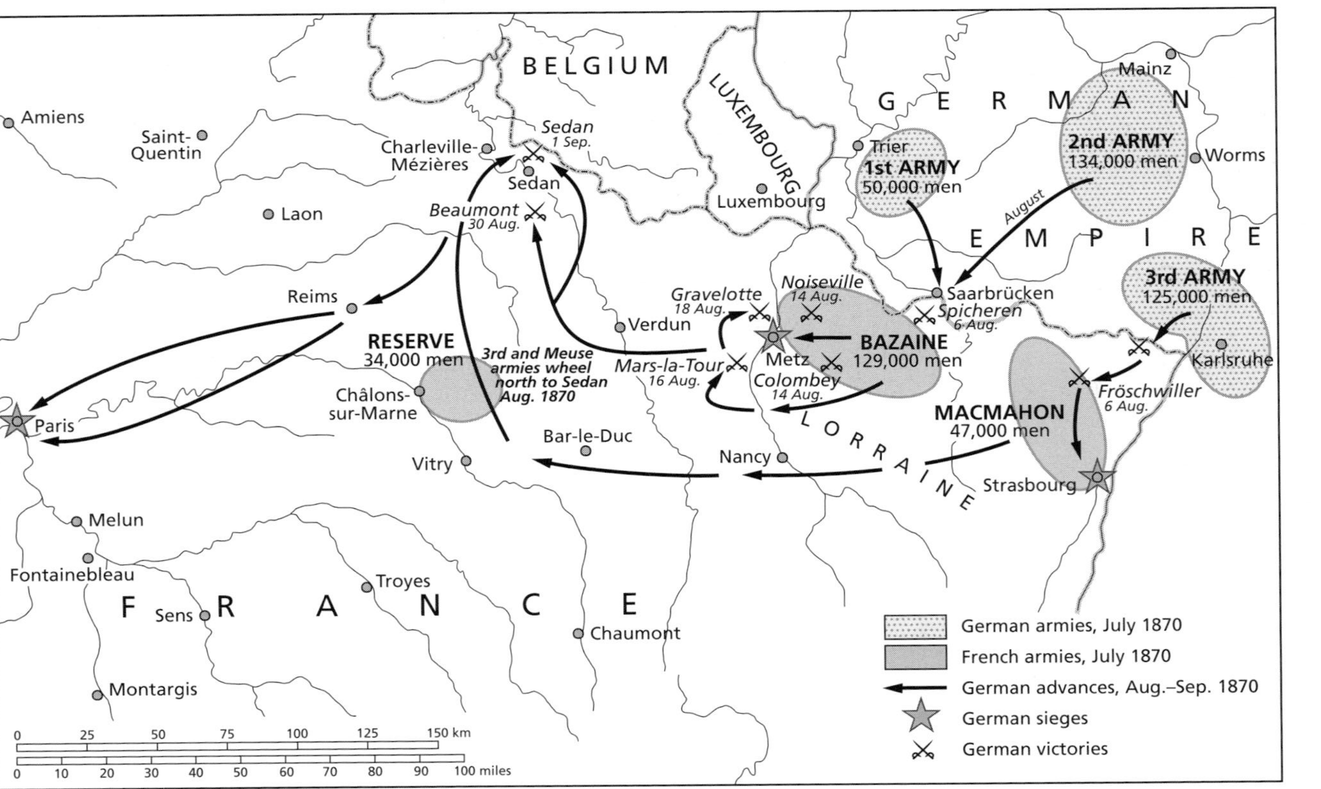

MAP 4. Franco-Prussian War, 1870–1871

observed after Prussian fall maneuvers in 1869. "Victory derives from marching and maneuvering."[8]

As the number of troops available to Prussia rose after 1866, the French needed to develop a reserve and national guard system. Napoleon III's war ministers tried after 1866 to introduce a *garde mobile* that would mirror the *Landwehr*, but the *garde mobile* was opposed and underfunded by the liberal *Corps Législatif*, which feared militarism and refused to consign more young Frenchmen to the "corrupting life of the barracks." War Minister Adolphe Niel's Military Law of 1868 called for the extension of French military service to nine years (five in active duty and four in the reserve) and the creation of 400,000 *gardes mobiles*, but the Legislative Body cut the guard's funding, so only 90,000 lightly trained *mobiles* were on the books in 1870. French efforts to build out their railways also stalled. Key strategic tracks to Verdun and Metz were never completed, and a northern line through Sedan remained single-tracked. Niel, who insisted on military control of France's railroads in wartime and speedy completion of the routes to Metz and Verdun, died in 1869; his successor returned the matter to the slow-moving Ministry of Public Works. France's efforts to mimic Moltke's general staff also failed. Staff officers in France were promoted by seniority, not merit, and showed little brilliance. The French general staff, one of its own members observed, had a reputation for "paper-pushing" and "bureaucratic servility." When assigned to regiments, French staff officers were reviled as *casanières* – shut-ins or convalescents – and given no authority to influence training or impose plans of campaign and battle.[9]

Technologically, the Franco-Prussian War was most notable for the massive deployment of Prussia's steel, breech-loading Krupp field artillery. Far superior to France's bronze, muzzle-loading four-pound guns, the Krupp six-pounders made the Franco-Prussian War altogether different from the Austro-Prussian War. They threw a heavier projectile further, faster, and more accurately than the French guns. The campaign in 1866 had been wrested from the Austrians by the Prussian infantryman, as Prussian artillery was outshot and outclassed. Prussian cannon fired on average only 50 rounds in 1866, Austrian cannon 118; much of the Prussian artillery consisted of smoothbores, while all the Austrian cannon were rifled. In 1870, Moltke turned the tables. Unable to procure both a new infantry rifle and field gun, he chose the

8 Dennis Showalter, *The Wars of German Unification* (London, 2004), 92–95, 100–05; Wawro, *The Franco-Prussian War*, 54–56.

9 Ibid., 46–49.

latter, and shaped every engagement with intensive accurate bombardments.[10] French after-action reports spoke of the ferocity of the Prussian artillery, which decided every battle. The Prussian guns were more modern and effective, and so were Prussian artillery tactics. Whereas French gunners remained in static lines behind their infantry, Prussian batteries pushed forward to shorter ranges and blasted the French out of cover. Sedan was the apotheosis of this tactic, as the French army was ringed by seven hundred Prussian guns and reduced to a panic-stricken rabble.

The mold for 1914 was cast in the wars of 1866 and 1870–71. Armies could no longer rely on the charisma of folk heroes like Blücher, Radetzky, Benedek, or Bazaine. They needed professionalism, rigor, organization, advanced technology, but also something of the Prussian "genius for war." The year 1870 showed that it was not enough to ape Prussian advances – to buy Prussian technology or imitate Prussian tactics; armies had to inculcate what the French called élan, the dashing spirit of war.

After 1870, every army – even the Prussians – wrestled with the dehumanizing implications of technological advance. If railroads, telegraphs, field guns, and rifles now determined success, what was the place of great captains? What incentives did soldiers have to attack and perform bravely on a fire-swept field?

The first theorist to grapple with these questions was the French Colonel Charles Ardant du Picq, who was struck down at Mars-la-Tour in 1870 by the very Prussian firepower that led him to postulate that troops must not defend – that they must, on the contrary, relentlessly attack in order to maintain morale in the face of fire. Ardant du Picq's posthumously published *Battle Studies* became the foundation of the Foch–Grandmaison school of *attaque à l'outrance* in 1914. The book, which was based on Ardant du Picq's interviews with French troops in 1868, concluded that the "moral action" of a briskly executed attack would overcome the "destructive action" of enemy rifle and shell fire. Troops became disheartened if forced to remain inert under artillery attack. It was better to unleash them, he wrote, even into deadly fire, than to watch them fall away as casualties or malingerers. Ferdinand Foch later took Ardant du Picq to heart. As he prepared French cadets for World War I, he wrote that the Prussians had won in 1870–71 because of "their pure morale and unswerving doctrine . . . their single-minded devotion to the capital idea: hit, and hit hard."[11]

10 Showalter, *Wars of German Unification*, 209–12.
11 Ferdinand Foch, *De la conduite de la guerre* (3rd edn., Paris, 1915), 181–82.

Foch's observation was fantasy, but it dovetailed with an outpouring of tactical doctrine from other army staffs and colleges, which appeared to defy developments elsewhere. The technological innovations of the 1860s became deadlier in the 1880s. Magazine rifles replaced the single-shot breech-loader. Small-caliber, smokeless metal cartridges replaced cardboard tubes of powder and ball. "Recoilless" artillery and high-explosive artillery shells made field guns more devastating to men and fortifications, and the machine gun replaced the *mitrailleuse* or revolver cannon, vastly increasing not only the firepower of the infantry, but also the dangers they faced. Hiram Maxim's machine gun, which was introduced in 1885, was water-cooled and fully automatic; it fired 600 rounds per minute, a devastating improvement over the 8 rounds per minute attained by Prussian infantrymen at the battle of Königgrätz in 1866. The new magazine rifles – the French Lebel, the Austrian Mannlicher, the German Mauser, the British Lee-Enfield – were loaded from vertically stacked clips of five cartridges, so infantrymen could fire fifteen or more aimed rounds per minute. The smaller bore, lighter, high-velocity metal cartridges were also easier to pack and carry. In the German wars of unification, soldiers had hesitated to lie prone on damp ground, lest they spoil their cartridges. The metal cartridges were waterproof, and troops could carry 200 of them, compared to about 60 in 1870. Moreover, smokeless propellant meant that troops could fire continuously without generating blinding clouds of gunsmoke and betraying their own positions to enemy infantry and artillery fire. The new infantry rifles were a force multiplier; French divisions, which had fired 40,000 rounds a minute in 1870, were firing 200,000 rounds a minute twenty years later. Recoilless artillery, which was mounted on a hydraulic slide that absorbed the recoil of the gun, so it did not jump out of position after every shot, brought much higher rates of aimed fire – fifteen to thirty rounds of shell or shrapnel per minute, compared to three or four rounds per minute in 1870.[12]

The implications of such a fire-swept field were lost on many generals, but other observers were more acute. In 1887 Friedrich Engels warned against a great European war, predicting "universal exhaustion" as the result – Europe reduced to "hunger, epidemics and general bankruptcy" by an attritional war fought by 10 million or more soldiers.[13] Jan de Bloch's *Future of War* in 1897 concluded that war had become all but impossible. Every army in Europe had instituted the draft. Despite the loss of 22 million emigrants at the end of the

12 Geoffrey Wawro, *Warfare and Society in Europe, 1792–1914* (London, 2000), 137–39, 152–54.
13 Willmott, *Faith in Reason*, 46–47.

nineteenth century, the population of Europe's seven leading states surged from 227 million in 1850 to 345 million in 1910. The rise of food imports from abroad, as well as the development of food processing and refrigeration, meant that peasants who would formerly have been needed to work the fields could now take up rifles instead.[14] Offensive operations appeared impossible against vast armies that were equipped with magazine rifles and machine guns and fired steel shells with high explosives. Fronts would be too long for Moltkean flanking operations, and the density of well-armed men per yard would make frontal attacks suicidal. Bloch did the math. Unless attacking armies could achieve a local advantage of eight-to-one (and resign themselves to massive casualties), he saw no prospect in offensive operations.[15]

Technological change married to the expansion of armies mandated rethinking the kind of industrial warfare that Moltke had perfected. The climactic battles of the American Civil War already prefigured trench warfare, as Confederates dug in before Richmond and the Union tried to root them out. The casualties at battles like Cold Harbor and Petersburg, where ninety thousand fell, were horrifying. The Russian experience in the trenches before Plevna in 1877 was also ghastly. In three great battles, which featured human waves advancing on a narrow front, the Russians attacked Turkish trenches in a horseshoe of hills. The Russian casualties were appalling – one-third of the troops engaged in the first assault, one-quarter of the troops engaged in the second and third.[16] Military journalists and correspondents pondered the changed face of war in the 1880s and 1890s. Every European great power possessed larger armies and better guns than Moltke had had at his disposal. Developments in infantry and artillery presaged the end of cavalry. A military arm already suffering in the industrial shift from horse to horsepower –"townbred men cannot scout like Buffalo Bill or ride like Cossacks," one British cavalier scoffed – now faced the prospect of annihilating fire on the battlefield.[17] European armies fashioned the very trap that they fell into in 1914, as Engels and Bloch discerned in the 1880s and 1890s. Vast, heavily armed armies were invincible in a conventional campaign. Only attrition could wear them down, and this process would exact a horrific toll on all sides.

14 Ibid., 51.

15 I. S. Bloch, *The Future of War* (Boston, 1903), xxvi–xxvii.

16 Bruce W. Menning, *Bayonets before Bullets: The Imperial Russian Army 1861–1914* (Bloomington, 1992), 60–71; Wawro, *Warfare and Society*, 127–29.

17 Stephen Badsey, *Doctrine and Reform in the British Cavalry, 1880–1918* (London, 2008), 232–34.

The great, blinding conceit of modern armies was that they could win by pluck and morale. The writings of Douglas Haig before and during World War I revealed that Ardant du Picq and Foch were not alone in subscribing to the "human-centered battlefield." Most leading generals did so too, for the simple reason that they could not bear to see soldierly virtues, like bravery and toughness, eradicated by machines. When Haig wrote the Field Service Regulations for the British cavalry in 1907, he insisted that "success in battle depends mainly on morale and a determination to conquer."[18] In Austria-Hungary, Franz Conrad von Hötzendorf disparaged the awful casualties inflicted by the Boers in their war with Britain, insisting that they were not so awful (the Prussians had lost a larger percentage of their troops at Gravelotte) and, anyway, since European conscripts would never shoot like Boers, they could be more effectively attacked, even if they were entrenched with rifles, machine guns, and artillery. Morale and a willingness to attack were still the decisive factors, Conrad argued.[19] Men like Conrad, Haig, Foch, and Pershing worried that reliance on machines – repeating rifles, machine guns, quick-firing artillery – would undercut the political, social, and cultural role of armies. If reduced to machine operators, troops would lose their grit and glory – the *sentiment du fer* – and, before long, officers would too.

This outlook doomed millions of troops in the wars of the early twentieth century. Well before World War I, however, it was obvious that industrial warfare had doomed the operational art of Moltke the Elder. In the Spanish–American War, American assaults on Spanish trenches and barbed wire in Cuba were repulsed with heavy casualties, often as high as 25 percent. Whereas the Spanish had rearmed with the Mauser magazine rifle and smokeless ammunition, some Americans still used an obsolete .45 caliber single-shot Springfield rifle, which fired charcoal ammunition that shrouded every US soldier in smoke. With such a rifle, a US general declared, "the charge is the safest form of attack."[20] Without adequate artillery, which they had left behind in their haste to reach Cuba, how else could the Americans come to grips with the Spanish? During the Boer War of 1899–1902, the British attempted to fight in the old Prussian style, as they scrambled in company

18 Tim Travers, *The Killing Ground: The British Army, the Western Front and the Emergence of Modern War, 1900–1918* (London, 1987), 49–50.

19 Wawro, *Warfare and Society*, 145–46.

20 Graham A. Cosmas, *An Army for Empire: The US Army in the Spanish-American War* (College Station, TX, 1994), 214–18; Perry D. Jamieson, *Crossing the Deadly Ground: United States Army Tactics, 1865–1899* (Tuscaloosa, 1994), 137–41; Wawro, *Warfare and Society*, 172–74.

3. Maxim machine gun used during the Boer War at Mafeking

columns to within 200 yards of the Boer positions, then charged with bayonets. The Boers, who could hold long frontages with few troops because of the defensive fire provided by Krupp artillery, Mauser rifles, and machine guns, cut down the British assaults. "The British," as Mark Twain smirked, "stand out in the open to fight Boers who are behind rocks."[21] The British assumed that they could use Prussian-style flanking attacks to roll up the Boers, but the Boers extended their own lines, demonstrating that one man with a Mauser was equivalent to half a dozen men with single-shot rifles, and beat the British back with high casualties at battles like Colenso, Magersfontein, and Spion Kop.

The Russo-Japanese War of 1904–05 confirmed the lessons of the Boer War. Here both the Russian and Japanese armies tried to maneuver in the Moltkean style, but they were unhinged by the new technologies, notably the heavy-caliber, high-angle howitzer, which proved so devastating in World War I. A hundred percent increase in caliber – made possible by improved steel casting techniques – permitted a 700 percent increase in shell weight. Since the shells

21 Ibid., 142–43.

were loaded with high explosives like trinitrotoluene ("TNT"), which yielded tremendous blast and scattered steel fragments at bullet speed across wide areas, attacking armies could be slaughtered and entrenched armies uprooted.[22] Five hundred and fifty pound shells, which descended from 11-inch (28-centimeter) howitzers and were put on target by new "indirect fire" techniques, explained the butcher's bill at Port Arthur, where one hundred thousand Russians and Japanese were killed or wounded. "Here," British observer Ian Hamilton scribbled, "the corpses do not so much seem to be escaping from the ground as to be the ground itself."[23] Japanese surgeons marveled at the wounds they treated, and often wrote off a corpse thus: "whole body honeycombed with gun wounds." By 1904, a single three-thousand-man brigade with rifles, machine guns, and artillery spewed more fire in 60 seconds than Wellington's army of sixty thousand had during the day-long battle of Waterloo. Some Japanese units that assaulted Port Arthur suffered 90 percent casualties. The battle at Mukden in early 1905 – putatively the war's climactic encounter on land – was not a climax at all. One hundred and thirteen thousand soldiers were killed or wounded in a battle that lasted three weeks and ended in stalemate. The Russians withdrew and the Japanese – staring into the vastness of Manchuria – dared not pursue. Bloch's conclusion was confirmed: "there will be no more victories of genius or military initiative, only of sums."[24]

There was still room for genius and initiative on the high seas. Naval warfare too had industrialized. The British used armored "floating batteries" and steamships in the Crimean War, in order to bottle up Russia's Baltic fleet and bombard the tsar's Crimean forts. The French had launched the world's first ironclad warship in 1858, a thinly clad wooden-walled vessel with sails and engines. The American Civil War featured the first clash between ironclads – the ten-gun Confederate frigate CSS *Virginia* against the USS *Monitor*, a twin-gunned "tower ship." Naval observers thereafter concluded that armored frigates and monitors represented the wave of the future. The sea battle of Lissa in 1866 pitted Austria's ironclad fleet against Italy's in the Adriatic. With little heavy industry, Italy had procured its frigates and monitors in British and American yards. Attempting to claim Dalmatia from the Austrians and to redeem their defeat on land at Custoza, the Italians hustled their eleven ironclads into battle against Austria's seven. Without the Prussian broadside

22 R. M. Connaughton, *The War of the Rising Sun and the Tumbling Bear* (London, 1988), 200.
23 Ibid., 201.
24 Wawro, *Warfare and Society*, 155–56; Bloch, *Future of War*, 50.

guns, which had been sold to the Austrians by Krupp but withheld once Prussia declared war on Austria, the Austrians were left with weak locally made smoothbores. These did not dent the 6-inch plates that protected the Italian ships. Out of options, the Austrian ships formed into three wedges, bulled into the Italian line, and miraculously sank the pride of the Italian navy, the New Jersey-built battleship *Re d'Italia*.

Commentators announced that naval warfare had changed radically. Guns were nothing against rams. In fact, the Austrians had been lucky. Most of their ram strokes had missed, for screw-driven warships could swerve away from the ram; and the *Re d'Italia* was pierced only because an Austrian broadside had smashed the ship's rudder and prevented it from evading the fatal stroke. Still, the ironclads that were adopted after 1866 were fitted with rams as well as guns. Naval designers wavered between rams and guns for forty years. Their indecision was sharpened by a large number of accidents on the high seas, in which warships blundered into the submerged ram of sister ships and sank.

The sea battle of Tsushima, which was in fact the climactic act of the Russo-Japanese War in 1905, settled conclusively the debate over rams and guns. After a voyage of eight months from their home ports in the Baltic, eleven Russian battleships, eight cruisers, and nine destroyers drove into the Strait of Tsushima between Korea and Japan. Here they were set upon by the entire Japanese navy – four battleships, twenty-seven cruisers, and twenty-one destroyers. Although most of the ships in the engagement still mounted the conventional ram bow, none used the ram. Instead, the Japanese made use of the great industrial improvements in warships, 8- and 12-inch rifled guns in rotating turrets. The 12-inch guns had a range of 4 nautical miles, which made ships invulnerable to a ram stroke. Advances in engines and metallurgy made ships faster and more maneuverable. Light steel alloys replaced heavy iron plates that had not only been cumbersome, but also ineffective against new time-fused, chrome-capped, armor-piercing shells. A battleship that required two feet of iron cladding in 1885 needed only 6 inches of light nickel steel ten years later.[25]

Steel armor did not protect the Russians against Japanese gunfire. The Japanese navy sank or seized the bulk of the Russian Baltic Fleet – all of its battleships, most of its cruisers, and most of their crews: five thousand Russian sailors were killed and six thousand captured. Japan did it with its guns, "crossing the Russian T" and obliterating the Russians with converging long-range fire

25 Michael Glover, *Warfare from Waterloo to Mons* (London, 1980), 170–78.

before the Russians could make their own guns effective. The battle contained a seed of the coming "dreadnought revolution." Japanese officers complained that they had difficulty correcting fire, since they could not distinguish between the faraway splashes of their 8- and 12-inch guns. The "all big-gun battleship" – with a single caliber to simplify fire control – was in the offing.[26]

War among the European great powers was also in the offing. Historians have studied the origins of World War I in detail, and most have concluded that the expansion of armies and the industrialization and professionalization of warfare after 1900 were chief causes of the World War I. The "lessons learned" from the Boer War and Russo-Japanese War, as well as growing tensions in Europe, where the Triple Entente (Britain, France, and Russia) and Triple Alliance (Germany, Austria, and Italy) competed for primacy, led armies to invest heavily in new technologies and infrastructure. German fears of "encirclement" by the Entente, Austro-Hungarian fears of eclipse or disintegration, Russian fears of a German-Austrian attack, French fears of Germany, and British fears of Germany's new High Seas Fleet and German global ambitions inclined every army to increase military spending after the Russo-Japanese War (a conflict that seemed for many years to remove Russia as a check on Germany).

Germany's notorious Schlieffen Plan, which the general-staff chief, Alfred von Schlieffen, put together between 1894 and 1905, was designed to break

4. German Navy at Kiel

26 David C. Evans and Mark R. Peattie, *Kaigun: Strategy, Tactics, and Technology in the Imperial Japanese Navy, 1887–1941* (Annapolis, MD, 1997), 116–29.

through the *Einkreisung* – encirclement – threatened by the Entente powers. Appointed chief of the general staff in 1891 at the age of fifty-eight, Schlieffen worried that the armies of France and Russia, whose warming relations were about to culminate in the alliance of 1894, would outnumber the German army by two to one. Rather than remain on the defensive, as Moltke the Elder had advised late in his career, Schlieffen sought to exploit Russian weaknesses – "the almost railwayless vastness of Russia" – by massing the German army in the west. France would be crushed in six weeks or less, whereupon the entire German army would be transported east to join the Austrians in crushing the slow-mobilizing Russians. A scheme as vast and ambitious as the Schlieffen Plan would have had no hope of success had it not combined Germany's material and manpower resources with industrial-age organization and infrastructure. "Mass armies," as Dennis Showalter has noted, required "mass administration," and the Germans were good administrators.[27] To skeptics in Austria-Hungary, who fretted that the Germans might arrive too late to turn back the Russian hordes, Schlieffen replied that "the fate of Austria will be decided not on the Bug, but on the Seine." The quick destruction of the French army would permit the Austro-German annihilation of the Russians.[28]

To beat the French, Schlieffen proposed a "right hook" through Luxembourg, Belgium, and the Netherlands, which would skirt France's state-of-the-art frontier fortifications, knife through British forces that might land to defend the Low Countries, and roll up the French army in a vast encirclement that Schlieffen likened to a "second Cannae."[29] Even if one accepts Terence Zuber's thesis that the plan was less inflexible than most historians believe and that it was in reality a ploy to goad the Reichstag into bigger military budgets, the fact remains that Schlieffen trusted German mobility to turn the flanks of the French and the Russian armies, and he never shrank from a war as grandiose as the one he sketched out in his formative memoranda.[30] Although a violation of Belgian neutrality was regarded as certain to bring in Great Britain on the French side, Schlieffen

27 Dennis E. Showalter, "Mass Warfare and the Impact of Technology," in Roger Chickering and Stig Förster, eds., *Great War, Total War: Combat and Mobilization on the Western Front, 1914–1914* (Cambridge, 2000), 80.

28 Paul M. Kennedy, ed., *The War Plans of the Great Powers, 1880–1914* (London, 1985), 224; Jack Snyder, *The Ideology of the Offensive* (Ithaca, 1984), 115–17.

29 Holger H. Herwig, *The First World War: Germany and Austria-Hungary, 1914–18* (London, 1997), 46–47.

30 Terence Zuber, *Inventing the Schlieffen Plan: German War Planning, 1871–1914* (Oxford, 2003).

and his successor after 1905, Helmuth von Moltke (the Younger), viewed the Belgian railroads as an essential link between the dense German railways on the lower Rhine and the rail network of northern France. German strategists also regarded Belgium as the only feasible route into France. After 1871, a chain of forts had sealed the French frontier from Verdun to Belfort, anchoring the country's northern flank in the wooded hills of the Argonne and its southern flank in the Vosges. Schlieffen and Moltke considered the Franco-German border too narrow to deploy Germany's army effectively and too well defended by forts and rivers – the Meurthe, Moselle, and Meuse – which coursed at right angles to any German advance.[31]

Geographical, technical, and logistical considerations thus overrode the cautions of policy. Russia's defeat in 1905 emboldened Schlieffen to strip forces from eastern Germany and to mass 2 million troops, along with their guns and implements, against a French army that, he reckoned, could not exceed eight hundred thousand troops. Indeed, had the first Moroccan crisis in 1905 culminated in the implementation of the Schlieffen Plan instead of a German diplomatic climb-down, the Germans would almost certainly have won. Convulsed by revolution and deprived of their navy and much of their exhausted army, the Russians would have been no help to the French and British.[32]

The Schlieffen Plan underlined the growing importance of fast deployments. Faster Prussian mobilization and movement had been a big part of the victories of 1866 and 1870. With railways improving – European rail capacity doubled and track length tripled between 1870 and 1914 – the fear spread, as Moltke the Younger put it, that a single day lost during mobilization could not be recouped in the entire war.[33] Joseph Joffre made the same point in a different way. Faced with the prospect of German invasion and the notorious Schlieffen Plan (the French knew its broad outlines thanks to the treason of Austria's Colonel Alfred Redl as well as Schlieffen's own public maunderings after his retirement), Joffre prophesied that each day of delay in summoning French reservists would mean the loss of 12–15 miles of French territory to the German juggernaut.[34]

31 C. R. M. F. Cruttwell, *A History of the Great War, 1914–1918* (2nd edn., Chicago, 2007), 7–8.

32 David G. Herrmann, *The Arming of Europe and the Making of the First World War* (Princeton, 1996), 45–51.

33 Willmott, *Faith in Reason*, 51.

34 Alex Marshall, "Russian Military Intelligence, 1905–1917: The Untold Story behind Tsarist Russia in the First World War," *War in History* 11 (2004): 397–401; Arden Bucholz, *Moltke, Schlieffen and Prussian War Planning* (New York, 1991), 310–11.

French measures to counter the Schlieffen Plan were half-industrial and half-spiritual. Like many others after 1870, the French generals – led by apostles of the "offensive spirit" like Louis Grandmaison and Ferdinand Foch – wanted to believe that a dauntless offensive would overwhelm the thickest defensive fire with its "moral action." The popular philosophical ideas of Henri Bergson seem also to have weighed on the French military thinkers.[35] In any case, France's general-staff chief, Joseph Joffre, began after his appointment in 1911 to reshape French war plans for a "brusque attack" into Germany. Crude studies of the Franco-Prussian War were used to justify an attack into the heart of German defenses in Lorraine and Alsace. Joffre reasoned that the Prussians had conquered France in 1870 despite heavy losses to the French chassepot and *mitrailleuse*. Moral action had triumphed over fire then. Pluck would trump technology again. Joffre's colleague, War Minister Adolphe Messimy, agreed in 1911 that "neither numbers nor miraculous machines will determine victory. This will go to soldiers with superior physical and moral endurance and superior offensive spirit."[36] France's Plan XVII, which embodied this thinking, was devised to move five French armies swiftly into position to recover Alsace-Lorraine and strike into Germany. Any German advance through Belgium would be severed from its base by French breakthroughs on either side of Metz. Joffre drilled French officers to believe that offensive spirit alone doubled the energy of attacking troops. "Victory," Foch intoned to cadets at St. Cyr, "equals will."[37]

Whereas Plan XVI had strung the French army out in defensive positions from the Channel coast to the Swiss border, Plan XVII massed 80 percent of the French army for a redemptive strike into Alsace and Lorraine. The French army had swelled to seven hundred thousand active-duty troops after the passage of the Service Law of 1913, which added a third year to French active service. This change increased the size of the army by a third with the stroke of a pen, and it made the French believe that they might overrun the German armies that stood in their path. Otherwise, Plan XVII contained no operational objectives, just the promise of a four-week push into Alsace-Lorraine and eastward. The plan featured foolhardy dogmatism. "Whatever the circumstances," it announced, "it is the intention of the commander-in-chief to advance with all forces united to the attack of the German armies."[38]

35 Cruttwell, *Great War*, 10.
36 Snyder, *Offensive*, 64–65.
37 Herwig, *First World War*, 65–67.
38 Cruttwell, *Great War*, 16.

The French assumed that the Russians would divert a large and growing fraction of German strength. Schlieffen had chuckled over the "railwayless vastness of Russia," but French and Russian planners had filled this vastness in the decade after the Russo-Japanese War with double and quadruple-tracked railways and detraining stations, as the industrialization of war advanced in eastern Europe. Knowing that France would be beaten without Russian help, the French and Russian general staffs synchronized their war plans. Russia's Plan XIX, which was finished in 1912, pledged to move three armies to the German border and four armies to the Austro-Hungarian border within fifteen days of mobilization. The Russian army was increased to 1.4 million men, and twenty-seven of its thirty-seven corps were deployed in European Russia for a *sokrushenie* – a short, Moltkean war of annihilation into Austria and Germany.[39] For the Germans, Plan XIX threatened disaster. Schlieffen had assumed that the Russians would require at least forty days to assemble large troop formations on the frontier. The Germans were now confronted with the prospect of Russian armies smashing into Posen and East Prussia, as well as Austrian Galicia, at the moment when the fighting in France, by the bulk of the German army, reached its climax.[40]

The British watched the escalation of troop strength and war plans uneasily. Their relations with Germany, which they had once considered a natural ally, had deteriorated after Germany's announcement in 1898 that it planned to build a battle fleet to rival the Royal Navy. This plan appeared to reverse the political course of Kaiser Wilhelm I and Bismarck, who had seemed content to make the German Empire a "satiated" European power and to consolidate the conquests of 1866–71. Kaiser Wilhelm II, who ascended the throne in 1888 at the age of twenty-nine, was taken with the arguments of A. T. Mahan's *The Influence of Sea Power on History*, which was published in 1890. Mahan argued that little England had become Great Britain by patching together a web of colonies, coaling stations, and strategic chokepoints such as Gibraltar, Suez, Aden, Cape Town, and Singapore. Britain's control of the sea lanes gave it control of the planet, for British trade, cash, resources, and troops could be rushed in and out of every hemisphere with a minimum of friction. Mahan's logic was both stunning and depressing. Wilhelm II felt cheated by his "satiated" predecessors; he hustled Bismarck into retirement in 1890 and resolved to lay down a big

39 D. C. B. Lieven, *Russia and the Origins of the First World War* (New York, 1983), 116–17; Menning, *Bayonets*, 222–27.

40 Ibid., 243–48, 270–71.

blue-water navy to make Germany a "world power" with colonies, resource areas, and coaling stations. "It will now be my task," he declaimed to a crowd in Hamburg, "to see to it that a place in the sun – *Platz an der Sonne* – shall remain our undisputed possession, in order that the sun's rays may fall promptly upon our activity and trade in foreign parts, that our industry and agriculture may develop within the state and our sailing sports upon the water, for Germany's future lies upon the water."[41]

The Anglo-German naval race revealed another dimension in the industrialization of warfare, as well as the stresses that it placed on finances, domestic politics, society, and foreign relations. For the Kaiser, a battle fleet was more than just a strategic asset. Wilhelm II's naval secretary, Alfred von Tirpitz, and his chancellor, Bernhard von Bülow, pushed shipbuilding at a fast clip – three battleships and two cruisers were projected every year for twenty years starting in 1898 – as a means to enrich and pacify German society and to weaken the parties of the left. "Naval policy," as the gambit was called, presumed that more jobs and rising wages in German industry would capture the loyalty of the working class and undermine German socialism. Higher employment and wages in the seaports and industrial regions would also permit the government to impose tariffs on foreign grains and raise the price of German bread (and beer), capturing the loyalty of German agrarians as well. This social and political function of shipbuilding was a new face of "industrialized warfare." It foreshadowed the "military-industrial complex" that emerged later.

The naval race coincided with the "dreadnought revolution," which rendered existing warships obsolete, spurred technological innovation, and drove the cost of seapower ever higher. In 1906, the British launched HMS *Dreadnought*, the world's first turbine-driven, all-big-gun battleship. With its 12-inch guns, *Dreadnought's* broadside was twice as powerful as that of any battleship afloat. Centrally controlled and electronically targeted, *Dreadnought's* 1,500-pound armor-piercing shells were also phenomenally accurate. They could strike from well beyond the effective range of pre-dreadnoughts, so the Germans (and every other navy) had to follow the British example, scrapping pre-dreadnoughts (many of which were of recent and expensive vintage) and pouring funds into a new class of battleships. Britain's First Sea Lord, Sir John "Jackie" Fisher, emphasized speed as much as firepower. "Speed is armor," he liked to say, and his dreadnoughts – pushed

41 Wawro, *Warfare and Society*, 177.

by 70,000-horsepower turbines – sped along at 21 knots when competitors were lucky to make 18.[42]

Fisher's "dreadnought leap" was controversial in Britain, for it rendered much of the Royal Navy itself obsolete. Fisher scrapped seventeen serviceable British pre-dreadnought battleships to make room in the budget (and to find crews and officers) for the dreadnoughts.[43] But the Germans felt most threatened. Tirpitz had worked out a "risk theory," which held that a German hundred-ship navy – sixty battleships and forty cruisers concentrated in the North Sea – would force the British to slacken their support for Russia and France and concede a redivision of colonies around the globe. Even at maximum strength, the German High Seas fleet would not be strong enough to defeat the Royal Navy, but it would confront the British with the risk of a battle that might so damage the Royal Navy to leave it vulnerable to poaching around the globe. This risk, the Kaiser and Tirpitz reasoned, would be too great for the British, who would have to worry about American, Russian, Japanese, French, and German naval power in areas vacated by British naval squadrons. Tirpitz assumed that the British would switch, not fight – that they would back German colonial claims and back out of their *entente cordiale* with the French and their warming relations with the Russians.

In the event, the British fought. Like their German counterparts, British fleet proponents ("navalists") were supported by the popular press, as well as by pressure groups and panicky "invasion literature" – stories about a German "bolt from the blue" toward Britain's shores. Tabloids like the *Daily Mail*, which had their equivalents in every European country, were a signal feature of the new urbanized, industrialized Europe. Like the pressure groups, they nurtured paranoia and xenophobia to drive newspaper sales. Thus the British government reached deep into its pockets to outbuild the Germans "two keels to one."[44] By 1911, the Germans had built only nine dreadnoughts to Britain's fifteen; they were losing the race, despite their own colossal expenditures. Industrialized warfare required capital, and the British had more of it for their

42 John Tetsuro Sumida, *In Defence of Naval Supremacy: Finance, Technology and British Naval Policy, 1889–1914* (London, 1989), 112, 256–7; Richard Hough, *The Great War at Sea, 1914–18* (Oxford, 1983), 10; Volker R. Berghahn, *Germany and the Approach of War in 1914* (2nd edn., New York, 1993), 90; Holger H. Herwig, *"Luxury Fleet": The Imperial German Navy, 1888–1918* (London, 1987), 61.

43 Nicholas A. Lambert, *Sir John Fisher's Naval Revolution* (Columbia, SC, 2002), 138–41; Herwig, *"Luxury Fleet,"* 49, 54.

44 Paul Kennedy, *The Rise and Fall of British Naval Mastery* (London, 1991), 216–18; Niall Ferguson, *The Pity of War: Explaining World War I* (New York, 1999), 2–3, 13–15; Ivo Lambi, *The Navy and German Power Politics, 1862–1914* (Boston, 1984), 316–21.

navy than the Germans did. Although Europeans feared German economic power, the Germans feared British financial assets – London's 800 million pounds of liquid foreign investments (nearly quadruple the German hoard), the returns they paid, and the spur they provided for British exports, work abroad, and national income.[45] "We just cannot *afford* a race in dreadnoughts against the much wealthier British," the director of the Hamburg-America Line, Albert Ballin, lamented.[46] And he was right, for, unlike the British, the Germans had to maintain a large land army as well. Forced to tag supplementary appropriations onto already bloated naval budgets in order to pay for the "dreadnought leap" and then – after 1910 – to finance the "super-dreadnought leap," to build even bigger battleships with even bigger guns, the German chancellor encountered opposition from the army, taxpayers, and the agrarians, who watched as the Russian army ran its railways up to the German border. With the supplements of 1906, 1908, 1911, and 1912, the German naval budget went from 20 percent to 25 percent of German military spending. The unit cost of dreadnoughts and battle cruisers doubled, adding 2 billion marks to the German national debt.[47]

Rising naval spending proved too much for Germany to bear. The Russian threat could not be ignored. Germany's humiliation in the second Moroccan crisis, when the dispatch of a German gunboat to Agadir in 1911 failed to persuade the British or the French to make substantial colonial concessions, prompted a reorientation in Berlin. Wilhelm II did not cut off funds to the navy – for Tirpitz assured him that German quality would overcome British quantity in the naval race – but the government did sweep larger sums back into the army. The German Army Law of 1912 was intended to accomplish five years of growth in a single year.

Its drafters set out to solve two problems that stemmed from the expansion and industrialization of warfare. The first was Germany's last reliable ally in Europe, Austria-Hungary, whose military weakness was a growing concern. The constitutional compromise (*Ausgleich*) between the Austrians and Hungarians in 1867 had weakened the Dual Monarchy militarily. Determined to reduce the power of Vienna, Hungarian leaders resolved every year after 1867 to cut funding for the joint army, which Hungarians viewed as a vehicle for repression and Germanization. While other armies

45 Ferguson, *Pity of War*, 31–39; Sumida, *Naval Supremacy*, 190; Herwig, *"Luxury Fleet,"* 65–68.

46 Berghahn, *Approach*, 90.

47 David Stevenson, *Armaments and the Coming of War: Europe, 1904–1914* (Oxford and New York, 1996), 101; Herwig, *"Luxury Fleet,"* 59; Berghahn, *Approach*, 90–96.

increased appropriations, the relative outlays of the Austro-Hungarian army steadily sank. In 1900, the Austro-Hungarian military budget stood at only 439 million crowns, a figure that equaled 35 percent of Britain's defense expenditures, 40 percent of Russia's, 41 percent of Germany's, and 45 percent of France's. The peacetime strength of the Austro-Hungarian army had sunk to three hundred thousand by 1912. One man in sixty-five was a soldier in France; the ratio in Austria-Hungary was 1:132. Nor did this army industrialize to the extent that its rivals did. Austria's arsenal of machine guns and light and heavy artillery was small. Whereas the French and German armies disposed of one field gun for every 195 soldiers in 1913–14, the ratio in Austria-Hungary was 1:338. The ratio in the Italian army was 1:295. To make matters worse, Austrian Emperor Franz Joseph I decided in 1906 to add a fleet of twelve dreadnoughts. The Hungarians refused to increase the pool of recruits to fulfill the navy's new demands. They agreed to increase the annual class of conscripts from 125,000 to 180,000, but they reduced the term of service from three years to two, so the army shrank even more.[48]

The German Army Law of 1912 and a follow-up the next year aimed to compensate for Austro-Hungarian weakness and to provide for the certainty that the Italians would not honor their treaty commitments to Germany and Austria-Hungary if war came. This was Germany's second problem. The Italians had used the backing of Berlin and Vienna to wrest Libya from the Ottoman Empire in 1911, but no one imagined a scenario in which Italy would send the five corps and two cavalry divisions that it had promised to Germany in a war with France.[49] The new German appropriations of 1912–13 thus aimed to give the Germans an immediate, decisive technological edge in what virtually everyone assumed was an imminent world war. Pessimistic in the long run, the Germans sensed opportunity in the short run. France's active-duty strength would not increase to 730,000 until 1916, and the Russian infantry, artillery, and aviation units that had been called into existence by the Great Army Program of 1913 would not be fully operational until 1917. Some of the strategic railways across Poland and Ukraine, which were funded by the Franco-Russian Railway Agreement of 1913, would not be complete until 1918.[50]

The gap between Germany's "front-loaded" readiness in 1913 and the Entente's unpreparedness, which was owed to the prudent spread of

48 Wawro, *Warfare and Society*, 201, 205–11; Stevenson, *Armaments*, 85–86; Norman Stone, *Europe Transformed, 1878–1919* (2nd edn., Oxford, 1999), 238–39.

49 Cruttwell, *Great War*, 4.

50 Herrmann, *Arming*, 197–208; Stevenson, *Armaments*, 322–23; Bucholz, *Planning*, 306–07.

expenditures over several budget years, made the Germans eager to strike before the military balance shifted against them. In May 1914, General Georg von Waldersee of the German general staff advised his colleagues to initiate a war immediately, "while the chances of achieving a speedy victory in a major European war are still very favorable for Germany and the Triple Alliance." Waldersee's recommendation was startling because of its prologue. "Germany," he wrote, "has no reason to expect to be attacked in the near future." Still, he concluded, there was no reason whatsoever to "avoid a conflict." Now was the time for war. Germany's infrastructure, artillery establishment, and trained manpower were momentarily superior to everyone else's. In May 1914, Moltke met with his Austro-Hungarian counterpart, Conrad von Hötzendorf, and insisted that Conrad find a pretext for a war with Serbia, which would draw in the Entente powers. "To wait any longer," Moltke said, "means a diminishing of our chances."[51]

Gavrilo Princip's assassination of Archduke Franz Ferdinand and Archduchess Sophie in June 1914 provided the pretext. "*Serbien muss sterben,*" the Austrian mobs chanted in front of the new war ministry building on the Ring. The "July Crisis" of 1914 has been thoroughly investigated by historians, who agree that the Germans did nothing to restrain Austro-Hungarian bellicosity. On the contrary, Berlin drove Vienna into the breach. Moltke overrode von Hötzendorf's last-minute worries that Austria was not ready for a wider war, assuring the Austrian leader that Germany was ready but that Germany's momentary superiority would not last: 3.5 million German and Austrian troops were ringed by 5.4 million Entente troops, whose advantage would increase as the modernization and expansion of these armies reached completion. And so the war began.

51 Ferguson, *Pity of War*, 16–20; Herwig, *First World War*, 20–21.

3

War and imperial expansion

BRUCE VANDERVORT

The purpose of this chapter is not to rehearse the history of the European and European-American colonial wars in the nineteenth century. Just giving the highlights of Britain's more than four hundred battles in some sixty colonial campaigns from 1837 to 1901 would fill a large volume. The aim of what follows is, rather, to explore the dynamics of colonial warfare in relationship to two grand, related themes in western military history during the long nineteenth century. These are the "second military revolution," a martial corollary of the still unfolding Industrial Revolution, and the related "totalization" of war, as whole populations were mobilized for conflict and became willing to accept that people in enemy lands, along with their economies and societies, had become legitimate targets of destruction. For the purposes of this chapter,

> [T]otal war, at least theoretically, consists of total mobilization of all the nation's resources by a highly organized and centralized state for a military conflict with unlimited war aims (such as the complete conquest and subjugation of the enemy) and unrestricted use of force (against the enemy's armies and civil population alike, going so far as the complete destruction of the home front, extermination and genocide).[1]

The first segment of the chapter will weigh the impact of the new weaponry and technologies, which were made available by industrialization, on imperial expansion in Africa, Asia, and America, with particular emphasis on innovations in communications and transportation. Assessing the extent to which colonial war approximated "total war" will be the task of the second part of the chapter. A final section will sketch out the profile of colonial warfare as practiced by western armies from roughly 1850 to 1914.

The long nineteenth century was the high noon of western imperialism. The pace of conquest became frenetic between 1850 and 1914, when all Africa

1 Stig Foerster and Joerg Nadler, eds., *On the Road to Total War: The American Civil War and the German Wars of Unification, 1861–1871* (Cambridge, 1997), 11.

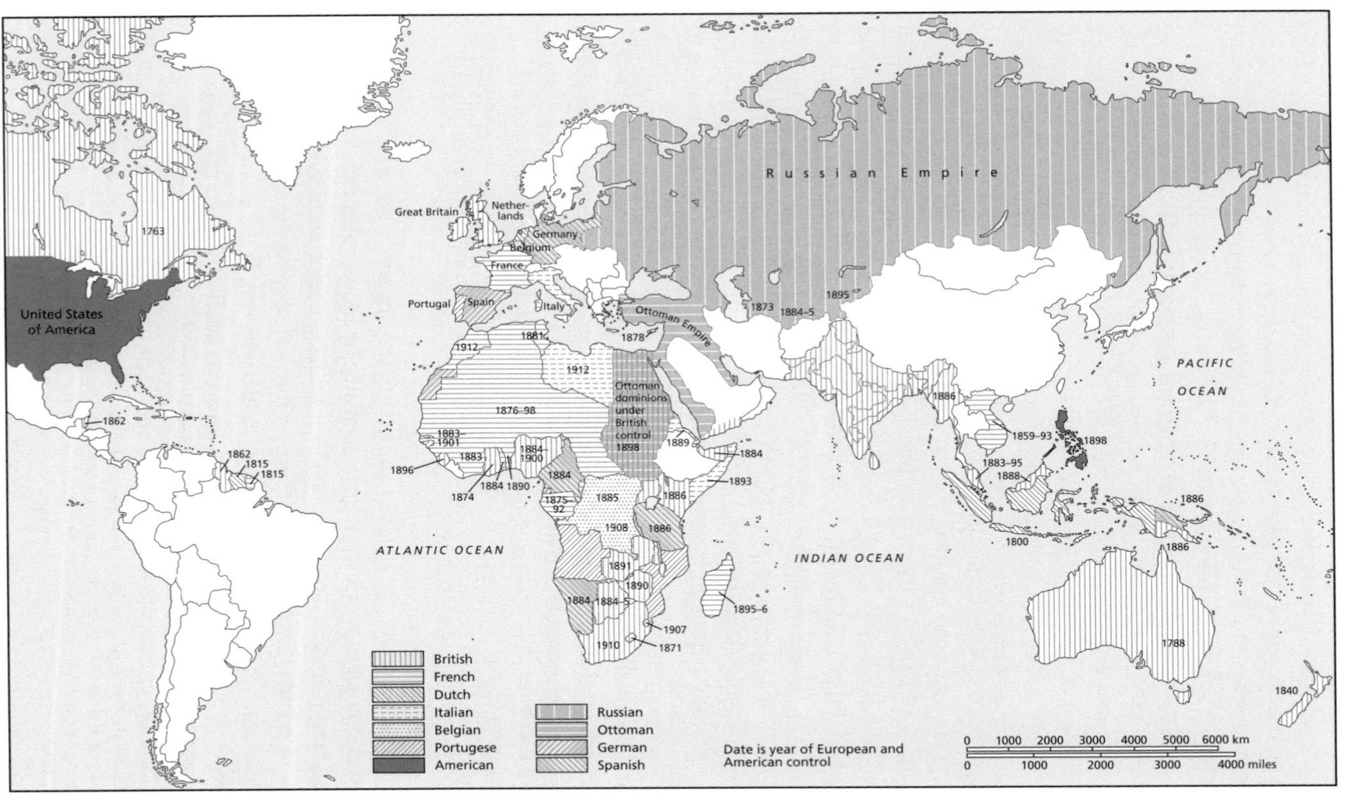

MAP 5. Growth of western empires after 1850

save Ethiopia and Liberia, large portions of Asia, all the Pacific Islands, and the "Indian country" of Argentina, Canada, Chile, Mexico, and the United States were brought under western rule. "The West had now arisen," writes Geoffrey Parker in his much-acclaimed work, *The Military Revolution: Military Innovation and the Rise of the West, 1500–1800*. "Thanks above all to their military superiority, founded upon the military revolution of the sixteenth and seventeenth centuries, the Western nations had managed to create the first global hegemony in history."[2] Buttressed by new developments in weaponry, communications, and transportation that emanated from the Industrial Revolution, the technological and organizational superiority of western armies was thought to have become so overwhelming that the campaigns of these armies outside Europe or against indigenous enemies in the New World were reduced to "wars against nature," in the phrase of the dean of Victorian theorists of colonial warfare, British Colonel Charles Callwell. These "small wars," it was believed, were fought only secondarily against human enemies; the real foes were climate, disease, distance, inhospitable terrain, and lack of food and water.[3]

While considerably different in their ways of war, the "savage" or "fanatical" enemies that European and European-American soldiers faced were nonetheless thought to be doomed to defeat by their lack of "the higher mental faculties," which provided western armies with unique powers to "co-ordinate, think strategically, and to innovate tactically and technically."[4] Thus the US military historian John Gates could argue that while North American Indians were "widely known for their stealth and ferocity," they possessed little knowledge of strategy and tactics. "They fought as they did because it was the only way they knew how to fight, and their success in keeping the field as long as they did resulted as much from the [US] Army's meager size as from the Indians' prowess as warriors."[5]

The belief that "small wars" were waged against nature and only peripherally against human enemies produced a remarkable spate of hyperbole among

2 Geoffrey Parker, *The Military Revolution: Military Innovation and the Rise of the West, 1500–1800* (Cambridge, 1988), 154. The "gunpowder revolution" of the fifteenth and sixteenth centuries enthroned the infantry as Queen of Battles in the western world, displacing the mounted arm.

3 Callwell, *Small Wars: Their Principles and Practice* (Lincoln, NE, 1996 [1896]), 21, 25, 57.

4 James Belich, *The Victorian Interpretation of Racial Conflict: The Maori, the British, and the New Zealand Wars* (2nd edn., Montreal and Kingston, 1989), 316.

5 John M. Gates, "Indians and Insurrectos: The US Army's Experience with Insurgency," *Parameters* 13 (1983): 61. Filipinos who resisted the US occupation of their country in the war of 1899–1902 were known as *insurrectos*.

European and European-American soldiers who were engaged in colonial campaigns. One of the more striking examples of this was the claim in 1854 by one Lieutenant John Grattan, fresh out of West Point and in command of troops at Fort Laramie, that "with thirty men, he could whip the combined force of all the Indians of the prairie."[6] By the end of the nineteenth century, sober experience had introduced an element of restraint into the campaign rhetoric of colonial soldiers, but they continued to be largely dismissive of their "native" opponents. In 1890 French Marine Captain Marie-Étienne Péroz, a veteran of a number of tough West African campaigns, wrote that "Two hundred energetic men, well commanded, amply supplied with ammunition and well in hand of a completely self-controlled leader who is knowledgeable in the various aspects of African warfare, should be able to cross Africa in any direction without being defeated."[7]

Although colonial soldiers in the Victorian era were aware of their edge in weaponry over the peoples of the lands they conquered – "Whatever happens, we have got / The Maxim gun, and they have not"[8] – they preferred to ascribe their victories to superior "moral force," a notion that often cloaked racist assumptions. Although the British troops who took the field in the Anglo-Ashanti War of 1873–74 in West Africa were equipped with the latest in weaponry, including a Gatling gun, their commander, Sir Garnet Wolseley, chose to believe that their greatest advantage over their foes lay in cold steel and the color of their skins. In his pre-battle exhortation, Britain's greatest Victorian soldier said that "Providence has implanted in the heart of every native of Africa a superstitious awe and dread that prevents the negro from daring to meet us face to face in combat. A steady advance or charge, no matter how partial, if made with determination always means the retreat of the enemy."[9] Callwell, the small-wars theorist, put the matter more bluntly. "The way to deal with Asiatics," he wrote, "is to go for them and cow them by the sheer force of will."[10]

6 On August 19, 1854, in a strange twist of fate, Grattan led a detachment of thirty troopers to a Sioux camp, bullied the Indians into a fight, and got himself and his whole force killed. Paul Hedren, *The Massacre of Lieutenant Grattan and his Command by Indians* (Glendale, CA, 1983), 50.

7 Marie-Etienne Péroz, *La Tactique dans le Soudan: Quelques combats et épisodes de guerre remarquables* (Paris, 1890), 52.

8 Hilaire Belloc, *Complete Verse of H. Belloc: Including Sonnets and Verse, Cautionary Verses, The Modern Traveller, etc.* (London, 1970), 184. Belloc's famous line about the Maxim gun appeared in his poem, "The Modern Traveller," in 1898, but was not written in celebration of European firepower, as is frequently assumed. It referred to the last line of defense of a pair of European freebooters against mistreated and rebellious porters in Africa.

9 Garnet Wolseley, "Memorandum on Bush Fighting," December 20, 1873, quoted in A. Lloyd, *Drums of Kumasi: The Story of the Ashanti Wars* (Harlow, 1964), 85.

10 Callwell, *Small Wars*, 72.

In the early years of imperial expansion, it was widely assumed that the moral superiority and military prowess of the west were evident enough that their occasional demonstration could overawe indigenous peoples and achieve bloodless victories. Warships were thought to be particularly useful in this regard. French officials were aware that Ahamadu Seku, the *khalifa* of the Tukolor empire in West Africa, which blocked expansion into the Western Sudan, had been told by his father that "when French gunboats sailed above Segu [on the Niger River], the collapse of the Tukolor Empire would be at hand." So the French hastened to bring a gunboat in sections overland from Senegal and reassembled it on the shores of the Niger.[11] Not long afterward, the *khalifa*'s empire duly collapsed, its demise helped along by French warships on the Niger.

There were also ways to cow the "natives" on land. One was the Gatling gun that Wolseley had taken along on his campaign against the Ashanti in 1873–74. As his army approached the enemy capital, Kumasi, Ashanti emissaries came out to inquire about peace terms. "I had them shown a Gatling gun in action," Wolseley wrote. "The sharp roar of its fire, the precision of its aim and the way in which its bullets threw up the water all around the target in the river impressed them."[12]

Western soldiers also believed that periodic parading through "native" territory dressed in martial finery and armed to the teeth would suffice to keep the peace and promote expansion. In 1856, during his stint as US secretary of war, Jefferson Davis argued that trying to intimidate the Western Indian tribes by building forts on the frontier was not working; instead he recommended the strategy employed by the French in their conquest of Algeria in the 1840s. The French had left "the desert region in the possession of the nomadic tribes," Davis wrote, and kept them in hand by sending

> expeditions into the desert regions as required. The marching columns are sufficiently strong to inflict punishment where it is deserved, [and] have inspired, it is said, the native tribes with such respect for their power that it has seldom been found necessary to chastise any tribe a second time.[13]

The notion that western victory in colonial warfare grew out of the barrel of a gun is recent, the product of a consensus between "technological

11 B. I. Obichere, "The African Factor in the Establishment of French Authority in West Africa, 1880–1900," in P. Gifford and W. R. Louis, eds., *France and Britain in Africa: Imperial Rivalry and Colonial Rule* (New Haven, 1971), 447.

12 Garnet Wolseley, *The Story of a Soldier's Life* (2 vols., New York, 1903), Vol. II: 320.

13 Senate Executive Document 5, 34:3, pt. 2, 3–26, "Annual Report of the Secretary of War to President Franklin Pierce, 1 December 1856," in Lynda Lasswell Crist and Mary Seaton Dix, eds., *The Papers of Jefferson Davis* (Baton Rouge, 1989), Vol. VI: 68–69.

determinists" among imperial historians and scholars in the developing world, who have sought explanations for defeat at the hands of western armies beyond traditionally cited factors, such as indigenous disunity, collaboration, and the proclivity to fight pitched battles. The prominent Ghanaian historian A. Adu Boahen has argued that "the most crucial [European advantage in the colonial wars] was military." "Above all," he contends, "technologically and logistically, African armies were at a great disadvantage in comparison with their invaders . . . What chance would such an army have against a well-trained, professional one armed with cannons and repeater rifles [and] maxim guns and enjoying naval and logistical support?"[14]

Until the mid nineteenth century, the technological gap between European and European-American armies and their colonial adversaries had not been large. A "military revolution" took place at this point, however, featuring, among other things, submarine telegraphy, steam-powered iron vessels, breech-loading, rapid-firing rifles and artillery, and the machine gun. Recent historians have argued that employment of this new technology, not the "moral force" dear to Victorian statesmen and generals, made possible the rapid conquest of large areas of Africa, the Americas, Asia, and the Pacific by expansionist western states between 1850 and 1914.

The machine gun, which made its appearance during the age of imperial conquest, has occupied a special niche in the accounts of historians of colonial warfare. The weapon had been available in a number of prototypes since the early nineteenth century. It was first used in combat, if sparingly, during the American Civil War, in the form of the Gatling gun. Subsequently, an array of models went on the market. The most famous was the invention of Hiram Maxim, which was first demonstrated to potential buyers in 1884. John Ellis argues that the machine gun came into its own as a weapon in colonial campaigning. It was, he wrote, "Absolutely crucial in allowing the Europeans to hang on to their tiny beachheads and give themselves a breathing space for further expansion . . . Without Hiram Maxim much of subsequent world history might have been very different."[15]

14 A. Adu Boahen, *African Perspectives on Colonialism* (Baltimore, 1985), 56–57. Boahen lists the failure of African peoples to form alliances against the European invader as a "not so crucial" factor in African defeat. Ibid., 57.

15 John Ellis, *The Social History of the Machine Gun* (New York, 1975), 17. Some historians still contend that General Custer would have lived to old age had he not left his Gatling guns behind when he rode off to the Little Big Horn in 1876. Roger Ford, *The Grim Reaper: The Machine Gun and Machine Gunners* (New York, 1996), 23.

The mid-nineteenth-century revolution in transportation and communications also improved the performance of European and European-American colonial armies. Land telegraphy had been in use since the 1840s and had been helpful to armies, such as those in the American West or on the North-West Frontier of India, whose centers of command lay in the not too distant hinterland. Land telegraphy could do nothing, however, to open a line of communication to overseas operations. This innovation came in the 1860s with the advent of submarine telegraphy, described by one author as the acme of Victorian inventiveness.[16] Submarine cables, writes Daniel Headrick, "were an essential part of the new imperialism."[17] A submarine cable hook-up in 1885 between Paris and Bamako on the Niger River, by way of the Canary Islands, cut the time required to get reinforcements from France to the Western Sudan from two months to a couple of weeks. For military officers in the colonies, however, who were used to virtual independence of action, this communications revolution came as a mixed blessing. With less than five hours separating the sending and receipt of messages, submarine telegraphy made it possible for government officials to intervene directly in colonial campaigns.[18] A bullying telegram from Prime Minister Francesco Crispi in Rome goaded a reluctant General Oreste Baratieri into launching a fateful attack on a much larger Ethiopian army at Adowa (or Adwa) in 1896. The result was the bloodiest battle in all the colonial wars and a disastrous defeat for Italy.[19]

The gradual introduction of steam-powered vessels into the arsenals of the colonial powers greatly aided imperial conquest. The new iron ships were less vulnerable to fire and rot, while steam propulsion meant that shipping was no longer dependent upon fickle winds. Steamships, civilian and military, carried European expeditionary forces around the world and kept them supplied with the necessities of war. Hospital ships took off the sick and wounded, and steam-powered gunboats moved up the rivers of Africa and Asia to provide fire support to ground troops on the march. In addition, naval landing parties were key elements in a number of colonial campaigns. Bluejackets from the Royal Navy could be found far inland in Africa, in the rain forests of Ashanti and on the savannah of the Anglo-Egyptian Sudan, manning machine guns, rocket tubes, and artillery pieces for the British Army. The most spectacular exploit of a naval landing team in the colonial wars was the seizure in 1893 of

16 Bernard S. Finn, *Submarine Telegraphy: The Grand Victorian Technology* (London, 1973).

17 Daniel R. Headrick, *The Tools of Empire: Technology and European Imperialism in the Nineteenth Century* (New York, 1981), 163.

18 Ibid., 130.

19 Nicola Labanca, *In marcia verso Adua* (Turin, 1993), 352.

the fabled city of Timbuktu, on the edge of the Sahara Desert, by sailors from two French gunboats on the Niger River.[20]

Some imperial states relied more on naval power than others. Dutch control of the far-flung Indonesian archipelago would have been unthinkable without ships of the Royal Netherlands Navy to ferry soldiers about and gunboats to support them up the rivers and along the coasts of Bali and Borneo, as well as to interdict arms smugglers from Singapore.[21] No imperial power benefited as much from naval power, however, as the potentate of the Congo Free State, the Belgian King Leopold II. Control over this immense region rested on mastery of its river system. Leopold's administrators achieved this control by assembling a large fleet of river-going steamboats, whose ability to shift troops around quickly was the deciding factor in the Arab War of the 1890s, during the most formidable challenge to the king's rule.[22]

The tropics of Africa and Asia continued for good reason to be known as the white man's grave for most of the nineteenth century. Before the middle of the century, the susceptibility of European soldiers to tropical diseases, such as malaria and yellow fever, produced "a rate of death at least twice that of soldiers who stayed home, and possibly much higher," and effectively ruled out European operations in the jungles and rain forests of Africa and Asia. Between 1819 and 1836, for example, British military deaths at the Sierra Leone station in West Africa, which were due almost exclusively to disease, averaged an astounding 483 per 1,000.[23]

Beginning in the mid 1800s, medical advances, such as the use of quinine to treat malaria, the discovery of the causes of cholera, the use of water filters, the availability of canned foods, and stricter enforcement of hygiene regulations among troops, reduced health risks to European soldiers in the tropics. Impressive gains were made between 1840 and 1860, as death rates began to slow among European troops in both Africa and Asia, thanks largely to success in treating malaria. The most significant improvements in the health of

20 D. Grévoz, *Les Cannonières de Tomboctou: Les Français et la conquête de la cité mythique (1870–1894)* (Paris, 1992), 128–66. The sailors slipped into Timbuktu just ahead of a much vexed column of marines and African *tirailleurs*.

21 Jaap A. de Moor, "Warmakers in the Archipelago: Dutch Expeditions in Nineteenth Century Indonesia," in Jaap A. de Moor and H. L. Wesseling, eds., *Imperialism and War: Essays on Colonial Wars in Asia and Africa* (Leiden, 1989), 62–63.

22 Headrick, *Tools of Empire*, 197. The Arab War was not against Arabs as such, but against Swahili-speaking slave traders and planters and their followers in the eastern Congo, who had originally come from Zanzibar and other city-states on the east coast of Africa, much of which had been ruled by the Arabian state of Oman until the 1880s.

23 Philip D. Curtin, *Disease and Empire: The Health of European Troops in the Conquest of Africa* (Cambridge, 1998), xii, 159.

European soldiers in tropical regions came in the decades before 1914, when "the germ theory of disease became an effective tool."[24]

Technology played a central role in the spectacular conquests of the long nineteenth century by European and European-American imperial armies, but it was hardly the decisive factor that "technological determinists" among historians of empire have claimed it to be. Some historians have assumed that because new weapons like magazine rifles and machine guns were available, they must have been deployed by European and European-American armies in colonial campaigns. Daniel Headrick, the leading historian of technology in European imperial conquest, has written that European colonial armies were "among the first beneficiaries of the gun [i.e. breech-loader] revolution."[25] The record on this score is, however, more mixed than Headrick assumes. While French marines in West Africa were the first to be issued the initial model of magazine rifle, the 1884 Gras-Kropatschek, their counterparts in other colonial armies were less fortunate. Horse soldiers of the US army fought the Indian wars in the west armed with single-shot breech-loaders, and on at least one memorable occasion, they were outgunned by their enemies.[26] The .30-caliber Krag-Jorgensen, the first magazine rifle adopted for use by the US army, was issued only in 1893, after the Indian wars were over.[27] In Asia, meanwhile, the military historian Jaap de Moor has observed that the introduction of the magazine rifle in the Dutch colonial army "proceeded very slowly and had in fact hardly begun when the Dutch conquest [of Indonesia] was completed" on the eve of World War I.[28]

"Native" troops in the colonial armies were the last to receive magazine rifles. To take but one example, while the British regulars in Kitchener's army at the battle of Omdurman in 1898 were equipped with the new Lee-Metford magazine rifle, the more numerous Egyptian and Sudanese troops who fought alongside them carried Martini Henry single-shot breech-loaders, a weapon that had first been issued to British soldiers in the 1870s.[29]

The use of machine guns in colonial warfare was also less extensive than some historians, among them John Ellis, have contended. During the last half of the nineteenth century, the French military conquered huge tracts of

24 Ibid., 229.
25 Headrick, *Tools of Empire*, 101.
26 That occasion was the battle of the Little Big Horn, when enough Indian warriors showed up with repeating rifles to sow panic in the ranks of Custer's troopers. See Robert M. Utley, *The Lance and the Shield: The Life and Times of Sitting Bull* (New York, 1993), 156.
27 Russell F. Weigley, *History of the United States Army* (New York, 1967), 290.
28 De Moor, "Warmakers in the Archipelago," 64–65.
29 I. H. Zulfo, *Karari: The Sudanese Account of the Battle of Omdurman* (London, 1980), 97.

North and West Africa, as well as Indochina, with only minimal use of the machine gun, although the weapon was widely available in a number of models. The German army started to take machine guns seriously as weapons of war only during World War I. Because German military leaders thought that the new weapons might be useful in scaring the "natives," a few were sent out to the colonies, where they were used to help put down insurrections in German Southwest Africa and Tanganyika in 1904–7.[30] Machine guns were irrelevant to the century-long struggle of the Dutch to bring the Indonesian archipelago under their control. Victory in the final lap of this contest, the battle for the province of Aceh in Sumatra in the early years of the twentieth century, came "when the *Korps Marechaussee* [colonial army] employed, not the Maxim gun, but that quintessentially primitive weapon, the naked saber."[31]

Although it proved useful in breaking into enemy fortresses or walled cities, artillery was used sparingly in European campaigns in Africa, because the big guns were difficult to transport across the trackless savannah or through the thick rain forests. An episode in the British West African Frontier Force's foray onto the plains of northern Nigeria in 1903, illustrated the problem.

> The 75-mm gun . . . required a carrier party numbering, with reliefs, thirty-two in all. One man carried all the spare parts, four carried the gun slung on a pole, two a wheel each, one the axle, four more the cradle, and another four the trail, both of which were slung on poles as well. The trail, the cradle, and the gun each weighed over 200 pounds.[32]

European troops faced similar difficulties in Asia. During the conquest of Tonkin (northern Vietnam) in the 1880s, French Foreign Legionnaires found that while artillery "terrified the natives" and was essential for reducing Chinese fortifications on Tonkin's northern border,[33] it was cumbersome

30 Ford, *The Grim Reaper*, 63–64.

31 H. L. Wesseling, "Colonial Wars: An Introduction," in de Moor and Wesseling, eds., *Imperialism and War*, 6. For more on this campaign, see de Moor, "Warmakers in the Archipelago," 69. Wesseling referred to the Dutch discovery that the *klewang*, the Malay world's equivalent of the machete, was the optimum weapon for fighting at close quarters in the rain forests of the East Indies.

32 D. J. M. Muffett, *Concerning Brave Captains: Being a History of the British Occupation of Kano and Sokoto and of the Last Stand of the Fulani Forces* (London, 1964), 114. Unwieldy though it was, the 1903 expedition needed artillery. The walls of the enemy city of Kano were 50 feet high in places and 40 feet thick at the base. It took the British big guns several hours to make a breach big enough to enable the infantry to take the city. Bruce Vandervort, *Wars of Imperial Conquest in Africa, 1830–1914* (Bloomington, 1998), 193.

33 The French invasion of Tonkin led to war with China, which had for centuries considered Vietnam a tributary. The Sino-French War (1883–85), which involved French shelling of

and required large numbers of coolies to haul through the jungle. Each gun was tied to two large bamboo logs roped together in an "X"; forty coolies were needed to carry it. "Sooner or later the bamboos break, sooner or later the porters fall and roll with the piece over a precipice or into an arroyo," recalled the Legionnaire Louis Carpeaux.[34]

Progress in military medicine was a boon to colonial campaigning, but it came slowly and had a greater impact on troops in barracks than in the field, as was shown by the fate of a French expeditionary force in Madagascar in the 1890s. In a ten-month-long campaign in 1895 to conquer the island, French troops lost 5,750 dead to disease, as against 25 to gunfire. In addition, some 1,200 "native" carriers and wagon drivers lost their lives. "[T]he main enemy was sickness, especially malaria," wrote historian Yvan-Georges Paillard. "[A]lmost 90% of the deaths were due to malaria and its complications."[35] As late as 1911–12, some two thousand Italian soldiers died of cholera during the invasion of Libya, many more than were killed by the Turkish and Arab enemy.[36]

It was fortunate that steam-powered vessels were available to confer greater mobility upon colonial armies, for the other great symbol of the Industrial Revolution, the railroad, made only the slightest of appearances in Africa and Asia during this period. In some areas, even roads that could support troop movements were nonexistent. And, in most of tropical Africa, sleeping sickness spread by the tsetse fly (*trypanosomiasis*) ruled out using beasts of burden, such as horses and mules. The result was that in the tropics colonial armies' baggage, food, tools of war, and much else had to be borne by columns of human beings, who were generally known as "carriers" in Africa and "coolies" in Asia. Large numbers of these people were needed to make a colonial expedition operable, with the result that men, women, and even children sometimes were press-ganged. Wolseley's march on the Ashanti

Chinese ports and an incursion into what is today Taiwan, as well as fighting along the Tonkin border, came to an end when the French Navy interrupted South China's crucial rice trade with the northern part of the country. On this conflict, see Lewis M. Chere, *The Diplomacy of the Sino-French War (1883–1885): Global Complications of an Undeclared War* (Notre Dame, IN, 1988).

34 Louis Carpeaux, *La Chasse aux pirates* (Paris, 1913), 37, quoted in Douglas Porch, *The French Foreign Legion: A Complete History of the Legendary Fighting Force* (New York, 1991), 229.

35 Georges Paillard, "The French Expedition to Madagascar in 1895: Program and Results," in de Moor and Wesseling, eds., *Imperialism and War*, 183–84. "The number of French deaths in those ten months," according to Philip Curtin, "was probably greater than their losses in the conquest of all the territory that was to become French West and Equatorial Africa." Curtin, *Disease and Empire*, 177.

36 V. G. Kiernan, *Colonial Empires and Armies, 1815–1960* (2nd edn., Montreal and Kingston, 1998), 131.

capital of Kumasi during the 1873–74 war required 8,500 carriers for 1,457 European troops and 483 soldiers of the West Indian Regiment.[37]

In 1901, Captain J. S. Herron of the US Second Cavalry, who had been sent around the world to visit European colonial armies in the field, explained what the British army sought to accomplish with its massive recruitment of carriers.

> In spite of their long tours of tropical service the British troops succeed in resisting the effects of the climate without excessive losses. This result is achieved by the system . . . of keeping the soldier a fighting man and, for all labor which is fatiguing, unhealthy or repugnant, employing natives paid by the state. In the field, the British troops are accompanied by numerous drivers, packers, laborers, etc. . . . it often happens that noncombatants are more numerous than the combatants.[38]

Mortality rates among these carriers was one of the scandals of the imperial era. While no good statistics exist for the late nineteenth century, when most imperial expansion took place, we do have data from World War I in Africa, where hundreds of thousands of carriers were engaged on both sides in the fighting. Geoffrey Hodges, who has devoted much of his life to a study of the Carrier Corps employed by the Allies in the East African campaign, concluded that well over a hundred thousand African carriers died during the war in British service alone, some from gunfire, most from overwork, disease, or malnutrition.[39]

The notion that small wars were "wars against nature" – that once western armies had overcome the environmental constraints of colonial campaigning, victory against their human foes became effortless – more than once proved a dangerous illusion for western governments and their colonial soldiers. From early in the history of western imperialism, European and European-American armies were obliged to undertake protracted campaigns, employing extreme measures, to overcome their "native" foes. It took French armies nearly two decades, from 1830 to 1847, to conquer Algeria, as they laid waste to parts of the country from end to end, in some cases repeatedly. By the time the war came to a close, the

37 David Killingray, "Colonial Warfare in West Africa, 1870–1914," in de Moor and Wesseling, eds., *Imperialism and War*, 163. The West Indians were brought over because it was assumed that, being of African descent, they would be immune to African diseases. They were not.

38 J. S. Herron, *Colonial Army Systems of the Netherlands, Great Britain, France, Germany, Portugal, Italy, and Belgium* (Washington, DC, 1901), 42. The US army hoped that Herron could provide them with ideas from his trip that would smooth the path to occupation of the Philippine Islands, then in progress.

39 Geoffrey Hodges, *Kariakor: The Carrier Corps: The Story of the Military Labour Forces in the Conquest of German East Africa, 1914–1918* (Nairobi, 1999).

French had committed nearly a hundred thousand soldiers, a quarter of their army, to the struggle.

But, as the Algerian example demonstrated, the equation "industrialization of warfare = modern war = total war" does not work well in the context of colonial warfare. To begin with, many of the largest western territorial gains and some of the most striking cases of "total war" in the colonial world occurred before the Industrial Revolution made a substantial impact on warfare. The whole of the Indian subcontinent came under British control before 1850. The First Opium War, which saw the initial defeat of the Chinese Empire by a western nation and brought Hong Kong to the British, was fought in 1839–42. The Dutch historian of *ancien régime* India, Dirk Kolff, contends that the transition to "total war" in India, and by implication elsewhere in the colonial world, took place earlier than is usually thought and that when it occurred, it was a product more of mindset than technology. The transition took place in India, he believes, in the late eighteenth and early nineteenth century,

> some fifty years *before* the revolution in communications and weapons technology – as indeed it did in Napoleonic Europe. . . . Warren Hastings and Arthur Wellesley[40] were as total in their objectives as was Bonaparte himself; and . . . they were successful for much the same reason: they were dealing with people whose aims were limited and who in consequence had no idea what they were up against.[41]

Furthermore, the total war that made Algeria French was won with the weapons – and tactics – of the Napoleonic era. This war proved immensely destructive, not because of new and more powerful weapons, but because classic European methods of securing victory, such as winning a decisive battle or seizing the enemy's capital, did not apply in places like Algeria. As Pierre le Comte de Castellane, one of the French commanders, explained.

> In Europe, once [you are] master of two or three large cities, the entire country is yours. But in Africa, how do you act against a population whose only link with the land is the pegs of their tents? . . . The only way is to take the

40 The reference here is to the first (1777–78) and second (1803–05) Maratha wars, in which British and allied indigenous forces under the command of, respectively, Governor-General Hastings and General Wellesley, the future Duke of Wellington, greatly expanded the boundaries of British India.

41 Michael Howard, "Colonial Wars and European Wars," in de Moor and Wesseling, eds., *Imperialism and War*, 218–19.

> grain which feeds them, the flocks which clothe them. For this reason, we make war on silos, war on cattle, [we make] the *razzia*.[42]

In the United States, meanwhile, a strategy similar to that employed by France in Algeria was implemented in the 1870s by Philip Sheridan, the commander of most of the army troops west of the Mississippi, to bring an end to the wars against the Plains Indians. His plan called for converging columns of cavalry to descend upon "hostile" villages, preferably in the dead of winter when the Indian ponies were weak from lack of forage, and to destroy the inhabitants' dwellings, food supply, and pony herds. He employed this strategy against the Comanche in Texas and the Sioux and Cheyenne on the Northern Plains, with the result that by the late 1870s most of the Plains Indians had been forced onto reservations. The victories of US soldiers in this "total war" on the Plains were due not to superior technology or armaments but to effective use of Indian scouts to find the camps, to the advantage of surprise, and, where possible, the application of overwhelming force.[43] As in Algeria, the strategy put in place by Sheridan was a response to the US army's difficulty in coming to grips with an elusive and mobile foe.

Until the decade preceding World War I, colonial campaigns did not require mass mobilization of resources and manpower. The first colonial war that featured anything comparable to a *levée en masse* was the closing, guerrilla phase of the second Anglo-Boer War (1899–1902), which saw Britain pour some five hundred thousand troops into the conflict, practically denuding the home islands of defenders. In the Turco-Italian War of 1911–12, the Italian army, bogged down in a seemingly endless guerrilla war in Libya, committed nearly a hundred thousand soldiers, including most of its elite troops and the bulk of its modern equipment, to the struggle. The deployment called into question Italy's commitment to the Triple Alliance. Had war broken out with France or Russia at this point, Italy would have been hard pressed, for practical reasons alone, to come to the assistance of its Austrian and German allies.[44]

42 Quoted in Douglas Porch, "Bugeaud, Gallieni, Lyautey," in Peter Paret, ed., *Makers of Modern Strategy: From Machiavelli to the Nuclear Age* (Princeton, 1986), 380. The Comte was referring to the French adaptation of the traditional Arab practice of the *razzia* or raid, which had been a means to obtain booty or remind the enemy of his vulnerability.

43 Bruce Vandervort, *Indian Wars of Mexico, Canada and the United States, 1812–1900* (London, 2006), 166–67, 175–77. Lance Janda, "Shutting the Gates of Mercy: The American Origins of Total War, 1860–1880," *Journal of Military History* 59 (January 1995): 7–26, argues that the policy used against the Plains Indians had its roots in Union Army depredations in the Shenandoah Valley of Virginia and in Georgia during the civil war, but that the attacks on Indian villages led to a proportionally greater loss of human life.

44 From 1892 to 1915 Italy was partnered with the Austro-Hungarian and German empires in an alliance against, eventually, Britain, France, and Russia (Triple Entente).

5. Scottish Highland Regiment of the British army

The British soldiers who took part in their country's colonial wars were drawn from the regiments of its all-volunteer regular army, supported on occasion by forces from the Dominions – Australia, Canada, New Zealand – and by the brown and white troops of the Indian army. Although its commanders were reluctant to allow its employment outside the subcontinent and there was resistance to foreign service among its Indian soldiers or sepoys, the Indian army, which was paid for entirely by the taxpayers of the colony, proved to be the empire's crucial reserve force – what the Marquess of Salisbury called "an English barrack in the oriental seas."[45]

The two major continental European imperial powers, France and Germany, had less flexibility than the British in fighting colonial wars, in that legislation forbade the use of conscripts outside Europe. In both cases, army conscripts could volunteer for colonial service, but the number who did so was negligible. The French got around this restriction by creating the Foreign Legion in the 1830s and, once their Algerian colony was transformed

45 Quoted in Brian Bond, "Introduction," in Bond, ed., *Victorian Military Campaigns* (London, 1967), 6.

into a department of France in 1848, by stationing the 19th Army Corps, better known as the *Armée d'Afrique*, at bases near Algiers, Constantine, and Oran. While the *Armée d'Afrique* was responsible for maintaining order in Algeria and, later, in the newly acquired colonies of Tunisia (1881) and Morocco (1912), French operations in West Africa and, initially at least, in Indochina were the exclusive province of the Marine Corps (*Troupes de la Marine*), a branch of the navy, which had had continuous overseas experience since the time of the Sun King and was composed of volunteers recruited in mainland France.[46] In 1900, following an extended debate over the creation of a special army for use in the tropics, the Chamber of Deputies decided that, rather than creating a new force, it could more cheaply and practically transform the Marine Corps into an *Armée coloniale* under the jurisdiction of the War Ministry.[47]

A similar debate had taken place in government and military circles in Italy in the 1880s. Emerging Italian ambitions in the Maghreb and the Horn of Africa seemed to demand a specialized colonial army. While Italian opponents of such a force included antimilitarists and anti-imperialists – the same kinds of people who opposed the creation of the *Armée coloniale* in France – they also included conservatives who charged that this force would drain troops from Europe, where Italy was already having difficulty meeting its obligations to the Triple Alliance. Debate also divided the Italian army itself. Some soldiers claimed that an army created for colonial service would function as a kind of elite. Since it was likely to be in combat more often than its metropolitan counterpart, promotions would come more rapidly to its personnel, and colonial soldiers would win most of the medals and decorations. Although younger officers, of course, lobbied for an independent colonial army, it eventually was agreed that colonial wars would be waged not by a colonial army but by expeditionary forces formed, when required, from among the units of the regular army. A permanent cadre was to be stationed in Naples, where units destined for colonial service would report to be outfitted with tropical gear and to receive their orders.[48] As a result, Italy was the only European imperial power to fight its colonial wars with conscripts.

46 The French Navy was responsible for the administration of all French colonies except for Algeria until the 1890s, when the newly created Colonial Ministry took charge.

47 The best source in English on the *Armée d'Afrique* and the *Armée coloniale* is Anthony Clayton, *France, Soldiers and Africa* (London, 1988). On the debate over creation of an *Armée coloniale*, see J.-C. Jauffret, *Parlement, gouvernement, commandement: L'armée de métier sous la 3e République* (2 vols., Vincennes, 1987), Vol. II: 657ff.

48 The Italian debate on the formation of a colonial army is summarized in Nicola Labanca, *Il Generale Cesare Ricotti e la politica militare italiana dal 1884 al 1887* (Rome, 1986), 191ff.

Compared to the armies that were deployed in Europe during the Napoleonic wars or World War I, the number of Europeans and European-Americans was minuscule in the armies that from 1850 to 1914 conquered most of Africa, vast swathes of Asia and the Pacific, and the "Indian country" of the Americas. While some 524,000 soldiers were on active duty in the Imperial German Army in 1900, only 2,871 were on duty in the Reich's colonies in Tanganyika, Southwest Africa, Cameroon, and Togo.[49] Ten years later, General Charles Mangin reported that three companies of French marines, some 450 men, were deployed in the whole of West and Equatorial Africa.[50] Meanwhile, the defense of the United States, as well as the conquest of the western half of its territory during the last thirty years of the nineteenth century, was entrusted to an army that never numbered more than twenty-five thousand men.[51]

Some twenty years ago, the historian David Killingray explained the remarkable lack of a European military presence in the colonial world by pointing out that in Africa, European empires "were gained principally by African mercenary armies, occasionally supported by white or other colonial troops."[52] When he made this assertion, it was hugely controversial. Today, it has become the orthodox view among military historians of the African colonial wars. And while indigenous soldiers bulked less large in European colonial armies in Asia, they were indispensable to imperial conquest and the maintenance of order in this part of the world too.[53]

European colonial armies recruited large numbers of soldiers among the "native" populations of Africa, Asia, and the Americas, but they did not do so indiscriminately. In fact, an elaborate body of argument was fashioned during the second half of the nineteenth century to explain a rigorously selective pattern of European recruitment of "native" soldiery – the so-called "martial races" theory. It originated among British soldiers and administrators in India, but it was was espoused by officials of other European colonial powers as well. It held that recruitment was to be limited to the extent possible to elements of the colonial population – typically characterized in the Victorian literature as

49 For overall German troop strength, see Paul Kennedy, *The Rise and Fall of the Great Powers: Economic Change and Military Conflict from 1500 to 2000* (New York, 1987), 203, table 19. Data on the German colonial army in Africa were taken from Herron, *Colonial Army Systems*, 115–18.

50 Charles Mangin, *La Force noire* (Paris, 1910), 175–76.

51 On the constraints on the US army during the nineteenth century, see Chapter 3 of Robert Utley's *Frontiersmen in Blue: The United States Army and the Indian, 1848–1865* (New York, 1967).

52 Killlingray, "Colonial Warfare in West Africa, 1870–1914," in de Moor and Wesseling, eds., *Imperialism and War*, 146.

53 See Karl Hack and Tobias Rettig, eds., *Colonial Armies in Southeast Asia* (Abingdon, 2006).

"races" – that had demonstrated a propensity for war. In Britain's Indian army, the largest of the colonial armed forces, this principle dictated a preference for the "martial" Gurkhas, Sikhs, and Muslim tribesmen from the North-West Frontier over "lazy, effeminate" Bengalis or "indolent" southern Indians like the Madrassis. Application of the "martial races" approach to recruiting proceeded apace throughout the last half of the century. By 1914, around 75 percent of some 120,000 "brown soldiers" in Britain's Indian Army were recruited in Nepal (Gurkhas) and the Punjab (Sikhs), and on the North-West Frontier (Pathans and other Muslim hill peoples).[54]

Britain's recruiting of its fighting men among the so-called "martial races" in India got its real start in the 1870s, when prominent figures in the British government and military began to fear that Russia, which was then winding up its conquest of Central Asia, was about to attack India by way of Afghanistan. Lord Frederick Roberts, the commander-in-chief of the Army of India, argued that the Army as it was then constituted might be capable of maintaining domestic order in India, but it would stand little chance against a European foe. Therefore, a new recruiting strategy, which was designed to bring "the best fighting material the country can supply" into the ranks of the Indian Army, was in order.[55]

Finding "the best fighting material" in India was not an easy task, wrote Sir George MacMunn, perhaps the most outspoken proponent of "martial races" theory. He wrote that "We do not speak of the martial races of Britain as distinct from the non-martial, nor of Germany, nor of France. But in India we speak of the martial races as a thing apart and because the mass of the people have neither martial aptitude nor physical courage . . . the courage that we should talk of colloquially as 'guts.'"[56] MacMunn estimated that perhaps 10 percent of the Indian population of some 350 million was capable of producing the warrior males the Indian army required. The rest of the population had been rendered unsuitable, he believed, among other things by religious diversity, juvenile eroticism, hookworm, malaria, and the "deteriorating effect of aeons of tropical sun on races that were once white and lived in uplands and on cool steppes."[57]

54 David Omissi, *The Sepoy and the Raj: The Indian Army, 1860–1940* (London, 1994), 19.

55 Ibid., 12.

56 George MacMunn, *The Martial Races of India* (London, 1932), 2. MacMunn was mistaken about the inapplicability of "martial races" thinking to Britain. Scots Highlanders had fulfilled this role in the minds of many Britons since the early nineteenth century, along with, to a lesser extent, the Irish. Omissi, *Sepoy and the Raj*, 24.

57 MacMunn, *Martial Races*, 2. MacMunn refers here to the notion that the progenitors of the Indian "martial races" were the so-called "Aryan" invaders, who came into India from the temperate north and imposed their culture and rule on the northern subcontinent after 1500 BCE.

However, as Heather Streets has pointed out in her seminal study of the question, there was more to the "martial races" theory than biological or geographical determinism.

> In India, authorities were overwhelmingly concerned to legitimate their exclusive recruiting strategies in terms of race and masculinity to keep politically suspect recruits out of the army ... [T]he memory of those [Indian] populations who remained loyal during [the Mutiny of 1857] was a critical factor in determining British perceptions about which men would make the best soldiers.[58]

Soldiers from Bengal, who could hardly be accused of unwarlike behavior, had formed the backbone of the mutiny and rebellion of 1857.[59] But if the British hid their discriminatory recruitment in India behind a theoretical façade, so did other European powers.

From the earliest attempts to achieve mastery over the sprawling East Indies archipelago, the Dutch had relied on indigenous soldiers. Although the Javanese were by far the most numerous of their colonial subjects, the Dutch preferred to recruit "native" soldiers from among the inhabitants of Ambon, a small island in the Moluccas group near New Guinea, far from the population center of the colony. A common reason given for this practice was that the Ambonese, unlike the Javanese, were a "martial" people. This was not the whole story, however. Of all of the Dutch subjects in the East Indies, the Ambonese had proved to be the most receptive to European civilization. By the end of the seventeenth century, most had become Christians; many were members of the Dutch Reformed Church. Consequently, the Dutch believed them to be reliable and loyal, unlike the Muslim Javanese. And, because the Ambonese identified with the Dutch, they were also more amenable to the Dutch way of war than were the Javanese, who disliked wearing European uniforms and boots and fighting in closed formation.[60]

The French colonial military was split over recruiting Muslim soldiers. Their decisions were partly a function of available alternatives. In North Africa, where the overwhelming majority of the population was Muslim, the French had little

58 Heather Streets, *Martial Races: The Military, Race and Masculinity in British Imperial Culture, 1857–1914* (Manchester, 2004), 4, 110.

59 Some writers have suggested that the British discrimination against the Bengalis was rooted in disdain for their Hindu religion. Not too much should be made of this claim, however. The Gurkhas were Hindus. The British also took recruits from the Hindu Rajputs in what is today Rajasthan, along the border with Pakistan.

60 Jaap A. de Moor, "The Recruitment of Indonesian Soldiers for the Dutch Colonial Army, c. 1700–1950," in David Killingray and David Omissi, eds., *Guardians of Empire: The Armed Forces of the Colonial Powers* (Manchester, 1999), 53–79.

choice in the matter, so they recruited thousands of Muslim soldiers to serve in the *Armée d'Afrique*, which was stationed in Algeria. In West Africa the situation was different. Although Islam was spreading rapidly in the region, there remained a large and militant animist population among the Bambara people, in what is today Mali. While the French proconsul in West Africa in the 1850s and 1860s, General Louis César Faidherbe, lauded Islam as a progressive faith and recruited Muslim soldiers for the *Tirailleurs sénégalais* (Senegalese light infantry), his successor, Colonel Joseph-Simon Gallieni, portrayed Islam as "the deadliest enemy of France's great work of penetrating the heart of Africa" and turned to animists like the Bambara for his soldiers.[61] According to the official view, however, the Bambara were not attractive because of their religion. They were attractive instead because they were "stocky, muscular and possessed of a powerful vigor," a warrior breed, but one that also demonstrated a "limitless confidence in [its] European superiors," in the view of Albert Ditte of the French Marines. They were also cheap. Ditte estimated that in 1900 it cost 2,127–2,540 Francs a year to keep a French marine in the field, but only 980.35 Francs to maintain a Bambara *tirailleur*.[62]

In Indochina the French invaders began to recruit indigenous troops only in the late 1870s, a decade or so after their conquest of Cochin-China, the southern part of the country. The first Vietnamese unit brought under the French colors was a regiment of Annamese infantry, which was formed in 1879.[63] The Annamese were peasant villagers from the south, who, in French eyes at least, lacked a martial tradition. Although praiseworthy for their "endurance, docility, and cheapness," Ditte remarked, they displayed little "penchant" for warfare and required much training and special care to turn them into soldiers. Other "native" populations existed, but they posed equally serious challenges to recruiters. The non-Vietnamese hill people of the north, the Montagnards, were unruly, independent, and thus best employed as irregulars. The Chinese, who inhabited the northern border region of Indochina, demonstrated fine soldierly qualities, including an aptitude for

61 Joseph-Simon Gallieni, *Mission dans le Haut Niger et à Ségou* (Paris, 1883), 205, quoted in Obichere, "The African Factor," 445. Gallieni's antipathy to Islam may have stemmed as much from his anti-clericalism as from islamophobia.

62 Albert Ditte, *Observations sur la guerre dans les colonies – organisation – exécution: conférences faites à l'École Supérieure de Guerre* (Paris, 1905), 52–53.

63 The term "Annamese" had two definitions. In the early years of their campaigning in Indochina, the French referred to all Vietnam as "Annam" since, in theory at least, all the country owed obedience to the king of Annam in Hue. Thus, all Vietnamese peoples could be called "Annamese." The French then began to distinguish between the populations of south and north Vietnam, referring to the latter as "Tonkinois" and the former as "Annamite." I use the second definition here.

6. Senegalese soldiers in the French army

maneuver, Ditte said, but they also displayed an inordinate "fear of being wounded and thus physically handicapped." Nor were they willing to fight far from home. "They also tend to want to be buried in their native soil, where their descendants can tend their graves and render them the honors due to ancestors."[64]

The crucial campaign for control of Indochina aimed at the conquest of its northern province, Tonkin. The war for Tonkin, which eventually drew in China, consumed most of the 1880s and continued into the final decade of the century. Although a large expeditionary force of Foreign Legionnaires and marines was dispatched from Africa, it was soon clear that indigenous troops would be required. Using the good offices of friendly mandarins and exploiting local ethnic and religious divisions, the French recruited three regiments of Tonkinese soldiers during the 1880s. These units were considered superior to the Annamese who had been recruited earlier, and they soon formed the backbone of France's Indochina army. Already by the mid 1880s, they made up one-fifth of the troops in French service in the peninsula.[65]

64 Ditte, *Observations sur la guerre dans les colonies*, 43–44.

65 Charles Fourniau, "Colonial Wars before 1914: The Case of France in Indochina," in Wesseling and de Moor, *Imperialism and War*, 79.

The recruitment of indigenous soldiers by the imperial powers served purposes other than providing cannon-fodder. It was demoralizing for "native" resistance to see indigenous people taking up the gun on behalf of the invader, particularly when the recruits came from one's own people, as they often did. Although all the imperial powers used this kind of psychological warfare, none was as practiced at it as the US army. The bluecoats of the US cavalry honed this stratagem in the Indian wars in the West, where General George C. Crook emerged as its most accomplished promoter. Crook brought along large numbers of Apache warriors, as combatants as well as scouts, in his successful pursuit of the great Apache leader, Geronimo, from Arizona Territory into the Mexican mountains in 1885. His column consisted of 193 Apache warriors and 48 white soldiers. "To polish a diamond there is nothing like its own dust," Crook said. "It is the same with these fellows. Nothing breaks them up like turning their own people against them."[66] The US army resurrected Crook's policy during the Philippine "Insurrection" early in the twentieth century, particularly in its campaign to bring the Muslim "Moros" on the southern island of Mindanao to heel. Robert A. Fulton's description of the Moro Constabulary, a body of soldiers hired to fight their own people, merits quoting at length.

> The Moro Constabulary was recognizable by its khaki uniform with red trim, wrapped puttees, and a distinctive red fez. The rimless fez permitted the Muslims to touch their foreheads to the ground during daily prayers. By choice and habit, the Constabulary soldier nearly always went barefoot ... The Constabulary uniform and membership accorded the new recruits a personal status and identity they did not enjoy in their villages and, even though meager by American standards, they received regular pay ... It was little wonder, then, that with few exceptions, the Constabulary was repaid in dogged loyalty and exceptional bravery. The Constabulary was the recruits' new family and the [American] officers their new *datus* [chiefs].[67]

Individually and collectively, women were probably more prominent in nineteenth-century colonial warfare than at any other time in history. They played important parts both in the colonial armies that were raised by Europeans and European-Americans and in indigenous movements that opposed imperial conquest. Two representatives of the latter phenomenon

66 Vandervort, *Indian Wars*, 8–9, 206–07. The Crook quote is from Charles F. Lummis, *General Crook and the Apache Wars* (Flagstaff, AZ, 1966), 17.

67 Robert A. Fulton, *Moroland, 1899–1906: America's First Attempt to Transform a Muslim Society* (Bend, OR, 2006), 274–75. Many of the Moros who fought alongside the Americans came from marginal elements of local society, such as slaves and "troublesome elements" in the villages. Ibid., 275.

were Lakshmi Bai, the Rani (queen) of Jhansi, a leader of Indian rebels against the British in the Mutiny of 1857,[68] and the medicine woman and warrior Lozen, who was companion in arms of two famous Apache Indian chiefs in the 1880s, her brother Victorio and Geronimo.[69]

In a category by themselves were the "Amazons" of Dahomey, elite women warriors who spearheaded resistance to French conquest of their kingdom, on the West African coast between Ghana and Nigeria, in the early 1890s. The world's only all-female combat unit during this period, some three thousand strong, they had their first taste of battle in the 1840s and

> soon became the most warlike, and the most feared, of all the Dahomean troops. It was they who bore the brunt of the fighting in a number of the most important of the nineteenth century Dahomean wars ... During the most desperately fought of all [these] wars, the struggle against the French, their losses were so severe that as a fighting force they were completely destroyed.[70]

The "unfeminine" nature of these women warriors fascinated Victorian observers, not the least of whom was the famed traveler and amateur ethnologist, Sir Richard Burton.[71] Observers seized on the claim that the members of the Amazon army were all royal wives and could have sex only with their king. Thus, their fierceness in combat, like that of their male counterparts in the Zulu *impis*, could be explained by repressed sexual desire.[72]

Warfare in the colonial world was often a family affair. African and Asian colonial soldiers insisted that their wives and children accompany them into the field, and although they worried that this practice might erode their troops' fighting spirit, European officers had no choice but to accept it. In time, European commanders came to see that the presence of their soldiers' families on campaign provided a bonus. The wives of *Tirailleurs sénégalais* in France's West African army carried gear, made camp, cooked meals, and

68 Tapti Roy, *Raj of the Rani* (New Delhi and New York, 2006).

69 K. M. Buchanan, *Apache Women Warriors* (El Paso, TX, 1986), 1.

70 D. Ross, "Dahomey," in Michael Crowder, ed., *West African Resistance: The Military Response to Colonial Occupation* (London, 1971), 149.

71 Richard Burton, *A Mission to Gelele, King of Dahome* (2 vols., London, 1864).

72 The idea that "Amazon" ferocity was the result of "enforced chastity" has had a long shelf life. Ross, "Dahomey," echoed it in the 1970s. A more recent student of the "Amazon" phenomenon, the anthropologist and historian Robert B. Edgerton, explains that the women's fighting spirit derived from a blood oath and ritual bonding. See his *Warrior Women: The Amazons of Dahomey and the Nature of War* (Boulder, 2000), 18. Another recent study of this subject is Stanley B. Alpern, *Amazons of Black Sparta: The Women Warriors of Dahomey* (New York, 1998).

mended clothes. In addition to looking after their husbands, the women often also saw to the needs of bachelor African soldiers in the army. The presence of the women also solved a thorny problem for the *Tirailleurs* Marine officers. Their African troops insisted on being served couscous in the field, rather than the bread or biscuit provided to white soldiers, but they refused to grind and cook the millet used to make it; this was women's work.[73]

The prodigious second "military revolution," which began around 1850 had a minor impact on the operations of colonial armies. New weapons were slow to arrive on the periphery and, when they did, they were often incompatible with the environment in which colonial wars were fought or the kind of warfare being waged. Because of the premium on mobility in colonial warfare, the new weaponry could be more of a burden than an aid. This was true of machine guns and especially artillery. The big guns were an essential ingredient in some colonial campaigns, such as the Russian conquest of the Caucasus, with its mountain fortresses (*aouls*). In others, however, the size and weight of these weapons held up fast-moving columns or diverted mule trains and human carriers from more crucial tasks, such as transporting ammunition, food, medical supplies, or wounded men. The development of submarine telegraphy had a considerable impact on colonial warfare, albeit not always salutary. Speedier communications between capitals and commanders in the field shortened the time needed to provide reinforcements and supplies, but also gave officials at home the ability to "micro-manage" military operations, sometimes with disastrous results. The introduction of steam-powered iron vessels into the fleets of the western powers was the greatest boon to colonial warfare. Expeditionary forces and war *matériel* now could be moved more quickly to distant theaters, and new steam-powered gunboats operated up rivers and along coasts to increase the fire support available to troops on campaign. Advances in medicine greatly increased the chances of survival of European troops in the tropics, although improvements came more quickly for soldiers in barracks than in the field.

In a sense, however, the impact of the Industrial Revolution on war diminished as one moved away from the western metropole. The cost of the new weaponry and innovations in communications and transportation did not endear them to members of parliament or metropolitan civil servants, who were determined that colonial expansion should be kept as cheap as possible. It was less expensive and, to the official mind, as effective to wage

73 J. Malcolm Thompson, "Colonial Policy and the Family Life of Black Troops in French West Africa, 1817–1904," *International Journal of African Historical Studies* 23 (1990): 427.

war on the periphery with "native" troops, who were equipped with weapons cast off by metropolitan armies and whose numbers were supplemented by hordes of irregulars who carried traditional weapons and were paid in booty and cheap alcohol. Wars in Africa and Asia were increasingly fought by soldiers recruited from the indigenous populations. In West Africa, the overwhelming majority of French troops on duty in 1900 were *Tirailleurs sénégalais*. Even fewer European soldiers were under arms in the German colonies at the turn of the twentieth century. Indigenous recruits took on a much larger role in the colonial armies of the French in Indochina and the Dutch in Indonesia. Two-thirds of the British Indian army was composed of sepoys. This critical reservoir of indigenous manpower experienced the effects of the Industrial Revolution on war more slowly and to a much smaller degree than did their western counterparts. On the eve of World War I, "native" soldiers in the Europeans' colonial armies were still carrying cast-off weapons from the first generation of the "breechloader revolution" – black-powder, single-shot rifles that had been issued to metropolitan soldiers in the 1870s. To the extent that the new automatic weapons and breech-loading, quick-firing artillery were to be found in their armies, "native" troops were not trained in their use – for fear that they might one day turn them against their colonial masters.

The question of "total war" must be seen in a different light in the context of the colonial world as well. The assumption that "total war" was inextricably linked to the impact of the Industrial Revolution is not valid with respect to the wars of imperial conquest in Africa, the Americas, or Asia. Some of the most prodigious European expansion took place here before the Industrial Revolution began to affect the way wars were fought, in the Indian subcontinent and North Africa, for example. Finally, "total war" on the periphery, the laying waste of villages and croplands, the slaughter of domesticated animals, and the massacres of men, women, and children, was practiced by western armies not because they now suddenly had the technical capacity to do so or because technology had become the basis for a new "way of war." Instead, it was the only means these armies had to defeat elusive, highly mobile peoples who were adept practitioners of guerrilla warfare.

4

The non-western world responds to imperialism, 1850–1914

JOHN P. DUNN

Nineteenth-century imperialism presented challenges and opportunities to the non-western world. To most states it was a threat, to several a role model. Embracing the "western way of war" required massive investments, plus dramatic political, educational, and social changes. Most attempts to do so were at best partially successful, many a waste of resources.[1]

A few states, like Ethiopia in the 1880s and 1890s, created new military systems that allowed powerful resistance to western imperialism. Elsewhere reformed armies enhanced the coercive powers of the state, reducing opposition to further change. Bandit leaders in the Balkans and Manchuria found their lairs less secure, Taiping rebels were mowed down by Ch'ing (Qing) soldiers who were armed with Enfield rifles, while in Morocco a few Krupp guns guaranteed that the sultan's annual *mahalla* would collect tribute quickly.[2]

China's *tzu ch'iang yun-tung* (*ziqiang yundong*), or Self-Strengthening Movement, is a good example of this proposition. A reaction to the the twin disasters of the First Opium War (1839–42) and the Taiping Rebellion (1850–64), this movement was the first sustained effort to improve the Ch'ing military. Self-strengthening represented more than the purchase of British rifles or hiring a few military advisors; it called for China to improve revenue collection, construct arsenals and shipyards, and to train more efficient soldiers and sailors.[3]

Although contemporary western attention focused on the colorful Frederick T. Ward and his replacement, Charles "Chinese" Gordon, more

1 For useful introductions see, Douglas Porch, *Wars of Empire* (London, 2000); David Ralston, *Importing the European Army: The Introduction of Military Techniques and Institutions into the Extra-European World, 1600–1914* (Chicago and London, 1990).

2 "Ch'ing" is the traditional Wade-Giles transliteration for 清; the modern Pinyin system converts these characters to "Qing." Readers relying on English language sources need be familiar with both systems, as many pre-1990 publications employ the former.

3 David Pong, *Shen Pao-chen and China's Modernization in the Nineteenth Century* (Cambridge, 1994); Mary C. Wright, *The Last Stand of Chinese Conservatism: The T'ung-Chih Restoration, 1862–1874* (Stanford, 1957).

lasting results came from gentry officials like Tseng Kuo-fan (Zeng Guofan), Li Hung-chang (Li Hongzhang) or Tso Tsung-t'ang (Zuo Zongtang). These men created new armies capable of ending the many rebellions that racked mid-nineteenth-century China. Their success came at a price, as self-strengthening required a buildup of local power. This presented a dangerous dilemma for Ch'ing leaders, who were a Manchu minority already troubled by Han proto-nationalists.[4] This dilemma was never solved, and self-strengthening went down in defeat during the Sino-Japanese War (1894–95). Ch'ing officials continued to experiment with military reforms up to the dynasty's collapse in 1911, but never in a consistent fashion that allowed China to defy the imperial powers.

China's story was far from unique. Morocco, Tunis, Egypt, Ethiopia, Iran, Afghanistan, and Korea made efforts to reform their armed forces. Each metamorphosis was, at best, partial. Only Japan and the Ottoman Empire made the complete transformation. The result was that both could fight European enemies with some chance for success, control internal dissidents, and even serve as regional role models for other non-western states engaged in military reforms.

Between 1850 and 1914, the "sick man of Europe" was an over-the-hill prize fighter barely capable of blocking Dame Fortune's many jabs. Religious and ethnic tensions, nationalism, corruption, and a host of foreign enemies were just parts of the problem. An economy based on agricultural production entering the new world market of the nineteenth century was another. Despite all, the "sick man" was capable of going the distance until World War I.[5]

Ottoman leaders had recognized the need for military reforms since the reign of Selim III (1789–1807). They also remembered that he was murdered by mutinous soldiers who resisted such change. His cousin, Mahmud II (1808–39), created more lasting reforms, but these only took off after the "Auspicious Event" (1826), when his new artillery corps massacred the reactionaries. Mahmud was also noted for instituting new uniforms, especially the *fes* (*tarboush*), which rapidly became the iconic headgear of

4 Good overviews of Chinese military history include: Bruce A. Elleman, *Modern Chinese Warfare, 1795–1989* (London, 2001); David A. Graff and Robin Higham, *A Military History of China* (Boulder, 2002), Peter Worthing, *A Military History of Modern China: From Manchu Conquest to Tian'anmen Square* (Westport, CT, 2007); and the introduction in Hans van de Ven, *Warfare in Chinese History* (Leiden, 2000).

5 For an overview of Turkish military history, see Mesut Uyar and Edward J. Erikson, *A Military History of the Ottomans: From Osman to Atatürk* (Westport, CT, 2009).

Ottoman soldiers. He and nearly every sultan thereafter were less successful in devising a system that could push talent into the officer corps.[6]

Men like Selim and Mahmud viewed European military forces as role models for their armed forces. Like Mehmet Ali of Egypt, they recognized that change required a combination of economic, educational, industrial, and military reforms. Unlike their rebellious vassal, Ottoman sultans seldom had the resources both to support extensive reforms and to defend the empire from its many enemies.[7]

After Ottoman authorities introduced conscription in 1848, Mahmud's soldiers morphed into the *Nizamiye*, a European-style army. It was much needed, both for internal security and foreign wars. Between 1850 and 1914, twenty major campaigns took Ottoman soldiers from Montenegro to Yemen. In the time between these conflicts, troops were regularly employed fighting "little wars" against rebels, terrorists, or bandits. Up to 1914, Ottoman soldiers were continually employed in *eşkiya takibi* ("brigand-chasing") campaigns. They also collected taxes and enforced the law, for outside major cities policemen were nonexistent.

These were far from minor events. For example, forcing the Jabal Druze to pay taxes and obey conscription in August 1910 required thirty-five battalions supported by three batteries of mountain guns. Even near the imperial nerve center, Istanbul, *Comitaji* bands were so numerous that the Ottoman Army in Macedonia conducted regular sweeps to disperse or destroy them until 1913. Colomar von der Goltz, the chief of the German training mission from 1883 to 1895, pointed to this as a major problem, which made Ottoman troops "more like a police than a modern army."[8]

6 Virginia H. Aksan, *Ottoman Wars, 1700–1870: An Empire Besieged* (Harlow, 2007); J. M. Bastelberger, *Die militärischen Reformen unter Mahmud II* (Gotha, 1874); Avigdor Levy, "The Officer Corps in Sultan Muhmud II's New Ottoman Army, 1826–1839," *International Journal of Middle Eastern Studies* 2 (1971): 21–39; Odile Moreau, *L'Empire Ottoman à l'âge des réformes: Les hommes et les idées du novelle ordre militaire, 1826–1914* (Istanbul, 2007); Stanford J. Shaw, *Between Old and New: The Ottoman Empire under Sultan Selim III, 1789–1807* (Cambridge, MA, 1971).

7 Erik. J. Zürcher, "The Ottoman Conscription System in Theory and Practice," in Erik J. Zürcher, ed., *Arming the State: Military Conscription in the Middle East and Central Asia, 1775–1925* (London and New York, 1999), 79–94. Mehmet (Muhammad) Ali's reforms are well covered by Khaled Fahmy, *All the Pasha's Men: Mehmed Ali, His Army and the Making of Modern Egypt* (Cambridge, 1997); and Afaf Lutfi al-Sayyid Marsot, *Egypt in the Reign of Muhammad Ali* (Cambridge, 1984).

8 Colomar von der Goltz, "Causes of the Late Turkish Defeat," *Military Review* (1913): 729. See also George Gawrych, *The Crescent and the Eagle: Ottoman Rule, Islam, and the Albanians, 1874–1913* (London, 2006); Jan Gordon, *A Balkan Freebooter: Being the True Exploits of the Serbian Outlaw and Comitaj Petko Mortich* (London, 1916); Eugene

This could not be helped. The army was vital for internal security and never completely replaced the police or gendarmerie. The constant need for "soldier-policemen" presented Ottoman leaders with a dilemma. Every time the army concentrated against a foreign enemy, troops were pulled from their constabulary duties, and local troublemakers were encouraged. Nearly every time reformers called for eliminating less competent units, war broke out. At this point "less competent" looked better than nothing.

A good example of these dilemmas was found during the reign of Abdul Hamid II (1876–1909). Within a year of his coronation, the Russo-Turkish War (1876–77) demonstrated Ottoman soldiers were just as potent as their fathers, while Ottoman generals were equally unchanged; they remained officers who could "snatch defeat from the jaws of victory." Although he was handicapped by an excessive fear of treason and by the search for an ideology that could strengthen his empire, defeat in 1877 made Abdülhamid a supporter of military modernization.[9]

In the early 1880s, Ottoman gold purchased Mauser rifles, Krupp artillery, and a team of German advisors. The latter were impressed with the raw material of the Ottoman army. "Mehmetçik," a Turkish version of "Tommy Atkins" or "Billy Yank," had long been praised as a first-rate fighting man. Throughout the nineteenth century, however, he was continually let down by poorly trained, incompetent, and corrupt leaders. By the 1880s, these men were split between two camps, the *alayli* and the *mektepli*. The former, who had been promoted from the ranks, were often illiterate, conservative, and elderly. The later, who had been trained in the academies, were more capable but suspect, as their better education might have infected them with anti-regime ideologies.

Abdülhamid played both groups, but always rewarded loyalty over efficiency. His "army of generals" contained 31 field marshals and 468 generals. *Alayli* remained in the ranks until 1909, when term-limits became law, and over ten thousand had to retire. This reform came at the wrong time, for eight thousand of these slots had not been replaced when the first Balkan War started in 1912.

L. Rogan, *Frontiers of the State in the Late Ottoman Empire: Transjordan, 1850–1921* (Cambridge, 2002); Albert Sonnichsen, *Confessions of a Macedonian Bandit: A Californian in the Balkan Wars* (New York, 1909).

9 Valentine Baker Pacha, *War in Bulgaria* (2 vols., London, 1879); Francis Greene, *The Russian Army and Its Campaigns in Turkey in 1877–1878* (New York, 1879); Frederick William von Herbert, *The Defence of Plevna, 1877* (London, 1911); Charles Ryan, *Under the Red Crescent: Adventures of an English Surgeon with the Turkish Army at Plevna and Erzurum, 1877–1878* (London, 1897).

The sultan could counter such criticism by noting that his army had won the so-called "thirty-day war" with Greece in 1897. The next foreign conflict, the Italian-Turkish War (1911) was less successful. Basically an instance of raw imperialism, this struggle came out of Italy's desire to grab Libya. Ottoman imperialism made this task easier, as thirty-five battalions drawn from Libya and Macedonia had just been sent to bolster the third Yemen campaign.[10]

Here was a strategic dilemma facing Ottoman decision-makers. The empire was large but contained a poor communications network. Getting troops from one end to the other took considerable time. In addition, provinces like Libya and Yemen produced limited revenues, were difficult to traverse, had topography that favored rebels, and thus required serious military assets to control. Ottoman imperialists added to these challenges, just like their French, British, Russian, and Italian counterparts, by their desire for conquests. Take, for example, the Hijaz, which contained Mecca and Medina. Could it be more easily defended if Ottoman forces advanced southward to dominate `Asīr? To control `Asīr, Ottoman troops should have captured a toehold in central Yemen. Not only would such expansion have created a large buffer zone around the "Holy Cities"; it would also have supported *"terakki ve temeddün"* ("progress and civilization"). The conquest of Arabia could be seen as an Ottoman version of the "civilizing mission."[11]

Yemen, and later next-door `Asīr, presented grave challenges to Ottoman generals. Both presented enemies united by religious leaders, mountainous terrain best understood by locals, and a price-tag for victory that far outweighed potential revenue flow. Yemen became a never-ending drain on Ottoman blood and capital. Three separate campaign medals were issued

10 Geroge F. Abbott, *The Holy War in Tripoli* (London, 1912); John Baldry, "The Turkish-Italian War in the Yemen, 1911–1912," *Arabian Studies* 3 (1976): 51–65; Ernst Bennett, *With the Turks in Tripoli* (London, 1912); David G. Herrmann, "The Paralysis of Italian Strategy in the Italian-Turkish War, 1911–1912," *English Historical Review* 104 (1989): 332–56; Italian General Staff, *The Italo-Turkish War (1911–12)* (Kansas City, 1914); Jafar Pasha al-Askari, *A Soldier's Story: From Ottoman Rule to Independent Iraq: The Memories of Jafar Pasha al-Askari (1885–1936)* (London, 2003); Enver Pasha, *Um Tripolis* (ed. Friedrich Perzyński, Munich, 1918); M. C. P. Ward, *Handbook of the Turkish Army* (London, 1900).

11 Saleh Muhammad al-Amr, *The Hijaz under Ottoman Rule 1869–1914: Ottoman Vali, the Sharif of Mecca, and the Growth of British Influence* (Riyadh, 1978); Frederick Anscombe, *The Ottoman Gulf: The Creation of Kuwait, Saudi Arabia and Qatar* (Columbia, 1997); Ann K. Bang, *The Idrisi State in `Asir, 1906–1934* (Bergen, 1996); Caesar E. Farah, *The Sultan's Yemen: 19th Century Challenges to Ottoman Rule* (London, 2002), 272; Robert Gavin, "The Ottoman Conquest of Arabia, 1871–1873," *History Today* (November 1963); Vincent S. Wilhite, "Guerilla War, Counterinsurgency, and State Formation in Ottoman Yemen" (Ph.D. dissertation, Ohio State University, 2004); A. J. B. Wavel, *A Modern Pilgrim in Mecca and the Siege of Sanaa* (London, 1912).

(1846, 1892, 1905), and even today *Yemen Türküsü* are popular folksongs that remind listeners of the high cost of subduing Yemen.

Repeated failures also sparked a revolution. Although military affairs were not its only cause, the army played a critical role in bringing the "Young Turks" into power. More formally known as the Committee for Union and Progress (CUP), this alliance of progressive politicians and junior army officers did not seek to dissolve the Sultanate, but rather to modernize it by restoring the 1876 Constitution, promoting Turkish nationalism, and speeding up army reforms.[12]

Ismail Enver (1881–1922), an army officer and CUP leader saw the latter goal as critical. Connected to things German by education and inclination, he was part of the triumvirate that dominated the empire during World War I. In a candid moment, Enver told a German friend "Your civilization is a poison, but a poison that awakens a people."[13]

Plenty of sleep, however, might have been a better prescription for the sick man, as the "Young Turks" were no better able to work the system than "Old Turks." This became clear during the first Balkan War (1912). Here an alliance of Greece, Montenegro, Serbia, and Bulgaria took advantage of Turkish preoccupation with campaigns in Libya and Yemen to launch a surprise attack against Ottoman holdings in the Balkans. Considering the fact that all but Montenegro had been part of the Ottoman Empire within the last century, the ability of these allies to field armies that totaled nearly twice the Ottoman forces in Macedonia was disturbing.[14]

Ahmad Izzet Paça, the Ottoman general who was most familiar with plans for the defense of Macedonia, was still in Yemen.[15] Nizam Paça, the minister of war, took command, but he lacked Izzet's knowledge of the prewar strategy and was hectored by the politically powerful "Young Turks." He thus opted for an aggressive stance that reflected his French military training. Accordingly, outnumbered and poorly led Ottoman armies were again placed in the worst possible tactical environment. Defeat followed defeat, as the

12 M. Şükrü Hanioğlu, *Young Turks in Opposition* (Oxford, 1995), and *Preparation for a Revolution: The Young Turks, 1902–1908* (Oxford, 2001); M. N. Tufan, *Rise of the Young Turks* (New York, 2000); V. Swenson, "The Military Rising in Istanbul 1909," *Journal of Contemporary History* 5 (1970): 171–84.

13 Cited in Şuhnoz Yilmaz, "An Ottoman Warrior Abroad: Enver Paşa as an Expatriate," *Middle Eastern Studies* 35 (1999): 44.

14 Edward Erikson, *Defeat in Detail: The Ottoman Army in the Balkans, 1912–1913* (Westport, CT, 2003); Wagner Hermengild, *With the Victorious Bulgarians* (New York, 1913); Handun Nezir-Akmese. *The Birth of Modern Turkey: The Ottoman Military and the March to World War I* (London, 2005).

15 *Paça* (*Pasha, Basha*) is not a name, but rather an Ottoman aristocratic title.

empire lost nearly all its European holdings. Then the Balkan League fell apart, and in the second Balkan War (1913) everyone ganged up on Bulgaria. Enver again pushed for an offensive, but with Bulgarian troops pulled out to fight former Greek and Serb allies, Ottoman forces advanced against almost no opposition. Enver even managed to join the lead column, which recaptured the culturally important city of Edirne (Adrianople).

Thus did Enver save his reputation and secure undeserved heroic status throughout the empire. He parlayed this status into yet more political capital, marrying the Sultan's niece, becoming minister of war, and getting promoted to *paça*. All these achievements empowered him to push the empire into World War I on the side of the Central Powers, where the "sick man" finally took a knock-out blow.[16]

In 1850 Japan was about as far removed from European and American power as was geographically possible. This situation played a role in protecting the nation from imperial sharks, which preferred to gobble up closer regions in central Asia, India, and China. After an initial lesson in "gunboat diplomacy," Japanese leaders recognized the threat of imperialism and quickly transformed their armed forces from antiquated to "state-of-the-art." Equally important, they initiated reforms that dramatically altered the nation's social, political, economic, and educational systems. These policies made Japan an exception in the story of the non-western world's reaction to nineteenth-century imperialism. By 1905, Japan was a world power with its own imperial aspirations.

Considering the situation in 1850, this change seems nothing less than miraculous. Self-isolated from most of the world by "maritime restrictions" that dated back to the 1630s, Japanese could not leave their country, and only a handful of foreigners could visit the port of Nagasaki. The Tokugawa *Bakufu*, or "Shogunate," an authoritarian regime that had been in power since 1603, viewed these restrictions as necessary for stability. Strict class differences, obedience to authority, and a small military also figured in government strategy. What passed for an army was more like a gendarmerie, with no general staff, nor even a structure to create brigade- or division-sized units. Even if the latter were possible, many Japanese soldiers still employed swords, spears, or bows, despite the presence of a Japanese firearms industry that dated back to the 1500s. Modernization was possible, but it required political

16 Edward Erikson, *Ottoman Army Effectiveness in World War I: A Comparative Study* (London, 2007); Alfred Nossig, *Die neue Türkei und ihre Führer* (Halle, 1916).

change, promised to be expensive, and required cuts in other government spending.[17]

These measures were difficult to enact, as the Shogunate was coming apart. It faced significant challenges in raising revenue, which were caused by the conversion from rice to a money-based economy, a silver-based currency that fared poorly when competing with the international gold standard, and taxation that had been unchanged in over two hundred years. This combination guaranteed tight budgets and economic hard times for Japan's warrior caste, the samurai. There were nearly 2 million samurai families in 1854, about 7 percent of the population. Although the males proudly carried their distinctive pair of swords, the military value of samurai was not significantly superior to that of the contemporary Ottoman Janissaries or Manchu Bannermen.

Samurai obtained support from either the Shogun or *Daimyo* (provincial leaders), but the stipends were not enough for the samurai to survive in Japan's changing economy. Fukuzawa Yukichi noted that many of his fellow warriors received only 50 to 75 percent of the minimum necessary to maintain a "respectable life." Late marriages, even infanticide, were suggested solutions. A few samurai spun silk or produced paper umbrellas, but work demeaned their class more than killing a child. By mid-century, the samurai represented an unhappy and potentially dangerous group.[18]

On the other hand, Japan had been at peace for over two centuries, enjoying growth in both population and agriculture. The country possessed a merchant-gentry class, with banks and capital, and skilled artisans who lacked only machines to become industrial workers. This combination of agriculture, capital, and a labor pool helped Japan's transition to a modern economy. Without them, the revolutionary changes of the 1870s and 1880s would have been far more difficult, if not impossible.

17 On the end of the Shogunate see, Harold Bolitho, *The Collapse of the Tokugawa Bakufu, 1862–1868* (Honolulu, 1980); Andrew Gordon, *A Modern History of Japan: From Tokugawa Times to the Present* (Oxford, 2003); Francis L. Hawks, *Narrative of the Expedition of an American Squadron to the China Seas and Japan under the Command of Commodore M. C. Perry, USN* (Washington, DC, 1856); William McOmie, *The Opening of Japan, 1853–1855: A Comparative Study of the American, British and Russian Campaigns to Force the Tokugawa Shogunate to Conclude Treaties and Open Ports to Their Ships* (Folkestone, 2006).

18 For accounts of samurai life in nineteenth-century Japan, see Katsu Kokichi, *Musui's Story: The Autobiography of a Tokugama Samurai* (Tucson, AZ, 1988); Fukuzawa Yukichi, *The Autobiography of Yukichi Fukuzawa* (New York, 2007). See also Eiko Ikegami, *The Taming of the Samurai: Honorific Individualism and the Making of Modern Japan* (Cambridge, MA, 1997); T. Sonada, "The Decline of the Japanese Warrior Class, 1840–1880," *Nichibunken Japan Review*, No. 1 (1990): 73–112.

Unhappy "barbarians" also featured in this mix. Centuries of isolation created an image of all outsiders as inferior and untrustworthy. Even if astute Japanese thought otherwise, this was the government's position and difficult to oppose. The Mito School, a movement that started in the 1840s, argued that China had been humbled by "barbarians," because of its contempt for foreign ideas. The school's members called for Japan to modernize its armed forces and for the reclusive Japanese emperor to utilize the respect that he enjoyed in order to unify the nation and make it stronger.

Elite opinion opposed this movement. Japan retained its maritime restrictions, which permitted only a heavily regulated Dutch factory in Nagasaki, and warned off or sank other foreign vessels that approached the coast. A good example of the obstacles to reform was the case of Takashima Shūhan, who purchased rifled muskets and field guns from the Dutch. He used these weapons to create a western-style infantry company and artillery battery. Using Dutch commands, he demonstrated their fighting value near Edo in 1841. Although the Shogun was impressed, conservative members of his court brought charges against Takashima. He remained under house arrest from 1846 to 1853.

A dramatic about-face came when Commodore Matthew Perry took a squadron of warships and forced Japan to open diplomatic relations and trade with the United States. Perry arrived in Tokyo Bay on July 8, 1853; his fleet included large black-painted steam frigates, such as the *USS Mississippi*, which were armed with 8- and 10-inch Paixhan guns. These "black ships" spread panic along the coast, until Perry departed on July 17. He returned with six ships in January 1854 and demanded access to the Shogun under threat of violence.

This demand resulted in the Kanagawa Convention (March 31, 1854), which established diplomatic relations, opened two Japanese ports to American ships, and granted "most favored nation status." A year later, Admiral Yevfimi Putiatin arrived with four Russian steamers, demanding similar terms. Next, the Americans gained extraterritoriality. In four more years, even Mexico possessed special privileges in Japan.

Perry's "gunboat diplomacy" opened Japanese eyes to the threat of military defeat and loss of independence. After his squadron left, Perry cruised to nearby Taiwan, and then returned home with charts, surveys, and a recommendation that Congress annex the island for naval bases and coal. The Bonin Islands were Perry's second choice. Six years later, the Second Opium War ended in further loss of territory and prestige for China. All these events opened Japanese eyes to the need for change.

Three options gained rapid support. First, the Shogun directed a large following that opted for opening the door a crack. Another faction, which was nearly as large and centered on the traditionally reclusive emperor, called for a return to total exclusion. Finally, a smaller group of *Daimyo* supported greater interaction with foreigners.

All these options came with political consequences and help explain the revolutionary turmoil of the 1850s and 1860s. Iyesada, the Shogun, initiated change. He asked Emperor Osahito to approve Kanagawa, not only implying that the emperor was his superior, but also accepting public blame for backing down in the face of Perry's warships. This step fueled the *sonnō jōi* ("Respect the Emperor, expel the barbarians") movement but also aided the Shogun's rivals. Iyesada further helped the opposition when he allowed *Daimyo* to import artillery, construct coastal defense batteries, and improve their domain's militia. He did so in order to spread the high costs of military modernization and in hopes of building a national consensus on dealing with the powerful foreigners. Instead, his actions fueled *sonnō jōi* and alienated top lieutenants, who resented sharing power with provincial leaders. The Shogun faced a "no-win" situation; he could be blamed for caving in to the foreigners, while these same foreigners could blame his regime were they to run into trouble with Japanese ultranationalists.

Between 1853 and 1866, two Shoguns and the emperor died of natural causes, as a complicated political struggle accompanied dramatic policy twists by all factions. Internal unrest flared among all classes. Young, mainly poor samurai became *shishi* ("men of high purpose"), who attacked foreigners and Shogunate forces. *Shishi* bands attempted to "free" the emperor in 1863 and 1864. Fleeing to the Chōshū Domain, where *sonnō jōi* support was strong, these disgruntled samurai helped fuel both a Shogunal invasion and domain-wide civil war.

The 1860s were also a time of frenzied training and the purchase of rifled muskets, modern artillery, and even Gatling guns by the Shogun and powerful domains like Satsuma, Saga, and Chōshū. Japanese tea and silk could pay for these expensive imports but barely, as the nation went through painful economic changes brought on by its reentry into world markets. Another change was the increased use of commoners as army personnel. Even the Shogun was training peasant riflemen in the 1860s, despite the fact that Tokugawa policy had long sought to monopolize weapons-training and ownership within the samurai class.

Fighting erupted on several fronts between 1863 and 1866, first when Japanese xenophobes murdered foreigners and burned their legations. These actions brought a response from US, French, Dutch, and British warships, which retaliated with attacks against the Shogun's new navy and coastal defense positions in the Satsuma domain. On August 15–17, 1863, a British flotilla bombarded the city of Kagoshima, destroying military stores and setting fire to over five hundred homes.

Unable to defend Japan, the Shogunate lost face while Chōshū and Satsuma, despite their support for the *shishi*, grew stronger. Chōshū military potential had dramatically improved because of efforts by Takasugi Shinsaku, who supervised numerous rifle companies, which were called *shotai* and comprised samurai and commoners. Although mainly armed with Enfield rifled muskets, some of these men had Spencer magazine rifles, which provided them with a considerable advantage over other Japanese military units.

The Chōshū–Satsuma alliance brought a final showdown with the Shogun in 1868. On January 3, the fifteen-year old Meiji emperor abolished the Shogunate and was "restored" to power. Next, pro-Shogun forces were shot to pieces at Toba-Fushimi (January 27–30). Fighting on land and sea continued until May 1869. It featured transitional military units, some of which were still armed with swords and spears, others with breech-loading rifles.

This year-long struggle, known as the Boshin War, ended with complete victory for the Meiji emperor and his Chōshū–Satsuma advocates, but military affairs still held high priority, as nearly all Japanese wanted to overturn the unequal treaties that had been forced on them during the 1850s and 1860s. War against the west was not a realistic option, even to the most rabid nationalists, so developing a strong, prosperous, and "respectable" country seemed the proper course. As Iwakura Tomomi put it in 1877, "Since the restoration, we have had to promote unprecedented reforms in order to confront foreign countries."[19] More resources, technology, industrialization, expert advisors, increased revenue, and compulsory education were required, all of which supported the government's primary goal of military expansion.[20]

A modern army was a central part of this strategy. The French advisor Albert Charles du Bousquet suggested that Japan build one on the European model. He recommended incremental steps to produce an effective fighting machine. First, military schools and academies were to train commissioned

19 Marlene Mayo, ed., *The Emergence of Imperial Japan: Self-Defense or Calculated Aggression?* (Lexington, MA, 1970), 2.

20 For interesting works on Meiji policy and politics, see Sydney E. Crawcour, "Industrialization and Technological Change, 1885–1920," in Kozo Yamamura, ed., *The Economic Emergence of Modern Japan* (Cambridge, 1997), 50–115; Marius Jansen, *The Emergence of Meiji Japan* (Cambridge, 2006); Donald Kean, *Emperor of Japan: Meiji and His World* (New York, 2005); Ernest Satow, *A Diplomat in Japan* (London, 1921); Richard Sims, *French Policy Towards the Bakufu and Meiji Japan, 1854–95: A Case of Misjudgment and Missed Opportunities* (London, 1998).

MAP 6. Meiji Japan and the Japanese empire

and noncommissioned officers (NCOs). Simultaneously, a compulsory national education system would guarantee a literate conscript pool. Next, the civilian economy was to support domestic production of modern weapons and ammunition. Finally, a conscript army could be established.

Returning from a study mission in Europe in 1873, General Yamada Akiyoshi agreed with the thrust of du Bousquet's plan, but he argued for a small, highly trained army at first. Japan could not afford a large army during the 1870s, he countered, but a small elite force would not strain the budget and could provide a cadre of officers and NCOs when more funding became available. Yamada also convinced the government to turn military drill into the main form of physical education in Japan's new public school system.[21]

Du Bousquet was one of nearly a hundred Dutch, German, British, Italian, and French nationals who served as military advisors to national or regional Japanese governments from the 1850s to the 1880s. At first, the French were the most influential. Organization and training along French lines continued even after the French defeat in the Franco-Prussian War, which many Japanese officers ascribed not to military defects but to a lack of French national will. Five years later, French advisors helped open the *Rikugun Shikan gakkō* (Army Officers' School), which was modeled after St. Cyr, and they themselves were among its first instructors. France also provided naval advisors, including Louis-Émile Bertin, who pushed Japanese fleet development toward a *Jeune École* model.

Although the French initially provided significant contributions to the Meiji armed forces, Britain became more influential with the navy and Germany with the army. The latter's influence was embodied in a charismatic Prussian, Major Jacob Meckel, who taught at the Army Officers' School from 1885 to 1888. Handpicked by Helmuth von Moltke at the request of the Japanese, Meckel connected with Japanese students, many of whom were more comfortable with

21 For more on the Meiji army, see T. F. Cooke, "Making 'Soldiers': The Imperial Army and the Japanese Man in Meiji Society and State," in B. Molony and K. Uno, eds., *Gendering Modern Japanese History* (Cambridge, MA, 2005), 259–94; James B. Crowley, "From Closed Door to Empire: The Foundation of the Meiji Military Establishment," in Bernard S. Silbermand and H. D. Harootunian, eds., *Modern Japanese Leadership* (Tucson, 1966), 261–85; R. F. Hackett, *Yamagata Aritomo in the Rise of Modern Japan, 1838–1922* (Cambridge, 1980); Leonard Humphreys, *The Way of the Heavenly Sword: The Japanese Army in the 1920s* (Stanford, 1995); Hyman Kublin, "The 'Modern' Army of Early Meiji Japan," *Far Eastern Quarterly* 9 (1949): 255–66; S. Lone, *Army, Empire and Politics in Meiji Japan: The Three Careers of General Katsura Taro* (New York, 2000); E. H. Norman, *Soldier and Peasant in Japan: The Origins of Conscription* (New York, 1943); Fukushima Shingo, "The Building of a National Army," in Tobata Seiichi, ed., *The Modernization of Japan* (Tokyo, 1966): 193–96.

imperial Germany than republican France. He stressed military education as a guarantee of an efficient army. His formula emphasized professional officers, staff work, a clear chain of command, and good logistics. He also supported those who favored an invasion of Korea, arguing that was "a dagger at the heart" of Japan if controlled by another power. After three years, Meckel had so impressed Japanese leaders that French influence dramatically declined. Save for uniforms, the army had opted for a German model.[22]

The administrative structure of the Japanese military also followed the German model. The Meiji regime created a *Hyōbushō* (military ministry), which had evolved into army and navy ministries by 1872. Unlike counterparts in other modernizing regimes, such as Manchu China or the Ottoman Empire, the Japanese military ministry was not troubled by infighting between line officers and administrators, because a large number of the latter had been serving officers with a shared view of how to build military power in Japan.

Dissension did not disappear, but it surfaced elsewhere. Technically, the Meiji emperor held great power, but he seldom employed it; and there was no Imperial Diet until 1889. Instead, Japan was dominated by clan leaders from Satsuma and Chōshū, the two domains that had provided the main forces behind the Meiji revolution. The most influential of these men, the *Genrō* (elder statesmen), "advised" the Meiji emperor, and because their advice was seldom rejected, they formed an oligarchy that dominated Japan well into the 1890s. After the Satsuma Rebellion (1877), they shared a vision of Japan that was captured in the Meiji slogan *"fukoku kyōhei"* (rich nation, strong military).

Initially, the implementation of this vision was hotly debated. One faction, led by Saigō Takamori, pressed for Japan's immediate entry into the world of empire via the conquest of Korea. They argued that a war with Korea could restore national pride, which had been lost in the last two decades; it would also employ samurai and provide resources for Japan's new industries. As Kirino Toshicki put it, "If we want to make our country equal to others, we must go overseas, fight, and make conquests."[23] Iwakura was spokesman for the opposition, and although he was not opposed to Japanese imperialism, he had just returned from an extensive study of Europe and believed that Japan was not ready for overseas adventures. He viewed the world in Darwinian terms and thought that "foreign countries are the natural enemies of our

22 Good sources on Meiji military connections with Germany include Georg Kerst, *Jacob Meckel: Sein Leben, Sein Wirken in Deutschland und Japan* (Göttingen, 1970); Ernst Presseisen, *Before Aggression: Europeans Prepare the Japanese Army* (Tucson, 1965).

23 Mayo, *Emergence*, 8.

imperial land."[24] He argued that Japan needed infrastructural development before imperial ventures.

These disagreements led to the *Seikanron*, or "debate over conquering Korea," which split the *Genrō*. Saigō failed to sell his plan for Japanese imperialism, and along with several key supporters, he resigned from government service. This development removed the most conservative of the original Meiji leaders and opened slots for new men. Thus *Seikanron* dramatically changed the makeup of the *Genrō*, affecting the development of the army and navy. It also ended a debate over conscription, which Yamagata and his fellow Chōshū clansman, Yamada Akiyoshi, promoted. Saigō had opposed any form of draft, and his resignation cleared the way for the first induction of peasant soldiers. In January 1873, the government was empowered to call on young men to perform three years of active duty, followed by an additional four years in the active reserve. No more than 3 percent of eligible youth were taken, both to cut costs and because of low literacy rates. As finances and the new educational system expanded, the percentage of those drafted increased in the 1880s and 1890s.

Charged with enforcing conscription, the *Kempeitai*, which was founded in 1881, illustrated how Meiji military reforms altered Japan. Another product of French influence, it was modeled after the *Gendarmerie nationale*. Within a decade, the *Kempeitai* had also become a military police force, which included a plainclothes branch. By 1907 it had detachments in Japan's overseas territories and had developed the brutal reputation which came to full blossom in the 1930s.

Japan's navy had a different tradition. It started nearly from scratch in the 1850s and, unlike the army, had no conservative clique of officers who distrusted change. Its leaders were more at ease with new technology and foreign advisors. In 1855, the Shogun authorized a naval academy in Nagasaki, with two hundred students and five Dutch instructors.[25] On the other hand, the navy had been starved for cash since the start of the Meiji revolution. This was partially due to infighting among Satsuma, Saga, and ex-Shogunate

24 Ibid., 20.

25 Meiji naval history is covered in Christian Dedet, *Les fleurs d'acier du Mikado* (Paris, 1993); Eugène Collache, "Une aventure au Japon," *Le Tour du Monde* 77 (1874): 49; David Evans and Mark Peattie, *Kaigun: Strategy, Tactics and Technology in the Imperial Japanese* Navy (Annapolis, MD, 1997); Ian Gow, "The Douglas Mission (1873–79) and Meiji Naval Education," in J. E. Hoare, ed., *Britain and Japan: Biographical Portraits* (2 vols., Tokyo, 1999), Vol. II: 189–204; John C. Pery, "Great Britain and the Emergence of Japan as a Naval Power," *Monumenta Nipponica* 21 (1966): 305–21; J. Charles Schencking, *Making Waves: Politics, Propaganda and the Emergence of the Imperial Japanese Navy, 1868–1922* (Stanford, CA, 2005); E. de Touchet, "L'Arsenal de Yokosuka de 1865 à 1882," *Ebisu* 26 (2001): 35–62.

officers, but it was also because Japan's leaders saw the rapid changes in naval technology as a reason for caution. In 1874, the navy obtained three British-built warships, which were the first to be added to the fleet since the 1860s.

Britain also provided most of the naval advisors, for the Japanese considered the Royal Navy their best model. "Officers are the heart of a warship," wrote Naval Minister Katsu Kaishū, and British-style leadership was advanced as the key to victory in the Meiji fleet.[26] A slight alteration marked the late 1880s, when Louis-Émile Bertin, the advocate of the *Jeune École* strategy, advised on ship procurement, helping to create the fast-moving fleet that devastated ponderous Chinese ironclads off the Yalu in 1895.

The Yalu was one of several contests fought by Japan's new armed forces. The Meiji military were involved in conflicts from the start. Once the Korea debate ended, the army was regarded not only as an instrument of protection against foreign enemies, but also as a guarantor of domestic tranquility. Drill for the first conscripts was mainly at the company and battalion level, and it featured skills that could be used to fight civil unrest. Training, discipline, and indoctrination ensured the army's loyalty. Every effort was made to isolate conscripts from political factions and to focus their attention on duty to the emperor.

These efforts paid off during the 1870s and 1880s, when the army crushed a variety of internal foes. The most formidable were the former samurai, who were already on the margins in the 1850s and were deprived of both status and salaries in the 1870s. A majority of them adjusted to the new system, serving the government or forming military colonies to increase the Japanese presence in Hokkaido. This second option not only removed potential troublemakers from the center of power, but also provided insurance against Russian designs on the island.[27]

Samurai who were unwilling to change found a spokesman in Saigō Takamori. Strong, tall, a skilled swordsman, and loyal to his friends, he seemed to embody the samurai ideal. Saigō was also a good tactician, who held important commands in support of the Meiji revolution. By the 1870s,

26 Cited in Schencking, *Waves*, 21.

27 For more on the military's role during Meiji internal unrest, see H. Bolitho, "The Echigo War, 1868," *Monumenta Nipponica* 34 (1979): 259–77; James Herold Buck, *Satsuma Rebellion: An Episode in Modern Japanese History* (New York, 1979); K. Meissner, "'General' Eduard Schnell," *Monumenta Nipponica* 4 (1941): 69–101; John M. Rogers, "Divine Destruction: The Shinpūren Rebellion of 1876," in Helen Hardacre and Adam L. Kern, eds., *New Directions in the Studies of Meiji Japan* (Leiden, 1997), 408–39; Shumpei Okamoto, "The Emperor and the Crowd: The Historical Significance of the Hibiya Riot," in Tetsuo Najita and J. Victor Koschmann, eds., *Conflict in Modern Japanese History: The Neglected Tradition* (Princeton, 1982), 262–70; Charles Yates, Saigo *Takamori: The Man behind the Myth* (London, 1995).

however, he had become a disgruntled revolutionary. His desires to improve samurai status via larger stipends or leadership in an invasion of Korea had come to naught. Instead, the government that he had helped create ordered samurai to cut off their distinctive top-knots in 1871, ended stipends in 1873, and in 1876 outlawed the public display of weapons by private individuals.

Saigō resigned from his government posts after the *Seikanron* debate in 1873. He returned to Kagoshima, his hometown, and established a martial-arts school that quickly established branches throughout the region. By 1875, he had built a significant paramilitary organization and dominated Kagoshima. Simultaneously, the government faced small-scale violent uprisings starting in October 1875. These featured bands of hundreds of samurai, who attacked government offices, forts, and troop barracks.

Although these revolts were crushed, Saigō's quasi-independent Kagoshima seemed connected to them, so government authorities investigated. Several botched efforts to gather intelligence and confiscate weapons followed, and in January 1877 thousands of Saigō's "students" attacked government centers. The Satsuma Rebellion began, the most significant internal conflict since the 1860s. Saigō quickly recruited fifteen thousand mainly ex-samurai and marched on Tokyo. His army multiplied during the march, and numbered about twenty thousand when it ran into the government stronghold, Kumamoto Castle. After several attacks were repelled, Saigō opted for a siege. This decision allowed Yamagata Aritomo to muster a force of thirty thousand conscripts for the decisive battle of Tabaruzaka. Fought between March 4 and 19, 1877, it featured artillery, Gatling guns, and amphibious landings by government troops, which not only attacked the rear of Saigō's command, but also struck farther afield, taking over Kagoshima's main arsenal. The result of the final battle – Shiroyama on September 24 – was a foregone conclusion, although Saigō and his followers fought so hard against incredible odds that they entered the world of popular culture as paragons of the samurai tradition.

Seven years later, the new army was called on to smash another internal uprising. Peasant farmers resented economic and social changes. During the first two decades of Meiji government, conscription centers were ransacked, and over a thousand schools were burned to prevent compulsory education. Rural rebellion had a long tradition in Japan. The last uprising of the Meiji era centered on Chichibu, a town not far from Tokyo. It featured over six thousand impoverished silk farmers, who formed a "Revolutionary Army" in November 1884. They attacked government records offices, the homes of the wealthy, and schools. Local police were overwhelmed, and the army took ten days to crush the rebellion.

Although government forces were never in danger of defeat, Japan's internal struggles of the 1870s and 1880s showed that both the army and the navy were loyal, capable of joint operations, and led by officers who understood modern warfare. Military actions had hardly been flawless. Poor staff work gave Satsuma rebels time to marshal their forces and launch an offensive. Yamagata cited these failings as justification for creating a general staff in 1878. He separated this body from the military administration, making the general staff answerable only to the army minister. Four years later, he convinced the Meiji emperor to issue the "Imperial Precepts for Soldiers and Sailors," which enjoined all servicemen to eschew politics, "but with a single heart fulfill your essential duty of loyalty."[28]

By then the *Genrō* had perfected their system and allowed the proclamation of a constitution in 1889. Styled after conservative Germany's, it allowed little power to the masses and ensured an independent military, mandating that both the army and the navy ministers be appointed by the emperor and selected from active-duty officers. This provision not only made civilian control of the armed forces nearly impossible, but it also allowed the service ministers to break civilian governments by withdrawing their support.

Now that Japan had a parliament, opposition parties sought to enhance their power via popular opinion. As in America and Europe, appeals to "jingoism" worked well in Japan. This fueled Japanese imperialism and benefited both ultraconservative forces like the *Genyōsha*, which promoted the emperor, and the *Jiyu minken undu* (Popular Rights Movement). For many of these men, the late nineteenth century seemed like an era in which countries grew bigger, controlled more resources, and expanded their military potential – or became targets for those who did. During the 1880s and 1890s, France expanded into Tonkin, the Russians mopped up central Asia, and Germany established bases in New Guinea and several Pacific islands.[29]

Yamagata viewed all powers as potential enemies. He believed that Asia was divided into "zones of sovereignty" like Korea, which Japan had to control, and "zones of advantage," like China, where Japan could use its power to gain access to markets and resources. Soejima Taneomi, who served both as foreign minister and later as home minister, argued that even with a

28 Ryusaku Tsunoda et al., *Sources of Japanese Tradition* (2 vols., New York, 1958), Vol. II: 198.

29 For more on Japanese imperialism, see W. G. Beasley, *Japanese Imperialism 1894–1945* (Oxford, 1987); Kenneth E. Boulding and Alan H. Gleason, "War as an Investment: The Strange Case of Japan," in Kenneth E. Boulding and Tapan Mukerjee, eds., *Economic Imperialism: A Book of Readings* (Ann Arbor, 1972), 240–61.

good navy it would be difficult for Japan to defend itself against a great power, but that bases on the Asian mainland would improve the odds.

Expansion overseas was a direct consequence of Meiji Realpolitik. The Japanese could swim with the sharks or watch nearby islands, Korea, and perhaps China become colonies that could be used as springboards to attack Japan. So the Japanese became sharks. In the best imperial style, a Japanese force landed on Formosa (Taiwan) and between 1871 and 1874 conducted raids against aboriginal tribes, which had attacked shipwrecked Japanese sailors. Five years later, the Japanese annexed the Ryukyu (Nansei) Islands, which had been a tributary state to both Japan and China since 1609, with little opposition.[30]

Korea came next, but it presented a greater challenge. It was a more valuable prize, thus more attractive to other powers. French and American landings had taken place in 1866 and 1871, proving that small foreign military units could take over Korean coastal islands or fortifications. Although some Japanese called for cooperation with other powers, most Meiji leaders held a contrary view. As Taneomi put it, "However civilized Korea becomes, do you think the great powers, who are as greedy as wild beasts, will decline to eat? On the contrary, the more civilized Korea becomes, the better feast it will make."[31]

Japanese diplomats and adventurers meddled in Korean affairs, until coups and counter-coups brought China and Japan to the verge of war in 1884. A study by the general staff in the same year showed Japan did not have the logistical capabilities to support an invasion of Korea. As a result, the Japanese agreed to a negotiated settlement via the Tientsin Convention of 1885. Two years later, the general staff began to plan an invasion of Korea and a subsequent operation against Manchuria. The fleet was enlarged, so in case of renewed conflict a military option would be available.[32]

China itself was of great concern to Japan. In Tokyo's perspective, the two countries held a "wheel-and-axle" relationship. The continued triumphs of western imperialists over the Middle Kingdom disturbed Japanese leaders. Fukuzawa Yukichi, a noted writer, argued that both Korea and China were

30 For more on the Taiwan Expedition, see Robert Eskildsen, "Of Civilization and Savages: The Mimetic Imperialism of Japan's 1874 Expedition to Taiwan," *American Historical Review* 107 (2002): 388–418; Leonard Gordon, "Japan's Abortive Colonial Venture in Taiwan, 1874," *Journal of Modern History* 37 (1965): 171–85; Edward H. House, *The Japanese Expedition to Formosa* (Tokyo, 1875).

31 Cited in Mayo, *Emergence*, ix.

32 On Japan's interests in late-nineteenth-century Korea, see Peter Duus, *The Abacus and the Sword: Japanese Penetration of Korea, 1895–1910* (Berkeley, 1995); A. Schmid, *Korea between Empires 1895–1919* (New York, 2002); Young-Woo Nam, "Japanese Military Surveys of the Korean Peninsula in the Meiji Era," in Helen Hardacre and Adam L. Kern, eds., *New Directions in the Studies of Meiji Japan* (Leiden, 1997), 335–42.

"foolish nations," which he compared to wooden houses awaiting a fire. Sugita Teiichi, a politician, suggested another analogy, arguing that Japan could not save either country without becoming "meat" for the great powers. It would be far better, he wrote, to join them "as a guest at the table."[33] Tokyo pulled up a chair to the imperialist table in 1894, when Tonghak rebels forced the deployment of four thousand Chinese regulars in Korea. Already incensed over the assassination of a political ally, the Japanese sent in a brigade and demanded China share control of Korea. Beijing refused, and the result was the Sino-Japanese War of 1894–95.[34]

This was the first real test for the Meiji armed forces. Like Japan, China had invested great effort to modernize its army and navy. Unlike Japan, China had failed to recognize all the changes needed for a modern military to function. The result was one disaster after another, as Japanese soldiers took over Korea and then advanced into Manchuria. It was no different on the high seas, where Japanese warships crushed the larger Chinese navy. When the fortress of Weihaiwei surrendered on February 12, 1895, the Japanese captured an intact Chinese battleship. China was not a "sleeping giant," as one Japanese journalist wrote, but "a sleeping pig."[35]

The Sino-Japanese War taught Japan several lessons. First, the army and navy were dedicated, efficient, and well led. Second, war could be profitable. Japan obtained a massive indemnity, which more than covered the cost of the war. The ¥364 million provided by China was about one-third of Japan's gross national product in 1895. Third, China surrendered Formosa and the Liaotung Peninsula. Finally, China renounced all rights over Korea. Another advantage, noted by Japanese leaders, was the cessation of internal political debates, as the nation rallied behind the war effort.

Another lesson came when France, Germany, and Russia ganged up on Japan, demanding Liaodong and Port Arthur be returned to China. This "Triple Intervention" reinforced the sense that predatory European powers were hostile to Japanese ambitions. As a contemporary journalist, Tokutomi Sohō, explained, this action had changed his worldview, for "sincerity and justice

33 Cited in Mayo, *Emergence*, 6. For more on early Japanese–Chinese military relations, see Li Tingjiang, "Zhang Zhidong and his Japanese Military Advisors: A Preliminary Analysis of Modern Japan's China policy," in A. Fogel, ed., *Late Qing China and Meiji Japan: Political and Cultural Aspects* (Norwalk, CT, 2004), 58–67.

34 The Sino-Japanese War is detailed in S. Lone, *Japan's First Modern War: Army and Society in the Conflict with China, 1894–95* (London, 1994); Philo N. McGiffin, "Battle of Yalu," *The Century* 50 (1895): 585–605; S. C. M. Paine, *The Sino-Japanese War of 1894–1895: Perceptions, Power, and Primacy* (London, 2002).

35 Cited in Duus, *Abacus*, 129.

did not amount to anything if you were not strong enough . . . Japan's progress would ultimately depend upon military strength."[36] Japanese nationalists saw the lease of this peninsula to Russia in 1898 as further proof of western cupidity. In addition, army and navy leaders shared a pessimistic view of the future of China and Korea. Japan, in their opinion, had limited time to expand onto the Asian continent, for, as Yamagata cautioned, soon "there will no longer be a Korea or a China, but the rule of the three powers."[37] Meiji leaders shared this vision, responding with increased military spending. The budget in 1896 doubled the size of the navy and increased the army to thirteen divisions. The nearly ¥300 million to pay for these expansions came from bonds raised against the Chinese indemnity – another sign that aggression paid big dividends.

China's "Boxer Rebellion" (1900–01), which Japanese authorities referred to as the Hokushin Incident, provided Tokyo with another chance to demonstrate great-power status. Japanese soldiers and sailors fought at Taku and Tientsin, in defense of the Beiing legations, and with the international force that relieved the legations. Komuro Jatarō, Japan's minister to Russia, argued that the Boxer Rebellion was a golden opportunity. "Our country," he wrote, "must always have a military and naval force equal to at least the strongest power in China."[38] Japan sent significant naval assets and an infantry division, and it was willing to send more ground units until Germany and Russia expressed their disapproval. Komuro had also advised a policy of cooperation, so no more troops landed in north China. Meanwhile, American and British observers noted the good cheer and determination of Japanese forces.[39]

These favorable reviews coincided with another turning point in Japan's efforts to attain equality, the Anglo-Japanese Alliance. A reflection of Japan's status, as well as changing British strategies for Asia, this connection originated in the 1890s, when, faced by American, Russian, and German competition, Britain looked for a junior partner. Ratified in 1902, the treaty of alliance called for Japan and the United Kingdom to join forces if either were attacked by more than one country. From a Japanese perspective, it was Japan's first international agreement concluded on the basis of equality, and it provided vital insurance against another "Triple Intervention."

36 Cited in Gordon, "Abortive Colonial Venture," 119.

37 Cited in Mayo, *Emergence*, 78.

38 Cited in ibid., 79.

39 For more on Japan and the Boxer Rebellion, see S. Lone, "Holding in the North: Japanese Policy toward Korea in the Boxer War, 1900," *Papers in Far Eastern History* 40 (1989): 79–94; Ian Nish, "Japan's Indecision during the Boxer Disturbances," *Journal of Asian Studies* 20 (1951): 241–50.

Russia had used the Boxer Rebellion to take over much of Manchuria, and it did not seem likely to depart even after the Boxer Protocols ended this conflict in 1901. In addition, Russian diplomats continued to push for greater influence in Korea. Despite a brief effort to arrange a trade-off, which would recognize Russian domination of Manchuria in exchange for Japan's control of Korea, Tokyo prepared for a war with Russia after 1902. Two years later, when Russian diplomats made clear their refusal to recognize Japan's position on Korea, Japanese torpedo boats launched a surprise attack on tsarist naval units in Port Arthur.[40]

War with Russia proved as popular as previous conflicts. Jingos stirred the people to new heights of patriotism. Conscripts cheerfully marched off to battle. Capitalists purchased war-bonds, and fashionable ladies soon sported "203 Meter Hill" hairdos – modeled on the position from which General Nogi's howitzers pounded the Russian garrison at Port Arthur.

Despite tremendous moral support, Japan faced a dilemma of scale. Although Japan had better trained, motivated, and directed soldiers, the tsar's army was much larger, and size mattered once the protagonists got bogged down in the slow and costly siege of Port Arthur. By 1905, the Japanese army had drawn nearly every available man of fighting age; Russia had just started to draw on its vast European reserves of manpower. Japan also had financial problems and was heavily in debt to banks in New York and London. Russia had its own financial issues, in addition to growing internal unrest that spilled over into the revolution of 1905, but the "Russian steamroller" could have held the Japanese in a stalemate. The decisive naval victory at Tsushima, along with the sober recognition that Japan needed to end the war, averted this possibility via the Treaty of Portsmouth. It required Russia to surrender the southern half of Sakhalin Island, its lease of the Liaotung Peninsula, and the South Manchurian Railroad. In addition, Russia recognized Japanese control of Korea.

Initially, the home front was delighted. The Yokohama coast witnessed a spectacular naval review on October 23, 1905, when Admiral Tōgō Heihachirō displayed his fleet and captured Russian vessels. It was a far cry from Perry's visit in 1854. In fact, it crowned a victory more significant than Adwa. A non-western power had mastered the tools needed to join the "first world." Japan's defeat of Russia proved that it was one of the great powers.

40 Much has been written on the Russo-Japanese War. A few good examples include I. H. Nish, ed., *The Russo-Japanese War, 1904–5* (8 vols., Folkestone, 2003); J. Steinberg et al., eds., *The Russo-Japanese War in Global Perspective: World War Zero* (2 vols., Leiden, 2005–2007).

7. Japanese soldiers before the attack on Fakumen (China) during the Russo-Japanese War

Russia's defeat also removed the last hope for an independent Korea. Japanese agents had assassinated Empress Myeongseong ("Queen Min") in 1895, removing a strong advocate of military modernization. When her husband, Emperor Gojong, proved obstinate after 1905, violence was no longer necessary. Japan simply annexed Korea in 1910. Despite low-level resistance, which sputtered off and on for the next few decades, Japan created a draconian colonial system that dominated the peninsula until 1945.

Still, victory in 1905 had been a close call. The fighting cost 370,000 casualties and ¥1.9 billion. These figures represented a third of all the men mobilized and seven times the national budget of 1904. The public soon concluded that these sacrifices had been poorly rewarded, especially once Japan failed to obtain an indemnity. One result was Tokyo's famous Hibiya Riots, in which thousands attacked police substations to vent their frustrations over the "humiliation" of Portsmouth. This "man-on-the-street" view, which was encouraged by military leaders, was that Japan had won the war but lost the peace. It was a failure of diplomacy, not the result of a close-fought military campaign that could easily have turned into disaster. As in 1895 and 1901, the Japanese public learned the wrong lessons in 1905.

These lessons reinforced a national consensus that aggression paid. The opportunities thus seemed boundless for Japan in the new century. The Chinese revolution of 1911, far from reviving this country, spun out of control, creating regional factions around various warlords. The question was whether Japan could benefit. The army and navy had to agree on a joint strategy. After 1905, this cooperation proved almost impossible, creating a major discrepancy between means and ends. Looking back from World War II, Admiral Shigeru Fukudome claimed that his navy was focused on the Pacific by 1907, viewing America as its "sole strategic enemy."[41] The army, however, which had Korea and Port Arthur to defend, saw China as an opportunity and Russia as a threat.

Japan could not afford to fight both America and Russia. This much was clear to Prime Minister Saionji Kinmochi, who refused to authorize funds to expand the Japanese army by two divisions in 1912. His decision led to a constitutional crisis when the army minister resigned and Yamagata convinced all serving generals to refuse service to a Saionji administration. The government fell, because the Meiji constitution allowed only general officers to serve as service ministers. A year later, Prime Minister Katsura Tarō suffered a similar fate, when, miffed over his refusal to fund additional dreadnaughts, the navy minister resigned. Created to protect the state and advance its interest, the military was now poised to take over and advance its own.

Thus did the Japanese shark enter the waters of the twentieth century. The *Genrō* who loosed this shark on China and Korea were mainly gone. In 1912 the

41 Cited in Mayo, *Emergence*, 44.

last vestige of foreign domination ended when Japan regained complete control of its customs revenue. In 1912 the navy minister also requested ¥350 million to expand the fleet in case of war with the United States. A year later, Japanese investments in China and Korea totaled $220 million; and a significant portion was focused in Manchuria. The road to Pearl Harbor had begun.[42]

42 On Japanese–American issues, see Akira Iriye, *Pacific Estrangement: Japanese and American Expansion, 1897–1911* (Cambridge, 1972).

5

War, society, and culture, 1850–1914: the rise of militarism

ROGER CHICKERING

The word "militarism" entered general usage in the 1860s. It initially carried several meanings, but the context was clear. At issue was the political and social place of armies and military values. The discussions of this issue were particularly intense in central Europe, where parliamentary struggles over the army in Prussia were the prelude to a series of wars that resulted in German national unification in 1871. The epithet "militarism" was hurled in the first place by south German democrats, Catholics, and other opponents of Prussian policies that eventually triumphed in the Franco-Prussian War. Across the Rhine, the same term was invoked meanwhile to criticize the emperor, Napoleon III, whose policies were said to invoke the specter of military conflict abroad in order to promote stability at home.[1] The term has spawned controversy ever since. Its most common connotations have been pathological.[2] On the one hand, they have focused on civil–military relations, on the failure of civilian control and the resulting intrusion of soldiers into policymaking institutions. Another common set of connotations has addressed broader questions of political culture – the pervasiveness of military patterns of thinking and behavior in civil society. Lawrence Radway, who wrote the original entry on "militarism" in the *International Encyclopedia of the Social Sciences* in 1929, captured both the institutional and cultural facets of the phenomenon when he defined militarism as a doctrine that "values war and accords primacy in state and society to the armed forces."[3]

1 Werner Conze et al., "Militarismus," in Otto Brunner et al., eds., *Geschichtliche Grundbegriffe: Historisches Lexikon zur politisch-sozialen Sprache in Deutschland* (8 vols., Stuttgart, 1972–97), Vol. IV: 22–29.

2 But see Dennis Showalter, "Army, State and Society in Germany, 1871–1914: An Interpretation," in Jack R. Dukes and Joachim Remak, eds., *Another Germany: A Reconsideration of the Imperial Era* (Boulder and London, 1988), 1–18.

3 Lawrence Radway, "Militarism," in *The International Encyclopedia of the Social Sciences* (London, 1968), Vol. X: 300. See John Gillis, "Introduction," in Gillis, ed., *The Militarization of the Western World* (New Brunswick and London, 1989), 1–10; Volker R. Berghahn, *Militarism: The History of an International Debate, 1861–1989* (New York, 1982).

The remarks that follow are not going to resolve the controversy. Mindful of the etymology of the word, they will argue that "militarism" best describes far-reaching cultural transformations that began after 1850 – first in continental Europe – to redefine the relationship between armed forces and society, even as both these concepts themselves underwent redefinition. In a narrower institutional sense, "militarism" does not do justice to these great transformations. Whether their names were Caesar, Tamerlane, Wallenstein, or Napoleon, warlords had long been potent forces in political councils around the world. Understood instead as a broader cultural phenomenon, militarism took root, primarily in the west, during the second half of the nineteenth century, in an era of universal military service, compulsory education, popular government, and furious industrial growth.

The dramatic series of events that began in Prussia in 1858, when the War Ministry introduced plans for wide-ranging reform of the army, presented the definitive resolution to a controversy that had raged among military planners and civilian leaders since the wars of the French Revolution. The triumphs of the French revolutionary and Napoleonic armies had left little doubt about the military superiority of the nation-in-arms – huge armies of soldiers who were committed to the cause for which they were fighting.[4] In the aftermath of these great wars, however, the virtues of such armies spoke with less force to European military leaders than did the problems that these bodies posed. Universal military service looked like a democratic principle, the military pendant to popular sovereignty. The political reliability of mass armies thus remained suspect in the eyes of monarchs who continued to cling to their own authoritarian powers. The other perennial difficulty with great popular armies was their expense; and to governments that faced the costs of reconstruction after the Napoleonic wars, this difficulty was formidable.

The search for a more suitable form of military organization after 1815 could draw on several alternatives. One was the militia, in which the principle of universal military service survived, but short terms of training and service promised to keep the costs low. In post-Napoleonic Europe the idea of militias appealed above all to the radical left, to Mazzinians and other democrats, who argued that these military bodies could be raised swiftly, deployed effectively for defensive warfare, and were unsuited to wars of aggression. In practice, however, only the Swiss instituted such a

4 See Alan Forrest, *The Legacy of the French Revolutionary Wars: The Nation-in-Arms in French Republican Memory* (New York, 2009).

system.[5] The more common alternative, which could be found from France to Russia, was an army in which selective conscription was paired with liberal exemptions. Political reliability was ensured by long terms of enlistment, which made these bodies effectively professional armies. Costs were kept low by limiting the size of the annual contingents. Among the European powers, only Prussia offered a major exception to this pattern. Here universal, short-term military service did exist in principle, as did a reserve body called the *Landwehr*, which remained largely autonomous from the regular army. The fact that conscription was not rigorously enforced after 1815 was due both to the penury of the Prussian government and the lingering political anxieties of the king and his leading soldiers.

The military reforms that were instituted in Prussia in the early 1860s – over the bitter resistance of the parliament – then molded universal service into a form of organization that was at once militarily, economically, and politically practical.[6] These reforms set the regular army on the foundation of a three-year term of active service, to which all able-bodied males were liable at the age of twenty. At the conclusion of this term, these soldiers returned to their peacetime pursuits; they also passed into a series of reserve levies, one of which was the *Landwehr* (now deprived of its autonomy). As reservists they continued to train for military service, albeit on a part-time basis, until the age of forty-five. The organization of the Prussian army was henceforth geared to the coordinated mobilization of active and reserve units. As a consequence, the peacetime army could be kept small, but it could expand rapidly with the incorporation of battle-ready reserves upon the outbreak of war. The mobilization of these units began at the local level, in the territories or *Wehrkreise* in which the seventeen corps of the Prussian army were recruited and anchored; mobilization proceeded, increasingly by rail, under the central direction of the general staff, whose officers were delegated to the major operational units.

The wars that followed laid bare the military superiority of the Prussian model.[7] Under the operational control of the general staff, the Prussian army defeated the ponderous professional army of Austria in the summer of 1866.

5 Hans Rudolf Fuhrer, "Das Schweizer System: Friedenssicherung und Selbstverteidigung im 19. und 20. Jahrhundert," in Roland G. Foerster, ed., *Die Wehrpflicht: Entstehung, Erscheinungsformen und politisch-militärische Wirkung* (Munich, 1994), 193–206.

6 Dierk Walter, *Preußische Heeresreformen 1807–1870: Militärische Innovation und der Mythos der "Roonischen Reform"* (Paderborn, 2003).

7 Dennis Showalter, *The Wars of German Unification* (London, 2004); Geoffrey Wawro, *The Austro-Prussian War: Austria's War with Prussia and Italy in 1866* (Cambridge and New York, 1996); Geoffrey Wawro, *The Franco-Prussian War: The German Conquest of France in 1870–71* (Cambridge and New York, 2004).

Four years later, as if in a "laboratory-setting" to test the several organizational alternatives, the Prussians and their German allies first defeated the professional army of imperial France, then the hastily assembled militias of republican France.[8]

Many factors figured in the breathtaking battlefield success of the Prussian forces, including fortune and, at critical points in the campaigns, superiority in weapons and tactics. Nevertheless, the lessons that were drawn almost universally from this spectacle emphasized the organizational foundations of the Prussian achievement. If properly put together and directed, an army of short-term conscripts seemed to hold the keys to mass and mobility in an era of popular government and industrialized warfare. In this belief, all the continental powers rushed to institute some version of the Prussian system, primarily in the form of short-term conscription (without exemptions), integrated reserve levies, territorial recruitment, and a general staff. Baden, Bavaria, Württemberg, and several other German states had reformed their armies even before the establishment in 1871 of the German Empire, whose military institutions then formalized Prussian hegemony in the new state. Austria drew the lessons in 1868 from its defeat at Prussian hands. The French republic did the same in 1872, when it introduced universal military service based initially on a five-year obligation. Russia and the new Kingdom of Italy quickly followed suit.

Several features of this new military order were of particular moment. For one thing, universal military service was a central dimension of state-building during the second half of the nineteenth century.[9] In France, Germany, Italy, and Austria-Hungary, this process accompanied administrative consolidation and the promulgation of constitutions that established government, at least implicitly, on the consent of the governed. They thus created a system of civic entitlements and obligations as the basis of government. New armies, however, were the symbols supreme of the new states. Outside Russia, military service became the counterpart to some form of male suffrage, while national systems of compulsory primary education joined these two institutions as the third "pillar of the modern state."[10] The connection between

8 Frank Becker, "'Bewaffnetes Volk' oder 'Volk in Waffen'? Militärpolitik und Militarismus in Deutschland und Frankreich 1870–1914," in Christian Jansen, ed., *Der Bürger als Soldat: Die Militarisierung europäischer Gesellschaften im langen 19. Jahrhundert: Ein internationaler Vergleich* (Essen, 2004), 159.

9 See James Sheehan, *Where Have All the Soldiers Gone? The Transformation of Modern Europe* (Boston and New York, 2008), 6–18.

10 V. G. Kiernen, "Conscription and Modern Society in Europe before the War of 1914–1918," in M. D. Foot, ed., *War and Society: Historical Essays in Honour and Memory of J. R. Western, 1928–1971* (London, 1973), 172.

8. School classroom, London

military service and public education was pivotal. Armies and compulsory schools provided millions of European males with a common national experience. The army was to be a "school of the nation," an institution in which civic values were taught along with military skills. At the same time, institutions of public learning became "schools of the army," and education became premilitary training. Military service was defined now as a civic obligation, but to be effective it had to be willingly embraced. The civic attitudes that defined this duty and gave it moral power incubated accordingly in the state's schools.

The new European military order was also dynamic. Armies – and soon navies as well – expanded in pace with the dramatic population growth of the late nineteenth century and, not coincidentally, with the expanding financial capacity of states to provide the industrial infrastructure to equip, supply, and transport massed armed forces. The wars of mid-century had been fought among armies that numbered in the hundreds of thousands; by the turn of the twentieth century every major power could, within weeks, put millions of soldiers onto the battlefield. Beyond magnifying their social presence, which could be measured alone in the number of men who wore military uniforms in public, the dramatic expansion of Europe's armed forces had important cultural consequences. The mobilization of these forces for war became an obsession among leading soldiers everywhere, a challenge that required vast feats of organization, bureaucratic coordination, and the precise planning of

9. Enlistment at Royal Army Service Corps HQ

troop movements. The obsessions of these soldiers were rooted in another lesson of the Prussian triumphs of mid-century. Prussian success emphasized the significance of rapid deployment for the first engagements, which henceforth figured, like Königgrätz and Sedan, to be the decisive moments in any future European conflict. These calculations in turn heightened the anxieties of professional soldiers toward potential enemies, which now threatened, with potentially catastrophic consequences, to steal the jump in the arduous race to mobilize.

As custodians of the nation's security, soldiers were trained to cultivate a salutary sense of suspicion. It was basic to what one might call "military virtues," a set of values, attitudes, and habits of mind and behavior – all coded male – that included toughness, heroism, discipline, unity of will, obedience to higher authority, and sacrifice in the nation's interest, as well as an acute sense of friend and foe.[11] These virtues in turn reflected a view of international relations that underwrote the elite roles of soldiers, the technicians of political violence.

11 Stefan Dudnik et al., eds., *Representing Masculinity: Male Citizenship in Modern Western Culture* (New York, 2007).

The same virtues ratified universal military service as a civic duty, emphasizing the inevitability, if not the desirability of warfare – *la patrie toujours en danger.* The term "militarism" described the salience of these virtues and the centrality of war in civic culture – the extent to which orientations that were historically indigenous to military institutions assumed the same role more generally. Militarism suggested the erasure of the line between male citizen and soldier, the fact that civilians were systematically encouraged to think and behave like soldiers, to embrace violent international antagonism as a natural or positive feature of human affairs.

Training in these virtues began in the public school systems that took root during the late nineteenth century in much of continental Europe. In France, where it was introduced in 1882, compulsory education was, like the military reforms that preceded it, conceived as a component of national renewal after defeat in war.[12] In fact, public education represented in part a response to the requirements of the new French army, an effort to relieve it of the need to train illiterate conscripts. The effectiveness of public education registered in the steady decline of illiteracy among these recruits. By 1914 their literacy rate had risen in France to 96 percent; in Germany it was virtually 100 percent.

While compulsory gymnastics promoted common "habits of order and discipline," the curricula in the public schools, particularly instruction in language, history, geography, and civics, were keyed to a common sense of national identity, belonging, pride, and an appreciation for the dangers that lurked in the wider world.[13] Eugen Weber has written of "a new patriotism beyond the limits naturally acknowledged" by French school children.[14] This loyalty encompassed the nation as a community, but its moral valences changed dramatically at the national frontier, where the realm of the "other" began. The first duty of teachers, counseled one French educator, was to make pupils "love and understand the fatherland." In this light the school was "an instrument of unity," an "answer to dangerous centrifugal tendencies," and "the keystone of national defense." "When France is threatened," schoolchildren learned, "your duty is to take up arms and fly to her

12 Jean-François Chanet, *Vers l'armée nouvelle: République conservatrice et réforme militaire 1871–1879* (Rennes, 2006); Forrest, *Legacy of the French Revolutionary Wars*; Richard D. Challener, *The French Theory of the Nation in Arms, 1866–1939* (New York, 1955).

13 Robert Gildea, *Education in Provincial France, 1800–1914* (Oxford, 1983), 264.

14 Eugen Weber, *Peasants into Frenchmen: The Modernization of Rural France, 1870–1914* (Stanford, 1976), 332.

rescue."[15] French schoolchildren learned as well from their study of the past that this threat historically resided across the Rhine.

Meanwhile, across the Rhine, German children were being schooled in similar civic virtues. Although it was less centralized than in France or Italy, public education in Germany was quickly nationalized in the aftermath of this country's birth in war; and it just as quickly took on military accents. As in France, compulsory gymnastics and corporal punishment were calculated to instill physical as well as mental discipline. Recent history was recast in the textbooks as Germany's triumphant military renewal after defeat at the hands of the French at the battle of Jena in 1806. "Is this a history book or a manual of war?" wondered one critic in 1904, after examining the texts in use in German schools. In this ambience, schoolchildren were taught to sing songs with "fresh patriotic and enthusiastic military content."[16]

In the case of young European males, the cultivation of these attitudes continued within the armed forces themselves, whose role now expanded exponentially to accommodate the hundreds of thousands of citizen-soldiers who were mustered each year. In principle at least, every able-bodied male spent from two to seven years of his early adulthood under direct military supervision, and the training he received transcended instruction in weapons and tactics. Particularly in Italy, Austria-Hungary, and Russia, where school systems were inchoate and poorly funded, significant numbers of conscripts were trained to read, as well as to understand languages of command that were previously unknown to them. Many in these countries also received their first formal civic training under the supervision of soldiers. Everywhere in Europe, military education emphasized discipline, obedience, and loyalty to the state as a matter of course. It also sought to heighten an awareness of threats both foreign and domestic, such as the socialist labor movement. Once they left active service, the civic education of European males continued under military auspices in the reserves – an experience that included participation in annual maneuvers. And even after reserve obligations were satisfied, veterans' associations, which were linked to the army, promoted civic virtue along with sociability in their ranks. In 1913 these ranks comprised almost three hundred thousand men in France and close to 2 million in Germany.

Most males on the European continent thus spent decades of their lives in institutions that systematically promoted military values. This was a social

15 Ibid., 333.

16 Roger Chickering, "Militarism and Radical Nationalism," in James Retallack, ed., *Germany, 1871–1918* (Oxford, 2008), 199–200.

fact. As several historians have recently counseled, however, its psychological repercussions are difficult, if not impossible, to gauge.[17] The degree and manner in which these men internalized the values to which they were massively exposed remains a matter of conjecture. Still, at the very least, the absence of any significant popular resistance to the outbreak of war in 1914 suggested that outside a handful of Russian Bolsheviks, virtually every European male of military age had accepted – many eagerly – the moral obligation to defend the nation-state with his life.

At all events, the civic socialization that these Europeans received provided them with reliable orientation to a broader cultural experience, which was pervaded by the symbols and images of international conflict. Tin soldiers, military uniforms, and board games to the theme of famous battles offered an early introduction to these symbols. Europe's armed forces were on constant, colorful display in mass-circulating magazines, newspapers, books, exhibitions, war monuments, and military museums. Military reviews and parades enjoyed enormous appeal. The ease with which these spectacles keyed into popular festive traditions has led some historians to speak of "folklore militarism."[18] Particularly on holidays like Bastille Day, the monarch's birthday, anniversaries of battles (like Austerlitz and Sedan), or in connection with the inspections of local regiments by heads of state, these festivals were the occasions of popular recreation (and, in the case of veterans' associations, popular participation), as well as military self-display. The "Kaiser parade" in Berlin was an annual German highlight. In Italy, where they featured both a parade and a military mass, the annual celebrations of Constitution Day documented the growing reconciliation of patriotism and popular Catholicism.[19]

Navies were objects of even more lavish display and celebration, above all in Germany and Britain. Here the fleet reviews and the increasingly frequent launching of warships scripted what Jan Rüger has recently called "naval theater." Growing cultural prominence accompanied the commodification of the navies in these two countries – the marketing of sailor-suits, model ships, board games, and cinematic extravaganzas – which, as Rüger writes,

17 Benjamin Ziemann, "Sozialmilitarismus und militärische Sozialisation im deutschen Kaiserreich 1870–1914," *Geschichte in Wissenschaft und Unterricht* 53 (2009): 148–64.

18 Jakob Vogel, *Nationen im Gleichschritt: Der Kult der "Nation in Waffen" in Deutschland und Frankreich 1871–1914* (Göttingen, 1997).

19 Ilaria Porciani, "Kirchliche Segen für den Staat: Das Verfassungsfest in Italian von 1851 bis zum Ersten Weltkrieg," in Sabine Behrenbeck and Alexander Nutzenadel., eds., *Inszenierungen des Nationalstaats: Politische Feieren in Italien und Deutschland seit 1860/71* (Cologne, 2000), 45–60.

10. Kaiser Parade, 1905

encouraged "a culture in which a triumphant intransigence and the preparation for war in the name of peace were critical features."[20]

The British case is of particular interest, for it suggests that compulsory popular education could alone, absent universal military service, breed a culture of international conflict. Although Prussian institutional influence was limited to staff reform in the British army early in the twentieth century, the school system that fitfully took shape after 1870 was designed to perform the same civic functions as its Prussian counterpart. Flag worship, patriotic songs, physical drill were central facets of British education, just as military tropes pervaded the readers used in the elementary schools. Both in the schools and more broadly, the navy was the central symbol of British patriotism, but the army, which was

20 Jan Rüger, *The Great Naval Game: Britain and Germany in the Age of Empire* (Cambridge, 2007), 247–48.

involved almost uninterruptedly in military operations overseas, also loomed large, thanks in no small part to the growing press coverage of its imperial exploits.[21] No less than their counterparts elsewhere, British schoolchildren devoured stories of military adventure, which writers like G. A. Henty had prepared for them. In the wake of the Boer War, the House of Commons debated the introduction of paramilitary training into the schools – a project that Robert Baden-Powell thereupon instituted, albeit on a smaller and voluntary basis, in the Boy Scouts.[22]

The establishment in 1910 of the Boy Scouts of America was one indicator that similar cultural forces were at work in the other side of the ocean. In the United States too, the absence of a conscript army deflected popular enthusiasm toward the burgeoning navy and the activities of a professional army that was often at war, whether on the western frontier or in colonies seized at the end of the century. Still, the subject of American militarism was a paradox already, given the insistence with which its own proponents deprecated the word. The US army taught Clausewitz at West Point and instituted staff and command reforms at the turn of the century, which owed inspiration to the Prussian model. Prussia figured more prominently, however, as the symbol of a civic authoritarianism that was known in the United States as "militarism" and was associated, in the American political discourse, with standing armies.[23] The problem of definition was well captured by Leonard Wood, the army's chief of staff. "We do not want to establish militarism in this country," he wrote. "But we do want to build up in every boy a sense that he is an integral part of the nation, and that he has a military as well as a civic responsibility."[24] Lacking the support of universal military service, the principal agents of this "unmilitaristic militarism" were the public school systems that sought to forge an American nation out of diverse immigrant populations in the aftermath of the civil war.[25] This great nation-building project rested to a significant degree on a vision of American exceptionalism or manifest

21 Hew Strachan, "Militär, Empire und Civil Society: Großbritannien im 19. Jahrhundert," in Ute Frevert, ed., *Militär und Gesellschaft im 19. und 20. Jahrhundert* (Stuttgart, 1996), 78–93.

22 Stephen Heathorn, *For Home, Country and Race: Constructing Gender, Class, and Englishness in the Elementary Schools, 1880–1914* (Toronto, 2000).

23 Irmgard Steinish, "Different Paths to War: A Comparative Study of Militarism and Imperialism in the United States and Imperial Gemany, 1871–1914," in Manfred Boemeke et al., eds., *Anticipating Total War: The German and American Experiences, 1871–1914* (Cambridge, 1999), 29–53.

24 Cited in Peter Karsten, "Militarization and Rationalization in the United States, 1870–1914," in Gillis, ed., *Militarization*, 44.

25 Ibid., 31.

destiny, which bred a sense of moral urgency that was militant, if not military, and resonated broadly in mass-circulation magazines and newspapers like those of the Hearst chain.[26] Military metaphors were basic to this missionary understanding of international politics. Even pacifists like John Dewey made this point clear when they advocated the "moral equivalent of war," an alternative form of international relations that would breed idealism, discipline, and sense of collective obligation but without the violence.

Both in Europe and in the United States, visions of conflict were systematized in the popular ideologies that underwrote military (or naval) buildup. Darwinism provided the most protean and pervasive template. The vision of violent struggle for survival adapted effortlessly to the claims of empire's champions, military leaders like Wood, navalists like Alfred Thayer Mahan and Alfred von Tirpitz, and racists on both sides of the Atlantic. The language of conflict was "hegemonic," in the sense that few significant political groups could speak anything else. The socialist labor movement, which in 1889 constructed the Second International as the countersymbol of the militant nation-state, fitted the vision of Marx and Engels into Darwinian categories.[27] Champions of free enterprise could likewise invoke Darwin to deprecate public intervention in the economy. The proponents of ethnic consolidation, Pan-Slavs and Pan-Germans, spoke a similar language of conflict, albeit in their own accents. So did the Zionists and other Jews who invoked the idea of the militant, "muscular Jew" in response to the racist anti-Semites. Nor was Dewey an eccentric figure in his search for a moral equivalent of war. Pacifists everywhere envisaged a world in which conflict would be banished from the battlefields and seas, but competition would otherwise continue in nonviolent forms to drive international relations.

The remarkable adaptability of this language of conflict suggests a broader social and political context for the analysis of militarism as a cultural phenomenon. The decades before World War I represented an era of tumultuous change in central and western Europe and in North America. The founding of modern nation-states coincided with the advance of industrial growth into steel and chemicals, a process that not only revolutionized the machinery of warfare, but also transformed economies and societies at a breathtaking pace. The state's own efforts to build a unified civic culture collided with

26 John Whiteclay Chambers II, "The American Debate over Modern War, 1871–1914," in Boemeke et al., eds., *Anticipating*, 241–79.

27 See Marie-Louise Goergen, "Militärische und 'militaristische' Einstellungen in der deutschen und französischen Arbeiterbewegung vor dem Ersten Weltkrieg," in Jansen, ed., *Der Bürger als Soldat*, 247–67.

confessional, regional, and ethnic loyalties. All these processes generated social conflict, which was mobilized politically both within nation-states and across borders. The development of a militant working-class movement was the most frightening by-product of this change, insofar as the class struggle that figured in revolutionary socialism was to eventuate in the disappearance of the nation-state itself. Meanwhile, the Catholic Church was the center of the "culture wars" that raged in France, Germany, and Italy, primarily over the claims of the secular state to shape the minds of schoolchildren.[28] Particularly in central and eastern Europe, where these same claims raised basic issues of language, internal conflict among ethnic groups was the result.

Understood as the prevalence of values that attached to international violence, militarism represented at once a dimension of a broader cultural phenomenon and a response to it. Domestic conflict traduced not only civic unity but also the discipline and order that military survival was said to require. Military leaders argued that war was the most basic mode of human conflict and that its imperatives transcended internal discord of every kind. Militarism was consequently about social control in an age of dynamic and rapid transformation. In the name of national security social conflict was to be contained, disciplined, deflected. Nowhere was this principle more dramatically inscribed than in France, where the new republican army was founded, in the shadow of the Paris Commune, to foster what one of its champions called "the triumph of the grand principles of obedience and submission."[29]

Militarism thus had basic social functions. It was in one sense a socially comprehensive phenomenon, and it informed a critical common civic experience. The values that it implied were taught to children of every social description, although children of the upper classes tended to encounter them in private rather than public schools (in "public" rather than board schools in Britain). Conscript armies collected young men of every social description, although the sons of the upper classes tended to enter with commissions. The participation of veterans' associations in military festivals demonstrated that these events, too, had broad social appeal. In another sense, however, the appeal of militarism was narrower. The vocal and articulate champions of what one might call the ideology of militarism, the most outspoken advocates of military preparedness and aggressive foreign policy, included retired military officers like Leonard Wood, military publicists, newspaper editors,

28 Christopher Clark and Wolfram Kaiser, eds., *Culture Wars: Secular–Catholic Conflict in Nineteenth-Century Europe* (Cambridge, 2003).

29 Quoted in John Whittam, *The Politics of the Italian Army, 1861–1918* (London, 1977), 113.

business, professional, and bureaucratic elites. Many of them congregated in patriotic societies of one description or another, such as the British Navy League and National Service League, the *Associazione Nazionalista Italiana*, the *Ligue de la patrie française*, the Pan-German League, or the Navy League of the United States. These organizations were home to men of property and education, whose anxieties about national security corresponded to their high stakes in the social order that the nation-state symbolized. People like them soon became such outspoken proponents of military values that some historians have wondered whether a term other than "militarism" – such as "bellicism" – might better capture the growing initiative of civilians in the militarization of Europe.[30]

Absent reliable measures, it is difficult to gauge the pervasiveness of the values and patterns of behavior that either term suggests. Although much of the evidence was anecdotal, the fortunes of the peace movement offered one possible comparative index, for the men and women who gathered in peace societies publicly promoted a vision of international relations that conflicted frontally with the premises of militarism. These pacifists, as they called themselves, insisted that a durable international peace was a practical project, that international political conflicts could be peacefully resolved by means of an international tribunal. To judge by the number and size of the peace societies, the social prominence and political influence of their adherents, there was a correlation between the prominence of the peace movement and the absence of a standing army. Peace societies were strongest in the United States and Britain, where the Protestant sects, particularly Quakers, provided a foundation. While the peace movement was weaker on the continent generally, Imperial Germany provided the most inhospitable soil – a problem that the pacifists themselves ascribed to the strength of this country's military traditions.[31]

Elsewhere on the continent, limited political integration made it more problematic to characterize political cultures as militaristic. In Italy, where neither universal manhood suffrage nor universal military service – let alone compulsory education – was effectively introduced until the eve of war in 1914, it was idle to speak of a nation in arms. Popular support for the army was constrained by regional, confessional, and social tensions, which helped turn the army into a more effective instrument of domestic repression than foreign

30 For example Jörn Leonhard, *Bellizismus und Nation: Kriegsdeutung und Nationsbestimmung in Europa und den Vereinigten Staaten 1750–1914* (Munich, 2008), 741–818.

31 Roger Chickering, *Imperial Germany and a World without War: The Peace Movement and German Society, 1892–1914* (Princeton, 1975).

policy. Admiration for martial values was confined in any case to *Italia legale*, the propertied and educated elites who ruled the country and repeatedly called out the army in their own defense.

Similar circumstances governed the situation in Austria-Hungary and Russia, neither of which resembled a nation-state. Ethnic strife became increasingly the defining mark of the Habsburg monarchy. It paralyzed parliamentary government, frustrated a uniform system of public education, turned the imperial army increasingly into an anomaly, and made militarism itself a subversive concept, insofar as effective nation-building would have destroyed the Habsburg state. The "apolitical nationalism" in whose name martial attitudes were cultivated in the Habsburg army was dynastic; it was oriented toward the multinational state whose principal symbol was the emperor himself. While the vitality of this symbolism was considerable, the army resembled, as Oskar Jászi wrote, an "artificial dynastic hothouse."[32] Ethnic conflict undermined a common civic culture to the point where Germans could protest in Graz against the garrisoning of soldiers whose regimental language was not German.[33] The most telling symptom of the problem, though, was the growing practical and symbolic autonomy of the Hungarian army (and reserves). The Hungarian project was in fact to turn an ethnic maze in east-central Europe into a militarized nation whose language was Magyar. As a direct consequence, more than 45 percent of the Croatians who were drafted into this army in 1910 failed to report.[34] This figure testified to the army's shallow roots in the civic culture outside the Hungarian crown land. It also spoke to the more general problem of political integration in both parts of the Habsburg monarchy, the fact that broad segments of the population, in this case the non-Magyar minorities, remained either estranged from or otherwise uninvolved in the civic culture. Much the same was true of Italy, and in both cases it was an effective block to the cultural coalescences between the military and civilian spheres that the word militarism implies.

It was true in Imperial Russia as well. None of the "pillars of the modern state" was in place here. Universal military service, popular government,

32 Oskar Jászi, *The Dissolution of the Habsburg Monarchy* (Chicago and London, 1964), 144–45; cf. Laurence Cole and Daniel L. Unowsky, eds., *The Limits of Loyalty: Imperial Symbolism, Popular Allegiances, and State Patriotism in the Late Habsburg Monarchy* (New York, 2007).

33 Christine Hämmerle, "Die K. (u.) K. Armee als 'Schule des Volkes'? Zur Geschichte der allgemeinen Wehrpflicht in der multinationalen Habsburgermonarchie (1866–1914/18)," in Jansen, ed., *Der Bürger als Soldat*, 210.

34 Ibid., 213.

and public education were either inchoate or nonexistent. Measured as a percentage of its eligible manpower under arms, the Russian army was the smallest in Europe. Conscription was diluted by a generous set of exemptions that were overseen by village communes and permitted more than two-thirds of the potential conscripts to avoid service.[35] Ethnic diversity and the state's limited administrative capacities consistently frustrated military reformers in their designs to found an army based on national loyalties.[36] So did the tsarist regime itself, which, with the Ministry of Internal Affairs in the lead, resisted the institutions on which militarism rested in western Europe. To the extent that militarism implied popular participation in civic as well as military institutions, it was subversive in autocratic Russia, too. Imperial Russia's last wars, in 1904 and 1914, were popular only among the tsarist elites.[37] Russian popular culture, at least as read in the popular *Lubok* literature, appears to have differed from its western counterparts, becoming, as Jeffrey Brooks writes, "more, not less cosmopolitan."[38]

Imperial Russia offers a case study in David Ralston's influential book on "importing the European army," where it figures alongside the Ottoman Empire, Egypt, and China.[39] Because Ralston's book emphasizes developments in the early-modern period – the adaptation of European weapons, tactical discipline, and forms of military organization and administration – the question is not central whether Russia belonged to Europe. "Importing the European army" became in any case a far more complicated global process in the late nineteenth century, in part because defining "the European army" had itself become a more dynamic problem.

In the present age of globalization, commercial metaphors like "importing" may be less useful than metaphors of translation, which emphasize the approximations and mutual appropriations in the process.[40] After 1871 the problem of military reform in much of the world revolved about the difficulty

35 Werner Benecke, *Militär, Reform und Gesellschaft im Zarenreich: Die Wehrpflicht in Russland 1874–1914* (Paderborn 2006).

36 Joshua A. Sanborn, *Drafting the Russian Nation: Military Conscription, Total War, and Mass Politics, 1905–1925* (DeKalb, IL, 2003).

37 Dietrich Beyrau, "Das Russische Imperium und seine Armee," in Frevert, ed., *Militär und Gesellschaft*, 141.

38 Jeffrey Brooks, *When Russia Learned to Read: Literacy and Popular Literature, 1861–1917* (Princeton, 1985), 239.

39 David B. Ralston, *Importing the European Army: The Introduction of European Military Techniques and Institutions to the Extra-European World, 1600–1914* (Chicago and London, 1990).

40 Dipesh Chakrabarty, *Provincializing Europe: Post-Colonial Thought and Historical Difference* (Princeton, 2000).

of translating European military institutions and practices without the attendant civic assumptions – or, to continue in the same metaphor, without employing the civic language of militarism. Many non-western societies had long emphasized violent intergroup conflict in their own cultural languages, but they lacked the size, administrative cohesion, and material infrastructure to withstand the western military challenge in the late nineteenth century. The superiority of European military institutions and practices was so transparent that many military reformers in other parts of the globe saw no alternative to remolding civic institutions as part of an urgent process of "self-strengthening."[41] The fact that most of them failed, that militarism took hold in so few places outside Europe, testified to the difficulties of this design, which foundered on the resistance and residual power of indigenous institutions and cultural traditions.

Military affairs were the most globalized dimension of human activity in the late nineteenth century. The world was linked in an intricate system of military communication whose centers lay in Europe. Its most dramatic features were periodic assertions of armed might, which had brought much of the globe under western imperial control by the turn of the twentieth century. Garrisons, military missions, naval bases, and coaling stations were nodes in an international network that spun out as well, via military academies and staff colleges, journals, military missions, student exchanges, and inspection tours, to keep the leaders of armed forces in nominally sovereign states outside Europe abreast of developments in Europe. Military technology, most of it German or French (or, in the case of navies, British), flowed around the world through the same network. The Franco-German rivalry remained intense, although the Franco-German War of 1870 redefined the European hierarchies of military repute and gave the advantage to German advisors, if not German military equipment.

German influence was but one of the forces that generated the most militarized state in the world outside Europe. What is commonly known as the Meiji restoration in Japan represented, as Jürgen Osterhammel has recently written, "the most radical and successful self-strengthening action of the nineteenth century."[42] The project that began in 1868 built Japan into an industrialized nation-state, which was geared for global competition according

41 See John Darwin, *After Tamerlane: The Rise and Fall of Global Empires, 1400–2000* (London, 2008), 269–94. See also the chapter by John P. Dunn in this volume.

42 Jürgen Osterhammel, *Die Verwandlung der Welt: Eine Geschichte des 19. Jahrhunderts* (Munich, 2009), 743.

to rules that were then being rewritten in western Europe. The central aspect of this effort was military reform, and it reflected European practices. Yamagata Aritomo and other Japanese leaders witnessed these practices firsthand during their visits to Europe, and then they brought French and German soldiers to Japan in order to train and advise the army they were building. The conscript army that was officially founded in 1873 at first reflected French advice, particularly in providing for exemptions and substitutions; but the decision in 1878 to establish a general staff on the German model portended a trend. Germans thereafter took over positions in the new army staff college and provided the guidelines on which the Japanese reorganized the army on a divisional basis in 1888.[43]

Insofar as they influenced both constitutional and educational reform, visits by Ito Hirobumi and Mori Arinori to Germany in 1883 helped root this army in the emergent Japanese civic culture. The Meiji constitution, which was promulgated in 1889, was modeled on the Prussian constitution of 1850. Like its model, it emphasized monarchical sovereignty and shielded the cabinet from parliamentary responsibility – a provision that in Japan, as in Prussia, kept the army beyond the control of the diet. Nonetheless, the parliament did enjoy significant budgetary and legislative powers; and popular consent, at least among the propertied males who could vote, was no mere formality. The Imperial Rescript on Education, which was issued a year after the constitution, provided the foundations for the national system of compulsory education that Mori was crafting. From the outset the ambience in this system was to be the parade ground. It governed discipline and curriculum alike. The pertinent section in the rescript, which schoolchildren were required to learn by rote, was that "should emergency arise," they were to offer themselves "courageously to the state."[44]

The educational system and the army were the complementary institutional props of a civic culture whose guiding principle was "collective patriotism" in a world of violent international struggle. Along with the emperor, whose public image was itself now militarized, the army and navy became the leading symbols of the new Japan. At the same time, however, Japanese militarism drew from indigenous cultural traditions – Buddhist conceptions of male superiority, Shintoist doctrines of the emperor's divinity, a Confucian social ethic of service and loyalty, and, above all, the warrior ethos of the

43 Ernst L. Presseisen, *Before Aggression: Europeans Prepare the Japanese Army* (Tucson, 1965), 118–19.

44 Marius B. Jansen, *The Making of Modern Japan* (Cambridge, MA, 2000), 409–10.

samurai.[45] There was no little irony here, insofar as the Meiji restoration led not only to the elimination of the samurai as a privileged warrior caste, but also to an attempt to make Japan into a nation of samurai.[46]

Japan's victory in its war with China in 1894–95 appeared to vindicate the new course. Defeat in the same war encouraged military reformers around Kang Youwei in China to emulate this course. The fortunes of their effort highlighted the extraordinary achievements of the Japanese, as it revealed the difficulties of building armed forces on the new European model. With the aid of German and Japanese advisors, Chinese reformers drafted proposals for a restructured central army, a general staff, a network of military academies, universal military service, reserve levies, parliamentary government, and a national system of education to prepare Chinese children for military duty.[47] Another Chinese military defeat, this time at the hands of an allied expeditionary force during the Boxer Rebellion in 1900, persuaded even the Qing rulers to embrace reform. The principal result was the founding of a central "new army" and the establishment in 1906 of the framework for a new educational system. An interim goal was an army of thirty-six divisions of volunteers, of whom 20 percent were to be literate.[48]

The project, which collided with the power of China's provincial armies, was burdened from the outset by forces that resisted the militarization of civic culture in the Qing Empire. The power of provincial elites was critical. It fed off the size and ethnic diversity of the empire, the administrative weakness of the central state, and its lack of financial resources. The country's central rulers were themselves anxious lest military reform raise more basic questions of political legitimacy. The advocates of reform found an institutional base in the new army itself, but growing obstructions from the Manchu leaders of the state and the old army made questions of political change difficult to circumvent. The revolution of 1911, which was spearheaded by divisions of the new army, brought a military reformer, Yuan Shikai, to power in the new republican state. The financial and administrative obstacles to reform were less overcome

45 Carol Gluck, *Japan's Modern Myths: Ideology in the Late Meiji Period* (Princeton, 1985), 138–42, 156, 269–70.

46 Jansen, *Making*, 399; cf. Wolfgang Schwendter, "Die Sammurai im Zeitalter der Meiji-Restauration: Elitenwandel und Modernisierung in Japan 1830–1890," *Geschichte und Gesellschaft* 28 (2002): 33–70.

47 Douglas R. Reynolds, *China, 1898–1912: The Xinzheng Revolution and Japan* (Cambridge, MA, 1993); Ralph L. Powell, *The Rise of Chinese Military Power, 1895–1912* (Princeton, 1953); cf. Ralston, *Importing the European Army*, 107–41.

48 Peter Worthing, *A Military History of Modern China: From the Manchu Conquest to Tian'anmen Square* (Westport, CT, and London, 2007), 80.

than transformed, however. The new government found it impossible to impose military, let alone civic unity in China, as a new age of fragmentation began, embodied now by the regional commanders of the new army itself.

In many respects the campaign on behalf of military reform in China resembled contemporary efforts in Russia, not least in the way that military defeat encouraged reform. In addition, both cases attested to the difficulty of separating military affairs from broader questions of civic structure in the vast, ethnically mixed "late empires" of the nineteenth century.[49] The Ottoman Empire fitted the same description. Military reform had begun here in the 1840s, during the *Tanzimat* era, when the Prussian army provided a model for introducing selective conscription, territorial organization, and a system of military academies into the Ottoman army.[50] Universal military service corresponded, however, neither to the designs of the reformers nor to the administrative capacities of the authoritarian but loosely structured Ottoman Empire. Military service was confined in practice to Muslims, if not Turks. Despite a durable connection to the German military, the Ottoman army could not prevent the progressive disintegration of the empire at its ethnic margins. Many of the military reformers who took power among the "Young Turks" in 1908 had, however, been educated in the reformed military academies; and the designs of these reformers did extend to universal military service, which they promulgated in 1909 as part of a broader plan to create a modern political system (and a modern school system) in the Ottoman Empire. The ethnic ramifications of this military project quickly became evident. The territorial reduction of the empire recommenced in 1911 and culminated in the establishment of an ethnically homogeneous but much-reduced Turkish state after World War I.

The fate of the Ottoman Empire testified anew to the structural tensions between old empires and new military institutions that appealed to civic loyalties. That such tensions did not emerge in newer western colonial empires in Africa and Asia was due in part to the political calculations of the colonial rulers. The areas brought under western control included several of the most martial peoples on earth. Some, such as the Ashantis and Zulus, had instituted forms of military organization that were based on powerful

49 Joseph W. Esherick, Hasan Kayalt, and Eric Van Young, eds., *Empire to Nation: Historical Perspectives on the Making of the Modern World* (Lanham, 2006).

50 Erik Jan Zürcher, "The Ottoman Conscription System in Theory and Practice," in Zürcher, ed., *Arming the State: Military Conscription in the Middle East and Central Asia, 1775–1925* (London and New York, 1999), 79–94; Ralston, *Importing the European Army*, 61–62.

collective loyalties and anticipated European patterns of the late nineteenth century. The Zulu kingdom put a tenth of its population into the field in 1879.[51] Recruitment systems in Africa were extraordinarily diverse, but most were based on some form of impressment (commonly slavery) or on militias that were reminiscent of European feudal levies.[52] Save only Ethiopia, whose levies were large, well equipped, and united by common religious and cultural loyalties, no African military system was remotely equal to the challenge of western technological superiority. After their imperial conquests, western leaders became inveterate opponents of indigenous militarism in the territories they governed, lest martial values encourage opposition to colonial rule. The military dynamics of colonial rule thus required a monopoly of military force and the subjection of indigenous armed bodies (to the extent to which they were allowed to survive) to colonial control. British rule in India rested on this principle, and the sepoy mutiny only underlined its importance.[53] Even in the Dominions, the British government was reluctant to concede autonomy to local institutions.[54]

The history of Latin America suggested, however, that establishing the institutional foundations of a militarized national culture remained a problem even in the successor states to colonial empires. The experience of major Latin American states in the late nineteenth century was similar enough in any case to suggest a number of general propositions. Military reform came in the name of state-building, constructing central governments that could exercise a monopoly over political violence – in many cases after decades of civil war among military forces that had been loyal to warlords, caudillos, or military adventurers. State-building was encouraged in the second half of the century by integration into the international economy and by the enduring spectacle of international violence in Latin America itself. Reform was part of a transition from what Alain Rouquié has characterized as "predatory militarism" to systems of fragile civilian preponderance.[55] Military reform now meant professionalization, particularly of officer corps. It featured reorganization, regularized recruitment of officers, and new institutions of military education

51 Jeff Guy, *The Destruction of the Zulu Kingdom* (London, 1979), 39.

52 Claude E. Welch, "Continuity and Discontinuity in African Military Organisation," *Journal of Modern African Studies* 13 (1975), 229–48; Bruce Vandervort, *Wars of Imperial Conquest in Africa, 1830–1914* (Bloomington and Indianapolis, 1998).

53 Stephen Peter Rosen, *Societies and Military Power: India and Its Armies* (Ithaca and London, 1996), 162–96.

54 "Imperial Defense," in E. A. Benians et al., eds., *The Cambridge History of the British Empire* (3 vols., Cambridge, 1929–59), Vol. III: 563–604.

55 Alain Rouquié, *The Military and the State in Latin America* (Berkeley, 1987).

on French or German models (and with French or German advisors). The results were officer corps that both looked and thought about international affairs much like their European preceptors. Latin American officers were also plentiful. The Mexican army had one officer for every five enlisted men in 1910, the Ecuadorian army one for every two.[56] These high proportions reflected the broader difficulties of recruiting common soldiers here and elsewhere in Latin America. Translating the European model of citizen armies foundered on familiar problems, the limited financial resources and administrative reach of the central state, ethnic and racial diversity, and the absence of public education, which turned armies in most Latin American lands into the only schools of the nation. As a result, the civic integration of the armed forces remained limited and left civilian governments vulnerable to periodic attack by their many professional officers.

There was no Latin American Japan. Chile was the closest approximation. The divisional reorganization of the army, the establishment of a *Colegio militar* and general staff, took place under the guidance of a German mission. Although universal military service was officially instituted in 1900, it provided for so many exemptions and exclusions that the army's ranks were filled as a rule by the illiterate and destitute (a category that was also disproportionately Indian), who could find no way short of desertion to avoid service. Despite its own pretensions, the army could make no credible claim to represent a nation in arms, if only because there was no Chilean nation to arm beyond the largely urban mercantile and professional middle classes that dominated the parliamentary institutions.[57] In basic respects, the Chilean situation resembled the Italian, as well as circumstances elsewhere in Latin America. French military advisors oversaw the professionalization of the officer corps in Peru, while Germans had supplanted their French rivals by the early twentieth century in Brazil, Argentina, and Bolivia.[58] The fact that military advisors from Chile played the leading role in reforming the armies in Ecuador, Columbia, Venezuela, and El Salvador was a further tribute to the prestige that German ideas and institutions enjoyed in this part of the world before 1914.

As a cultural phenomenon, militarism was rooted at the end of the nineteenth century in the European nation-state, in which civic and ethnic loyalties

56 John J. Johnson, *The Military and Society in Latin America* (Stanford, 1964), 72.

57 William F. Sater and Holger H. Herwig, *The Grand Illusion: The Prussianization of the Chilean Army* (Lincoln, NE, and London, 1999).

58 See Frederick M. Nunn, *Yesterday's Soldiers: European Military Professionalism in South America, 1890–1914* (Lincoln, NE, and London, 1983), 100–53.

largely coincided. The power of European armies rested on the capacity of these states to mobilize enormous armed forces without crippling their peacetime economies. The success of this project reflected the consonance, defined here as militarism, between armed forces and civic cultures. Universal military service was understood as a civic obligation, the price of civic entitlements like public education and political participation. Militarism remained largely confined to western Europe and Japan, until the material and ideological tools became available to forge nations out of multiethnic empires. They did so after World War I, that vast European struggle to which militarism was first geared.

6

War-making and restraint by law: the formative years, 1864–1914

JEAN H. QUATAERT

Recent historical research in international and transnational history claims that a new international order developed in the later nineteenth century.[1] Often framing it as an inquiry into the making of the contemporary global age, historians have pointed to the emergence of a "new internationalism" of sentiments, institutions, and intergovernmental agreements. The growing transnational circulation of people, ideas, technology, and information was met by the establishment of permanent international institutions and organizations, which coordinated a variety of reforms and social agendas across borders, as well as by intergovernmental cooperation that set uniform rules for international postal, telegraph, and sanitary services. These changes brought new public and private actors into the international arena, which was still dominated by the sovereign powers of states and empires. For Akira Iriye, these developments presaged a growing consciousness of a global community over and above the designs of the imperial and territorial state.[2] The focus on global interconnections in the face of continuing national tensions and antagonisms has not gone unchallenged. But these debates have brought renewed attention to the characteristics of the international order during the half-century before World War I.

On an independent track, legal scholars have pinpointed significant changes in the sphere of international law, starting in the mid nineteenth century. As part of the remarkable growth in state interdependence, formal canons of law began to govern many aspects of interstate relations, from commerce and trade to copyright, transportation, and war. Spearheading this shift was the movement to codify the laws of war, which had long been regulated by customary norms and ad hoc bilateral agreements. First written as multilateral

1 I want to thank the German Marshall Fund, USA, for supporting the research for this essay under its Senior Research Fellowship, 2001–02.

2 Akira Iriye, *Global Community: The Role of International Organizations in the Making of the Contemporary World* (Berkeley and Los Angeles, 2002), 6, 9, 37.

treaties and agreements around the middle of the century, these new instruments became the hallmark of modern international law. In the words of Arthur Nussbaum, an early but influential legal historian, the shift to written multilateral law inaugurated a "new era" in legal history, although it remained in its "early stages" on the eve of World War I.[3]

A distinct branch of the law of armed conflict, known today as International Humanitarian Law, also emerged in this period. This step, too, marked a new beginning in intergovernmental efforts to formulate rules and regulations for the conduct of war. Codification, however, took place against the backdrop of continuing warfare on the European continent, as well as in territories that had been subjected to imperial conquest and incursion, notably in Africa and Asia. War-making remained an essential attribute of states' sovereign prerogatives. Yet law-making, which sought the regulation of these prerogatives, continued apace. Legal scholars subsequently subsumed it into two broad, iconic models for the restraint of war, which reflected the geographic places of their origins – Geneva and The Hague.[4] While it was fluid at the outset, this distinction is useful for analytical purposes.

Succinctly stated, the Geneva Conventions of 1864 (and their subsequent revision in 1906) gradually extended legal protections to categories of *individuals* who were deemed particularly vulnerable to the "calamities" of war: wounded enemy soldiers, the medical personnel needed for their care, and prisoners of war. "Geneva" gave legal protections to discrete groups of people in armed conflict. It thus moved beyond the standard practices of international law, which had regulated the duties and responsibilities of *states* in their mutual interests, but had only incidentally covered individuals, as in provisions for diplomatic immunities or the safeguarding of "alien" (non-national) property. "The Hague" model was named for the conferences that met in 1899 and 1907. These drew on several earlier precedents in multilateral law, seeking restraints on the conduct of war on land (primarily in 1899) and redefining them to the seas (in 1907). Article 22 of the 1899 convention formulated the enduring concept of limited war, declaring "[t]he right of belligerents to adopt means of injuring the enemy is not unlimited."[5] The convention listed a series of actions in wartime that contravened this principle, declaring illegal, among

3 Arthur Nussbaum, *A Concise History of the Law of Nations* (New York, 1950), 191, 198.

4 Frits Kalshoven, *The Laws of Warfare: A Summary of Its Recent History and Trends in Development* (Leiden, 1973), 24.

5 "Annex to the Convention: Regulations Respecting the Laws and Customs of War on Land," in Adam Roberts and Richard Guelff, eds., *Documents on the Laws of War* (Oxford, 1989), 52.

11. The Geneva Convention

other practices, the use of poisons, asphyxiating gases, and expanding bullets, as well as the murdering of an enemy who had laid down his arms.

These laws did not prohibit war, but they sought a new Faustian bargain between what their architects called the "necessities of war" and the "requirements of humanity." The Hague authors embraced the same definition of legitimate warfare that was found in the St. Petersburg Declaration of 1868; it asserted that the "only legitimate object which States should endeavour to accomplish during war is to weaken the military forces of the enemy," and it sought to prohibit all other actions that resulted in "excess suffering."[6] Following earlier philosophical precepts that differentiated between morality and law, these authors moved from the moral principle of excess to a set of legally prohibited behaviors. This effort to delineate a humanitarian sphere of protection for all those who were caught in the exigencies of war accounted for the new label of *humanitarian* law. It sought a new basis of international cooperation, which the architects affirmed in a separate convention that established a Permanent Court of Arbitration to settle international disputes.[7]

6 In Roberts and Guelff, eds., *Documents*, 30–31.

7 For additional perspectives on these laws, A. Pierce Higgins, *The Hague Peace Conference and Other International Conferences Concerning the Laws and Usages of War: Texts of Conventions with Comments* (Cambridge, 1909).

The movement to codify the laws of war operated in a social field that affected the very processes of law-making. Codification was closely tied into national and international civil society and increasing public interest in peace and arbitration. Starting in the 1870s, international law became a distinct branch of academic study, typically migrating from faculties of philosophy and theology to faculties of law. Themselves part of growing contacts across territorial borders and the seas, these lawyers founded the first international associations to promote the scientific codification of law, such as the International Institute of International Law and the International Law Association (both established in 1873), and they supported specialized journals, among them the *Revue de Droit International*. These associations attracted a wide membership, including many government officials, military and naval officers, and leading pacifists in the transatlantic world.

The supporters of codification operated in a climate that was receptive to the claims of "science" to provide clear moral and practical foundations for the social order. In this "positivist" atmosphere, many lawyers adhered to the corollary that a scientific process that led to better law would lead to a better world. With close ties to state authorities, international lawyers dominated the Second Committee at The Hague, which was responsible for codifying the laws of war on land in 1899, and they remained prominent at subsequent congresses. In their ranks were such respected lawyers and publicists as Feodor de Martens from St. Petersburg, the Parisian lawyer Louis Renault, Philipp Zorn from Königsberg, and T. M. C. Asser, the Dutch lawyer who was president of the Institute. Although it was weighted heavily toward European influences, international law began to shed its character as "European public law," as it had been known to early legal positivists in the seventeenth and eighteenth centuries. Open, multilateral, and written law – an innovation implemented in the 1856 Paris Declaration Respecting Maritime Law – allowed for accession by states. As more states signed on, the law became more "universal," at least in the eyes of the professionalizing international law community. The codification movement established the formal norm of universal law.[8]

To a growing public, the movement also seemed to promise peace. The work at The Hague was followed avidly by a growing reading public in national and transnational networks, including members of peace societies

8 Irwin Abrams, "The Emergence of the International Law Societies," *Review of Politics* 19 (1957): 361–80; Calvin DeArmond Davis, *The United States and the First Hague Peace Conference* (Ithaca, 1962), 126–27 mentions the lawyers on the drafting committee; cf. Roberts and Guelff, eds., *Documents*, 23–27; Nussbaum, *A Concise History*, 186.

and many feminists, who believed that women's suffrage, by bringing the values of caring into state decision-making, would herald a more peaceful era. International lawyers developed close ties to activists in the peace movement, whether these were Quakers, members of the Universal Peace Union in the USA, or affiliates of the International Peace Bureau, which was headquartered in Berne after 1891. Peace societies demanded a permanent arbitration court and gradual disarmament; they found sustenance in the concrete steps taken toward arbitration that also seemed to define their era. These included an Anglo-American arbitration treaty, which was adopted in 1874, and the twenty-nation Inter-American Conference in 1889, which was called to write a convention (never ratified) requiring arbitration. Many international lawyers were prominent in adjudicating disputes among nations. In this context, the Hague Conferences became known widely as the Peace Conferences. Negotiation and codification, however, found little resonance among socialists, who branded as "illusory" any effort to set legal curbs on imperialist wars, which they saw as an inevitable component of the international capitalist order of states. The men at The Hague were well aware of public interest, both positive and negative, which they greeted with ambivalence. Representatives of the highest diplomatic and military ranks, as well as the new guild of law professionals, distrusted popular mobilization even as they sought to authorize their own efforts by appealing to the public interest and conscience. The day-to-day deliberations of the working committees at both Hague Conferences were closed to journalists and the public.[9]

This chapter examines law-making as a dynamic process and sets the formulation and revision of law at international congresses in their wider social contexts. On the one hand, analysis at the international level of law-making gives an aura of inevitability to the development of this law. Its parts seem to fit a logical progression. The original Geneva Conventions of 1864, for example, were extended to maritime conflicts in 1868 but never ratified, leaving the law unsettled. Their formulations nonetheless fed the larger international movement to address the general laws of war, first unsuccessfully in Brussels in 1874 and subsequently at The Hague in 1899. In turn, the Hague Conference incorporated the Geneva Conventions into its regulations (Art. 21) but expressed the "wish" for an additional conference to clarify and revise the Conventions,

9 Davis, *The First Hague Peace Conference*, 11–12, 18; Calvin DeArmond Davis, *The United States and the Second Hague Peace Conference: American Diplomacy and International Organization 1899–1914* (Durham, 1975), 191–97; Abrams, "Emergence," 371–72; Jean H. Quataert, *The Gendering of Human Rights in the International Systems of Law in the Twentieth Century* (Washington, DC, 2006), 6–7.

which took place in 1906. In addition, the First Hague Conference called for a subsequent international gathering to extend its protections to maritime law, and thus the Second Hague Conference met in 1907. Dissatisfied with the outcome on maritime practices, notably with the continuing disagreements over blockades, contraband in wartime, and prize law, the great naval powers (Britain, the United States, Germany, France, and Russia) called their own conference and issued the Declaration of London in 1908, the last major proclamation of multilateral law on armed conflict before World War I.

On the other hand, law-making was a contingent process, reflecting the distinct political, diplomatic, and military events of the era. It was shaped as much by the "lessons" of the numerous wars fought during the period as by any legal logic. The Geneva Conventions were implemented immediately in the theaters of war, opening new spheres of action in medical services at home and on the battlefield. Reports on the ground then became grist for new debates about extending legal protections and ways to engage many highly charged issues of the day, including membership in the international community, notions of humanitarianism, "civilized" warfare, and neutrality, as well as conceptions of public and private spheres of activity. As a new universal legal discourse that was tied to action at home and abroad, law-making became a site of struggle over the terms of inclusion, opening claims from a variety of new actors, including women, who forged new roles in medicine, philanthropy, and patriotic defense, and from representatives of Islamic states and empires, which demanded accommodation of their symbols of identity. These fields of action, furthermore, created permanent structures that coordinated the implementation of the law. Through trial and error, the International Committee of the Red Cross (ICRC), which was founded in 1863, established increasingly clear rules and regulations for the formal acceptance of the Geneva Conventions by belligerents at the outbreak of war. The ICRC served, too, as the mediator between the law's intent and the responses undertaken in the chaotic circumstances of battle. As an international clearing house, the ICRC brought a wealth of experience to the authorities and lawyers who codified law at international congresses.

Reflecting the grass-roots perspectives of voluntary medical associations on the battlefield, the German reformer Gustav Münzel offered valuable insights in 1901 into contemporary understandings of international law and sovereign power. Addressing the concern that the ratification of treaty law would curtail sovereignty, he anchored international law in states' mutual interests. As he put it, "all states must have an equal interest" (*ein gleichmässiges Interesse*) in protecting wounded soldiers from the "horrors" of lingering on the battlefield – a principle that applied equally to one's own soldiers and enemy combatants. On more ambiguous legal terrain, he also acknowledged that this law could not impinge on areas within the sovereign "discretion" of the parties; yet it had to provide clear rules that "command or prohibit action" (*die etwas positives gebieten oder verbieten*).[10] As a representative of wartime medical services on the ground, Münzel was part of a movement that pushed for revisions of the Geneva Conventions.

He was also part of a wider milieu, whose concerns provide additional insight into why state and military authorities around mid-century were receptive to movements to safeguard wounded soldiers and codify the customs and laws of war. Münzel's critique underscored the imperatives of "people's wars," even if his own understanding of the changes implied by this term was less precise than the analyses of subsequent military historians. Münzel understood that since the Napoleonic era, the waging of war, anchored now in the male citizen's duty of military service, required mass public support, the mobilization of technology, resources, and public morale. It also needed expanding medical services in order to provide the most up-to-date medical aid on the battlefield as well as at home, including social investments in veterans' care. Many historians now speak of a new gendered bargain, which was struck between state authorities and their people over the shared sacrifices of war. This bargain was based on a transnational model of service and relief, which extended, however unevenly, to most sovereign states across the globe in the decades prior to World War I. Although the idea of a "bargain" was beyond Münzel's worldview, the *Ungewissheit der Familie*, the strain on families who did not know the fates of their soldier fathers, brothers, or sons, was fundamental to his defense of the Geneva Conventions, which rested on their inherent necessity, fairness, and universality.[11]

Münzel was not alone in tying state interests and public expectations. According to Albert Love, US authorities were well aware of public outrage at the "unnecessary human suffering and loss of life during the Crimean War [1853–56] and at the bloody fields of Solferino" (during the Italian wars of independence against Austria in 1859). At the time, many influential people had been "indignant and horror-stricken" when they learned of the failure of their governments to provide even minimal medical care on the battlefield.

10 Gustav Műnzel, *Untersuchungen über die Genfer Konvention: Eine Darstellung und Kritik des nach diesem Verträge geltenden Land-Kriegsrechtes* (Freiburg, 1901), 103, 111.

11 Műnzel, *Untersuchungen*, 107. On the new gender bargain, see Stefan Dudink, Karen Hagemann, and John Tosh, eds., *Masculinities in Politics and War: Gendering Modern History* (Manchester, 2000).

Concern about public opinion traversed the seas and made, Love wrote, the organization of the Sanitary Commission "of sharp necessity" at the outbreak of the American Civil War. In his view, this concern also accounted directly for the Red Cross movement's pushing for the Geneva Conventions.[12]

Subsequent treaties that banned the use of certain types of weapons in wartime likewise reflected mounting fears about the proliferation of new and ever more deadly technologies. These treaties were the only concrete products of the wider agenda to limit armaments, which had animated the original call for the Hague Conference. Proposals to curb armaments, however, contravened the jealously guarded sovereign "discretion" of state authority, which Münzel had readily acknowledged. The US representatives were told in 1899 that "the question of limitation could not be profitably discussed."[13] A consensus among the delegations defeated efforts to impose limits on armaments and military expenditures in 1899. The topic was not even included on the agenda of the Second Hague Conference.

By contrast, the leading military officers agreed with little controversy to examine the lawfulness of certain kinds of weapons. In effect, they moved the issue of weaponry from the confines of battle into the arena of public law, seeking precise quantitative measurements by which to judge a weapon's capacity to inflict unnecessary suffering. As one leading scholar of the laws of war notes, these "military experts . . . were only too anxious to believe . . . that 'the progress of civilization' brought with it not only efficient weaponry but also . . . inhumanity in warfare."[14] Nonetheless, the principle of banning weapons according to such subjective criteria has remained legally confusing and arbitrary.

The thorny question of enforcing international law, which has fed legal theorists' interest in why states adhere to law in the first place, was not fully applicable to this early era of law-making. There were no effective mechanisms to ensure adherence to international legal principles or to mandate punishment for states and armies that breached the laws. Only in 1906 did the revised Geneva Conventions (Article 28) call on states to pass legislation forbidding "pillage and maltreatment" of the wounded, if the prohibitions in the states' military codes were insufficient. Similarly, in 1907 the revised Convention (IV) governing the laws and customs of war on land included the first provisions on "accountability" (Article 3). It suggested that a

12 Albert G. Love, "The Geneva Red Cross Movement: European and American Influence on its Development," *Army Medical Bulletin* 62 (1942): 1, 6–7.

13 Davis, *The First Hague Peace Conference*, 78, 110.

14 Geoffrey Best, *Humanity in Warfare: The Modern History of the International Law of Armed Conflict* (London, 1980), 160.

belligerent party that "violates the prohibitions of the said Regulations shall, if the case demands, be liable to pay compensation ... [and that such responsibility applies to] all acts committed by persons forming part of its armed forces."[15] Authors of reports and letters from the field began more insistently to press the issue of responsibility, particularly during the widespread violence against civilians in the Balkan Wars of 1912–13. But only gradually did compliance become part of the debates among members of the organizations that were responsible for overseeing and implementing the law.

For many contemporaries, then, the law's authority did not elicit the most commentary. More striking were the permanent institutional arrangements that accompanied the law, which, because its new treaty form extended far into the future, itself seemed "permanent." This proposition applied as well to the many associations that emerged to promote and extend the Geneva idea.

"Geneva" was the brainchild of Henry Dunant, a citizen of the Swiss city and one of a number of continental philanthropists who took up the cause of Europe's wounded soldiers once they had become the mid-century symbol of suffering humanity. Present at Solferino, he wrote a searing exposé, which electrified public opinion and prompted five compatriots to found the *Societé genévoise d'Utilité publique* to spread his ideas. Dunant traveled to many European capitals, winning over high dynastic and military officials, as well as government leaders and prominent philanthropists. Unlike his contemporaries, the Italian reformer Fernando Palasciano and the French pharmacist Henri Arrault, who proposed competing agendas, Dunant had a unique proposal: He called for a permanent network of voluntary relief societies to supplement the existing medical services of armies (and subsequently navies). His supporters convoked an international congress in October 1863 in Geneva, which thirty-six official and unofficial representatives of states and their military leaders attended. This congress formally proposed the founding of national relief committees everywhere to aid military medical services. The congress also made the ad hoc Geneva committee the "intermediary" body to coordinate the work of the newly founded national committees, and it envisioned future international assemblies to discuss strategies and share information. The congress recognized that the dangerous work on the battlefield had to be protected by a universally acknowledged sign of neutrality and hence inviolability – which they designated the Red Cross.[16]

15 Higgins, *The Hague Peace Conferences*, 213.

16 Münzel, *Untersuchungen*, 26–30; John F. Hutchinson, *Champions of Charity: War and the Rise of the Red Cross* (Boulder, 1996), 31–37.

These representatives acknowledged, however, that safeguarding medical personnel who aided friend and foe alike on the battlefield required the full support of the belligerent states. It required, in short, a treaty that would be binding on the ratifying states and open to adherence by others. But there was an irony in this outcome. Reflecting the viewpoint of the high commands, the representatives of the sixteen sovereign states that negotiated what became the Geneva Conventions were skeptical that "voluntary" relief societies could operate independently on the battlefield. In formal terms, the Geneva Conventions of 1864 thus excluded voluntary associations from its own rules, which protected ambulance services and military hospitals, as well as the medical military staffs (including the chaplains) that ministered to the wounded soldiers.

The volunteer model initiated by Dunant nonetheless developed as one of the first and longest-lasting transnational humanitarian movements. It was an early example of an NGO (non-governmental organization) network, although this term was not known at the time, and Dunant's organizations subsequently gained extensive governmental backing. Private national relief societies proliferated after 1864 and, as Münzel's report showed, they increasingly sought formal inclusion in the legal system established by the Geneva Conventions – an effort that was led by the newly designated International Committee of the Red Cross. In this context, law and humanitarianism fed one another. Both invoked impartiality and full neutrality, and both claimed to stand above the messy world of political self-interest. Humanitarian values informed the law's dominant self-representation, as it claimed, by means of newly authorized humanitarian spheres of activities, to provide impartial guidance for states in the international arena.

From uncertain beginnings, the ICRC put in place procedures and rules that covered the outbreak and course of war and secured the organization's own role under international humanitarian law. In a private capacity, the ICRC became indispensable to the implementation of treaty law. In the decades before 1914, its members were a homogeneous group of male Protestant burghers of conservative to liberal views, who were conscious of their standing as the only aid society that was truly entitled to the "honorable" name of "international," as they put it in 1867, after receiving an award at the International Exhibition in Paris. Claiming a universal mandate to spread the "charitable spirit" (*élan charitable*), they employed the language of humanitarianism in their cause. In their own definition, the ICRC acted "exclusively" for humanitarian purposes and "absolutely" removed from politics. Their vision translated in national contexts into activity "without political aim or object," the "righteously" helping of "sufferers on all sides."[17]

During its early years, the ICRC carved out vital tasks. These centered on promoting voluntary aid societies to supplement governmental medical services, a mission that it carried throughout the so-called "civilized" world, employing a readily available language of global differentiation that made its way into the law. By this account, "civilized" nations subscribed to the laws of war and, in peacetime, provided institutionalized relief services for their armed forces – in both official and private capacities. Starting in 1869, the ICRC published an information bulletin, soliciting reports from member societies, although its press releases were constrained by the organization's emerging practice of official neutrality. While appealing for public support, the ICRC grappled with the problem of press coverage of wartime operations. In addition, at the imminent threat of war, the ICRC ensured the acceptance of the Geneva Conventions by the belligerents for the duration of hostilities and brokered necessary relief services, including reduced rates for its own surgeons to travel to the field of battle.[18] Figure 11 captures this important intermediary role. It represents an Ottoman receipt for money collected by the Spanish Red Cross to aid wounded Ottoman soldiers during the second Balkan War; it was sent to the empire via the ICRC. Committee members also pushed for further codification and revision of the laws of war. Much of this administrative work became routinized over the decades, but behind the rules and procedures were deep and continuously contested issues, such as the definition of war (or the level of armed conflict at which the Geneva Conventions were to be activated) and the boundaries of state sovereignty. In these tense negotiations with state governments and agencies, the humanitarian mantle served the ICRC well.

Establishing national aid societies in sovereign territories around the globe followed distinct trajectories. In the German states of central Europe, the new Red Cross movement relied on preexisting patriotic women's associations, which had provided various forms of aid for disabled veterans and a range of working poor since the Napoleonic wars. Dunant found considerable support

17 Geneva Red Cross Archives (hereafter ACICR), AF (Ancien Fonds), 21, Travaux du CICR, 1863–76, letter June 12, 1867; AF, 21, File 5, "L'insurrection dans L'Herzégovine," *Bulletin International*, No. 25 (January 1876); British Red Cross Archives, Lord Wantage Papers, D/Wan/2/3/1 Press Cuttings Turco-Servian War 1876, *The Times*, August 16, 1876.

18 ACICR, 21, File 5, Papiers diverse concernant le Comité international, overview, 1863–78; ibid., RUTU, Guerre russo-turque (Agence de Trieste), 1877–78, File 3, Correspondance Médecin et Infirmiers.

among the female dynastic patrons of these organizations: representatives of Baden, Prussia, Hesse, and Württemberg had been instrumental in drafting the Geneva Conventions. German unification in 1871 created a more centralized Red Cross Society, headquartered in Berlin, although the day-to-day planning in peacetime remained under the jurisdiction of seven distinct state organizations. By contrast, the British National Aid Society emerged during the Franco-German War of 1870–71 to raise funds, materials, and medical personnel for both sides. As part of an empire that was geared less to land than naval warfare, the British voluntary association grew out of wars in which Britain was neutral. The first use of voluntary medical personnel to aid British troops occurred in the colonial theaters of war. Early on, the society also relied on domestic Ladies' Committees, which pushed for the expansion of medical training, including the first scientific courses for nurses who eventually were sent to hospitals near the front. Nurses were originally trained under government auspices, but by 1881 the society was supervising a small cadre of volunteers, although the suitability of women for battlefield roles remained contentious.[19]

Other societies quickly followed. Although the ICRC was skeptical at the start about expanding the charitable impulse beyond Europe, believing its rules more suitable to the higher moral development of the Christian heartland, success in Japan opened new options in the "Far East." The first overtures occurred in 1873, when post-Meiji reformers traveled to the capitals of Europe. They also met with the ICRC and took the Geneva idea back home. A Japanese Red Cross Society was founded in 1886, the same year in which Japan adhered to the Geneva Conventions. Efforts in Montenegro embroiled the Geneva Committee in matters of sovereignty. The outbreak of the insurrection in Bosnia-Herzegovina in 1875–76, which was part of an increasing number of separatist movements in the Ottoman Balkans, led to a wave of wounded refugees fleeing to nearby Montenegro. Against the vociferous protest of authorities in Istanbul, who insisted that the instability was a domestic matter, the ICRC sent a delegation to Montenegro, headed by the physician Frédéric Ferrière, with instructions to create an official aid society and gain the country's adherence to the Geneva Conventions. This step assumed an independent status for

19 Jean H. Quataert, *Staging Philanthropy: Patriotic Women and the National Imagination in Dynastic Germany, 1813–1916* (Ann Arbor, 2001), esp. 74–89; A. K. Loyd, *An Outline of the History of the British Red Cross Society from Its Foundation in 1870 to the Outbreak of the War in 1914* (London, 1917), 5–16.

Montenegro in international law, which it did not acquire until the Congress of Berlin in 1878.[20]

Although independent and autonomous, the national relief societies that constituted the international movement increasingly adopted shared features: name, sign, strategies, and goals. The precondition for internationalism, as well as for thriving international institutions such as the socialist Second International and the women's internationals, was a high level of national autonomy. In the case of the Red Cross movement, government recognition became the basis for continuing development. Known in the idiom of the day as "centralization," this principle was the cardinal point made by Clara Barton in her effort to mobilize public support for a relief society in the United States. Writing in 1878, four years before the US Senate ratified the Geneva Conventions, she described the necessity of centralization and coordination. Recognizing the need for efficiency in wartime, she explained: "Relief Societies have a common central head to which they send their supplies, and which communicates for them with the seat of war or with the surgical medical authorities, and it is through this central commission [that] they have governmental recognition." While she mentioned their training in peacetime, which lent a "permanence they could not otherwise have," as well as their humanitarian impartiality, she stressed the importance of government support for the central leadership.[21] In Germany, among other countries, the Red Cross societies were included in the medical mobilization orders for the armed forces in 1878. The British Aid Society, which merged with other groups to form the Red Cross Organization in 1905, was given a virtual monopoly to transmit "all voluntary offers of assistance in aid of the wounded and sick" to the Army Council. In the best case, Red Cross organizations worked with their governments, a linkage facilitated early by the ICRC's close ties to the ruling houses and state authorities. Red Cross delegations consistently received the support of the highest leadership; and their reports mirrored the perspectives of the dominant elites.[22]

Incorporation of the Red Cross movement into government medical war agendas – as well as the movement's role in national disaster-relief

20 AICRC, AF 21, File 5, "L'Ambassade japonaise," *Bulletin*, no. 17, October 1873; Hutchinson, *Champions of Charity*, 205–6; AICRC, AF, 21, File 13, Monténegro et Herzégovine, 1875–1876, no. 10 "Project," the proposals for a Montenegro Red Cross Society; and December 1875, no. 13 "instructions générales" for the delegation.

21 Clara Barton, *The Red Cross of the Geneva Conventions: What It Is* (Washington, DC, 1878), 4–5.

22 Quataert, *Staging Philanthropy*, 178–88; Loyd, *An Outline*, 25; and AICRC, 21, PFF4, detailed report of Dr. Ferrière, "Briefe aus Montenegro," translated and reprinted in full in the *Allgemeine Zeitung*, Augsburg, May–June 1876.

planning – addressed the major concerns of high officials, who had refused in 1864 to include volunteers under the Geneva Conventions' protections. In Münzel's eyes a shift in opinion already had taken place by 1901. Earlier, he said, volunteering had been too new an idea; but now this volunteer movement had proved itself. Reflecting a growing consensus among decision-makers, he described the state of affairs: "the Red Cross societies are widespread, well organized and, due to their constant preparation in peacetime, well suited to provide relief on the battlefield when the official medical personnel and hospital staff are not able fully to fulfill their tasks."[23] Mounting pressure from below pushed the legal changes. As revised in 1906, the Geneva Conventions protected the work of volunteer societies. Article 10 placed the "personnel of Voluntary Aid Societies, duly recognized and authorized by their Government," under the same protections as the military medical corps. If captured, they were not to be considered prisoners of war – a legal status that had first formally been defined in the codified laws of land warfare in 1899 – but were required to continue their services until it was safe to repatriate them. Furthermore, the revisions to the Conventions no longer used the term "neutral" to designate impartial humanitarian medical service, affirming its inviolability instead. This shift returned neutrality to its original place in the laws of war, as a designation for states (and their newly instituted medical services) that were neutral in a particular armed conflict. Finally, the revisions also affirmed the Red Cross as the distinctive universal sign for medical services for armies and navies, outlawing its use as a trademark for commercial purposes by any individual or organization independent of the official Red Cross movement.

The affirmation in 1906 of the Red Cross as the *unique* emblem for medical services that were tied to the state, however, spoke to the limitations of the universalist project. In general, this project underscored a fundamental paradox of codification, which asserted universal rules even as it excluded more diverse understandings of the law. More specifically, codification masked an alternative practice that had been evolving on the ground over the past thirty years, which reflected deep social tensions over membership in the human community that was envisioned through humanitarian service. The cultural theorist Pierre Bourdieu has offered a critical assessment of the language of universality. In terms that are applicable to humanitarian universalism, he has noted that universality is produced "only by instituting social universes which, by the effect of the social alchemy of their specific laws of functioning, tend to

23 Münzel, *Untersuchungen*, 165–66.

extract the sublimated essence of the universal from the often merciless clash between particular interests." This process of extraction allows the universal to become a "collective enterprise."[24]

The collective enterprise to remake international law involved similar mechanisms of exclusion. Neither the Hague treaties nor the associated arbitral institution were extended to colonial conflicts, which literally formed the historical backdrop to the work of codification, notably the Philippine rebellion against the United States in 1899, the Southern African (Boer) War between 1899 and 1902, the Boxer Rebellion in China in 1900–01 and the German campaign against the Herero and Nama peoples of Southwest Africa in 1904–07. The great powers saw these struggles as internal matters of empire, outside the jurisdiction of the emerging legal regime for warfare. Britain had kept the Boer republics out of the Hague negotiations in 1899, just as the delegates refused to admit Korea to the table in 1907, acquiescing in Japanese imperial claims a year before this country formally annexed its Korean "protectorate" in 1908. The Geneva Conventions, however, were implemented during the Boer War by the medical personnel of the belligerent as well as neutral powers, perhaps because the war was fought between recognizable "state" entities and involved mainly the so-called "white races." But when the Chinese delegate Colonel Ting called in 1907 for clarification on the definition of "war" – and alluded to the invasion of China by the great powers under the verbal subterfuge of an "expedition" – he was ignored. Similarly, the representatives of Japan, who with Cuban delegates had favored broadening the scope of international oversight for prisoners of war in the revised code, failed to extend the obligations of neutral powers to ensure neutralization of territories that they controlled beyond their formal borders. The proponents of this extension had sought to redress the perceived misuse of French ports by the Russian army during the Russo-Japanese War of 1904–05.[25]

Tensions over the emblem that signified the work of impartial battlefield service posed a different challenge. Looking back in 1873, the ICRC claimed that it had always intended to spread its mission beyond Europe, hoping to transplant Europe's enlightened, humanist culture abroad through work symbolized by the cross, which, the committee claimed, evoked not Christianity but Switzerland by inverting the colors of the Swiss flag. The ICRC admitted that it expected incomprehension from "savages" and

24 Pierre Bourdieu, *The Field of Cultural Production: Essays on Art and Literature*, ed. Randal Johnson (New York, 1993), 190–91.

25 Davis, *The Second Hague Peace Conference*, 37–40, 211–12.

"barbarians" (*aux sauvages ou aux barbares*), alluding to the law's presumption of "civilization," although the committee also toyed with the idea of an emblem that featured different symbols on a shared white background. Within a year of its formation, the ICRC took its message to the Ottoman Empire, which had been admitted to the European diplomatic community by the Treaty of Paris in 1856. The Porte acceded to the Geneva Conventions in July 1865, although it did not establish a functioning aid society for well over a decade.[26]

The Ottomans, for whom late-nineteenth-century warfare was a familiar experience, forced the first confrontation over the sign of inclusion, insisting that Ottoman sovereignty be symbolized by a Red Crescent, to reflect the Muslim identity of the dynasty. According to Ottoman reports, an earlier effort to establish an official society had foundered on the issue of the cross. In 1876, the Ottoman committee sent the constitution of its new Red Crescent Society to the International Committee for recognition. Simultaneously, Sultan Abdul Hamid asked the ICRC to call the signatory states together to accept the crescent in a formal revision of the Geneva treaty, a proposal that remained on the diplomatic table for decades. Impending war between the Russians and the Ottomans forced a decision in 1878. After wide consultation, the International Committee accepted a compromise offered by Bernhard Ernst von Bülow, the Prussian state secretary: reciprocal recognition of cross and crescent for the duration of this war alone. As Bülow explained in his proposal, it seemed like a reasonable accommodation of the sensibilities of wounded Muslim soldiers. This practice became standard fare in the Russo-Ottoman (1877–78), Tripolitanian (1911–12), and Balkan Wars (1912–13). Although it hung like a shadow over negotiations concerning the rules of war in 1899, 1906, and 1907, the sultan's proposal, which was supported by states, such as Persia and Siam, that wanted their own distinct symbols, failed to become formal international law before 1914.[27]

This compromise sat uneasily with medical providers on the ground, for whom the humanitarian rhetoric of the Geneva Conventions invited ruminations about the "proper" ordering of self and others in a wider community

26 *Bulletin*, no. 17, October 1873.

27 For details on the controversy from the perspective of the International Committee, see *Procès-verbaux des Séances du Comité International de la Croix-Rouge, 1863–1914*, ed. Jean-François Pitteloud (Geneva, 1999), 292–93, 398; and, from the Ottoman side, AICRC, AF, 19, 2 "Appel à l'humanité pour l'organisation d'une Societé de Secours aux blessés dans l'Empire Ottoman," 1868; ibid., 19/2/ Project Moynier, "La Croix-Rouge et l'Islamisme."

bound by service. It allowed, however, many patterns of inclusion and exclusion.

By far the most contentious issue was the presumed divide between Christians and Muslims. In the idiom of European medical relief, this gap meant that even the crescent could not turn "Muslim cruelty" into "Christian brotherly love." This problem pervaded the ICRC's published and private correspondence during its early decades, and it surfaced in the reports of its official delegates, whether they were sent to Montenegro in 1876 (Frédéric Ferrière), to Istanbul in 1878 (the Austrian baron Jaromir Mundy), or to the five major states involved in the first Balkan War in 1912 (the Swiss doctor Carle de Marval). Ferrière's biweekly reports showed how the medical needs of locals pushed Red Cross work beyond the formal jurisdiction of the law, which was limited to wounded soldiers. He helped many sick villagers who flocked to his makeshift mobile clinic. Helping civilian victims increasingly characterized the work on the ground, as volunteer medical staff began to aid refugees and migrants who were fleeing war, wounded civilians who had been caught in the crossfire, and other destitute people; at times, the medical personnel sought ICRC sanctions for their actions. These activists were coming to understand that the need for "humanitarian relief" would exceed both the law's reach and the war's duration. But this expansive interpretation of the humanitarian impulse coexisted with crass stereotypes, one-sided accusations of Muslim fanaticism and its "deep-seated hatred" (*haine invétérée*) for Christians.[28]

Similar, if more subtle, sentiments percolated up from the Ottoman side. At the moment when the Ottoman Empire was losing large numbers of Christian subjects, members of the Ottoman aid society struggled with their own different loyalties, as they sought to promote the Geneva vision. In 1877, in a letter (marked highly confidential) to Gustav Moynier, the president of the ICRC, Dicran Pechedimaldji repeated unfiltered accusations of "Turkish" cruelty as he pleaded for the crescent in order to promote the shared work on behalf of wounded soldiers. At the time, he was one of ten Christians on the fifteen-member board of the Ottoman society. Acknowledging the ongoing controversy over the sign, Münzel was less generous in 1901. He invested the cross with sacred meaning for the peoples of Europe. Yet, he claimed, over the past thirty years, it also had become "sacrosanct"

28 *Sanitäres über den türkisch-montenegrinisch-serbischen Feldzug i. J. 1876*. Separat-Abdruck aus der Deutschen militäirärzlichen Zeitschrift von 1877, CICR Library, no. 2746, 57; *Bulletin*, no. 35, January 1876; Ferrière, "Briefe," 7, 23, 45.

throughout the "civilized" world. Even the Japanese, he noted, had given up their opposition to the emblem. Thus he warned that adopting the crescent would threaten unity and, whether because of ignorance or confusion, endanger the protective aura of the cross. Letters from the Tripolitanian and Bulgarian theaters during the second Balkan War captured ongoing tensions on the ground. Ameer Ali, the head of an English Red Crescent society that was aiding Ottoman soldiers, described the situation. "I found ignorance on both sides, antipathy against the crescent armband among Muslims and among Bulgarian officers of lower ranks and ordinary soldiers, an entire failure to understand the purposes of the crescent." He noted that "whatever the origins of the red cross, it has been constantly associated with The Cross in the minds of the world, both military and civilian." In late July 1914, drawing on notions circulating among medical volunteers, he pleaded with the International Committee to adopt a new, universal emblem consisting of a horizontal bar and a vertical crescent.[29] His proposal faded into the din of world war.

Matters of membership, however, were never simple. Military attachés who covered the Russo-Ottoman War as correspondents drew other divides. For most observers, Russians and Ottomans represented quintessential "others" – backward in organization, transport, and sanitary preparations, inherently "submissive" (Russians) or religiously "fanatical" (Turks). As the US minister to Constantinople summed up the indictment, "[r]eligious fanaticism, antipathy of race intensified by ages of oppression and misrule, traditional national hostility . . . all combined in relentless merciless carnage."[30] With near unanimity, these observers concluded that the conflict was no western European war and thus of little long-term strategic interest. Confined within stereotypes about presumed national characteristics, they failed to recognize the technological changes in weaponry that spawned the trench warfare of World War I. Other participants used voluntary humanitarian services to highlight the unique characteristics of their own compatriots and strengthen national pride. Deepening national identity through transnational activities was a goal of the detailed accounts that were sent back to leading newspapers for public consumption; so was the solicitation of private money. A report of the British Stafford House during the Russo-Ottoman War made the point. The authors described the pride that readers would feel over the

29 AF, 19, 2/73, Constantinople, September 12, 1877; Münzel, *Untersuchungen*, 140–44; AF, 24, Travaux du CICR, 1911–14, File 7, July 28, 1914.

30 Maureen P. O'Connor, "The Vision of Soldiers: Britain, France, Germany and the United States Observe the Russo-Turkish War," *War in History* 4 (1997): 287–88.

"courage, devotion and resolution displayed by hospital and ambulance staff" – veritable "English characteristics" they noted – and over how the work redounded to the honor of the "English nation."[31]

Coordinating the Red Cross movement, the ICRC became the hub in the widening circulation of letters, reports, documents, and official government complaints about the fate of the Geneva Conventions in wartime. As an outside body with no legal standing, it took on a vital supervisory role, gradually establishing a customary right to initiate inquiries. No similar outside agent had emerged to oversee the Hague Conventions' regulations.

Ferrière set an early precedent. Unable to respond to the entreaties of the Montenegran government for aid in 1875 – "the main organ by design is not able to intervene" – the ICRC sent him with instructions to inquire about the treatment of the wounded. Similarly, Mundy took an activist role in Istanbul, pressuring Ottoman commanders to let in supplies of medicines, sending envoys to oversee sick Russian and Romanian prisoners, and raising private monies through Austrian and German newspapers to support the medical services of the Ottoman Red Crescent Society.[32]

Aid society reports from the battlefield showed growing observance of the Geneva Conventions, although the "powers" of these societies varied greatly. Dr. Barrington-Kennett, a member of the Stafford House, moved around the battlefield relatively freely "under the protection of the Red Crescent" during the Russo-Ottoman War. Threatened by incendiary weapons and roving Ottoman irregular forces near Barardjik, another staff member, Dr. Sandwith, wrote with satisfaction: "the Stafford House flag was able to afford protection for the night to many frightened women and children." By contrast, Dr. Attwood, who was surrounded by Cossack troops in the same area, admitted that when he made "references to the Geneva Conventions" in his effort to continue on to Edirne, he merely "provide[d] amusement." For the medical staff, infractions of the Conventions were serious, and records gave detailed evidence of the crimes, as in the charge that the Russians had deliberately bombarded a Stafford House hospital in Rustchuk in December 1877. "Our hospital was totally destroyed and untenable and in twelve hours we had removed all the patients and property of the hospital (except the wooden bedsteads), along with private goods, etc., into the town," complained

31 *Report and Record of the Operations of the Stafford House Committee for the Relief of Sick and Wounded Turkish Soldiers, Russo-Turkish War, 1877–78* (London, 1879), 2–4.

32 AF, 21, 13, *Journal de Genève*, December 23, 1875; ibid. 19, 2/94–95, letter November 3, 1877; ibid. 21, 1/116, letter February 8, 1878.

Dr. Stivens. Subsequently, after he saw a Russian report that denied culpability, he issued a detailed rejoinder of "such an utterly false statement."[33]

In time, reports about infractions circulated beyond the printed page. One doctor telegraphed the President of the Orange Free State in December 1899, during the Boer War; his complaint was translated and sent on to all diplomatic consuls in the territory, as well as to the ICRC. It cataloged the mistreatment of a British ambulance crew that had been taken captive. "Our treatment was fully illegal and contrary to the Geneva Conventions," charged Dr. Van Niekerk, who detailed his efforts to negotiate the crew's rights, as war prisoners, to proper rations, modes of travel, and the return of their seized mobile hospital, which was being improperly held as a "prize of war."[34] Within the framework of the law, the ICRC became the institution of first – and last – resort. Between 1911 and 1913, in particular, it was used heavily by belligerents to lodge formal, well-documented complaints of atrocities and other legal breaches. Reflecting mounting concerns on the ground about the level of brutality and violence, medical witnesses increasingly demanded that the ICRC speak out. As one distressed doctor put it, reflecting broader sentiments, the committee had to take a stand and openly "deplore" massacres. Guarding its neutrality, the ICRC remained cautious. After wide consultation, it exhorted the signatory powers repeatedly to follow the letter of the law; but it refused to make charges public.[35]

The years 1864–1914 were the formative period in the codification of laws that governed the conduct of war (*jus in bello*) and protected categories of people who fell into the hands of adversaries. Not yet established as a formal legal regime with powers to indict and punish, these early laws nonetheless subjected many aspects of warfare to normative regulation. They circumscribed war-making on land and sea (and in the air), defined its scope and proper objectives, and created international institutions such as the Permanent Court of Arbitration and its record-keeping body, the International Bureau, which gave concrete identity to new legal values. Of vital importance for the law's future jurisdiction, the preamble to the Fourth Hague Convention of 1899 affirmed the continuing authority of international customary law in armed conflicts. It stated that behavior not explicitly

33 *Report* (Stafford House), 15, 50–51, 67.

34 AICRC, AF, 25, Guerres Balcaniques, File 3, Hans Daae, "Notes et impressions de la dernière guerre truco-grecque"; telegram, Dr. Boris Lajos, November 21, 1912.

35 Ibid., letter from the German Central Committee of the Red Cross, Berlin, November 27, 1912. The collection contains many charges and counter-charges of infractions of Geneva Convention rules.

prohibited by a treaty might not be permitted because of the continuing authority of international customary law. Known as the Martens Clause for its author, Fedor Federovitch Martens, the Russian delegate who proposed it, the principle provided in part that

> [u]ntil a perfectly complete code of the laws of war is issued, the Conference thinks it right to declare that in cases not included in the present arrangement, populations and belligerents remain under the protection of . . . principles of international law, as they result from the usages established between civilized nations, from the laws of humanity, and the requirements of the public conscience.[36]

Recognizing that the new code was not exhaustive, the clause declared that states remained bound by a higher law (the "laws of humanity"), which had enduring validity. It thus laid the legal foundation for new notions of crimes "against humanity" as grave breaches of international customary norms.

Emerging around mid-century in the context of people's wars and the public's new interest in international arbitration and peace, the language of the law deployed new humanitarian sentiments, positing a shared fate that bound humanity and, via the legal innovation of open accession, underpinned the movement toward more "universal" law. Codification sustained newly professionalizing fields in law and medicine, and it opened gendered spheres of work at home and in battlefield service. Conversely, the law and its implementation drew sustenance from its basis in humanitarian claims to impartiality and disinterest. This linkage, furthermore, strengthened the work of the ostensibly private International Committee of the Red Cross, which established a customary right to supervise the implementation of the laws. Expansion of the Geneva idea deep into national societies also stimulated public involvement in humanitarian service. Despite the ambivalence of the early architects, public opinion has become vital to the ongoing fate of the laws of war.

36 "Convention (IV)," in Roberts and Guelff, eds., *Documents*, 45. In their introduction, the editors also provide a useful discussion of customary law in the origins and development of the laws of war. See ibid., 4–6.

7

The arms race: qualitative and quantitative aspects

ANTULIO J. ECHEVARRIA II

Analyses of the arms race that preceded World War I typically focus on quantity, and with good reason.[1] The numbers of weapons and personnel which each alliance could mobilize were enormous indeed, and numbers always matter. As Clausewitz noted, numerical superiority is the "most common element" in tactical and strategic victory, while pointing out it is not always decisive.[2] Although it is common practice to represent the arms race in terms of quantitative comparisons, doing so overshadows the race's qualitative dimensions, which are just as important to an accurate understanding of the nature of military competition during this period. The quarter-century before the war saw more qualitative advances, defined as technological innovations, than any previous era. The industrial revolution, for all its emphasis on mass production and efficient distribution, also created numerous opportunities for innovation, many of which were actively sought by military establishments. In fact, the pursuit of technological and tactical innovations had become integral to the dynamics of military competition by the turn of the century. Qualitative advances are, in other words, as much hallmarks of the prewar arms race as are its unprecedented numbers of weapons and personnel. As a result, this chapter gives equal attention to the quantitative and qualitative aspects of the prewar arms race.

An arms race is defined here as a competition between two or more parties for military supremacy, which is sought by amassing a greater quantity or

1 See Craig Etcheson, *Arms Race Theory: Strategy and Structure of Behavior* (New York, 1989); Paul M. Kennedy, ed., *The War Plans of the Great Powers, 1880–1914* (London, 1985); *The Rise of the Anglo-German Antagonism, 1860–1914* (London, 1980); Robert K. Massie, *Dreadnought: Britain, Germany and the Coming of the Great War* (New York, 1992); David Stevenson, *Armaments and the Coming of the War: Europe, 1904–1914* (New York and Oxford, 1996); David G. Herrmann, *The Arming of Europe and the Making of the First World War* (Princeton, 1996).

2 Carl von Clausewitz, *On War*, trans. and ed. Michael Howard and Peter Paret (Princeton, 1984), 194.

quality of weapons, or both. There is an ongoing debate as to whether such competitions tend to become ends in themselves, and the extent to which they then lead to war.[3] An examination of the events of the arms race that preceded World War I suggests the race neither became an end in itself, nor led directly to war. Admittedly, the major competitors at times seemed to embrace the basic impulse to outpace their rivals militarily, thereby giving apparent credence to the idea that arms races tend to become ends in themselves. However, this basic impulse still generally served each of the major powers' larger political goals, which were as vague as they were inherently competitive. These broader goals typically consisted of either maintaining or reordering the existing balance of power, which in turn required that each state continually seek ways to enhance its political influence. That was frequently done through the practice of armed diplomacy, that is, intimidation. Influence itself is difficult to measure, requires constant nurturing, and is generally only acknowledged when exercised.

To be sure, military power is a critical component of political influence; however, as the first (1905) and second (1911) Moroccan crises demonstrated, neither the limits nor the negative effects of armed diplomacy were well understood. Achieving military supremacy, or at least trying not to fall too far behind, did not become an end in itself, per se; rather, it was a tool of a larger dynamic, one that was symptomatic of an age in which war was considered a legitimate continuation of political intercourse by other means. That intercourse was without a definable end. Military supremacy (or at least respectability) was, thus, tantamount to guaranteeing one's right to exercise power freely, even if supremacy itself required as much effort to maintain as to achieve.

The prewar arms race was actually a combination of three separate, but interrelated competitions for mastery of the sea, land, and air power domains. The last domain was almost entirely new, and it was not clear how achieving air supremacy would affect, or be affected by, the other two. This uncertainty was compounded by the fact that, even though the races overlapped, they also unfolded at different rates, partly because of the nonlinear nature of technological change. Innovations in the realm of sea power, for instance, took place at a much

3 Compare Niall Ferguson's, *The Pity of War: Explaining World War I* (New York, 1999), 82, which argues that it was Germany's perception that it had lost the arms race which precipitated World War I; see also Herrmann, *Arming*, and Stevenson, *Armaments*. Scholars have debated the relationship between arms races and war at least since the beginning of the nuclear buildup during the Cold War; see Samuel Huntington, "The Arms Race Phenomena," *Public Policy* 8 (1958): 1–20 and Lewis F. Richardson, *Arms and Insecurity* (Pacific Grove, CA, 1960); see also the classic works by A. J. P. Taylor, *War by Time-Table: How the First World War Began* (London, 1969) and *How Wars Begin* (London, 1979).

faster rate initially than for land and air power. That changed abruptly in 1906, when one aeronautical record after another was broken, and again in 1909, when air power moved from being the subject of unbridled speculation, as it is in H. G. Wells's *War in the Air* (1908), to a practical combat arm.

In addition, the arms race was made more complex as each of the major competitors – France, Britain, Germany, Russia, the United States, and Japan – entered it at different times in the quarter-century before 1914. Each brought additional variables into play in the form of different interests and capabilities. The rise and fall of their fortunes caused shifts in the general balance of power: Russia's defeat in Asia at the hands of the Japanese, for instance, affected the balance of power in Europe after 1905, though this shifted again in 1911–12; similarly, the fact that France and Britain built a number of ships for the Japanese navy facilitated Japan's growth as a naval power in the East. Thus, the arms race was truly global in aspect.

The four decades before 1914 are rightly referred to as the age of mass; for they saw the introduction or continued emergence of mass politics, mass culture, and mass production, all of which helped define the social and political fabric of the west.[4] However, this was also clearly an era of unprecedented technological discovery and invention, a period that some scholars have called the age of the second industrial revolution, or the technological revolution.[5] It was during this era that inventions such as the telephone (1876), electric street car (1879), steam turbine (1884), motorcycle (1885), automobile (1885), subway (1863), wireless telegraph (1895), dirigible (1900), and airplane (1903) appeared or were developed into forms suitable for mass production. This surge of innovation was largely facilitated by the widespread availability of machinery from the industrial revolution proper; with little modification such machinery could also manufacture prototypes. Also, the economic rise of Germany, the United States, and Japan, as well as the continued commercial growth of France and Great Britain during this era, generated substantial capital for investment in new enterprises.

As a result, while the major players in the arms race routinely assessed their military strength in quantitative terms, they also increasingly had to take into account the possible effect that new inventions or technological improvements

4 Mikulás Teich and Roy Porter, eds., *Fin de Siècle and Its Legacy* (Cambridge, 1990); Richard Hamilton and Holger Herwig, eds., *The Origins of World War I* (New York, 2003), 30–31, remind readers that little of the mass sentiment of the period is based on anything more than anecdotal evidence.

5 Melvin Kranzberg and Carroll W. Pursell, Jr., eds., *Technology in Western Civilization*, Vol. II: *Technology in the Twentieth Century* (New York, 1967).

might have on military operations. These qualitative enhancements took several forms, including improved torpedoes, submarines, magazine-fed rifles, smokeless power, machine guns, rapid-firing artillery, more effective munitions, heavier (dreadnought-class) battleships, "lighter-than-air" vessels, and fixed-wing aircraft. These, in turn, gave rise to a number of tactical innovations, such as the reintroduction of *guerre de course* (a form of commerce raiding) by the *Jeune École* (Young School) in France.[6] Nor were such tactical innovations simply focused on applications of new material: some included efforts to gain a decisive edge within the realm of psychological motivation, such as attempts to revitalize the warrior spirit so as to instill a greater will to win in one's soldiers.[7]

The nature of military competition in the age of innovation was described by Germany's former chief of the great general staff, Alfred von Schlieffen, in an article entitled, "War in the Present Day" (1909):

> If one side invented a faster-firing rifle, a longer-range cannon, or a more effective shell, it could be sure that the other side would quickly develop a rifle that fired even faster, a cannon with an even longer range, and a shell that was even more effective . . . Each party was endeavoring to create a situation similar to that of 1866, when one enemy entered the arena armed with the needle-gun and the other armed with only a muzzle-loader.[8]

Schlieffen was clearly referring to a dimension of military competition that involved more than achieving quantitative advantages. His remarks concerning how difficult it was to obtain an enduring or truly decisive advantage are telling evidence of how important the competition had become. Since Germany could not count on achieving sufficient numerical or technological superiority, Schlieffen made a case for tactical and operational innovations in the form of flank attacks and envelopments. The extent to which such doctrinal innovations could have succeeded is debatable; but the point is that the search for a qualitative advantage manifested itself in several ways in the years before World War I, and thus was never far from the minds of military planners and strategists.[9] In short, military thinking had begun to consider new ways of achieving qualitative advantages without necessarily losing sight of the importance of material superiority.

6 Arne Roksund, *The Jeune École: The Strategy of the Weak* (Leiden, 2007).

7 Antulio J. Echevarria II, "The Cult of the Offensive Revisited: Confronting Technological Change before the Great War," *Journal of Strategic Studies* 25, no. 1 (March 2002): 199–214.

8 Alfred von Schlieffen, "Der Krieg der Gegenwart," *Deutsche Revue* (January 1909): 13–24; see also *Alfred von Schlieffen's Military Writings*, trans. and ed. Robert T. Foley (London and Portland, 2003).

9 Some of those innovations are discussed in Antulio J. Echevarria II, *After Clausewitz: German Military Thinkers before the Great War* (Lawrence, KS, 2001).

Given the impressive variety and frequency of technological innovation during this period, it is hardly surprising that military strategists thought increasingly along qualitative lines. Nonetheless, as Schlieffen implied, the problem for military strategists was that qualitative advantage was often fleeting: as the value of one advance became apparent, rival powers copied the technology, improved it, or developed any number of countermeasures. As a result, for perhaps the first time in the history of military thinking, strategists had to consider not just whether, but when, to purchase or "buy into" large quantities of a particular technology. As Germany's failed sortie with the semi-recoilless 77-millimeter field gun in 1897–98 demonstrates, technological obsolescence came much more swiftly in this period than ever before; the French fully recoilless "model 75" that came out in 1898 fired twenty rounds per minute without re-aiming, whereas the German gun could manage only five to nine rounds per minute, and required re-aiming.[10] Paradoxically, the pace of technological change and the speed at which innovations were reproduced and distributed also worked against the search for military supremacy in qualitative terms; this in turn contributed the impression that the arms race was more quantitative than qualitative. That notwithstanding, the search for qualitative advantages remained as active and relentless as the push for greater quantities.

The arms race at sea can be viewed in terms of two quantitative and two qualitative turns. The race began in earnest with Great Britain's formal adoption of the "two-power standard" in the naval defense bill of 1889, which declared that the Royal Navy would establish and maintain a fighting power "at least equal to the strength of any two other countries."[11] The bill called for the production of ten battleships, forty-two cruisers, and eighteen torpedo gunships over a period of five years. At the time, the Royal Navy was already as strong as the next two largest navies, the French and Russian. Nevertheless, the two-power standard was ambitious because even a conservative naval expansion by either France or Russia would require a redoubled effort on the part of Britain. British naval expenditures after 1889, in fact, doubled compared to the previous ten-year period.[12]

Not surprisingly, the bill defined naval strength explicitly in quantitative terms, that is, by the total number of capital ships (battleships and battle cruisers).

10 Eric Dorn Brose, *The Kaiser's Army: The Politics of Military Technology in Germany during the Machine Age, 1870–1918* (Oxford, 2001), 65–68.

11 Lawrence Sondhaus, *Naval Warfare, 1815–1914* (New York, 2001), 161; Roger Parkinson, *The Late Victorian Navy: The Pre-Dreadnought Era and the Origins of the First World War* (Woodbridge, 2008).

12 Paul M. Kennedy, *The Rise and Fall of British Naval Mastery* (London, 1991 [1976]).

In so doing, it reversed the decision made three years earlier to suspend the building of battleships due to the growing threat posed by new technological innovations in the form of underwater mines, submarines, torpedoes, and fast torpedo boats. By the late 1880s, it seemed obvious that large, expensive capital ships could be severely damaged, or worse, by relatively inexpensive mines and torpedoes. Indeed, it was chiefly because of these developments that the French *Jeune École* argued that the day of the battleship had ended. States could now avoid major sea battles altogether, and concentrate on attacking a nation's merchant vessels and sea lines of communication; likewise, underwater mines, coastal artillery, and small torpedo boats seemed ideal for enhancing coastal defense. These views gained ground swiftly, with Germany, Austria-Hungary, Italy, Spain, and Japan entertaining the idea of maintaining maritime security with fleets of small, highly maneuverable vessels.[13]

However, additional qualitative innovations occurred during the next decade in the form of improved propulsion for larger ships, rapid-firing cannon, better fire-control mechanisms for engaging smaller craft, and torpedo-boat destroyers. These essentially nullified the advantages associated with small vessels armed with torpedoes. Put differently, a series of later technological innovations offset the threats posed earlier, and shifted the balance back in favor of capital ships.

By the late 1890s, France and Russia had either renewed or expanded their building programs in response to the British actions, and the United States had begun to build a capital fleet as well. Thus, instead of deterring naval competition, as the British bill was surely intended to do, it intensified the race. While the United States did not explicitly set an adversarial course with Britain, France and Russia did. The expansion of their programs, in turn, forced Britain to push the quantitative dimension of the naval arms race further, adding three more battleships to its original target of ten, and to implement a new five-year plan, which was to add twelve more battleships and twenty cruisers by the end of the century.[14]

As a by-product of this expansion, several European-built warships found their ways into the Japanese and Chinese navies, which eventually caused a shift in the balance of power in the East. Japan's decisive defeat of China in the first Sino-Japanese War (1894–95) introduced another competitor into the arms race. The Japanese navy destroyed over 90 percent of the Chinese Beiyang fleet in a mere handful of engagements. The imperial Japanese navy, which was established on the model of the British Royal Navy, numbered just over a

13 Roksund, *Jeune École*.
14 Kennedy, *British Naval Mastery*.

dozen cruiser-class warships, mainly of British and French construction, as well as about two dozen torpedo boats. The Beiyang fleet, one of four in the Chinese navy, had been roughly the same size as the entire Japanese navy at the time, and it included two battleships of German construction. In 1890 it was considered the best fleet in Asia. However, corruption, logistical problems, and poor discipline were endemic, and cooperation between the Beiyang fleet and the other three Chinese fleets was virtually nonexistent. The military reforms instituted by the Japanese during the Meiji period proved vastly more effective than those implemented by the Chinese during the Self-Strengthening Movement.[15]

Japan's naval victory established it as Asia's preeminent power. The Japanese acquired Taiwan and the Penghu islands as a result of the war, but had to relinquish portions of the Liaodong Peninsula and Port Arthur due to pressure from the Triple Intervention (by Russia, France, and Germany). Even so, US Secretary of the Navy Hilary A. Herbert, subsequently remarked that "Japan had leaped, almost at one bound, to a place among the great nations of the earth."[16] Russia's efforts to increase its sphere of influence in the Far East, especially in Korea, now had to reckon with the modernization and continued expansion of the Japanese military. The Russians and Chinese entered into a secret security treaty in 1896, while the British concluded an alliance with the Japanese in 1902, which remained in effect until 1921. Japan also supplied the bulk of the naval and land forces which, along with contingents from the United States and the major European powers, suppressed the Boxer Rebellion in 1900.[17] This role was further evidence that the balance of power had shifted in Asia.

Japan and Russia were the major players, but the redistribution of power between them was far from complete. After the war with the Chinese, the Japanese began a ten-year naval expansion program, which, by 1905, resulted in the construction of six battleships, eight armored cruisers, nine cruisers, two dozen destroyers, and over sixty torpedo boats.[18] While most of these vessels were built in Britain, an increasing number were constructed in Japan, reflecting her growth as an industrial power.

15 S. C. M. Paine, *The Sino-Japanese War of 1894–1895: Power, Perceptions, and Primacy* (Cambridge, 2003); Benjamin A. Elman, "Naval Warfare and the Refraction of China's Self-Strengthening Reforms into Scientific and Technological Failure, 1865–1895," in Andrew Lambert, ed., *Naval History 1850–Present* (Aldershot and Burlington, 2007).

16 Cf. Paine, *Sino-Japanese War of 1894–1895*, 3.

17 Diana Preston, *The Boxer Rebellion* (New York, 2000).

18 David C. Evans and Mark R. Peattie, *Kaigun: Strategy, Tactics, and Technology in the Imperial Japanese Navy, 1887–1941* (Annapolis, MD, 1997).

The next turn in the naval arms race was quantitative; it came with Germany's naval bill of 1898, which appropriated some 400 million marks to build a navy of nineteen battleships, eight coastal armored ships, twelve large and thirty small cruisers, along with a number of supporting vessels.[19] It was a direct response to the threat posed by the expansion of the British Royal Navy. This response was quickly followed in 1900 with a bill that established a seventeen-year deadline for completing the construction of a fleet that was to comprise two flagships, thirty-six battleships, eleven large, and thirty-four small cruisers.[20] The timing could not have been better for Germany, as Britain was embroiled in the second Boer War (1899–1902).

Underlying both bills was the so-called risk theory (*Risikogedanke*) introduced by Grand Admiral Alfred von Tirpitz, secretary of state of the Imperial Naval Office. The theory aimed at posing an unacceptable risk to Britain in the form of a fleet so strong that the Royal Navy would have to consider withdrawing vessels from the Mediterranean and Far East to retain its supremacy, leaving British interests there exposed. Tirpitz calculated that rather than accept the risks of reducing its presence in either the Mediterranean or the Far East, the British would recognize Germany's arrival as a legitimate power, and enter into some sort of power-sharing relationship – perhaps achieving "concessions" in the form of bases and access to certain markets – that would ultimately enhance German influence and prestige.[21] The first step, however, was to build a fleet so strong that the Royal Navy would want to avoid doing battle with it. Thus, the Reich's initial strategic goal was not naval supremacy in its own right, but a "place in the sun," which would translate into greater political influence abroad.

Tirpitz's theory was based upon assumptions that were not so much flawed as dependent upon relationships that were dynamic, and thus in need of constant reassessment and adjustment. The first assumption was that Germany's growing shipbuilding capacity could challenge Britain's. This was not an unreasonable

19 Annika Mombauer, "German War Plans," in Richard F. Hamilton and Holger Herwig, eds., *War Planning 1914* (Cambridge, 2010), 65–66; Michael Epkenhans, "Wilhelm II and 'His' Navy, 1888–1918," in Annika Mombauer and Wilhelm Deist, eds., *The Kaiser: New Research on Wilhelm II's Role in Imperial Germany* (Cambridge, 2003); and *Die Wilhelminische Flottenrüstung, 1908–1914: Weltmachtstreben, Industrieller Fortschritt, Soziale Integration* (Munich, 1991).

20 Rolf Hobson, *Imperialism at Sea: Naval Strategic Thought, the Ideology of Sea Power, and the Tirpitz Plan, 1875–1914* (Boston, 2002).

21 Paul M. Kennedy, "Tirpitz, England, and the Second Navy Law of 1900: A Strategical Critique," *Militärgeschichtliche Mitteilungen* 8 (1970): 38; Cf. Mombauer, "German War Plans," 66.

belief at a time when Britain was involved in the second Boer War and faced a substantial drain on its defense budget. Germany's economic growth to this point had been phenomenal. While steel production grew by 350 percent in Britain, it increased almost 1,500 percent in Germany (and by more than 8,600 percent in the United States); coal output rose by 650 percent in Germany, compared to 250 percent in Britain.[22] In Germany and America, steel production had started from a smaller base, so increases were more dramatic. Nonetheless, from 1889 to 1913 Germany's gross national product doubled, while that of the British grew by only two-thirds.[23] By 1914, Germany was the most powerful industrial nation in the world after the United States. It is worth noting that a number of influential German industrialists and bankers purportedly counseled against war, insisting that "Germany becomes stronger with every year of peace."[24]

Tirpitz's second assumption was that the British would grow weary under the burden of ever-increasing naval expenditures. This assumption became more reasonable after the Liberals took office in Britain in 1905, as they favored an agenda of reduced defense spending; however, that did not last. A third assumption was that Britain would not seek an alliance with another naval power, given its desire to maintain naval supremacy, and particularly in light of the two-power standard. A fourth assumption was that the European naval race would be unaffected by events in other parts of the globe or by other dimensions of military competition, such as land and air power. Again, each of these assumptions called for periodic reevaluation and adjustment to reflect changes in the strategic situation.

The Russo-Japanese War (1904–5) demonstrated the tenuous nature of Tirpitz's scheme. The Japanese navy defeated the Russian Baltic and Pacific fleets, thereby causing a further shift in the balance of power not only in Asia, but also in Europe. At the battle of Tsushima, Japanese Admiral Togo annihilated the main Russian fleet of thirty-eight ships, sinking, disabling, or capturing all but four. Notably, Togo's fleet was the first to use wireless telegraphy while carrying out a naval maneuver, "crossing the Russian T" at Tsushima, under battle conditions; a recently developed technological advantage thus helped win a battle at sea.[25]

22 S. B. Clough, *The Economic Development of Western Civilization* (New York, 1959), 377, 385; W. O. Henderson, *The Rise of German Industrial Power, 1834–1914* (Berkeley, 1975), 233–34.

23 B. R. Mitchell, *European Historical Statistics 1750–1970* (London, 1975), 818–26.

24 Richard F. Hamilton and Holger H. Herwig, "World Wars: Definitions and Causes," in Hamilton and Herwig, eds., *Origins of World War I*, 32.

25 R. M. Connaughton, *The War of the Rising Sun and the Tumbling Bear: A Military History of the Russo-Japanese War 1904–5* (London, 1988); J. N. Westwood, *Russia against Japan, 1904–1905: A New Look at the Russo-Japanese War* (Albany, 1986).

However, the cost of the Russo-Japanese War and the military expansion that preceded it was staggering. Japan had borrowed heavily from the United States and Great Britain to finance her naval expansion and the conduct of the war itself, and thanks to the intervention of the great powers she had received little financial compensation from the Russians, who were reeling from the military defeat and from domestic uprisings and mutinies within the officer corps. The Russians subsequently engaged in a formal entente with the British in 1907, a development that, not unlike Britain's treaty with Japan in 1902, the risk theory had not foreseen. While the arrangement provided Russia much-needed assurance strategically, it also compromised Tirpitz's calculations, thereby reducing the likelihood that Germany could achieve its goals.

The next major turn in the naval arms race was qualitative. It came in 1905, when the British began building HMS *Dreadnought*, which was commissioned in 1906. Until this point, a state-of-the-art battleship displaced some 13,000 tons and was typically armed with four 12-inch guns (along with several smaller quick-firing guns for close-in defense) with a range of 6,000 yards. The *Dreadnought* was almost 50 percent larger, displacing nearly 18,000 tons, and it was armed with two and a half times as many guns – ten 12-inch guns, each of which had a range of up to 13,000 yards, more than twice that of earlier guns. Moreover, a new type of steam-turbine engine allowed the *Dreadnought* to reach speeds of 21 knots, 2–6 knots faster than those of existing battleships. Dreadnought-class vessels rendered obsolete all existing battleships, including some fifty capital ships in Britain's own fleet.[26] The 1906 edition of *Jane's Fighting Ships* ranked Britain first among naval powers, followed in order by the United States, France, Japan, Germany, Russia, Italy, and Austria-Hungary.[27] This ranking, however, was the last of the pre-dreadnought era.

Battleships were not the only vessels to benefit from the qualitative turns associated with development of the dreadnoughts. Battle cruisers and destroyers also doubled in size, speed, and firepower. A state-of-the-art destroyer in 1905 displaced less than 500 tons and was armed with a few 3-inch quick-firing guns and small-diameter torpedoes. By 1914 destroyers displaced nearly 1,000 tons, could reach speeds of 35 knots, and were typically armed with four 4-inch guns and several 21-inch torpedoes. Thus, the qualitative turn was far-reaching.

Meanwhile, the effect on coastal artillery was adverse. Coastal guns had generally been powerful enough and of sufficient range to force capital ships

26 D. K. Brown, *Warrior to Dreadnought: Warship Development 1860–1905* (Annapolis, MD, 2003).
27 Fred T. Jane, *Jane's Fighting Ships* (New York, 1906–7).

to remain a respectful distance from shore. Once wooden ships began to yield to armored vessels, and once steam began to replace sail, the advantage began to shift to warships, which could now close more quickly to within effective range of coastal targets. Coastal defenses responded by introducing underwater minefields, land-based torpedoes, dispersed batteries, disappearing gun platforms, and ever heavier ordinance. In short, the costs of coastal defense rose astronomically; yet, the advantage remained with seaborne vessels since they could now mass superior firepower at specific points more readily.

A few years before the outbreak of war, the qualitative dimension of the naval arms race turned yet again. In 1910, dreadnought-class battleships were themselves rendered obsolete by the production of so-called "super dreadnoughts," typified by HMS *Orion*, which carried ten 13.5-inch guns. These massive ships were in turn superseded in 1913 by yet another generation of battleships – the Queen Elizabeth class – which was armed with eight 15-inch guns.[28] This class of warship continued to serve throughout World War II, although its value diminished as the power of aircraft carriers grew.

Germany's production of heavy battleships declined dramatically after 1912, as the focus of German armaments shifted to land power. At this time, the Reich ranked second overall in naval power with a navy that was 40 percent the size of Britain's; the United States ranked third, and France and Japan were tied for fourth.[29] By the time war broke out in 1914, Germany had forty-three capital ships (seventeen dreadnoughts, twenty pre-dreadnoughts, and six battle-cruisers), compared to Britain's 74 (twenty-four dreadnoughts, forty pre-dreadnoughts, and ten battle-cruisers). The Kaiser's navy had failed to achieve the desired 2:3 ratio of capital ships with the Royal Navy. Moreover, it had failed to keep pace with the development of other naval weapons, such as submarines, which could be seen as a qualitative – or asymmetric – component in the race for naval superiority. Between 1900 and 1914, for example, the French navy commissioned seventy-six submarines; Britain had eighty-eight by the time the war began, the United States thirty-two, but Germany only twenty-two.[30] More significantly, Germany had no ally to help close the naval gap; instead this technological innovation went quickly from qualitative to quantitative, but not in the favor of the Central Powers.

28 Siegfried Breyer, *Battleships and Battlecruisers of the World, 1905–1970* (London, 1973).

29 Fred T. Jane, *Jane's Fighting Ships* (New York, 1912–13).

30 Robert Hutchinson, *Jane's Submarines: War beneath the Waves from 1776 to the Present Day* (New York, 2005).

Although historians have rightly criticized Tirpitz's ambitious plan, his calculations were not the principal problem with the scheme.[31] The primary fault lay in the Reich's general failure to reexamine its assumptions, as well as in the inability of key statesmen and military professionals to define their strategic goals clearly and to adjust them as the situation changed. Opportunities for formal arms-control agreements between Germany and Britain arose several times between 1906 and 1912; these included the 1907 Hague Conference, British efforts to negotiate an understanding from 1908 to 1911, and the Haldane mission of 1912.[32] However, as is so often the case when one senses that a better bargain can be had by holding out, no formal agreement was ever reached, even as a starting point for further negotiations. Instead, both sides tended to misread the overtures of the other. Although no formal agreement was reached, an informal understanding did essentially occur during the final two years before the war, as evidenced by the fact that the naval arms race basically ended in 1913.[33]

The land-power race was more qualitative than quantitative until 1911, when key decisions resulted in a more dramatic increase in the size of European armies. The most critical technological innovations up to 1914 came in the form of magazine rifles, machine guns, quick-firing artillery, better fortifications, and heavy artillery. Magazine-fed rifles appeared in the 1880s and were quickly adopted by all the European powers, especially France and Germany. By the late 1890s the German Mauser Model 98 had a range of 2,000 meters and a higher muzzle velocity and flatter trajectory than its predecessor, the Model 88. It remained the German army's standard infantry rifle through the end of World War II. Machine guns also became more reliable and practical in the late 1890s. The Maxim machine gun fired between 480 and 600 rounds per minute and had a range of more than 2,000 meters. However, the fielding of machine guns proceeded slowly until the Russo-Japanese War, which demonstrated their value, particularly as defensive weapons.[34] The British, who were looking for ways to augment their small expeditionary force, held the lead in the fielding of machine guns until 1904. Despite recurring problems with mechanical failures and ammunition

31 A recent comparative critique is Hobson, *Imperialism at Sea*, 215–45.

32 John H. Maurer, "Arms Control and the Anglo-German Naval Race before World War I: Lessons for Today?" *Political Science Quarterly* 112 (1997): 285–306.

33 Kennedy, *Anglo-German Antagonism*.

34 One of the best books on weapons technologies of the period is Hans Linnenkohl, *Vom Einzelschuss zur Feuerwalze: Der Wettlauf zwischen Technik und Taktik im Ersten Weltkrieg* (Koblenz, 1990).

re-supply, all armies adopted some form of machine gun after 1905. The goal, which was largely achieved before the summer of 1914, was to have one two-gun section for every battalion.

The development of recoil-absorbing mechanisms created a new generation of artillery pieces, known as "quick-firers," the most famous of which was the French 75-millimeter gun, fielded in 1897. As mentioned earlier, it could fire between twenty to thirty rounds per minute, while improved munitions, such as long-range shrapnel, made each round more effective. The 75-millimeter gun gave the French the advantage in the arms race on land until about 1906, when the Germans finally overcame internal bickering and bureaucratic friction to answer with a truly recoilless cannon.[35] Again, this case illustrates the problem of purchasing a weapon too soon. The Russians and British began to field their own versions of the quick-firer in 1904 and 1905, while the efforts of the Austro-Hungarian and Italian armies to do the same stalled for lack of funding.

The Germans took the lead in heavy artillery, particularly after 1903, when they began fitting their 150-millimeter howitzers for full recoil-absorption. Part of the reason for the German emphasis on heavy artillery was Schlieffen's appreciation of the difficulties of cracking the improved fortifications that had sprung up in Belgium, the Netherlands, and along the French frontier. The resultant distribution in the German army was one heavy-artillery battalion (of sixteen to eighteen guns) per army corps. Between 1904 and 1908, the French began to equip their army corps with heavy guns as well, but only with one battery (of six guns) per corps. By 1911, this decision had left the French (with 120 heavy guns) significantly outgunned by the Germans (who had 380) – a ratio that did not include the German advantage in heavy mortars and siege artillery.[36]

As mentioned earlier, efforts to obtain advantages in the qualitative dimension also extended to human material. Despite increasing reports regarding the physical and psychological degeneration of modern human material, each of the major powers tended to see its citizens as "racially" superior to those of their likely foes. Such self-perceptions were clearly products of the era's penchant for stereotyping ethnic groups in terms of a few simple characteristics which were as decidedly vague as they were self-reflexive. Even as each power spared no effort in convincing itself that its national character was superior to those of its competitors, each also took the so-called degenerative

35 Brose, *Kaiser's Army*.
36 Bruce I. Gudmundsson, *On Artillery* (Westport, CT, 1993).

forces of modernization seriously. These forces were thought to introduce a certain nervousness and anxiety into the psyches of modern peoples, causing debilitating mental and physical disorders. Studies conducted in Britain, France, Germany, and the United States purportedly confirmed the onset of modern "nervousness."[37] It was not at all clear whether individuals affected by this malady would have the psychological and physical fortitude to withstand the horrors and hardships of modern war.

The threat of physical debilitation could be addressed through vigorous training. However, psychological debilitation required a certain training of the mind and a strengthening of the character; these goals were to be accomplished by inculcating martial values and a warrior spirit within society as a whole, and especially among those populations approaching military age. A wave of professional and semi-professional military literature as the century turned helped set the stage for the rise of numerous youth groups, such as the Boy Scouts and the Young German League, and military instruction in the so-called school of the nation; public debates against the principal doctrines of socialism and pacifism ensued, though their genuine effectiveness is difficult to measure.[38] The Japanese soldier was held up as a model for modern troops; he was seen as the embodiment of a time-honored warrior code, was considered well trained, disciplined, and skilled in the use of modern weapons, including machine guns and artillery. If the state of military technology were roughly equal among combatants, so went the logic, a strong military spirit would make the difference, as it had in the war of 1904–05. All of these efforts should be seen as a larger struggle to achieve, or at least avoid losing, a qualitative edge in the human dimension. Ironically, the extent to which the so-called "lost generation of 1914" endured the war's horrors and hardships suggests that attempts to restore the warrior spirit were either remarkably successful or patently unnecessary.[39]

The quantitative dimension of the arms race on land unfolded incrementally until 1911, when the embarrassment of the second Moroccan crisis apparently convinced some among the German leadership that the Reich's military might needed to be stronger to avoid similar humiliations in the

37 George M. Beard, *American Nervousness: Its Causes and Consequences* (New York, 1881); Willy Hellpach, *Nervosität und Kultur* (Berlin, 1902); Gabriel Hanotaux, *L'Energie française* (Paris, 1902).

38 Echevarria, *After Clausewitz*, 112–13, 125–27.

39 Michael Howard, "Men against Fire: The Doctrine of the Offensive in 1914," in Peter Paret, ed., *Makers of Modern Strategy from Machiavelli to the Modern Age* (Princeton, 1986).

future.[40] One result of this logic was the German army bill of 1912, which also complemented the desire to limit the naval arms race by redirecting funds toward the army. One reason for the army bill of 1912, then, was the determination to redress a perceived imbalance of power on land; the Russian military appeared to have recovered from the war with Japan, so the threat of a two-front war for Germany had returned. A third reason for the bill was the Reich's hope of deterring potential foes while at the same time preparing itself for war, which military planners, and especially the chief of the general staff, General Helmuth von Moltke (the younger), appear to have taken as a question of *when* rather than whether.[41]

The bill added some twenty-nine thousand men to the peacetime strength of the German army and provided for a number of technological, organizational, and logistical improvements. Almost immediately after its passage, the bill came under criticism for being inadequate, especially given the rapid rate of the Russian army's reform and expansion. After much debate in the Reichstag, another army bill was passed in the summer of 1913. This one added 137,000 more men to the peacetime strength of the army.[42] The growing attitude within Moltke's general staff was that war was inevitable, and that it ought to occur as soon as circumstances were favorable.

The Entente's reaction to the two German army bills was as predictable as the Reich's intentions were obvious. In the winter of 1912–13, the Russian Defense Minister Vladimir Sukholminov told the French military attaché, General de Laguiche, accurately: "Germany is in a very critical position. It is encircled by enemy forces: to the west France, to the east Russia – and it fears them."[43] The Entente believed that it had maneuvered the Central Powers, Germany in particular, into a position of disadvantage. Even as the German public was being prepared for the additional burdens entailed in the army bill of 1913, the French introduced a plan to return to three-year military service, which would keep more trained men on active duty longer. The Russians, too, promised further expansion of the tsar's army, but bureaucratic delays prevented progress until the summer of 1914. To be sure, the Entente's growing power on land contributed to the spread of pessimism among the Reich's war planners; then again, optimism has hardly any place in military thinking.

40 Herrmann, *Arming*, 161–66. For a broader context see Hew Strachan, *The First World War*, vol. I: *To Arms* (Oxford, 2001), 1–34.

41 Annika Mombauer, *Helmuth von Moltke and the Origins of the First World War* (Cambridge and New York, 2001).

42 Gordon Craig, *Germany 1866–1945* (Oxford, 1978).

43 Herrmann, *Arming*, 191.

The arms race in the air started much later than the struggle for military supremacy at sea or on land. However, its pace was breathtaking, and its qualitative and quantitative elements were tightly intertwined. The qualitative challenges were substantial, for the first recorded flight of heavier-than-air aircraft occurred only in 1903. Then, between 1905 and 1913, one aeronautical record after another was broken, particularly by the French, who led in nearly every category of aviation development. Even with such swift progress, however, both airships and fixed-wing aircraft had difficulty meeting military specifications after 1903.[44] When *Jane's All the World's Airships* published its first volume in 1909, there were hardly any military aircraft to report, although the military value of flight had long been the subject of speculation and scientific romance (as science fiction was known at the time).[45]

The years 1910 and 1911 saw the breakout of military aviation, particularly fixed-wing aircraft. A few airplanes and dirigibles participated in French and German military maneuvers in 1910, delivering valuable intelligence to ground commanders and proving their worth. Dirigibles were still unstable at high altitudes, so airplanes quickly took center stage. German investment in fixed-wing aircraft increased from 36,000 marks in 1909 to almost 26 million marks by 1914, a phenomenal, but not unrepresentative increase in terms of percentage.[46] A report published in 1913 by the US secretary of war compared aeronautical appropriations for that year in US dollars: France led the way with expenditures of $7.4 million dollars, followed by Germany and Russia with $5 million each; Britain and Italy trailed with $3 million and $2.1 million respectively.[47]

Whereas military aircraft were absent in the 1909 edition of *Jane's All the World's Aircraft*, they dominated the volume published in 1913. This volume, which regrettably relied exclusively on official sources, reported that the British had 142 fixed-wing aircraft in military service and seven dirigibles. It also reported that the French had some 421 military airplanes and fourteen dirigibles, while the Germans, whose appreciation for the military value of fixed-wing aircraft had come later, had some 200 airplanes in service and another 200 on order or under construction, along with ten dirigibles.[48] These numbers were approximate. They changed almost daily, as new aircraft entered service, were retired, or became otherwise inoperable. The figures

44 Lee Kennett, *The First Air War, 1914–1918* (New York, 1991).

45 Fred T. Jane, *Jane's All the World's Airships* (New York, 1909).

46 John H. Morrow, *German Airpower in World War I* (Lincoln, NE, 1982), 7.

47 I. B. Holley, Jr., *Ideas and Weapons* (Washington, DC, 1997), 29.

48 Fred T. Jane, *Jane's All the World's Aircraft* (New York, 1913).

also did not reflect the number of civilian aircraft, or the pilots who were active in the many national aviation societies and clubs that had sprung up across Europe and the United States. These societies provided a ready source of experienced pilots and supplemental aircraft in time of war.

As shown, the three interrelated arms races before World War I included important quantitative dimensions, but also critical qualitative ones. To concentrate on the former is to overlook a characteristic that distinguished this particular arms race from previous ones. At no earlier time in history were

12. Bomb dropped by hand from a German plane (1915)

technological innovations so prevalent as in the quarter-century before 1914: change reached literally every facet of life. The range of doctrinal innovations that appeared in this period was also richer, and more hotly contested, than in any era hitherto. It is worth remembering as well that Moltke's desire that the war begin sooner rather than later was, in his mind, justified by qualitative as well as quantitative assessments, however flawed or pessimistic. Quantity without quality does not equal a threat, just an excuse. Intelligence estimates indicated that both the Russian and the French armies had shown significant qualitative improvements. Thus, it was not only the size of the Entente's armies, per se, but the quality of their equipment, their level of training, and their morale and readiness to fight.

Nevertheless, World War I was not inevitable; but some kind of armed conflict probably was. The habit of tying political influence too closely to demonstrations of military might almost guaranteed it. Take the arms race out of the picture, and a war still occurs at some point, and probably in the Balkans. Certainly, the dynamics of intimidation set in motion by an arms race can contribute to the mishandling of a crisis. That there were misjudgments on both sides no one disputes. However, it is worth noting that war was avoided in 1905 and 1911, and contained in 1912–13, despite the fact that a complex and expensive arms race was well underway. For all the political tensions and increased expenditures caused by the naval arms race, the war did not start at sea. Nor did it start in the air. So, if arms races are causes, they are decidedly unreliable ones. Rather, what seems defensible is that the arms race of the prewar era was part of the deliberate and all too familiar practice of armed diplomacy, or using military production, mobilizations, and deployments to obtain concessions or to force changes in a rival's policies. What was really at issue in the crisis of 1914, then, was the larger goal of political influence and how far a state would go to preserve or enhance it. At that time it was clear, at least to the Reich's leadership, that armed diplomacy did not go far enough.

Hindsight says that pursuing more patient avenues of political influence, such as continued economic growth and expanded trade, almost surely would have brought more favorable results for the German Empire, and Europe as a whole. Of course, hindsight, by definition, is always right.

PART II

⋆

THE ERA OF TOTAL WAR, 1914–1945

Introduction to Part II

ROGER CHICKERING

The war that began in 1914 in Europe quickly took a direction that few observers had anticipated. The failure of the great German offensive in northern France in September 1914 triggered tactical and strategic dynamics that produced an ineluctable stalemate in the central theater of conflict. The sheer scale of fighting produced similar results in other theaters and suggested a terrible conclusion: this war could not be won on the battlefield. As the generals struggled with the new dimensions of combat, the belligerent states were compelled to mobilize their civilian societies to sate the war's vast appetites for material and human resources. The war's demands began to encompass everyone in the belligerent states.

The results were not only unanticipated but also profoundly disorienting. The challenge now faced by participants of all descriptions was to make sense of these developments, to find the proper terms with which to endow them with historical significance, once words like "battle," "heroism," "sacrifice," and "progress," and "triumph" began to fail as guides to events. The desperate search for tactical innovation and strategic alternatives to overcome the stalemate was a central part of the story. Meanwhile, civilian leaders struggled to build not only a managerial, but also a conceptual apparatus that would be equal to the new challenges they faced. It bespoke the magnitude of these challenges that few civilian leaders from the war's first days were still in office when the great "remobilizations" took place late in the conflict, bringing resolute and ruthless men to power whose understanding of "war" itself had been honed in the bitter circumstances – the surprises, disappointments, disillusionments, and paradoxes – of the great struggle.[1]

1 See John Horne, "Introduction: Mobilizing for 'Total War,'" in John Horne, ed., *State, Society and Mobilization in Europe during the First World War* (Cambridge, 1997), 1–17.

Georges Clemenceau was cut of this mold. When he presented his new government to the French Chamber of Deputies in November 1917, he announced his determination to pursue the logic of the present conflict to its extremes. For all its allusions to the traditions of the French Revolution, Clemenceau's was the language of a new kind of war. He baptized it *"la guerre intégrale,"* and he defined it as "war, nothing but war."[2] That this terse definition had comprehensive implications was immediately clear from his other remarks, as he described a war that no longer drew distinctions between soldiers and civilians. "The obligations of the front and the obligations of the home front," he announced, "let them be the same [*confondu*]." "These silent soldiers of the factory, deaf to evil insinuations, these old peasants bowed to their soil, these solid working women, these children who provide them the aid of their own basic weakness: these are our *poilus*." Clemenceau's promise was thus to mobilize all the resources and energies of the French nation, civilian and military, and to pursue victory without compromise. Clemenceau not only reenegerized the French war effort, but his speech to the French parliament also injected a term into the discourse of twentieth-century warfare, which then took on a life of its own. The comprehensive unity of which he spoke – the *intégralité* – struck a chord, particularly on the French political right, where within months it had metamorphosed into "totality," spawning the term "total war."[3]

The wartime developments that inspired this nomenclature were by no means limited to France, nor was the nomenclature itself. Nonetheless, despite its clear bearing on the war that had just ended, the emergence of "total war" as the key term in a new language of war followed a circuitous route after 1918. General agreement prevailed in the European military journals that the dynamics of the next war would be largely the same as in the last, that the next great war would be long, comprehensive, and limitless. Discussions in Italy were pivotal. Here the terms "*totale*" and "*integrale*" were both early employed – the latter by Giulio Douhet, the theorist of air power, to describe a war that would bring military violence home to the civilians by means of strategic bombing.[4] Of broader significance was the fact that the new Fascist state in Italy used the term "totalitarian" to characterize itself,

2 Annales de la Chambre des Députés, November 20, 1917: www.assemblee-nationale.fr/histoire/clemenceau/clem3.asp.

3 Léon Daudet, *La Guerre totale* (Paris, 1918); cf. Daniel Segesser, "Nur keine Dummheiten: Das französische Offizierskorps und das Konzept des Totalen Krieges," in Stig Förster, ed., *An der Schwelle zum Totalen Krieg: Die militärische Debatte über den Krieg der Zukunft 1919–1939* (Paderborn, 2002), 113.

4 Giulia Brogini Künzi, "Die Herrschaft der Gedanken: Italienische Militärzeitschriften und das Bild des Krieges," in Förster, ed., *Schwelle*, 69–72.

announcing that the comprehensive mobilization of society by the state had in the twentieth century become a basic principle of politics, in peace as well as war. This term quickly attached as well to the new regime in the Soviet Union, whose leaders had made no secret of their admiration for the Hindenburg Program – the highlight of Germany's remobilization of the home front in World War I – as a guide to rule.[5] In Germany itself, the Italian experiment generated a broad "discourse of totality." Its principal protagonists were a group of Hegelian scholars, particularly Carl Schmitt, who stood out for his advocacy of an all-comprehensive "total state." Ernst Jünger's book on *Total Mobilization*, which appeared in 1930, drew this discourse directly into the realm of military thinking, stressing the political (and metaphysical) implications of wartime mobilization in 1914–18.[6] By 1935, when Erich Ludendorff published his treatise, *Der totale Krieg*, the term "total war" already enjoyed general currency in the German military literature; and it soon did elsewhere, too.[7]

Once the German armored offensives stalled in the Soviet Union, World War II thus offered fewer conceptual surprises than World War I. "Totality" already offered a compelling historical narrative and an analytical language to fit the events. The two world wars were in this light governed by similar dynamics, which dictated the ever-growing purview and relentlessness of warfare – to the point of global conflict. The differences lay chiefly in scope. The second war was merely "more total" than the first – longer, more global, more radical in its claims, more unlimited in the goals of the belligerents, more monstrous in its violence. Participants on both sides understood the war in just these terms. Goebbels made this point dramatically in February 1943 when he posed the question "Do You Want Total War [*Wollt Ihr den totalen Krieg*]?" in hopes of remobilizing the German home front to still greater exertions in Feburary 1943.[8]

The idea of total war entered its heyday in 1945. As a means to chart the historical significance of recent developments, it had evidently been ratified in World War II. In addition, the conclusion of this vast struggle itself suggested

5 Abbott Gleason, *Totalitarianism: The Inner History of the Cold War* (New York and Oxford, 1995), 13–30.

6 Thomas Rohkrämer, "Strangelove, or How Ernst Jünger Learned to Love Total War," in Roger Chickering and Stig Förster, eds., *The Shadows of Total War: Europe, East Asia, and the United States, 1919–1939* (Cambridge, 2003), 179–96.

7 Markus Pöhlmann, "Zur Etymologie des totalen Krieges," in Förster, ed., *Schwelle*, 346–51.

8 Martin Kutz, "Fantasy, Reality, and Modes of Perception in Ludendorff's and Goebbels's Concepts of 'Total War,'" in Roger Chickering and Stig Förster, eds., *A World at Total War: Global Conflict and the Politics of Destruction, 1937–1945* (Cambridge, 2005), 189–206.

a terrifying, nuclear culmination to war's totalization. During the half-century after 1945, this specter lent compelling force to the concept of total war, which now invaded textbooks and monographs as the organizing principle of a "master narrative" of modern military history. Political scientists, sociologists, economists, journalists, and film-makers like Stanley Kubrick joined historians in portraying military history since the French Revolution as the relentless march of warfare toward totality.

Only toward the end of the twentieth century did this vision begin to lose its purchase, once the collapse of the Soviet Empire and the end of the Cold War reduced the likelihood of a third world war. In the meantime, however, the idea of total war had become increasingly implausible as a guide to the history of warfare after 1945. In an era that is preoccupied with the challenges of asymmetric warfare, the terror of nuclear weaponry has itself escaped the limits of a Strangelovean scenario. New concepts or paradigms, like "Revolutions in Military Affairs" promise more comprehensive guidance to the history of war.[9]

Another reason why the concept of total war lost purchase was that it was itself riddled with ambiguities, contradictions, and methodological confusion.[10] No one has yet produced a convincing definition of total war. Perhaps the most useful approach to the problem has been to treat total war as a Weberian "ideal type," as a set of attributes, characteristics, or ingredients of warfare, which have never been historically realized, because they can never be fully achieved. Instead, they represent analytical markers, points toward which developments might be shown historically to converge. A number of such attributes have commonly been identified in connection with total war.[11] The broadest and most basic (and most persuasive) has been the deliberate and systematic erasure of distinctions between soldiers and civilians, although it is debatable whether this state of affairs was unique to the wars of the twentieth century.[12] In the great wars of that century, at any rate, civilians were arguably no less important than soldiers in determining the outcome; they were essential to keeping vast armies supplied in the field and

9 Macgregor Knox and Williamson Murray, eds., *The Dynamics of Military Revolution, 1300–2050* (Cambridge, 2001).

10 Roger Chickering, "Total War: The Use and Abuse of a Concept," in Manfred F. Boemeke et al., eds., *Anticipating Total War: The German and American Experiences, 1871–1914* (Cambridge, 1999), 13–28.

11 See Stig Förster, "Introduction," in Roger Chickering and Stig Förster, eds., *Great War, Total War: Combat and Mobilization on the Western Front, 1914–1918* (Cambridge, 2000), 1–15; Stig Förster, "Das Zeitalter des totalen Krieges," *Mittelweg* 36, no. 8 (1999): 12–29.

12 See Mark Grimsley and Clifford J. Rogers, eds., *Civilians in the Path of War* (Lincoln, NE, and London, 2002).

to supporting them morally. This vision of total war has paradoxically less to do with soldiers than civilians on the home front; and it emphasizes an essential new dimension of warfare – the fact that war now requires the commitment of everyone in the belligerent states. The corollary of this proposition is that no one in the belligerent states is immune from military violence, be it in the form of starvation encouraged by naval blockade, bombardment from the air, or premeditated genocide.

A second commonly cited attribute of total warfare is oriented more, although not exclusively, toward the operations of military forces. In this reading, total war is distinguished by its erasure of every restraint on military violence, whether geographical, legal, moral, or political. Total war is global. Armies, navies, and air forces know no limits in the selection of their targets or the intensity of the violence they employ. Warfare in these circumstances cannot be settled by compromise; because it plays on elemental hatreds, it must end in the total defeat, the "unconditional surrender" of one side or the other. This feature of total war is reflected in the increasingly extravagant character of war aims, which are necessary as well to sustain the morale of home fronts that have themselves become theaters of combat.

The benefit of defining total war in these terms lies in the comparative analysis that it makes possible. Total war offers a set of indices with which to study wars, to construct comparisons among them, and to venture generalizations about historical patterns of development. The disadvantage is the price that this comparative exercise can exact in imprecision, anachronism, and teleological thinking. "Total" was an extravagant word for an extravagant time when it was first attached to war. The word remains a problem, insofar as it discourages analytical nuance. To call the wars of the French Revolution or the American Civil War the "first total war" arguably obscures more than it reveals.[13]

Analyzing the era of the two world wars in the light of total war is not without its own pitfalls, but it can lay claim to a certain historical legitimacy.[14] It does speak powerfully to themes and developments that culminated in the first half of the twentieth century. Participants in these two industrial wars used the term "total" to describe what they themselves were doing. By

13 This is not to deny the powerful insights toward which this question can, in the right hands, lead. See David A. Bell, *The First Total War: Napoleon's Europe and the Birth of Warfare as We Know It* (Boston and New York, 2007); Mark E. Neeley, Jr., "Was the Civil War a Total War?" *Civil War History* 37 (1991): 5–28.

14 Roger Chickering, "Are We There Yet? World War II and the Theory of Total War," in Chickering and Förster, eds., *A World at Total War*, 1–18.

practically any index one might choose, these two wars were the two most monstrous ever fought, although the comparative question (not to say the "conundrum") persists as to whether the second of these conflicts was in fact "more total" than the first. In all events, the authors of the chapters in this section are all sensitive to the analytical problems with which they must contend in using the term "total" to write about this era. Each of them has set out to analyze dimensions of warfare in the period that was bounded by Sarajevo and Hiroshima. The idea of total war represents no more than a working hypothesis, whose claims have to be tested. And to anticipate, not in all cases can these claims be verified.

The chapters by Michael Neiberg and Gerhard Weinberg provide the bookends to this section, whose coverage of the era between 1914 and 1945 is organized thematically. The two authors have performed the Herculean service of distilling the operational history of the two world wars into two chapters. Neiberg undercuts one common assumption about the first war that has colored interpretations of total war. Trench warfare did not produce the greatest casualty figures; these came instead at the beginning and end of the conflict, during the moments of the greatest operational mobility. His chapter emphasizes nevertheless the profound changes that set in during this war, particularly on the western front (the "most modern" theater of this war), as armies undertook slow and painful adjustments to the new imperatives of defensive warfare, whose dominance on the battlefield was inescapable. His chapter also documents the expansion of the war into Africa and Asia, as well as onto the home fronts of the belligerents. The militarization of societies, economies, and politics was the consequence. In the end, the war proved a contest of productive capacities; and the Allied victory was due to their material superiority, which by 1918 was insuperable.

Gerhard Weinberg's feat of condensation is even more remarkable, for he describes a conflict in which Europe was only one of the principal theaters of operations and in which naval operations were a more salient dimension of the conflict. His account raises questions about some of the claims commonly made to support the proposition that World War II was a total war. His chapter insists that the expansion of German power was a singular phenomenon; it was more radical than either the Italian or the Japanese war efforts (and, for that matter, the German war effort in World War I). In the second war, the Germans not only planned the conquest of vast expanses of European territory and the annihilation of all the Jews in the world, but also began in the late 1930s to prepare for a global naval war against the United States. Still, Weinberg's chapter shows that the dynamics of production familiar from the first war were again at work in the second. Germany and Japan ultimately lost to a coalition whose operations were better coordinated and whose productive capacities were more effectively mobilized.

One of the alleged markers of total war has been its growing intensity, which played out in several ways, notably in the inhumanity with which belligerent states treated enemy armed forces who fell prisoner. Iris Rachamimov looks carefully at this problem in the era of the two world wars. Her findings confirm that the lot of prisoners of war was on the whole much more difficult during World War II, particularly on the eastern front and in east Asia, at the hands of Nazi Germany, Soviet Russia, and Imperial Japan. The mortality rates of prisoners, including those who were held in Allied camps, were significantly higher than during World War I, when agreements on inspections and relief packets were worked out among the belligerent states even as hostilities raged. Still, Rachamimov cautions against easy generalizations. The treatment of prisoners in both conflicts was a complex story, contingent on a variety of considerations, including the supply of food in the capturing power and the fear of reprisals. In any case, the Geneva Convention of 1949 sought to repair the breakdown of humanitarian guarantees during World War II, so her story has, in this respect at least, an encouraging end.

The next two chapters in this section, by Sophie De Schaepdrijver and Pierre Purseigle, confront the central dimension of total war, the integration of civilians into the war effort. The fact that their chapters do so in radically different contexts suggests the complexity of this problem. De Schaepdrijver examines the treatment of civilians by a hostile power in an occupied land, while Purseigle analyzes the efforts of belligerent states to mobilize their own civilian populations. As De Schaepdrijver emphasizes, military occupation was complicated in both world wars by longer-term visions of conquest, although Germany and Japan were particularly devoted to this imperial project during the second war. As long as either war continued, however, the occupying powers faced the challenge of exploiting, at minimal cost, the human and material resources of the occupied areas – labor in particular. Although foreign occupation was used to raise morale on the home front, the fundamental difficulty was what De Schaepdrijver calls the "fundamental deficit of legitimacy" of the occupying regimes in the lands that they occupied. Here, although collaborators could be found, indigenous resistance of many varieties frustrated the mobilization of resources. It speaks moreover to the "totalization of war" that radical visions of empire and the determination of the occupiers to exploit the areas under their control made occupation regimes far more brutal in the second war. The fact that more than 50 percent of the casualties in this war were civilian is grim evidence of this process.

Purseigle's chapter appears to describe a different situation altogether. Along three axes – cultural, material, and political – he charts the effective efforts of belligerent states to mobilize their own home fronts. He, too, writes of the "totalizing logic" of war in the twentieth century, but he notes that the attendant blurring of lines between soldiers and civilians set in during both world wars. Most significantly, however, he emphasizes that in both wars the problem of legitimacy was potentially as acute on home fronts as it was in occupied areas. In these circumstances, the political dimension of mobilization was critical. Even in dictatorial regimes like Stalinist Russia and Nazi Germany, mobilization was self-mobilization. It depended on constant negotiations between state and civil society. Purseigle thus argues forcefully that the Anglo-American Allies enjoyed an advantage over the Axis powers, insofar as their political systems were better able to accommodate the "social negotiation" on which "social mobilization" ultimately depended for its success.

The next four chapters deal with the interwar period, as states and societies sought to assimilate the experience of World War I, some with an eye to another war. As Carole Fink notes in her chapter on the search for alternatives to war, the peace settlement after World War I was itself deeply divisive, and the mechanisms that were devised to guarantee it failed to win the support of most of the major powers. She then provides a lucid survey of efforts in the 1920s to construct the machinery to resolve international disputes by means other than war. Principal among these was the League of Nations, whose achievements in promoting economic, social, and humanitarian cooperation were by no means insignificant. In the critical area of collective security, however, the League's champions were frustrated by lingering suspicions among the great powers, several of which, including the USA and the USSR, were not members of the League. Significantly, the era of greatest international stability, which began with the Locarno Pact in 1925, was overseen by a new concert of Europe, a short-lived return to great-power management, before the onset of the Depression and the radicalization of politics in Europe and Asia paralyzed the League and defeated hopes to avert another great war.

These hopes figured prominently in the massive memorialization of World War I, which is the theme of Jay Winter's chapter. Military cemeteries, museums, battlefield memorials proliferated after 1918. However, the messages that they conveyed were, as Winter emphasizes, never free of controversy. The symbolism of the war's commemoration was itself, as Winter writes, polyvalent.

To take a notable example, the politics of memory in veterans' movements was on display every year on Armistice Day; and it ran the range from militarism to militant pacifism. Winter also notes that the experience of World War II altered memorial traditions in Europe. For one thing, an unalloyed narrative of heroism was inappropriate to the experience of much of Europe. For another, as Picasso's famous portrayal of Guernica announced, civilians now occupied a much more prominent place among the victims of war. In this way even commemorative practices adjusted to the totalization of warfare.

The next two chapters examine military affairs in the interwar period. If the grand narrative of total war needs World War II as a telos, if it requires that military planners reflected systematically on the experience of World War I to frame doctrines appropriate to a new and more destructive war, it will find little support in the rich and provocative chapter by Eugenia Kiesling. Instead, she argues, the formation of military doctrine was a complex, contingent process, which reflected the interplay of social, political, cultural, and institutional circumstances that varied from country to country. Military *Alltagsgeschichte* mattered. Even in the case of Germany, where the most successful doctrinal adaptation is commonly thought to have taken place, her analysis demonstrates that military planning was riddled with tensions, contradictions, and fortuitous developments. The doctrinal transition from the one war to the next was nowhere smooth.

Roger Reese dilates on an aspect of this problem. His chapter examines the armies in the one-party "revolutionary states" of the early twentieth century in Russia, China, Italy, Germany, and Spain, each of which represented, in its own way, a legacy of World War I. Like Kiesling, he relates a complex story. He analyzes how professional soldiers sought to contend with the aggressive ideologies of these "total" regimes, which offered not only the prospect of military action (which the soldiers welcomed), but also the subordination of the armed forces to the revolutionary party or state (which the soldiers did not welcome). Reese suggests that the left-wing regimes in the Soviet Union, China, and Republican Spain were more thoroughgoing in their efforts to bring the armed forces under political control, but civil–military relations were difficult in Fascist Italy and Nazi Germany as well. The only exception to this pattern was Nationalist Spain, where the army constituted the core of the regime. Reese concludes, however, that nowhere did ideology leave a significant imprint on operational developments. "All the armies of revolutionary states," he writes in this respect, "were remarkably non-revolutionary."

8

World War I

MICHAEL S. NEIBERG

Even among specialists of World War I, images of the battlefield remain dominated by iconic western-front battles such as Verdun, the Somme, and the third Battle of Ypres (Passchendaele). The mass suffering and horrific conditions of these battles make such prominence understandable. It might, therefore, come as a surprise that the highest casualty rates of the war occurred when the war was at its most fluid and open, in its first months in 1914 and its final months in 1918. This chapter examines the experience of war from 1914 to 1918 at the operational level. It begins by underscoring the shocking casualty rates of the war's opening months and characterizes trench warfare as a reasonable response, even if many senior commanders resisted it. The chapter then examines solutions to the stasis of trench warfare that generals sought around the globe, with varying degrees of success.[1]

Although one compares catastrophes at one's own risk, a few points illuminate the general pattern. The French suffered their highest casualty levels in the opening phases of the war, during the so-called "Battles of the Frontiers," especially during their invasion of the mountainous terrain of Alsace and Lorraine. The French historian Michel Goya calculates that the 13th Infantry Division, a representative unit, took 11,903 casualties in the first seventy-five days of the war. These losses effectively amounted to 100 percent casualties. On average, this division suffered 230 casualties per day of combat in the war's first months. By contrast, even at Verdun, where the division again suffered badly, its loss rate was 113 casualties per day.[2] Stunning as the latter figure is, it is not half of the former.

1 Good general introductions to the war include Hew Strachan, *The First World War*, Vol. I: *To Arms* (Oxford, 2001); David Stevenson, *Cataclysm: The First World War as Political Tragedy* (New York, 2004); Michael S. Neiberg, *Fighting the Great War: A Global History* (Cambridge, MA, 2005); and Michael Howard, *The First World War: A Very Short Introduction* (New York, 2007).

2 Michel Goya, "Le Processus d'évolution tactique de l'armée française de 1871 à 1918" (Ph.D. thesis, Université de Paris IV–Sorbonne, 2007), 482–83.

The same pattern held true for Germany. Germany's highest casualties occurred during the war's early weeks and during the offensives of the spring of 1918, which witnessed a return to mobile warfare. From August 1 to November 30, 1914, the German army on the western front suffered 678,000 casualties. During the return to mobile war from March 1 to July 1, 1918, the German army suffered another 688,000 casualties. These figures were significantly higher than estimates of total German casualties during the murderous battles of Verdun (428,000) and the Somme (538,000). Similarly, the highest British casualties occurred during the opening phases of the German 1918 offensives – 317,000 in March and April 1918.[3]

The great battles cannot be ignored. However, comprehending the bloody nature of open warfare in the war's initial and closing months is essential to understanding what soldiers hoped to achieve by resorting to trench warfare. Only in this light can one understand the frustrations that they experienced in trying to break free of the limits of trench warfare. Fighting from trenches was far from an ideal method of warfare, but as a reaction to the enormous losses suffered in 1914, it was reasonable, even if most generals assumed that it was a temporary expedient. The return of mobility to the western front in 1918 did indeed hasten the end of the war, but not, as the Germans expected, by restoring movement to the operational level of war; instead, the mobility of the battlefield in 1918 caused such enormous casualties in the German army that it could no longer fight the war to a successful conclusion.

From the perspective of 1918, the war of 1914 might well have struck some as having been fought in another world. This almost antediluvian age of war had featured the belief in the battlefield efficacy of human will, cavalry, and the cold steel of the bayonet.[4] The age had yet to see the full destructive power of heavy artillery, airplanes, and tanks. It had also yet to see the sinister, personal nature of poison gas, the explosive power of underground mines, or other terrifying features of modern warfare, such as shell shock.

Nevertheless, war in 1914 did not require such weapons to kill men at unprecedented rates. A war with brightly colored uniforms, mobile field artillery, and drawn sabers could still produce carnage, as the casualty figures

3 James McRandle and James Quirk, "The Blood Test Revisited: A New Look at German Casualty Counts in World War I," *Journal of Military History* 70 (2006): 676–77.

4 Malcolm Brown, *The Imperial War Museum Book of 1914* (London, 2004) provides some first-hand accounts from soldiers who lived through the first months of the war. Annika Mombauer, *Helmuth von Moltke and the Origins of the First World War* (Cambridge and New York, 2001), analyzes the frustrations of 1914 from the view of the German high command.

demonstrated. All the armies of 1914 brought with them an aggressive spirit and placed faith in the offensive as a way to impose one's will on the enemy. All these armies rejected the defensive as a form of warfare that ceded the initiative to the enemy and ran the risk of losing key economic assets to enemy occupation. Combined with an eagerness to win the war quickly, in order not to disrupt their nations' social, political, and economic patterns, offensive doctrine led the armies of 1914 to attack, even when doing so defied logic.[5]

All the armies benefited from the enthusiasm and willingness of their men to take enormous risks. Soldiers in all European armies went into battle singing and waving flags. French soldiers advanced into Alsatian towns amid scenes of jubilation appropriate to liberation. The photographs of eager young men of all nations joining the military perhaps overstate their enthusiasm, but the morale of front-line units was high in the war's early months.

The élan of the soldiers could not overcome their inexperience and ignorance of the nature of modern warfare. The problem was only partly technological. At least in theory, all armies understood the destructive power of machine guns, which could theoretically fire 450 to 600 rounds per minute.[6] However, few officers had seen machine guns in combat, and most assumed that it was possible to compensate for their rates of fire. In 1914, moreover, machine guns were still in short supply and were not well integrated into battalions and platoons. As with any new technology, many officers dismissed the impact of machine guns, assuming that the will of their soldiers would overcome the increased rates of fire.

Officers soon found that war in 1914 did not match their expectations. Inexperienced soldiers, led by inexperienced officers, had to advance into terrain that most of them had never seen, often with poor maps, unreliable communications, and tenuous supply lines. Maneuvers that had been possible on the parade ground or in war games proved immensely difficult in the stressful conditions of war. The results were confusion and chaos.[7] Commanders lost contact with their subordinates, who had to improvise. When they did not know what else to do, officers commonly went back to their training and attacked, often with disastrous results. Even when they succeeded, as the Germans did in many engagements in Belgium and

5 Holger Herwig, *The Marne, 1914: The Opening of World War I and the Battle that Changed the World* (New York, 2009) effectively analyzes one of the 1914 battles on the western front.

6 John Ellis, *The Social History of the Machine Gun* (Baltimore, 1986).

7 See Nikolas Gardner, *Trial by Fire: Command and the British Expeditionary Force in 1914* (Westport, CT, 2003); Tim Cook, *At the Sharp End: Canadians Fighting the Great War, 1914–1916* (Toronto, 2007).

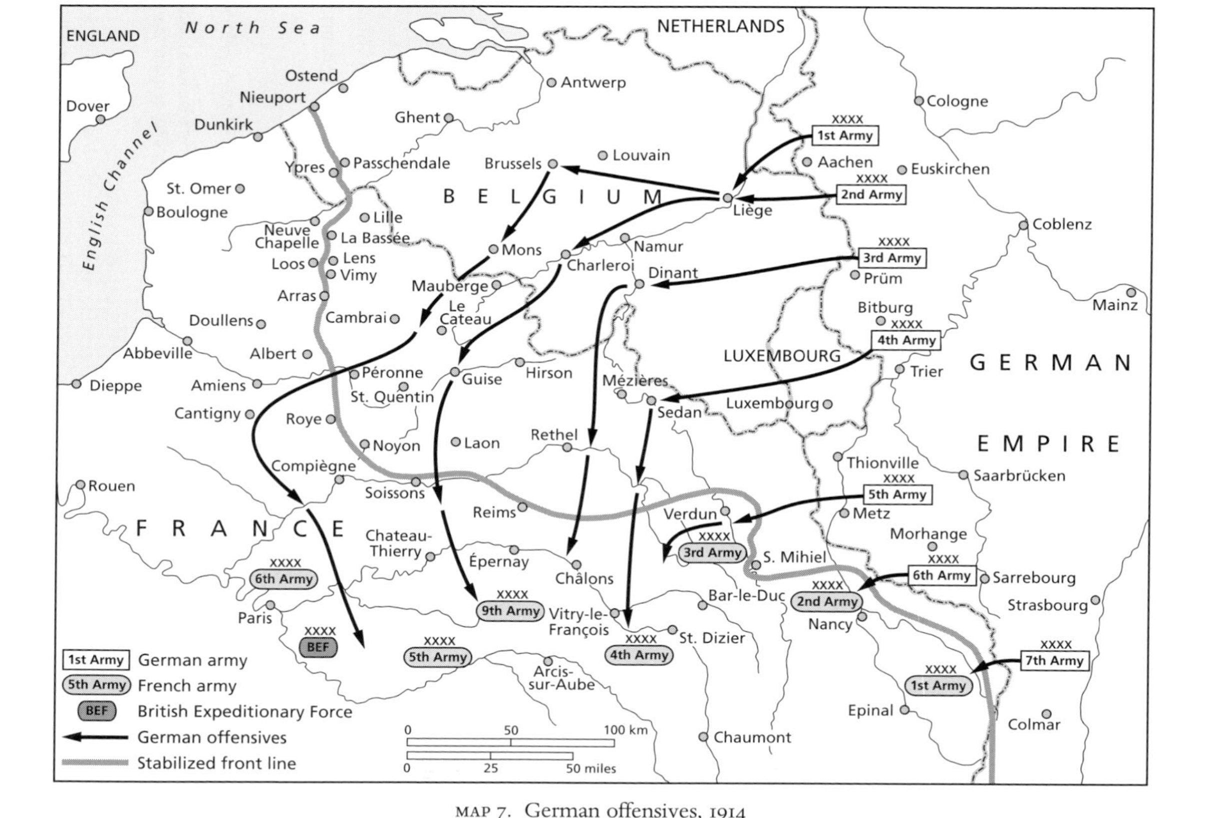

MAP 7. German offensives, 1914

Lorraine, the casualty rates were prohibitive. Similarly, the brave stands of the British Expeditionary Force (BEF) at Mons and Le Cateau have justifiably gone down as one of the British army's greatest moments, but their costs were dear. Mobile warfare proved deadlier than almost anyone had dared to fear.

The fluidity of the battlefield itself caused large numbers of casualties. In the west, these resulted from confused and disorganized charges that melted away in the face of heavy enemy fire. In the east, greater room for maneuver allowed the better-organized German armies to envelop the more disorganized Russian armies. The results were enormous numbers of prisoners of war. At the battles of Tannenberg and the Masurian Lakes in August and September 1914, the Russians lost more than 250,000 men, the majority of them as prisoners.[8]

Given the staggering casualties during the war's first months, the recourse to trench war was a sound response.[9] All belligerent armies had lost unprecedented numbers of men, including critical NCOs and junior officers, many of whom had died leading charges. The BEF was gone for all intents and purposes, well on its way to becoming the "heroic memory" to which the journalist Philip Gibbs had relegated it by the middle of the war.[10] The British, who had resisted conscription in favor of a volunteer professional army, were an extreme case, but they were not alone. All armies lost their prewar cadres and leaders. They needed to replace them with hastily called reservists, draftees, and new volunteers, all of whom were even less experienced than the men whom they replaced.[11]

Equipment was also in short supply, as all armies went through artillery pieces, shells, and bullets at a pace that no one could have anticipated.[12] Ideas about equipment had to be rethought, as brightly colored uniforms and soft hats gave way to more muted tones and steel helmets. Larger armies also meant that these items had to be produced in enormous numbers, so fundamental changes in the economies of the belligerent states were required.

8 Dennis Showalter, *Tannenberg: Clash of Empires* (Dulles, VA, 2003) remains the classic treatment of the battle and one of the best battle studies of the war.

9 Tony Ashford, *Trench Warfare, 1914–1918: The Live and Let Live System* (London, 1980) and John Ellis, *Eye-Deep in Hell: Trench Warfare in World War I* (Baltimore, 1989) remain two standard accounts of trench warfare.

10 Philip Gibbs, *The Battles of the Somme* (New York, 1917), ix.

11 On how these armies managed to maintain cohesion, see Alexander Watson, *Enduring the Great War: Combat, Morale and Collapse in the German and British Armies, 1914–1918* (Cambridge, 2008).

12 On technological changes see Albert Palazzo, *Seeking Victory on the Western Front: The British Army and Chemical Warfare in World War I* (Lincoln, NE, 2000); Mark E. Grotelueschen, *Doctrine under Trial: American Artillery Employment in World War I* (Westport, CT, 2000).

13. British artillery officers at rest

States with predominantly agricultural economies, such as Austria-Hungary and Russia, felt the strain more quickly than advanced industrial states, but all belligerent nations had to adapt to the new economic realities.[13]

On the battlefield, trenches provided protection from machine guns and artillery shells, while the armies retooled and trained new men. Generally speaking, German trenches were deeper and stronger than French and British trenches, because the Germans defended occupied territory and needed to conserve manpower for a war on two fronts. The French and British, by contrast, needed to resume the offensive if they were to reclaim lost territory, liberate Belgium (as well as Alsace-Lorraine), and win the war. Consequently, in 1915 and 1916 most French and British generals regarded the trenches as temporary measures, not harbingers of a new paradigm of modern warfare.

In the east, distances were too great and resources too scarce to allow the trench networks that characterized the war in the west.[14] Soldiers still dug in where they could, but most trench systems were shallow. Defensive warfare instead focused on fortifications, which guarded strategic locations like railroad crossings. Without unfettered access to rail networks, the movement of

13 See Avner Offer, *The First World War: An Agrarian Interpretation* (New York, 1991).

14 Graydon A. Tunstall, *Blood on the Snow: The Carpathian Winter War of 1915* (Lawrence, KS, 2010).

supplies across the great spaces of the east became nearly impossible. Sieges of the east's great fortress complexes were long and bloody, if less dramatic than the big battles. The Russian siege of Przemysl in 1914–15 lasted 194 days and resulted in the surrender of 110,000 Austro-Hungarian soldiers. The Russians also captured Lemberg (L'viv), taking sixty thousand Austro-Hungarian soldiers and 637 heavy artillery pieces. The terrible conditions of most prisoner-of-war camps in the east meant that these men were less likely to survive the war than if they had participated in major battles.[15]

The obvious differences between fortifications and trenches have not prevented scholars from labeling both as forms of siege warfare. Both required a great deal of patience and immense quantities of artillery shells, if carefully prepared enemy defenses were to be destroyed. Neither shells nor patience were in adequate supply in 1915. Artillery tended to be too small in caliber; the most common types of artillery pieces were light guns of 75-millimeter (French) or 77-millimeter (German) caliber and were intended to advance with attacking infantry, not to destroy enemy fortifications. Shells that were filled with shrapnel and designed to kill men in the open were less useful for killing men in trenches or otherwise fortified positions. These guns also fired shells on a flat trajectory, which was inappropriate for hitting targets underground. Armies realized the problem, but the manufacture of sufficient quantities of larger guns (and the ammunition they fired) took time to achieve.

Time was as precious a commodity as high-explosive artillery shells. World War I generals have received much criticism (some of it deserved) from historians for conducting hasty and ill-prepared offensives. These officers were under tremendous pressure, however, to bring the war to a successful conclusion. All states felt the need to avoid a long war that would drain treasuries, disrupt what the British called "business as usual," and kill unknown numbers of young men. French and British generals faced added urgency to expel the Germans from the territories they occupied, lest they impose further economic exploitation and cultural dominance. For their part, the Germans felt the pressing need to win quickly on at least one front, in order to avoid the exhausting two-front nightmare they all feared. Thus no general could expect to remain passive and keep his job.[16]

15 See Alan Kramer, *Dynamic of Destruction: Culture and Mass Killing in the First World War* (Oxford, 2007), 62–68; Heather Jones, "The Enemy Disarmed: Prisoners of War and the Violence of Wartime, Britain, France, and Germany, 1914–1920" (Ph.D. thesis, University of Dublin, 2006). See also the chapter by Iris Rachamimov in this volume.

16 Recent biographies of some important generals include William Astore and Dennis Showalter, *Hindenburg: Icon of German Militarism* (Dulles, VA, 2005); Michael S. Neiberg,

Nor did most generals want to remain passive. Despite the challenges of attacking positions defended by barbed wire, pre-sighted machine guns, and concrete or steel reinforcements, most officers expected that success could be achieved. In most cases they were wrong. Machine guns proved hard to locate, harder to destroy. Each had the firepower of up to eighty infantrymen, and the number of these weapons increased. Many attacks simply withered. Observers described how machine guns killed attacking troops like scythes cutting through wheat. Nor could artillery cut sufficient holes in barbed wire.

There were, therefore, a number of titanic, costly failures in 1915. One of the worst occurred in Champagne, where French troops made slight advances at a cost of more than a hundred thousand casualties. The French also attacked the strategic Vimy Ridge near Arras, losing nearly a hundred thousand additional men for no practical gains. They did inflict terrible losses on the Germans, but this dynamic was cold comfort to French generals, who were aware of the population disparity between France and Germany and were hence reluctant to embrace a strategy of attrition.

Next to the horrific losses of 1915 were notable successes. The most important was in the east in May, when German and Austro-Hungarian forces tore a 28-mile hole in the Russian lines near the towns of Gorlice and Tarnow.[17] Retreating Russian units panicked, exposing flanks and giving the Germans an opportunity to exploit their successes. A few months of campaigning followed in open country, until the Germans had taken the fortresses of Przemysl and Lemberg, chased the Russians east of the Dniester, and conquered all of Poland. Germany's success seemed to prove that trench networks could be broken if conditions were favorable.

More modest successes in 1915 included two breakthroughs by British forces, at Neuve Chapelle in March and at Loos in September, although the attackers were unable to exploit their success. The Germans broke into the Allied line at the second battle of Ypres, terrorizing Algerian soldiers during the first employment of poison gas on the western front.[18] Like the British at Neuve Chapelle, however, the Germans failed to take advantage of their local success and soon saw their opportunities evaporate. Still, most generals, including Great Britain's Douglas Haig and France's Joseph Joffre, focused on what had worked rather than what had not. As a result, they believed that

Foch: Supreme Allied Commander in the Great War (Dulles, VA, 2003); Andrew Wiest, *Haig: The Evolution of a Commander* (Dulles, VA, 2005); and Keith Jeffrey, *Field Marshal Sir Henry Wilson: A Political Soldier* (New York, 2006).

17 Richard DiNardo, *Breakthrough: The Gorlice-Tarnow Campaign, 1915* (Westport, CT, 2010).

18 On gas see Ulrich Trumpener, "The Road to Ypres: The Beginnings of Gas Warfare in World War I," *Journal of Modern History* 47 (1975), 460–80.

they were close to solving the problem of trench warfare. Their solutions included targeting ineffective units, overwhelming the battlefield with artillery fire, and creating numerical mismatches on specific parts of the battlefield. All these ideas and many more were tested in the war's second half.

The entry of the Ottoman Empire into the war was a catalyst as the European conflict expanded into a world war.[19] The reasons for the Ottomans' entrance were complex, rooted largely in the desires of Turkish modernizers to "hitch Turkey's star to a Triple Alliance victory as quickly as possible," in order to neutralize the Russian threat to Constantinople and gain a free hand to pursue pan-Turanic policies in Central Asia.[20] The Ottomans fought a brutal campaign against the Russians in the Caucasus mountains; this campaign laid the seeds for the removal of the Armenian population and, with it, the deaths of almost 1 million civilians in what many scholars consider the twentieth century's first genocide.[21]

The conflicting interests of the Ottoman and British empires took the war to the four corners of the globe. The British sent Indian troops to Egypt and Mesopotamia, Australian and New Zealand troops (known as ANZACs) to Gallipoli. The reverberations of these campaigns were powerful and long-lasting. An Indo-British army in Mesopotamia also surrendered at Kut al Amara, representing the largest British force ever to surrender. The fate of the Australians and New Zealanders at Gallipoli accelerated the development of nationalism in these two parts of the British Empire. The ANZACs suffered more casualties on the Somme and at Passchendaele and they played a major role in the triumphs of 1918, but Gallipoli retains its hold on Australian national consciousness. April 25, Anzac Day, remains Australia's day of national commemoration.

Campaigns far from the western front, like Gallipoli, looked less modern. Stalemate on the western front permitted the construction of a vast, sophisticated infrastructure of medicine and supply.[22] In the farther-flung theaters (and in areas where the lines shifted too frequently to permit such infrastructures), the war resembled conflicts of centuries past. Men in the Middle East, Salonica, and the Caucasus were as likely to die from diseases as they were from enemy fire. The inability of armies to provide men in distant theaters with suitable clothes and shoes led to many deaths from exposure and frostbite.

19 Edward Erickson, *Ordered to Die: A History of the Ottoman Army in the First World War* (Westport, CT, 2000). See also F. A. K. Yasamee, "The Ottoman Empire," in Keith Wilson, ed. *Decisions for War, 1914* (London, 1994).

20 Hew Strachan, *The First World* War, Vol. I: To *Arms* (Oxford, 2001), 671.

21 See Jay Winter, ed., *America and the Armenian Genocide of 1915* (Cambridge, 2003).

22 Ian M. Brown, *British Logistics on the Western Front, 1914–1919* (Westport, CT, 1998).

14. Russian battlefield, 1915

Italy, which joined the war effort in 1915, embodied the paradox.[23] A modern nation with advanced technology and industry, Italy should have been able like the French, British, and Germans to care for its men. Much of Italy's war, however, was fought in the high altitudes and rugged terrain of the Julian Alps, along the banks of the Isonzo River.[24] Despite stalemate on the Isonzo front, difficulties of climate and the inaccessibility of small-unit outposts meant that supplies often came by mule and, when they did arrive, they were inadequate.

By the end of 1915, Allied and German generals had come to different conclusions about the future of trench warfare. Joffre and Haig supported a plan to conduct multiple, simultaneous attacks on the German trench networks in the summer of 1916. They hoped to create one or more breakthroughs, which would prevent the Germans from concentrating their efforts against either of the Allied armies. The operational approach of the French and British involved saturating the battlefield with the largest artillery barrages of the war to date. Hundreds of thousands of artillery shells, they presumed, would neutralize whatever resistance the German trench networks could offer.

23 Mark Thompson, *The White War: Life and Death on the Italian Front, 1915–1919* (New York, 2008).

24 John Schindler, *Isonzo: The Forgotten Sacrifice of the Great War* (Westport, CT, 2001).

Before the Allied generals could carry their vision to the battlefield, the Germans implemented a different vision. Erich von Falkenhayn, the chief of the German general staff, had concluded that a breakthrough of the enemy's trench system was not possible. He had therefore conceived of a massive battle of attrition, which would, in his famous phrase, "bleed the French army white."[25] Then, without the French army to do its fighting, Falkenhayn reckoned that the British would have to accept peace on Germany's terms.[26]

The grisly battle of Verdun became Falkenhayn's laboratory. The battle remains to many French and Germans the icon of the war, the symbol of heavy casualties for minimal gains. This formula suited Falkenhayn's wishes, however. He hoped to use the dynamics of trench warfare to grind the French army down, forcing it into hasty and costly attacks. At one level his plan worked, as the French did conduct numerous offensives at high cost. Falkenhayn failed, however, to appreciate that the French attacks would wear down the Germans to a degree that he could not control. Especially in the later phases of the Verdun campaign, the French introduced new artillery methods and infantry tactics, which recovered strategic ground and compelled the Germans to counterattack more than Falkenhayn had planned. As a result, both armies were bled white, and Falkenhayn was relieved of his position.[27]

The impact of Verdun reverberated for the rest of the war. Among the most important changes that it prompted was the rise to power of a group of modernizers in the French army, led by Henri-Philippe Pétain.[28] They argued against the aggressive infantry tactics that had proved so costly in 1914 and 1915. Instead, the modernizers advocated battles that would be conducted methodically by artillery and other machines of war. Infantrymen would attack only after the battlefield had been prepared by the artillerists, and they would aim only for small, short-range goals.[29] The new methods promised to reduce the numbers of French casualties, but they also offered no quick fixes to a long war.

25 Although new research is underway that should change our view of the meanings of Verdun, Alistair Horne, *The Price of Glory: Verdun 1916* (London, 1962) remains the standard treatment.

26 Holger Afflerbach, *Falkenhayn: Politisches Denken und Handeln im Kaiserreich* (Munich, 1994).

27 Robert T. Foley, *German Strategy and the Path to Verdun: Erich von Falkenhayn and the Development of Attrition, 1870–1916* (Cambridge, 2005).

28 Robert Bruce, *Pétain: Verdun to Vichy* (Dulles, VA, 2008) and Charles Williams, *Pétain: How the Hero of France Became a Convicted Traitor and Changed the Course of History* (London, 2005) are two recent treatments.

29 Robert Doughty, *Pyrrhic Victory: French Strategy and Operations in the Great War* (Cambridge, MA, 2005); Michel Goya, *La Chair et l'acier: L'invention de la guerre moderne, 1914–1918* (Paris, 2004).

French losses at Verdun also forced the British to take a more active role in the joint Franco-British offensive along the Somme River.[30] Like Pétain, Haig believed that artillery could clear the way for his infantry, but unlike Pétain, he believed that a decisive breakthrough of the German lines was possible. The preparatory artillery bombardment that began on June 24, 1916 was the heaviest in history. Still, in the view of many soldiers then and historians now, it was too thin, given the great depth and breadth of the German positions, as well as inadequate fire control and ammunition.[31]

Another failure of British artillery on the Somme had to do with the rolling barrage. The idea was to train infantrymen to follow a moving curtain of fire at a carefully choreographed pace. In theory, the shelling would destroy enemy opposition or at least force enemy soldiers into their underground bunkers, so advancing soldiers could move safely forward. The rolling barrage had been used throughout 1915, but at the Somme it received its fullest test yet. Commanding and controlling artillery in the heat of battle required that the artillery fire be preset and that the infantry keep pace. On the Somme, inexperienced, terrified soldiers had trouble advancing over damaged ground, while artillerists erred on the side of caution, firing shells too far in order to avoid killing their own men. So the barrage got away from the men, leaving them with insufficient cover against German machine gunners and riflemen. Thus the artillery failed to protect the largely untested volunteers of the British "Pals" battalions, so called because the men had been permitted to join units with their pals. Battalion after battalion of Pals went over the top between the Somme and Ancre Rivers on July 1, 1916, expecting little resistance. British artillery had failed, however, to eliminate German barbed wire, trench defenses, and machine-gun positions, so advancing British infantry faced the full fury of German defenders. The consequence was the bloodiest day in the history of the British army. Sixty thousand casualties, including twenty thousand battle deaths, resulted within hours.

The Somme campaign ground on into November, but the British gained little territory despite enormous human costs on both sides. The British did, however, change their tactics and, by some accounts, their rationale for the battle. While Haig held stubbornly to the belief that a breakdown in German morale would permit the British to break through German lines, he began to

30 Coalition concerns figure prominently in William Philpott, *Bloody Victory: The Sacrifice on the Somme and the Making of the Twentieth Century* (London, 2009).

31 This is the view of one of the battle's foremost historians, Gary Sheffield, in his *The Somme* (London, 2003). For a scathing view of British errors, see Robin Pryor and Trevor Wilson, *The Somme* (New Haven, 2005).

conceive of the battle as an instrument of attrition, which would "wear out" the Germans and prepare victory at some point in the future.[32] The most famous British innovation was the introduction of tanks on the battlefield in September. Like the French, British generals concluded that the war would be won as much by machines as men.

German failures at Verdun, British failures at the Somme, and continued Italian failures on the Isonzo contrasted with a surprising Russian success in the east. In early June General Alexei Brusilov attacked a substandard Austro-Hungarian unit with a brief but ferocious artillery bombardment, which led to the surrender of two hundred thousand Austro-Hungarian soldiers within a few days. Brusilov had created conditions for open warfare, of which generals on the western front dreamed, but he could not exploit his gains because of the losses that his own men had suffered, the inadequacies of the Russian supply system, and the unwillingness of flanking Russian armies to advance. Nevertheless, his success encouraged generals to focus in 1916, as they had in 1915, on features of warfare that suggested that victory was eventually possible.

By 1916 all but the most optimistic generals had stopped promising quick victories. Those who, like France's Robert Nivelle, did make such promises failed spectacularly. The short-war illusions of 1914 were replaced by predictions of up to thirty years of war, in which neither side would muster the strength to defeat the other. A satirical French postcard from this period showed a French baby being born with a rifle in hand and asking "*Y a-t-il encore de Boches*?" (Are there any Germans left?).

The militarization of children reflected the ways in which the logic of total war had come to dominate thinking. Another French postcard of the era featured a painting by Jean-Jacques Waltz (better known as Hansi) that showed a mother handing a baby boy a toy French soldier. The caption read: "His first toy." The colors in the room were the blue, white, and red of France and the mother wore an Alsatian dress. Hansi also painted a famous scene of children reenacting the first Battle of the Marne. In Germany, too, the militarization of children became a theme for artists, as Max Beckmann's apocalyptic *Children Playing* demonstrated. The painting depicted children "fighting in a savage game of face-to-face combat."[33] Even unborn children became part of the aesthetic of the war, as *La Dernière Guerre* showed.

32 David French, "The Meaning of Attrition, 1914–1916," *English Historical Review* 103 (1988): 385–405.

33 Kramer, *Dynamic of Destruction*, 263.

This drawing featured a pregnant widow who was sobbing over the fresh grave of her husband.[34]

Artists were concerned with the impact of war on children, but politicians and generals were more concerned with other matters. In all the belligerent nations, they demanded the militarization of industry in order to provide the masses of weapons that were required. The most far-reaching programs came into being in Germany in the summer of 1916, in response to the German losses on two fronts during the first two years of the war. The goal of the so-called Hindenburg Program was to double the production of munitions and to triple the supply of machine guns and artillery pieces in less than a year. To accomplish this feat, every able-bodied man in Germany was to be mobilized, while the army agreed to demobilize soldiers who had relevant industrial skills. The Hindenburg Program also involved the ruthless exploitation of European territories under German control, as civilians were deported to work in German industry. German workers suffered less coercion but found their rights to change jobs curtailed.

The political realm was militarized, too. Soldiers in Germany, particularly the new team of Paul von Hindenburg and Erich Ludendorff, arrogated political decisions to themselves, even in areas that were once considered civilian. By the end of 1916 they had isolated or neutralized the chancellor, Theobald von Bethmann-Hollweg, who eventually resigned in favor of a more pliable successor. In France and Britain, elected officials retained power, but both states marked a decline in the power of legislatures in favor of more powerful executives, which were personified by Britain's David Lloyd George and, by the end of 1917, France's Georges Clemenceau.

A principal goal of the Hindenburg Program was to mobilize manpower, which had become scarce in all armies after the carnage of the war's first three years. This pressure bore on German operational thinking in 1917. On the western front the Germans used prisoners of war to construct a massive network of super-trenches known as the Hindenburg or the Siegfried Line. This "line" was actually a system of five linked fortified zones, as deep in places as 8,000 yards. It featured reinforced concrete dugouts and pillboxes, barbed wire coils up to 8 feet tall, and preregistered artillery zones. The line enabled the Germans to shorten the front by some 25 miles, although they devastated the land that they gave back, felling trees, flooding coal mines, and poisoning wells. In exchange for the territory they gave up, the Germans eliminated an exposed salient and, most importantly, freed up thirteen divisions, because the

34 Image in the temporary exhibit "Amours, guerres, et sexualité, 1914–1945," Musée de l'Armée, Les Invalides, Paris, 2007.

new positions required fewer men to defend. The soldiers released from static defense duties were placed in a mobile reserve, transferred to other theaters of the war, or taken out of the line for training in new tactics. Soldiers with industrial skills could be furloughed in line with the economic goals of the Hindenburg Program.

Germany's implementation of "Operation Alberich," the withdrawal to the Hindenburg Line, also removed much of the justification for France's major campaign in 1917. The new French commander, Nivelle, had planned a massive operation against German positions on the high ground along the Aisne River. The attack was to center on a narrow ridge called the Chemin des Dames. Heavily defended atop steep cliffs, the ridge was a particularly uninviting target, especially because the Germans were likely to abandon it as part of Alberich. Nivelle nevertheless pressed on, promising that the new artillery and infantry methods that had been perfected at Verdun would pierce the German line and bring victory.

Even if Nivelle had been less careless in his preparations and more modest in his goals, it is unlikely he would have succeeded. His plan was no more sophisticated than the one that had resulted in so many French deaths in nearby Champagne in 1915. All three of Nivelle's army commanders in the Chemin des Dames theater (including Pétain) warned the prime minister, Paul Painlevé, that the attack would fail, as did the highly respected general Ferdinand Foch and the war minister, the colonial hero General Louis Lyautey, who was so pessimistic that he resigned his post and returned to Morocco rather than have his name associated with the disaster he foresaw.

The troops at the front were not privy to these doubts. They saw mountains of ammunition, imposing tanks, and confident staff officers, all of which created a sense of overpowering optimism. Artillery would prepare the ground and tanks would advance alongside the men, providing heavy and mobile fire support. Infantry units were trained in the new relay methods of attack, whereby one unit advanced while another rested and regrouped. The success of British diversionary attacks on April 9 (including the great Canadian triumph at Vimy Ridge) and the announcement of the United States' decision to enter the war further boosted morale.

As in 1914, however, high morale could not overcome the material and organizational problems of trench warfare. German positions on the ridge offered excellent observation of the French below and strong defenses against artillery. These defenses featured the subterranean complex known as the Caverne du Dragon, in the center of the ridge, and the formidable Fort de Malmaison on its western end. Poor weather grounded French observation planes in the days before the attack and turned the ground into a mucky morass, which wreaked havoc with carefully prepared artillery timetables.

The result, as the doubters had predicted, was disaster. The rolling barrage failed miserably. The Germans had such excellent observation of the battlefield that they had moved men and weapons away from the artillery fire. They counterattacked in the afternoon of the first day, April 16. French medical staff had to treat six times the number of wounded they had been told to anticipate. Nivelle stubbornly kept the attacks going, blaming his subordinates for the failure and breaking a promise to stop after forty-eight hours if the offensive did not produce the expected results. By the time the offensive did stop (owing in part to the extraordinary intervention of the French president, Raymond Poincaré), Nivelle's army had suffered 120,000 casualties for gains so minimal that they could not be registered on maps. As a sign of their opposition to the foolishness that had led to the slaughter, French soldiers began to refuse orders to return to front-line trenches. They were careful not to let the Germans know what was happening, but in perhaps a majority of the French divisions, men refused orders and, in some divisions, ridiculed their officers and condemned the war.[35] The country now faced a crisis in discipline and morale that, coming on the heels of the first Russian Revolution, terrified French leaders.

Nivelle soon lost his job, to be replaced by Pétain, who brought a measure of calm and a steady hand to the crisis. Perhaps more importantly, he replaced the crude offensive mindset of previous French commanders with his more methodical approach to warfare. He ordered the French army to conduct only limited offensives in 1917, in order to buy time for French industry to provide heavier artillery, tanks, and new airplanes. He also sought to conserve French manpower, implementing new tactics more appropriate to a war of *matériel*. With these tools at his disposal, as well as the arrival of hundreds of thousands of fresh American troops, Pétain hoped to win the war in 1919 or 1920.

Haig did not want to wait that long. He sought to win the war in 1917 and ordered another massive offensive, this time in Flanders. He believed that Pétain's inaction in 1917 signaled the French army's unwillingness to resume the offensive in the foreseeable future. Haig might well also have wanted to win the war before the Americans could arrive *en masse* and so to take credit for a victory that he believed belonged to the British. The resulting offensive, known as the third Battle of Ypres or Passchendaele, was one of the operational low-points of the war. Almost nothing went right, from poor planning by the

35 Leonard V. Smith, *Between Mutiny and Obedience: The Case of the French Fifth Infantry Division during World War I* (Princeton, 1994).

army's commanders and problems in replacing manpower to abysmal weather. As on the Somme, the British relied on a heavy artillery bombardment to clear the way for the infantry. Although the barrage used at Passchendaele was significantly heavier and more accurate than that used at the Somme, it failed to destroy the German defenses, in part because the Germans had turned to a system of defense in depth, which placed much of German forces beyond the range of British guns. From late July until November, the British army hammered away at the German positions, making minimal gains for such enormous losses that the campaign has become a synonym for futility ever since.

The unimaginative British approach at Passchendaele contrasted with the innovations that they used in another offensive, near Cambrai in November 1917. This one featured the first attempt systematically to coordinate the efforts of artillery, armor, and infantry. Tanks were to break through the German trenches, crushing wire, causing panic, and opening gaps through which the infantry could advance. The British amassed 476 tanks for the operation, but, unwilling to gamble everything on an untested technology, they limited logistical support for the tanks to 48 hours of operations. Although 170 tanks were disabled by enemy fire or broke down, the British created gaps in the German lines and captured more ground in a single day than they had in three months at Passchendaele. However, the British decision not to gamble with the tanks at Cambrai meant that the resources did not exist to exploit the gains. As a result, the Germans moved reinforcements into the gaps and halted the British advance. Haig urged renewed attacks, which resembled the futile action at Passchendaele more than the first day's at Cambrai. Soon the British found themselves defending their own positions against vigorous German counterattacks. In the end, nearly a hundred thousand British casualties paid for minimal gains. It was a fitting end to 1917.

The Germans knew that they needed to restore strategic mobility to the battlefield in 1918. Most German leaders had concluded that time was working against them, as the British blockade cut more deeply into the German economy and Germany's allies showed increasing signs of weakness. Two additional factors compelled the Germans to seek a decision in 1918. The collapse of the Russians and the ensuing Bolshevik revolution made mass German troop-transfers possible from the eastern to the western front. For the first time in the war, Germany could focus its strength on one front. On the other hand, hundreds of thousands of American soldiers would soon arrive on the western front. Although senior German leaders dismissed the likely impact of the inexperienced Americans, the need to win the war before their arrival *en masse* played a critical role in the German decision to gamble

15. Tank in West Flanders

as soon as the spring weather permitted. Germany's goals for 1918 were total. As David Zabecki has argued in the most complete analysis yet of the 1918 offensives, the German goal was "to achieve a decisive and unconditional victory" in the west, not to "establish a position of relative strength from which to negotiate a conclusion to the hostilities that would be favorable to Germany on the balance sheet." In other words, Germany would crush its enemies in 1918 in a "battle of annihilation."[36] If the German armies fell short of this aim, Germany would lose the war.

The quest for the battle of annihilation followed the same strategy as it had in 1915, now though with new methods. The Germans aimed to replicate the success of Gorlice–Tarnow, to open a hole in the enemy's line where it was defended by weak units. Ludendorff chose the British, who not only were numerically weaker than the French but were also licking the wounds of Passchendaele. The first German offensive was to strike the British Fifth Army, which had an unsteady commander and was stretched thin over a long front line. Once they had "punched a hole," in Ludendorff's words,

36 David Zabecki, *The German 1918 Offensives: A Case Study in the Operational Level of War* (London, 2006), 5, 40.

German forces would fight in circumstances that favored them. They would force the British to the north, in hopes of protecting the ports on the English Channel, and the French to the south in order to protect the approaches to Paris. The Germans could then force their way between the Allied armies and exploit the classic military advantages of a central position to destroy the one, then the other.

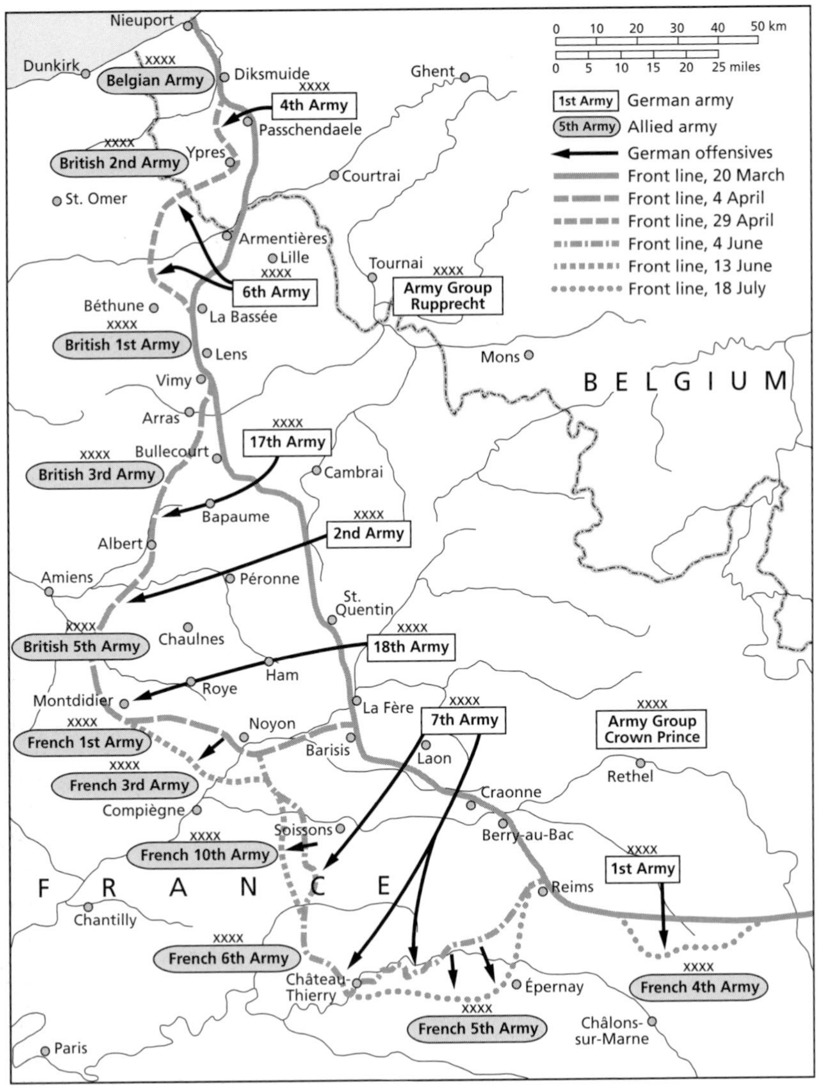

MAP 8. Ludendorff offensives, 1918

The tactics that were calculated to produce this result had only recently come into being. They involved large-scale exploitation of the infiltration tactics that virtually all armies had been developing. The tactics were complex and involved a devolution of command authority to lower-ranking personnel, so soldiers could make quick decisions and capitalize on local successes. Artillery and poison gas would protect infantry advances, isolating enemy centers of resistance. The infiltration units (sometimes called storm troops) would then destroy enemy command-and-control posts, allowing conventional infantry units to deal with isolated British forces.[37]

The system had worked well in 1917 against the Italians and the Russians, but in 1918 the Germans faced the more formidable British and French armies. Still, the first offensive, which was code-named "Operation Michael," struck the British Fifth Army in March with a ferocity never before seen. The Germans fired 3,200,000 shells on the first day of the offensive; more than one-third of them carried "yellow cross" or mustard gas. German troops destroyed the British communications system and so broke the Fifth Army that for a time Ludendorff thought that he would win the war.

The Germans had prepared a dynamic offensive that failed to win the war, for three reasons. First, the Allies reacted unexpectedly as a single entity, not as separate French, British, and American components. At the height of the crisis, they agreed to create a general reserve and a single commander for the western front. This was Foch, whose deft movement of units plugged gaps in endangered sectors. His infectious optimism and ability to divine Germany's next moves helped to restore calm and confidence.[38]

Second, the German attacks lacked a master plan. As a result, German actions lost coherence at both the large- and small-unit levels. After "Michael," the Germans undertook four more offensives, none of which was successful. The attacks were launched so far from one another that the German logistical system could not support them all. Foch remarked to a British colleague "I wonder if Ludendorff knows his own craft."[39] As one offensive failed, Ludendorff started another, with no apparent idea of what it was supposed to accomplish.

37 Bruce I. Gudmundsson, *Stormtroop Tactics: Innovation in the German Army, 1914–1918* (Westport, CT, 1995).

38 Elizabeth Greenhalgh, *Victory through Coalition: Britain and France during the First World War* (Cambridge, 2005).

39 General Sir Charles Grant, "Some Notes Made at Marshal Foch's Headquarters, August to November, 1918," Grant Papers 3/2, p. 5, Liddell Hart Centre for Military Archives, King's College, London.

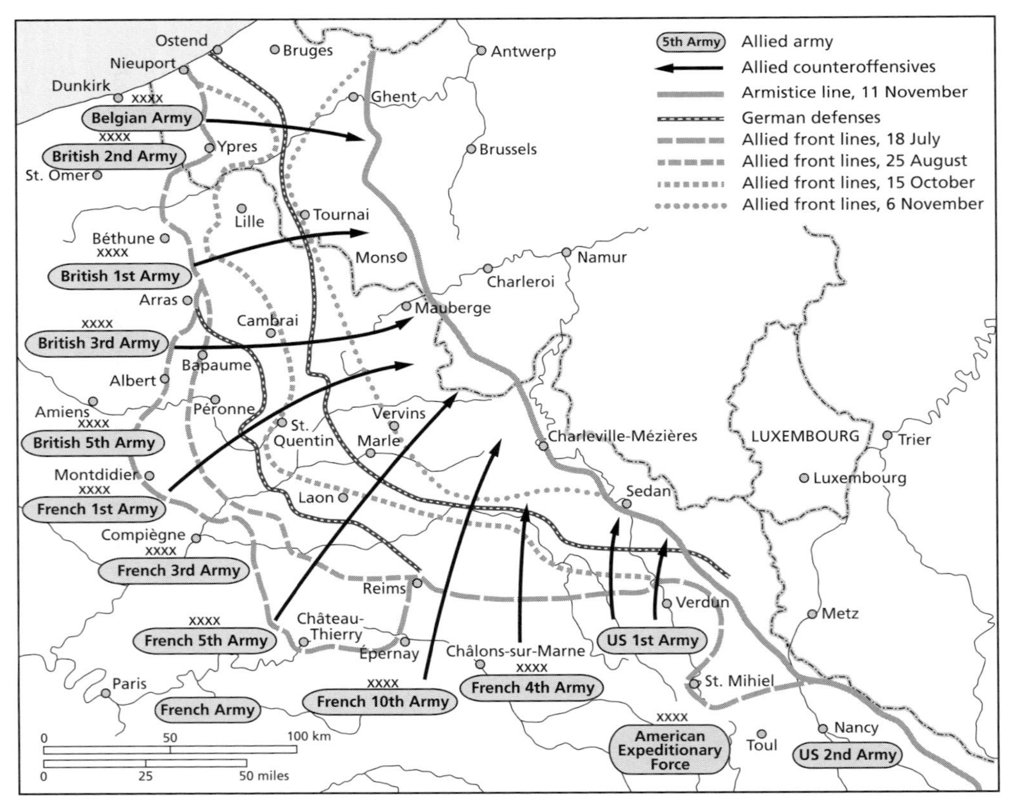

MAP 9. Allied counteroffensives, 1918

Finally, the German offensives produced diminishing returns because they inflicted tremendous casualties on all parties. "Michael" cost the Germans 239,800 casualties; "Operation Georgette" cost 325,800, and "Operation Blücher" 105,370. The Germans inflicted high casualties on their enemies as well, but the Allies now had American replacements; the Germans had no such options. Nor did they have the bountiful supplies that German soldiers found (and often stopped to loot) in Allied camps. Ironically, the new German tactical system did restore mobility to the battlefield, but its effects were more costly than the stalemate battles that the German had fought in 1915, 1916, and 1917.

The Allies stopped the German advance in July 1918 and responded with their own style of war, the set-piece battle.[40] Using massive artillery, armor, and aviation, they relied on new weapons for which the Germans had no answers. Even the strongest German defenses, like those on the Hindenburg Line, were no longer a match for the sustained pressure of Allied *matériel*, which was now in the hands of skilled soldiers who combined them into a war-winning system. The Americans showed their inexperience, but they learned; and their sheer numbers allowed Foch and the Allied commanders to put sustained pressure on multiple sectors of the line, convincing the Germans to seek an armistice before the Allies invaded the German homeland.[41]

The great irony was that the central operational challenge of the war was to achieve mobility in order to avoid mass casualties. This quest flew in the face of hard evidence that casualty rates were higher during periods of greatest mobility. That generals could have persisted in their quest despite this evidence was testimony to the horrors of massive stalemate battles in the minds of soldiers who had been trained to think of speed and maneuver. Their hopes that, thanks to new technologies, mobility would reduce casualty rates awaited another test in another war.

40 Michael S. Neiberg, *The Second Battle of the Marne* (Bloomington, 2008) and Tim Cook, *Shock Troops: Canadians Fighting the Great War, 1917–1918* (Toronto, 2008).

41 Mark E. Grotelueschen, *The AEF Way of War: The American Army and Combat in World War I* (Cambridge, 2006).

9

Military captivity in two world wars: legal frameworks and camp regimes

IRIS RACHAMIMOV

Military captivity was one of the most pervasive experiences in both world wars. In World War I an estimated 8 million soldiers became prisoners of war (POWs), while in World War II the number was perhaps as high as 35 million.[1] If one adds the number of soldiers captured in the multitude of wars that occurred between the signing of the Hague Convention of 1899 (the first major international treaty relating to the treatment of POWs) and the signing of the Geneva Convention in 1949, the number of captured soldiers approximated 50 million.

The difficulty of assessing the number of POWs during this period stems not only from the general unreliability of wartime statistics during the first half of the twentieth century, but also from the deliberate obfuscation by some armies of their casualty figures.[2] Moreover, because the designation "prisoner

I would like to thank the Israel Science Foundation (ISF) for supporting this research. This chapter was written during my fellowship year at the Stanford Humanities Center. I am extremely grateful to the center and to its director, Aron Rodrigue, for providing such an intellectually stimulating environment. The initial draft was presented at the Law and History Workshop at Stanford. I would like to thank Richard Roberts, Amalia Kessler, Helen Stacy, Dina Moyal and Binyamin Blum, who provided valuable comments. Many thanks also to my friend and mentor István Deák for his advice.

1 On the problems of estimating POW numbers, see Alon Rachamimov, *POWs and the Great War: Captivity on the Eastern Front* (Oxford and New York, 2002), 34–44. See also Niall Ferguson, *The Pity of War: Explaining World War One* (New York, 1999), 368–69; Rotem Kowner, "Imperial Japan and Its POWs: The Dilemma of Humaneness and National Identity," in Guy Podoler, ed., *War and Militarism in Modern Japan: Issues of History and Identity* (Folkestone, 2009); G. F. Krivosheev, *Soviet Casualties and Combat Losses in the Twentieth Century* (London, 1997), 231 (I thank Dina Moyal for this reference); S. P. MacKenzie, "The Treatment of Prisoners of War in World War II," *Journal of Modern History* 66 (1994): 487–520; Pavel Polian, "First Victims of the Holocaust: Soviet-Jewish Prisoners of War in German Captivity," *Kritika: Explorations in Russian and Eurasian History* 6 (2005): 763–87; Mark Spoerer, "The Mortality of Allied Prisoners of War and Belgian Civilian Deportees in German Custody during the First World War: A Reappraisal of the Effects of Forced Labour," *Population Studies* 60 (2006): 121–36; Christian Streit, *Keine Kameraden: Die Wehrmacht und die sowjetischen Kriegsgefangenen 1941–1945* (Stuttgart, 1978).

2 See Krivosheev, *Soviet Casualties*, 231–34.

of war" came to be applied only to interstate warfare (rather than intrastate or non-state warfare), many *de facto* combatants did not acquire this legal designation at all (or lost it for various reasons). In other words, the evolving legal codification of POW treatment in the period 1899–1949 affected not only the treatment of military captives, but also the framing of captivity itself.

The aim of this chapter is to examine the development of this legal framework and to analyze its complex historical interaction with regimes of treatment during both world wars. The chapter argues that although the story of captivity offers some of the most harrowing and murderous episodes in modern warfare, an internationally recognized standard of treatment had evolved by the middle of the twentieth century. This established standard became a binding reference point, which exerted moral and political pressure even on belligerent countries that objected to its "western" provenance or the liberal values that were encoded in it.

Cultural definitions of what is permissible in warfare existed long before the first multilateral conventions of the nineteenth century.[3] Whether inspired by religious, economic, racist, or moral considerations, belligerents have always waged war according to certain norms, or, to use Geoffrey Best's words, they have generated "their own codes of conflict behavior."[4] Throughout history the treatment of POWs has accordingly included killing, enslavement, incarceration, release on parole, and unconditional release. These practices reverberated in different guises after the formalization of laws of warfare in the nineteenth and twentieth centuries.[5]

However, after the mid seventeenth century, the emergence of the European state system with the institution of standing armies anchored the modern premise of treating prisoners: that POWs were in the power of the state whose army had captured them, not in the possession of the individual or group to whom they had

3 Michael Howard, "Constraints on Warfare," in Michael Howard, George Andreopoulos, and Mark Shulman, eds., *The Laws of War: Constraints on Warfare in the Western World* (New Haven, 1994), 1–11; Joan Beaumont, "Rank, Privilege and Prisoners of War," *War and Society* 1 (1983): 68.

4 Geoffrey Best, *War and Law since 1945* (Oxford, 1994), 14.

5 See Joan Beaumont, "Protecting Prisoners of War, 1939–1995," in Bob Moore and Kent Fedorwoich, eds., *Prisoners of War and Their Captors in World War II* (Oxford and Washington, DC, 1996), 277–97; Beaumont, "Rank"; Best, *War and Law*, 135–42; Howard S. Levie, *Prisoners of War in International Armed Conflict* (Newport, RI, 1977); Adam Roberts, "Land Warfare: From Hague to Nuremberg," in Howard et al., eds., *Laws of War*, 116–39; W. Michael Reisman and Chris Antoniou, eds., *The Laws of War: A Comprehensive Collection of Primary Documents on International Laws Governing Armed Conflict* (New York, 1994), ch. 4; "The Hague Conventions," and "Geneva Convention," in Jonathan F. Vance, ed., *The Encyclopedia of Prisoners of War and Internment* (Santa Barbara, CA, 2000), 148–50, 171–72.

fallen prisoner.[6] The history of international legal thinking about the treatment of POWs can be seen as the elaboration of this premise under changing circumstances. The evolving international standards of treatment all adhered to the basic notion that "legitimate warfare" was fought between the "properly" organized forces of sovereign states. Because modern history – particularly in the first half of the twentieth century – provided plentiful examples of *de facto* combatants who were engaged in other forms of warfare (such as civil wars or guerrilla fighting), a large number of men and women were given neither the designation nor the protections that attached to the status of "POWs." The history of POWs is thus only a partial history. It relates foremost to captured enemy combatants who fought in wars between states.

Attempts to codify the treatment of POWs in multilateral treaties began in the late nineteenth century and continued with increased vigor during the first half of the twentieth. These attempts drew from two main traditions. These were embodied in the Geneva Convention, which dealt with the treatment of war victims, and the Hague Convention, which related to the conduct of hostilities. The fact that the most important treaties dealing with prisoners of war were signed in The Hague (in 1899 and 1907) and Geneva (in 1929 and 1949) attests to the dual status of POWs, as both neutralized combatants and potential victims.[7]

The first multilateral treaty on the treatment of POWs – the 1899 Hague Convention – was a modest affair, encompassing just seventeen articles.[8] Yet these delineated a vision of treatment that in many respects still underpins the laws of war. This vision prescribed fundamentally different treatment for officers and men, allowing, for example, the use of rank-and-file prisoners as labor by the captor state but prohibiting the use of officers in this way. It allowed the internment of prisoners in a range of places and facilities. It guaranteed POWs the rights of free postage, freedom of religion, proper burial, and death notification. It called for the establishment of two crucial services – inquiry offices to coordinate and communicate information regarding individual prisoners, and organizations to channel relief to places of internment. Finally, it stipulated – in what became known as the Martens Clause – that POWs "must be humanely treated" and that "[U]ntil a more complete code of laws of war is issued . . . populations and belligerents remain under the protection of the empire of the principles of international law, as

6 Levie, *Prisoners of War*, 5.

7 See Jean Quataert's chapter in this volume.

8 The text of the convention can be found in numerous publications. See Vance, *Encyclopedia*. It is also online: www.icrc.org/ihl.nsf/FULL/150?OpenDocument (1899); www.icrc.org/ihl.nsf/0/1d1726425f6955aec125641e0038bfd6 (1907).

they result from the usages established between civilized nations, from the laws of humanity and the requirement of public conscience."[9]

The Hague Conventions of 1899 and 1907 did, however, contain a few formulations that proved unfortunate to captive combatants in the twentieth century. These included qualifications of who constituted a legitimate combatant (and who by extension did not) and the decision not to set minimum standards for treatment of POWs, but rather to use the formula that "prisoners of war shall be treated as regards board, lodging and clothing on the same footing as the troops of the government who had captured them."[10] Finally, the conventions included the call to repatriate POWs "after the conclusion of peace" rather than after the cessation of hostilities, a difference that meant years of additional internment to some POWs.[11]

Because the Hague Conventions were sparse and general, representatives of four belligerent eastern-front states – Russia, Germany, Austria-Hungary, and Turkey – met during World War I in Stockholm to work out the specifics of acceptable treatment. The main paragraphs of the Stockholm Protocol, which these four belligerents ratified in May 1916, spelled out in detail the privileges and obligations of prisoners of war and the agencies that assisted them. Thus, for example, the protocol sought ways to improve registration methods, to streamline the transfer of money to POWs, and to expand the activity of relief organizations.[12] It also set precise standards for clothing, lodgings, and hygienic infrastructure. At the same time, on the western front bilateral agreements resolved the practical difficulties of internment.[13] Although these ad hoc arrangements did not have the same international standing as the Hague Convention, they constituted a repository of amendments that were used during the next major revision of POW law in 1929.

The 1929 Geneva Convention attempted to fill in blank spaces and loopholes that the experience of World War I had exposed.[14] It encompassed ninety-seven articles, which specified in much greater detail what the signatories hoped would be a universal standard of humane treatment. The

9 See Roberts, "Land Warfare," 122.

10 Hague Convention, Article 7.

11 Hague Convention, Article 20.

12 Ernst Streeruwitz, "Die Stockholmer Konferenz 1915," in Hans Weiland and Leopold Kern, eds., *In Feindeshand: Die Gefangenschaft im Weltkriege in Einzeldarstellungen* (2 vols., Vienna, 1931), vol. II, 331–35; Elsa Brändström, *Among the Prisoners of War in Russia and Siberia* (London, 1929), 186–88; Heinrich von Raabl-Werner, "Österreich-Ungarns offizielle Kriegsgefangenen Fürsorge," in Weiland and Kern, eds., *Feindeshand*, vol. 2, 324–31.

13 Beaumont, "Rank," 70.

14 The text of the 1929 Geneva Convention is in Vance, *Encyclopedia*, and online: www.icrc.org/ihl.nsf/52d68d14de6160e0c12563da005fdb1b/eb1571b00daec90ec125641e00402aa6.

convention was divided into parts, sections, and chapters, each of which covered aspects of POW treatment. By following the different stages of captivity – from the moment of "Capture" to "Liberation and Repatriation at the End of Hostilities" – the convention showed a deep understanding of the difficulties and dangers encountered by POWs at various junctures of their internment. It covered in detail questions of discipline, labor, hygiene, and relief operation, providing for the first time a recognized role to the International Red Cross and to a neutral "Protecting Power" that represented a belligerent.

Whereas the Hague Conventions had envisioned internment in diverse locations, such as a "fortress, town, camp or other place," section II of the Geneva Convention acknowledged that "Prisoner of War Camps" were now the main places of internment.[15] These "fenced camps" were expected to be located away from the "fighting zone" and were "as far as possible [to] avoid bringing together in the same camp prisoners of different races or nationalities."[16] The call for racial and national segregation boded ill for the idea of universal standards of treatment. The Geneva Convention also accepted for the first time the concept of women combatants, stating, albeit vaguely, that "women shall be treated with all consideration due to their sex."[17]

The 1929 Geneva Convention was signed and ratified by over forty states before World War II. However, two important future belligerents did not become contracting parties. Japan signed the convention in 1929 but did not ratify the section that dealt with POWs (it did ratify the part that dealt with the sick and wounded in the field). The USSR neither signed nor ratified the convention. However, as Charles Roland pointed out in the Japanese case, both countries had ratified the 1907 Hague Convention and were theoretically "bound to honour that agreement."[18]

The 1929 Geneva Convention had mixed results during World War II. Although it ensured decent protections for Anglo-Saxon POWs in Axis lands and Axis prisoners held by the western Allies, it was shockingly ineffective on the eastern front, in the Balkans, and in east Asia. The fact that over 5 million POWs did not survive captivity during this war led to further elaboration of POW law in the 1949 Geneva Convention, which made prisoners of war, according to

15 Hague Convention, Article 5; 1929 Geneva Convention, Article 9.

16 1929 Geneva Convention, Article 9.

17 1929 Geneva Convention, Article 3.

18 Charles G. Roland, "Allied POWs, Japanese Captors and the Geneva Convention," *War and Society* 9 (1991): 85.

Geoffrey Best, "the most favored category of war victim."[19] This convention fleshed out in even greater detail the specifics of POW treatment.[20] Encompassing 143 articles and five annexes, it sought to resolve ambiguities that had been encoded in international law since the 1899 Hague Convention.[21] It required that food "shall be sufficient in quantity, quality and variety to keep POWs in good health and to prevent loss of weight or development of nutritional deficiencies."[22] This provision stood in contrast to the two previous conventions, which had linked the quantity and quality of food to that received by depot troops of the captor state. On the issue of prisoners as laborers, the 1949 Geneva Convention reversed earlier formulations, defining the kinds of work that were permissible, rather than those held impermissible. Captor states were now permitted to use only six categories of labor (in addition to camp maintenance) and were forbidden to use POWs to clear minefields laid by an enemy.[23]

The two most important amendments made in 1949 dealt with repatriation and the definition of combatants. The convention now stipulated that repatriation should commence "without delay after the cessation of active hostilities."[24] This provision did not, however, cover POWs "against whom criminal proceedings for an indictable offence are pending," opening the door for the incarceration of war criminals.[25] Nor did the 1949 convention prohibit forced repatriation of POWs to their mother countries, despite pressure from the International Committee of the Red Cross (ICRC) to do so. Nevertheless, as Jonathan Vance points out, because of the ideological conflicts of the Cold War era, many POWs were not forced back to their home states, and the ICRC was allowed to conduct interviews with POWs – without witnesses – to ensure that they desired to be repatriated.[26]

The most striking change in the 1949 Geneva Convention applied to the definition of legitimate combatants. Previous conventions had covered members of armed forces who belonged to a belligerent state (including militias,

19 Best, *War and Law*, 135.

20 The text of the 1949 Geneva Convention is in Vance, *Encyclopedia*, and online: www.icrc.org/ihl.nsf/7c4d08d9b287a42141256739003e636b/6fef854a3517b75ac125641e004a9e68.

21 Beaumont, "Protecting," 280

22 1949 Geneva Convention, Article, 26.

23 1949 Geneva Convention, Article 50.

24 1949 Geneva Convention, Article 118. This paragraph also provided that in the absence of an agreement to cease hostilities, "each of the Detaining Powers shall itself establish and execute without delay a plan of repatriation in conformity with the principle laid down in the foregoing paragraph."

25 1949 Geneva Convention, Article 119.

26 Vance, "Geneva Convention," *Encyclopedia*, 107–09; Beaumont, "Protecting Prisoners," 282–83.

volunteer units, and citizens conscripted in a *levée en masse*), as long as they fulfilled certain conditions.[27] The 1949 convention broadened definitions to include "resistance movements" and "members of regular armed forces who profess allegiance to a government or authority not recognized by the Detaining Power."[28] These two additions incorporated lessons drawn from World War II, during which partisans and "non-recognized" armed forces, such as Marshal Badoglio's Italian Army, had been denied the status of POWs. Nevertheless, as István Deák has pointed out, partisan warfare could not, by its very nature, adhere to the conditions stipulated in the 1949 Geneva Convention, whose new provisions only closed loopholes that pertained to regular armed forces. Thus, although the 1949 convention inched toward a broader definition of captivity in war, the framework created in 1899 still defined the contours of the story.

The history of captivity in the twentieth century offers many examples of decent treatment, as well as a plethora of brutal regimes. Historians who have analyzed captivity have recognized that the reasons for different treatment can rarely be reduced to simple parameters, such as the nationality of the captors or the captives, the ideology of the regimes involved, the kind of warfare practiced, or the duration of the conflict. During the same war, an army might violate international law at one point and observe the standards of treatment at another. An army that observed international standards in one conflict could commit atrocities in another. Ideological goals and local customs could fit international laws in one context and be diametrically opposed to them in another. Thus although assessments of POW treatment during the world wars emphasize that POWs on the whole fared better in World War I than World War II, broad generalizations oversimplify complex dynamics. As a result, historians of captivity have generally identified a combination of factors that contributed to proper treatment or abuse of POWs.

Explicit, a priori dismissal of international standards often – though not always – heralded mistreatment of POWs. Dismissal could take the form of opposition to liberal-bourgeois ideals, which were encoded in multilateral conventions, or hostility toward the western provenance of international law. The rejecting powers signaled their intention to mete out harsher regimes than prescribed by international conventions or to allow the exigencies of war to

27 These conditions were: (1) To be commanded by a person responsible for his subordinates. (2) To have a fixed distinctive emblem recognized at a distance. (3) To carry arms openly. (4) To conduct their operations in accordance with the laws and customs of war. Hague Convention (1907), Article 1. See also Beaumont, "Protecting Prisoners," 283.

28 1949 Geneva Convention, Article 4, sections 2 and 3.

determine treatment. Conversely, belligerents that accepted a commitment to international standards at the commencement of hostilities recognized a binding reference point by which to resolve problems and solve specific issues.

At the outbreak of World War I all belligerent countries restated their commitment to the Hague standards in either their 1899 or their 1907 form.[29] Nonetheless, no country possessed the infrastructure or experience to deal with the massive influx of POWs, whose capture began during the first days of the war. The problem was acute on the eastern front, where at least a quarter of a million soldiers were captured during the first two months, and close to 5 million during the next three years. Abysmal conditions prevailed in internment facilities for the rank and file in Russia, Turkey, Romania, Bulgaria, Austria-Hungary, and Serbia.[30] POWs found themselves in a wide array of structures that had been haphazardly arranged for human habitation. Factories, hotels, circuses, castles, ship hulks, and monasteries were all used for long-term internment. Work detachments made these sites even less likely to resemble what historian Gerald H. Davis has called "a POW camp of the classic mold."[31] Russia (and France) relied on a variety of structures to house prisoners, many of which were inappropriate for human occupancy.

Despite such dismal conditions, belligerents acknowledged both a standard of treatment and the authority of neutral observers (be they representatives of protecting powers or Red Cross delegates) to ascertain the discrepancy between standards and their implementation. As both internal and diplomatic correspondence of captor states attested, inspection tours by neutral observers brought pressure to ameliorate conditions.[32]

These inspections also created a twofold dynamic that facilitated improvements. First, they cleared the way for parcels and other forms of support to be

29 A number of states that had signed and ratified the 1899 convention did not ratify the 1907 convention. Among these were Bulgaria, Italy, Montenegro, Serbia, and Turkey: www.humanlaw.org/hague1907.html.

30 See Rachamimov, *POWs and the Great War*, ch. 3; Hannes Leidinger and Verena Moritz, *Gefangenschaft, Revolution und Heimkehr: Die Bedeutung der Kriegsgefangenenproblematik für die Geschichte des Kommunismus in Mittel- und Osteuropa 1917–1920* (Vienna, 2003), part II; Reinhard Nachtigal, *Russland und seine österreichisch-ungarischen Kriegsgefangenen, 1914–1918* (Remshalden, 2003), ch. 2; Richard B. Speed, *Prisoners, Diplomats and the Great War: A Study in the Diplomacy of Captivity* (New York, 1990), part 2; Yücel Yanikdağ, "Ottoman Prisoners of War in Russia 1914–1922," *Journal of Contemporary History* 34 (1999): 69–85.

31 Gerald H. Davis, "The Life of Prisoners of War in Russia 1914–1921," in Samuel Williams and Peter Pastor, eds., *Essays on World War I: Origins and Prisoners of War* (New York, 1983), 167.

32 See, for example, US National Archives, Records of the Department of State Relating to World War I and Its Termination, 1914–1929. Record Group 59; Microfilm number M367. Department of State / File Number 763.72114 (European War, Prisoners of War).

sent from home states to interned soldiers. Blankets, boots, clothing, and medicines were now transported to prisoners in large quantities via neutral countries such as Denmark, Sweden, Switzerland, China, and the Netherlands. Moreover, as inspections by neutrals became regularized, Red Cross delegations from warring states – headed usually by aristocratic nurses – were also allowed to visit interned compatriots and to distribute aid. Thus, for example, six German and Austro-Hungarian nurses – each heading a delegation – visited 123 camps in Russia in the winter of 1915–16 and distributed relief to close to 325,000 prisoners of war.[33] Second, visitations by neutral observers and relief societies led to the ad hoc elaboration of the Hague articles. The fact that all belligerents in World War I had reiterated their commitment to a standard set in this convention, albeit generally, made its concretization during the war achievable and desirable. The result was not only to improve conditions for many POWs, but also to create a repository of tested measures that found their way into the 1929 Geneva Convention.

In contrast to World War I, three of the major belligerents in World War II – the USSR, Nazi Germany, and Japan – rejected international law in part or in full. Furthermore, during the final weeks of this war, the United States and Great Britain rejected parts of the Geneva Convention with regards to the treatment of captured German soldiers. In each case, rejecting the Geneva standards reflected the intention to subject POWs to a harsher regime than stipulated.

Unlike Tsarist Russia, which had been a leading advocate of international humanitarian law at the end of the nineteenth century, the USSR did not sign the 1929 Geneva Convention. It promulgated instead in 1931 its own "Statute on POWs," which rephrased into Marxist–Leninist terms forty-five of the ninety-seven Geneva articles, discarding more than half of the others as "too specific."[34] In July 1941, shortly after the German attack on the Soviet Union, the "Statute on POWs" was further revised to give the NKVD – not the Red Army – control over POW affairs.[35] Upon the outbreak of the second Sino-Japanese War in 1937, the Japanese government, which had ratified only parts of the 1929 Geneva Convention, decided to classify this conflict as an "incident" (*Shina jihen*), not a war, so – according to the Japanese

33 See Alon Rachamimov, "'Female Generals' and 'Siberian Angels': Aristocratic Nurses and the Austro-Hungarian POW Relief," in Nancy M. Wingfield and Maria Bucur, eds., *Gender and War in Twentieth-Century Eastern Europe* (Bloomington, 2006), 23–46.

34 Pavel Polian, "The Internment of Returning Soviet Prisoners of War after 1945," in Bob Moore and Barbara Hatley-Broad, eds., *Prisoners of War, Prisoners of Peace* (Oxford and New York, 2005), 124–26.

35 Polian, "Internment," 125–27.

interpretation – even the laws that Japan had ratified were "inapplicable."[36] The most notorious example of a priori rejection of international law was German action on the eastern front during World War II. Even as he prepared the invasion of the Soviet Union, Hitler made it clear that he "did not consider this a formal battle between two states, to be waged in accordance with the rules of International Law, but as a conflict between two philosophies."[37] The implications of this statement for Soviet POWs were conveyed to *Wehrmacht* soldiers by their immediate superiors at the outset of operation Barbarosa. As one soldier recalled:

> Our Captain Finkelberg gave us a speech about the Red Army two days after the campaign began. We soon understood that the signs had changed, because he told us we did not need to take any prisoners. They would just be extra mouths to feed; and in general this was a race that should be destroyed in the name of progress.[38]

The Germans' refusal to abide by international law manifested itself as well in their finding ways to circumvent it. They used various legal arguments to retain hundreds of thousands of Polish, French, Belgian, and Italian POWs as forced laborers after the cessation of active hostilities.[39] Similarly, when the Third Reich disintegrated in May 1945, western Allied powers refused to give German soldiers the status of POWs, arguing that the 1929 Geneva Convention did not apply to them. Instead, German POWs were named "Surrendered Enemy Personnel (SEP)" by the British forces and "Disarmed Enemy Forces (DEF)" by the Americans, and they received treatment that was well beneath the standards prescribed by the 1929 Geneva Convention and harsher than Axis POWs had received during the war.[40]

In its most severe manifestations, rejection of international standards contributed to the direct or indirect murder of 2.5 million out of 5.7 million Soviet POWs in German hands,[41] 1 million out of 3.15 million Germans captured by

36 MacKenzie, "Treatment," 513–14; Kowner, "Imperial Japan," 10–11.

37 Keitel testimony in International Military Tribunal, *Trial of the German Major War Criminals* (23 vols., Nuremberg, 1946–49), Vol. XI: 33, quoted in MacKenzie, "Treatment," 505.

38 Gosudarstvennyi arkhiv Rossiiskoi Federatsii (GARF) f. 7021, op. 148, d. 44, ll. 15a, 15b, quoted in Polian, "First Victims," 777.

39 MacKenzie, "Treatment," 497–99.

40 Beaumont, "Protecting Prisoners," 279; Günter Bischof and Stephen Ambrose, eds., *Eisenhower and the German POWs: Facts against Falsehood* (Baton Rouge, LA, 1992); MacKenzie, "Treatment," 502–3.

41 This estimate is in Polian, "Internment,"123–24. Other estimates put the mortality figure as high as 4.7 million, while Germany acknowledged 670,000. See John Barber and Mark Harrison, *The Soviet Home Front: A Social and Economic History of the USSR in World War II* (London and New York, 1991), 40; Krivosheev, *Soviet Casualties*, 236.

the Soviets,[42] as many as 90,000 of 594,000 Japanese captured by the Red Army at the end of the war,[43] and 35,756 Anglo-Americans out of 132,134 captured by the Japanese army.[44] In all these cases the mortality of POWs exceeded the rate in any belligerent state during World War I. In a few notorious instances, these three powers executed thousands of POWs to send a political message. The Japanese army executed tens of thousands of Chinese soldiers in Nanjing in 1937. The NKVD executed 22,000 Polish officers in Katyn in 1940, and the *Wehrmacht* executed more than five thousand Italian POWs in September 1943, following the armistice between Italy and the Allies.

The exact number of German soldiers who died in Allied custody after the end of hostilities has been hotly debated by historians, but even conservative estimates acknowledge 56,285 deaths in American camps, 21,800 in French hands. In the latter case, German POWs were employed in clearing mines without proper safeguards. French administrative records suggest that two thousand POWs were maimed or killed each month. Although the estimated mortality rates in these cases are low (1.1 percent of German POWs detained by the US army and 2.3 percent by the French)[45] and cannot be equated with those on the eastern front or in east Asia, there is truth to S. P. Mackenzie's claim that "callous self-interest and a desire for retribution played a role in the fate of these men."[46]

Explicit a priori commitment to multilateral conventions was an important indicator of treatment in all twentieth-century wars. However, it did not ensure decent living conditions for POWs. The material circumstances within captor states also affected treatment, regardless of intentions. The length of warfare in both world wars and the pressures on belligerent economies over extended periods meant that material resources were often allocated according to the military usefulness of groups of people. Sections of the population that were deemed deserving received a larger share of an often dwindling pie, while others experienced a decline in their living conditions, resorting often to

42 Andreas Hilger, "Re-Educating German POWs: Aims, Methods, Results and Memory in East and West Germany," in Moore and Hatley-Broad, eds., *Prisoners of War*, 62. See also Hilger, *Deutsche Kriegsgefangene in der Sowjetunion 1941–1956: Kriegsgefangenenpolitik, Lageralltag und Erinnerung* (Essen: 2000), 137; Rüdiger Overmans, "German Historiography, the War Losses and the Prisoners of War," in Bischof and Ambrose, eds., *Eisenhower*, 155–69.

43 Yoshikuni Ingrashi, "Belated Homecomings: Japanese Prisoners of War in Siberia and Their Return to Post-War Japan," in Moore and Hatley-Broad, eds., *Prisoners of War*, 105.

44 Kowner, "Imperial Japan," 13; MacKenzie, "Treatment," 515–16.

45 Albert Cowdrey, "A Question of Numbers," in Bischof and Ambrose, eds., *Eisenhower*, 92; Overmans, "Historiography," 150–51.

46 MacKenzie, "Treatment," 503.

black markets to supplement official rations.[47] During World War I, Germany, Russia, and Austria-Hungary all suffered immense shortages in food, clothing, and fuels, which reached disastrous levels in the final two years of the war. Under these conditions, POWs – especially rank-and-file – were routinely placed at the bottom of the pecking-order, suffering in some cases extreme malnutrition.[48] Although material conditions for POWs in Imperial Germany were usually better than those in Austria-Hungary and Russia, food rations for POWs in all three countries fell during the final two years below the prescribed 2,700 calories a day. Prisoners who regularly received food parcels from their home states – primarily America, Belgium, Britain, France, and Germany – suffered less malnutrition than Austro-Hungarian, Italian, Russian, Romanian, and Serbian POWs, who received few or no food parcels.[49]

The two hundred thousand British and one hundred thousand American POWs in Nazi Germany during World War II relied on Red Cross parcels to supplement their diets. Although these English-speaking prisoners benefited from the protections of the 1929 Geneva Convention, their calorie intake fell well below the requirement that food provided by the detaining power be equal to that provided to its own depot soldiers. When the flow of parcels dwindled dramatically during the last six months of the war, American and British POWs suffered from malnutrition. The rations given by the Japanese army to Allied POWs were likewise inadequate, reaching starvation levels toward the end of the war, when the Allied blockade greatly reduced the amount of food reaching Japanese hands.

Even when material circumstances were generally adequate, hazardous conditions prevailed in specific locations or during particular phases of captivity. Local shortages plagued the first few months of captivity during both world wars, particularly during evacuation from the front line to the rear. This crucial period, during which soldiers were transformed from combatants to captives, frequently involved rushed marches over long distances with little food, sleep, or medical provision. The journey often consisted of train rides in cramped and unsanitary conditions, before POWs reached assembly camps to be properly registered and counted. During World War I, POWs in Russia spent between one and three months on the road. They marched on average 25 kilometers a day, but some marches exceeded 45 kilometers. To underfed, tired, bewildered, and often wounded prisoners, these distances were difficult to endure.

47 Verena Moritz, *Zwischen Nutzen und Bedrohung: Die russischen Kriegsgefangenen in Österreich 1914–1921* (Bonn, 2005), 180.

48 Ibid., 183–84; Speed, *Prisoners*, 72–74.

49 Ibid.

16. Defeated Russian soldiers marching to internment

In even harsher and more punitive conditions, a similar ordeal awaited Axis soldiers who were captured during World War II by the Red Army. They endured long marches on foot without sufficient food or clothing, followed by cramped train rides together with sick, wounded, and dying comrades. In May 1943 the commander of the Saratov Camp reported to NKVD-GUPVI headquarters in Moscow that out of 8,007 POWs sent to the camp in three transports, 1,526 had perished along the way; 4,663 additional prisoners died in the first six weeks after their arrival.[50]

One of the most notorious evacuations during World War II became known in US collective memory as the "Bataan Death March."[51] Following the surrender of some 66,000 Filipino and 12,000 American troops on April 9, 1942, the Japanese army evacuated the captives from the southern tip of the Bataan peninsula to internment facilities in Central Luzon. Having expected fewer than half of this number of prisoners and having underestimated the malnourishment and demoralization of the captured soldiers, the Japanese army rushed the evacuees on excruciating marches, often without food,

50 Stefan Karner, *Im Archipel GUPVI; Kriegsgefangenschaft und Internierung in der Sowjetunion 1941–1956* (Vienna and Munich, 1995), 41.

51 Robert S. La Forte, "Bataan Death March," in Vance, ed., *Encyclopedia*, 23–24.

water, or proper shelter. To exacerbate matters, Japanese soldiers beat the stragglers, executing many at the slightest pretext – some in gruesome fashion. Estimates vary of how many perished during the Bataan march. The lowest cite six thousand American and five to ten thousand Filipino soldiers. Lieutenant-General Masaharo Homma, the Japanese commander of the invasion of the Philippines, was executed in 1946 by the International Military Tribunal for war crimes, including this episode.

The use of POWs as laborers also affected their living conditions, improving their treatment in some cases, worsening it in others. Both the 1907 Hague Convention and the 1929 Geneva Convention authorized the use of rank-and-file soldiers in labor that was not "excessive and . . . [with] no connection with the operation of the war."[52] Both conventions prohibited the forced labor of officers, and both called for remuneration based (with deductions for maintenance) on the existing pay-rates of soldiers who worked in the captor army. This authorization translated into massive employment of POW labor in both world wars, which tempered the military's demand for indigenous labor forces.

France and Germany began to employ POWs in the winter of 1914–15, and Austria-Hungary, Russia, and Britain followed suit within a year.[53] Although all captor states wished to pair their captives' civilian expertise with allotted tasks, the great demand for labor meant that most work was assigned randomly. POWs were to be found in agriculture, industry, transportation, and a host of other occupations, as well as in vast construction projects. "All Europe's major belligerents," argues Richard Speed, "became heavily dependent on war prisoners to replace workers who had been sent to the front."[54]

As a rule, prisoners who were employed on private farms or in small firms fared better than those who worked for states, large enterprises, or great estate owners. Although the rates of pay were usually determined by administrators and employers, small private employers offered additional incentives in the form of food, pocket change, tobacco, and alcohol. Working on small farms also integrated prisoners into peasant households with their traditions of paternalism and hard work. Germany and Austria-Hungary employed about half their prisoners on farms or in small enterprises. Here they also lived, according to one Austro-Hungarian report, "as though restrictions of movement virtually did not exist."[55]

52 1907 Hague Convention, Article 6; 1929 Geneva Convention, Article 31.
53 Speed, *Prisoners*, part 2.
54 Ibid., 103.
55 Moritz, *Nutzen und Bedrohung*, 120.

In contrast, POWs who worked in factories and mines rarely received benefits in kind, although their base wages tended to be higher. These prisoners were discouraged from "fraternizing" with local inhabitants, and armed sentries kept a watchful eye on them during all times.[56] German and Austro-Hungarian POWs worked in French locomotive and automotive factories, stone quarries, ports, and quays. In August 1915 a French inspection team found 618 prisoners living in tents and warehouses on the outskirts of Rouen, where most of them were employed as stevedores on barges or ships. They worked between forty-eight and fifty-four hours a week, and like most prisoners, received their wages as coupons that were redeemable in the camp canteen. Living conditions in these work detachments seldom exceeded official norms, and they dipped well below when scarcity prevailed in captor states.

The worst conditions of World War I prevailed along the Murman railway line, which connected the Petrograd region to the ice-free port of Murmansk.[57] Traversing Karelia and the Kola Peninsula, the Murman railway was a top priority of the Russian army at the beginning of the war, when the Central Powers cut the supply routes across the Baltic and Black Seas. To expedite the construction of the railway, the Russian government sent some seventy thousand prisoners of war between July 1915 and October 1916 to reinforce the existing workforce. Although funds had been allocated by the Russian government for housing, maintaining, and clothing the prisoners, Russian guards and engineers embezzled much of the money. Thus the laboring prisoners lacked proper accommodations and often slept in branch huts or on the bare ground. The great distances along the line (over 950 miles) and its limited accessibility meant that fresh food rarely reached the prisoners. Hard labor in these conditions led to many deaths among the POWs. Elsa Brändström estimated that 25,000 died on the Murman railway, although the official Russian figures admitted only 379. The historian Reinhard Nachtigal, who has published the most detailed monograph on the subject, found Brändström's account more plausible, calling the project "the epitome of the horror of captivity."[58]

During World War II all major belligerents, particularly Nazi Germany, used POW labor. The Germans employed an estimated 10 to 15 million civilians, POWs, and concentration-camp inmates as forced laborers in the

56 Speed, *Prisoners*, 102.
57 Brändström, *Among the Prisoners*, 137.
58 Reinhard Nachtigal, *Die Murmanbahn: Die Verkehrsanbindung eines kriegswichtigen Hafens und das Arbeitspotential der Kriegsgefangenen (1915 bis 1918)* (Grunbach, 2001), 16.

period 1939–45, of whom some 4.5 million were prisoners.[59] In the first two years of the war, Germany used POWs primarily in agriculture, inaugurating a more extensive and brutal policy at the end of 1941. According to Fritz Sauckel, the German plenipotentiary for labor, POWs were "to be fed, sheltered, and treated in such a way as to exploit them to the highest possible extent at the lowest conceivable degree of expenditure."[60] With the exception of British, Commonwealth, and US POWs, who were generally protected by international law, all POWs in Germany were deprived of their rights. Polish, Serb, French, and Italian prisoners were ostensibly "released" and converted to the status of civilian workers who were attached permanently to their places of work. Germany also blackmailed the Vichy government to send skilled French workers to Germany in exchange for the release of unskilled French prisoners. Such formalistic maneuvers were deemed unnecessary in the case of Soviet and Jewish-Polish POWs, who, in the words of Mark Spoerer and Jochen Fleischhacker, were treated as "less-than-slave laborers."[61]

The Soviet Union began to use Axis POWs in large numbers during the winter of 1942–43. Until this time, captured soldiers had often been shot on the spot or interned in horrific conditions. After the battle of Stalingrad, however, the large number of Axis prisoners and the acute manpower shortages in the USSR created an incentive to employ these men. Like Soviet prisoners in Germany, Axis POWs worked for long hours and were abysmally fed and sheltered. At the end of the war, the Soviet Union retained 3.5 million Axis prisoners to rebuild the devastated country. Most of these prisoners had been repatriated by May 1950, but the last batch, who had been branded "war criminals" by Soviet courts, returned only in 1956.

Although Great Britain and Japan never relied on POW labor to the same extent as Germany or the USSR, they employed prisoners in significant numbers. In Britain and the Commonwealth countries, plans for large-scale employment of POWs were formulated only in the first months of 1941, after the capture of some two hundred thousand Italian soldiers in North Africa. Although the War Office at first believed these POWs to be a security hazard, the increasing demand for labor, coupled with the perception that most Italians were "apolitical peasants," made their employment a more attractive

59 Mark Spoerer and Jochen Fleischhacker, "Forced Laborers in Nazi Germany: Categories, Numbers, and Survivors," *Journal of Interdisciplinary History* 33 (2002): Table 5.

60 MacKenzie, "Treatment," 499.

61 Spoerer and Fleischhacker, "Forced Laborers," 176.

proposition.[62] As Churchill wrote in May 1941, "it might be better to use these docile Italian prisoners of war instead of bringing in disaffected Irish over whom we have nothing like the same control."[63] By the end of the war, Britain and Commonwealth countries had put five hundred thousand Italian prisoners of war to work. Although Britain treated working Italian prisoners according to the Geneva norms, their continued employment after October 1943, when Italy officially became a co-belligerent against Germany, was problematic. Like Germany and the Soviet Union, Imperial Japan employed millions of forced laborers during World War II. However, most of these laborers were civilians from occupied areas in east Asia (mainly China and Korea), rather than captured Allied troops. Still, the Japanese employed an estimated 193,000 allied POWs in heavy manual labor, and, contrary to international law, in war-related projects. The biggest of these was the construction of the Burma–Thailand railway, which ran 261 miles across inhospitable climes from Ban Pong in Thailand to Thanbyuzayat in Burma. Some 64,000 Allied POWs (mainly British, Dutch, Australians, and New Zealanders) worked here, seven days a week in extreme privation, between June 1942 and October 1943. According to Colonel Yanagita, an area commander in the Japanese Railway Administration, "we were told that though there [was] an international Law . . . there might be some cases which must be handled in accordance with the circumstances and not exactly according to International Law."[64] In practice, this policy translated into meager rations, habitual brutality from the mostly Korean guards, and a lack of medical care. Prisoners were made to sign parole forms, in which they promised not to escape, and were told that those who did escape "could be shot on the spot."[65] Overall, twelve thousand POWs perished on the project, succumbing to dysentery, beriberi, malaria, or murder by their captors. According to some accounts, as many as 125,000 indigenous workers died as well.

The fourth factor that influenced the treatment of POWs is what S. P. Mackenzie has called the "mutual hostage factor."[66] This term describes the principle that if a belligerent state mistreated – or appeared to mistreat – enemy prisoners, a dynamic of reprisal and counter-reprisal was unleashed,

62 Neville Wylie, "Prisoners of War in the Era of Total War," *War in History* 13 (2006): 225.

63 Bob Moore, "British Perceptions of Italian Prisoners of War, 1940–1947," in Moore and Hatley-Broad, eds., *Prisoners of War*, 29.

64 Sibylla Jane Flower, "Captors and Captives on the Burma–Thailand Railway," in Bob Moore and Kent Federowich, eds., *Prisoners of War and Their Captors in World War II* (Oxford, 1996), 235.

65 Ibid.

66 MacKenzie, "Treatment," 516.

which could be resolved only through third-party mediation. To avoid a reprisal cycle, both sides had an interest in adhering to mutually acceptable standards. However, this interest might wane in certain circumstances, such as a marked discrepancy in the number of POWs, the disavowal of captive soldiers by their home states, or the prioritization by belligerents of war aims over the lives of prisoners. Thus, the mutual-hostage factor is best understood as a latent phenomenon, which worked in conjunction with others.

During World War I the mutual-hostage factor was a significant stabilizing force. Nevertheless, on a few occasions belligerent governments did become embroiled in quid pro quo measures against certain categories of prisoners. The building of the Murman railway line, for example, led in the autumn of 1916 to a reprisal cycle between Germany and Russia. The Germans began the cycle by downgrading the privileges of Russian officers to those of rank-and-file prisoners.[67] The Russians retaliated with the same measure, prompting the intervention of neutral Sweden and the eventual extrication of German POWs from the Murman project. Likewise, a French protest over the caloric value of rations provided by German authorities set off a retaliatory cycle between France and Germany in 1916–17. Although regulations in Germany stipulated that POWs were – like German depot soldiers – to receive 2,700 calories a day, local authorities were given considerable latitude to decide the makeup of the diet. As quantities of foodstuffs decreased generally in Germany, so did the proportion of meat in the French prisoners' diet. In retaliation, the French created the *régime réciproque*, a special diet for German POWs, which provided significantly less meat than the *régime normal*. These measures remained in force until the end of the war, even though both countries found ways to ameliorate the conditions of prisoners, whether through food parcels from home or the purchase of extra food in official camp canteens.[68]

Retaliatory dynamics came into play on several occasions during World War II. One of the best-known incidents involved the shackling of some 5,500 British, Commonwealth, and German POWs during the autumn of 1942.[69] The spark for the retaliatory cycle was the Germans' discovery that Canadian and British forces had tied the hands of captured *Wehrmacht* soldiers during the raids on Dieppe in August 1942 and then, in October, on the Island

67 Nachtigal, *Murmanbahn*, 73–82.

68 Speed, *Prisoners*, 72–74, 87–89.

69 Jonathan F. Vance, "Men in Manacles: The Shackling of Prisoners of War, 1942–1943," *Journal of Military History* 59 (1995): 483–504; Arieh J. Kochavi, *Confronting Captivity: Britain and the United States and Their POWs in Nazi Germany* (Chapel Hill, 2005), 40–52.

of Sark.[70] In response to what it called "wild-west methods," the German high command ordered the shackling of some thirteen hundred Allied prisoners whom the Germans had captured in Dieppe, stating that these prisoners would remain shackled until assurances were given that German prisoners were not to be bound again.[71] This step prompted the British and Canadians to order that a similar number of German POWs be put in manacles, which in turn led to the shackling of an additional four thousand British and Commonwealth prisoners in Germany. The British government wished to retaliate further, but opposition in Canada, Australia, and the United States led to the unshackling of German POWs in December 1942. Although the Germans did not rescind the order to shackle POWs, they implemented it only randomly throughout 1943, agreeing discreetly to end it in November 1943 at the request of Carl Burckhardt, the president of the ICRC.[72]

More ominous was Hitler's secret "Commando Order" (*Kommandobefehl*) of October 18, 1942, which instructed German troops that "all enemies on so-called commando missions in Europe and in Africa . . . whether armed or unarmed, in battle or in flight, are to be slaughtered to the last man."[73] Alleging Allied violations of the 1929 Geneva Convention, the German military leadership put the order into action until April 1945. The order contravened the 1929 Geneva Convention, which prohibited acts of violence and reprisal, but the German leadership was willing to use violence against POWs to exact revenge. The same logic also worked during the mass air raids on German cities by the Allies, as Goebbels led the calls to execute Allied POWs in retaliation for German civilian losses. However, "the mutual hostage factor, supplemented in the last months of the war on the German side by fear of personal indictment [was] a powerful factor in preventing the collapse of the Geneva Convention in the West."[74]

The Geneva Convention did not collapse on the western front during World War II. However, it did so on the eastern front and in east Asia, resulting in the deaths of some 5 million POWs. If mortality figures be taken as the ultimate test of international law, POW regulations were hardly an unequivocal success during World War II. In fact, given the comparative

70 Vance, "Manacles," 485–88; Kochavi, *Confronting Captivity*, 40–41.

71 Vance, "Manacles," 485.

72 Ibid., 497.

73 Vasilis Vourkoutiotis, "Commando Order," in Vance, *Encyclopedia*, 62. See also Vourkoutiotis, *Prisoners of War and the German High Command: The British and American Experience* (New York, 2003).

74 MacKenzie, "Treatment," 496.

efficacy of the Hague Convention during the Russo-Japanese War and World War I, disregard for the Geneva Convention during World War II suggested a retreat from common humanitarian standards.[75]

However, developments during the first half of the twentieth century indicated a more complex trajectory. Alongside flagrant violations of international conventions, all belligerents adopted, to some extent, the public rhetoric of compliance. Even the USSR declared its intention in the summer of 1941 to abide by the 1907 Hague Convention.[76] Likewise, at the beginning of 1942 Japan indicated to the Allies its willingness *mutatis mutandis* to accept some the 1929 Geneva Convention's provisions on the basis of reciprocity.[77] These declarations did not represent full acceptance or sincerity, but they signified that the language of the convention had at least become the starting point for international discussions of war captivity.[78] Following World War II, all major powers found it in their interest to refine POW law in the 1949 convention.

Still, despite the negotiation of a new, comprehensive convention in the postwar era, POWs were hardly "the most favored category of war victim."[79] Interstate arrangements constituted – and still constitute – only one side of the ordeal of captivity. Arrangements within home countries also played – and still play – a central role in determining the well-being of repatriated POWs. The most notorious example of harsh post-repatriation treatment occurred in the USSR, where Stalin's Order No. 270 of August 16, 1941 set the tone.[80] It equated war captivity with treason. Soviet prisoners who returned alive from German captivity encountered a hostile reception from their government.[81] One Red Army nurse and POW in Germany, Sofia Anvaer, escaped a Nazi death march and fled eastwards toward advancing Soviet forces. Upon reaching her comrades, she was handed over to the Soviet military counterespionage service (known as SMERSH or "death to spies") for detention and "special interrogation." Accused of being a Nazi collaborator, a traitor, and a "German whore," she spent the next year in prison and was denied all contact with her family. At one point in the investigation, her survival was cited as proof of her treason: "A Jewess? Jews don't come back alive from there," she was told by an

75 See Kowner, "Imperial Japan," 8–9.
76 MacKenzie, "Treatment," 510.
77 Flower, "Captors and Captives," 234–35.
78 I thank Helen Stacy for suggesting this formulation.
79 Best, *War and Law*, 135.
80 Polian, "Internment," 126.
81 Ibid.

17. German POWs listen to a speech by Vice-Chancellor Franz Bluecher

investigator, who added, "only cowards were taken prisoner, in the worst circumstances people shot themselves." Anvaer was released only in March 1946, four and a half years after being captured by the *Wehrmacht*.[82] She was luckier than most of her comrades. Many of them were remobilized into the notorious work battalions or sent for years to *spetsposelenie* (special settlements) to perform forced labor in areas of extremely harsh climate. In 1951 some of these ex-POWs were given "supplementary sentences," which extended their banishment. Those who were finally discharged were forbidden to reside in certain areas of the USSR, including Moscow, Leningrad, and Kiev. Only after the demise of the Soviet Union could ex-POWs publish their stories in full in Russia. German prisoners, on the other hand faced, a different reception upon their return. Whether in the eastern or the western parts of Germany, POWs served as a central trope in the discourse of German victimization. In western Germany they were portrayed as victims of Soviet camps,

82 Roger Markwick, "An 'Indelible Stain': Memoirs of a Red Army POW Nurse, 1941–46," paper presented at the AAASS Convention, Philadelphia, November 2008. I thank Roger Markwick for allowing me to quote from his paper.

in eastern Germany as victims of National Socialist megalomania. Their reintegration into civilian life during the 1950s and their transformation into productive citizens reflected, in the words of Frank Biess, a widespread desire "to create a distance from unprecedented experiences of violence, suffering and deprivation."[83]

Thus their rehabilitation reflected a yearning in the 1950s for social renewal and political reconstruction, as well as lack of moral accountability. Their tales became a quintessential expression of German anguish.

83 Frank Biess, *Homecomings: Returning POWs and the Legacies of Defeat in Postwar Germany* (Berkeley, 2006), 228.

10

Military occupations, 1914–1945

SOPHIE DE SCHAEPDRIJVER

This chapter examines the rule and exploitation of conquered lands by highly mobilized states that waged "totalizing" or total wars in 1914–18 and 1937–45. The occupations of the world wars in many ways resembled other modern occupations during peacetime or low-intensity conflicts, and they shared many dynamics with regimes of imperial expansion.[1] This chapter, however, will concentrate on the specific nexus between high-intensity warfare and military occupation. It will start by charting the military occupations of World War I and World War II. For reasons of space, some occupations will remain unexamined, such as the Entente's occupations during World War I, the Soviet occupation of the Baltic in 1940–41, and occupations by Romania, Hungary, and Bulgaria during World War II. The first issue addressed regards the aims of occupying powers – both the long-term and the immediate, wartime aims. The next issue is the practice of occupation, the quest for order and compliance with minimal troop deployment. This part of the chapter touches on the problem of imperial "overstretch." The following section addresses occupation from the perspective of the occupied; it focuses on the diminishing realm of "ordinary" life under occupation, addressing questions of civilian compliance and defiance. The chapter ends with a reflection on the differences between the occupations of the two world wars.

The belligerent occupations of World War I were mainly confined to Europe. When the offensive operations on the western front ground to a halt in November 1914, Germany found itself occupying almost all of Belgium

1 Eric Carlton, *Occupation: The Policies and Practices of Military Conquerors* (London, 1992); Alexander Cooley, *Logics of Hierarchy: The Organization of Empires, States, and Military Occupations* (Ithaca, 2005); David Edelstein: *Occupational Hazards: Success and Failure in Military Occupation* (Ithaca, 2008); Alfons Lammers, *Vreemde Overheersing: Bezetters en Bezetten in sociologisch Perspectief* (Amsterdam, 2005); Karma Nabulsi, *Traditions of War: Occupation, Resistance, and the Law* (Oxford, 1999). See also Chapters 3 and 17 in this volume.

and all or part of nine northeastern French departments – in all, ruling over some 10 million people in one of the world's most industrialized, urbanized areas.[2] A year later, when the front line in the east extended from the northern tip of Courland (Lithuania) to East Galicia, the Central Powers were in control of large swaths of eastern Europe, including Russian Poland, most of the Baltic territories, which were now renamed *Ober Ost* (Supreme Headquarters East), Serbia, and Vardar-Macedonia.[3] Montenegro and most of Albania were occupied shortly later. A year and a half after the outbreak of the war, Germany controlled the equivalent of 28 percent of its home population and just under half the inhabitants of the French Empire; Austria-Hungary had enlarged its population by nearly a tenth, and Bulgaria by as much as 50 percent. During subsequent stages of the war, the Central Powers' control expanded further. In December 1916, the three Central Powers, with Ottoman aid, jointly occupied more than two-thirds of Romania.[4] After the Italian debacle at Caporetto in October–November 1917, German and Austrian troops penetrated 100 kilometers into the northern Italian region of Friuli-Venezia Giulia.[5] The treaty of Brest Litovsk in March 1918 enormously expanded the Central Powers' sphere; the Russian Empire lost a third of its territory and an estimated 50 to 55 million people. German control over the Baltic expanded

2 Annette Becker, *Oubliés de la Grande Guerre: Humanitaire et culture de guerre* (Paris, 1998); Sophie De Schaepdrijver, *La Belgique et la Première Guerre mondiale* (Frankfurt, 2004).

3 Werner Basler, *Deutschlands Annexionspolitik in Polen und im Baltikum 1914–1918* (Berlin, 1962); Werner Conze, *Polnische Nation und Deutsche Politik im Ersten Weltkrieg* (Cologne, 1958); Mark von Hagen, *War in a European Borderland: Occupations and Occupation Plans in Galicia and Ukraine, 1914–1918* (Seattle, 2007); Julie Jacoby, "Lublin in World War I," AHA presentation, January 2008 (with thanks to Julie Jacoby for sharing this and other unpublished work). On the Baltic, Vejas Gabriel Liulevicius, *War Land on the Eastern Front: Culture, National Identity and German Occupation in World War I* (Cambridge, 2000); Aba Strazhas, *Deutsche Ostpolitik im Ersten Weltkrieg: Der Fall Ober Ost 1915–1917* (Wiesbaden, 1993). On Serbia, Jonathan Gumz, *The Resurrection and Collapse of Empire in Habsburg Serbia, 1914–1918* (Cambridge, 2009); Jovana Knežević, "The Austro-Hungarian Occupation of Belgrade during the First World War: Battles at the Home Front" (Ph.D. dissertation, Yale, 2006). On the Bulgarian occupation of Macedonia, Björn Opfer, *Im Schatten des Krieges: Besatzung oder Anschluss – Befreiung oder Unterdrückung? Eine komparative Untersuchung über die bulgarische Herrschaft in Vardar-Makedonien 1915–1918 und 1941–1944* (Münster, 2005).

4 Lisa Mayerhofer, "Making Friends and Foes: Occupiers and Occupied in First World War Romania, 1916–1918," in Heather Jones and Jennifer O'Brien, eds., *Untold War: New Perspectives in First World War Studies* (Leiden, 2008), 119–50; Harald Heppner, "Im Schatten des 'Grossen Bruders': Österreich-Ungarn als Besatzungsmacht in Rumänien 1916–1918," *Österreichische Militärische Zeitschrift* 45 (2007): 317–22.

5 Gustavo Corni, *Il Friuli occidentale nell'anno dell'occupazione austro-germanica 1917–1918* (Udine, 1993); Gustavo Corni, "La società veneto-friulana durante l'occupazione militare austro-germanica 1917–1918," in Z. Cimprič, ed., *Kobarid/Caporetto, 1917–1997* (Ljubljana, 1998), 221–51.

by over 300 kilometers; in the south, Austro-German control expanded 1,250 kilometers to the Don River, including the Crimea. Until November 1918, the east seemed wide open.[6]

The Entente's European holdings were, in the main, more purely strategic, such as the "occupation" of Salonika behind the Macedonian front from 1916 to 1918. Russia's occupation of East Prussia in 1914 and its intermittent control over Galicia from 1914 to 1916 reflected the mobility of warfare on the eastern front.[7] Longer-term domination, which led to long-lived postwar "mandates," was established by British imperial troops in the Middle East, in Palestine and Mesopotamia. Jerusalem was taken in December 1917, ending four hundred years of Ottoman life, and Baghdad was taken in March 1918.[8] In Africa, the Entente (including the Union of South Africa) occupied German African possessions, substituting one form of colonial rule for another.

Preceding the general outbreak of World War II, the Axis powers' initial conquests testified to the breakdown of international cooperation in peacetime. Fascist Italy's invasion of Abyssinia, a fellow member of the League of Nations, was followed by five years of rule over *Africa Orientale Italiana*, which comprised Ethiopia, Eritrea, and Italian Somaliland (1936–41), a colony of 11.5 million inhabitants.[9] In the summer of 1937, Japan, which in 1931 had occupied its "sphere of influence" in northeast China and created the puppet state of Manchukuo, sent the Kwantung Army to invade the Beijing and Shanghai

6 See Liulevicius, *War Land*, 206–20; also Winfried Baumgart, *Deutsche Ostpolitik 1918: Vom Brest-Litowsk bis zum Ende des Ersten Weltkrieges* (Vienna and Munich, 1966). On the occupation regimes succeeding each other in Galicia and Ukraine over the course of World War I, von Hagen, *Borderland*.

7 Von Hagen, *Borderland*; Laurie Cohen, "Everyday Life in Times of War and Occupation at Border Towns in Galicia, Podolia, and Volhynia" (Presentation at the Fourth Conference of the International Society for First World War Studies, Washington, DC, October 2007.) On Lemberg (L'viv), see Christoph Mick, "Nationalisierung in einer multiethnischen Stadt: Interethnische Konflikte in Lemberg 1890–1920," *Archiv für Sozialgeschichte* 40 (2000): 130–33; Christoph Mick, "Besatzung und interethnische Beziehungen in Lemberg 1914–1945," Presentation at Seminar "Expériences et violences d'occupations en Europe (1900–1950): Approches comparées et croisées," Paris, June 2006 (with thanks to Christoph Mick for sharing his paper).

8 Anthony Bruce, *The Last Crusade: The Palestine Campaign in the First World War* (London, 2002); Cyrill Falls, *Armageddon, 1918: The Final Palestinian Campaign of World War I* (Philadelphia, 1964) on Palestine; on Mesopotamia, A. J. Barker, *The Bastard War: The Mesopotamian Campaign of 1914–1918* (New York, 1967) and F. J. Moberly, *The Campaign in Mesopotamia* (4 vols., London, 1923–27).

9 Angelo Del Boca, *Gli Italiani in Africa Orientale*, Vol. II: *La conquista dell'Impero* (Bari, 1981); Giulia Borgini Künzi, "Total Colonial Warfare: Ethiopia," in Roger Chickering and Stig Förster, eds., *The Shadows of Total War: Europe, East Asia, and the United States 1919–1939* (Cambridge, 2003), 313–26; Haile M. Larebo, *The Building of an Empire: Italian Land Policy and Practice in Ethiopia, 1935–1941* (Oxford, 1984); Alberto Sbacchi, *Ethiopia under Mussolini: Fascism and the Colonial Experience* (London, 1985).

regions. In Europe, Austria and the Sudetenland were amalgamated into Germany in March and October 1938 respectively. The Czech parts of Czechoslovakia, which were redefined as the German "protectorate" of Bohemia and Moravia, were directly ruled by Germany after March 1939. In the next month Italy invaded Albania; it too was turned into a "protectorate."

These acquisitions were dwarfed by Axis conquests once the conflict started. At the end of 1942, Germany controlled one-third of the European landmass and nearly half its inhabitants, plus sizeable parts of northern Africa. Its domination extended from the Channel Islands to the Kalmyk steppe and from Norway to the Sahara.[10] Italy had acquired large Mediterranean territories, from the Grenoble region in France through parts of Croatia, the Dalmatian coast, and western Macedonia to a large area of Greece and its islands.[11] The Japanese ruled directly or indirectly over 340 to 350 million people – five to six times the population of the prewar French and Dutch empires, or some three-quarters of the population of the British Empire – in an area that reached from the Solomon Islands in the mid-Pacific to the Burmese–Indian border, and from New Guinea to the Aleutian Islands.[12]

In 1914, the Central Powers did not enter the war in order to create European empires. Their goal was continental or regional dominance, not a redrawing of the map. By contrast, territorial expansion was the reason why Japan and Germany went to war in 1937 and 1939, following years of piecemeal acquisitions. Likewise, the creation of a Mediterranean empire was a central purpose of the Italian Fascist regime. But in 1914–18 conquest bred its own logic: permanent control over conquered territories became a war aim. This was particularly the case in Germany, where lobbies formulated far-reaching demands as early as September 1914, and protest against the possibility of a peace without annexations gave rise to a mass movement, the *Deutsche Vaterlandspartei*, in 1917–18.[13] Following Germany's vast conquests in the east, the outcome of the war, which entailed the loss of the Prussian Polish provinces and the Entente's occupation of the Rhineland, lent further appeal to geopolitical, social Darwinist thinking in Germany afterwards. Germany's need for *Lebensraum* in the east was the centerpiece of Hitler's worldview and the reason why he went to war. Italy, which signed the "Pact of Steel" in May 1939, decided to engage in a "parallel war." For all the extravagance of Fascist

10 Mark Mazower, *Hitler's Empire: How the Nazis Ruled Europe* (New York, 2008).

11 Davide Rodogno, *Fascism's Italian Empire: Italian Occupation during the Second World War* (Cambridge, 2006).

12 Peter Duus, et al., eds., *The Japanese Wartime Empire, 1931–1945* (Princeton, 1996).

13 Fritz Fischer, *Germany's Aims in the First World War* (New York, 1967).

rhetoric, Italy's territorial claims were ad hoc, and Germany decided in any case which territories would be Italy's to rule.[14] The Japanese wartime empire was in part opportunistic in nature. The Japanese first took advantage of the absence of unified authority in China, then, after 1940, exploited the Nazi conquest of Europe's colonizing states.[15]

In both wars and in both the European and Asian theaters, plans for long-term gain included agricultural colonization, the creation of subordinate economies, and the suppression of uncongenial ideologies – even of ideologies altogether. In 1915–18 the Habsburg state aimed to return conquered Serbia to an "apoliticized" state of vassalage.[16] More generally, the occupations of World War I opened possibilities to create ethnically homogeneous territories, but these remained, by and large, no more than possibilities – plans for what a contemporary called "a kind of 'ethnic territorial cleansing'" – which never left the blueprint stage.[17] One exception was Bulgaria's policy of forced transfers and even the mass murder of Serbs, Greeks, Vlachs, and other minorities in occupied Serbia and Macedonia.[18]

World War II was more basically a war of empire. For all three Axis powers, it was not a war against nation-states so much as a war to conquer putatively unstructured "spaces," which were inhabited by congeries of disparate, subaltern peoples. Such views had been adumbrated during World War I, particularly with regard to the German-occupied Baltic.[19] During World War II, millions of civilians were subjected worldwide to forced migration of one kind or another – expulsion, internment, or compulsory labor. The Italians, who had undertaken mass deportations and internment in Cyrenaica in 1930, returned to these methods in the occupied Balkans. Between November 1941 and May 1942 alone, in the newly created "Province of Ljubljana" (which had 340,000 inhabitants) 25,000 Slovenes, including children, were interned in camps.[20] By the end of March 1941, 408,000 Poles and Jews had been expelled from Germany's newly annexed

14 Rodogno, *Fascism's Empire*, 80.
15 See Wen-hsin Yeh, ed., *Wartime Shanghai* (London and New York, 1998).
16 Gumz, *Resurrection and Collapse*.
17 Heinrich Class, as quoted in Wolfgang Mommsen, "Der 'polnische Grenzstreifen': Anfänge der 'völkischen Flurbereinigung' und der Umsiedlungspolitik," in Mommsen, *Der Erste Weltkrieg: Anfang vom Ende des bürgerlichen Zeitalters* (Frankfurt, 2004), 120. See also Imanuel Geiss, *Der polnische Grenzstreifen 1914–1918: Ein Beitrag zur deutschen Kriegszielpolitik im Ersten Weltkrieg* (Lübeck and Hamburg, 1960); Isabel V. Hull, *Absolute Destruction: Military Culture and the Practices of War in Imperial Germany*, (Ithaca, 2005).
18 Opfer, *Im Schatten*.
19 Liulevicius, *War Land*.
20 Rodogno, *Fascism's Empire*, 84, 334, 348.

Polish territories; a comparable number of Poles had been sent to Germany proper as forced laborers.[21] Parallel mass deportations occurred in Russian-occupied Poland. But Nazi Germany was the only Axis power to entertain dreams of expanding into empty lands or lands made ethnically "pure." Neither Italy nor Japan had the equivalent of the SS (*Schutzstaffel*) with its racial obsessions. In both states, to be sure, imperialists wanted the conquered domains to be settled by racially superior imperial elites (including fondly imagined contingents of sturdy farmer-settlers).[22] However, these were to settle alongside the vanquished populations, without the latter's systematic deportation, let alone their decimation or extermination.[23]

Who formulated these long-term goals and who lobbied for them? In the *Führerstaat*, this question is easily answered: even for a totalitarian state the concentration of powers in Hitler's hands was exceptional. *Il Duce*, too, enjoyed wide-ranging powers in matters of imperial expansion.[24] In the cases of Wilhelmine Germany during World War I and *tennō* Japan during World War II, wartime empire was not the work of the emperor, nor of the army alone, but rather of an ever-wider coalition of pro-expansionist forces that pushed the agenda onward and left no imperialist claim unheeded. In both cases, the changes wrought by industrialization (which had generated anxieties about overpopulation, "degeneration," agricultural self-sufficiency, and dependence on imported raw materials) and a diminished sense of limitations among the political and bureaucratic elites created the basis for a broad coalition in favor of expansion.[25]

The more immediate goals of the occupying regimes – what these states wanted from their conquests to support the wars that they were then waging – were threefold. The first and most immediate was the establishment of order, as occupied territory was being transformed into a hinterland for a fighting army. This goal translated into different needs, depending on the shape and mobility of the fighting front, as well as on the terrain. Occupying powers preferred to commit as few troops as possible to policing occupied lands. In practice, this

21 Mazower, *Hitler's Empire*, 97.

22 Many of the considerable number of Japanese who migrated to the Chinese mainland were not farmers, but urban *petits bourgeois* – shop-keepers, company employees, and minor officials. In the empires of Italy and Germany, settlement by farmers was equally disappointing.

23 See John Docker, "Are Settler-Colonies Inherently Genocidal? Re-Reading Lemkin," in Dirk Moses, ed., *Empire, Colony, Genocide: Conquest, Occupation, and Subaltern Resistance in World History* (New York, 2008).

24 Rodogno, *Fascism's Empire*.

25 Duus et al., eds., *Wartime Empire*, xiv; see Louise Young, *Japan's Total Empire: Manchuria and the Culture of Wartime Imperialism* (Berkeley, 1999).

design prescribed two courses of action, which were not mutually exclusive: immediate terrorization of the populace and enlisting local forces of order. The German troops that invaded Belgium in 1914 killed over five thousand civilians and burned tens of thousands of houses in a savage reaction to alleged civilian sniping.[26] The violence subsequently gave way to a wary *modus vivendi* between occupiers and occupied. This arrangement included some common policing. As elsewhere, the occupied had a stake in maintaining order, for they themselves were made to bear the brunt of disturbances.[27]

The second goal was the exploitation of material resources, including labor. Requisitionings, then levies for "occupation costs" were imposed on invaded lands. Revenue was siphoned off through the establishment of monopolies on crucial resources, such as opium in occupied central and northern China.[28] Markets were rigged, as occupying regimes and ordinary soldiers bought goods at forced exchange rates, if they did not engage in outright looting, as did Hans Frank, the notorious Governor General of Nazi-occupied Poland. Other depredations included the "sequestration" and takeover of noncooperative manufacturing firms and utilities, as well as the hauling off to the homeland of industrial facilities (such as machinery and driving-belts), transportation infrastructure (railway lines and rolling stock), and agricultural resources (such as wood and livestock). In addition, the spoliation of Jewish property across Nazi-dominated Europe was a significant source of revenue.

One major resource, which occupying powers exploited with increasing ferocity as their military fortunes declined, was labor – either of the more-or-less voluntary variety or of coerced, even slave labor. In August 1914, the German authorities forced half a million seasonal agricultural workers from Russian Poland to remain in Germany. Forced labor was introduced in the General Governments of Belgium and Poland in 1916. The measure was rescinded a year later, but it continued in areas under direct German military rule in northern France, western Belgium, and the Baltic.[29] Forced labor was

26 John Horne and Alan Kramer, *German Atrocities 1914: A History of Denial* (New Haven, 2001).

27 Benoît Majerus, *Occupations et logiques policières: La Police bruxelloise en 1914–1918 et 1940–1945* (Brussels, 2007). On the *modus vivendi* see De Schaepdrijver, *La Belgique*.

28 Timothy Brook, "Opium and Collaboration in Central China, 1938–1940," in Timothy Brook and Bob Tadashi Wakabayashi, eds., *Opium Regimes: China, Britain, and Japan, 1839–1952* (Berkeley and Los Angeles, 2000), 323–43.

29 Jens Thiel, *"Menschenbassin Belgien": Anwerbung, Deportation und Zwangsarbeit im Ersten Weltkrieg* (Essen, 2007), 31–33; Christian Westerhoff, "Zwangsarbeit im Ersten Weltkrieg: Rekrutierung und Beschäftigung osteuropäischer Arbeitskräfte in den von Deutschland besetzten Gebieten," Ph.D. dissertation, Erfurt, 2009 (with thanks to Dr. Westerhoff for sharing his unpublished work).

also imposed on civilians under Bulgarian and Habsburg rule.[30] During World War II, the number of foreign workers in Germany rose prodigiously, to 4.6 million at the end of November 1942. By then, Fritz Sauckel, Hitler's Labor Plenipotentiary, was running one of the largest forced-labor programs in history. As ever more German men were sent to the Russian front and millions of Russian prisoners of war starved to death, coercion was stepped up. In the west the so-called Mandatory Labor Service (*Service du Travail Obligatoire*) was introduced in France in August 1942. In the east it was more brutal. Entire villages were burned down if workers failed to show. One German official compared the recruiting drives in the east to "the blackest periods of the slave trade."[31] After 1942, an ever-increasing number of concentration-camp inmates were set to work; from the Channel Islands to Majdanek, German and German-controlled territories were dotted with an archipelago of "subcamps," which engaged in one industrial activity or another. In the last year of the war, over a quarter of the German workforce was foreign – nearly 8 million workers.[32] Likewise, as Japan's war effort grew desperate, the Japanese authorities began to requisition labor with increasing ruthlessness.[33] Working under harsh supervision, underfed, and without adequate medical care, hundreds of thousands of men in labor-service battalions in Southeast Asia and Korea built infrastructure for the war effort – roads, airstrips, and railway lines. An estimated hundred thousand Burmese and Malay Indian workers died building the Burma–Siam railway. In addition, an estimated fifty thousand to two hundred thousand "comfort women" from Korea, China, the Philippines, Burma, and elsewhere were shipped to Japanese military brothels.[34]

The exploitation of resources benefited not only the military, but also the home front. Because he was obsessed with the "stab in the back," which had allegedly been administered to German troops by war-weary German civilians in 1917–18, Hitler regarded keeping the home front supplied as a top priority. In addition, SS officials hoped that cruel measures against Russian workers would "co-opt" the skeptical German working class into the regime's ideology, "enrolling them in the master-race in their dealings with Russians."[35] This

30 Opfer, *Im Schatten*, 114–29; Gumz, *Resurrection and Collapse*.

31 Otto Bräutigam, cited in Mazower, *Hitler's Empire*, 299.

32 Adam Tooze, The *Wages of Destruction: The Making and Breaking of the Nazi Economy* (London, 2006). See also Richard Evans, *The Third Reich at War* (New York, 2009), 348–67.

33 See Nicholas Tarling, *A Sudden Rampage: The Japanese Occupation of South-East Asia, 1941–1944* (Honolulu, 2001).

34 Duus et al., eds., *Wartime Empire*. See also George Hicks's contribution to the same volume, "The 'Comfort Women,'" 305–23.

35 Evans, *Third Reich*, 355.

18. Poster used by German occupying forces in France

19. Portrait of Marius Jonker Roelants, painted on a wooden bread plate by a fellow inmate at Camp Amersfoort, the Netherlands, just before his removal to first an SS Concentration Camp at Vught, and then Rheinbach Prison in Germany. Marius died from disease on 1 May 1945 in Salzwedel, shortly after the city was liberated.

practice related to the third goal of occupiers vis-à-vis their conquered territories. The prestige of conquest was to be harnessed for domestic use, in order to promote the ongoing mobilization of the home population, which was itself a crucial resource in an industrial war. In Italian town squares, giant maps were displayed, which showed the Fascist state's conquests (until they vanished after mid-1941). During World War I, Germany's possessions in the west and east had generated much enthusiastic rhetoric, which centered on the idea of Germany's regenerating mission. Likewise, during World War II, images of harvesting settlers and splendid new cities in Manchuria impressed the Japanese public.[36]

The need to ensure domination while fighting a war led occupying powers to seek stability beyond coercion. Achieving some kind of self-replenishing authority over conquered lands promised maximum return for a minimal expenditure of troops. At a basic level, occupying powers did enjoy at least some temporary legality, given the existing "laws" of belligerent occupation. In addition, occupying powers could highlight the end of the violence and the

36 Young, *Japan's Total Empire*.

upheaval of invasion to foster an atmosphere of "normalcy" and acceptance. In occupied Belgium in the summer of 1915, Governor General von Bissing convened a group of German architects to discuss rebuilding cities that had been damaged during the invasion. He believed, as his son later wrote, that "One day the German army in the occupied territories will be honoured for having endeavored everywhere . . . to heal the wounds it had to make."[37] A memoir published in 1939 by a Japanese "pacification agent," who had been sent to the city of Zhenjiang two weeks after its atrocious treatment at the hands of invading troops in November 1937, also stressed reconstruction and regeneration.[38] Fostering acceptance was easier where the violence of the invasion had spared civilians or the deposed regime had been discredited, as was the case in both France and French Indochina in 1940.

Although occupying powers tried everywhere to reach a degree of co-operation with indigenous authorities, levels of indigenous autonomy differed markedly. During the occupations of World War I, no national or provincial authorities were enlisted as "partners." A native, countrywide relief organization was allowed in Belgium, if grudgingly and under international pressure; but in Poland Governor General von Beseler dismantled a similar organization.[39] Habsburg occupiers took over the administration in Serbia even at the local level.[40] In areas under direct military occupation, such as northern France, the Belgian coast, and the Baltic, even local indigenous authority was greatly whittled down. In *Ober Ost* no locals were allowed to work with the occupation administration. Not altogether paradoxically, however, the intensification of warfare begat vassal states and statelets. The Central Powers created a kingdom of Poland in November 1916 in hopes of raising an army against Russia. The Germans declared Flanders independent in December 1917. Baltic countries such as the "Duchy of Courland and Semigallia" were born in 1918. In April of the same year a German-backed military coup produced the Ukrainian Hetmanate.[41]

37 Friedrich Wilhelm von Bissing, introduction to August Grisebach et al., *Dinant: Eine Denkschrift. Bearbeitet im Auftrage Seiner Exzellenz des Generalgouverneurs in Belgien Generaloberst Freiherrn von Bissing im Jahre 1916* (Munich, 1918), 5.

38 Timothy Brook, *Collaboration: Japanese Agents and Local Elites in Wartime China* (Cambridge, MA, 2005), 103–21.

39 Sophie De Schaepdrijver, "A Civilian War Effort: The *Comité National de Secours et d'Alimentation* in Occupied Belgium, 1914–1918," in De Schaepdrijver et al., *Remembering Herbert Hoover and the Commission for Relief in Belgium* (Brussels, 2007), 24–37. On the abolition of the Polish *Centralny Komitet Obywatelski*, see Conze, *Polnische Nation*, 116–19. A more critical judgment is in Basler, *Deutschlands Annexionspolitik*, 113.

40 Knežević, "Belgrade," 33.

41 Von Hagen, *Borderland*, 94.

Japan's empire during World War II relied heavily on local elites, devolved arrangements, and puppet states, although Taiwan was governed by Japanese officials. Collaborationist governments administered Manchuria and occupied China. A Manchu dynast was appointed in Manchukuo. In Nanjing, the Japanese set up an "occupation state" in the guise of Liang Hongzhi's "Reformed Government" (1938–40), followed by the "Reorganized National Government" of Wang Jingwei, a Nationalist who had fallen out with Chiang Kai-shek (Chiang Chieh-shih). Much of the local administration remained intact, as village elders and notables were enlisted to assist in administration. Burma and the Philippines declared independence in August and October 1942, respectively; both were led by champions of the Greater East Asia Co-Prosperity Sphere. French Indochina (Vietnam, Laos, and Cambodia) technically remained under Vichy colonial administration until March 1945. To the chagrin of Indonesian nationalists, the Japanese considered the Dutch East Indies too close to the front in New Guinea to be allowed self-rule. Nor did Japanese plans for the region envision independence in the long run. Strategically crucial areas, such as Hong Kong, Singapore, Timor, Borneo, and occupied New Guinea, were annexed to the Japanese empire and ruled by the military.

In Nazi-occupied Europe, indigenous autonomy and the devolution of power were largely restricted to the west. Denmark kept its government until 1943 under the supervision of the German Foreign Office. In France, the Vichy government retained civil administrative authority throughout the country even after November 1942, when the *Wehrmacht* extended its occupation into the "Free Zone." The "autonomy" of Vichy was exemplified in the regime's ability to prosecute and, in a few dozen cases, to execute spies who had worked for the Germans. Even in the occupied zone of France, the Germans were not initially thick on the ground; in the spring of 1941, no more than two hundred German officials were in Paris.[42] The civil administrations of Norway, the Netherlands, and Belgium remained in place. In the east and southeast, by contrast, little autonomy was left to local authorities, with the exception of puppet regimes in Slovakia and Croatia. The *Wehrmacht* ruled Serbia, Greece, and the parts of Russia immediately behind the battlefront. The area termed *Ostland*, which comprised eastern Poland, White Russia, and the Baltic states, was run, together with the Ukraine, by Reich commissioners as a kind of colony. Rump Poland, the General Government, was directly ruled by Germany. As a result of the Germans' refusal to work

42 Mazower, *Hitler's Empire*, 238.

with Polish elites, who had in any case been decimated in an effort to kill Polish nationalism, tens of thousands of German officials and large numbers of German troops were needed to ensure German rule.[43]

Fascist Italy annexed parts of Slovenia and Dalmatia to form two new provinces. In the Ionian Islands, civil commissioners prepared the way for annexation, and local authorities were deposed. Local civilian authority was kept in place in the Cyclades and southern Sporades, but these islands were ruled by the military, as were the parts of the Greek mainland that the Italians occupied, in spite of their intention to create an independent state there. The strip of French land that fell under Italian control witnessed the introduction of the full array of Fascist forces of order – the *carabinieri*, police, customs forces, border militia, forest and revenue officers, and *Fasci di Combattimento*. On July 12, 1941, Montenegro, which had been detached from Serbia, became a kingdom under the "protection" of Rome.[44]

This new kingdom lasted one day. Within hours, a revolt broke out, and the territory had to be turned over to military rule. Montenegro offered an extreme example of the difficulties inherent in creating puppet states in wartime. As the war intensified, nowhere did the arrangement of occupation yield sufficient resources to address the needs of occupying powers; the resulting increase in coercion further eroded cooperation and the legitimacy of the occupying powers. In 1942, the introduction of obligatory labor in France created centers of partisan activity where there had been none, depressing productivity in French factories that worked for the German war effort. During World War I, in Habsburg-occupied Serbia, increased repression bred armed civilian resistance, which was otherwise rare in this war.[45] In areas where cooperation or legitimacy was never a priority of the occupying power, as in Nazi-occupied eastern Europe, the brutality of rule undermined the exploitation of conquest. But for Hitler's murderous contempt for the Slavs, nationalist and anti-Bolshevik sentiments in these lands could have been put to profitable use.[46] The more convincing and genuine notion of "panasianism" allowed the Japanese to enroll nationalist, anticolonial elites in Southeast Asia during World War II. But even here, harsh exploitation,

43 Jan Tomasz Gross, *Polish Society under German Occupation: The General Government 1939–1945* (Princeton, 1979); Czeslaw Madajczyk, *Die Okkupationspolitik Nazideutschlands in Polen 1939–1945* (Berlin, 1967).

44 Rodogno, *Fascism's Empire*, 9–11; 80–108; 121.

45 Gumz, *Resurrection and Collapse*.

46 Mazower, *Hitler's Empire*, 245–48, 457, 464.

coupled with Japanese priorities and racial contempt, taxed the sympathies of occupied populations.[47]

Compared to colonial or commercial empires, the wartime empires were unwieldy weapons. They could not make good a conqueror's military-industrial deficiencies. In fact, the maintenance of empire weakened military fortunes. Japan's spectacular wartime expansion rested on a slim material base. Conquest was difficult to sustain, hegemony only apparent, and the costs exceeded the benefits. Moreover, Japan's pursuit of empire created an opposing alliance of superior forces.[48] Likewise, during World War I Germany's enormous land gains after Brest-Litovsk rendered impossible a negotiated peace that would have left the country with at least some of its spoils.[49] Fascist Italy had no basis for imperial dreams. The Ethiopian campaign and participation in the Spanish Civil War had bankrupted the state even before the outbreak of World War II.

In addition, occupations were disorderly affairs, which further compromised the bureaucratic efficiency of belligerent states. During World War I, the German Emperor William II's "personal regime" was replicated by the Prussian career officers who ruled the occupied territories. They felt no accountability to the government in Berlin and administered their lands like fiefdoms, imposing opaque and capricious structures of command.[50] During World War II, Japan's empire, which was administered through the Greater East Asia Ministry in Tokyo, maintained a certain bureaucratic ethos. In Nazi Germany's occupied lands, the civil service was sidelined to the benefit of the party, whose leading men were to constitute, in Hitler's view, "a breed of viceroys" – rulers, not administrators. A centralized imperial bureaucracy was abhorrent to the Führer and his *alte Kämpfer*. The SS, which represented a much more centralized vision, did force its way into occupied Europe – especially in the east – in 1941, when the invasion of the USSR and uprisings in Yugoslav lands raised the issue of resistance. The agency's leader, Heinrich Himmler, became minister of the interior in 1943. However, this change

47 Tarling, *A Sudden Rampage*.

48 Edward J. Drea, *In the Service of the Emperor: Essays on the Imperial Japanese Army* (Lincoln, NE: 1998).

49 See Sebastian Haffner, *Die Sieben Todsünden des Deutschen Reiches im Ersten Weltkrieg* (Hamburg, 1964).

50 I owe this insight to Christoph Roolf (Düsseldorf), whose dissertation-in-progress elaborates this point with regard to the occupation of Belgium in 1914–1918. On the "personal regime," see Isabel V. Hull, *The Entourage of Kaiser Wilhelm II, 1888–1918* (Cambridge, 2004).

neither brought centralization closer nor put an end to tensions between party and state.[51]

In both world wars, occupied populations sought mainly to survive. The range of "normal" activities available to them differed over time and by location, but it was limited everywhere. Mobility was much restricted. Ordinary economic activities endured longer in some countries and in some sectors than in others, but as a rule the impeded flow of people and goods, monetary difficulties, requisitioning of goods, tools, and labor, war levies, expropriations, expulsions, destructions, and other calamities wrought by occupation increasingly restricted economic life. Illegal gains, obtained on black markets of many varieties, became correspondingly important. While it did not grind to a halt (contrary to pious postwar myths), public life did shrink. Private lives were affected, as marriage and birth rates dropped even in privileged areas.

At the same time, occupations offered allurements to the occupied, sometimes in the context of diminished expectations. To the extent that the establishment of an occupation regime signaled an end to open violence, it could occasion relief. Occupation regimes could offer opportunities for advancement. Quisling governments needed clerks, compliant newspapers needed copy. The arrival of a new population of occupation personnel (sometimes with their families) offered opportunities as well. Paris was a lively literary and entertainment hub during World War II. Even much-depressed Belgrade saw a surge in café life under occupation in World War I.[52] During the same war, intellectuals of varying renown wrote for newspapers and journals that the occupiers had launched in Serbia, Romania, northern France, and Belgium.[53] Under Nazi occupation some intellectuals, like the novelists Robert Brasillach in France, openly endorsed the regime. Knut Hamsun in Norway went so far as to offer his Nobel Prize to Joseph Goebbels.[54]

51 Mazower, *Hitler's Empire*, 224–56.

52 Olivier Corpet and Claire Paulhan, *Collaboration and Resistance: French Literary Life under the Nazi Occupation* (Minneapolis, 2010); Patrick Buisson, *1940–1945 Années érotiques: De la Grande Prostituée à la revanche des mâles* (Paris, 2008); Jovana Knežević, "Persuasion over Coercion: The Austro-Hungarian Occupation of Belgrade during the First World War," presentation at the Third Conference of the International Society for First World War Studies, Dublin, September 2005.

53 Maria Bucur, "Romania: War, Occupation, Liberation," in Aviel Roshwald and Richard Stites, eds., *European Culture in the Great War: The Arts, Entertainment, and Propaganda, 1914–1918* (Cambridge, 1999), 243–66; Sophie De Schaepdrijver, "Occupation, Propaganda, and the Idea of Belgium," in ibid., 267–94; Knežević, "Belgrade."

54 Alice Kaplan, *The Collaborator: The Trial and Execution of Robert Brasillach* (Chicago, 2000); Ingar Sletten Kolloen, *Knut Hamsun: Dreamer and Dissenter* (New Haven, 2009); Monika Zagar, *Knut Hamsun: The Dark Side of Literary Brilliance* (Seattle, 2009).

Occupation regimes nevertheless faced a fundamental deficit of legitimacy. It was difficult to ground a regime imposed by violence in continuity and consent. Enlisting local elites was thus crucial.[55] To many within these elites, occupation regimes held out the promise of maintaining existing social hierarchies. Other pledges addressed national aspirations. A "Council of Flanders" was established in occupied Belgium in 1917, and similar bodies emerged in Poland and the Baltic. In Japanese-occupied Indonesia, the leaders of the Indonesian nationalist movement, Sukarno and Muhammad Hatta, who had spent years in Dutch colonial prisons, proffered "hearty cooperation to our military administration."[56] For these, as for other national leaders, cooperation with a victorious Asian power was the best route to independence; and the alternatives appeared to be destruction or submission. Such figures had no choice but to define forced labor at the hand of the occupier as a liberating measure. In 1917, the Council of Flanders declared that forced labor was the price of German victory, hence Flemish independence. Similarly, in 1945, Sukarno explained in occupied Java that "the sweat of the forced laborers is poison for the Allies."[57]

In 1918 the same Council of Flanders drafted plans to create a gendarmerie to help police the occupied population and quell Belgian resistance to *its* authority. The plan remained a blueprint. More generally, armed assistance to occupying powers was rare in Europe during World War I. It was more widespread, though still more the exception than the rule, during World War II. In the final days of the war, members of the French SS Charlemagne defended Hitler's bunker in Berlin. One hundred and twenty-five thousand west Europeans joined the Waffen-SS. So did many more from eastern Europe. As Germany lost the war, ethnic standards for taking up arms on behalf of the Reich relaxed; by the end of the war nearly half a million eastern Europeans had volunteered or had been impressed into the Waffen-SS. Among them were ethnic Germans, Hungarians, Romanians, Estonians, Ukrainians, and even Bosnian Muslims, whom Himmler decreed to be Aryan.[58] Occupation made possible the violent settling of scores by armed collaborators, such as the *Milice* in Vichy France. Militias helped implement extreme policies throughout the occupied territories, corralling forced laborers, arresting resisters, deporting Jews.[59]

55 Brook, *Collaboration*; Philippe Burrin, *La France à l'heure allemande 1940–1944* (Paris, 1995).

56 In the words of Japanese authorities, referring to "Indonesian people" in general: Ken'ichi Gotō, "Indigenous Elites," in Duus et al., eds., *Wartime Empire*, 274–301, 281.

57 Ibid., 282; De Schaepdrijver, *La Belgique*, 277.

58 Mazower, *Hitler's Empire*, 455–460.

59 See Lieven Saerens, *De Jodenjagers van de Vlaamse SS: Gewone Vlamingen*? (Tielt, 2007).

Militias were not the only indigenous forces that assisted occupying regimes. Ordinary police forces did so as well. Under military occupation the boundaries of "normal" policing were under constant pressure, as maintaining public order and safeguarding the citizenry shaded into complicity with the occupier.

"Normal" activity could also shade into forms of resistance. Across occupations, an array of forms of noncompliance, unarmed defiance, or armed confrontation arose. Unarmed activities included administrative and industrial obstruction, the publication of underground protest literature, sabotage, establishing escape networks for "enemy" troops, sheltering people who had been targeted for arrest or deportation, and military intelligence. Armed resistance could target collaborators or members of the occupation regime, or it could transform into more open, albeit guerrilla-like forms of battle. The varieties of resistance depended on many factors, such as geography – the nature of the terrain or access to a neutral frontier – the depth and rigor of the occupation regime, and indigenous traditions of defiance of central authority.

Some forms of noncompliance, such as shirking labor obligations or hiding requisitioned goods, became daily strategies of survival, but when local authorities engaged in it, it took on overtones of defiance. In occupied Belgium in 1917, the city of Tournai refused to submit lists of the unemployed whom the Germans had targeted for forced labor, declaring its unwillingness to "provide arms against its own children."[60] Another form of civilian defiance was discursive. Clandestine newspapers and pamphlets were disseminated in great variety; they ranged from the high-brow, such as Albert Camus's magazine *Combat* during World War II, to more popular forms, like the dramas and cartoons that were addressed to rural audiences in China.[61] Practical varieties of unarmed resistance encompassed networks to hide and facilitate the escape of enemies of the occupying regime. These networks were ad hoc creations but deeply embedded in civilian society. Like other forms of organized resistance, they relied on preexisting professional, political, or confessional contacts. Clandestine communist cells in Nazi-occupied western Europe were an extreme example.[62] To assist a core of activists, many networks relied on large numbers of occasional helpers – neighbors, couriers, people who were willing to lend out space or "mailboxes" or to

60 De Schaepdrijver, *La Belgique*.

61 Chang-Tai Hung, *War and Popular Culture: Resistance in Modern China, 1937–1945* (Berkeley and Los Angeles, 1994).

62 Bob Moore, "Comparing Resistance and Resistance Movements," in Moore, ed., *Resistance in Western Europe* (Oxford and New York, 2000), 249–64, 251–52.

provide food and other supplies. By virtue of this commitment, the occasional participants themselves effectively entered the world of illegality. Intelligence networks, too, could only survive on the strength of local knowledge and goodwill, in addition to professional savvy. In Belgium during World War I, the dense railroad network that ferried German troops between the western and eastern fronts was the focus of spying activities by Belgian railway professionals, who were, as a result, disproportionately likely to become "martyrs" of the resistance.[63] In World War I armed resistance to an occupier was virtually nonexistent; Serbia was the only exception. The *franc-tireurs*, whose specter prompted the massacres of the summer of 1914 in Belgium and northern France, were a figment of the invading armies' imagination. Assassinations of collaborators were rare, of occupation personnel rarer still. The killing of General von Eichhorn in the Ukraine in July 1918 occurred as occupation shaded into civil war, as the rudimentary Ukrainian state could claim no monopoly of armed violence.

Armed resistance was more prevalent during World War II, although only a small proportion of people were involved. Partisan warfare needed propitious (or, rather, unpropitious) terrain. Lines were blurred between armed resistance and banditry. Under the Japanese occupation in China, particularly in rural Chongming in the Yangzi Delta, armed bands posed as resisters to feed off the rural populace; in Shanghai, gangster and "resistance" activities occasionally merged.[64] On the other hand, as in Marseille, the line between collaboration and gangsterism also blurred.[65] Resistance engagement could be fueled by desperation, when the occupied saw no other way out of imminent destruction, as well as by hope, when victory for the occupying power ceased to be certain. Thus across Europe in World War II, the intensification of repression and the battle of Stalingrad (which gave rise to visions of liberation) gave impetus to resistance movements. The numbers of Europeans who were engaged in armed resistance against Nazi regimes remained small (an estimated 2 percent of the population in France,

63 Laurence Van Ypersele et al., *De la guerre de l'ombre aux ombres de la guerre: L'espionnage en Belgique durant la guerre 1914–1918 – histoire et mémoire* (Brussels, 2004), 31–35.

64 For Chongming, see Brook, *Collaboration*, 215; for Shanghai, see Frederic Wakeman, Jr., *The Shanghai Badlands: Wartime Terrorism and Urban Crime, 1937–1941* (Cambridge, 1996).

65 Paul Jankowski, *Communism and Collaboration: Simon Sabiani and Politics in Marseille 1919–1944* (London and New Haven, 1989). Jankowski has argued against blurring the lines, maintaining that choosing resistance could mean taking the longer, "civic" view: "In Defense of Fiction: Resistance, Collaboration, and Lacombe, Lucien," *Journal of Modern History* 63 (1991): 457–82.

rather more in Serbia), although the informal networks that supported them were much more extensive, if hard to quantify. Defiance, like compliance, was deeply rooted in the societies out of which it emerged.

Among the dead of World War I, an estimated 10 percent were civilians. The proportion in World War II was 50 percent. The occupations of both wars show similar contrasts: the conquered populations of 1914–18 inhabited a more separate civilian sphere. The range of civilian reactions to occupation during World War I remained by and large more *civilian* – unarmed – particularly in western Europe, where the continued fighting of the population's "own" army encouraged a stricter division of labor between armed forces and civilian populations under occupation. Both collaboration and resistance to occupying regimes remained, in this sense, civilian phenomena. Another difference between World War I and II lay in the scale of repression. Although spies were shot and "unwanted persons," such as notables who were suspected of influencing the population against the occupying power, sent away to prisons in the imperial homeland (Germany or Austria), no collective reprisals took place after 1914 in the vein of World War II.

Civilians in the occupied territories of World War I did suffer heavily. From Lille to Vilnius, many endured mass flight, malnutrition, forced labor, and daily repression. In fact, with the exception of Jews, occupied populations in western Europe were probably worse off in World War I than in World War II. Moreover, there were foreshadowings of ethnic cleansing during World War I. The ethnic violence of Bulgaria's occupation not only continued a tradition from the Balkan Wars; it also foreshadowed later developments. However, the massacres of 1914 and the introduction of forced labor shocked international public opinion, which testified to standards that still held. That these standards lowered during the interwar period was due largely to the coarsening wrought by the war of 1914–18 itself. The scale of conquest in World War II and the scale of violence directed against civilians – the level of destruction, the return of torture, and the enormous violence among the occupied – then testified to the totalization of war.

So did the destruction of the European Jews. This crime was intimately bound to occupation and empire. The mass exterminations started in Poland and accelerated after the invasion of the Soviet Union. The murderous targeting of Jews affected the practice of occupation across Europe. For the occupied, routine compliance with administrative rules, such as the keeping of registers, became a form of *de facto* complicity. Whether the occupied wished to acknowledge it or not – and many refused to do so for decades – because of the Shoah, the realm of "normal" governance was

20. Deportation of Jews from Warsaw

smaller than it had been in 1914–18.[66] During the first war, the upholding of indigenous authority under occupation was uncontroversial; it could in fact be defined as the patriotic defense of civilians' interest in avoiding instrumentalization by the enemy military. Maintaining domestic order was considered to be a part of this task, and armed resistance seemed like the reckless, unpatriotic endangerment of fellow citizens. By contrast, in 1939–45, indigenous authority was suspect by definition, as exemplified by the laden term "war burgomasters," which would have been unconceivable in 1914–18.[67]

After the armistice in 1918, the memory of occupation was overshadowed by that of the battlefield. Occupation had been a marginal experience, far from both front and home front. In addition, the "pacifist turn" of the 1920s fostered skepticism about civilian suffering under occupation, which was

66 For a valuable contrasting view, see Brook, *Collaboration*, 244.

67 See Bruno De Wever et al., eds., *Local Government in Occupied Europe (1939–1945)* (Ghent, 2006). See also Nico Wouters, *Oorlogsburgemeesters 40/44: Lokaal bestuur en collaboratie in België* (Tielt, Lannoo, 2004), a shortened version of his unpublished Ph.D. dissertation of 2004, which offered a comparison of local government in Belgium, northern France, and the Netherlands (with thanks to Nico Wouters for sharing his unpublished work).

retrospectively defined as a product of war propaganda, as was the notion, briefly put forward by French and Belgian liberals, that German occupation had had ideological dimensions. By contrast, after World War II, occupation by the totalitarian powers was widely defined as a theater of ultimate civic choices, both in Europe and in China. This was a "moral" reading of occupation, which served the legitimacy of postwar states.[68]

68 See Pieter Lagrou, *The Legacy of Nazi Occupation: Patriotic Memory and National Recovery in Western Europe, 1945–1965* (Cambridge, 2000).

11

Home fronts: the mobilization of resources for total war

PIERRE PURSEIGLE

Scholars customarily mock the naïve assumption that World War I would be over by Christmas 1914. However, a close examination of opinion in the belligerent states reveals a general understanding that wars, even those projected to be short, now required the comprehensive mobilization of societies. Still, the extent to which the current conflict would transform life on the home front was poorly understood.

After the guns fell silent in 1918, politicians, soldiers, and scholars attempted to make sense of an experience that had challenged conventional understandings of the relationship between war and civil society. Two examples might be cited. In *Der totale Krieg*, which was published in 1935, Erich Ludendorff, Germany's First Quatermaster-General during World War I, argued that only a military dictatorship could ensure the necessary mobilization of the nation's resources in another war.[1] A year later, the French scholar Elie Halévy observed that the "Era of Tyrannies"

> dates from August 1914, that is, from the time when the belligerent nations turned to a system which can be defined as follows:
>
> a. In the economic sphere, greatly extended state control of all means of production, distribution and exchange; – and at the same time, an appeal by the governments to the leaders of workers' organizations to help them in implementing this state control hence syndicalism and corporatism along with étatisme.
>
> b. In the intellectual sphere, state control of thought, in two forms: one negative, through the suppression of all expressions of opinion deemed unfavorable to the national interest; the other positive, through what we shall call the organization of enthusiasm.[2]

1 Hew Strachan, "Total War in the Twentieth Century," in Arthur Marwick, ed., *Total War and Historical Change: Europe, 1914–1955* (Buckingham and Philadelphia, 2001), 261

2 Elie Halévy, *The Era of Tyrannies: Essays on Socialism and War* (London, 1967), 181, 205.

Halévy's and Ludendorff's political frames of reference could hardly have been more different. Yet both stressed the centrality of the state in the process of mobilization. That is the theme of this chapter, which will address ways in which the dynamic of social mobilization in both world wars revealed the changing character of warfare itself.

The "totalizing logic" of World War I blurred the boundaries between combatants and non-combatants, between "soldier and civilian."[3] Mass armies, supported by industrialized economies, demanded the commitment of the nation's material and technical resources. The meaning of wartime mobilization thus shifted from its original military definition to encompass civil society, whose human, financial, and cultural resources were expected to support the armed forces in the field. The wars of German unification, the Franco-Prussian War in particular, had given the word *Heimatfront* wide currency in the newly unified Germany.[4] In Italy during World War I, *il fronte interno* became the term of choice among interventionists and nationalists. As Antonio Gibelli has pointed out, the term conjured up an internal enemy, whose activities were to be met as resolutely as those of the enemy at the front.[5] To meet the challenges of "total war," belligerent societies thus mobilized cultural, material, and political resources – ideas, wealth, and power – in specific and sometimes idiosyncratic ways. Despite the complexity of this process, these categories highlight the dynamics of social mobilization in both world wars.

Historians of World War I have rejected the proposition that the populations of Europe enthusiastically welcomed the outbreak of the conflict.[6] Although it was sincere, the nationalist fervor that was witnessed in towns and cities in the belligerent countries in August 1914 belied broader attitudes. Resigned to a conflict whose consequences they dreaded. Most people saw this war "as one of legitimate self-defence."[7] This conviction undermined

3 John Horne, ed., *State, Society, and Mobilization in Europe during the First World War* (Cambridge, 1997), 3; Roger Chickering and Stig Förster, eds., *Great War, Total War: Combat and Mobilization on the Western Front, 1914–1918* (Cambridge, 2000), 8; Jean-Jacques Becker, "Retour sur la comparaison et réflexion sur les héritages," in *La Violence de guerre, 1914–1945* (Brussels, 2002), 336–37.

4 Alexander Seyferth, *Die Heimatfront 1870/71: Wirtschaft und Gesellschaft im deutsch-französischen Krieg* (Paderborn, 2007).

5 Antonio Gibelli, *La Grande Guerra degli italiani* (Milan, 1998), 174.

6 Jean-Jacques Becker, *1914: Comment les Français sont entrés dans la guerre* (Paris, 1977); Jeffrey Verhey, *The Spirit of 1914: Militarism, Myth, and Mobilization in Germany* (Cambridge, 2000); Adrian Gregory, *The Last Great War: British Society and the First World War* (Cambridge, 2008).

7 John Horne, "Public Opinion and Politics," in Horne, ed., *A Companion to the First World War* (Oxford, 2010), 280.

nascent opposition to the war, which was hampered as well by legislation that the belligerent states adopted to restrict political and civic rights in the name of national defense.[8] The conflict was immediately invested, however, with existential significance. Intellectuals, artists, and scholars rallied behind the flag, portraying their states as defenders of lofty ideals and articulating a language of mobilization that soon swept the warring societies.[9] This war was couched in similar terms across the lines of battle. In the words of the Oxford scholar Alfred Zimmern, this was "a conflict between two different and irreconcilable conceptions of government, society and progress."[10] In a manifesto addressed "to the world of culture [*An die Kulturwelt*]," ninety-three German scholars set out in similar terms to defend the actions of German armies, which had been vilified for atrocities committed during the invasion of Belgium and France.

As churches in each country proclaimed God to be on their side against their co-religionists in other countries, political movements ignored ideological contradictions as they justified national defense. The international socialist movement failed to organize a response to the war, which its national constituent groups were likely in any case to support. In the belligerent states, working-class organizations had by and large adopted the dominant vision of the war. Nationalism provided the grammar of cultural mobilization, but this language was accentuated by secular and religious teleologies. In Japan, Marquis Inoue Kaoru welcomed the outbreak of the war as "the divine aid of the new Taishō era for development of the destiny of Japan."[11] Japanese elites aimed to seize the opportunity offered by the war to revive the "national essence."

Despite comprehensive external pressure, the commitment of civil societies to national defense is best described as self-mobilization. This "defensive acquiescence" in both military engagement and social mobilization was made possible by the force and durability of nation-building in the decades before.[12] Long before the war, nation-states had been endowed with

8 Hew Strachan, *The First World War*, Vol. I: *To Arms* (Oxford, 2001).

9 Christophe Prochasson and Anne Rasmussen, *Au nom de la Patrie: Les Intellectuels et la Première Guerre mondiale (1910–1919)* (Paris, 1996); Martha Hanna, *The Mobilization of Intellect: French Scholars and Writers during the Great War* (Cambridge, MA, and London, 1996).

10 Alfred Zimmern, "German Culture and the British Commonwealth," in R. W. Seton-Watson et al., *The War and Democracy* (London, 1915), 348.

11 Frederick Dickinson, *War and National Reinvention: Japan in the Great War, 1914–1919* (Cambridge, MA, 1999), 239.

12 Stéphane Audoin-Rouzeau and Annette Becker, "Violence et consentement: La 'Culture de guerre' du premier conflit mondial," in Jean-Pierre Rioux and Jean-François Sirinelli, eds., *Pour une histoire culturelle* (Paris, 1997), 112.

"immense positive expectations," which reinforced nationalist sentiments in the language and images of the sacred.[13] The enemy was therefore seen as a threat to one's own culture, identity, and way of life. The struggle was for life and death. The supporting narrative was constantly reconfigured to commit social identities to the war effort. The dynamics of wartime representations reflected the social history of each belligerent society and produced a diversity of war cultures to sustain the mobilization of the home fronts. The defense of the nation was commonly articulated in communitarian terms, in the language of local, class, or religious solidarity.[14] This war of national defense was construed as a battle for the safety of family and home. Thus the conventional, mundane nature of national sentiment accounted for much of its resilience in the face of industrial warfare.

Defensive nationalism also stood at the core of cultural mobilization during World War II. While propaganda played a role in shaping peoples' understanding of the conflict, nations "drew heavily upon the reserves of traditional belief."[15] Public opinion again echoed political leadership; the nation's strategic imperatives required military action. In countries like France, where the population had struggled to deal with the upheaval and losses of World War I, Nazi aggression simplified things. In contrast, the nationalization of the Italian masses remained incomplete. Mussolini's wavering and late commitment to the conflict did nothing to consolidate national sentiment, which was weakened, despite Fascism, by the persistence of regional identities.[16] National grievances over the "mutilated victory" in World War I had not convinced the country of the case for war in 1940.[17]

The Soviet Union provided a clearer example of the force of defensive nationalism. Based on the principles of international proletarian solidarity, the Soviet state had striven to redefine the political culture of its constituent

13 Jay M. Winter, "Propaganda and the Mobilization of Consent," in *The Oxford Illustrated History of the First World War* (Oxford, 1998), 218.

14 Pierre Purseigle, "Beyond and Below the Nations: Towards a Comparative History of Local Communities at War," in Jenny Macleod and Pierre Purseigle, eds., *Uncovered Fields: Perspectives in First World War Studies* (Boston and Leiden, 2004), 95–123; Stefan Goebel, "Forging the Industrial Home Front in Germany: Iron-Nail Memorials in the Ruhr," in ibid., 159–78; Roger Chickering, *The Great War and Urban Life in Germany: Freiburg, 1914–1918* (Cambridge, 2007), 364–65; Pierre Purseigle, *Mobilisation, sacrifice, et citoyenneté: Angleterre and France, 1914–1918* (Paris, Forthcoming).

15 Raymond Aron, *The Century of Total War* (Lanham, MD, 1985), 84; Jay M. Winter, *Sites of Memory, Sites of Mourning: The Great War in European Cultural History* (Cambridge, 1995).

16 Toby Abse, "Italy," in Jeremy Noakes, ed., *The Civilian in War: The Home Front in Europe, Japan and the USA in World War II* (Exeter, 1992), 104–25.

17 Gerhard L. Weinberg, *A World at Arms: A Global History of World War II* (Cambridge, 2005), 484.

republics through political education, propaganda, and coercion. Yet, in the face of the German invasion, whose success promised enslavement, the population of the USSR rallied behind the state. This was a "Great Patriotic War." The defense of the fatherland not only featured in governmental propaganda but also synergized with the population's feeling.[18] In a country in which the state had done little to endear itself to its citizens, national sentiment sustained the mobilization of Soviet society. Its capacity to withstand the shocks of total war rested on the personal and collective commitment of citizens to accepting the requirements of war and, most importantly, to enduring the terrible deprivations that it entailed.

In this respect, the Allies enjoyed an advantage over the Axis powers. While all belligerents resorted to propaganda and the control of information in order to impose their views of the conflicts, the aggressive policies of the Nazis and their allies narrowed the field of options available to the Allied populations and allowed their governments to take the moral high ground, facilitating the mobilization of cultural and political resources. As Richard Overy has put it, this moral dimension of warfare is "inseparable from any understanding of the outcome."

> Allied populations were sustained by the simple morality of defending themselves against unprovoked assault; Axis populations knew in their hearts that they had been led into campaigns of violence which the rest of the world deplored.[19]

In both conflicts, war cultures were grounded in the moral superiority that each camp claimed to embody. The ethics of mobilization helped define and regulate social relations within the belligerent societies. Here, too, the cultural dynamic of mobilization reflected the transformation of warfare. The totalizing logic of the two world wars generated norms of wartime social life. The mobilization of the home fronts thus bred new divisions, new social categories, within the belligerent citizenry, whose positions were defined by duty and the wartime "social relations of sacrifice."[20] The front-line soldier stood out as the role model in a wartime narrative that prescribed civilian comportment in the light of duty, sacrifice, and solidarity. The material comfort of home-front populations was expected to become a casualty of the war, deprivation a gesture of solidarity with front-line soldiers. Material

18 John Barber and Mark Harrison, *The Soviet Home Front, 1941–1945: A Social and Economic History of the USSR in World War II* (London and New York, 1991), 68–73.
19 Richard Overy, *Why the Allies Won* (London, 2006), 28.
20 Jay Winter and Jean-Louis Robert, eds., *Capital Cities at War: Paris, London, Berlin, 1914–1919* (2 vols., Cambridge, 1997–2007), Vol. I: 10.

deprivation also compounded military losses to foster a growing sense of victimization on the home front. The dialectical interaction of victimization and participation thus structured the perceptions and behavioral patterns that determined the level and forms of social mobilization.[21]

As the wars dragged on, a series of distinct "characters," dominated by the towering figure of the soldier-in-arms, came to embody the ethic of mobilization, creating a "language" of social morality – a sense of what was "fair" or "unjust," acceptable or unacceptable – that regulated "relations between social actors."[22] The munitions worker, the nurse, the shirker, to name but a few, presented additional distinctive figures of mobilization, positive or negative depending on their levels of participation in the war effort. In both conflicts and across the belligerent societies, one figure, the "profiteer," became a paradigm. Suspicions were first likely to attach to those who had been spared from military service. Even in countries where conscription was in place, men whose age or physical fitness prevented them from serving at the front were not always immune from recriminations about their lack of patriotism. As women's contributions to the war effort challenged conventional gendered definitions of patriotic service, the demands of mobilization bore heavily on all sections of society.[23]

Alongside military service, the issue of fair access to foodstuffs and other material resources bred accusations of profiteering. The unequal distribution of food, coal, petrol, and other vital goods – which was often compounded by forced or planned internal migrations – put national solidarity to the test. In many cases, the relations between urban dwellers and rural populations exacerbated these tensions as soon as access to foodstuffs became problematic.[24] Aerial bombardment of home-front populations in World War II contributed further to "resentment at what looked like an unequal sharing of burdens."[25]

The radicalization of warfare accompanied the radicalization of war cultures. This development was rooted in World War I. The hatred of the enemy already loomed large in representations of the war, and it encouraged the cultural and moral commitment of each nation to fight until the capitulation of

21 Pierre Purseigle, "'A Wave onto Our Shores': Exile and Resettlement of Western Front Refugees, 1914–1918," *Contemporary European History* 16 (2007): 427–44.

22 John Horne, "Social Identity in War: France, 1914–1918," in Horne, ed., *Men, Women and War* (Dublin, 1993), 119–35.

23 Janet S. K. Watson, *Fighting Different Wars: Experience, Memory, and the First World War in Britain* (Cambridge, 2004).

24 Jill Stephenson, *Hitler's Home Front: Württemberg under the Nazis* (London and New York, 2006), 205.

25 Weinberg, *World at Arms*, 480.

21. Women workers in British munitions factory

the enemy, who was depicted as uncivilized, if not inhuman.[26] Even in liberal democratic societies like France and Britain, war cultures focused on the evil of the enemy, the "Boche" or the "Hun."[27] In this way, the geopolitical tensions that the belligerents' leadership had set out to resolve through war were naturalized and made more intractable, since a moderate settlement would compromise civilization itself. By 1918, however, the survival of civility itself was in doubt.[28]

Cultural historians of World War I have built on George L. Mosse's concept of "brutalization" to stress the centrality of violence in the belligerent societies, although no straightforward link has been demonstrated between the experience of war and the brutalization of politics.[29] Nonetheless, in addressing how

26 Stéphane Audoin-Rouzeau and Annette Becker, *14–18: Retrouver la guerre* (Paris, 2000).

27 Michael Jeismann, *La Patrie de l'ennemi: La notion d'ennemi national et la représentation de la nation en Allemagne et en France de 1792 à 1918* (Paris, 1992), 301.

28 Olivier Compagnon, "1914–18: The Death Throes of Civilization: The Elites of Latin America Face the Great War," in Macleod and Purseigle, eds., *Uncovered Fields*, 279–95.

29 George Mosse, *Fallen Soldiers: Reshaping the Memory of the World Wars* (New York and Oxford, 1990); cf. Antoine Prost, "The Impact of War on French and German Political Cultures," *Historical Journal* 37 (1994): 209–17; Jon Lawrence, "Forging a Peaceable Kingdom: War, Violence, and Fear of Brutalization in Post–First World War Britain," *Journal of Modern History* 75 (2003): 557–89.

the war continued in the minds of former belligerents, Mosse opened up an area of research that is now being explored in light of cultural demobilizations in interwar Europe.[30] The political culture developed by French veterans of World War I rested on an ambivalent combination of patriotism and pacifism.[31] Recent studies of transnational counterrevolutionary networks in central Europe have also shed light on the links between the war and the subsequent brutalization of politics. The legacy of defeat and revolution mobilized veterans, as well as younger men with no direct experience of combat, to fight in the streets of Germany, Austria, and Hungary against Bolsheviks, Jews, and feminists.[32]

To these fighters, violence had become a legitimate political instrument, and warfare now stood as their guide to politics.[33] Although the complexity of demobilization across the former belligerent societies sheds doubt on Michael Geyer's sweeping notion of the "habitualization of war," his work rightly highlights the importance of wartime mobilization in interwar politics.[34] World War I had revealed the state's capacity to mobilize resources, irrespective of the outcome of the war.[35] Technological advancements (particularly in air power) and strategic thinking indicated a shift toward mobilization for war as the organizing principle of social life. In his analysis of the Abyssinian war in the mid 1930s, the British strategist and fascist sympathizer J. F. C. Fuller predicted that the next conflict would "be an absolute war in which the political lives of the nations will be staked in a death struggle between two contending ideas"[36]

The means of modern war were becoming the instruments of warfare's totalization, which political movements across the former belligerents

30 John Horne, ed., "Demobilisations culturelles après la Grande Guerre," *14–18 Aujourd'hui, Today–Heute* 5 (2002): 55–70.

31 Antoine Prost, *Les Anciens Combattants et la société française (1914–1939)*, Vol. III (Paris, 1977); Prost, *Republican Identities in War and Peace: Representations of France in the Nineteenth and Twentieth Centuries* (Oxford and New York, 2002).

32 Robert Gerwarth, "The Central European Counter-Revolution: Paramilitary Violence in Germany, Austria and Hungary after the Great War," *Past & Present* 200 (2008): 175–209.

33 Michael Geyer, "The Militarization of Europe, 1914–1945," in John R. Gillis, ed., *The Militarization of the Western World* (New Brunswick and London, 1989), 70.

34 Michael Geyer, "War and the Context of General History in an Age of Total War," *Journal of Military History* 57 (1993): 145–63; Pierre Purseigle, "Warfare and Belligerence: Approaches to the First World War," in Purseigle, ed., *Warfare and Belligerence: Perspectives in First World War Studies* (Boston and Leiden, 2005), 1–37.

35 Geyer, "Militarization," 75.

36 J. F. C. Fuller, *The First of the League Wars: Its Lessons and Omens* (London, 1936) quoted in Strachan, "Total War," 262. Strachan points out, however, that air power was conceived not only as an instrument of terror, but also as a way to impose limits on warfare. Ibid., 268.

advocated with increased urgency. In Japan military-bureaucratic elites triumphed who favored institutional and political change modeled on the Kaiserreich. The language of Japanese imperial expansion took on racial overtones and featured a likely confrontation with the United States.[37] Most significantly, as Louise Young has brilliantly demonstrated, the "total imperialism" that was implemented after 1931 in Manchuria was defined not only by the exploitation of colonial territories but also by the kind of mobilization this exploitation required.[38] The Pacific War also illustrated the role of racial stereotypes in mobilizing a liberal democratic society, such as the United States. Isaiah Berlin, who was then working at the British Embassy in Washington, noted that the American public had reduced the Japanese to a "nameless mass of vermin."[39] Racial tropes were popularized in the American press, which evoked a "war of oriental races against occidental races for the domination of the world."[40]

Despite the differences between the American and Japanese political systems, the language of race offered a powerful way to construe and radicalize war in both countries. Nowhere, however, did the language of race speak more powerfully than in Nazi Germany, where the national community was redefined as a "community of struggle [*Kampfgemeinschaft*]," whose mobilization resulted in the conquest of *Lebensraum* and the elimination of the nation's enemies.[41] Here the regime's biopolitics drove the radicalization of mobilization. During World War I, antisocial behaviour was denounced as antipatriotic, but this war laid the foundations of German policies in World War II, when the Nazi regime designated entire social groups in Germany and the occupied territories for destruction.[42] The "barbarization of warfare"

37 Dickinson, *War and National Reinvention*, 115, 151, 201–02, 235–36; Erez Manela, *The Wilsonian Moment: Self-Determination and the International Origins of Anticolonial Nationalism* (Oxford, 2007).

38 Louise Young, *Japan's Total Empire: Manchuria and the Culture of Wartime Imperialism* (Berkeley, 1999), 13–14, Part II.

39 John Dower, *War without Mercy: Race and Power in the Pacific War* (New York, 1986), 90.

40 Quoted in ibid., 161; Masahiro Yamamoto, *Nanking: Anatomy of an Atrocity* (Westport, CT, 2000), 189, n. 83.

41 Jeremy Noakes, "Hitler and the Nazi State: Leadership, Hierarchy, and Power," in Jane Caplan, ed., *Nazi Germany* (Oxford and New York, 2008), 74; Richard Evans, *The Coming of the Third Reich* (London, 2004), 69–76; Avraham Barkai, *Nazi Economics: Ideology, Theory, and Policy* (New Haven, 1990); Adam Tooze, *The Wages of Destruction: The Making and Breaking of the Nazi Economy* (London and New York, 2006).

42 Vejas Gabriel Liulevicius, *War Land on the Eastern Front: Culture, National Identity, and German Occupation in World War I* (Cambridge, 2000); Donald Bloxham, *The Great Game of Genocide: Imperialism, Nationalism, and the Destruction of the Ottoman Armenians* (Oxford, 2005).

produced its own dynamic of cultural mobilization.[43] While nationalism retained its defensive dimension (as the determination of the German armies demonstrated in the last months of the war), the dehumanization of the enemy was now combined with internal terror.[44] This radicalized mobilization also impinged on the strategic calculations of the Nazi leadership. Even though most German observers underestimated the the USSR's resources and fighting capabilities, the case for invading the country was far from compelling. According to Hitler's racial worldview, however, the Slavic enemy had to be crushed. Ideology trumped operational imperatives.

The system of representations that gave rise to total war also promoted the mobilization of the material resources that industrialization had made available. Like the mobilization of ideas, the mobilization of wealth revealed the nature of both conflicts and invites reflection on the relationship between the totality and the modernity of warfare in the twentieth century. As war redefined social relations, it reconfigured the economic priorities. The industrialization of warfare also redefined the nature of victory, because the outcome on the battlefield depended on the productive apparatus of the home front. As a result, one question has come to dominate the historiography of the war economies. Was the outcome of both wars determined alone by the balance of material resources and productive capacities?[45]

The answer is negative.[46] While it was critical, the advantage conferred by American economic production provides only a partial explanation for the victories of the Allies in the two world wars. These wars affected belligerent economies in two ways. First, they disrupted essential economic processes. Production suffered; supply was adversely affected by the mobilization of men, which created a range of shortages, by the disruption of the activities of states and enterprises alike, by the blocking of trade routes, the impairment of distribution networks, and uncertain consumption. Second, belligerent economies also had to meet the demands of mass armies on the battlefield. Total war was not an external liability; it was the main determinant of the economic life of the home fronts.

Most of the countries that went to war in August 1914 were industrial societies. Industrialization made possible the mobilizing and equipping of

43 Omer Bartov, *The Eastern Front, 1941–1945: German Troops and the Barbarization of Warfare* (Basingstoke, 1985).

44 Strachan, "Total War," 266.

45 Cited in Mark Harrison, "Resource Mobilization for World War II: The USA, UK, USSR, and Germany, 1938–1945," *Economic History Review* 41 (1988): 171.

46 This is the central thesis of Overy, *Why the Allies Won*.

military forces of unprecedented size. Industrialized warfare also created its own pressures. The armies of 1914 had to be supported by dense logistical networks. Anchored by railways, well-developed supply lines allowed armies to survive without exhausting the resources of the land on which they were fighting. Because it also required technological and scientific know-how, as well as organizational skills, mobilization meant a swift and profound, if temporary, transformation of national economies. Total war was indeed "the largest enterprise hitherto known to man, which had to be consciously organized and managed" and could only be pursued by highly specialized industrialized societies.[47]

The transformation of the French armament industry during World War I revealed the challenges faced by businesses and government. At the outbreak of the conflict, France produced ten to twelve thousand shells a day; by 1918, this figure stood at two hundred thousand.[48] Military mobilization initially deprived the war industries of their most-needed workers. By January 1916, however, the metallurgical sector had returned to prewar levels of employment. The mobilization of women, young people, and foreigners, as well as POWs and colonial subjects, placed 1.7 million workers at the service of the French armaments industry in 1918.[49] In June 1941, the Soviet economy was producing 230 tanks, 700 military aircraft, 4,000 guns and mortars, 100,000 rifles, and more than a million shells every month, while 7.5 million Soviet citizens, 10 percent of the working population, were serving in uniform. A year later, the Soviet economy moved to full mobilization.[50] The "storm of steel" that Ernst Jünger wistfully evoked in his reminiscences of World War I had first gathered in the home-front factories.[51]

Military and economic mobilization differed during the two wars because of prewar preparations. In 1914 governments expected the disruption to industry to be minimal. The realities of war soon convinced them and business leaders that "business as usual" was no adequate response to the situation. The surprise that greeted the acceleration of the diplomatic crisis in July and August 1914 betrayed a critical lack of economic preparation. The economic response to the war was therefore determined by the degree of

47 Eric Hobsbawm, *The Age of Extremes: A History of the World, 1914–1991* (New York, 1994), 44.

48 Ibid., 45.

49 Pierre-Cyrille Hautcoeur, "Was the Great War a Watershed? The Economics of World War I in France," in Stephen Broadberry and Mark Harrison, eds., *The Economics of World War I* (Cambridge, 2009), 174–75.

50 Barber and Harrison, *Soviet Home Front*, 17, 153, 215.

51 Weinberg, *World at Arms*, 489.

industrialization and the sophistication of the productive apparatus in each belligerent country. World War I also brought a challenge to economies that remained largely dependent on agriculture. Russia, Italy, Austria-Hungary, and the Ottoman Empire found it difficult to mobilize their economies and societies.[52] As political intervention, including rationing, further disrupted the situation, rural communities tended to revert to a subsistence economy, to the detriment of the urban populations, while richer, industrialized countries could support higher agricultural prices.

Economic mobilization in World War II was largely determined by strategic choices and rearmament policies that preceded the declarations of war. During the interwar period the former belligerents reflected on the lessons of the previous conflict. But their economic preparations were also a function of attitudes toward war in the interwar period itself. For this reason preparations were extensive in Germany, much less so in the United Kingdom, and almost nonexistent in the United States. The economics of mobilization belied the notion of a general militarization of interwar Europe. In France and Britain, defense expenditures decreased until the mid 1930s. At no point between 1918 and 1938 did they match their pre-1914 levels. The same pattern marked the numbers of military personnel. Britain's "ten-year rule" stipulated that financial planning exclude the possibility of a major war over this period of time. This rule was renewed annually until 1936, when Japan and Germany were identified as potential strategic threats.[53] Until this time, however, as Mark Harrison has put it, "the fears of financial instability still exceeded the fear of external aggression."[54]

By contrast, the USSR prepared for war. In 1940, 20 percent of its national income was devoted to national defense.[55] However, Soviet strategic planners had not yet defined the kind of conflict that they expected to face (see Chapter 14). The absence of clear strategic options translated into unfocused and costly preparations. Although the Spanish Civil War had revealed the mediocre quality of Soviet equipment and munitions, spurring a new effort, Soviet rearmament was hampered by the low productivity of the economy. Defense output had nonetheless doubled and Red Army force levels tripled by 1940.

While his rivals were hoping for the continuation of peace, Hitler was committed to an imminent conflict, as Germany's preparations showed. Germany's strategic choices defied the country's material inferiority to a

52 Peter Gatrell, "Poor Russia, Poor Show: Mobilising a Backward Economy for War, 1914–1917," in Broadberry and Harrison, eds., *Economics of World War I*, 256–57.

53 Peter Clarke, *Hope and Glory: Britain 1900–1990* (London, 1996), 136.

54 Harrison, "Resource Mobilization," 174.

55 Ibid.

western coalition. The success of blitzkrieg prevented Germany's enemies in the west from mobilizing their greater resources, but the invasion of the Soviet Union revealed that Hitler's strategic choices had grown out of the Nazi obsession with *Lebensraum*.[56] Germany had been dependent on the Soviet Union for raw materials, fuel, and food, so the first consequence of the invasion was to block this source of supply. Once they declared war, the Allies opted to maximize their economic superiority and to provide their armed forces with weapons of higher quality. Despite the intensification of its own effort and its support of Japan, Germany could not plug the resources gap; in fact, its brutal policies of conquest and occupation drew resources away from the military effort.

In both world wars, the material balance favored Germany's opponents and was critical to the mobilization of the home fronts and the outcome of both conflicts. However, the ratio of resources does not fully account for the wars' outcomes. Another critical factor was the way in which the belligerent countries balanced – with varying degrees of success – the demands of the armed forces and the civilian economies.

The financing of World War I highlighted the tensions, as well as compromises that were necessary. In 1914, the fiscal structure of the belligerent states remained rudimentary, and taxation raised only a minor portion of the revenue needed to finance the war effort. As a result, war finances depended on borrowing, in particular domestic borrowing, which accounted for over 70 percent of the belligerents' wartime revenue. The success of this effort documented the continued civilian support for the war, because victory in the field was necessary to repay the borrowed money. If civilians altered their consumption to help finance the war, they did so as well in response to inflationary pressures that were generated by the costs of war and governments' monetary policies. Prices doubled in Britain, France, and Germany; they had multiplied three- to fourfold in Russia and sixfold in Austria-Hungary by the end of 1916. Inflation encouraged both lending and borrowing, as businesses and consumers responded to the movement of prices.[57]

More significantly, inflation threatened civilian living standards and, as a result, the resilience of home-front morale. Across the belligerent nations, the organized working class managed to maintain and, in some cases, improve its purchasing power, as industrial mobilization increased its bargaining position.

56 Alan Milward, *The German Economy at War* (London: Athlone Press, 1965), 1–28.
57 Theo Balderston, "Industrial Mobilization and War Economies," in Horne, ed., *Companion to the First World War*, 223–34.

A significant section of the middle classes suffered disproportionately from inflation, as their fixed incomes could not keep pace, while governments controlled rents and other middle-class sources of revenue. In Britain, rationing was not established until 1918, but the evolution of prices, wages, nutritional practices, and health policy brought a noticeable improvement in living conditions and life expectancy.[58] In this respect, the contrast was stark between France and Britain on the one hand, and the Central Powers on the other. Although the rationing of bread was introduced in January 1915, living standards in Germany were soon undermined by inflation and shortages. Although the German people did not starve, their diets were dramatically affected, as hunger soon became the defining feature of civilian hardship.[59] The incapacity of the state to feed the population or to regulate supply and consumption during the infamous "turnip winter" of 1916–17 threatened Germany's social compact and war effort.[60] In Petrograd in 1917, hunger fed revolution.

The significance of inflation and food shortages did not escape governments that were anxious to maintain morale during World War II. They paid particular attention to food consumption. Scarred by the experience of interwar inflation as well, policymakers tried to control this apparently inevitable feature of wartime economies. In this respect at least, Germany did well. Taking 1936 as the base (100), retail prices reached only 113 in 1944. However, as Jeremy Noakes has pointed out, civilian consumption was a better indicator of the "extent of the sacrifices made by the populations." On this measure, the difficulties of both Germany and Japan were apparent. Compared to prewar levels, civilian consumption fell in these countries respectively by 24 and 31 percent; by contrast, it fell by only 16 percent in Britain, and it rose by an equal percentage in the United States.[61]

Labor shortages strengthened the economic position of women during both wars. In the face of sexual prejudices and the opposition of trade unions, which feared dilution, women compensated for the conscription of male workers. In France, the proportion of women in the workforce rose from 32 percent in 1914 to 40 percent in 1918; in Britain, it rose from 26 to 36 percent.[62] In World War II the proportion of women in the workforce also increased significantly – by

58 Jay M. Winter, *The Great War and the British People* (London, 2003), 280.

59 Avner Offer, *The First World War: An Agrarian Interpretation* (Oxford, 1989), 45–53.

60 Roger Chickering, *Imperial Germany and the Great War, 1914–1918* (Cambridge, 1998), 146.

61 Noakes, *The Civilian in War*, 4–5.

62 Margaret Darrow, *French Women and the First World War: War Stories of the Home Front* (Oxford, 2000), 185; Gail Braybon, *Women Workers in the First World War: The British Experience* (London, 1981).

32 percent in the United States; in Soviet Russia, it rose from 38 percent in 1940 to 53 percent in 1942.[63] Although the fascist regimes were more reluctant to mobilize them, women made up 51 percent of the German civilian workforce in 1944. Ideologically committed to the exploitation of conquered territories and populations that were deemed racially inferior, both Nazi Germany and Imperial Japan relied on foreign workers. In Germany, they made up almost 20 percent of the workforce in 1944 (up from 11.7 percent in 1942), while Japan employed 1.4 million Korean workers in July 1945.[64] Providing labor to industry was the central balancing act in the economic mobilization for total war. Governments walked a tortuous path between insufficient and excessive commitment of labor to the war. The economics of modern warfare imposed material limitations on mobilization for total war. In this respect the mobilization of Nazi Germany was "ultimately unsustainable."[65]

In both world wars, the mobilization of home fronts reflected the strategic positions of the belligerents – in particular their access to global markets for raw materials, capital, and labour. Strategic and economic imperatives turned World War I of 1914 into a global conflict.[66] The advantages that Britain derived from global empire and naval predominance illustrated this truth. British shipping had placed the United Kingdom at the heart of the global economy and offered the country access to most trade routes, control of which was critical in both world wars. Belligerents also competed for access to international financial markets.[67] Here again, Britain had a great advantage, thanks to its favored position on the American financial market. Britain's access to US credit not only financed its war effort, but also allowed the country to support the rest of the Entente.

Global trade also afforded access to new sources of food during World War I. Western European belligerents made up for their dependence on food imports with external supplies. In this respect, the German situation underlined the significance of access to overseas markets. For all the country's military strength before the war, German agriculture suffered from the Allied blockade, which restricted access to critical inputs like fertilizers and fodder. Price controls, requisitions, and the regulation of production by the government failed to

63 Weinberg, *World at Arms*, 496.

64 Noakes, *The Civilian in War*, 3; Jeremy Noakes, "Germany," in *The Civilian in War*, 39, 42.

65 Harrison, "Resource Mobilization," 187.

66 Hew Strachan, "The First World War as a Global War," *First World War Studies* 1 (2010): 3–14.

67 The best synthetic treatment of the financing of World War I is to be found in Hew Strachan, *The First World War: To Arms* (Oxford, 2001), ch. 10.

22. Shipyard in Britain

provide the relief needed and expected by the population. The exploitation of conquered territories like the Ukraine also failed to bring the expected relief to the food supply.[68] Agricultural output also fell in France, not only because men had been mobilized, but also because northeastern France was occupied or devastated. Yet France's strategic alliances allowed the country privileged access to the international markets. In 1916, 43 percent of the wheat consumed by the French population was imported.[69]

68 Albrecht Ritschl, "The Pity of Peace: Germany's Economy at War, 1914–1918 and Beyond," in Broadberry and Harrison, *Economics of World War I*, 57–59.

69 Balderston, "Industrial Mobilization and War Economies," 228.

Coalition warfare allowed belligerents not only to extend their commercial networks but also to pool their resources, to contribute to one another's war effort. In this respect, the Entente was again at an advantage. Forty percent of the shells used by the Russian army were imported. While France relied on British and American steel to sustain industrial mobilization, the country was the Entente's largest arms producer, and it equipped the American Expeditionary Force for battle in 1918. Forty percent of Britain's munitions came from the United States. The Allied blockade meant that while Germany, Austria-Hungary, and Russia depended on domestic or conquered resources to meet the demands of industrial warfare, Britain and France could rely on imports to make up for their domestic limitations. The United States' entry into the war and its formal commitment to the Entente's cause spurred a reorganization of the alliance's economic warfare. The coordination of allied purchases, which had been previously overseen by a private agent, J. P. Morgan, now fell to inter-governmental agencies like the Inter-Allied Control Boards. More than the United States' direct military contribution, the financial dimension was decisive. Keen to rationalize a bidding process that limited competition and therefore contributed to inflation, the United States encouraged cooperative purchases. As Hew Strachan has remarked, "by 1917–18 the alliance was the most powerful economic bloc in the world's commodity markets, and its ordering created what were virtually global monopolies in the purchasing of major foodstuffs."[70]

The globalized nature of warfare and the importance of combined resources were even more evident during World War II. The balance of resources was neither fixed nor stable, but with the exception of the United States, all belligerent economies were externally dependent. The annexationist strategy of the Axis demanded the coercive exploitation of conquered territories and populations. This strategy was predicated on the Axis states' ability to utilize fully the productive capacity of these regions. It also assumed that the Allies would fail to mobilize their domestic resources effectively. Both assumptions were wrong.[71] Still, Germany's income rose as the country's armies extended their reach across Europe. In 1942–43, resources from outside the Reich accounted for a sixth of German national income. Britain and Russia also relied on external support. In 1943, a quarter of the supplies of the Russian aircraft industries were imported; in the same year, two-thirds of British tanks were produced overseas, and by 1944, the Lend-Lease agreement with the

70 Strachan, *First World War*, 222.

71 Mark Harrison, "The Economics of World War II: An Overview," in Mark Harrison, ed., *The Economics of World War II: Six Great Powers in International Comparison* (Cambridge, 1998), 6.

United States had accounted for 40 percent of Britain's armaments. By the end of 1941, Britain had received 5,012 aircraft from the United States; by contrast, German conquest had yielded seventy-eight planes from France and the Netherlands.[72]

The German and Japanese imperial projects were both founded on a racial understanding of politics and society. The underlying ideologies justified mobilizing resources by military expansion. These ideologies radicalized conventional imperial practices, turned colonial extraction into racial exploitation, and conflated the economic and racial challenges posed by the United States' emergence on the global stage. The exploitation of POWs and foreign workers denoted a dramatic shift in emphasis from World War I. The domestic economy of Nazi Germany relied on 7.5 million forced laborers, whose contribution allowed the Third Reich to limit the industrial mobilization of German women. From 1942 onwards, the exploitation of Russian and Polish prisoners and civilians freed German men to fight on the eastern front. The omnipresence of slave workers on the German home front also signaled the new racial order, which the war was meant to establish across Europe. Different degrees of mistreatment and violence testified to the hierarchical nature of this New Order. Europe's material and human resources were to be exploited for the aggrandizement of Nazi Germany. Japan also resorted to forced labor, while the Soviet dictatorship exploited 4.3 million German and Japanese prisoners of war.[73] Forced labor, which was based on ideas of racial inequality, embodied the conflation of culture and economics in total war.

In both conflicts, the Allies' material advantage was supported by greater integration into international markets. Yet the experience of World War II invites two qualifications. The British experience during this conflict suggested that the success of mobilization did not rest alone on size and scale. Britain's highly sophisticated industrialized economy compensated for the country's small size and dependence on international markets; and Britain achieved efficient mobilization of relatively limited resources. The degree of economic development mattered a great deal. The Allied coalition was able to coordinate the efforts of its members to play to their collective strengths and to mitigate their weaknesses. The British economy teamed with the large but less-developed Soviet economy, thanks to the material, financial, and technological support that both received from the United States. Interallied

72 Weinberg, *World at Arms*, 490; Harrison, "Resource Mobilization," 189; Tooze, *Wages*, 410.
73 Harrison, "Resource Mobilization," 190; Weinberg, *World at Arms*, 475–78.

cooperation underlined the critical link between the politics of coalition warfare and the economics of total war.

The politics of the belligerent states were integral to economic mobilization. States entered into new relationships with businesses and civil society in order to meet the challenges of industrial warfare. In August 1914 many commentators doubted that the liberal democratic states could mobilize their economies effectively. In World War II, the uncontested authority that was claimed, if not always enjoyed, by authoritarian states was often thought to be key to economic mobilization. Nazi Germany and Soviet Russia, both of which had placed the command of the economy at the heart of their political projects, were thus considered to be better suited to industrial warfare than their liberal counterparts. In both world wars, however, liberal democratic regimes proved equal to mobilizing their resources while maintaining the living standards of civilian populations. Liberalism harnessed the techniques of business management as well as the tools of the state to meet the demands of total war.

The mobilization of resources pitted national bureaucracies as well as armies against one another. Fabienne Bock has observed of World War I that the wartime state was distinguished by its exuberance.[74] To a degree, however, the observation mischaracterizes the nature of the wartime relationship between the state and economic agents, for the experience of both world wars emphasized the limitations of the state, even as it demonstrated the state's capacity to steer the economy for national defense. Both wars gave rise to new forms of cooperation among the state, businesses, and civic organizations, as they "engendered new forms of corporatist cooperation between civil servant and businessman."[75]

The guises of this cooperation were determined in part by political and business cultures. Cooperation or innovation was not the preserve of liberal democratic regimes alone. In both world wars, the German leadership attempted to translate the idea of a national community into economic terms. The role of Walther Rathenau at the helm of the War Raw Materials Office in the summer of 1914 was to guide an effective attempt by the state to combine capitalism and socialism in the interest of mobilization. As the head of AEG (the German General Electric company), Rathenau could build on his

74 Fabienne Bock, "L'Exubérance de l'état en France de 1914 à 1918," *Vingtième Siècle: Revue d'Histoire*, no. 3 (1984): 41–51.

75 Mark Roseman, "War and the People: The Social Impact of Total War," in Charles Townshend, ed., *The Oxford Illustrated History of Modern War* (Oxford and New York, 1997), 250.

business experience in providing for the material needs of the armies; the experience of his French counterpart, Albert Thomas, a socialist who performed a similar role in cooperation with business leaders, mirrored the German experiment.

The war compelled states and markets alike to overcome their own limitations in producing war material. The key to economic mobilization, though, was managerial and organizational effectiveness. State bureaucracies provided the regulatory structures to ensure the coherence of an effort to which the private sector had consented. In Britain, joint-committees ensured that the interests of the armed forces and businesses were served. Communication was essential. For all its wealth, the US economy required central oversight. It came in World War II with the creation of the Office of War Mobilization in May 1943. In the economic realm, as in military affairs, the direction of the war remained the preserve of the state, which exercised its coercive powers with little hesitation. Even in countries that remained committed to economic liberalism, such as the United Kingdom in 1914, the state did not hesitate to impose its control over essential industries, including railways (1914), steel (1916), and coal (1917).

The management of manpower was more problematic. By 1914, conscription was increasingly associated with modern citizenship (see Chapter 5). In the eyes of many Anglophone liberals, conscription still appeared to contradict the liberal case for war.[76] By 1915, however, the demands of mass warfare had exposed the limitations of volunteerism. Despite the political and organizational acumen that had allowed the raising of Kitchener's Armies, Parliament resorted in January 1916 to conscription, which came to symbolize the wartime state's coercive powers. In all the belligerent societies, conscription documented the critical role of coercion in extracting resources (in this case human) for total war. It also emphasized the role of the state's coercive powers in managing the often competing demands of the armed forces and war economies. In both world wars, the state could adjust recruitment policies to reconcile the military and civilian dimensions of the war. The role of the state was therefore to adjudicate as well as to extract, to guarantee that mobilization comported with the social relations of sacrifice

During World War I, France and Germany sought to allocate skilled labor to the military and critical civilian sectors. They also had to address the social tensions generated by perceptions of injustice in a system that seemed to

76 R. J. Q. Adams and Philip Poirier, *The Conscription Controversy in Great Britain, 1900–18* (Basingstoke, 1987).

protect some categories of workers from military service.[77] Laws passed in France in 1915 and 1917 brought industrial workers under the authority of the military, in an effort to address the political and ethical unease aroused by perceptions of unequal sacrifice.[78] Coercion required legitimacy. To maintain it, authorities depended on many partners, the trade unions in particular. In Germany, the Hindenburg Program of August 1916 aimed to intensify industrial mobilization by means of comprehensive state control. The Auxiliary Service Law of December 1916 expanded state control of workers' mobility, but it also increased the trade unions' role in industrial relations.

Wartime taxation was central to the dynamic of state intervention in the economy. Essential to the funding of the war effort, taxation doubled during the war years. The introduction of an income tax marked a defining moment in the fiscal history of many belligerent states. Equally significant was the imposition of a tax on excess profits, which was designed to address ethical as much as financial concerns. Such taxes were also a response to the wartime triangulation of state coercion, business interests, and trade-union pressure, as war rearranged the relations between the state and the market.

During the interwar period the popularity of state planning grew in policy-making circles, not only in Nazi Germany and Soviet Russia, but also in the liberal democracies. However, the experience of the Axis powers and the Stalinist regime, whose political systems hinged on the coercive exercise of state authority, warrants special consideration. For despite their profound differences, these regimes were all predicated on state intervention into social and economic life. Dominant political cultures, state ideologies, and institutional structures reflected this fact, as they extolled the mobilizing capacity of the state. Yet these regimes paradoxically experienced difficulties in harnessing the power of the state to mobilize resources for industrial war. Historians have highlighted the political tensions and administrative inconsistencies that undermined the effective management of the war effort. These "homegrown failures" themselves derived from the political cultures and structures of these countries. In Italy, administrative incompetence was compounded by corruption, while in Japan tensions between the armed forces and their business partners combined with institutional rivalry between the army and navy to undermine mobilization. In Germany tensions between state and the Nazi

77 On the gendered dimensions of such debates, see Nicoletta F. Gullace, "White Feathers and Wounded Men: Female Patriotism and the Memory of the Great War," *Journal of British Studies* 36 (1997): 178–206.

78 John Horne, "'L'impôt du sang': Republican Rhetoric and Industrial Warfare in France, 1914–1918," *Social History* 14 (1989): 201–23.

party, and between the party and the military establishment, also affected the mobilization of industrial and technological resources.

The Nazi regime offered a striking illustration of the paradox of dictatorship. Although it hinged on the person of the *Führer*, who embodied the will of the nation, the regime did not so much concentrate power in Hitler's hands as it built a fragmented political system oriented around him. Administrative chaos was the result, as state and party agencies competed for political and material resources.[79] The internal dynamic of the regime, this "authoritarian anarchy," hindered wartime mobilization.[80] Through its role in the new *Volkssturm*, for example, the Nazi party interfered with the mobilization of manpower. Other party actors, such as the SS (*Schutzstaffel*), expanded into the economic realm, particularly in occupied Europe, setting a collision course not only with conventional economic actors, but also with organs of the state that were responsible for mobilizing and allocating resources. The "polycratic" nature of the Nazi regime allowed the proliferation of agencies at the cost of administrative coherence.[81] The Ministry of Economics, the War Economy Office, and the Office of the Four-Year Plan, as well as twenty-seven other national offices, took part in this process. When in 1942, Albert Speer became minister of armaments and war production (which had been established only in 1940), he set out to centralize the direction of the war effort. By September 1943 he had taken control over most of the economy, except for the management of labor and the equipment of the SS.[82] Speer's effort to rationalize mobilization challenged a division of responsibility that was favored not only by Hitler, but also by party agencies like the SS, as well as the lower ranks of the leadership.

Another part of the problem was ideological. In keeping with the party's ideas about race, Nazi war effort relied to an unsustainable extent on forced labor. When the conscription of domestic labor was forced on the regime in the final year of the war, it was insufficient to reverse the tide. The occupation of western Europe also undermined Germany's capacity to exploit the lands that it had conquered. The agricultural sector in Denmark, the Netherlands, and France suffered from shortages of manpower, fertilizers, and other

79 Ian Kershaw, "'Working towards the Führer': Reflections on the Nature of the Hitler Dictatorship," *Contemporary European History* 2 (1993): 103–18.

80 Walter Petwaidic, *Die autoritäre Anarchie* (Hamburg, 1946).

81 On Nazi "polycracy," see Martin Broszat, *The Hitler State: The Foundation and Development of the Internal Structure of the Third Reich* (London and New York, 1981).

82 Werner Abelshauser, "Germany: Guns, Butter, and Economic Miracles," in Harrison, ed., *Economics of World War II*, 156.

essential resources, so occupying forces were unable to remobilize these economies to their own benefit. Because it was governed by the racial obsessions of the Nazis, exploitation of the fabled *Lebensraum* in the east was as difficult as it was in the western occupied lands.

Nor could the other Axis states overcome limitations imposed by their own political systems. In Italy, Mussolini's management of the war was erratic and misguided, and it led him to promote officials on the basis of their ideological or personal loyalties, not their professional competence. In Japan, which went to war in 1937 in Manchuria, the strains of mobilization were apparent by the time of Pearl Harbor in December 1941. The wartime leadership could not impose its vision on the country's elites. The bureaucracy resisted the attempt to mobilize state and society under the authority of the army and prime minister. Civilian elites prevented the creation of mass organizations under the aegis of the army. General Tōjō never enjoyed the authority of other wartime leaders and had to conduct coalition politics within both the armed forces and the civilian government.[83]

Dictatorships were determined from the start to mobilize states effectively for a global conflict. Yet the example of the Soviet Union demonstrates the danger of hasty generalizations about the relationship between coercion and mobilization. Economic historians of World War II have established the significance of the Soviet economy's transformation, which entailed the relocation, under intense military pressure, of essential industries to Central Asia and the Urals. Here, safe from Hitler's armies, the real "armaments miracle" of World War II occurred.[84] Dictatorship enabled the Soviets to meet the Nazis' challenge. Survival demanded pragmatism, however. Despite the regime's authoritarianism, it accommodated the "individualization of authority and responsibility," which came to characterize its wartime administration. This relative autonomy of action initially promoted the mobilization of local resources. The pace and conditions of mobilization soon created imbalances, however; and major problems emerged at the end of 1941. The transformation of the armament industry was obtained at the expense of the rest of the economy; and it soon threatened mobilization itself. The allocation of raw materials, energy, and manpower proved problematic, as did the housing and food supply. To address these issues, the state had undertaken a "reassertion of bureaucratic order" by the end of 1942, after the centralization

83 Ben-Ami Shillony, *Politics and Culture in Wartime Japan* (Oxford and New York, 1981).
84 Tooze, *Wages*, 588.

of management in the Operations Bureau.[85] Political will and coercion in all events resulted in an extraordinary relocation and transformation of the war economy, which allowed the Soviet Union to contribute decisively to the Allied war effort.

The "remarkable revival of Soviet military and economic power" counts among the most dramatic aspects of World War II.[86] As a result, the Soviet Union soon outproduced its enemy and provided its armies with better weapons and equipment. From mid 1941 to mid 1944 "Soviet resources were employed in the cause of Germany's military defeat with far greater intensity than those of the United Kingdom."[87] The capacity of the economy to withstand the strain of war was also due to the resilience of the Soviet population. But there were limits to the intensity of mobilization that belligerents could sustain. While Britain never mobilized more than 50 percent of its wealth for the war effort during World War II, Russia mobilized 61 percent in 1942–43. Although levels of economic development accounted for this difference, neither Britain nor the Soviet Union could strain its economy much further, lest it collapse under the burden. The Soviet case also demonstrated the importance of the balance of forces in each theater of operations. On the eastern front, the opposing forces were closely matched and required the most intense mobilization. Furthermore "it was the nearness of combat conditions, and the blurring of the distinction between the fighting front and the home front, which stimulated national feeling and promoted economic mobilization."[88] Wartime mobilization once again reflected the character of warfare in the first half of the twentieth century.

During both world wars, economic mobilization revealed the importance of productive capacity. The intensity of economic mobilization was constrained, however, by the political issues that it itself raised. The German mobilization in World War I was limited by growing discontent on the home front. Material resources, know-how, and the authority of the state were essential to mobilization, but success and sustainability depended on the ongoing legitimacy of the war effort. The authority of the wartime state required legitimacy for the effective use of coercion. Here lay the fundamental link between the authority of the state and the legitimacy of the war.

It is therefore difficult to disentangle the mechanics of social mobilization from the evolution of public opinion. The nature, scale, and duration of both

85 Harrison, "Resource Mobilization," 178–79.
86 Overy, *Why the Allies Won*, 23.
87 Harrison, "Resource Mobilization," 191.
88 Harrison, "The Economics of World War II," 23.

world wars account for the difficulties that historians have had in charting the evolution of public opinion.[89] John Horne has convincingly suggested three phases of mobilization, which corresponded to three different articulations of state and civil society – self-mobilization, remobilization, and demobilization. Downplaying the conventional emphasis on coercion, Horne stresses that the success of remobilization in 1917–18 depended ultimately on the continuing legitimacy of the state and the war effort.[90]

Psychological mobilization on the home front was a complex and dynamic process. Neither coercion nor ideological enthusiasm accounted for the resilience of populations that constantly renegotiated their contributions to the war effort. Existing political cultures offered the framework for such negotiations, in which the state was only one, albeit the dominant actor among many.[91] The significance of these negotiations was revealed in the mechanisms and institutions that were set up to allocate essential resources, such as manpower. In Britain the Military Service Act of 1916, which established conscription, stipulated the creation of local military service tribunals. Arbitrating between the demands of the military and the interests of local communities, these bodies provided a site where agents of the state raised military manpower despite individual opposition and local economic interests. Representatives of civil society thus adjudicated conflicts that reflected wider debates over the extraction of the means of war-making.[92] These debates highlighted the significance of the constant negotiation in which civil society attempted to limit the claims of the state. Likewise in Germany, the implementation of the Hindenburg Program had to concede the growing importance of organized labor and a "certain parliamentarisation of the German system of government."[93] The key, however, was the "state's ability to secure the consent of key groups in civil society."[94] As General Groener put it in November 1916, "the war could in any case not be won against the opposition of the workers."[95]

89 Pierre Laborie, *Les Français des années troubles: De la Guerre d'Espagne à la Libération* (Paris, 2001).

90 Horne, "Public Opinion and Politics," 289–90.

91 On political cultures as framework for political and social conflicts, see Keith M. Baker, "Introduction," in Baker, ed., *The French Revolution and the Creation of Modern Political Culture* (Oxford and New York, 1987), xi–xxiv.

92 See Charles Tilly, *Coercion, Capital, and European States, AD 990–1990* (Oxford and Cambridge, MA, 1990), 97.

93 Jürgen Kocka, *Facing Total War: German Society, 1914–1918* (Leamington Spa, 1973), 130.

94 James Cronin, "The Crisis of State and Society in Britain, 1917–22," in Leopold H. Haimson and Charles Tilly, eds. *Strikes, Wars, and Revolutions in an International Perspective: Strike Waves in the Late Nineteenth and Early Twentieth Centuries* (Cambridge and Paris, 1989), 459.

95 Kocka, *Facing Total War*, 136.

Policymakers and military leaders nevertheless regularly drew the wrong lessons from World War I. Throughout World War II they remained wary of labor agitation and grass-roots social movements, equating them with opposition to the war effort. In Italy, the privations of war had by 1942 largely undermined the legitimacy of both the conflict and the Fascist regime. American and British bans on wartime strikes likewise failed to stifle social unrest; Britain experienced more strikes during the war than it had in the 1930s. In both countries workers gained concessions and greater access to state authority. The secretary general of the British Transport and General Workers Union, Ernest Bevin, served as minister of labor in the wartime coalition, while the American government exerted pressure on employers to implement social legislation. Both wars thus illustrated how the changing character of warfare contributed to the gradual, if limited empowerment of the citizenry. The war experience reinforced the terms of the social contract to which "citizenship" referred. Popular consent to the war effort came as much through struggle as outspoken support.[96] Even in the Nazi and Soviet dictatorships, coercion did not suppress all discontent; in Germany, party institutions and officials could be blamed, so criticism could be vented without challenging the *Führer*'s rule.

World War I demonstrated the transformative power of total war. It brought down the Russian, German, Austro-Hungarian, and Ottoman empires and brought the birth of nations throughout central and eastern Europe. In Japan the war redefined national identity.[97] Across the belligerent world, from Washington to Beijing, social movements challenged political, social, racial, and gendered hierarchies.[98] In the eyes of protesters, World War I had demonstrated the need to redefine the contours of the nation. Home-front mobilization lay at the heart of the relationship between war and social change.[99] In both world wars, the belligerent states called upon the resources

96 Charles Tilly, "The Emergency of Citizenship in France and Elsewhere," in Tilly, ed., *Citizenship, Identity and Social History* (Cambridge, 1996), 229.

97 Dickinson, *War and National Reinvention*, 81–83, 114–15, 151, 153.

98 Rana Mitter, *A Bitter Revolution: China's Struggle with the Modern World* (New York, 2005); Susan R. Grayzel, "Across Battle Fronts: Gender and the Comparative Cultural History of Modern European War," in Deborah Cohen and Maura O'Connor, eds., *Comparison and History: Europe in Cross-National Perspective* (Abingdon and New York, 2004), 71–84; Jennifer D. Keene, "Protest and Disability: A New Look at African-American Soldiers during the First World War," in Purseigle, ed., *Warfare and Belligerence*, 177–203; Michael Lewis, *Rioters and Citizens: Mass Protest in Imperial Japan* (Berkeley, 1990).

99 One stimulating recent exploration of this question pays little attention to wartime social mobilization: Sandra Halperin, *War and Social Change in Modern Europe: The Great Transformation Revisited* (Cambridge and New York, 2004).

of civil society, which responded in accordance with the terms of the social compact that defined national solidarity. The emergence of welfare states after 1945 represented a continuation of the social negotiation that had defined social mobilization during the war.[100]

In the wake of World War II, Raymond Aron offered a bleak analysis of the retrenchment of liberalism in the age of "total war":

> The citizen puts on a uniform just as he goes to the polling booth. Here and there the equality of individuals, who at law are interchangeable, is respected. But the citizen-soldier is integrated in an immense machine over which he loses all control. Group autonomy, freedom of judgment, the expression of opinion become luxuries which the country in peril finds it difficult to safeguard. Material wealth accumulated during the years of peace is squandered; the privileges which were accorded generously to individuals are economized. Liberal bourgeoisie abdicates; soldiers and organizers rule over the masses. Total mobilization approaches the totalitarian order.[101]

The mobilization and victimization of the home fronts were also the two pillars of what John R. Gillis and others have described as "militarization" – the emergence of warring societies in which the dissolution of the civil–military distinction rendered the meaning of "home front" literal.[102] The idea of militarization suggests a profound change in the nature of the belligerent societies. It understates, however, the significance of the role of civil society in this process. Neither militarization nor victimization captures the complexity of civilian participation in the war effort.

In the face of industrial warfare, belligerent societies were compelled to commit most of their human, material, and cultural resources. Technological developments and operational imperatives underlined the link between the modernization of warfare and the totalizing logic of both conflicts. Yet, as Hew Strachan has pointed out, the ideological foundations of total war lay in the political revolutions of the eighteenth century, and they preceded the invention of the material means of modern war.[103] In the nineteenth century,

100 John Horne, *Labour at War: France and Britain 1914–1918* (Oxford, 1991); José Harris, "War and Social History: Britain and the Home Front during the Second World War," *Contemporary European History* 1 (1992): 17–35.

101 Aron, *Century of Total War*, 88.

102 Gillis, ed., *Militarization*; Michael Geyer, "Gewalt und Gewalterfahrung im 20. Jahrhundert – Der Erste Weltkrieg," in Rolf Spilker and Bernd Ulrich, eds., *Der Tod als Maschinist: Der industrialisierte Krieg, 1914–1918* (Bramsche, 1998), 241–57.

103 Strachan, "Total War," 271; Daniel Moran and Arthur Waldron, eds., *The People in Arms: Military Myth and National Mobilization since the French Revolution* (Cambridge, 2002).

national ideals were translated in military terms by the *levée en masse* and the inexorable association of citizenship and national defense.[104] Enhanced in the twentieth century by the industrial means of warfare, "total war" redefined belligerence. Waged on a global scale, World War II was defined physically by atomic weapons and morally by the Holocaust; it thus undermined the association of modernity and progress. This war affected every aspect of social life. The unprecedented level of military casualties, as well as the demands of the armies in the field, brought the total mobilization of the home front. World War I had already demonstrated that the modern state could achieve an unprecedented degree of social mobilization. World War II proved that the fate of belligerent nations "depended as much on the successful mobilization . . . of the nation as it did on the fighting itself."[105]

The totalizing logic of the two world wars demanded the mobilization of all financial, material, and human resources. Belligerents managed the mobilization of ideas, wealth, and power in accordance with their political systems. Organization, extraction, and exploitation defined the wartime relationship between state and society. The resulting war cultures narrowed the policy options available to leaders of the belligerent states and transformed both conflicts into zero-sum games, in which there could only be winners and losers. Compromise with the enemy became unthinkable. The price of "victory" in most belligerent societies was bankruptcy and physical exhaustion. That these were preferred to defeat reflected collective adaptations to the war effort, which remained nonetheless conditional and contested. Social negotiation on the home front represented an important pendant to the totalization of warfare, and it speaks to the *rapprochement* of the military and social histories of warfare.

104 Michael Howard, "Total War in the Twentieth Century: Participation and Consensus in the Second World War," in *War and Society: A Yearbook of Military History* (London: Croom Helm, 1977), 217. See also Jörn Leonhard, *Bellizismus und Nation: Kriegsdeutung und Nationsbestimmung in Europa und den Vereinigten Staaten 1750–1914* (Munich, 2008).

105 Overy, *Why the Allies Won*, 21.

12

The search for peace in the interwar period

CAROLE FINK

> War has not only escaped direction and control, it involves all civilization and its elimination is a question of practical politics.[1]
>
> It wasn't worth it.[2]

World War I ended on an ominous note, with divided victors, unrepentant losers, and a shattered global economy. After unprecedented military and civilian casualties and huge physical destructiveness – followed by brutal armed conflicts in eastern Europe, the Near East, and Northern Asia – history's first total war came to an official end almost a decade after the shots in Sarajevo. Throughout the war anguished combatants and neutrals had made proposals to prevent future explosions of violence, and they expected a more peaceful world to emerge. The length, ferocity, and inconclusive outcome of World War I guaranteed, however, that the quest for a permanent peace would be arduous.

Ultimately, it was also unsuccessful. There is now a scholarly consensus that its failure was due to the punitive peace treaties, the victors' unwillingness or inability to enforce or revise these documents in the 1920s, and their craven surrender to aggressive states in the 1930s.[3] Underlying this failure were the postwar national realities: Germany's drive to regain world power, France's futile efforts to maintain a costly victory, imperial Britain's obsession with maintaining a power balance in Europe, the United States' withdrawal from the obligations of treaty enforcement, the Soviet Union's destabilizing influence, Fascist Italy's adventurism, disunity in the new east-central and southern

1 James T. Shotwell, "Plans and Protocols to End War," *International Conciliation*, No. 208 (March 1925): 7.

2 Harry Patch (last British Army Veteran of World War I) statement in 2007, quoted in *New York Times* obituary, July 26, 2009, 21.

3 This consensus spans the work of A. J. P. Taylor, *The Origins of the Second World* War (2nd edn., Greenwich, CT, 1967) to Zara Steiner, *The Lights that Failed: European International History, 1919–1933* (Oxford, 2005).

Europe, and the increasingly volatile non-western world. With a massive supply of diplomatic and political records, scholars have now examined the goals and methods of statesmen, private figures, and organizations that spoke in the name of peace but failed to forge a durable order. Scholars have also investigated the alliances that were more provocative than effective, the role of ideology in international affairs, the procession of abortive international conferences, and the putative turning points (such as Locarno, Manchuria, and the Rhineland occupation). They have painted a full, if grim picture of what became a "twenty-year truce."[4]

Another way of examining the interwar period has been to study the impact of peace ideas, movements, and initiatives. At the center of this discussion is the work of the newborn League of Nations, which, despite its limited membership and power, made significant attempts to achieve international collaboration and arbitration, collective security, and disarmament.[5] In the League lay the hopes of the small states and many pacifists, who sought a new means to conduct international politics based on justice, equality, and democracy. This organization failed, however, to inspire the great powers to apply concerted, consistent measures toward rebuilding a war-torn world and securing an enduring peace.[6]

Most scholars acknowledge that the treaties that were signed with Germany (June 28, 1919), Austria (September 10, 1919), Bulgaria (November 27, 1919), and Hungary (June 4, 1920) were punitive settlements, dictated by the victors. So was the Treaty of Riga (March 18, 1921) between Poland and the new Soviet Union. The sole exception was the Lausanne agreement between the Allies and Turkey (July 24, 1923), which replaced the treaty of Sèvres with a negotiated settlement.[7]

To be sure, losers rarely accept the terms of defeat. After it had achieved an overwhelming victory in the east in March 1918 and then launched a major offensive in the west, only to sue seven months later for an armistice based on Woodrow Wilson's opaque Fourteen Points, Germany was unprepared for the tough terms of the Versailles treaty. These stipulated the loss of 10 percent

4 See especially Sally Marks, *The Illusion of Peace: International Relations in Europe, 1918–1933* (2nd edn., New York, 2003); Andrew J. Crozier, *The Causes of the Second World War* (Oxford, 1997).

5 Susan Pederson, "Back to the League of Nations," *American Historical Review* 112 (2007): 1091–117.

6 F. Walters, *History of the League of Nations* (London, 1960); F. S. Northedge, *The League of Nations: Its Life and Times, 1920–1946* (Leicester, 1986).

7 Alan Sharp, *The Versailles Settlement: Peacemaking after the First World War, 1919–1923* (2nd edn., Basingstoke, 2008) is brief, thorough, and balanced.

of Germany's population, 13 percent of its territory, a million square miles of its colonial possessions, an unspecified sum of reparations, and its unilateral disarmament.[8] Born in collapse and revolution, the new Weimar Republic inherited the burden of undoing Versailles.[9]

Soviet Russia, another defeated state, lost 15.4 percent of its European territory and 23.3 percent of its prewar population. After barely surviving civil wars and foreign intervention, it faced in 1922 a still hostile west and a *cordon sanitaire* of east European buffer states, which had been created or enlarged from former tsarist territories. Consequently, to mask its enormous losses, the Soviet government pursued a dual-track diplomacy of old-fashioned Realpolitik combined with the machinations of the new Communist International.[10] Kemalist Turkey, on the other hand, which had profited from its postwar military success and Allied disunity, now entered a period of national consolidation and international seclusion.[11]

The most volatile element in the peace settlement was the region between Berlin and Moscow, which had been created more by arms than diplomacy. Reborn Poland, the new Finland, Estonia, Latvia, Lithuania, Czechoslovakia, and Yugoslavia, the greatly enlarged Greece and Romania, as well as the heavily reduced Austria, Hungary, and Bulgaria all emerged from World War I with border conflicts, minority problems, and severe economic difficulties, which were caused both by wartime disruption and by the erection of postwar barriers to trade, transportation, and investment. Heavily militarized, nationalistic, and anti-communist – and fiercely opposed to any form of post-imperial federation – east-central and southern Europe lay vulnerable to German and Soviet irredentism, Allied neglect, and its own disunity.[12]

The overseas provisions of the treaties also planted the seeds of unrest. At almost the start of their deliberations, the victors divided Germany's former

8 The victors had restricted the Reich's army to a hundred thousand long-term volunteers and its navy to fifteen thousand men, and banned a general staff, air force, and offensive weapons. It also turned the Saar coal mines over to France, ordained the permanent demilitarization of the Rhineland and a fifteen-year Allied occupation, demanded the trial of war criminals, and excluded Germany from the League of Nations.

9 Peter Krüger, *Versailles: Deutsche Aussenpolitik zwischen Revisionismus und Friedenssicherung* (Munich, 1986).

10 Jon Jacobson, *When the Soviet Union Entered World Politics* (Berkeley, 1994).

11 According to the Lausanne treaty, the new republic regained Thrace and the Straits (although it accepted their demilitarization), was relieved of the foreign capitulations, and spared the punitive economic and military clauses that had been imposed on the Central Powers; it was also allowed to eliminate its large Greek minority through forced population exchange. Bülent Gökay, *A Clash of Empires: Turkey between Russian Bolshevism and British Imperialism, 1918–1923* (London and New York, 1997).

12 Magda Ádám, *The Versailles System and Central Europe* (Aldershot, 2004).

African colonies among Great Britain, France, Belgium, and South Africa, and its Pacific possessions among Australia, New Zealand, and Japan – all under the cloak of "mandates" of the League of Nations. This new device, which was designed by the South African soldier and statesman Jan Smuts to transform old-fashioned imperialism into modern, altruistic, and purportedly transitory western rule, not only quashed the hopes of pan-African leaders but also disappointed annexationists in Canberra, Wellington, and Tokyo.[13]

The division of the former Ottoman territories in the Middle East proved even more explosive. After the United States withdrew from peacemaking, and following long and difficult negotiations between French and British diplomats, Syria and Lebanon, Palestine and Iraq all become "A" mandates of the League in 1922, subject to ostensibly short-term French and British control. The borders that the Allies drew infuriated Arab nationalists and intensified the Arab–Jewish struggle in Palestine. Moreover, the Allies' reach did not extend to Armenia or Kurdistan, both of which were eventually devoured by more powerful neighbors.[14]

The entire peace settlement – the separate treaties that were hammered out under changing military, diplomatic, and political conditions – had few supporters and many opponents. While the winners battled over the spoils, the losers complained of vengeance and hypocrisy. Even before the Versailles treaty was signed, British liberal and socialist intellectuals pleaded for a fairer treatment of Germany, and subject peoples protested against the newest division of colonial spoils. Japan smarted over the American and British rebuff of its efforts to guarantee racial equality in the League Covenant, and China, outraged by the victors' refusal to guarantee the return of Kiaochow, refused to sign the treaty.

Once the diplomats left Paris, the revisionist voices became loud, passionate, and pervasive.[15] Stirred by the writings of John Maynard Keynes, critics in the Allied camp condemned the peacemakers for economic ineptitude, ubiquitous violations of self-determination, and vindictive treaty articles that impeded reconciliation between victors and vanquished. On the other side, the official German propaganda machine attacked the "war-guilt lie" and

13 Quincy Wright, *Mandates under the League of Nations* (Chicago, 1930), 3–126; cf. Susan Pederson, "The Meaning of the Mandates System: An Argument," *Geschichte und Gesellschaft* 32 (2006): 560–82.

14 David Fromkin, *A Peace to End All Peace: The Fall of the Ottoman Empire and the Creation of the Modern Middle East* (New York, 2001).

15 Carole Fink, "Revisionism," in Gordon Martel, ed., *A Companion to Europe, 1900–1945* (Malden, MA, 2006), 326–31.

all the violations of Wilson's Fourteen Points. Former neutrals blamed the Big Three for a "peaceless" Europe which lay under a cloud of disillusion, divided by new borders and plagued by inflation, unemployment, and stagnation.[16] The leaders of peace movements, which had emerged as a significant international presence before World War I, almost unanimously denounced the treaties for fostering revanchism and threatening a new war.[17]

Among the few defenders of the Paris Peace settlement was Czechoslovakia's first president, T. G. Masaryk. The scholar-politician, the son of a Moravian coachman, celebrated the peacemakers for liberating small nations like his own and urged the end of "chauvinism" and the cultivation of "humaneness" and "internationality."[18]

The League of Nations, the world's first international organization, was born on January 16, 1920, six days after the Versailles treaty came into force. It was thus irretrievably linked to the contested peace settlement. This progeny of almost a half-century of idealism and specific proposals was an entirely new entity, a permanent institution to promote collective action among sovereign states to maintain peace. Unlike the old Concert of Europe, it had a home in the tranquil setting of Geneva; it also had an annual budget, held periodic meetings, and included small as well as great powers.

The League was also laced with contradictions. Among them was the promise of universality, which clashed with its limitation of membership to the victor states. Membership was voluntary and withdrawal easy. Moreover, the Covenant did not abolish war but simply provided a deliberative apparatus (Articles 11–15), including a three-month cooling-off period. Article 16, which called for economic and military sanctions against aggressors, bound neither members nor non-members. And underlying the League's birth was an inherent clash between its great-power members, which still preferred old-style diplomacy, and small states that pressed for a more robust League.[19]

Peace advocates were divided over the new organization, whose creation was embedded in the reviled Versailles treaty. Those who acknowledged a promising, if flawed institution worked to enlarge the reach of international law, strengthen the League's arbitration procedures, expand its membership,

16 See, for example, John Maynard Keynes, *The Economic Consequences of the Peace* (London, 1922); Francesco S. Nitti, *Peaceless Europe* (London and New York, 1922); Graf Max Montgelas, *The Case for the Central Powers: An Impeachment of the Versailles Verdict* (New York, 1925).

17 David Cortright, *Peace: A History of Movements and Ideas* (Cambridge, 2008), 58.

18 Thomas Garrigue Masaryk, *The Making of a State* (London, 1927), 385–90.

19 Zara Steiner, "The League of Nations and the Quest for Security," in R. Ahmann et al., eds., *The Quest for Stability: Problems of West European Security, 1918–1957* (London, 1993), 38.

23. Celebrations at the first assembly of the League of Nations in Geneva

and accelerate decolonization and world disarmament. These "conservative" pacifists, who were in organizations like Britain's huge League of Nations Union (whose numbers reached four hundred thousand in the early 1930s) or the sixteen national branches of the International Federation of League of Nations Societies, prodded the League to fulfill its Wilsonian ideals.[20] On the other hand, the naysayers, who represented more radical political viewpoints, not only accused the League of bolstering the status quo, but also doubted the will and ability of its dominant members to protect smaller countries from aggression.[21]

The initial portents were nonetheless promising, especially in the creation of the League Secretariat. The first secretary-general, Sir Eric Drummond, a cautious veteran of the British Foreign Office, pledged to create an international civil service independent of national authorities. Although this ideal occasionally clashed with political realities – especially in the assignment of

20 Donald S. Birn, *The League of Nations Union, 1918–1945* (Oxford, 1981), 13–14.

21 Cortright, *Peace*, 59, 64–65. See also Jill Liddington, "'Wars Will Cease When . . .': Feminism and Anti-Militarism in Britain," in Guido Grünewald and Peter van den Dungen, eds., *Twentieth-Century Peace Movements: Successes and Failures* (Lewiston, 1995), 81–97.

directorships – and although officials in the Secretariat were often encumbered by League members' jealous defense of their own sovereign rights, Drummond's youthful, energetic staff developed an internationalist *esprit de corps*, which was driven by their commitment to expand the League's membership and international reach.[22]

The League's most successful efforts were its promotion of international economic, social, and humanitarian collaboration. Technically called into action and supervised by the Council and Assembly – and bound by tight budgets – the League's special agencies, which were guided by the Secretariat, left their mark throughout the world. The League's most visible achievement in the 1920s was the resettlement of almost 2 million refugees. Faced with a humanitarian crisis in the wake of revolution and civil war in Russia, the Council created the world's first High Commissioner for Refugees in August 1921 and appointed the Norwegian scientist, polar explorer, and diplomat Fridtjof Nansen, who had earlier directed the repatriation of 425,000 prisoners of war and mobilized famine relief in eastern Europe. Nansen, who viewed his mandate as an opportunity to enlarge the League's reach, traveled the world convening conferences of specialists, raising private funds, coordinating non-governmental organizations, and mobilizing local and national governments to aid in the relocation of Russians and also of Greek and Armenian refugees from Asia Minor. He devised the special certificate (the so-called "Nansen passport") that allowed stateless persons to traverse international boundaries until they acquired another nationality.[23]

Yet there were practical and ideological limits to these ambitious projects. Nansen's activities were greeted with indifference in the United States, suspicion in Soviet Russia, and scant cooperation in Great Britain and France, which disliked Nansen's dealings with Moscow. His appeals for financial burden-sharing received a cold response from most League members. When Nansen died in 1930, the great powers abolished his office on the eve of a new refugee crisis. Moreover, his achievements had obscured the refusal of the international community to confront the right of individual states to expel unwanted people or the rights of refugees to asylum.[24]

Another innovation was the League's Health Organization. Directed by the energetic Polish physician Ludwik Rajchmann, this body represented a

22 James Barros, *Office without Power: Secretary-General Sir Eric Drummond, 1919–1933* (Oxford, 1979); Walters, *League*, 76–80.

23 Claudena M. Skran, *Refugees in Inter-War Europe: The Emergence of a Regime* (New York, 1995).

24 J. M. Scott, *Fridjof Nansen* (Geneva, 1971), 237–38.

significant expansion of prewar international efforts. It extended its own mandate beyond the control of epidemic disease to disease-prevention, the protection of children and invalids, and improving education in nutrition. Rajchmann's organization, which enjoyed the cooperation of Soviet Russia, Germany, and the United States, raised funds from private US foundations and dispatched large medical units to China. The Health Organization also compiled public health records, produced and circulated medical bulletins, and set international standards for medicines and medical procedures, facilitating safer travel throughout the world. Yet here, too, the League was constrained by inadequate funding and the suspicions of the great powers.[25]

The League also distinguished itself in controlling drugs and traffic in women. Dame Rachel Crowdy, who (although she was never named a director) headed the Section on Opium and Social Questions, gathered massive data about the extent and profits of international drug trafficking and the ineffectiveness of local policing. Her efforts spurred the Council to adopt two conventions, in 1925 to strengthen League control over illicit traffic and in 1931 to limit drug manufacture and set up two supervisory bodies with authority over signatories. Crowdy, too, found her efforts blocked by political realities. Enforcement of the Council's tough opium-control measures depended on the good faith of governments, while poppy cultivation never came under international control. Crowdy's advocacy of the rights of women and children in poor lands outside Europe provoked criticism, especially from Great Britain, over her meddling in the sovereign rights of governments.[26]

The League's last-born agency, the Committee on Intellectual Cooperation, was given a practical mandate to improve the conditions of intellectual workers and to promote international contacts, as well as the visionary task of strengthening the idea of peace. Its membership included notables such as Henri Bergson, Albert Einstein, H. G. Wells, Aldous Huxley, and Marie Curie, who submitted an ambitious agenda to the Assembly in 1922, only to have their hopes and budget curtailed. Consequently, the committee's work shifted in 1924 to Paris, where the French government had established an International

25 Marta Balinska, *A Life for Humanity: Ludwik Rajchman, 1881–1965* (Budapest and New York, 1998); Paul Weindling, ed., *International Health Organizations and Movements, 1918–1939* (Cambridge and New York, 1995).

26 Rachel E. Crowdy, "The Humanitarian Activities of the League of Nations," *Journal of the Royal Institute of International Affairs* 6 (1927): 153–69; Barbara Metzer, "Towards an International Human Rights Regime during the Inter-War Years: The League of Nations' Combat of Traffic in Women and Children," in Kevin Grant et al., eds., *Beyond Sovereignty: Britain, Empire, and Transnationalism, c. 1880–1950* (Basingstoke and New York, 2007), 54–79.

Institute of Intellectual Cooperation under its own direction.[27] Still underfunded and weakly organized, the Committee on Intellectual Cooperation nevertheless boasted several accomplishments, among them a project to reform French and German history textbooks. Also, under its direction forty-four national committees linked scholars, translators, librarians, archivists, and museums, promoted the preservation of antiquities and monuments, and fostered collaboration among journalists, radio broadcasters, and film-makers.[28]

Yet this project was one of the League's weakest endeavors. Lingering wartime memories made collaboration among intellectuals more difficult to establish than among physicians, economists, or social workers. Relations between the institute and the committee were always tense, resources modest, and political cooperation among members and non-members of the League inadequate. Moreover, the gulf between the communist and western worlds, between the western hemisphere and Europe, and between colonial powers and their subjects could not be bridged. Nominated by the Council, the committee remained an elite organization, distant from the public it was intended by serve. In the end, the political and economic crises of the 1930s snapped French will to support the enterprise, rending the fragile bonds of European cultural cooperation.[29]

The League undoubtedly made contributions in the humanitarian realm. Armed with copious data, the Secretariat and the technical organizations set new international standards and, with the utmost discretion, occasionally altered national legislation and administrative practices. Their global efforts were resurrected after World War II by the United Nations in the form of the High Commissioner for Refugees, the World Health Organization, and UNESCO. However, the energy, dedication, and expertise that the League mobilized were outweighed by the scope of its tasks, the paucity of its funding, and divergent national and colonial interests, to say nothing of a western sense of cultural and scientific superiority and the immense difficulties of coordinating private national and international groups. In addition, the League's work to promote peace through practical, compassionate, and collaborative ventures was hindered by inadequate supervision and coordination in Geneva itself.[30]

27 Henri Bonnet, "La Société des Nations et la coopération intellectuelle," *Cahiers d'histoire mondiale* 10 (1966): 198–209.

28 Paul David, *L'Ésprit de Genève: Histoire de la Société des Nations* (Geneva, 2000), 305–9.

29 Jean-Jacques Renoliet, *L'UNESCO oubliée: La Société des Nations et la coopération intellectuelle (1919–1946)* (Paris, 1999), 323–33. A second institute in Rome, which dealt with educational aspects of the cinema, lasted until 1937.

30 Victor-Yves Ghébali, *La Société des Nations et la Réforme Bruce, 1939–1940* (Geneva, 1970).

The Secretariat was also responsible for two of the League's major political undertakings – mandates and the protection of minorities. Both extended the League's reach in an unprecedented manner, and both required deft balancing among aggrieved persons, their governments, and a vigilant international public opinion.

The Permanent Mandates Commission (PMC), which reported directly to the Council, had more independence and authority than any other agency of the League. According to Article 22 of the Covenant, mandatory governments were obliged to promote the "well being and development" of the population in the mandated territory as a "sacred trust of civilization." The PMC's nine members, of whom a majority were to be nationals of non-mandatory powers, were nominated by the Council and barred from direct dependence on their governments (although this ban was difficult to enforce in practice); and at least one member had to be a woman.

The PMC's task was to examine annual reports from the governments that administered the fifteen diverse mandatory territories, as well as petitions from the inhabitants of these territories. During its eighteen-year existence, the PMC conducted painstaking investigations of major international issues, from liquor traffic to forced labor and slavery, from conscription to local uprisings. This regular scrutiny was manifest in the PMC's public reports to the League Council; and it led to sometimes heated exchanges with the representatives of the mandatory powers. This was thus a significant innovation: international scrutiny of the two greatest imperial powers, Great Britain and France, in the new territories they had acquired.[31]

To be sure, the PMC had only limited resources and power to implement its findings. Barred from on-the-spot investigations, the commissioners relied on the mandatory governments for information and cooperation. They could not recommend sanctions, and they were constrained by age-old attitudes as well as an unquestioning support for the moral basis of colonialism: the west's obligation to improve the lot of backward peoples. On the other hand, if the PMC did not substantially ease the yoke of imperialism during the interwar period, it raised questions of its durability. Much to the chagrin of governments in Paris and London, the commission encouraged the voices of native populations and their advocates, reinforcing the growing challenge to the west's global dominance. Its efforts, too, were revived and expanded after

31 Michael D. Callahan, *Mandates and Empire: The League of Nations and Africa, 1914–1931* (Brighton and Portland, OR, 1999), 58–59, 199–200.

World War II by the UN Trusteeship Council, whose charge was to bring the mandated territories to independence.[32]

One of the Secretariat's smallest sections oversaw the League's most delicate and controversial political activity, the protection of minorities in a dozen states in east-central and southern Europe. To mitigate the perils faced by millions of newly transferred people, as well as the danger of their exploitation by irredentist neighbors, the peacemakers devised the unprecedented minority treaties and assigned enforcement to the League Council. However, the states with the ethnic minorities resisted interference in their domestic affairs, and Council members were reluctant to accuse fellow governments of treaty violations.

Sensitive to the broad public interest in the minority question, the Secretariat took charge. Under the leadership of the Norwegian diplomat, Erik Colban, the League's Minorities Section examined every minority petition and disposed of all but a few. Colban then guided the deliberations of the ad hoc council committees charged with deciding whether treaty violations had occurred, conducted confidential negotiations with government officials, and, in the rare unsolved cases, appeared at the Council discussions as well. The League's procedures, which were designed to fulfill the treaties without provoking the new states, placing major burdens on the guarantors, or encouraging exaggerated expectations from minorities and their defenders, did produce some positive results. Under Colban's prodding and the threat of public censure, some accused governments reduced their property confiscations and their restrictions on language use, religious practice, educational opportunities, and citizenship rights, and even liberalized other aspects of their legislation and administrative practices. But predictably Colban's judicious diplomacy drew criticism from minorities and their spokesmen, who complained about the "dark room" in Geneva, where their voices were excluded and their petitions buried.[33]

Minority protection stirred a major international debate once Germany entered the League in September 1926. Kin country to millions of *Auslandsdeutsche*, the Weimar Republic vowed to "reform" the League system. Although it was supported by other revisionist states and the neutrals, Germany encountered strong British, French, and Italian resistance, as well as the

32 R. N. Chowdhuri, *International Mandates and Trusteeship Systems: A Comparative Study* (The Hague, 1955).

33 Erik Colban, "The Minorities Problem," *The Norseman* 2 (1944): 310–36; Pablo de Azcárate, *League of Nations and National Minorities: An Experiment* (Washington, DC, 1945); Christoph Gütermann, *Das Minderheitenschutzverfahren des Völkerbundes* (Berlin, 1979).

Secretariat's determination to block all but minor changes. The German crusade ended abruptly in 1933, when the Third Reich began to persecute its own Jewish minority, left the League, and helped destroy the minority-protection system, only to distort the issue in 1938 with its threats to Czechoslovakia. Thus in the aftermath of World War II and the Holocaust, the League's minority-protection system – which had been harshly judged for both its restrictiveness and its vulnerability to abuse – was not revived by the United Nations.[34]

Two other new institutions, the International Labor Organization (ILO) and the Permanent Court of International Justice (PCIJ), were connected to the League. The ILO, which was inscribed into the Covenant, linked international peace with "social justice." Although it was funded by the League, the ILO was an autonomous body whose membership included representatives of governments, employers, and labor. Under its first director, the moderate French socialist Albert Thomas, and with a staff of almost a thousand, the ILO developed a global reach. This highly centralized, activist organization collected data, held frequent meetings, developed eighty conventions on labor protection, furnished technical assistance to governments, and gave labor a voice in League forums. Even during the Depression, the ILO continued to hold meetings and issue recommendations; and it kept Germany and Japan, as well as the United States, as members. Overcoming the peacemakers' skepticism over its relevance, the ILO became a powerful organization that not only helped trade unions expand and raised standards for the treatment of workers, but refuted communist propaganda about the west's indifference to the proletariat.[35] The organization exists to this day.

Written into the Covenant and founded in 1922, the Permanent Court of International Justice was the world's first independent standing tribunal. Its eleven (later fifteen) members were elected by the Council and the Assembly. It convened annually at its permanent home in The Hague. The court was empowered to render judgments and give advisory opinions to the League; although not legally binding, the latter had moral and political weight. Peace advocates saw the PCIJ, like the ILO, as a means to change the conduct of international relations, a facility to settle disputes through legal procedures.[36]

34 Carole Fink, "The League of Nations System of Minority Protection, 1920–1939," in Marta Petricioli and Donatella Cherubini, eds., *Pour la paix en Europe: Institutions et société civile dans l'entre-deux-guerres* (Brussels, 2007), 41–56; cf. Martin Scheuermann, *Minderheitenschutz contra Konfliktverhütung? Die Minderheitenpolitik des Völkerbundes in den zwanziger Jahren* (Marburg, 2000).

35 Edward J. Phelan, *Albert Thomas et la création du B.I.T.* (Paris, 1936).

36 Manley O. Hudson, *The Permanent Court of International Justice, 1920–1942: A Treatise* (New York, 1943).

24. Permanent court of International Justice, The Hague

The court was active. Between 1922 and 1939 it heard sixty-six cases, of which twenty-eight were requests for advisory opinions. Many of these cases arose from disputes over the peace treaties, and the court did not shrink from establishing precedents. It rendered judgments in several significant cases, among them a high-profile dispute between Germany and Poland over language-testing by Polish authorities in Upper Silesia.[37] By 1939 the court's jurisdiction had been recognized in some six hundred international agreements. The PCIJ strengthened the League, demonstrating the importance of a legal system, developing a body of jurisprudence, and occasionally straying from conventional interpretations of international law.[38]

The PCIJ's authority nevertheless faced severe limitations. Referrals were restricted to governments; and individual citizens could not plead before the court. Initially, the Council's decisions for referral were unanimous; but

37 Manley O. Hudson, ed., *World Court Reports* (Washington, DC, 1934), 268–319.

38 In 1928 the PCIJ made a "revolutionary pronouncement," which upheld the rights of individual citizens under international law: Hersh Lauterpacht, *The Development of International Law by the International Court* (London, 1958), 173–76.

Germany's entry in 1926 made this procedure impossible. Although an American jurist always sat on the bench and leading Americans urged adherence, the United States never signed the PCIJ's statute.[39] Moreover, the great and small powers disagreed over compulsory jurisdiction. Britain, in particular, feared restrictions on its naval freedom of action and distrusted "continental" jurists who were thought likely to side with Germany.[40]

In sum, the League's fulfillment of its humanitarian, legal, and political mission produced a credible record, and many of its tasks were revived by the United Nations. The League's deficiencies were also manifest. It was always short of funds. The largest single contributor, Britain, which paid 11 percent of the League's budget, was the most outspoken critic of waste and "unnecessary expenditure."[41] Especially among the most powerful members, there was a deficit of support for the Secretariat's initiatives. Paradoxically, the growth of non-governmental organizations may well have undermined the practical peace work of the League of Nations.[42] International organizations such as the World Federation of League of Nations Societies, the Inter-Parliamentary Union, the Socialist International, and the Women's International League for Peace and Freedom, all of which had supported the League's creation and collaborated with its agencies, scrutinized its activities, issuing continual criticisms and demands for reform. The League's fledgling efforts to promote international cooperation thus provided a lightning-rod for a great variety of interests – victor and vanquished, colonial and anti-colonial, capitalist and socialist, rich and poor – that had achieved global audience through the non-governmental organizations.

The League of Nations was, above all, a security organization. Its principal mandate was to maintain peace in two ways: by resolving disputes between governments and by responding collectively to breaches of the rules by aggressor states. This dual responsibility for arbitration and collective security was encumbered by two key articles in the Covenant. Article 10, which Wilson had advocated on the model of western hemisphere defense, defined the

39 Michael Dunne, *The United States and the World Court, 1920–1935* (New York, 1988).

40 Lorna Lloyd, *Peace through Law: Britain and the International Court in the* 1920s (Bury St. Edmunds, 1997), 9–11. Britain finally signed the optional clause under the second Labour government in 1929, and the reluctant Dominions soon followed.

41 Between 1920 and 1946 the League's annual budget, including that of the ILO and PCIJ, was just $5.5 million. Northedge, *League*, 71.

42 In 1929 the League's *Handbook of International Organizations* listed 478 international organizations, of which 90 percent were private; by 1932 this number had risen to 560. Akira Iriye, *Global Community: The Role of International Organizations in the Making of the Contemporary World* (Berkeley and Los Angeles, 2002), 28.

League's primary task "to respect and preserve as against external aggression the territorial integrity and existing political independence of all Members of the League." Article 8, drawing on widespread pacifist sentiment, called for the reduction of the armaments of all League members "to the lowest point consistent with national safety and the enforcement by common action of international obligations." Joining collective security with the peace treaties, on the one hand, and with disarmament on the other was a major incongruity.

The principal obstacle to realizing the goals enunciated in the two clauses was the disagreement between the two victor powers, France and Great Britain, over both the origins of World War I and the means to prevent another conflict. Twice invaded in the past half-century and faced with immense war losses and a vengeful Germany, France sought peace through the strict enforcement and expansion of Article 10. Thwarted by its ex-allies from creating a military force under the League or obtaining an Anglo-American guarantee, France insisted that the League function as a protective instrument, in which members were automatically bound to come to the aid of a threatened state. In this view, France was supported by the new, enlarged states that were wedged between Germany and Soviet Russia.[43] Britain, on the other hand, had not been invaded but had been economically damaged by the war and still had a vast global empire to defend. Like France, Britain had failed at the peace conference, in this case either to water down Wilson's guarantee of the territorial status quo in Article 10 or to dilute it with a clause providing for revision of the settlement.[44] British leaders thus pursued the dual, often contradictory quest to limit their obligations to the League and to promote the prompt "pacification" of Europe.

At the core of their beliefs, Britain and its Dominions were convinced that World War I had been a terrible blunder caused by rampant militarism and a rigid alliance system. Consequently, they also viewed the peace treaties as a disaster, which had created unsustainable borders, and France's postwar policy as a drive for European hegemony and a threat to the British Empire. The British attitude matched the sentiments of former neutrals, such as the

43 Marks, *Illusion*, 40.

44 On February 6, 1919, Lord Robert Cecil, the British delegate on the League of Nations Commission, attempted to dilute Article 10 by substituting the more passive formulation: "respect other members' independence," but he was stopped by Wilson, who feared the League would become "hardly more than an influential debating society," which was precisely what Britain preferred. On February 11, Cecil launched another challenge to Article 10, proposing that the League Assembly periodically revise "treaties which have become obsolete." Contrary to his intention, this proposal became the separate Article 19 of the Covenant. Sharp, *Versailles Settlement*, 56–58.

Netherlands and the Scandinavian countries, and the League's Latin American members, as well as Germany, the Soviet Union, and the United States, all of which strove for a thorough revision of the Versailles system.[45]

The result was stalemate in Geneva between the League's two strongest members.[46] France and Britain had only reluctantly supported the League's creation as a concession to Wilson. Now, bereft of America's support, the two countries conducted their cold war in an unfamiliar, uncongenial site in front of smaller powers (which had their own desiderata), Secretariat officials who had an ambitious international agenda, and a highly concerned public.[47] The main casualty was the League itself, whose ethos, ordained by Wilson, was always contested.[48]

The League also had formidable rivals. The victors had reserved the mechanisms for enforcing the peace treaties to the Supreme Council, the Conference of Ambassadors, and the Reparations Commission, as well as to the various boundary and disarmament commissions; and in the United States' absence France's vote was often decisive in these bodies. Moreover France, unconvinced that the gaps in the Covenant would ever be filled, promptly created its own security network through military alliances with Belgium, Poland, and Czechoslovakia, although it failed to obtain the most prized pact of all, with Britain.[49]

Despite the Secretariat's conciliatory efforts, the League's link with the peace treaties aroused antagonism in Germany, the Soviet Union, and the United States. Consequently, the League was excluded from major international gatherings, including the Washington Conference (1921–22), which set limits on the great powers' naval strength, and the Genoa Conference (1922), a thirty-four-nation summit that attempted to reintegrate Germany and the Soviet Union and promote the economic restoration of Europe. The first

45 Ruth Henig, "Britain, France, and the League of Nations in the 1920s," in Alan Sharp and Glyn Stone, eds., *Anglo-French Relations in the Twentieth Century: Rivalry and Cooperation* (London and New York, 2000), 139–57.

46 Described graphically in Salvador de Madariaga, *Disarmament* (New York, 1929).

47 This public was also divided, especially in Britain, between "pure pacifists," who demanded the reduction of international obligations that might lead to another war, and "true Leaguers," who accepted coercive action to thwart aggression. Keith Robbins, "European Peace Movements and their Influence on Policy after the First World War," in Ahmann et al., eds., *Quest for Stability*, 78–82.

48 For example, at each of the first four assemblies of the League the Canadian delegation proposed to eliminate Article 10 from the Covenant or adopt a highly restrictive interpretation.

49 On the *mésentente cordiale* see Alfred Fabre, *La Crise des alliances: Essai sur les relations franco-britanniques depuis la signature de la paix (1919–1922)* (Paris, 1922); Arnold Wolfers, *Britain and France between Two Wars* (New York, 1966).

conference was an apparent success, the second a glaring failure, but the League's absence at both had diminished its stature.[50]

The League's record of resolving interstate conflicts was mixed. During its first decade the Council mediated seventeen disputes. Among these were (over Soviet objections) the dispute between Finland and Sweden over the Åaland Islands in 1920, the partition of Upper Silesia in 1922, the award of Mosul to Iraq in 1924, and a border clash between Greece and Bulgaria in 1925. However, on more difficult problems, such as Vilna and Corfu, the Council deferred to the Conference of Ambassadors. The obstacles to a larger role by the League lay not only in the Council's unanimity rule and the obligatory presence of the accused government during mediation, but also in British opposition to applying sanctions under Article 16.[51]

Yet the League of Nations became popular among Europeans, especially in Britain. There the growing League of Nations Societies cheered each League accomplishment, however small, as testimony to a new style of diplomacy. Thus, not unexpectedly, the organization's principal security initiative emerged in the League's most democratic forum, the annual Assembly. This initiative represented an attempt to reconcile the small powers' need for security with the universal desire for disarmament.

The catalyst for the League's action was the Ruhr invasion in 1923, through which France attempted to compel Germany to pay reparations. Britain had been opposed, Germany resisted, and Europe confronted its first postwar crisis.[52] In an extraordinary act of cooperation, British and French negotiators in Geneva produced a draft treaty of mutual assistance, which the Assembly adopted in September 1923. The treaty contained guidelines for collective League action against aggression, including the coordination of military forces, along with a call for general disarmament.[53]

This first foray by the League Assembly was abortive. The British government refused to sign the treaty because it threatened to place a disproportionate burden on its armed forces. The Dominions, especially Canada, as well

50 League of Nations Archive, Geneva, Directors Meetings, Drummond remarks, June 8, 1922,

51 Balfour reminded the Council in August 1920 that the absence of Germany, the Soviet Union, and the United States made Article 16 unenforceable and represented an intolerable burden on Britain (League of Nations, *Official Journal*, 4th meeting, 8th session [1920], 25); cf. Undated Memorandum [April 1926] on the Foreign Policy of His Majesty's Government, with a List of British Commitments in their Relative Order of Importance, *Documents on British Foreign Policy*, Ser. 1A, 1 (London, 1966): 846–48.

52 Conan Fisher, *The Ruhr Crisis, 1923–1924* (Oxford, 2003).

53 Steiner, *Lights that Failed*, 379–80.

as the Dutch and the Scandinavians, were also opposed to giving the League coercive powers, as were the three most significant non-members. Even France was unwilling to accept the prospect of disarmament, even as vaguely presented in the treaty, without ironclad security guarantees.[54]

Once the Ruhr crisis had been settled through US intervention, Britain attempted to reshape the security debate in the League. The Labour prime minister, Ramsay MacDonald, who envisaged a more vigorous League – with Germany, if not the United States as a member – confronted the demand by Édouard Herriot, the French premier, for future protection. Both leaders appeared before the Assembly in September 1924 to present their visions of peace. Then, following extraordinary negotiations, the Assembly adopted the Geneva Protocol for the Pacific Settlement of International Disputes.[55] The protocol represented the climax of four years' effort to fill the Covenant's gaps and to set the League in a new direction.[56] It addressed the triad of arbitration, security, and disarmament. It required adjudication of all disputes (including those involving non-members) by the Permanent Court of International Justice, the Council, or an ad hoc tribunal. It labeled as an aggressor any state that refused to submit to judgment, and it mandated collective action against the offender. It also required, however, that a disarmament agreement be concluded before the protocol came into force. Moreover, the Geneva Protocol excluded matters within a state's domestic jurisdiction and left the decision to impose sanctions to individual members.[57]

Despite the cautious formulation of its requirements, the protocol failed to persuade opponents in London, Ottawa, Washington, and Berlin, not to mention among the former neutrals that feared the dangers of increasing the League's authority and power. Rejection of the protocol by Britain's new Conservative government in March 1925 delivered the *coup de grâce* to this, the League's last attempt to devise a comprehensive security and disarmament system on the basis of existing treaties.[58] A return to the old ways of great-power diplomacy lay ahead.

The struggle inside the League between victors and losers – between proponents of the status quo and critics of the new order – was completely

54 Ibid.

55 Patrick O. Cohrs, *The Unfinished Peace after World War I: America, Britain, and the Stabilisation of Europe, 1919–1932* (Cambridge, 2006), 202–3.

56 P. J. Noel Baker, *The Geneva Protocol for the Pacific Settlement of International Disputes* (London, 1925).

57 Walters, *League*, 268–76.

58 Carolyn J. Kitching, *Britain and the Problem of International Disarmament, 1919–1934* (London and New York, 1999), 81–85.

altered in 1925 by the resurgence of Germany. Under the deft leadership of the converted nationalist foreign minister Gustav Stresemann, the Weimar Republic offered a solution outside the League to the security conundrum – a return to managing European affairs by the great powers. The Locarno treaties, a regional arrangement that was negotiated without League participation, represented a "clear retreat from the concept of the 'indivisibility of peace.'"[59] Signed by five states, Belgium, Britain, France, Germany, and Italy, these treaties guaranteed Germany's western borders but were silent about its eastern frontiers with Poland and Czechoslovakia. Hailed at the time by a public that was hungry for signs of international reconciliation – the British, French, and German foreign ministers all won Nobel peace prizes – the Locarno system created a new Concert of Europe, in which German participation was essential.[60]

Germany's readmission to the ranks of the great powers, which was promoted eagerly by Britain and accepted reluctantly by France, came at a high price for the League. Supported by the United States and the Soviet Union, the Weimar Republic insisted on a new version of European pacification, which was based on the erosion of the peace treaties, presumably by peaceful means. Through skillful diplomacy, Germany capitalized on Anglo-French differences, as well as on public opinion that favored revision of the treaty, to remove the shackles of Versailles. Stresemann's intent was apparent. He ended Allied military control, obtained a permanent seat in the League Council, and freed Germany from having to apply Article 16 against the Soviet Union. Stresemann's next major goals were aimed at his Locarno colleagues. He wanted to reduce reparations further and end the Allied occupation of the Rhineland, which had been demilitarized by the Treaty of Versailles. In the meantime the League provided a useful forum for the world's foremost revisionist power, where Germany could challenge its eastern neighbors, demand the return of its colonies, and clamor for universal disarmament.[61]

Thus, the Locarno era was scarcely a golden age. The "Geneva tea parties" among Aristide Briand, Austen Chamberlain, and Stresemann masked a host of unsolved problems behind the aura of détente. One was disarmament. In 1925 the League achieved a marked success in a protocol that banned the use of poison gas in war and was ratified by thirty-six states

59 Steiner, "League," 49.

60 Gaynor Johnson, ed., *Locarno Revisited: European Diplomacy, 1920–1929* (London and New York, 2004).

61 Christoph M. Kimmich, *Germany and the League of Nations* (Chicago and London, 1976), 76–149.

(but not by the United States or Japan). Despite high public expectations, however, there was no progress in implementing Article 8 of the Covenant. Aside from the technical and political complexity of general disarmament, the Anglo-French debate continued, muddied now in the Locarno era by German demands for "equality," America's resolute detachment from European affairs, and Soviet grandstanding.[62]

The security gap thus remained unfilled. The Kellogg–Briand Pact of 1928, which sixty-three states signed, renounced war but contained no enforcement procedures against aggressors. Critics in the peace movement also noted the lack of impediments to the use of force by great powers within their spheres of influence. The victors continued to clash over the terms of a European peace. When the League sought to revive arbitration and expand security guarantees along the lines of Locarno, France insisted on maintaining Article 10 of the Covenant, while Britain demanded a comprehensive disarmament agreement as the price of further financial or military commitments. Indeed, the British greeted Briand's plan for a Federal European Union, a potential security arrangement, with almost as much skepticism as did the Germans.[63]

Dark clouds outside Europe underscored the League's limits in preserving peace. Aspiring to a dominant role in East Asia, Japan viewed the League as an "annoyance."[64] Its neighbor China, split by the clash between the Guomindang and the Communists, lay open to intervention by outsiders, as well as to the ravages of the trade in opium and arms, which the League was helpless to stop.[65] In Latin America the long, bloody Chaco War between Bolivia and Paraguay emphasized the costs of the League's failure to gain US cooperation.[66]

Anticolonialism also grew, buttressed by the words and deeds of Gandhi and Kemal. Revolts took place in Persia and Egypt, as well as in the British and French mandates of Iraq and Syria. In North Africa, the Franco-Spanish

62 B. J. C. McKercher, "Of Horns and Teeth: The Preparatory Commission and the World Disarmament Conference, 1926–1934," in B. J. C. McKercher, ed., *Arms Limitation and Disarmament* (Westport, CT, and London, 1992), 173–80.

63 R. W. Boyce, "Britain's First 'No' to Europe: Britain and the Briand Plan, 1929–30," *European Studies Review* 10 (1980): 17–45.

64 Sydney Gifford, *Japan among the Powers, 1890–1990* (New Haven, 1994), 57.

65 Hans J. Van de Ven, *War and Nationalism in China, 1925–1945* (London and New York, 2003), 74–75. Responding to a plea by League of Nations Union leader Lord Robert Cecil in February 1927, British Foreign Secretary Austen Chamberlain informed the League of the dispatch of British forces to China, adding "there was no way in which the League could be of assistance." Walters, *League*, 329–30.

66 Barros, *Office without Power*, 251–57; J. Barros, *Betrayal from Within: Joseph Avenol, Secretary General of the League of Nations, 1933–1940* (New Haven, 1969), 47–51.

suppression of the Moroccan revolt represented a brutal demonstration of western power. Moreover, in Palestine, where Britain sought to reconcile the Balfour Declaration with Arab national claims, the violence that erupted in 1928 and 1929 showed the looming danger of competing local ambitions that would attract worldwide attention.[67]

The Locarno era in Europe ended abruptly with the onset of the Great Depression and the radicalization of German politics after Stresemann's death. By then the peace treaties had fallen into a web of myth and vituperation, and their defenders had produced scant results. Thus, the struggle opened in the 1930s between forces that were determined to topple the postwar order and its weakened, divided guardians.

In the decade before World War II, there were two major challenges to peace. The first were the direct military assaults on League members – by Japan in Manchuria and China and Italy in Ethiopia – as well as the intervention by the two fascist powers in Spain. The second challenge was Nazi Germany's systematic diplomatic assault on Versailles. The German démarches included unilateral rearmament in 1935, the reoccupation of the demilitarized zone of the Rhineland in 1936, and the annexation of Austria and parts of Czechoslovakia in 1938. Also, the Third Reich destabilized the international order by driving tens of thousands of its impoverished Jewish citizens into exile and overturning France's security system through a series of pacts with Poland (1934), Italy and Japan (1936), and Soviet Russia (1939).[68]

Britain and France remained the League's only pillars. The United States' continuing hostility toward Geneva placed the burden of responding to treaty violations on these two overextended powers, which were more divided than ever as they faced economic misery and social unrest at home and agitation within their empires. Although antiwar sentiments persisted in the 1930s, the mainstream peace organizations now saw the need to bolster the League, not only by working for general disarmament but also by endorsing collective security.[69] But the governments in London and Paris were opposed to both.

67 Bernard Wasserstein, *The British in Palestine: The Mandatory Government and the Arab-Jewish Conflict, 1917–1929* (London, 1978).

68 Gerhard L.Weinberg, *Hitler's Foreign Policy, 1933–1939: The Road to World War II* (New York, 2005).

69 Martin Ceadel, *Pacifism in Britain, 1914–1945: The Defining of a Faith* (Oxford, 1980); Mona Siegel, *The Moral Disarmament of France: Education, Pacifism, and Patriotism, 1914–1940* (Cambridge and New York, 2004); Cecilia Lynch, *Beyond Appeasement: Interpreting Interwar Peace Movements in World Politics* (Ithaca, 1999).

Either piecemeal or deliberate, appeasement thus became the order of the day.[70] The pattern was set in 1931 with the League's feeble response to Japan's conquest of Manchuria. From the outset, League members were unable to agree whether an act of aggression had occurred and whether the organization's reach extended to East Asia. The League's cumbersome structure impeded a prompt investigation, and the prevailing suspicion among the powers prevented coordinated action either in Geneva or outside. Consequently, on February 24, 1933, seventeen months after the invasion, the League Assembly adopted a report that avoided condemning Japan or invoking sanctions under Article 16. Nonetheless, one month later an irate Japan left the League, created the puppet state Manchukuo, and suffered no punishment other than the world's non-recognition of its actions.[71]

At the same time, Hitler's arrival in power in January 1933 cast a spotlight on the League's deadlocked Disarmament Conference in Geneva, where delegates were attempting anew to solve old disagreements. Suddenly, Britain, France, Germany, and Italy resumed the old Locarno pattern when they signed a pact in Rome, pledging to coordinate their European policy in "conjunction with the League." Not unexpectedly, the Third Reich, which had already been censured by the Council and Assembly for its anti-Semitic legislation and faced a wall of opposition to its demands for military "equality," followed Japan out of the League in October, now that the organization had ceased to serve German purposes.[72]

The League was by now foundering financially, politically, and morally because of the world economic crisis, the exodus of its most talented officials, and the debacles over Manchuria and disarmament. It was thus unprepared in March 1935 to respond to Ethiopia's plea for aid against Fascist Italy. Once again, the League faced difficulties in defining the nature of aggression, as there were uncoordinated responses by the powers, delays in launching a League investigation, and doubts over the wisdom of operating outside Europe. Nonetheless, in November, in response to public clamor, the Assembly, for the first time in its history, condemned the invasion and voted sanctions.[73]

70 Wolfgang Mommsen and Lother Kettenacker, eds., *The Fascist Challenge and the Policy of Appeasement* (London and Boston, 1983).

71 Christopher Thorne, *The Limits of Foreign Policy: The West, the League, and the Far Eastern Crisis of 1931–1933* (London, 1972).

72 Kimmich, *Germany and the League*, 150–207.

73 The Peace Ballot in the summer of 1935, which was sponsored by the League of Nations Union, registered substantial British sentiment in favor of the League and collective security: Lynch, *Beyond Appeasement*, 112–18.

Still, the British and French governments recoiled from collective action. Seeking Italy's collaboration against a rearming Nazi Germany and fearing retaliation by Rome, London and Paris sought a solution outside the framework of the League. The resulting Hoare–Laval Pact offered Mussolini a virtual victory. Apprised of the details, however, an aroused British public forced Hoare's resignation from the Foreign Office. Although the League's decision to invoke sanctions prevailed, key members gave virtually no financial assistance to Ethiopia. The sanctions were unevenly and incompletely applied. In July 1936, two months after Ethiopia's resistance collapsed, the Assembly voted, on Britain's recommendation, to lift them.[74]

The demise of treaty enforcement was also evident in the League's tepid response to Germany's coup in the Rhineland. In March 1936 Hitler, who was heartened by Mussolini's impending victory in Africa and hoped to exploit the clamor over the Franco-Russian treaty, sent troops into the demilitarized zone in violation of the Versailles and Locarno treaties. Pressed by their alarmed publics, the French and Belgian governments reluctantly called an emergency session of the Council.[75] The edgy debate that took place in London in April 1936 centered on whether there had been a "clear-cut" violation of Locarno that required sanctions. The Soviet Union, now a permanent member of the Council, urged a stiff response. Denmark, representing the European neutrals, acknowledged Germany's dereliction but cautioned against plunging into a war; Chile asked for an advisory opinion from the Permanent Court of International Justice, and Australia questioned the League's responsibility in a regional issue. Germany's presence at the deliberations further clouded the discussion. Permitted by League rules to speak, the Third Reich's representative announced that with the shackles of Versailles now removed, his government was prepared to join a long-term guarantee of European peace. In the end the League took no action. After Britain, France, and Italy failed in private to find a conciliatory formula, a divided Council dropped the Rhineland dispute.[76]

With echoes of 1914, Europe had now divided into two camps: the combative Rome–Berlin axis on one side and the despondent treaty-defenders on the other. Between them the smaller European states, despairing of the League's protection, adopted a *sauve qui peut* mentality. Belgium retreated into neutrality, while several east European governments gravitated toward the Third Reich. After the Ethiopian debacle, reform of the League was in the air. The

74 George H. Baer, *Test Case: Italy, Ethiopia, and the League of Nations* (Stanford, 1976).
75 Walters, *League*, 693–94.
76 Northedge, *League*, 244–54, links the Rhineland and Ethiopian crises.

major proposals included separating the Covenant from the peace treaties, removing Article 10, and forging regional agreements instead of universal obligations.[77]

As European conditions deteriorated, the global situation grew darker. Confronting the Arab revolt in Palestine and a growing independence movement in India, an overstretched Britain sought to come to terms with Mussolini and Hitler. London and Paris disregarded the League in responding to Mussolini's brazen intervention in Spain, Japan's assault on China, and Hitler's seizure of Austria. The Geneva organization was also ignored when, at the end of September 1938, the Locarno powers met in Munich and, to avert Hitler's threats of war, agreed to the mutilation of Czechoslovakia[78]

In autumn 1938 the League Assembly assessed the damage. Following Britain's lead, most delegates abandoned the Wilsonian dream of collective security and renounced their obligations under the Covenant. Only Litvinov, soon to be replaced as foreign minister when the Soviet Union abruptly abandoned its collective-security campaign, pleaded for the preservation of Articles 10 and 16.[79] Until the outbreak of World War II, the League maintained a shadow-existence, diminished in membership, poorly attended, and starved for funds. However, it continued to fulfill some of its functions until the end. In one of its boldest final acts, the Permanent Mandates Commission censured Great Britain in June 1939 for issuing a White Paper that violated its Palestine mandate; but the outbreak of war prevented a hearing in the Council.[80]

Chamberlain's Britain reluctantly adopted old-style security measures in 1939. Facing growing public outrage over the Third Reich's destruction of Czechoslovakia, the pogroms against the Jews, and the threats to Poland, it stepped up rearmament, issued unilateral guarantees to Hitler's small neighbors, commenced negotiations with France, and initiated desultory talks with the Soviet Union. It was too late. Hitler's next victim was unwilling to be sacrificed for peace; the old Entente had been frayed by two decades of mistrust and noncooperation; and Stalin preferred a pact with Hitler. Moreover, this time Hitler wanted more than simply to overturn the treaties

77 J. M. Yepes and Pereira da Silva, *La Question de la réforme du pacte de la Société des Nations* (Paris, 1937).

78 Hermann Raschhofer, *Völkerbund und Münchener Abkommen* (Munich and Vienna, 1976).

79 Teddy J. Uldricks, "Soviet Security Policy in the 1930s," in Gabriel Gorodetsky, ed., *Soviet Foreign Policy, 1917–1991: A Retrospective* (London, 1994), 65–74; Walters, *League*, 777–88

80 League of Nations. Permanent Mandates Commission, *Minutes* (1939), 95–98, 275–89; League of Nations, *Official Journal* (1939), 107, 501.

and destroy the League; he now intended to make Germany the master of Europe and large parts of the world.[81]

It is easy to point out the interwar failures that were due to a defective international structure, weak and unimaginative political leadership, and a widely ambivalent public opinion, which both opposed war and championed their governments' national and imperial interests. From this perspective, politics, culture, and economic frailty combined to thwart the efforts for a lasting peace after World War I. It is more difficult to see how things could have turned out otherwise. However imperfect, the peace treaties could not have been maintained without concerted commitment from the world's strongest governments; nor could the treaties have been altered in a conciliatory manner – even to a slight extent – without the courage and vision of the strong and the acquiescence of all parties concerned. None of these conditions existed.

Peace activists who supported the League worked tirelessly in the 1920s for a more vigorous organization; but they themselves were split in their politics, methods, and goals. Their rallying to the banner of collective security in the 1930s foundered on European imperialism, US noninvolvement, and Anglo-French appeasement, to say nothing of the determination of the "pure pacifists" and their right-wing compatriots to avoid war at any cost.

The League of Nations was a noble attempt to maintain peace, promote international cooperation, and protect its members from aggression. Despite the many achievements of its collaborative ventures, it failed to establish the two key elements on which its effectiveness depended: robust political machinery and a universally accepted concept of collective responsibility – goals that peace advocates seek to this day.

81 Christian Leitz, *Nazi Foreign Policy: The Road to Global War* (London and New York, 2004).

13

Commemorating war, 1914–1945

JAY WINTER

In all combatant countries, remembering the two world wars was not a choice; it was a ubiquitous and enduring necessity. Given the staggering toll that the wars took in life and limb, this fact is hardly surprising. While commemoration was an integral part of mourning practices, it went beyond the personal level – the accommodation of individuals and families to loss – to shape in fundamental ways the physical, political, and cultural landscapes of the world in which we live.

No one has an accurate count of the number of memorials in Europe and beyond that commemorate the two world wars. This chapter considers only those that were constructed in the period 1914–45. In Britain and France alone, over sixty thousand local memorials adorn public squares and other sites. Similar monuments were built in towns and villages in Belgium, Italy, Yugoslavia, and throughout central and eastern Europe. These memorials were carefully built and tended in politically stable countries. In unstable states – in Ireland, for instance – they were destroyed, displaced, or simply left to be hidden by overgrown weeds.

In the Soviet Union revolution occluded the war, leaving the 2 million Russian men who had died for the tsar without commemoration. The bodies of Tsar Nicholas II himself and his family, who were murdered in 1918 by revolutionary soldiers, remained hidden in shallow graves near Ekaterinburg, where they were found after the fall of communism eighty years later. In Poland and other successor states, those who died in civil war against Bolshevism were honored, while those who had died between 1914 and 1918 for one of the three empires that had occupied their national territory – the German, Austro-Hungarian, and Russian – were quickly forgotten.

Outside Europe commemorative sites and war memorials appeared by the thousands. In Australia, Canada, New Zealand, India, Iraq, Palestine, Turkey, and the United States, construction of many prominent local war monuments took place in the interwar years. Churches and churchyards had them, as did many other public buildings – schools, universities, railway stations. The Australian war memorials are unusual, in that they frequently list those who served alongside those who died. Theirs was a volunteers' war, and conscription was voted down twice. War memorials are, therefore, chastening reminders to passers-by of those who went, and by inference, those who did not join up.

In Protestant countries, war memorials were both public and utilitarian. They provided a sense of meaning through public works to benefit the survivors – war-memorial hospitals and highways, cricket pitches and water troughs, scholarships and halls of residence. Catholic countries had fewer such useful sites, which were named for individuals or groups who had died in the war; Catholic commemoration was more sacred than secular.

In countries on whose soil fighting had taken place, war cemeteries served (and still serve) as powerful memorial sites. The Imperial (later Commonwealth) War Graves Commission designed and maintained cemeteries wherever British soldiers had fallen. The British practice was to group soldiers in small sites near where they died. Most are arrayed in individual graves. These are marked by stelae on which are inscribed their names, regiments, ages, and a brief message, chosen by their families. There are also mass graves and graves of unidentifiable soldiers, "whose names are known but to God."

British war cemeteries all have an altar of remembrance in the form of a long, rectangular white stone, on which is inscribed a line from Ecclesiastes, "Their name liveth for evermore." The words were chosen by the British poet Rudyard Kipling, who lost his son in the war of 1914–18. The choice was more than a literary flourish, for the names are the heart and soul of these sites. They are arrayed in equality; rank is irrelevant. Each of the millions of lives lost is marked with the same ceremony.

These war cemeteries all have a prominent bronze sword of sacrifice, which is encased in stone and placed in the center or toward the rear of the site. This feature, which was designed by Sir Reginald Blomfield, is not a Latin cross, but rather a chivalric form; it recalls in medieval terms the honor and courage of individual soldiers in wars that claimed millions. Consequently, the cemeteries of the British Empire are more ecumenical than Christian. They honor equally men of all faiths or none. Other nations adopted the Latin cross as the standard marker for individual graves. This was the case in France and the United States, despite the fact that church and state are separate by law in these two countries. Honoring war dead has erased the divide. Jewish stars are used for Jewish graves. In Commonwealth war cemeteries, crosses are carved on the face of the rounded stelae. The grounds are well kept and have the air of an English garden cemetery. They are places of beauty, order, and tranquility.

German war cemeteries in France and Belgium are different from those of the Allied countries. The bitterness that was engendered by the war spilled over into negotiations in 1919 over the space allotted to German war cemeteries in countries that Germany had invaded. There is still no full study of this matter, but the space allocated to German war cemeteries was limited. They are densely packed and have more mass graves than do Allied cemeteries. In addition, German gravestones – either in rough crosses or Jewish stars – give the sites a somber coloration, for they were made of dark, unpolished stone, different from the light, polished stone used in the stelae of Commonwealth war graves or in French and American crosses.

In many German cemeteries large trees evoke German traditions of the *Heldenheine*, heroes' groves. Some cemeteries have additional statuary. A notable example is the granite statues that the German sculptress Käthe Kollwitz carved to honor her son Peter, who was killed in Belgium in 1914. In 1932 the statues were placed in the war cemetery where her son's body lay. The sculpture portrays herself and her husband, separate and on their knees, begging forgiveness from the young men who, like their son, never had the chance to live out their lives (see Figure 25).

After World War I a new symbolic form appeared, which was appropriate to a war in which 70 million men had been mobilized from every walk of life, of whom approximately 9 million were killed. This was the tomb of the unknown soldier. Its emergence reflected the enormous destructive power of modern weapons. The unprecedented ravages of artillery fire accounted for the fact that roughly half the men who were killed in the 1914–18 war have no known graves. Consequently, in both winning and losing countries, efforts were made to construct a symbolic site to honor loved ones who had vanished without trace.

In Britain this effort took two forms. The first was the Cenotaph, which was designed by Sir Edwin Lutyens for the Allied victory parade of July 1919. It is an empty tomb in the center of official London on Whitehall, between Downing Street and the Houses of Parliament, and it quickly became the symbolic site for all those who wanted to honor the war-dead buried overseas, identified or not. A year and a half later, a second site opened in Westminster Abbey – a tomb at the entrance, which every visitor has to pass. In it is the coffin of one unknown warrior – the term comprehended soldiers, sailors, and airmen – to represent them all. A similar tomb was constructed under the Arc de Triomphe in Paris and in other sites, including Arlington National Cemetery, just outside Washington, DC.

Like cemeteries, war museums sprang up while the conflict was raging. In 1917 a British Imperial War Museum was established. It settled a decade later

25. Vladslo monument, Belgium

in Lambeth, in a home for collecting and preserving the ephemera of war, from weapons to correspondence. Ironically, the museum was located on the grounds of the former "Bedlam" lunatic asylum.[1] In France, a similar wartime

1 Gaynor Kavanagh, "Museum as Memorial: The Origins of the Imperial War Museum," *Journal of Contemporary History* 23 (1988): 77–97; Alan Borg, *War Memorials: From Antiquity to the Present* (London, 1991), 140; Charles Ffoulkes, *Arms and the Tower* (London, 1939).

26. Cenotaph, London, Armistice Day, 1920

initiative to preserve traces of World War I produced a great library and archive that is still in use, the *Bibliothèque de documentation internationale contemporaine* in Nanterre, on the outskirts of Paris. The Australians established a War Museum (now the Australian War Memorial) in October 1917. Soldiers were invited to submit objects for display. The historian of Australian commemoration, Ken Inglis, reports one "Digger's" reply: "The GOC recently made a request for articles to be sent to the Australian War Museum, especially those illustrating the terrible weapons that have been used against the troops in the war. Why not get all the Military Police photographed for the Museum?"[2] Twenty-five years later, in 1941, the Australian War Memorial opened in the nation's capital, Canberra. Charles Bean, the official Australian war historian, had been with ANZAC troops at Gallipoli and in France. He directed the construction and design of the museum, which merged into the national war memorial. The core of the main building is designed in the form of Hagia Sofia in Istanbul, and its extended walls, which point to the Australian parliament, list the names of all the Australian men who died in the two world wars. Within the museum are dioramas, scale-models of battlefields in Gallipoli, Palestine, and France. These installations are powerful renderings of the physical landscape of battle, showing dead and wounded men on both sides. They are both heroic and anti-heroic representations; they show the ugliness of war alongside the courage of the men who endured it.

War museums were themselves memorials, but the balance between display and preservation was different in the two cases. The private initiative of a German industrialist, Richard Franck, led to the creation of the *Kriegsbibliothek* (now the *Bibliothek für Zeitgeschichte*) in Stuttgart.[3] The director of the Historical Museum in Frankfurt was responsible for another German collection of documentation and ephemera related to World War I.[4] The Cambridge University Library invited readers and dealers to send in books and pamphlets on the war; these are now preserved in the Cambridge War Collection.[5] Similar efforts produced a war collection in the New York Public Library. The Canadian War Museum was formally established in 1942 and now houses both archives and objects related to Canada's war experience.

War museums were tributes to the men and women who endured the tests of war. These facilities had little room for recording the history of antiwar movements. In their presentations of weapons and battlefield scenes, most, though not all, tended to sanitize war; the dioramas of the Australian War

2 *Aussie* (16 February 1918), cited in Ken Inglis, "A Sacred Place: The Making of the Australian War Memorial," *War and Society* 3 (1985): 100.

3 R. Franck, "Eine Bitte," *Mitteilungen von Ihrer Firma und Ihren Kollegen*, 13 (November 1915).

4 Detlef Hoffmann, "Die Weltkriegssammlung des Historischen Museums Frankfurt," in *Ein Krieg wird ausgestellt. Die Weltkriegssammlung des Historischen Museums (1914–1918): Themen einer Ausstellung* (Frankfurt, 1976).

5 This collection is now available on microfilm from Adam Matthew Publications, Marlborough, Wiltshire.

Memorial did not. In the first decades after the Armistice of 1918, the fear of offending those who were still in mourning governed the selection of "appropriate" representations of war. The gigantic naval guns at the entrance to the Imperial War Museum tell a conventional story of war and the hardware used in it. In this and many other cases, the hardware is German. After the Armistice, German field guns of various calibers were distributed as trophies to Allied communities, where they were stored in public places and mostly forgotten.

During the interwar years the pacifist Ernst Friedrich criticized powerfully such collections and the bravado that attached to the war. He set up an antiwar museum in Berlin in 1924. This collection of documents and gruesome photographs showed everything that the official collections omitted. With images of savage brutality, Friedrich demonstrated the selectivity of war museums, their censorship of disturbing images of war.[6] His museum was destroyed once the Nazis came to power. In 1982, his grandson reopened the museum in Berlin. Still, this museum was the exception; the rule was to gather weapons and images of war in a sanitized form.

Still other sites – the sites of battles themselves – stand halfway between cemeteries and museums. Sections of the trench system on the western front have been preserved, as have sites of decisive battles of World War II. One of the most moving marks the place where the Newfoundland Regiment was massacred at the tiny hamlet of Beaumont-Hamel on the Somme on July 1, 1916. This unit had paid for their own uniforms, equipment, and training. In a few minutes they lost everything in a suicidal advance against German machine-gun fire. The site of the massacre remains sacred for Canadians, into whose country Newfoundland was incorporated in 1949. It is a cemetery as well as a preserved battlefield. An information center helps visitors understand what happened. A bronze caribou stands above a mound of rocks. From here visitors can survey the point, marked by an ossified tree that Canadians call the "danger tree," toward which the Newfoundlanders marched to their deaths. Their trenches are virtually intact. So are German emplacements 200 yards away. It took Allied troops six months to cover this ground.

This triad of cemeteries, memorials, and preserved battlefield sites can be found elsewhere, too. The Chemin des Dames to the east of Paris has them; French soldiers mutinied here in 1917, after their commander refused to call off an offensive that was going nowhere. The huge pentagonal fort of Douaumont remains as it was during the terrible battle of Verdun in 1916. In 1927, a clergymen, Monseigneur Ginisty, led a movement to create an

6 Ernst Friedrich, *War against War!* (Seattle, 1987).

ossuary on the site of the battle. Here he consecrated a chapel, which was covered by a tower with a beacon that could be seen for miles. Under the building are casements covered by glass, through which observers can gaze at the mixed remains of thousands of German and French soldiers.[7] This was a holy site to German as well as French veterans. After the failure of the plot to kill Hitler in 1944, one of the conspirators, General von Stülpnagel, asked his Gestapo guards, who were taking him back to Germany and certain death, to let him stroll around Verdun for a few moments. Here, he said, was where he should have died. He raised his revolver, fired it, but only blinded himself. He was transported back to Germany, where he was duly executed.

Both world wars left scars on the landscape that memory-activists – those who did the work of remembrance – preserved, so later generations could see what happened there. One British community in Northumberland bought land at La Boisselle, near Albert in northern France, in order to preserve a giant crater that was created when a mine exploded under German positions on July 1, 1916, at the beginning of the Battle of the Somme. A plaque on a bench here captures the sentiment of those who preserved the site: "From the men of Northumberland who came home to the men who stayed behind."[8] Many of these battlefield sites were dangerous places, littered with unexploded ordnance. The French conducted a *moisson de fer*, a harvest of iron, every summer, to collect the detritus of war before it could take more lives. Most land went back to farming, although the fields around Verdun were turned into a national forest, in which every tree was planted after 1918.

Commemorative activity is never politically neutral. Most sites of remembrance are hotly contested domains. They are sacred for millions of men and women. Museums are the cathedrals of the twentieth century, places set aside for contemplating eternal themes – life, death, sacrifice, and redemption. So are battlefields and cemeteries. Those who visit these sites encounter not one, but many contradictory messages: solace and disorientation, staggering inhumanity as well as compassion and dignity, silences and patriotic affirmations. In the interwar years, these were sites of pilgrimage, as families sought to tread the ground where their loved ones had died. In 1928 a delegation of Gold Star mothers from the United States traveled to Europe to do so. Others came with particular memories and sadness. In pilgrimages to war memorials and war cemeteries, women entered centrally into the narrative of war and its

7 Antoine Prost, *Republican Identities in War and Peace* (Oxford, 2000), chs. 1–2.
8 The bench was put next to the huge crater under German lines at La Boisselle. It is part of the Lochnagar Crater Memorial.

aftermath, which could no longer be a story only about or among men. It was about everybody. The message of commemorative sites is never simple or fixed, however; it is always in the eye of the beholder.

Commemoration marked the political as well as the physical landscape of the countries that engaged in the two world wars. The politics of forgetting accompanied the politics of remembering. The loss of life of 2 million men in the Russian army from 1914–17 was an inconvenient fact for the new Bolshevik regime. Only now, after the collapse of the Soviet Union and the Soviet empire in eastern Europe, have these "unknown soldiers" of World War I been brought back into the story of war remembrance.

The terms of the peace in 1919 complicated the framing of remembrance in a host of ways, insisting on the moral as well as military superiority of the winners. According to Article 231 of the Treaty of Versailles, which the German delegation signed reluctantly, war guilt rested on the losers alone. This provision was galling to those who had fought for Germany or Austria-Hungary. However, remembering the end of the war provided the losers with a rallying point. In Germany, a majority of the population was convinced that the Treaty of Versailles was unjust. Many veterans insisted that the treaty be revised, through diplomatic means if possible, through force if necessary after the Nazi seizure of power in 1933.

Veterans were privileged actors in the commemorative politics of the combatant countries. They knew war in ways that only they could express, and they claimed to speak on behalf of the men who had died. Yet within this commemorative mission, no single political viewpoint predominated. Millions of men joined veterans' associations. Some of these organizations were on the extreme right of the political spectrum. The fascist movements in Italy and Germany embodied military values; they used uniforms, military discipline, sacred flames, and ceremonies to link their mission to that of their fallen comrades. Veterans were active on the political left too, although they were less numerous or vocal than their adversaries on the right. Some veterans, like those in Henri Barbusse's *Association républicaine des anciens combattants*, became part of the international communist movement. The majority of veterans' associations, though, steered toward the political center, and worked primarily to win adequate pensions for disabled men and the families of dead soldiers.

Some veterans' groups, particularly among French veterans, worked within the League of Nations and developed a form of soldiers' pacifism. The *Union Fédérale* of disabled men, a million strong, sought to create an international veterans' movement, which would include men who had fought on both sides. They shared information on developments in prosthetic medicine, and they worked with the International Labour Organization to assure fair treatment and access to the labor market for veterans. Other veterans, such as members of the British Legion and the American Legion, wanted nothing to do with their former enemies or the League of Nations.[9] They were disgusted when some French internationalists claimed that they could talk to Hitler and Mussolini – men like themselves, who knew how terrible war was. But as the situation in Europe worsened in the 1930s, the hopes of these internationalists were dashed. After World War II, fascist veterans' groups vanished. So did the organizations of pacifist veterans, many of whom now championed human rights as a shield against war and state tyrannies.

Historical scholarship on interwar commemoration is still divided about the extent to which remembering war was (and remains) an instrument of dominant political elements in a society. One school of opinion emphasizes the usefulness to political elites of honoring those who serve in war, whose service and sacrifice help establish the legitimacy of rule by these elites.[10] Some commemorative events are observed no matter who is in power – witness Bastille Day in France or Independence Day in the United States. Other events are tied to the establishment of a new regime and the overthrow of an older one: November 7 marked the Bolshevik revolution and the establishment of the communist regime in Russia, symbolizing a new order and its challenge to its enemies around the world.

This top-down approach emphasizes commemoration as a grammar of national, imperial, or political identity, which political leaders and their epigoni cultivate. There is much to support this argument. Anzac Day, April 25, is celebrated as the moment when the Australian nation came of age. It commemorates the landing of the Australian and New Zealand Army Corps in Turkey as part of the British-led expeditionary force in 1915. The fact that the landing was a failure has not diminished the iconic character of the date.[11] Modern Turkey was born at the same time and in the same place. Mustafa Kemal, who was later known as Atatürk, commanded Turkish forces that held the heights overlooking Gallipoli. The first monument that leads from the Australian War Memorial in Canberra to the national parliament was placed there by Ataturk. Its inscription reads in part: "Rest in peace . . . you, the

9 Jay Winter and Antoine Prost, *René Cassin: Un soldat de la Grande Guerre* (Paris, 2010), ch. 3.
10 Jay Winter, *Sites of Memory, Sites of Mourning: The Great War in European Cultural History* (Cambridge, 1995), ch. 4.
11 Ken Inglis, "World War One Memorials in Australia," *Guerres mondiales et conflits contemporains* 167 (1992): 51–58.

mothers, who sent their sons from faraway countries wipe away your tears; your sons are now lying in our bosom and are in peace. After having lost their lives on this land, they have become our sons as well."[12] Here compassion crossed the battle lines; in many other instances, however, bitterness predominated. With images of Hitler and Mussolini in mind, many people concluded during the interwar years that commemorating war was a militarized exercise, which honored not only those who died in war but also war itself.

This functionalist interpretation, the view that commemoration was useful to right-wing nationalist and imperialist opinion, is widely held today, but it is not unchallenged.[13] A second school of scholarship emphasizes that public commemoration can allow dominated groups to contest their subordinate status. However much political leaders or their agents try to choreograph commemorative activity, there is space for subversion or creative interpretation of the official script. For different groups Armistice Day on November 11 was a moment for both celebration and denigration of military values. Pacifists announced their message "Never Again" at commemorative ceremonies; military men used these moments to glorify the profession of arms and demonstrate the duty of citizens to give their lives, if necessary, for their country in war. Like the contradictions in war itself, the contradictions in these simultaneous forms of expression have never been resolved.[14] This alternative interpretation of commemoration's meaning emphasizes its intrinsically multivocal character. De-centering the history of commemoration recognizes its polyvalence.

Occasionally, dissonant voices joined in a consensus about what was being remembered. Between 1919 and 1938 in Britain, a two-minute silence was observed throughout the country. Telephonists pulled the plugs on all conversations. Traffic stopped. The normal flow of life was arrested in the moment of national reflection. During World War II a disruption like this to war production was not in the national interest, so the two-minute silence was moved to the Sunday nearest November 11. During the interwar period, "Mass Observation," a pioneering social-survey organization, asked hundreds of British people what they thought about during the silence. They replied that they thought not of the nation, victory, or armies, but of the men who were not there. Their silence was a meditation on absence. It moved remembrance from political orchestration into the realm of family history.

12 www.skp.com.au/memorials2/pages/00012.htm.

13 George L. Mosse, *Fallen Soldiers: Reshaping the Memory of the Two World Wars* (New York and Oxford, 1990).

14 Adrian Gregory, *The Silence of Memory: Armistice Day, 1919–1946* (Leamington Spa, 1994).

Using shared language and gestures, families commemorated their own within wider social and political frameworks, but a level of intimacy remained in family remembrance. Käthe Kollwitz kept her son's room as it had been before he volunteered for service in 1914. The family celebrated Christmas here long after he died.[15] This braiding together of the public and the private, the macrohistorical and the microhistorical, gave war commemoration its power and rich repertoire of forms in the twentieth century.

Some of these forms were religious; others were more iconoclastic. There was in every combatant nation after 1914 an efflorescence of spiritualism, the belief that it was possible to communicate with the dead in a collective séance, led by a medium. Families took comfort from messages conveyed from their loved ones that they were safe and in the company of the army of the dead. The living could thus go on with their lives – freed, if they were fortunate, from some of the crushing burden of bereavement.[16]

Commemoration has always been a business. It costs money; it requires specialists' services and needs funding and, over time, re-funding. Two kinds of expenditure figure in the history of war commemoration. The first is capital expenditure; the second is recurrent expenditure.

The land for commemorative sites has to be purchased. Appropriate symbolic forms have to be designed, then constructed as a focus for remembrance activities. The first step requires money – sometimes substantial sums – whether public money or private. Especially in urban areas, private land has come at a premium. Then there are architects' fees, especially when a public competitive tender has been offered, as it was on many occasions after 1914, and professionals submitted proposals. Once the symbolic form is chosen, it has to be finished according to the architect's or artist's designs.

When these projects were national in character, production was in the public eye. National art schools and bodies of "experts" had to have their say. Standards of taste and decorum were proclaimed, though not necessarily observed *au pied de la lettre*. Professional interests and conflicts came into play. Professional infighting in national commemorative projects is well studied, but the same complex procedure occurred on the local level too, without the same level of attendant publicity. Local authorities usually took charge of these projects and occasionally deflected plans toward their own particular visions, whatever public opinion might have thought.

15 Jay Winter, "Communities in Mourning," in Jay Winter and Emmanuel Sivan, eds., *War and Remembrance in the Twentieth Century* (Cambridge, 1999), ch. 2.

16 Winter, *Sites of Memory*, ch. 3.

In thousands of commemorative projects, public funding covered only part of the costs. Public subscriptions were critical, especially in Protestant countries where the concept of utilitarian memorials was dominant. In Catholic countries the notion of a "useful" memorial was a contradiction in terms; symbolic language and utilitarian language were deemed mutually exclusive. Given traditions of volunteerism in Protestant countries, the rule of thumb was that private citizens picked up most of the tab. The state provided subsidies and occasional matching grants, but most of the money came from ordinary people. The same was true in Britain, at least with respect to a widely shared form of public commemoration: the purchase of paper poppies, the symbol of World War I's lost generation. These poppies are still worn on lapels, and the Royal British Legion and other charities use the proceeds of their sale to aid disabled veterans and their families.

The financial headaches of commemoration have left traces one can still see. In Cambridge a war memorial was constructed en route from the railway station to the center of the town, in order to mark the way along which the men who went to war returned victorious four years later. An undergraduate from the university served as a model, and his proud stride, that of the returning hero, replete with olive wreath, can be seen to this day. The problem was that the war memorial committee ran out of money during construction, so it remains lopsided. The figure has the legs suitable to an 8-foot statue, but the committee had enough money for only a 6-foot construction. The torso, too small for its legs, betrays the sculptor's economizing. Thousands of other local monuments were adjusted to the purse of their commissioners, but in Britain the most popular commemorative form was also the least expensive – the obelisk.[17]

The global scope of war meant that the business of remembrance entailed international travel. The voyages started as pilgrimages; many were mixed with tourism, although usually not in equal measure.[18] In either case, there were train and boat journeys to take, hotel rooms to reserve, guides to hire, flowers to lay at graves, trinkets and mementos to purchase. Museums told more of the story that pilgrims had come to share. Here, too, money was exchanged along with the narratives and symbols of remembrance. This mixture of the sacred and the profane was hardly an innovation. Pilgrimage

17 Ken Inglis, "The Homecoming: The War Memorial Movement in Cambridge, England," *Journal of Contemporary History* 27 (1992): 583–606.

18 David Lloyd, *Battlefield Tourism: Pilgrimage and the Commemoration of the Great War in Britain, Canada and Australia, 1918–1939* (Oxford, 1994).

to war cemeteries represents public commemoration over long distances. It was impossible to judge where pilgrimage stopped and tourism took over.

Veterans' associations dealt with financial questions of a different kind. Some ex-servicemen were so severely wounded that they shocked their own family members as well as passers-by. Such was true of the "*gueules cassées*," the men with broken faces. Disfigured veterans formed their own associations, and they joined together to buy land on which they could build summer cottages, taking their holidays in peace. They bought beach fronts, too, and gave their members a semblance of normalcy that they otherwise lacked most of the time.[19]

Other French soldiers gave a start in life to war orphans who had been adopted informally by the state. Veterans provided them with smallholdings, so they could marry and raise families as independent farmers. In other ways, too, veterans stood in for their brethren-in-arms, providing avuncular advice and money when possible. Family life was again the hidden site of commemoration. The costs of war were most frequently and anonymously remembered within families. The caretakers, particularly wives, sisters, and mothers, tended the wounded for decades after the war. The business of remembering was every day etched on their faces.

War remembrance is not only a set of political gestures and material tasks. It is also an art form, which arranges and interprets signifying practices. This field of action can be analyzed on two overlapping levels, the semiotic and aesthetic.

Some commemorative symbols are nationally distinctive; others are shared in many countries. The sculpture of a Gallic cock or common soldier (*poilu*), which were found on many French war memorials, could not be used in German or British sites. The Iron Cross on German commemorative plaques was out of place in Allied sites. Still, one country's symbolic repertoire sometimes overlapped with that of others, even when they had been adversaries. After World War I, the first war fought among fully industrialized nations, many commemorative forms used medieval notation. Images of knights and saintly warriors recaptured a time when combat took place between individuals, rather than as an impersonal, unbalanced duel between artillery and human flesh. In particular, the war in the air took on the form and romance of chivalry. On the losing and the winning sides alike, medievalism flourished.[20]

19 Sophie Delaporte, *Gueules cassées de la Grande Guerre* (Paris, 2004).
20 Stefan Goebel, *The Great War and Medieval Memory: War, Remembrance, and Medievalism in Britain and Germany 1914–1940* (Cambridge, 2007).

The human form survived on interwar war memorials. In some instances, classical images of male beauty marked the "lost generation"; other memorials adopted more stoic poses of men in uniform. In most cases, victory was either partially or totally eclipsed by a sense of overwhelming loss. Within this aesthetic landscape, traditional Christian motifs were commonplace. The form of the grieving mother – *Stabat Mater* – brought women into the local and national constellation of grief.[21]

In Protestant countries, the debate over aesthetics took on a quasi-religious character. War memorials with crosses offended some Protestants, who believed that the Reformation had precluded such "Catholic" notation. Obelisks were aesthetically preferable (as well as cheaper). In France, war memorials were restricted by law to public rather than church grounds, although many parishes in Catholic regions, such as Brittany, found ways around this proscription. In schools and universities, the location of memorials touched on similar issues. Some were placed in sacred space, such as chapels (as in New College, Oxford), semi-sacred space near chapels (as in Pembroke College, Cambridge), or secular space. Public thoroughfares and train stations also housed lists of names of those who had died in war.

This practice of naming set the pattern for commemorative forms after World War II and beyond. After 1945, names were simply added to World War I memorials. This practice recognized the links between the two twentieth-century conflicts; it was also a matter of economy in postwar austerity. Naming still mattered after the Vietnam War, and World War I forms inspired its memorials, most notably Maya Lin's Vietnam Veterans' Memorial in Washington. Her work drew on Sir Edwin Lutyens's memorial to the missing on the River Somme at Thiepval, which was inaugurated in 1932.

Most commemorative forms in the interwar years reflected the widespread hope that a catastrophe such as World War I could never happen again. One of the singular ironies of the period between the wars is that many believed at the same time that war was both unthinkable and just around the corner. This uneasy feeling, the sense that staggering sacrifices had been in vain, then made it difficult to return to the symbols of heroic national service after World War II. In addition, the tendency for artists to explore abstraction drew them away from the figurative domain, which had been central to the commemorative art of World War I. For these reasons, the story of war commemoration between 1914 and 1945 stands at the end of a longer story of mimesis and artistic representations of the human form. The vast array of commemorative art

21 Winter, *Sites of Memory*, ch. 4.

that was created during the first half of the twentieth century was like a nova, a flaring up before the extinction of a long tradition of religious, romantic, and classical forms, which had been explored in many ways to provide a framework of understanding, a sense of meaning, in an age of total war.

Before the 1930s, war remembrance focused on those who had served and died while in uniform. From the Spanish Civil War on, this activity extended to the remembrance of civilians who had suffered and died in war. Well over half the 50 million people who died in the war of 1939–45 were civilians. Nearly all 6 million victims of the Holocaust were. So were the ordinary people of Guernica, the Basque city that was bombed in 1937, whose suffering was captured in Picasso's painting. This painting, simply entitled *Guernica*, is a landmark in the shift of war remembrance from soldiers to civilians, the innocent victims of war.

The lethal reach of air power separated the killing of the two world wars, although civilians did perish in air bombardments during the first conflict. As the nature of war changed, so did commemorative language and gestures.[22] Picasso's mural shows this change in sharp relief. This painting is shocking in a host of ways. It is a cry of outrage, an accusation against the crimes of the German Condor Legion, whose bombers experimented in terror bombing, obliterating the center of this ancient Basque town. But it is more. It has iconic images of cruciform figures and broken statues, as well as a curious light bulb at its center. Commentators have interpreted this light bulb in different ways. A good guess is that it is what just it seems to be, a light bulb, a direct reference to the theme of "Illuminations," which was the leitmotiv of the 1937 Paris exhibition of the arts of everyday life. Picasso's mural was completed at staggering speed; after hearing of the attack on Guernica and seeing newsreels of the damage, he produced the painting in two weeks. It hung in the Spanish pavilion of the Parisian exhibition. Not far away at the same exhibition was the "House of Electricity," in which the French painter Raoul Dufy had painted *La Fée electricité*, the largest painting ever produced. It was a panegyric to science in general and electricity in particular. Picasso's light bulb showed the other face of science, its capacity to turn electricity into killing power. The victims in Guernica – the men, women, and animals that were torn apart – testified to the dark side of enlightenment, science turned into butchery.[23]

22 Jay Winter, "Pacifism, *Guernica*, and the Spanish Civil War," in Martin Baumeister and Stefanie Schüler-Springorum, eds., *"If You Tolerate This . . ." The Spanish Civil War in the Age of Total War* (Frankfurt, 2008), 267–92.

23 Jay Winter, *Dreams of Peace and Freedom: Utopian Moments in the Twentieth Century* (New Haven, 2007), ch. 3.

Picasso's *Guernica* was in many ways the most important work of commemorative painting of the twentieth century. After the fall of the Spanish Republic in 1939, it migrated from Paris to New York, before it was eventually installed in its present home, in the Reina Sofia Museum in Madrid. It not only commemorates the suffering of the Spanish Civil War, but also evokes the madness of armed conflict *tout court*.

Before 1945 commemoration was framed in the multiform languages of hope. The purpose was not only to imbue war with redemptive meaning, but also to renew and repair the symbols of civilization itself. Much of the work of remembrance had an implicit or explicit pacifist message: war on this scale must never happen again. Soldiers had died by the millions so their sons would not follow them into combat. This vision was by no means the only one to come out of World War I. Some veterans, like Hitler, dreamed of revenge and reversing the defeat of 1918. Another, Mussolini, strutted around the stage of interwar politics, seeking a grandeur that Italy had failed to find in either World War I or the ensuing peace. Partly because of the weakness of the League of Nations, which was designed to offer collective security to the world, partly because of the erosion of democratic regimes in the world economic crisis, partly because the horror of another conflict disposed peace-loving people to appease dictators in hopes of avoiding war, these warmongers won the argument.

During World War II, discussion focused on how its commemoration would differ from that of World War I a generation earlier. Nazi occupation and collaboration made straightforward national narratives of heroism on the battlefield unacceptable. In addition, the centrality of air power created so many ruins that preserving them became a challenge of a different magnitude. Coventry Cathedral was left precisely as it was on November 15, 1940, the morning after a Luftwaffe raid. The scale of the devastation made ruins the iconic landscape of World War II. That was as true of Dresden as it was of Warsaw or Tokyo. After the vast commemorative efforts and hopes that attended World War I, it was impossible simply to repeat the messages of redemption that had been imbedded in war memorials throughout the world. New forms and images were needed to give meaning to the second total war of the twentieth century and to later conflagrations.

14

Military doctrine and planning in the interwar era

EUGENIA C. KIESLING

Twentieth-century military studies commonly treat the period 1919–39 as one of preparation for World War II.[1] Apart from its teleology, this orthodox narrative is limited by a technological emphasis. The interwar years become a Eurocentric historical laboratory, in which historians assess how well the participants combined past experience, evolving technology, and prognostications. Who demonstrated the highest level of military effectiveness in preparing for World War II? In the process, who offered the best model from which successor military organizations should learn?[2]

This chapter looks beyond this narrative and the telos of World War II in three contexts. One is social, in this term's broad sense. To say, for example, that "the German and Soviet militaries had spent the previous twenty years imagining future conflict and arming their nations to win the coming war of technology" is to obscure the nature of doctrinal development.[3] Doctrine, the stated subject of this chapter, does not derive cleanly from a synergy of military theory and weapons' capabilities, but results instead from the complex interaction of political, economic, cultural, and other factors.

The second context of this chapter is institutional. A contemporary American artillery officer, Captain John K. Christmas, observed that peacetime military "developments are often deflected by traditions, immediate expediencies, peace requirements, and the political and financial factors involved." While the notion is so obvious as to approach cliché, it highlights the broad range of things – those "immediate expediencies" – that soldiers do

1 Thanks for editorial advice from Greg Daddis and Randy Papadopoulos and for significant revisions by Dennis Showalter.

2 See especially Allan R. Millett and Williamson Murray, eds., *Military Effectiveness* (3 vols., Boston, 1988) and Harold R. Winton and David R. Mets, eds., *The Challenge of Change: Military Institutions and New Realities, 1918–1941* (Lincoln, NE, 2003).

3 Mary R. Habeck, *Storm of Steel: The Development of Armor Doctrine in Germany and the Soviet Union, 1919–1939* (Ithaca, 2003), ix.

on a routine basis.[4] Theory is important, but a more accurate understanding of wartime practice comes from the study of the minutiae of peacetime military activity – the military historian's *Alltagsgeschichte*.

The chapter's third context is geographic. Doctrine is the focus of the chapter, but armed forces exist for purposes ignored in studies of doctrine. In much of the world, armies were too engaged in state-building to have time for war-planning. And the military instruments of state-building were usually anything but technological.

For an illustration of this point, one can look at the experience of interwar Brazil. In 1916, Brazil emulated nineteenth-century European states by introducing a conscript army as a means to promote national cohesion and create "conscientious and dignified Brazilians."[5] While most Brazilian officers were comfortable with the liberal government, an energetic minority claimed to represent the national interest when they demanded social reform as well as military modernization.[6] Revolution and civil war in the 1930s ended in a coup by Getúlio Vargas, who, pursuing his generals' vision of national defense requirements, established an authoritarian government in 1937. The soldiers' repeated interventions in politics did not significantly involve issues of doctrinal or material innovation. Absent a modern armaments industry, French military advisors struggled to bring the Brazilian army, which had been at peace since 1870, up to the standards of 1918, let alone 1939.[7] Laurels, however dubious, won during its brief engagement on the Italian front during World War II made the army the unifying national symbol that its founders had sought three decades earlier. The soldiers who returned from Europe played an important role in the removal of Vargas's autocratic regime in 1945. If this action had little to do with traditional military effectiveness, the Brazilian army's example is more generally relevant to the history of nation-building than is the lurid history of the *Wehrmacht*.[8] The armies of Latin America serve

4 John K. Christmas, "The Mechanization of Armies," *Military Engineer* (July–August 1929), 340, quoted in George F. Hofmann, *Camp Colt to Desert Storm: The History of US Armored Forces* (Lexington, KY, 1999), 111.

5 Peter M. Beattie, *The Tribute of Blood: Race, Honor, and Nation in Brazil, 1864–1945* (Durham, NC, and London, 2001), 230.

6 Frank D. McCann, *Soldiers of the Patria: A History of the Brazilian Army, 1889–1937* (Stanford, 2004), 262–63.

7 Robert L. Scheina, *Latin America's Wars*, vol. II: *The Age of the Professional Soldiers, 1900–2001* (Washington, DC, 2003), 166–69.

8 For another, equally instructive case, see William F. Sater and Holger H. Herwig, *The Grand Illusion: The Prussianization of the Chilean Army* (Lincoln, NE, and London, 1999), 201.

as a reminder that armies operate in their own unique circumstances, while studies of military effectiveness beg the question "effectiveness for what?"

The interwar experiences of other countries offer additional insights into doctrinal formation without shedding any light on World War II. Like many more recent military actions, General Augusto C. Sandino's revolt in Nicaragua in 1926 was a personal power play against a president whose election had been secured by US Marines. Sandino claimed to be fighting not against his own government but the US intrusion into Nicaraguan affairs. His army's incompetence proved irrelevant to the outcome, since its regular defeats, at least as reported by the Sandinista press, inspired Nicaraguans with a vision of heroic resistance. Far from building a disciplined army, Sandino encouraged his peasant recruits to plunder their own people. At every level, loot was a major objective of the exercise, which represented an example of the Latin American phenomenon of "revolution" as "a valid economic alternative for those who are unable or usually unwilling to obtain more traditional employment."[9] The turning point of the campaign against the Americans occurred when eight marines were killed or wounded in an ambush, after which the US Senate voted to withdraw all US forces.[10] After the withdrawal of these forces and the election in November 1932 of another liberal general, Sandino agreed to retire.[11] The Nicaraguan insurgency's origins in personal ambition and Sandino's methods of raising combatants and resources from the countryside have plenty of parallels, past and present. So does Sandino's exploitation of his primary asset, which was the effect of American operations, especially aerial bombing, on Nicaraguan and international opinion.[12]

In the conventional interwar military historiography, the war in Spain appears as a doctrinal proving-ground for foreign armies. Seen on its own terms, however, the Civil War of 1936–39 was the formative experience of modern Spain. It is less interesting as a precursor of World War II than for its parallels with modern conflicts that combine foreign war with internal political, ideological, and religious struggles. Most of the weapons tested in Spain were early or interim models, whose effectiveness was difficult to assess because they were employed by or against unskilled Spanish troops. From

9 René de la Pedraja, *Wars of Latin America, 1899–1941* (Jefferson, NC, and London, 2006), 309–18, citation 318.
10 Ibid., 320.
11 Ibid., 322–24.
12 Richard Hallion, *Strike from the Sky: The History of Battlefield Air Attack 1911–1945* (Washington, DC, and London, 1989), 71–74.

the results, foreign armies learned what they or – in the Soviet case – their political masters wished. For example, the effectiveness of antitank guns against primitive tanks confirmed most armies' preferences for using armor only in cautious combination with infantry. Although bombings of Madrid and Guernica offered a shocking foretaste of air warfare against civilian targets, they did not resolve disagreements about whether air power was best used in direct support of ground and naval forces or for independent, strategic missions.

The Spanish Civil War was more significant as a demonstration of war as a political contest. The combatants fought to impose competing visions of economy, society, and culture, and the struggle within the government coalition of republican, anarcho-syndicalist, socialist, and communist groups proved as important as the civil war between the government and the Nationalists. Military analysis alone, however, cannot explain a war whose outcome so depended on support from outside, especially since the Soviet Union modulated its aid to the Republican side in pursuit of policy-objectives that were opaque to idealists in the antifascist ranks. Three interconnected struggles – international, national, and factional – were conducted largely in the realm of propaganda. Posters, radio broadcasts, newspapers, and sermons fired ideological and religious broadsides of the sort now disseminated via television, the Internet, text-messages, and fatwa.

Connections between warfare and political mobilization were also explicit in the Chinese Communist Party's twin struggles against internal rivals and the invading Japanese. Mao Zedong insisted that the army be a tool of the Chinese Communist Party, an integrated political and military instrument. Party-political officers promulgated ideology to the soldiers, who disseminated it throughout the country. The soldiers were meant to be volunteers, paid only their basic expenses to live the egalitarian life for which they fought.[13] Mao's theory of revolutionary war, in which political education was both a means and an end in the struggle for liberation, proved one of the most influential developments of the interwar period. Indeed, given the uncertain future of the People's Republic of China, the historical significance of Mao's military doctrines remains incalculable.

Brazil, Nicaragua, Spain, and China illustrate the value of examining interwar military events in broad contexts and on their own terms. The importance of military *Alltagsgeschichte* and military culture in the

13 Xiaobing Li, *A History of the Modern Chinese Army* (Lexington, KY, 2007), 34–35, 39, 45, 51–55.

development of doctrine is highlighted in three of the interwar era's other military powers, Japan, the United States, and Germany.

The military history of interwar Japan offers an especially sharp challenge to the conventional analytical model, which assumes a technologically inspired synergy among policy, strategy, operations, and tactics. More than in the case of any other power, the Japanese army and navy competed intensely with one another in their claims to interpret Japan's national interest. Although either China or the Soviet Union could have occupied the attention of the Japanese army, neither potential adversary aroused the interest of the navy, which was keen to exploit its position after 1918 as the world's third largest navy. Disputes over strategy between army and navy, and within each service, encouraged less strategic reflection than competitive actions, such as the invasions of Manchuria and China. A culture that justified insubordination, if it was committed in the name of Japan's warrior spirit, led junior officers from the army to murder a prime minister in 1932 and to attempt to overthrow the government in 1936.[14]

The navy had little interest in the war in China, but the army's failure to bring the ground campaign to a satisfactory conclusion sparked the navy's effort to bomb the Chinese people into submission with long-range aircraft, which had been designed to cooperate with the fleet. The ensuing terror-bombing campaign typified the chaotic policies that emanated from immediate concerns with little strategic direction. Although it raised the navy's status in relationship to the army and provided useful combat experience for its pilots, participation in China diverted the navy from its maritime mission. It increased the navy's investment in land-based bombers and pilots at the expense of the carrier fleet. It distracted naval planners from the strategic requirements of a war against the United States, which the navy's aspirations and thinking rendered increasingly likely. The navy ignored the strategic purposes of air warfare, treating it as a technical and tactical problem. Small numbers of good aircraft and superb pilots proved inadequate, however, to the demands of a war against the United States.

In a broader context, the Imperial Japanese Navy disdained logistics in pursuit of technology. Condemned by the terms of the Washington Naval Treaty to numerical inferiority to both Great Britain and the United States, but committed to a Mahanian effort to destroy any fleet that ventured into the western Pacific, Japan determined to beat greater tonnage with superior weapons manned by highly trained crews. Prior to decisive fleet action, the

14 Ben-Ami Shillony, *Revolt in Japan* (Princeton, 1973).

unfavorable balance of tonnage was to be lessened in an offensive campaign of attrition, which would employ fleet submarines, cruisers, and destroyers that had been trained for night battle and equipped with revolutionary oxygen-propelled torpedoes.[15] This action was to be followed by strikes by carrier-aircraft against the US carriers. The Japanese reliance on quality over mass was further embodied in the 18-inch-gunned super-battleships *Yamato* and *Musashi*, which Japanese naval planners had begun to design even before Japan abrogated the Washington Treaty.

In the Soviet Union, the Japanese army itself faced an enemy that was far superior in material resources. Unlike the navy, the army did not seek technical solutions to material deficiencies; instead it embraced the belief that the warrior spirit would prove as indomitable as it had been in 1905. That the newest Japanese light machine guns incorporated bayonet mounts symbolized the conviction that courageous infantrymen could overcome technological disadvantages. But the Arisaka rifle proved so poor a weapon that many soldiers preferred the hand grenade. Japanese artillery lacked the range and projectile weight to compete against Soviet guns. In the absence of an effective antitank weapon at the Battle of Nomonhan, Japanese infantry improvised Molotov cocktails from soft-drink bottles filled with sand and gasoline.[16] Japan's armored force featured diminutive two-man, infantry-support tankettes. Defeat at Nomonhan in August 1939 taught the Japanese that *bushido* had to be buttressed by modern weapons.[17] Until these could be produced, however, willpower inculcated through rigorous, ferocious training had to suffice.

Wishful thinking was even more pronounced at the operational level. An army that disdained logistical personnel did not concern itself with the inadequacies of its supply arrangements. In the short run, the Japanese soldier's ability to fight for days on nothing but the rice in his pack gave the army extraordinary freedom of movement, but the inability to supply soldiers with adequate rations, let alone ammunition or fuel, proved a devastating weakness in a war against an industrial giant (in this case, too, the United States).

The army created by the United States National Defense Act of 1920 suited a country that was wary of militarism, fortunate in the width of its saltwater moat,

15 David C. Evans and Mark R. Peattie, *Kaigun: Strategy, Tactics, and Technology in the Imperial Japanese Navy 1887–1941* (Annapolis, MD, 1997), 217–29, 220–23.

16 Alvin D. Coox, *Nomonhan: Japan against Russia, 1939* (Stanford, 1985), 310.

17 Edward J. Drea, "Tradition and Circumstances: The Imperial Japanese Army's Tactical Response to Khalkhin-Gol, 1939," in *In the Service of the Emperor: Essays on the Imperial Japanese Army* (Lincoln, NE, and London, 1998), 11.

and determined to avoid another bloody foreign adventure. This small, professional force, which was largely isolated from the national culture, provided an instructive case study of soldiering in a strategic and financial vacuum.[18] The army's most striking aspect was the disregard of technological innovation in favor of professional study and mobilization-planning. Shrunk to numbers inadequate even for training, let alone for fighting a modern war, the US army compensated by educating its officers to handle practical, organizational problems – on paper. While only a small percentage of the officer corps could advance beyond branch schools, they established a model for the rest, and the army rewarded their credentials with key command and staff positions during World War II.[19]

While planners in the War Department developed schemes to man and equip a mass army, graduates of the Army Industrial College drafted legislation that provided a peacetime framework for incorporating civilian resources into the nation's arsenal.[20] None of these ideas had immediate practical consequences in the isolationist environment, but they justified the assertion that American soldiers understood "that major wars were 'total wars' comprehending the whole of the warring nations' economy and manpower."[21] Within the War Department, these exercises encouraged the vision of war as a strategic whole and, at least at the planning level, heightened an appreciation for the material bases of victory.

The emphasis on *matériel* did not result in a craving for new weapons. Although the United States led the world in civilian applications of the internal-combustion engine, tank development remained a cottage industry. American soldiers saw warfare as a test of human rather than technological prowess. Interwar preparations emphasized the eventual mobilization of large numbers of infantrymen. Chief of Staff Douglas MacArthur warned against spending scarce funds on *matériel* at the expense of "the human element."[22]

18 Budget constraints limited the army's total strength to less than 138,000 of an authorized 298,000 for most of the interwar period: Edward M. Coffman, *The Regulars: The American Army 1898–1941* (Cambridge, MA, and London, 2004), 234.

19 Peter Schifferle, *America's School for War: Fort Leavenworth, Officer Education, and Victory in World War II* (Lawrence, KS, 2010). Other laudatory studies of the CGSS are Timothy K. Nenninger, "Leavenworth and Its Critics: The US Army Command and General Staff School, 1920–1940," *Journal of Military History* 58 (1994): 199–231, and Harold R. Winton, *Corps Commanders in the Bulge: Six American Generals and Victory in the Ardennes* (Lawrence, KS, 2007).

20 On the public outcry against the mobilization law, which was similar to the reaction in France, see Marvin A. Kreidberg, *History of Military Mobilization in the United States Army 1775–1945* (Washington, DC, 1955), 493–94.

21 Ibid.

22 David E. Johnson, *Fast Tanks and Heavy Bombers: Innovation in the US Army, 1917–1945* (Ithaca and New York, 1998), 113.

The signature US weapon of World War II, the M1 Garand rifle, symbolized the American belief in individual marksmanship in a period when other armies saw riflemen as handmaidens of the light machine gun.

The army's interwar experiments with tanks and tank-destroyers provides additional evidence that in shaping technological choices, institutional culture tends to trump both strategic vision and operational planning.[23] Only in June 1940 did the War Department overrule objections from the rival infantry and cavalry branches to mandate the creation of an armored force. Its new medium tanks were to carry a low-velocity, general-purpose 75-millimeter main gun, which was mediocre as an antitank weapon.[24] The antitank mission fell instead to the artillery branch, whose solution was the "tank-destroyer." Created by mounting a 75-millimeter gun on a medium-tank chassis, the tank-destroyer was supposed to close rapidly, strike from cover, and withdraw before the enemy could react. Aggressiveness, skill, and independent action would make tank-destroyers as lethal to massed armor as American riflemen – and their bayonets – were to enemy infantry. However, sometimes called "the artilleryman's solution to the problem posed by a mobile, armored target," the tank-destroyer was an orphan; it was given up by the field artillery for eventual development under a separate command.[25]

The field artillery branch's rejection of the tank-destroyer reflected its confidence in towed artillery, as well as its preference for offensive, infantry support over a defensive, antitank role.[26] As late as 1938 about half of the US light artillery was horse-drawn. While artillerymen eventually accepted the idea that guns ought to be towed by tractors, which were replaceable by horses in time of need, they balked at self-propelled guns.[27] Given its grudging abandonment of the horse, the interwar field artillery was hardly a model of peacetime innovation. Even the official branch historian, Boyd L. Dastrup, has found little improvement in equipment or tactics over the methods of World War I.[28] But Dastrup's tale of "conservatism, limited funds, and pacifism" pays too little attention to the prosaic processes by which US ordnance became a war-winning weapon.

23 For a good introduction see ibid.

24 For a short, useful discussion of technical issues in tank design, see M. Ogorkiewicz, *Design and Development of Fighting Vehicles* (Garden City, NY, 1967), 25–41.

25 Johnson, *Fast Tanks*, 152.

26 Boyd L. Dastrup, *King of Battle: A Branch History of the U.S. Army's Field Artillery* (Washington, DC, 1993), 199–201.

27 Constance McLaughlin Green et al., *The Ordnance Department: Planning Munitions for War* (Washington, DC, 1955), 203–4. The statistic applies to German artillery as well.

28 Dastrup, *King of Battle*, 190.

An inquiry in 1919 into the army's performance during World War I produced plans for new light, medium, and heavy guns and howitzers, all of which were ready for action by the end of 1942.[29] Thanks to technical innovations that remain underappreciated, the new field pieces fired superior shells, which were detonated by sophisticated fuses. Fire-control procedures, which were based on improved communications and new methods to compute trajectories, allowed massed fire at the battalion and later division level. When the air corps refused to disperse control over air assets to help find targets and adjust fire, field artilleryman bought their own aircraft.[30] The result was the ability to fire the "time on target" (i.e. simultaneous detonation) barrages, that were feared – and unmatched by – Axis combatants. American political circumstances in the interwar period dictated a small professional army, which was unsuited for world war, but whose ethos favored the creation of the artillery that won the battles in western Europe, as well as the industrial organization that won the war.

Germany's stunning successes in the period 1939–41 seem to have been the fruits of two decades of assiduous preparation. Received wisdom is that the small army that the Treaty of Versailles allowed Germany laid the foundations for successes in World War II, developing a military culture that dictated professional training to the exclusion of external matters. In fact, in interwar Germany the armed forces were shaped by "immediate expediencies." By throwing the army's support behind Friedrich Ebert's socialist government on November 9, 1918, General Wilhelm Groener helped stabilize a disintegrating country.[31] Hans von Seeckt, the chief of staff from 1919 to 1920 and then commander-in-chief until 1926, had exploited weaknesses in the Weimar constitution to pursue independent policies, such as secret military collaboration with the Soviet Union.[32] His pretense to political neutrality promoted an army that could claim to represent the true interests of Germany and "save Germany from the ravages of the politicians."[33] His tacit approval of right-wing sentiments legitimated an enduring anti-republican tone within the

29 Ibid., 183, 206.

30 Edgar F. Raines, Jr., *Eyes of Artillery: The Origins of Modern US Army Aviation in World War II* (Washington, DC, 2000), 15–16.

31 Gordon A. Craig, *The Politics of the Prussian Army, 1640–1945* (Oxford, 1955), 377.

32 In general, Seeckt's pro-Soviet policy conflicted with Gustav Stresemann's efforts to reconcile Germany with the West. See Gordon A. Craig, *Germany 1866–1945* (Oxford, 1981), 520

33 Matthew Cooper, *The German Army 1933–1945: Its Political and Military Failure* (London, 1978), 10.

army.[34] Collaboration with Adolf Hitler in 1933, which was rationalized as a disinterested effort to solve the ills of the Weimar government, put the army in the service of a political vision.[35]

Seeckt was not an apolitical general, nor did German military doctrine grow in an apolitical environment.[36] Officially an imposition of the Versailles regime, the new professional army suited Seeckt. Well-armed, highly trained, long-service professionals could outmaneuver, envelop, and destroy the large but indifferently trained armies of the traditional European pattern. "Mass," he observed, "becomes immobile: it cannot maneuver and therefore cannot win victories, it can only crush by sheer weight." Smaller forces brought fewer logistical constraints and more rapid adaptation to changes in technology. A full-time professional army could maintain a higher and more uniform level of training than a reserve-based army.

Doctrinal choices had deep political roots in this army. Led by Lieutenant Colonel Joachim von Stülpnagal, some officers argued that World War I had erased distinctions between soldier and civilian and that the logical outcome of this fact was a *Volkskrieg*, a people's war of terror against an invading army.[37] To Seeckt, who was eager to reassert the army's monopoly over armed conflict, this vision implied the chaos of socialist militias and *Freikorps*.[38] When in 1928 war games based on the scenario produced a comprehensive German defeat, the minister of war, Wilhelm Groener, demanded a new strategy based on deterrence, defensive warfare, and international cooperation. Defenders of Reichswehr planning – and culture – countered by decrying national submission to "military rape."[39]

The same mentality that made the Reichswehr hostile both to people's war and to defensive-strategy war fostered an enthusiasm for tanks, whose mechanized firepower promised to multiply the offensive operational potential of a small army. Treaty prohibitions whetted appetites for armored

34 Craig, *Politics*, 353–56.

35 Manfred Messerschmitt, "German Military Effectiveness between 1919 and 1939," in Millet and Murray, eds., *Military Effectiveness*, Vol. II: 222.

36 For Seeckt's dabbling in treason, see Craig, *Germany*, 431, 460, 463. Groener complained that Seeckt's public espousal of *Überparteilichkeit* challenged his subordinates to guess which political line would foster their careers: Craig, *Politics*, 435.

37 Michael Geyer, "German Strategy in the Age of Machine Warfare, 1914–1945," in Peter Paret, ed., *Makers of Modern Strategy: From Machiavelli to the Nuclear Age* (Princeton, 1986), 557–61.

38 James Corum, *The Roots of Blitzkrieg: Hans von Seeckt and the German Military Reform* (Lawrence, KS, 1992), 63–64.

39 Geyer, "German Strategy," 561–62. Groener also preferred a conscript army to Seeckt's wholly professional force and advocated a form of the *Krümper* system in 1932, Corum, *Roots of Blitzkrieg*, 53, 181.

fighting vehicles, even as they prevented wasteful expenditure on primitive models. Germany had little need to test tanks, as long as reports of foreign exercises with the world's most modern models were in public circulation.[40] British maneuvers in particular convinced the Germans that, in the words of Werner von Fritsch, "armoured, quickly moving tanks most probably will become the operationally decisive offensive weapon. From an operational standpoint, this weapon will be most effective if concentrated in independent units like tank brigades."[41]

New machines, however, did not come with instruction books or a new operational vision. Well before World War I, the fear that a European war would escalate in magnitude and violence – with corresponding disruptions to German political institutions – led Germany's professional soldiers to emphasize the decisive battle (*Vernichtungsschlacht*). Their grail was the rapid destruction of enemy armies, in order to secure victory before the exigencies of national mobilization wrested strategic leadership from their hands.[42] In the German military tradition, decisive battle meant the *Kesselschlacht*, the sort of encirclement that Helmuth von Moltke had achieved against the Austrians at the battle of Königgratz in 1866 and against the French at Sedan in 1870. The encirclement of the French armies on a much larger scale had failed in 1914, but mechanization promised the mobility that would have made Alfred von Schlieffen's concept a success. In the interwar period dominant German doctrine treated armored divisions as partners with infantry and artillery units in a combined-arms effort to encircle and destroy enemy armies. Instead of changing German military thought, tanks contributed firepower and mobility to plans that were rooted in a military culture still dominated by the figures of the Elder Moltke, Schlieffen, and Seeckt.[43]

Competing with *Vernichtungskrieg* was another vision, which was propounded most notably by Generals Oswald Lutz and Heinz Guderian and based on the so-called "indirect approach" of the British theorist B. H. Liddell Hart. The proponents of annihilation conceived of armored units as

40 For a discussion of homegrown German armor theory and an argument for the primacy of Liddell Hart's views over those of Fuller in shaping the creation of the German Panzer divisions, see Azar Gat, *British Armour Theory and the Rise of the Panzer Arm: Revising the Revisionists* (New York, 1999).

41 Cited ibid., 54; Geyer, "German Strategy," 559.

42 Ibid., 531.

43 Here I disagree with Corum's identification of Seeckt as the father of the Blitzkrieg and with Willmott's admittedly sophisticated analysis of Blitzkrieg as a component of the *Vernichtungsschlacht*, as well as with Wilmott's assumption that the *Vernichtungsschlacht* required mass: H. P. Willmott, *When Men Lost Faith in Reason: Reflections on War and Society in the Twentieth Century* (Westport, CT, 2002), 104–12.

elements of combined-arms operational forces. The "armored idea" recast the tank as a strategic tool.[44] Rather than destroying an enemy army, which took time, the armored idea called for paralyzing it. For this purpose, however, numbers could be counterproductive, and firepower was less important than mobility.

In the dispute between the *Vernichtungsgedanke* and the "armored idea," National Socialism proved paradoxically to be a conservative force. Although they were pleased by restored conscription and growing budgets, senior officers did not share Hitler's timetable for rearmament. Seeckt's Reichswehr had favored mobility over mass; his heirs sought a calibrated expansion of the army, in order not to flood it with unassimilable numbers.[45] In the face of threats to their autonomy and a disruptive surge in military manpower, these officers sought uniform standards of equipment and training throughout the army, and they resisted diverting scarce resources to a separate armored force. The apparent affinity between blitzkrieg and National Socialism disguised the Nazis' adherence to the more traditional *Vernichtungsgedanke*. Even after expansion flooded the *Wehrmacht* with young men who were steeped in party propaganda, the conservative officer corps hardly welcomed the intrusion of ideology into military life, and they resented colleagues, many of whom were associated with the idea of independent armored forces, whose attachment to the party fostered their careers.[46]

In any case, the material bases for conversion to the armored idea did not exist. Germany was deficient in military equipment of all types, as well as oil. That between 1937 and 1941 only 5 percent of the *Wehrmacht*'s budget went to tanks and motor vehicles, while the fact that almost a third went to traditional infantry weapons, artillery tubes, and ammunition spoke volumes about German doctrine.[47]

44 Cooper, *German Army*, 143–44. Cooper accepts Liddell Hart's claim to have influenced Heinz Guderian. This claim was demolished in John J. Mearsheimer, *Liddell Hart and the Weight of History* (New York, 1988) but revivified in Gat, *British Armour Theory*. On Liddell Hart's influence on Erwin Rommel, see Cooper, *German Army*, 145.

45 Ibid., 120; Craig, *Politics*, 485.

46 James S. Corum, *The Luftwaffe: Creating the Operational Air War, 1918–1940* (Lawrence, KS, 1997), 121. War Minister Werner von Blomberg, a senior officer with a rare enthusiasm for Hitler, added National Socialism to the training program in 1933, mostly to gain Hitler's support in the army's competition with the *Sturmabteilung* (SA): Craig, *Politics*, 473–76. By the time the war started, the *Wehrmacht* was wholly, in Omer Bartov's words, "Hitler's Army." See Omer Bartov, *Hitler's Army: Soldiers, Nazis, and War in the Third Reich* (New York, 1991); Geoffrey Megargee, *Inside Hitler's High Command* (Lawrence, KS, 2002).

47 Adam Tooze, *The Wages of Destruction: The Making and Unmaking of the Nazi Economy* (London and New York, 2006), 212.

German success in Poland was due not to a new "armored idea," but instead to good training in traditional combined-arms warfare, an institutional culture that fostered aggression and initiative, and the strategic advantage of an envelopment campaign launched from both Polish flanks. Had the *Wehrmacht* executed its original plan for the invasion of France, the operation would have reiterated the German commitment to the *Vernichtungskrieg*. It would also have suited French defensive arrangements and might well have failed, making impossible the claim that the interwar German army "solved the problem of operational indecisiveness."[48]

Like the mechanization of the *Wehrmacht*, the Luftwaffe's doctrine is easily misunderstood by those who seek the roots of a technologically driven blitzkrieg in the interwar period. In the 1920s the Reichswehr had taken cooperation between air and ground operations for granted, integrating aircraft, albeit imaginary ones, into maneuvers. Once the new Luftwaffe came into being, however, it showed less interest in joint operations, demanding a four-engine bomber – aviation's new icon and the surest demonstration of an air force's institutional autonomy. The Luftwaffe's version of ground support was air-interdiction, the bombing of troop-assembly areas and lines of communication. However, mesmerized by the actions of German JU-87 Stukas in Poland and France, historians have exaggerated the Luftwaffe's interest in close-air support by the end of the 1930s. Even the Stuka was initially regarded as a tactical bomber more than a close-support aircraft.[49]

Luftwaffe doctrine drew little from the writings of the Italian air-power prophet, General Giulio Douhet. In fact, the Luftwaffe rejected the terror-bombing of cities on principle.[50] Germany lacked the financial and industrial resources to build an air force capable of achieving the air superiority that Douhet envisaged, let alone to relegate the army and navy to a secondary role.[51]

Discussions of a doctrine of "total war" have further diverted attention from the practical roots of German doctrine. The book most often credited with publicizing the concept of total war, Erich Ludendorff's *Der totale Krieg*, which appeared in 1935, contained less military theory than incoherent ranting.

48 Robert M. Citino, *Blitzkrieg to Desert Storm: The Evolution of Operational Warfare* (Lawrence, KS, 2004), 27

49 Corum, *Luftwaffe*, 230–31. Against Corum's argument (p. 268) that the decision reflected a preference for close air support, Richard Muller points out that in 1939 even the Stukas were assigned to strategic bombing: Muller, *The German Air War in Russia* (Baltimore, 1992), 19.

50 Corum, *Luftwaffe*, 89.

51 Ibid., 143–44, 238–39.

Ludendorff was less interested in the organized mobilization of national resources than he was enraptured by an unreasoning surge of the "national soul" under the guidance of a charismatic leader.[52] In treating "total war" as a shortcut to victory rather than a recipe for outlasting the enemy in a modern war of attrition, Ludendorff shared a lot with Douhet, who advocated the destruction of cities in the interest of a rapid decision, but little with the proponents of the *Vernichtungskrieg*. For the *Wehrmacht*, "total" war implied unwanted civilian intrusion into the military realm. As Michael Geyer puts it, the primary concern of German military planners in the interwar years was to limit war in order to make it once again the purposeful use of force under elite control.[53]

France, Great Britain, and the USSR had in common two decades of opportunity to make military preparations for war in stable, albeit not static contexts. The French army, a self-appointed defender of the social and political order, had a conflicted relationship with the French civilian government. The tension reflected the experience of World War I, the lesson that victory required the mobilization of national resources for what Georges Clemenceau had dubbed *"la guerre intégrale"* or "total war." Military leaders, too, recognized the need to ensure the infrastructure that sustained France's army, navy, and colonial empire. "Total war" was the French answer to Germany's demographic superiority and France's own postwar overstretch. France maintained a professional cadre to train a mass army based on universal male conscription – *la nation armée*. French generals had to believe that war would see the whole country rally behind the tricolor.

The theory that modern wars would be tests of national endurance was reassuring to the leaders of a country that was unwilling to support a large peacetime army. It led to the adoption of a "long-war" strategy and a defensive military doctrine, but it also engendered concerns within the army about the political culture of France. Victory in "total" war required France to retain the patriotic spirit that had supported the horrendous sacrifices of World War I. But what if France ceased to be a cohesive country? In the immediate

52 For Ludendorff's role in orchestrating German "total war" from 1916 to 1918, see Gerald D. Feldman, *Army, Industry, and Labor* (Princeton, 1966), 150. Roger Chickering offers the observation about authorship of the Hindenburg Program in "Sore Loser: Ludendorff's Total War," in Roger Chickering and Stig Förster, eds., *The Shadows of Total War: Europe, East Asia, and the United States, 1919–1939* (Cambridge, 2003), 172. Chickering argues that the lack of interest in Ludendorff's book on the part of the German government, National Socialist Party, and *Wehrmacht* signifies not its irrelevance but the depth to which Germans had embraced an ideology, however inchoate, of "total war": ibid., 177–78.

53 Geyer, "German Strategy," 554.

aftermath of World War I, a prostrate Germany seemed to be a more distant problem to many French officers than was domestic communism.

Insubordinate rumblings within the officer corps, reinforced by the army's history of repressing political and labor unrest, not to mention the matter of Alfred Dreyfus, led the French left, though it was not unmoved by arguments based on the imperatives of national security, to sponsor a series of measures, which were popular in war-weary France, to diminish the army's influence over the population.[54] The period of conscript service fell from three years to eighteen months in 1923 and to one year in 1926. In 1928, the annual intake was divided into two parts, forcing the professional cadres to renew the cycle of basic training every semester and to abandon the second-semester conscripts to make-work employment. Although lawmakers spoke of regular reserve training as compensation for the attenuated period of active military service, they proved reluctant to fund such impositions on their fellow citizens.[55]

Such measures reinforced the beleaguered officers' belief that the government no longer protected the country's values.[56] General Maximé Weygand made so little secret of his disdain for republican politicians that they required him to swear an extraordinary oath to the republic upon assuming the position of commander-in-chief designate in January 1931.[57] Opinions differ as to the competence of Weygand's successor, General Maurice Gamelin, but even his most sympathetic biographer acknowledges the role that political adroitness and a reputation as "a republican general" played in his ascent.[58]

This political environment did not promote reasoned debate over military doctrine. When the French parliament debated a proposal in 1935 to create a mechanized striking force on the model that had been outlined by Charles de Gaulle in his *Vers l'armée de métier*, arguments over the value of independent armored units were drowned out in the uproar over de Gaulle's insistence, which was anathema to French republicans, that the armored units be manned exclusively by professional soldiers. In the long run, de Gaulle will be remembered not as the prophet ignored, but as a figure who retarded the development of French armor by unnecessarily linking mechanization to a

54 See Richard D. Challener, *The French Theory of the Nation in Arms* (New York, 1965), 150.

55 See Eugenia C. Kiesling, *Arming against Hitler: France and the Limits of Military Planning* (Lawrence, KS, 1996), 63–68.

56 See Paul Marie de la Gorce, *The French Army: A Military-Political History* (trans. Kenneth Douglas, Paris, 1963), 185–96 on the army's growing distrust of parliamentary institutions.

57 Martin S. Alexander, *The Republic in Danger: General Maurice Gamelin and the Politics of French Defence, 1933–1940* (Cambridge, 1992), 396–7.

58 Ibid., 17.

professional army.[59] Ironically, because France lacked the money to hire professionals and because volunteers were already scarce, conscription was probably the only realistic basis of an armored force.

Even if de Gaulle's proposals had been politically palatable, they were out of place in the larger constellation of the nation's force-structure, strategy, and doctrine. France had no expansionist aims in Europe; its national security depended on defensive alliances. The greatest problem was that a new armored force would undermine French commitments to a long-war strategy and the doctrine of methodical battle. The theory of *la guerre intégrale* called for France to exploit its national resources, popular patriotism, colonial manpower, and alliances while avoiding the bloody mistakes of World War I. Should Germany attack, France intended to mount a parsimonious defense, using firepower to preserve manpower. Building the Maginot Line along the French frontier, from Switzerland to Luxembourg, contributed to this strategy by encouraging the Germans to seek an easier invasion route via Belgium. In order to meet the invaders in Belgium, which was the preferred ground for a static defensive war, the army motorized several infantry divisions. During their rapid advance, these units would require screening and reconnaissance forces. For this mission, which had traditionally been performed by cavalry, France created the world's first armored divisions, the *Divisions légères mécaniques*, combining fast tanks with a regiment of tracked infantry. These divisions differed only slightly in composition from Germany's later Panzer divisions, but their screening and reconnaissance mission has led historians to underestimate their combat power.[60]

In this French vision of war, French soldiers, who were dug in and amply protected by antitank guns, would allow Germans to exhaust themselves in futile attacks, while they themselves massed the resources for an allied counterattack. Offensive operations would then take the form of what French doctrine called "*la bataille conduite*" or "methodical battle," the method that had proven itself against the Germans in August 1918. It called for a series of short, phased advances, which were to be punctuated by pauses to maintain the careful choreography among the artillery barrage, advancing infantry, and

59 Martin Alexander, "Liddell Hart and De Gaulle: The Doctrines of Limited Liability and Mobile Defense," in Paret, *Makers of Modern Strategy*, 614–16.

60 See Jeffrey A. Gunsburg, "The Battle of the Belgian Plain, 12–14 May 1940: The First Great Tank Battle," *Journal of Military History* 52 (1992): 207–44. In spite of its similarity to the Panzer divisions, historians resist calling the DLM an armored division: Williamson Murray, *The Change in the European Balance of Power 1938–39: The Path to Ruin* (Princeton, 1984), 103.

lightly armed, slow-moving infantry-support tanks. The doctrine, especially the use of light tanks as infantry-support weapons, was a logical choice for an army that was composed of inadequately trained reservists and led largely by reserve officers. While most American soldiers would have recoiled at the thought, *la bataille conduite* resembled their own army's reliance on central control of devastating firepower in World War II.

Defensive aims, the nation-in-arms, motorized infantry, light mechanized divisions, antitank artillery, battalions of infantry-support tanks, and "methodical battle" composed a coherent package. Oblivious of the capabilities of the *Divisions légères mécaniques* and uninterested in the asymmetry of French and German strategic objectives, historians have decried the lack of heavy armored divisions in the French army. Given French doctrine and war plans, however, what is more surprising is the French decision to field new medium-tank divisions, called *Divisions cuirassées de réserve*, at the end of 1939. The first German Panzer divisions had evoked concerns in France about the validity of a doctrine that was based on the proposition that horse-drawn antitank guns could be effective. In October 1936 General Gamelin ordered the *Conseil Supérieur de la Guerre* to evaluate the merits of medium-tank divisions to counter a German armored offensive. The ensuing discussions concluded with only a call for further analysis, and large-scale tests scheduled for 1937 were canceled because the necessary machines had not yet been built. Fearing that the presence of powerful armored divisions might tempt commanders to independent operations, the *Conseil Supérieur de la Guerre* proposed to harness them to the methodical battle by denying them organic infantry or other support.

While the four armored divisions that were finally activated in 1939 and 1940 did contain small mechanized infantry, artillery, and other supporting elements, they were labeled *Divisions cuirassées de réserve* because the qualifying "reserve" denied them an independent offensive role and reaffirmed their subordination to corps or army control.[61] Uncertainty about the place of these units in French doctrine frustrated effective training. Their rapid destruction in the spring of 1940 was due not least to the fact that their commanders, with the possible exception of Colonel Charles de Gaulle of the half-formed 4th Division, had no idea what to do with them.

Medium-tank divisions were an anomaly in an army that was committed to a doctrine of passive defense, but more serious divergences between theory and practice had already vitiated France's long-war strategy. Political discord

61 Kiesling, *Arming*, 161–67.

and a commitment to *laissez-faire* economics defeated a legislative framework for national mobilization.[62] Averse in principle to political action and cool toward specific governments, generals failed to insist upon this foundation of their strategy and continued to preach the doctrine of methodical battle. Only during the "phony war" did French leaders, military and civilian, acknowledge the inadequacy of the long-war strategy in the face of growing German strength, American neutrality, and Soviet participation in Germany's destruction of Poland. Besides, what government would impose the hardships of a long war on its civilian population if it were possible to win a short one? Thus the failure to follow through on planning for a long war contributed to Gamelin's startling revision of French operational planning in search of a rapid victory in Belgium in 1940.[63]

Historians have explored the failure of the British army to exploit the lead in armor development with which it had emerged from World War I. British soldiers, they note, invented the tank during this war; then interwar British theorists developed ideas that were exploited by Germany and the Soviet Union in the next war. However, given Britain's strategic requirements and political institutions, the surprise is not that armored experiments proved abortive, but that they took place at all. In fact, J. P. Harris has persuasively explained the deficiencies in British armor at the outbreak of World War II as the result of ill-conceived innovation.[64]

For Britain, the end of World War I did not introduce a quiet period of reflection. Although the army reverted immediately to the long-service, professional structure of the prewar years and budgets shrank, responsibilities did not. British soldiers were soon engaged in civil wars in Ireland, Iraq, and Afghanistan, unrest in India, and garrison duties throughout an expanded empire. While armored cars (and the Royal Air Force's aircraft) proved useful in repressing insurrection in the new mandate in Iraq, tank units were an expensive irrelevance in other imperial operations. Nor did a country that was protected from the European continent by a twenty-mile antitank ditch regard armored divisions as a cost-effective tool for home defense.

62 Ibid., 14–35.

63 Don W. Alexander, "Repercussions of the Breda Variant," *French Historical Studies* 8 (1974): 479–81.

64 J. P. Harris, *Men, Ideas, and Tanks: British Military Thought and Armoured Forces, 1903–1939* (Manchester and New York, 1995), 306. See also Tim Travers, *How the War Was Won: Command and Technology in the British Army on the Western Front, 1917–1918* (New York, 1992); Paddy Griffith, *Battle Tactics of the Western Front: The British Army's Art of Attack, 1916–1918* (New Haven, 1992).

The bulk of scarce financial resources went to the navy, which was charged with the protection of the home islands and overseas interests.

While the army's daily missions focused on small wars overseas, the writings of J. F. C. Fuller and his self-proclaimed disciple, B. H. Liddell Hart, offered radical ideas that were suited to a major conventional war on the European continent. While their ideas differed in detail, Fuller and Liddell Hart agreed that a modern army could best be defeated by rapid penetrations deep into its rear areas and the destruction of its command posts. The idea was to bypass enemy armies altogether; the strategic objective was to paralyze not only front-line forces but the enemy's ability to resist.[65]

Aiming at paralysis rather than destruction would allow a small mechanized army to defeat a mass army at minimal cost in lives, before Britain's civilians again experienced the burdens of "total" war. However, even a small armored force would be vastly expensive and useful only in a continental war; it would also require an improbable change in the British army's strategic mission and the exchequer's budgetary priorities.[66] Nevertheless, in spite of financial limitations, obsolescent equipment, the continuing absence of a mission, and jealousy among the traditional arms, the Royal Tank Corps executed intermittent tests over several years, to be rewarded in 1931 with the establishment of the Tank Brigade.[67] Experiments in combining tanks, armored cars, artillery, infantry, and aircraft impressed the Germans. They also increased the confidence of the Royal Tank Corps itself, whose leaders generally rejected combined arms, deprecating supporting elements on the grounds that only small, mobile, all-tank formations could survive the aerial threats of the modern battlefield.[68] Further experiments led to the authorization of a Mobile Division in 1937, although its purpose – either to fulfill cavalry functions or to act as an independent strike force – remained disputed; so, as a consequence, did its composition.[69] Even as the army innovated beyond the apparent requirements of this division, armor's leading propagandist began to worry about the consequences of creating units suitable for the kind of continental operations that he also insisted Britain ought to avoid.

65 Liddell Hart's writings obscure the differences between his strategic employment and Fuller's tactical employment of armour, see Gat, *British Armour Theory*, 5–9.

66 Michael Howard, *The Continental Commitment: The Dilemmas of British Defense Policy in the Era of the Two World Wars* (London, 1972); see also Harold R. Winton, *To Change an Army: General Sir John Burnett-Stuart and British Armored Doctrine, 1927–1938* (Lawrence, KS, 1988), and Harris, *Men, Ideas, and Tanks*.

67 Ibid., 238–41.

68 Ibid, 245–48.

69 Ibid., 282–87.

Liddell Hart therefore tempered his enthusiasm for armored divisions with admonitions not to commit them to Europe – indeed, given the weaknesses of Britain's air defenses, to avoid war entirely.[70]

Britain's armor experiments contrasted not only with the strategic priority of home and imperial defense over continental intervention, but also with the belief, which loomed large in politicians' minds and popular fears, that the next war would feature aerial attacks against defenseless cities. In an effort to justify its own postwar existence, the Royal Air Force (RAF) insisted that even though raids on civilian targets had produced little damage during World War I, their psychological impact had been significant.[71] Confusion reigned in this service, which claimed to seek a "knockout blow" against Germany but made no serious effort to develop the aircraft, doctrine, or navigational techniques appropriate to this mission. Moral uncertainties about attacking cities fostered further confusion. Although enemy morale was the target of choice, "terrorizing the enemy civilian population" was not acceptable, according to the commandant of the RAF Staff College.[72]

The reciprocity of civilian vulnerability was at the heart of British doctrine. The air staff provided shocking calculations of the retaliation that would follow a British strike against German cities and placed no faith in defensive preparations. Because "the bomber will always get through," deterrence became Bomber Command's *raison d'être*.[73] Political leaders, who were committed to a deterrent force to guarantee peace, discounted the dangers of advertising a strategic bombing mission while maintaining an inadequate bomber fleet. By announcing that bombing was a terrifying but legitimate tool of war, British policy merely tempted foes to act before the RAF could equip to modern standards.

This theoretical debate ignored the fact that most of the RAF's equipment was designed for imperial policing and small-scale colonial wars. Moreover, as Tami Biddle points out, the RAF had inherited from the army a cavalry culture more interested in field sports than in the technological shape of future warfare.[74] Another social factor, however, underpinned the RAF's success in World War II. More than any other government during the interwar period, the British worked with civilian scientists and intellectuals. The radar program

70 Ibid., 292.

71 Tami Davis Biddle, *Rhetoric and Reality in Air Warfare: The Evolution of British and American Ideas about Strategic Bombing, 1914–1945* (Princeton, 2002), 72, 76–81.

72 Ibid., 93.

73 John D. Buckley, *Airpower in the Age of Total War* (Bloomington, 1999), 114–17.

74 Biddle, *Rhetoric and Reality*, 82.

operated quietly behind the scenes. Even more important was the development of command-and-control mechanisms and protocols that allowed the RAF's Fighter Command to win the Battle of Britain. In this respect, economics trumped the offensive ethos. Fighter aircraft were cheaper and easier to build than bombers; hence they were the first outcome of the rearmament program that began in 1937. Just enough of them were on line in 1940 to give "the few," who so earned Churchill's praise, a fighting chance.

Doctrinal debate was nowhere more heated or consequential than in Russia, where "Soviet military science formed in the course of a fierce armed conflict of the young socialist state against internal counterrevolution and imperialist intervention."[75] Doctrinal uncertainty was seemingly incongruous in a system governed by the Marxist–Leninist principle that, in Frunze's words, doctrine derived "from the class essence of the state and … the level of development of the country's productive forces."[76] Socialist theory notwithstanding, however, arguments over military doctrine remained part of the internal struggle for power – and personal survival.[77]

When Frunze and Leon Trotsky, the people's commissar for military and navy affairs, disputed the relative merits of offensive and defensive warfare or the utility of Frunze's demand for "unified military doctrine" and "uniquely proletarian military art," the substance of the argument was less important than power within the Soviet military hierarchy. Frunze couched his military claims in ideological terms, identifying offensive warfare as the "basic form of actions [*sic*] of the Red Army." He insisted that maneuver suited "the class nature of the Red Army" and "the spiritual attributes of the proletarian elements leading it."[78] Although he was no less committed a communist or confident of the martial qualities of the working class, Trotsky had to champion the unproletarian position that objective military conditions might not respond solely to Marxist arguments.[79] Trotsky's military logic won an ephemeral victory at the Party Congress in 1922, but he lost the political battle to Frunze in January 1925.[80]

During his own brief tenure as people's commissar for military and navy affairs in 1925, Frunze moderated his commitment to offensive warfare but

75 V. Y. Savkin, *The Basic Principles of Operational Art and Tactics* (Washington, DC, 1972), 39.
76 Frunze, quoted in Richard W. Harrison, *The Russian Way of War: Operational Art, 1904–1940* (Lawrence, KS, 2001), 124.
77 Mark von Hagen, *Soldiers in the Proletarian Dictatorship: The Red Army and the Soviet Socialist State, 1917–1930* (Ithaca, 1990), 40–41.
78 Savkin, *Operational Art*, 40–41.
79 Harrison, *Russian Way*, 123.
80 Ibid., 123–25.

continued to predict that Soviet economic expansion would eventually support a truly proletarian – and therefore offensive – military doctrine.[81] His nuanced positions reflected a more "sober" and "realistic" appraisal of the situation, which was remarkably similar to the one advocated by the now disgraced Trotsky.[82] If affirming his belief in a communist military theory represented an effort to ward off charges of ideological unorthodoxy, his worries were not unreasonable, as Stalin encouraged him to undergo the elective surgery that killed him. His successor, Kliment Voroshilov, was Stalin's henchman.

Frunze had justified his military ideas in terms of party orthodoxy. Once Stalin and Voroshilov defined the communist position, ambitious soldiers were safer offering technical arguments. In his study of the development of Soviet operational art, Richard Harrison cites the tsarist pedigrees of the originators of this crucial doctrinal idea as evidence of the continuing influence of the imperial ideas in Russian military thought, but these men, such as M. N. Tukhachevsky, A. A. Svechin, V. K. Triandafillov, and N. E. Varfolomeev, were responding as well to the dangerous internal dynamics of the Soviet state.[83] Tainted by their tsarist past, they were doomed to lose ideological contests, so they needed to shift the locus of argument from the political to the technical realm. Thus Tukhachevsky called for serious study of the military lessons of World War I rather than citing clichés about the civil war.[84]

Things had not changed in 1937, when the curriculum of the new General Staff Academy focused on operations and its commandant was denied permission to institute a course on strategy.[85] This situation reflected the Red Army's definition of a new level of war between tactics and strategy – a project that looked to be technical, safely divorced from rhetoric about proletarian armies. As defined by Svechin in 1924, operational art "organizes the separate tactical activities into the operation, proceeding from the criterion of the operation as a whole."[86] Operational art quickly came to refer not simply to the new level of war but also to the exploitation of this level through "deep

81 Savkin, *Operational Art*, 41.

82 Harrison, *Russian Way*, 133.

83 Ibid., 125, 141–42. Harrison notes that Tukhachevsky's tsarist background might have driven him to become "redder" than the average Red Army commander, but he does not consider the proposition that because men with his background could only go so far – or survive so long – in an ideological struggle, Tukhachevsky had an incentive to emphasize technical arguments.

84 Ibid., 133.

85 Ibid., 216.

86 Quoted in ibid., 140.

operations." The triumph of operational-level analysis cemented the victory of the short-war "destructionalists" over the advocates of attrition and positional war. Proponents of deep operations denied, as did the "positionalists," that modern military conditions allowed the destruction of armies in single, decisive victories. "Cannaes," wrote Triandafillov, "cannot be realized through a single operation."[87] Rather than acknowledging that wars of attrition had thus become inevitable, proponents of operational art posited that destruction of the enemy would occur in a series of consecutive battles.[88] A single operation would flow forward from one battle to the next over distances of hundreds of kilometers, as enemy reserves were attacked before they could reconsolidate the broken front. Deep operations were to take the form of an attack in echelon; each echelon was constituted for a specific purpose, and it burned itself out in accomplishing its objective. Although echelons necessarily moved sequentially, a fast tempo of operations ensured that the enemy was engaged throughout the entire depth of its defense.[89]

More than in the German case, Soviet doctrine developed in the absence of the military hardware necessary to employ it. As H. P. Willmott notes, "The main features of the Deep Battle were in place by the end of the 1920s, at which time the Soviet Union had about 90 tanks and the same number of armored cars."[90] Only a decade later did the Red Army have the weapons suitable for any kind of "deep operations," and these weapons originated in economic policies outside the army's control.

The purpose of the Five-Year Plans was to catapult the Soviet Union into the industrial age, creating modern industrial infrastructure and a loyal proletariat. The resources that shifted from agriculture to factories produced lavish *matériel* for the army.[91] By 1935, when the Reichswehr had only a few Panzer Mark I's to its name, the Red Army had acquired thousands of tanks and airplanes.[92] These weapons had been built to stimulate Soviet industry, impress rival nations, and reward the Red Army for its role in rural collectivization – not, however, to fulfill the doctrinal visions of "deep operations."

87 Quoted in ibid., 154.

88 David M. Glantz and Jonathan House, *When Titans Clashed: How the Red Army Stopped Hitler* (Lawrence, KS, 1995), 6–8. Modern armies adopted the Soviet terminology in the 1980s, and one finds it anachronistically applied to the campaigns of Napoleon, but the credit for adding "operations" to the classic duo of strategy and tactics properly belongs to the Soviet Union in the interwar period.

89 Savkin, *Operational Art*, 45.

90 Willmott, *Faith in Reason*, 116.

91 See Roger Reese's chapter in this volume.

92 Harrison, *Russian Way*, 173.

The tanks that were still in service in 1941 proved hopelessly inferior to German models, but producing them had fulfilled Stalin's major purpose in creating a modern industrial economy.

In the mid 1930s, however, military theory and industrial production intersected. Maneuvers in 1935 and 1936 featured practical experiments with deep operations.[93] Maneuvers with large numbers of primitive tanks stimulated technical development, which eventually led to the superb T-34 medium and KV-1 heavy tanks. But then the evolution of operational art halted abruptly, because this ambitious concept went far beyond the Red Army's human and material capabilities. Skilled leadership was lacking at every level. Appropriate tanks did not exist. The theory that aircraft could function as flying artillery could not be tested until the Ilyushin Il-2 ground-attack aircraft appeared in 1941. The Red Army lacked trucks to support mobile operations; and the logistical demands of operations remained largely unexplored. Radios were rare, and few Soviet conscripts had the skills to maintain modern equipment. The fact that the Red Army developed a doctrine that it eventually could execute speaks to the contingent origins of military ideas.[94] So does the repression of "deep operations" in 1937, when Stalin, whose economic policies had begun to make "deep battle" feasible, purged the army of the leading proponents of this doctrine, most notably Chief of Staff Marshal Tukhachevsky. Tukhachevsky's replacement, Stalin's crony Voroshilov, promptly reinstituted political officers at the corps level and above as a sign of the army's renewed subservience. Discussion of operational art ended; the mechanized corps were broken up and their tanks distributed among infantry and cavalry units.[95] Still, the seeds of the most effective military doctrine of World War II had been sown. While Soviet skill in "deep operations" contributed greatly to the Soviet victory over Germany, this victory would have been impossible without the dramatic modernization of the Soviet economy.[96]

Historical epochs are not laboratories for discovering universal military theories. The historian is more like the naturalist, who observes a range of species and acquires insights into behavior – some species-specific, some suggestive of general principles. Interwar military forces were complex organisms, each shaped by a complicated combination of domestic political

93 Ibid., 216–17.

94 The realization of deep operations in 1944–45 required trucks provided by the United States; Willmott, *Faith in Reason*, 126.

95 Glantz and House, *Titans*, 12; Harrison, *Russian Way*, 220–44.

96 See Tooze, *Wages*, 511.

circumstances, historical precedents, organizational cultures, technological opportunities, service rivalries, and personal interactions. The interplay of these forces surfaced in day-to-day behavior, and quotidian concerns often discouraged strategic thinking. Understanding the military history of the interwar period (or any other period) requires the painstaking study of the minute details of individual military forces. To make this point is not to invoke the style of military history that is sometimes disparaged as "button-collecting." The color of collar tabs on parade uniforms does not matter. Other seemingly trivial questions do. How much autonomy accompanied the red trouser stripes of the German general staff officer? How often did infantry units train with antiaircraft guns? Did generals join admirals for lunch? Arguably more than analyses that parse military theory, questions like these explain nations' wartime performance. As the interwar period recedes further into the past, our perspective widens to take in an expanse of events whose interest to the military historian goes far beyond the story of World War II.

15

The military and the revolutionary state

ROGER R. REESE

The rise to power of radical political groups in the early twentieth century in China, Russia, Italy, Germany, and Spain posed particular challenges to the military establishments in these countries. In analyzing these challenges, this chapter will focus on questions that Geoffrey Best has raised: "whose armed force really is it? Whose work is it doing? And to what social group or class's idea is it answering?"[1] The chapter will also pose several additional questions. How did revolutionary states view their armies? How did the regimes define the purpose of their armies? How did these armies view themselves in their service to the revolutionary states? And in what ways, if any, were the armies revolutionary? In all five countries, revolutionary states sought to take over existing armies or to create new ones, but in either case they sought to force them to do the work of the new government and to answer to the social group or class that had created the revolutionary party and the government.

All the revolutionary regimes except Franco's feared military institutions to a degree. In addition, the regimes in Germany, Nationalist Spain, and Italy sought to erase the autonomy of traditional military institutions, while regimes in the USSR, Communist China, and Republican Spain sought to prevent it. Simultaneously, all these armies sought at one time or another to create or protect their own institutional autonomy. Conversely, subverting the military's autonomy, revolutionary regimes sought to harness the armed forces to their domestic social and foreign policies.

Right-wing movements – Italian Fascists, German National Socialists, and the military-led movement in Spain, which eventually took on fascist trappings – all allied with existing armed forces, but the Bolsheviks and democratic, leftist parties in Republican Spain had more conflicted relations with the military. The Soviets and Spanish Republicans had ideological misgivings about national military organizations. In contrast, the Chinese Communist

1 Geoffrey Best, *War and Society in Revolutionary Europe 1770–1870* (Leicester, 1982), 17.

27. Communist soldiers in Shanghai

Party (CCP) had itself become militarized in its early years of struggle, and its army was stamped by the party's efforts to prevent conflict between party and army. One difference between left and right revolutionary regimes was their approach to civilian control of the military. Unlike the leftist revolutionary regimes, which sought institutional control over the armed forces, rightist revolutionary states sought personal control.

While the leaders of right-wing revolutionary parties, Benito Mussolini and Adolf Hitler, allied themselves with standing armies and sought their support, they also endeavored to harness these armies to their own revolutionary purposes – a design that clashed with the outlook and agenda of these armies. Simultaneously, right-wing leaders had created private, quasi-legal armies of followers, who were loyal to the party: Mussolini's Black Shirts and Hitler's SA (*Sturmabteilung*, also called Brown Shirts) and SS (*Schutzstaffel*). In Spain the opposite occurred. Right-wing elements of the army created the revolution, brought one of their own, General Francisco Franco, to power, created the new state, and brought the right-wing nationalist political parties – the Falange (Blue Shirts) in particular – to heel. In Germany and Italy, the new revolutionary states dominated the existing armed forces without achieving their trust or loyalty. The Italian army machinated against Mussolini in 1943, while members of the German armed forces (*Wehrmacht*) attempted on several occasions to assassinate Hitler, most famously on July 20, 1944. Franco, a highly popular general, had no trouble with the army, but the various right-wing political parties presented a challenge, which his standing with the military proved crucial in overcoming.

On the left the relationship with the military was more problematic. China, Russia, and Spain all faced civil war after revolution. The Chinese created an army for their party. The Bolsheviks first disbanded the old regime's regular army and attempted to rely on an armed citizenry. Then they tried to create a new army along class and ideological lines, co-opting elements of the old army to train and lead it. When this effort failed, too, they fell back on conscription and coercion for the rest of the civil war. Only in peacetime did they address the problem of a standing army in a revolutionary socialist state. The Spanish Republic inherited much of the standing army after the revolt of rightist elements in 1936, but it was reluctant to rely on loyal elements as a base for a new army to fight the insurgency, which grew into civil war. Instead, under pressure from leftist political organizations, the Republic disbanded the old Spanish army in areas under its control and created a new army, which comprised former officers, Soviet military advisors, and volunteer units formed along political, regional, and trade-union lines. However, the relationship between the Republic's military and political leadership was never satisfactory.

With the exception of Republican Spain, these were all one-party states or movements that aspired to statehood. The one-party state, a phenomenon of the twentieth century, first appeared in the aftermath of the October Revolution. The role of the party and its ideology was crucial not only to governing but also to civil–military relations, and it distinguished the experience of the military in previous revolutions, such as the American or French, from the military experience of "totalitarian" revolutions after World War I. The influence of the party, state, and military varied from case to case. In the Soviet Union the Communist Party held preeminent power over the state and the armed forces. In Communist China the party was also dominant; it fashioned both an army and a state to its needs. In Italy and Germany the ruling parties were the strongest elements, but not by much. Both co-opted state apparatuses and military institutions that had strong identities; the military they neither fully penetrated nor controlled. In Nationalist Spain the army dominated, at least for the first decade, because it had made the revolt and won the civil war, building a state to suit its needs and co-opting political parties to mobilize popular support.

Although it represented the exception, the Spanish Republic deserves particular notice because it oversaw the rebuilding of the state and the military during the civil war. The state was the leading element, as it was in "normal" states, but this Spanish state was, like its army, under tremendous pressure from strong and assertive leftist political parties, especially the Spanish Communist Party (PCE, *Partida Comunista de España*). Despite its small numbers, and thanks to its connection with the Republic's main benefactor, the USSR, the PCE exerted great influence over the state and the military.

Soviet Russia's Workers' and Peasants' Red Army (*Raboche Krest'ianskaia Krasnaia Armiia*, RKKA) was the first army of a revolutionary state in the twentieth century. Almost everything the Soviet state did in creating a military set precedents, although few of these applied to other revolutionary situations. The Bolsheviks had not created an armed wing in preparation for their seizure of power in October 1917. From the party's birth, it had ideological objections to the idea of a standing army. Leftists in general saw armies as repressive organs of the state, and they feared "Bonapartism" – a military dictatorship that emerged from the chaos of revolution. For a time the Bolsheviks thought that they could do without an army at all, depending instead on an armed citizenry in times of emergency. Such thoughts proved illusory. World War I, a disintegrating empire, civil war, and foreign intervention proved that an army was needed, at least in the short run.

Even before the new regime achieved peace with the Central Powers at Brest-Litovsk in March 1918, the Bolsheviks had begun disbanding the Imperial Russian Army. They did so for ideological and practical reasons. They regarded the army as a reactionary organization that was controlled by their class enemies. In anticipation of civil war, they feared the army might serve their enemies. Instead, they planned to consolidate their power on the strength of a voluntary militia of class-conscious workers. However, this citizens' army, which began to form in January 1918, failed to attract sufficient numbers of men, and it performed disastrously in its first battle with the Germans at Narva in February 1918.

In the aftermath of Brest-Litovsk, Vladimir Lenin ordered Leon Trotsky to organize a regular army. In order to conduct a civil war against their enemies on the left and right, and then a war with Poland in 1920, the Bolsheviks contradicted everything they had professed to believe about armies. They now relied on conscription rather than volunteers, on peasants rather than workers, on former NCOs, and on officers from the old regime, whom they coerced to administer, train, and do much of the leading. As a safeguard against counterrevolution, the Bolsheviks assigned commissars to co-command with the officers, so officers' orders were not official until their commissars had countersigned them. Draconian punishment was prescribed for treason.

At the end of the civil war, the party confronted the issue of whether the new revolutionary state should keep a standing army. Ideological purists were opposed. After intense debate, the Tenth Party Congress compromised with a "mixed system," which retained a small – by Russian standards – standing army of 548,000 men from all services, backed up by a much larger territorial militia of citizen soldiers. The compromise was hailed as "an army of a new type." Relations between officers and enlisted men would be "brotherly," discipline would be "revolutionary," and an eight-hour day would be maintained. The state mandated universal adult male military service, but conscripted for active service primarily those from the working class, because they were thought to be more politically reliable, and indoctrinated the peasantry through part-time service in the militia.

The leadership of the peacetime army lay in the hands of reliable party stalwarts, such as Mikhail Frunze and Kliment Voroshilov, who had pursued military careers after participating in the civil war. Few in the army's new leadership had both revolutionary credentials and military experience prior to the civil war. Those who had experience had served overwhelmingly in the ranks. They won their rank in the civil war through battlefield success, party loyalty, and connections. For about a decade, the army relied on officers of the old army, who were labeled "military specialists" (*voenspetsy*), to administer, teach and train, and supervise staff work. Few of them served in command positions. There was a concerted and ultimately successful effort to replace the *voenspetsy* with new "Red Commanders." By 1932 few *voenspetsy* remained on active duty, and of those who did, over half had joined the Communist Party.[2]

Even though the majority of officers had joined the army after the revolution, the party, in an effort to maintain political control over "its" army, maintained the system of commissars and dual command in military units. As a check to the danger of "Bonapartism," commissars answered to the party through the Main Political Administration of the Red Army (PUR), which in turn answered to the Central Committee of the Communist Party – not to the People's Commissariat of Defense, which was part of the state apparatus. Eliminating dual power became an intense issue in the immediate post-civil war years. A faction within the army argued for one-man command (*edinonachalie*) and a large degree of military autonomy. It also proposed disbanding PUR. By removing organized party activity from the army, military traditionalists hoped to depoliticize the armed forces and make military considerations the sole basis of military

2 Roger R. Reese, *Stalin's Reluctant Soldiers: A Social History of the Red Army, 1925–1941* (Lawrence, KS, 1996), 105.

decision-making. Immediately, however, stiff opposition emerged from the civilian party organization. Its proponents argued against professional autonomy, that the Red Army was the party's army; the party was entitled to control the military's organization, and political considerations were a vital aspect of military decision-making. The Fourteenth Party Congress in December 1925 resolved the issue. It approved *edinonachalie* but limited the army's autonomy, deciding to maintain PUR and to redefine the role of commissars, who were henceforth in charge of political affairs, morale, and discipline.[3]

The decision reflected less a fear of military counterrevolution than the determination to use the army for political purposes.[4] The RKKA was to be politically, socially, and economically integrated into the party and state. The party saw the army as a vehicle to indoctrinate a new generation into socialism through military service and to promote the regime's social and economic policies. Commissars conducted classes on Marxism and other themes that related to political education. Party cells in military units recruited soldiers into the party. Commissars organized communist soldiers to help civilians, mostly peasants, with farm work and to proselytize on behalf of the party. Entire divisions were used as industrial labor during the five-year plans, as well as to sow and harvest on collective farms.

Political education and activity failed in the end, however, to produce revolutionary soldiers. With few exceptions, soldiers proved apathetic to indoctrination and passively accepted the transformation to a socialist society. The major exception to this rule was the forced collectivization of agriculture in the 1930s, which engendered opposition within the ranks of peasant soldiers. When the Soviet state found itself *in extremis* in 1941–45, it fell back on traditional themes of Russian nationalism to motivate soldiers, rather than call on them to defend the revolution and socialism.

Conscription policies reflected the party's goal of a revolutionary transformation of society. The army could draw men and officers only from the working class, the poor and middle peasantry, and white-collar workers. Military promotion depended more on political considerations than aptitude. Party membership was never formally required, but few officers were promoted much beyond the rank of captain without a party card. Officers who were party members had their political merits scrutinized as part of their annual reviews.

3 Roger R. Reese, *Red Commanders: A Social History of the Soviet Army Officer Corps, 1918–1991* (Lawrence, KS, 2005), 76–77.

4 Mark von Hagen, *Soldiers in the Proletarian Dictatorship: The Red Army and the Soviet Socialist State, 1917–1930* (Ithaca, 1990), 210–20; Dmitrii Voropaev and Aleksei M. Iovlev, *Bor'ba KPSS za sozdanie voennykh kadrov* (Moscow, 1960), 91.

The officer corps of the RKKA never accepted the idea that the standing army should remain small or that the territorial militia should bear the main burden of defense. Officers put constant pressure on the party to increase the size of the armed forces. The party resisted the pressure on grounds of economic insufficiency until the start of the five-year plans in 1928, when Joseph Stalin decreed the gradual expansion of the armed forces and the upgrading of its armament.

Stalin's power over the army did not rest with state authority. His dictatorial power came instead through his position as general secretary of the Communist Party, the party's monopoly on power, his membership of the party's Defense Council, and his power to appoint people's commissars and to dictate state policy. He had no constitutional power over the armed forces, but this technicality had no practical bearing. Leaders of other revolutionary states, by contrast, sought to legitimize their control of the military through constitutional means.

Stalin's relationship to the army was like his relationship to all other Soviet institutions – uneasy. Stalin appointed his toady Voroshilov to the post of commissar of defense in 1925, on the death of Frunze, who had been appointed by Lenin. Stalin divided the high command between Voroshilov and a cohort of untalented Bolshevik stalwarts, such as Kulik and Shtern, and a group that had military talent and vision, among them Tukhachevsky, Svechin, and Triandafillov. This practice kept the army faction-ridden. Stalin had a keen interest in military affairs and followed military developments closely, but he guided the army with a light hand until the terror purges. Because the army had been configured to acceptable social and political forms before his rise to power, Stalin had no need to manipulate its recruiting base or structure. Instead, he sought by means of the terror and the cult of personality to make it loyal to himself personally.

The advent of Stalinism was a mixed blessing for the Soviet military. The army was showered with money for research and development of new weapons, allowed steadily to increase the number of men and units, and permitted to integrate the territorial militia into the standing army. But Stalinism also meant intrusive civilian control and the intensified politicization of military life. Political repression of army officers began in 1926, when 26,000 supposed "Trotskyite" officers were dismissed from service, as struggles within the party played out in the army.[5] From this point until Stalin's

5 Iu. I. Korablev, *KPSS i stroitel'stvo vooruzhennykh sil SSSR* (Moscow, 1959), 276.

death, civilian authorities dismissed thousands of officers for political reasons.[6] The infamous terror purge of the army in 1937–39 represented an extreme extension of political processes that had begun in the 1920s. Altogether, by May 1940, 22,705 officers and commissars had been executed, imprisoned, or dismissed, but 11,596 had been rehabilitated. Stalin rehabilitated several thousand more officers in 1941 and 1942, reducing the numbers lost during the terror to fewer than 10,000.[7] Still, the attendant reshuffling of the high command and rapid promotion of new cadres produced a major change. The RKKA was no longer the party's army; it was Stalin's.

The army's limited autonomy evaporated after the German attack on June 22, 1941. On June 23, Stalin created the *Stavka* of the High Command of the Armed Forces to supervise the military aspects of the war. Its twenty members included Stalin, eleven officers, and nine civilians. All the civilians were members of the Communist Party's Central Committee or the Council of People's Commissars.[8] On June 30, Stalin created the State Committee for Defense (GKO) in order to coordinate decision-making in all aspects of the war. It comprised party, state, and military officials, and its resolutions had the force of law. Assuming the posts of people's commissar of defense and supreme commander-in-chief of the armed forces for the duration of the war, Stalin, like Hitler, made himself the focal point of military decision-making, to the point of making decisions at the operational level.

Sun Yat-sen intended that the revolution of 1911 would overthrow the Qing dynasty, establish a republican form of government, and introduce a new socio-economic system.[9] In this effort he inadvertently sowed the seeds of a clash between two revolutionary armies, which have opposed one another to this day. These were the Communist Chinese Army (CCA) and the National Revolutionary Army of the Guomindang Party (GMD).[10] Upon Sun Yat-sen's death in 1925, Chiang Kai-shek took over both the Guomindang Party and its army. As a result of the Bolsheviks' success in 1917, a Chinese communist movement came into being to challenge the GMD for control of the revolution. At first the two movements cooperated against their common enemies, the numerous warlords, but after 1927 they fell into fighting each other, until

6 Sergei T. Minakov, *Sovetskaia voennaia elita 20-kh godov* (Orel, 2000), 513–18.

7 Reese, *Stalin's Reluctant Soldiers*, 143.

8 "O stavke glavnogo komandovaniia vooruzhennykh sil Soiuza SSR," *Izvestiia TsK KPSS* no. 6 (1990), 196–97.

9 George T. Yu, "The 1911 Revolution: Past, Present, and Future," *Asian Survey* 31 (1991): 895–904.

10 Hans van de Ven, "The Military in the Republic," *The China Quarterly* 150 (1997): 353.

1936 when they became allies once again, this time against the Japanese invaders. After the defeat of the Japanese in 1945, the final stage of the conflict between the CCA and the GMD ended in 1949 in communist victory on the mainland and the GMD's flight to Taiwan.

The Chinese Communists, unlike their Bolshevik mentors, had few misgivings about a military establishment, because the Communist Chinese Army grew organically out of the party. The official birthday of the CCA was August 1, 1927. At its inception it was called the Workers' and Peasants' Red Army, although independent regional party military units had existed as early as 1924. The party created the army for the Nanch'ang uprising in 1927, in which the Communists split from Chiang Kai-shek and the GMD. This uprising led to a ten-year period of armed conflict between the CCP and the GMD. The issue of party control of the military was settled at the origin. Party leaders were the first military leaders. They assumed this role as part of their political duties in making the revolution. The party controlled the army through the Military Commission of the Central Committee of the Chinese Communist Party, also called the Central Military Commission (CMC), which had been established in 1925. The army answered to the CMC, which answered to the party's Central Committee and the Politburo. The CMC was in charge of military policy and management in accordance with the guidance of the CCP. The army pledged its allegiance to the party, not the state or constitution.

The Long March of 1934–36, during which the CCP fought for survival against Chiang Kai-shek's GMD, was a milestone in communist Chinese military-political history.[11] Initially, the army divided into three columns, which later merged into two over a two-year period, commanded by the party's highest leaders. Although they were in charge of military operations, the Communist leaders did not identify themselves as soldiers, but saw themselves as party men who undertook military operations. During and after the Long March, they were highly political, bickering and maneuvering in the CCP and CMC to get their way. The Long March forced the question of how best to achieve a revolution. One faction preferred conventional warfare and conducted their operations accordingly, with little success. The other major faction, which was led by Mao Zedong, opted for guerrilla war until conditions allowed general insurrection and large-scale military operations. The struggle over revolutionary military doctrine was won by Mao as part of his political victory, which resulted in his domination of the CCP. During

11 John M. Nolan, "The Long March: Fact and Fancy," *Military Affairs* 30 (1966): 77–90.

World War II the CCA operated as a guerrilla army in an uneasy alliance with Chiang Kai-shek against the Japanese invaders. After the defeat of the Japanese, however, it went over to conventional operations as the civil war against the GMD resumed from 1946 to 1949.

While the Soviets relied on officers of the old army to train and administer the new army, the Chinese Communists had fewer worries about the army's loyalty or leadership. The Chinese party built the army from the ground up with its own members, without the help of class enemies or the professional military. As the army grew, the party ensured its anti-bourgeois and anti-aristocratic class character. During the first years soldiers' committees strengthened morale and let the soldiers police their own ranks. In late 1929, Mao dissolved these committees and replaced them with party cells at the company level and, in imitation of the Red Army, with commissars at higher levels. This move enabled the party to influence the rank and file, keep tabs on political morale, and establish the party as a presence in soldiers' lives. Over the objections of some field commanders (all of whom were ranking party men), the Central Committee ultimately decided against a professional, institutionally separate military.[12]

Established in 1931, the General Political Department managed the political commissars. Commissars served as the equals, rather than as subordinates of commanders, and they were responsible for political affairs, political indoctrination, education, personnel matters, internal security, and discipline. They also recruited soldiers into the party. Like its Soviet counterpart, the Chinese Communist Party regarded political work in the military as a means to support the army in its mission, to oversee the reliability and efficiency of cadres, to monitor the effectiveness of training, enforce legal norms, and enhance troop discipline.[13] In the service of the party-state, the army became a mechanism for agitation, organization, and control of the masses. In many ways the army served as a model for the organization and operation of the increasingly militarized CCP.[14]

Europe's first revolutionary regime on the right took root in Italy in the early 1920s and provided the first example of a military institution's response to it. Despite the martial air that he assumed – his designs on empire and military glory – Mussolini's relationship with the Royal Italian Army (*Regio*

12 Van de Ven, "Military in the Republic," 363.

13 James C. Mulvenon and Andrew N. D. Yang, eds., *The People's Liberation Army as Organization*, Vol. X (Santa Monica, 2002), 229.

14 Samuel B. Griffith, *The Chinese People's Liberation Army* (New York, 1967), 5; van de Ven, "Military in the Republic," 364.

Esercito) was never easy. Throughout the Fascist era, the high command and most of the officer corps retained a traditional outlook, were monarchist in sentiment, held themselves aloof from the party, and contained many anti-Fascists, although six generals had participated in the March on Rome in 1922.[15] The army then came to a quick accommodation with Mussolini, who promised extensive autonomy and indulged the army's hopes for modernization.[16] In the enlisted ranks and among junior officers, by contrast, the Fascists found enthusiastic support.

Because the military leadership was not an eager ally of the Fascist state, Mussolini reneged on his promise of autonomy and sought to make the army an instrument of his will. He placed General Pietro Badoglio, a nominal supporter, in charge of the high command in 1925. Mussolini also made him a marshal, appointed him chief of the supreme general staff (*Comando Supremo*), a powerless advisory and coordinating body, but left it at that. Badoglio accommodated the Fascist regime without complaint, but sought to protect the officer corps from party interference, especially in matters of personnel. He served until he was sacked in 1940 as the scapegoat for the debacle in Greece. General Ugo Cavallero, who replaced him, was pro-Fascist but for this reason was not well liked among his peers. Whether under Badoglio or Cavallero, most Italian officers remained dubious of the Fascist government, and as an institution the army served as a brake on Mussolini's rash ideas of challenging Britain and France with military and naval force in the 1920s and 1930s. Only in the mid 1930s did Mussolini get the upper hand, forcing the military to intervene in the Spanish Civil War.

The conservative army did prevent attempts by the Fascist Party to indoctrinate soldiers and place ideological prerequisites on recruitment, promotion, and assignment. Despite the army's division into two blocs – one traditional and monarchist, the other pro-Fascist and innovative – the conservatives defeated attempts to subvert its social hierarchy, maintaining rigid distinctions among the enlisted, noncommissioned, and officer ranks.[17] The army continued to rely on the apolitical peasantry for the bulk of its manpower. The true believers in Fascism were drawn largely from urban areas and found their way into the Black Shirts' militia, the *Milizia volontaria per la sicurezza nazionale* (Voluntary Militia for National Security, MVSN).

15 F. L. Carsten, *The Rise of Fascism* (Berkeley and Los Angeles, 1980), 62.

16 Brian R. Sullivan, "The Italian Armed Forces, 1918–1940," in Allan R. Millett and Williamson Murray, eds. *Military Effectiveness*, Vol. II: *The Interwar Period* (Boston, 1990), 169.

17 Ibid., 169, 175–86, 190, 200.

During the fifteen years of Badoglio's tenure, Mussolini controlled the armed forces. He appointed himself minister of all three armed services. In 1940, he created the rank of First Marshal of the Empire, which only he and the king held. Finally on May 29, 1940, he had the king delegate the royal power of wartime command to him.[18] Mussolini took seriously his office of commander of the armed forces; in no way did he regard himself as a figurehead. He invested time and energy in his responsibilities, but not because he was enamored of things martial. As a young socialist before World War I, he had had a jaundiced view of the army, and he never dropped his wariness of military professionals and their class. He remained skeptical of the high command's loyalty and held their opinions suspect.[19] On the other hand, he respected military tradition and rebuffed those in his party who urged him to reform the military.

As dictator, Mussolini, *Il Duce*, put on militaristic airs, often wore a uniform, and ordered invasions of Ethiopia, Libya, Albania, and Greece. These actions, however, spoke more to the militarism of his Fascist ideology and his goal of a new Roman Empire than to any internal desire to be a soldier. As head of state, he favored the military with large budgets and new equipment, but these funds were neither sufficient nor well spent. The wars in Africa ate up much of the funds, while corruption took its share, leaving less than necessary for upgrading armaments and *matériel* for an expanding army.[20] Despite Fascism's martial façade, the army fell behind other armies during the 1920s in armor and mechanization. The problem was that most of the leadership in all the services resisted tactical and technological innovation. The army was devoted to the infantry and mules. It had no armored divisions, nor did it want them.[21] The Italian army was in no sense revolutionary if strategy, tactics, or weaponry be the standard of judgment.

Mussolini did intend to challenge the army's monopoly on armed force. His vehicle was the Fascist Party's armed wing, the Black Shirts, whom he reorganized in 1923 into the MVSN. The MVSN was to serve alongside the army but answer to the party. This institution regularized local "squadronism" and the thuggery associated with it, legitimizing the Black Shirts and putting

18 Howard McGaw Smyth, "The Command of the Italian Armed Forces in World War II," *Military Affairs* 15 (1951): 40.

19 Ibid., 45–46.

20 Sullivan, "Italian Armed Forces," 170–75; R. J. B. Bosworth, *Mussolini's Italy: Life under the Fascist Dictatorship, 1915–1945* (New York, 2005), 444–45, 456–57, 464–66.

21 MacGregor Knox, *Hitler's Italian Allies: Royal Armed Forces, Fascist Regime, and the War of 1940–1943*, (Cambridge, 2000), 53–56.

them on the government payroll. At first, members of the MVSN swore personal loyalty to Mussolini, then, in 1925, also to the king, while the army swore loyalty to the king alone.[22] Until 1941, the MVSN's commander (the chief of staff of the militia) answered to Mussolini, not to the armed forces. The MVSN oversaw the pre-induction military training of Italian youth, but it promoted Fascist ideology better than it prepared men for military service.[23] At the beginning of World War II, three of Italy's seventy-five infantry divisions were MVSN. Regular army officers looked on the MVSN with justified disdain. All three Black Shirt divisions were destroyed in North Africa in February 1941 and never reconstituted. The MVSN continued to recruit, but after late 1941 its men were grouped into brigade-sized formations of "M" (for Mussolini) battalions.[24]

Although he was loyal to Mussolini and enamored of the Fascist movement, Cavallero was a professional officer and thought that the armed forces would be better off with him, not Mussolini, as their operational commander. He consequently changed the command relationship in 1940, making the chief of the supreme general staff into a command, not an advisory position and requiring the chiefs of the three services to answer to him. Although he still held his ministerial positions, Mussolini now had to go through Cavallero to interact with the field armies, navy, and air force.[25] Cavallero also extended his control over the field armies. From December 1940 to February 1943, he took direct charge of the Italian armies in Africa, Russia, Greece, and the Balkans. In 1941, he also took command of the MVSN.

In a prelude to Mussolini's overthrow in February 1943, the army orchestrated Cavallero's replacement by General Vittorio Ambrosio. The continuing significance of the military to the stability and continuity of the Fascist state was evident in the fact that Mussolini's downfall was only complete when the conspirators convinced King Victor Emmanuel III to revoke the dictator's command of the armed forces. The Black Shirts were in no position to save their patron, and at the army's behest, the new government abolished the MVSN and absorbed its men into the *Regio Esercito*.[26]

22 Carsten, *Rise of Fascism*, 67.

23 Brian R. Sullivan, "The Italian Soldier in Combat, June 1940–September 1943: Myths, Realities and Explanations," in Paul Addison and Angus Calder, eds., *Time to Kill: The Soldier's Experience of War in the West 1939–1945* (London, 1997), 179.

24 Ibid., 179–80, 187, 189, 191; Salvatore Vasta, "'M' Battalions: The Duce's Own," *Coorte: Italian Military History Journal* 1 (2006): 12–13.

25 Smyth, "Command," 43–45.

26 Ibid., 50–52.

The Royal Italian Army did not turn on Mussolini, for it had never accepted him or the Fascist Party. It served the king, and the king had allowed Mussolini and the Fascist Party to run the country. Fascism had not been kind to the Italian army. It gave soldiers opportunities to excel, but many of these had ended in failure or humiliation. Even the few victories left a bad taste in the mouths of many army leaders. It took too long to conquer Ethiopia; the campaign in Greece was saved only by German intervention, while 85,000 soldiers and members of the MVSN became casualties in Russia alongside the *Wehrmacht*. The army was never properly funded or equipped for its tasks, and politicized decision-making at the top exacerbated the problems.[27] Remaining loyal to the letter of the law, the Royal Italian Army served the Fascist state but not the Fascist Party. It answered not to ideology but to the officer class, which sought to rescue both the army and the state in 1943.

Like Mussolini, Hitler sought personal control over the armed forces, but he was more determined to make fundamental changes to the social structure of the *Wehrmacht*'s officer corps. Furthermore, he took greater pains to ensure that his will was carried out in the armed forces and that the army remained subservient, if not completely loyal.

The fact that Hitler owed his consolidation of power in large part to the high command did not deter him from bringing the armed forces to heel. The considerations that constrained him in 1934 were the challenge to his power from Ernst Röhm, the leader of the *Sturmabteilung* (SA), the Nazi Party's army of nearly 2 million Brown Shirts, and Hitler' own desire for military conquest. To win the internal power struggle with the SA and to wage war he needed the legitimacy, power, skill, and organization of the regular army. Fortunately for Hitler, the high command feared Röhm and was as ready as Hitler to avenge the Treaty of Versailles.

The army's fear of Röhm was due to his desire to abolish the old army, much as the Bolsheviks had done in Russia, and to create a revolutionary army to match the revolutionary society envisioned in Nazi ideology. Röhm regarded the SA as the foundation of this future army and as leverage for political power in the Nazi regime. Hitler was always cool to Röhm's scheme, but indulged him until he felt powerful enough to strike him down. In these circumstances, the German army high command became

27 MacGregor Knox, "The Italian Armed Forces, 1940–3," in Allan R. Millett and Williamson Murray, eds., *Military Effectiveness*, Vol. III: *The Second World War* (Boston, 1988), 136–79. It was Mussolini's, not Hitler's idea that Italy send men to Russia in order to be in line for rewards after the defeat of the USSR.

political. It supported Hitler on the condition that he deprive the SA of its arms and secure the army's role as the nation's sole bearers of arms.[28] Hitler made the deal; the army took an oath of loyalty to him, but from this point on, Hitler sought to erode the autonomy of the officer corps both personally and institutionally.

With the complicity of the army, Hitler and his paramilitary force, the SS (*Schutzstaffel*), murdered Röhm and about eighty other opponents during the "Night of the Long Knives" on June 30, 1934. This action ended the SA's threat to Hitler and the army. Hitler used the occasion to bring the high command more under his control by murdering two retired senior officers (Kurt von Schleicher and his assistant General Kurt von Bredow), who had opposed his efforts to dominate the armed forces.[29] Believing that a greater good had been served, the army looked the other way.

Despite their postwar denials, even at the highest ranks of the Junker aristocracy, professional soldiers embraced elements of Nazi ideology that they believed would strengthen the internal cohesion of the army. The last act in Hitler's establishing control over the armed forces came on February 4, 1938, when he announced his reorganization of the defense administration, so he could exercise direct control. Hitler took this last, decisive step to power over the armed forces in the aftermath of the "Fritsch–Blomberg Crisis." General Werner von Blomberg had been Hitler's minister of war, and General Werner von Fritsch the commander-in-chief of the *Wehrmacht*, but each had insisted on defending the military's autonomy and had resisted the idea of military action as a solution to Germany's growing economic problems. In January 1938, Blomberg was forced to resign after evidence was produced that his new wife (he had been a widower for five years) had in her youthful past posed for obscene photographs. Days later Heinrich Himmler, chief of the SS, and Hermann Göring, the head of the Prussian police, fabricated evidence of Fritsch's homosexuality and forced his resignation.[30] Hitler thereupon reorganized the high command, giving himself the legal power to command the armed forces. The officer corps, though skeptical about the charges against both generals, stood by.

Hitler maintained the SS as his personal armed force. Within this organization arose a branch called the Waffen-SS, which, under Himmler, was

28 Bernd Wegner, *The Waffen-SS: Organization, Ideology and Function* (Oxford, 1990),

29 Robert J. O'Neill, *The German Army and the Nazi Party, 1933–1939* (New York, 1966), 49–51; David Jablonsky, "Röhm and Hitler: The Continuity of Political-Military Discord," *Journal of Contemporary History* 23 (1988): 367–82.

30 O'Neill, *German Army*, 139–50.

intended to act as a military organization. Himmler created the Waffen-SS incrementally between 1933 and 1939. It initially shared many of the demographic and political attributes of the SA but was loyal to Hitler, who eventually brought order to its revolutionary tendencies and professionalized its fanaticism.[31] Eventually, however, as an armed force proven in combat, the Waffen-SS did challenge the army's monopoly on armed force.

To a degree the Waffen-SS embodied the revolutionary army that Röhm had envisioned. Like the SA and a plethora of other right-wing paramilitary groups dating from 1919, the Waffen-SS recruited anti-bourgeois, anti-democratic, fascist, and chauvinistic revolutionary soldiers. As an organization, it promoted violence as an act of personal and national liberation. Its mission was to crush the left, whether this was embodied in a revolutionary movement or a state. Its command structure was hierarchical, but it sought to be egalitarian.[32] As the embodiment of the Nazi social order, the Waffen-SS drew most of its officers from the masses and brought them up through the ranks, in contrast to the social elitism of the regular army's officer corps. Over time, the Waffen-SS became a disciplined army of romantic revolutionaries, marginally professional, and elitist within the framework of Nazi ideology. Its war-fighting methods were unoriginal, however. It employed tactics taught by the *Wehrmacht*, adding ruthlessness, ferocity, and fanaticism, often at the expense of expertise and thoroughness. Its legitimacy came through its service to Hitler; but in the eyes of the *Wehrmacht*, it never became a legitimate military organization. In combat the Waffen-SS depended on the *Wehrmacht*, just as Mussolini's MVSN depended on the Italian army. The *Wehrmacht* trained it, equipped it, and had strategic control over it.

Hitler would neither disband the regular army nor replace it with the Waffen-SS. Instead, he sought to transform it into a "professional-political" army, much like the Soviet Red Army. For its part, the German high command accepted that the regular army would be the servant of the Nazi state but refused to make it the servant of the Nazi Party. As minister of defense, Blomberg shaped the army's policy of teaching the soldiery the basics of Nazi ideology, loyalty to a militant *Volksgemeinschaft* – a unified "people's community" of duty and destiny. Like the Red Army, the *Wehrmacht* established

31 Wegner, *Waffen-SS*, 60–105.

32 Amos Perlmutter, "The Romantic Revolutionary: The Storm Troopers and the Waffen-SS," in Amos Perlmutter and Valerie Plave Bennett, eds., *The Political Influence of the Military: A Comparative Reader* (New Haven, 1980), 105.

political indoctrination classes as part of officer training in 1935, although these were not systematically institutionalized until 1938. Officers were in turn supposed to transmit the ideals of National Socialism to the soldiers by example.[33] Eventually, the equivalent of political commissars appeared in the German army after the attempt on Hitler's life on July 20, 1944. Despite a certain aloofness toward Nazi ideology, officers could not prevent the rank and file from becoming "Nazified," if only because draft cohorts had imbibed this ideology from their youth. As Stephen Fritz has shown, Nazi ideology was as instrumental as nationalism and military tradition in maintaining bonds among soldiers.[34] In this sense, the *Wehrmacht* soldier was not much different from his Waffen-SS counterpart.

In matters of personnel, Hitler less resembled Mussolini, who took a hands-off approach, than he did the Bolsheviks. He, too, sought to alter the class composition of the officer corps, favoring the common man at the expense of the old elites. Although he had great respect for the army – a reflection of his experience as a *Frontkämpfer* during World War I – Hitler was opposed to the elitist social traditions of the Prussian aristocrats who ran the German army. He had did not abandon his determination to remake the armed forces in light of Nazi social principles, nor was he content to see these principles isolated in the Waffen-SS. He intended ultimately to promote officers by merit, proven in combat, rather than by seniority or social credentials. He planned to replace the Prussian aristocracy with a new generation of Germans who were steeped in Nazi ideology. The army's personnel office resisted his designs until late 1942, when Hitler finally replaced its chief with a loyal follower, Rudolf Schmundt, who forced through an egalitarian promotion policy against the wishes of the general staff.[35]

By the start of World War II, the German army was, as Omer Bartov has written, Hitler's army.[36] It was Hitler's tool of social and racial policy. It was also instrumental to Hitler's foreign policy, which led to the conquest of Europe. Its development of the blitzkrieg had nothing to do with Nazi ideology, but the army's professional competence made possible the imposition of this ideology on most of Europe for nearly six years. Hitler's powers,

33 Jürgen Förster, "Motivation and Indoctrination in the Wehrmacht, 1933–45," in Addison and Calder, eds., *Time to Kill*, 265, 267–68.

34 Stephen Fritz, *Frontsoldaten: The German Soldier in World War II* (Lexington, KY, 1995), 156–218.

35 MacGregor Knox, "1 October 1942: Adolf Hitler, Wehrmacht Officer Policy, and Social Revolution," *Historical Journal* 43 (2000): 801–25.

36 Omer Bartov, *Hitler's Army: Soldiers, Nazis, and War in the Third Reich* (New York, 1992).

like Stalin's, eventually extended even to operational decision-making. Finally, as a component of the Hitler state, the *Wehrmacht*, from the general staff to the common soldiers, was complicit in the Holocaust.[37]

The Spanish Civil War of 1936–39 produced the last of the interwar revolutionary armies. In fact, for a short time it produced two, but in the end Franco's Nationalist army destroyed the Republic's army. The Spanish Civil War began as a revolt within the army against the Popular Front government of the Spanish Republic. The army, however, split almost evenly between those who remained loyal to the Republic and those wished to destroy it and create a conservative, authoritarian state. While ideology divided the army, practical issues also played an important role. The Spanish army officer corps had been divided since the 1920s over personnel policy, which had offered rapid promotions to officers of one branch of the service. Promotion was governed by seniority and merit, but at a time when infantry officers were engaged in North Africa and gaining rapid promotions, artillery and engineer officers felt disadvantaged. To protect their interests, these officers wanted promotions to rest on seniority alone. After the dictatorship of Primo de Rivera had sided with the infantry during the 1920s, many artillery and engineer officers turned against him and the right, and in 1936 they chose the Republic.[38]

The fact that roughly half the army sided with the Republic caused the initial military uprising in 1936 to fail. Nonetheless, the Republic found itself in a precarious military position, primarily because it was ideologically suspicious of the army. Close to 70 percent of the generals remained loyal to the Republic.[39] In 1938, however, only 14 percent of the prewar officer corps still served the Republic. Only 10 percent of the naval officers (not counting specialists such as engineers) remained in the service of the Republic.[40] Many of those who did not go over to Franco were arrested, dismissed, executed, or murdered. There were admittedly instances of betrayal by officers, but the majority of the Republic's government comprised anarcho-syndicalists, liberal republicans, socialists, and communists, most of whom distrusted the officer corps. Consequently, the Republican government decided to follow the Soviet precedent, so shortly after the insurrection it

37 Geoffrey Megargee. *War of Annihilation: Combat and Genocide on the Eastern Front, 1941* (Lanham, MD, 2005).

38 Paul Preston, *Franco: A Biography* (New York, 1993), 54–55.

39 Ibid., 146.

40 Michael Alpert, "The Clash of Spanish Armies: Contrasting Ways of War in Spain, 1936–1939," *War in History* 6 (1999): 345.

28. Popular Front Army parade in Spain

disbanded the regular army and created a new armed force that would support the revolutionary goals of the Popular Front.

The new army was created in October 1936. It served under the president of the Republic, Largo Caballero, who was also minister of war. He established a committee under the fanatical communist, Major Eleuterio Diaz Tendero, which was charged with classifying officers as Fascist, Republican, or indifferent, and with keeping those who could be trusted as the nucleus of a new officer corps.[41] Despite this vetting, the Republican leadership always felt a measure of distrust toward the new army. It was organized on a volunteer basis. It was divided into the Popular Army (*Ejército Popular*), militias that were controlled by political parties such as the anti-Stalinist socialist POUM (*Partido Obrero de Unificación Marxista)* and the anarcho-syndicalist CNT (*Confederación Nacional de Trabajo*), and the International Brigades. The militias formed among untrained trade unionists who volunteered in the first days of the rebellion to fight insurgent garrisons in their locales. The militias were highly politicized, and they sought to maintain democracy within their formations, which varied in size from regiments to brigades. The Republican government attempted to control the armed forces, which remained undisciplined, the object of distrust and political machinations.[42] In November 1937, the head Soviet advisor in Spain, Kachelin, reported to Voroshilov, the Soviet commissar of defense, that "Each party is striving to consolidate its own influence within the army and the command staff is under the constant pressure of its own parties."[43] Because they represented the most disciplined element on the Republican side, the government reluctantly grew to rely on Spanish Communist officers and Soviet advisors to coordinate the activities of the army.

The Popular Front government thus turned to its only foreign benefactor, the USSR, not only for arms and ammunition, but also for qualified military leaders. Some 2,100 Soviet military advisors served in Spain. For a time, in 1936, Soviet officers directly commanded some brigades of the Popular Army.[44] The Republic sent many men to the Soviet Union for training as pilots, while Russians set up schools in Spain to train the Popular Army's NCOs. Soviet advisors were often domineering, so military training was fraught with political and cultural tensions.[45] Stanley Payne has described the Popular Army, a "Spanish variant of the Red Army."[46] At its founding five Communists served on the general staff, two of whom were the deputy chief and the chief of operations. Three of the first six brigade commanders were

41 Paul Preston, *The Spanish Civil War 1936–39* (Chicago, 1986), 111–12.

42 Alpert, "Clash," 345.

43 Kachelin to Voroshilov, Document 59, in Ronald Radosh et al., eds., *Spain Betrayed: The Soviet Union in the Spanish Civil War* (New Haven and London, 2001), 290.

44 Stanley G. Payne, *The Spanish Civil War, The Soviet Union, and Communism* (New Haven and London, 2004), 170.

45 Alpert, "Clash," 338, 350; Payne, *Spanish Civil War*, 171.

46 Payne, *Spanish Civil War*, 161.

Communists or affiliated with the PCE. A Communist in the War Ministry controlled army personnel, *matériel*, and supply. Following the Red Army's precedent, the Popular Army employed commissars for political indoctrination under a central command, which was in turn dominated by Communists.

The desire of Spanish Communists to dominate the officer corps complicated military affairs in the Republic. There was constant friction between the PCE and Largo Caballero, who sought to limit Communist influence. Nevertheless, by 1938, during the second government of Negrin, Communists ran virtually all aspects of the war effort. Most newly promoted division and corps commanders were Communists, some of whom had trained in the USSR. Thirty-nine of forty-two command positions in the air force and navy were in Communist hands. During the war many Republican officers joined the PCE for ideological or practical reasons. Others sympathized with the Communists. On the Central Front around Madrid in 1937, nearly 90 percent of officers were members of the PCE or the Communist-dominated JSU (*Juventud Socialista unificada*, United Socialist Youth), as were 125 of 186 battalion commissars and 62 of 68 brigade commissars. Leaders of the large CNT complained that of the Republic's seventy divisions, their own members commanded only nine.[47]

The military effectiveness of the Popular Army suffered for a variety of reasons. Because the Republic did not trust the officers from pre-revolt days, the government hesitated to give them latitude to improvise. The Republican high command was decentralized, so it had difficulty in coordinating operations on several fronts or the movement of militias, the Popular Army, and the International Brigades. Furthermore, while many colonels and generals remained on the Republican side, few mid- and lower-level officers from the pre-revolt army did, and few of them had combat experience. In addition, when Soviet advisors controlled front-line operations, their own training discouraged initiative among their officers. Their distrust was not misplaced, for most battalion-level officers were working-class men who were new to military life, hastily trained, and rapidly promoted. Many had come up through the militias, which had selected their own officers before they were absorbed into the Popular Army.

The conservative Nationalist Army, which was based on the half of the army that had revolted against the Republic, differed in most respects from the Popular Army. It also had little in common with the armies of other right-wing governments. Like the Italian and German armies, it sought to stay out of politics, but like the Nationalist Chinese Army, it had political intentions.

47 Ibid., 171, 176, 210–11, 252, 260.

These were to halt the revolutionary tendency of the Republic, which was exemplified by the Popular Front and its radical social reform, and to replace this government with a conservative, authoritarian state.[48] The officers who led the coup had no political organization, which was probably a factor in their initial failure. The coup on July 18, 1936 thus failed to unseat the government of the Republic and led to an unanticipated civil war.

The military leader of the coup, General Sanjurjo, was killed in an airplane crash the day after the coup began. The leader of the monarchist party, Calvo Sotelo, had been murdered just before the coup, and the leader of the Fascist party or Falange (Blue Shirts), José Antonio Primo de Rivera, was captured, tortured, and executed during the initial phase. General Mola, who had organized an alliance among the various groups that had conspired against the Republic, did not seek leadership after the failure of the coup. So this role fell almost by default to General Francisco Franco, who was not at the time a Fascist but had brought his army from Africa to support the rebels.

On September 21, 1936, a "temporary junta" voted in Salamanca to name Franco commander-in-chief and to give him supreme authority for military affairs. A week later the junta also gave Franco responsibility for all matters of public policy for the duration of the conflict. These decisions made him not only leader of the army, but also the chief of government and potentially the head of the Spanish state.[49] Franco then adopted the title *Caudillo* (warlord). The resulting situation was unlike any other revolutionary state and its army in the interwar era. Here was a rebelling army that created a revolutionary state to fulfill ill-defined but passionately held political goals.

For almost the first ten years of Nationalist Spain's existence, the state was an instrument of the army.[50] The army was the instrument not only for winning the war, but also for administering the emerging new state. For the duration of the civil war the army and state were one; an independent state apparatus did not emerge until after the victory. In running the war and the state, Franco had an advantage that his adversaries lacked – a battle-tested, trustworthy, and committed army. He led the army's best operational unit, the Army of Africa. Although few generals rallied to the Nationalist side, they turned out to be the better ones. The Nationalists also attracted most of the field-grade officers, lieutenant-colonels and majors, and junior officers,

48 Ibid., 109.
49 Jean Grugel and Tim Rees, *Franco's Spain* (London and New York, 1997), 6.
50 Ibid., 10.

captains and lieutenants, many of whom had had combat experience in Morocco.[51]

The Nationalists were not monolithic. They, too, had militias with independent political aspirations – Carlist militias in the north in Navarre and randomly located Falangist militias. However, in December 1936, Franco absorbed the militias into the regular army.[52] The idea of a crusade to save Spain from the left united the Nationalist factions, while the left itself remained factionalized. To achieve this unity, Franco realized that the nascent military state needed a political arm to mobilize the masses. Accordingly, in April 1937, he promulgated the Decree of Unification, which united all political parties and into the *Falange Espanola Tradicionalista y de las JONS* (FET). Institutionally the FET was separate from the state. Its program, which set the tone for the political and social order, was largely Fascist. Franco's brother-in-law, Ramón Serrano Suñer, guided the Falange and its politics until December 1937, while Franco served as its nominal leader.

The Falangists were pro-Nazi and became a threat to Franco in the 1940s. They tried to push him into an active alliance with Hitler. In an effort to pay Hitler back for his support during the civil war, but also to deflect the militancy of the Falangists without committing Spain to the European war, Franco formed the "Blue Division" to serve with the German army in Russia. Falangists were heavily recruited to volunteer for this division. Nearly fifty thousand of them did so, many in the same anti-communist spirit that animated the SA and SS.[53] The Blue Division was the closest approximation of a special politicized military organization that Franco could countenance. Throughout his tenure as *Caudillo*, Franco had to balance the generals and the FET to maintain his dictatorship. Some of the generals were disappointed that the monarchy was not restored, and many senior army officers exhibited an indiscreet anti-Falangist sentiment.

Because he was *Caudillo*, the head of a unified effort, Franco prosecuted the civil war without the difficulties that plagued the politically diverse Republic. He dictated Nationalist strategy. Although his Italian allies criticized him for being too slow and methodical, he designed a strategy not only to defeat the Republic, but also to eliminate institutions and political forces that could challenge his government afterwards. Behind the front lines, his *reconquista*

51 Preston, *Spanish Civil War*, 111–12.

52 Grugel and Rees, *Franco's Spain*, 10.

53 Arnold Krammer, "Spanish Volunteers against Bolshevism: The Blue Division," *Slavic Review* 32 (1973): 388–402; Wayne H. Bowen, "Spanish Soldiers in the German Army and *Waffen-SS*," *WWII Quarterly* 4 (2007): 25–26.

destroyed trade unions, outlawed opposition political parties, and restored land to the church and landowners. A speedy end to the war, brought on by the early capture of Madrid (which Mussolini and others advocated), would have made his consolidation of power in a revolutionary state far more difficult than it was as a dimension of the war.

In contrast to the Republican government, Franco trusted his army. Within bounds he gave latitude to the initiative of his subordinates. His centralized command and logistics coordinated efforts across fronts. He also received more effective support from his Italian and German allies than the Republicans received from the Soviets. The Nationalist Army was used more imaginatively than the Republican; front-line officers were allowed to improvise in combat. So were airmen and sailors.[54] Because he had brought over a large force of Moors from Africa, and because he could call on Italian soldiers and MVSN units, Franco did not need to introduce conscription until the spring of 1937.[55]

The Spanish Civil War ended in the victory of a right-wing revolutionary army over a left-wing revolutionary army. The Spanish army had not been inherently extremist. Many officers would have preferred a middle ground, but in 1936 there was none. The insurgents had not sought to create a fascist regime but came to live with one in which one of their own was head of state and commander-in-chief. The officers who served the Republic grew disenchanted with social and political radicalism; they feared the penetration of the Soviet Union and domination of the government by the PCE.

When it came to fighting wars, all the armies of revolutionary states were remarkably non-revolutionary. The interwar period was rife with creative military thinking and technological innovation without regard to ideology. The most revolutionary change in war was the German development of combined-arms warfare in the blitzkrieg. Here, coordinated, swift-moving forces of armor, mechanized infantry, motorized artillery, and tactical air support were to overwhelm the enemy at the point of attack and then to smash deep into his rear. However, the blitzkrieg was a response not to ideological ferment, but to the stalemate warfare of 1914–18. The *Wehrmacht* had begun experimenting with these ideas well before the Nazis came to power. The Italian Giulio Douhet had begun writing about the strategic use of military aviation before Mussolini conceived of the march on Rome, yet under the Fascist regime the Royal Italian Air Force failed to exploit his thinking.

54 Alpert, "Clash," 331–51.

55 Gabriel Jackson, *The Spanish Republic and the Civil War 1931–1939* (Princeton, 1965), 428.

If political revolution affected military thinking anywhere, it was in the Soviet Union. In the immediate aftermath of the Russian civil war, there was some dizzy talk of a new way of warfare, which would be based on "revolutionary mobility" and use machine guns mounted on horse-drawn carts with little artillery or logistical support. Once these fantasies (which Trotsky had ridiculed) were cast aside, serious military thinking blossomed, thanks not to the insights of Marxism but rather to the casting off of the fetters that had frustrated thinking and experimentation in the hidebound Imperial Russian Army. Led by a new generation of military theorists, such as Mikhail Tukhachevskii, the Red Army, too, began to look at the potential of armor, air power, and combined operations.

The Spanish Civil War offered an experimental battlefield for Europe's five revolutionary armies, yet no revolutionary way of war was even attempted. Franco's strategy for winning the war was traditional, reminiscent of his experience in Morocco and integral to his state-building project. The Germans deployed only small numbers of light tanks. They had no intent to test their ideas of blitzkrieg, satisfying themselves instead with experiments in terror bombing and testing combat aircraft. The Italian forces in Spain, including the MVSN, stuck to conventional infantry tactics. The Red Army, which tested tank units in Spain, concluded that large, independent tank formations were of little use and that tanks would serve better in small groups, as support for infantry. The Republic's army, with its large numbers of committed leftists, often exhibited revolutionary élan but otherwise introduced no military innovation of note. Mao's little red book was less about how to wage war than how to wage revolution short of all-out war. Once the time came for all-out war, the Chinese Communist Army fought it in conventional style.

In the end, the armies of revolutionary states were not revolutionary, and for good reason. Military institutions are geared for war, which requires professional autonomy, hierarchy, discipline, subordination, organizational predictability, consistency, and devotion to honor, duty, and country. All these attributes can be characterized as conservative; and they have historically been antithetical to revolutionaries. Even though some armies were harnessed to revolutionary social and political causes, especially in China, the USSR, and Nationalist Spain, they did not become revolutionary institutions.

Other than as means to serve the defense of their countries or movements, the revolutionary elites saw their armies as instruments to advance revolutionary social agendas, as vehicles of indoctrination and loyalty-building, avenues of social mobility, or as tools to fulfill aggressive foreign-policy goals. The German and Italian armies accepted their military missions, but in their efforts to preserve their professional autonomy, they resisted the social agendas set for them. The other armies accepted the political and social roles prescribed for them. Spain's Nationalist Army under Franco was the extreme example of a military force that dominated politics and government.

One general conclusion can be drawn from the history of revolutionary armies in the interwar period. They answered, for the most part, to revolutionary elites and the ideas these elites represented. Revolutionary elites sprang from all strata of society, but once they assumed power, they sought to speak for the state that they were trying to create. In some cases, the revolutionary elite commanded the army through a party, in others through the state, but only in Nationalist Spain did the army high command co-opt the revolutionary elite. Finally, in no way did the revolutionary elites transform twentieth-century warfare to reflect their ideology.

16

World War II

GERHARD L. WEINBERG

After the Munich Conference, Adolf Hitler regretted having recalled his order to initiate hostilities. His "lesson" from Munich was never to pull back from war again, but to initiate hostilities in 1939. To keep his eastern border quiet while fighting Britain and France, he wanted the countries in the east to subordinate their policies to Germany. In the winter of 1938–39, he succeeded with Hungary and Lithuania. Poland's leaders, though they considered substantial concessions in serious negotiations, were unwilling to surrender this country's recently regained independence without a fight. Early in 1939 Hitler therefore decided to attack Poland in the fall and not to become involved in negotiations that might make it difficult to initiate hostilities, as he believed had happened in 1938. If Britain and France held to Poland, they would be fought at the same time; if not, their turn would come the following year. To avoid any danger of a peaceful settlement, his ambassadors in London, Paris, and Warsaw were kept from their posts in the critical days of August; and the final demands on Poland, designed to rally the German public, were withheld until they could be declared lapsed.[1]

Rather than the initiatives of Japan in seizing Manchuria in 1931 or Italy in attacking Ethiopia (Abyssinia) in 1935, the war initiated by Germany on September 1, 1939 is taken as the beginning of World War II, because Japanese and Italian actions were continuations of prior expansionist policies, not the implementation of truly new policies. As Hitler had explained to his military commanders days before the invasion of Poland, this was a war for the annihilation of Poland and its people, not the attainment of some new border. His backdating his October 1939 authorization for the systematic killing of the handicapped and his moving forward the January 1939 public announcement of the intent to murder the Jews, in both cases to September 1,

1 For the immediate background, see Gerhard L. Weinberg, *Hitler's Foreign Policy 1933–1939: The Road to World War II* (New York, 2005), chs. 26–28.

1939, illuminate how Hitler saw the conflict as the beginning of the demographic revolution on a German-dominated globe. Neither the Italians nor the Japanese understood that this was not a war for specific pieces of land, bases, colonies, or status, like prior global conflicts such as the Seven Years War or World War I. This discrepancy in the purpose of the war contributed to the unwillingness and inability of the three nominal allies to develop substantial coordination in military operations and diplomacy.[2]

In the 1930s Joseph Stalin had repeatedly signaled Berlin a willingness to work out an agreement, but he had been rebuffed. Since the Soviet Union had no common border with Austria or Czechoslovakia, his first targets, Hitler saw no point in a deal with Moscow. When Stalin gave signs of interest in agreement with Germany early in 1939, Hitler changed his attitude. The Soviet Union had a border with Poland and could help break any blockade of Germany that the western Allies might impose. Whatever concessions were made to Stalin for the quick crushing of Poland and economic assistance thereafter would be reclaimed by the speedy defeat of the Soviet Union after Germany's victory in the west. Hitler's thinking explains why Joachim von Ribbentrop, the German foreign minister, was authorized to give Stalin whatever he wanted – including things the latter did not request.

The timing of the German–Soviet agreement of August 23, 1939 had an enormous impact on the war. In World War I, the Soviets had made a separate peace with Germany early in 1918. This enabled Germany to move forces from the eastern to the western front for major offensives there. By then, however, Germany had been so weakened by prior years of fighting, while the British and French were being reinforced by a growing stream of American soldiers, that the effort to defeat the Allies failed. In World War II, the Soviets made a deal with Germany just before rather than years into the war. The agreement enabled the Germans to drive the Allies off the continent in the north, the west, and the south, and it left the Soviet Union alone with the Germans in the east. As a result, the Soviet Union would be first in a poor position for defense against Germany, then in a good position for offense across the same land area, while the same agreement left the western Allies first in a good defensive position, protected by the Channel and the North Atlantic, then in a poor position for offensives: the water was equally wide in both directions.

2 See the entry "Axis Strategy and Co-operation," in *The Oxford Companion to the Second World War* (Oxford, 1995), 97–99.

The German invasion of Poland had been carefully prepared. Fake attacks in Germany by concentration-camp inmates, who had been murdered in Polish uniforms, provided the incidents to justify war. Once hostilities opened with a German air attack on a Polish town and bombardment of the Polish base in Danzig (Gdansk), German forces struck across the territory that Prussia had annexed from Poland in 1772 and returned in 1919. Major German units invaded Poland from East Prussia in the north and Silesia in the south. Having delayed their mobilization to avoid blame for a new war, lacking modern military equipment, and trying to defend a long border, the Poles were defeated rapidly in spite of spirited resistance at several points.[3] Some Polish soldiers escaped to the west via Romania to continue fighting; several Polish warships escaped, and Polish intelligence shortly before the war had provided the British and French with equipment and information about their success in breaking into the German enigma coding system. Polish hopes of continuing resistance through the winter from eastern Poland were crushed by the Red Army, which invaded Poland from the east. German and Soviet soldiers met and moved to an agreed partition line.

The British government of Neville Chamberlain had warned Berlin that an attack on Poland would lead to war. When the Germans refused to withdraw, Britain declared war, followed by France and the dominions of Canada, Australia, and New Zealand. The Union of South Africa took longer because of division among the white population, while the Irish Free State declared neutrality. The war at sea began immediately, but the French and British did not believe that they could mount a major offensive in the west until their forces, especially the British army, were much stronger. In spite of massive German air attacks on cities in Poland, the Royal Air Force faced rigid restrictions. Instead of bombs, it dropped leaflets on German cities, hoping that the German people might resist their government. Although there were a few doubters in the Third Reich, and a tiny minority in the military and political elite did attempt to overthrow the Hitler regime later in the war, the bulk of the German population held to the government until the end.[4]

Hitler hoped to launch an attack in the west through Holland and Belgium in the late fall of 1939, but the need for clear weather (so the German air force could support the advancing troops) and doubts among German military commanders led to postponements through the winter. During this interval,

3 A fine recent account is Alexander B. Rossino, *Hitler Strikes Poland: Blitzkrieg, Ideology, and Atrocity* (Lawrence, KS, 2003).

4 For a general survey of the war on all fronts, see Gerhard L. Weinberg, *A World at Arms: A Global History of World War II* (rev. edn., New York, 2005).

four important developments altered the situation. The Soviet Union began to annex the three Baltic States, but Finland refused to make the territorial and diplomatic concessions that Moscow demanded. Anticipating a campaign of a few days, the Soviets attacked Finland at the end of November but ran into trouble, as effective Finnish resistance caused heavy casualties. A massive onslaught early in 1940 caused Finland to sue for peace. Stalin abandoned the puppet government that he had intended to install and agreed to terms in March 1940. This conflict had two effects that were significant for the wider war. First, it drove Finland into the arms of Germany in 1941, in hopes of recovering territory lost by the peace treaty and perhaps of acquiring more. Second, it confirmed the German perception of a weak Red Army, as Hitler and his generals saw the checks it had received but not that its soldiers had fought on in the face of losses, inadequate training and equipment, and terrible weather.

The second important development during what was called the "phony war" was a series of soundings by some in Germany about their overthrowing Hitler and making peace if the Allies would make peace on reasonable terms. These soundings went through several channels, including the Vatican. The Allies gave hints of interest in an arrangement, but the Germans did not act against the regime. Since some of those who had been thought to oppose the Nazi regime were subsequently active in preparing the invasion of the two neutral Scandinavian countries and then the three neutral Low Countries, no British government thereafter listened to such soundings unless the German opposition first acted at home.

The third development during the winter was the preparation of German plans for invading Norway and Denmark. The commander-in-chief of the German navy, Admiral Erich Raeder, began urging an invasion of Norway in October 1939 (assuming that Denmark would be occupied to assure communication with Norway) for two main reasons. He was anxious to avoid the situation that Germany's navy had faced in World War I, when it was confined to the North Sea without secure access to the Atlantic. Secondly, in the winter, when the Baltic Sea was frozen, Germany depended on the transportation of Swedish iron by train to the Norwegian port of Narvik and then by ship to Germany. Hitler rejected Raeder's simultaneous advice to initiate hostilities with the United States, since Germany had neither completed building its own navy to fight the US navy nor did it have an ally with such a fleet. After some consideration, Hitler agreed to invading Norway and Denmark. Plans were made for a combined operation with most of the German surface fleet, substantial air units, and army forces transported by parachute and ship.

The fourth development during the winter was a change in the German plan for attack in the west. As Hitler had explained in 1938, this campaign was to begin with a strike through the Netherlands, as well as Belgium and Luxembourg – not only through the last two, as in World War I. The original concept was for a sweep with an emphasis on the right flank. However, the western Allies prepared for such a thrust. Doubt was thrown onto the German design when a German plane made an emergency landing in Belgium with material on the original plan. Thereafter, primarily at the insistence of German intelligence officers, who correctly anticipated what the French and British would do, the concept was changed. Now the Germans planned to thrust through the Ardennes on the left flank of the attack and cut toward the English Channel. Relying on a slow reaction by the western Allies to this attack, the Germans would entrap whatever forces the Allies sent into the Low Countries.[5]

Before the clearing of the weather made the western offensive possible, the Germans struck in Scandinavia. In early April 1940 German warships with troops aboard secretly left for Copenhagen, Oslo, and additional Norwegian harbors, including Narvik. While the Danish government surrendered, the Norwegian government refused to do so. Its guns sank a German heavy cruiser on the approaches to Oslo. The king and his government left to continue the fight rather than surrender to Germany or the Norwegian Nazi, Vidkun Quisling, who gave his name to traitors thereafter. Allied forces tried to aid the Norwegians, but with the temporary exception of Narvik, which they abandoned once the Germans struck in the west in May, they operated in such confused fashion that the Germans took over the country. The Allied troops were evacuated, and in London the fiasco ironically brought to power its architect, Winston Churchill.

Two other aspects of the fight for Norway had significant repercussions. First, although during the naval battles accompanying the struggle for Norway the British took substantial losses, including the aircraft carrier *Glorious*, the losses of the German navy proved more significant. The Germans lost several cruisers and numerous destroyers, and their only two battle cruisers, the *Scharnhorst* and the *Gneisenau*, were damaged. Both were out of commission during the critical months of the summer and early fall of 1940. While the victory of the British in the Battle of Britain was won in the air, the German failure to attempt an invasion was due at least as much to their naval losses in the Norwegian campaign.

5 Ernest R. May, *Strange Victory: Hitler's Conquest of France* (New York, 2000).

The second aspect of long-term significance concerned the Soviet Union. The Soviets had assisted the German invasion of Norway, especially by providing a naval base on Soviet territory from which the Germans shipped essential material to Narvik. German control of Norway's naval and air bases had a major impact on Allied efforts to send supplies to the Soviet Union once the Germans attacked this country. Both the great losses suffered by Allied supply convoys to Russia's northern ports and the periodic interruptions in sending such convoys resulted partly from the prior Soviet policy of helping Germany.

On May 10, 1940, the Germans began their invasion of Holland, Belgium, and Luxembourg with parachute drops at critical points and armored thrusts at the southern portion of the new front. The French and British tried to assist the invaded neutrals by moving forward, as they had planned and the Germans anticipated. Furthermore, the French supreme commander, General Maurice Gamelin, sent the major French reserve forces into Holland. So when the Germans broke through in the Ardennes and headed for the Channel, no substantial Allied forces were available to plug the gap.

With no effective attack on the German thrust from both flanks, hopeless confusion in the French command structure, and the surrender of the Dutch and Belgian forces, the British commander, Lord Gort, saved the British and part of the French units that had been cut off, ordering a retreat to Dunkirk for evacuation. The German commander, Gerd von Rundstedt, wished to maintain a strong armored force to attack southward against new defenses that the French were developing, and, with Hitler's agreement, he temporarily halted the armored divisions that were headed for Dunkirk. Hitler hoped that Hermann Göring's promise to destroy the Allied force from the air could be implemented. Because the area was close to the bases of the Royal Air Force, this proved impossible. Although the Allies suffered heavy losses and left their vehicles and other equipment, over two hundred thousand British and over one hundred thousand French soldiers were carried to England, where the former played a significant role in rebuilding the British army.

The German thrust south quickly broke through the dissolving French army. Against those who wanted to continue the fight from North Africa, the new French leader, Marshal Henri-Philippe Pétain, requested an armistice on June 17. Eager to finish the fighting in the west in order to turn east, Hitler arranged terms that involved the occupation of much of France – including its Atlantic coast – but he did not include the more extravagant conditions that Italy demanded. Pétain's government would be called after the small town of Vichy where it resided in unoccupied France. It was allowed to keep a small army at home and larger forces in the colonies.

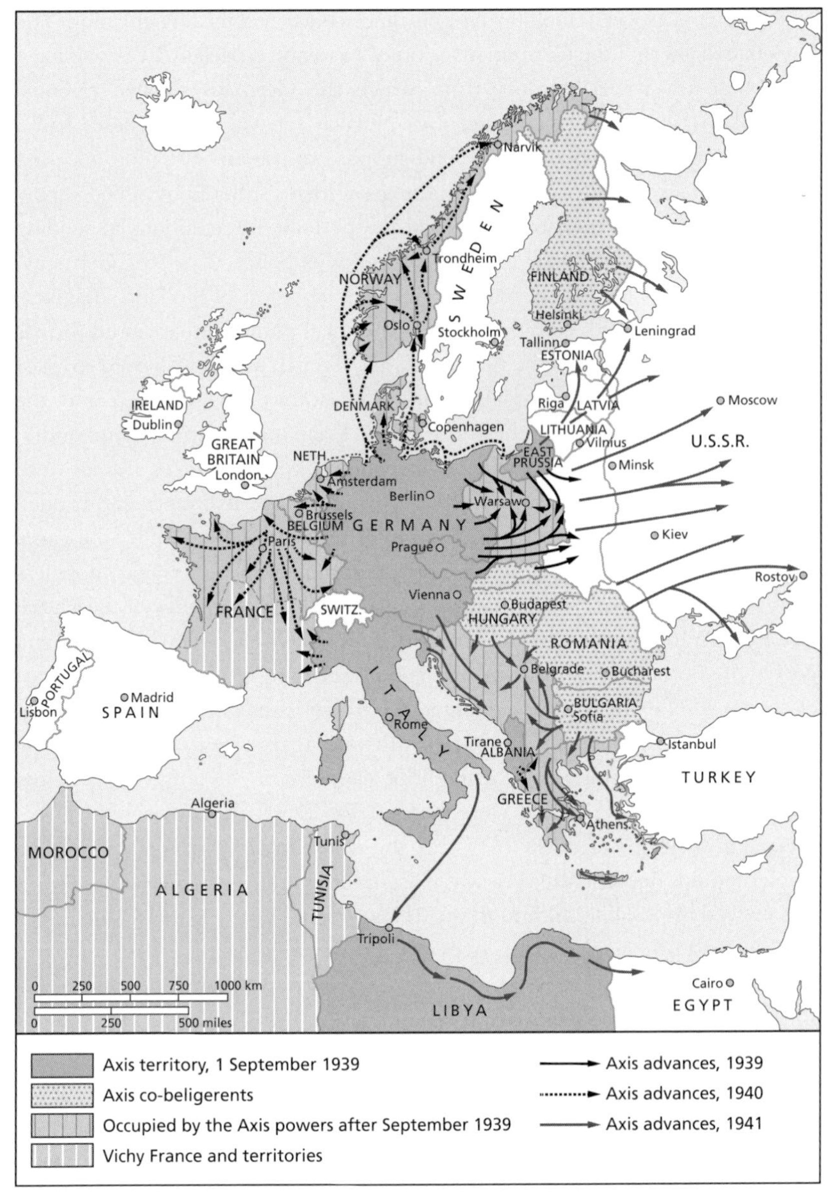

MAP 10. Axis advances, 1939–1941

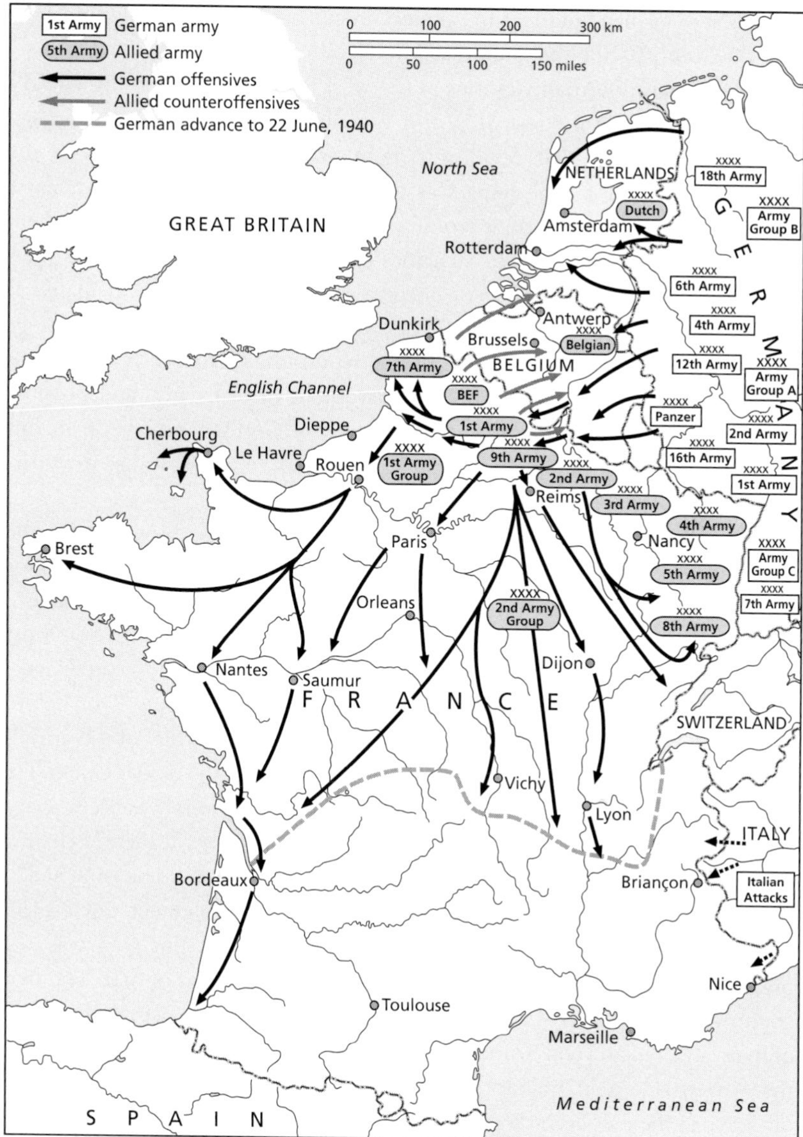

MAP 11. German offensive, May–June 1940

There, at the marshal's orders, they fought the British, the Free French, and the Americans, but never the Germans, Italians, or Japanese, whenever any moved into French territories. The Free French were those who followed General Charles de Gaulle in refusing to cease fighting. They did so from the basis first of his headquarters in London, then from French colonies in Africa and the South Pacific that supported de Gaulle.

The dramatic German victories in the west led to decisions in the world's capitals that framed the rest of World War II. Under Churchill's leadership, the London government decided to fight on, and it had the bulk of the population behind it. The hope was that Britain could hold off or defeat a German invasion but, if not, it would continue the war from Canada (where the country's gold and foreign securities reserves were shipped), while guerrillas made the occupation forces uncomfortable. Victory was anticipated at the end of a long war, in which blockade was to combine with uprisings among the conquered peoples of Europe, whom the Germans' policies were certain to antagonize, substantial bombardment of Germany, and possibly help from the United States. A major feature of German actions up to this point, the bombing of cities and strafing of civilian refugees, reduced restrictions on the Royal Air Force in 1940.

In Germany, a major repercussion and three decisions flowed from the victories. The repercussion was enormously increased public enthusiasm for the regime. The lengthy and eventually unsucessful struggle on the western front in World War I appeared to have been replaced by a quick victory. Most of the doubting minority now rallied to those who were already convinced.

The new decisions involved both the eastern and western fronts. Even before the French request for an armistice, General Franz Halder, chief of the army's general staff, had begun to draft plans for an invasion of the Soviet Union. He understood that in Hitler's thinking the campaign in the west was preliminary to the seizure of vast lands in the east. Other German military leaders also drew up such plans. Hitler hoped, like Halder, that the invasion could be launched in the fall of 1940. Examination of the steps needed to implement this project convinced Hitler by the end of July 1940, however, that this plan was not practical. He set the invasion for late spring or early summer of 1941. The two countries that the Soviet Union had, with German assistance, deprived of parts of their land, Finland and Romania, were expected to join Germany in attacking the Soviets. German military and diplomatic preparations for a combined offensive in the east accordingly began in the late summer of 1940.[6]

The second German decision was to try to crush Britain quickly before turning east. The islands were to be invaded and occupied. Detailed arrest lists were compiled. These would be implemented by police headed by the same person who was later designated for Moscow, Alfred Six. An invasion

6 Gerhard L. Weinberg, *Germany and the Soviet Union 1939–1941* (Leiden, 1972).

MAP 12. Operation Barbarossa, 1941

presupposed control of the air. In the ensuing Battle of Britain, the British won because of a combination of excellent fighter planes and pilots, the skilled utilization of radar, and inadequate numbers of German planes and pilots. Without a substantial navy to shield a landing force, the Germans turned to bombing British cities in the hope of forcing surrender. Although it caused casualties and damage, this effort from August 1940 to May 1941 failed to lessen the determination of the British public and government.[7]

7 Richard Overy, *The Battle of Britain: The Myth and the Reality* (New York, 2000).

The third decision, which was ordered and temporarily implemented before all the others, was to prepare for war with the United States. Armaments preparations for such a conflict had begun in 1937, and keels for the first of the super-battleships believed needed had been laid down in early 1939. Construction was halted when Germany started the war. Now that war in the west was believed over, construction on the blue-water navy was ordered resumed on July 11, 1940. German insistence on ownership of air and naval bases in Northwest Africa for war against the United States led to Spain's refusal to enter the conflict, and the German naval building program was again halted in the fall of 1941, but for a while it looked as if the wars that Hitler intended would be carried out according to his preferences.[8]

The Italian dictator Benito Mussolini had reluctantly refrained from entering the conflict in 1939. As he saw Germany winning in early 1940, he decided to join in order to assure Italy part of the spoils. Although he had talked loudly about the benefits of war, he had not prepared the Italian military for a major conflict. Once they entered the war, Italian forces made no substantial advances against the French, contributed minimally to the bombing of Britain, added a bit more to German submarine operations in the Atlantic, and failed dismally in Africa. The brief Italian drive into British Somaliland was soon reversed, as British forces overran Italian Northeast Africa in the winter of 1940–41. A delayed minimal offensive from Libya into Egypt was soon reversed by the victory of numerically inferior British troops, who thereupon advanced into Libya. Fearful that Germany's moving troops into Romania (as part of plans to attack the Soviet Union, which Hitler had not shared) would threaten Italian aspirations in the Balkans, Mussolini ordered an ill-prepared and soon blocked invasion of Greece. The war that Mussolini imagined almost over was just beginning, and his German ally had to bail Italy out in Africa as well as the Balkans.[9]

Spain's dictator Francisco Franco also wanted to enter the war quickly, before it ended, hoping for great colonial expansion in Africa. When he discovered that the Germans expected full ownership of bases on and off the coast of Northwest Africa – and began to see that the war might not be over – Franco decided not to enter the conflict. He subsequently assisted the

8 Norman J. W. Goda, *Tomorrow the World: Hitler, Northwest Africa, and the Path toward America* (College Station, TX, 1998).

9 There is a series of books on Italy's role in the war by MacGregor Knox, beginning with *Mussolini Unleashed 1939–1941: Politics and Strategy in Fascist Italy's Last War* (Cambridge, 1982); *Hitler's Italian Allies: Royal Armed Forces, Fascist Regime, and the War of 1940–1943* (Cambridge, 2000).

German submarine campaign and German intelligence, and was eager to help the Germans in other ways, but he refrained from entering hostilities.

The first Soviet response to Germany's victories was quickly to gather in anything that Berlin had promised earlier, lest peace break out. The Baltic states were formally annexed, as was a large part of Romania, some of it once Russian, some once Austrian. There were hopes of further gains, but these were thwarted by Germany. Stalin never grasped that the Germans' changed policy toward Finland and Romania was part of a plan to attack the Soviet Union. He hoped to continue the alignment with Germany, sent Foreign Commissar Molotov to Berlin to work out a new arrangement, and devoted the following months to forging an agreement with Berlin. Neither his own intelligence agency's securing a copy of the German invasion plan in December 1940 nor a confirming summary of it provided by the United States in February 1941 could awaken Stalin. He made many conciliatory gestures to Berlin, but he never understood the reason behind the silence these evoked.

Having suffered defeat by Soviet forces at Nomonhan in 1939, the Tokyo government decided that it was time to seize European colonial possessions in South and Southeast Asia. Japan took the first steps in this direction in September 1940, joining an alliance with Germany and Italy and moving troops into northern French Indochina. Concern about striking before the United States left its bases in the Philippines in 1946 was relieved by Berlin's assurance that it would join war against the United States, should the Japanese believe that war with this country was a prerequisite to moving south earlier. From Hitler's perspective, an allied Japan would provide the large surface fleet that Germany had not yet built.[10]

The government in Washington found support among an increasing portion of the population for measures to rearm the country and assist Britain. For the first time, a coalition government of sorts emerged in Washington. The Congress voted for a massive increase in the navy, and for the first time conscription was introduced in peacetime. The building up of an air force had been ordered in late 1938 and was pushed forward. Years passed before substantial American forces could be deployed, but the shock of German victories affected the country dramatically. One of the most dramatic effects was the reelection of Franklin Roosevelt to a third term in November 1940; another was public support for the exchange of fifty older American

10 James W. Morley, ed., *Japan's Road to the Pacific War: The Final Confrontation* (New York, 1994); Nobutaka Ike, ed., *Japan's Decision for War: Records of the 1941 Policy Conferences* (Stanford, 1964)

destroyers for bases in British possessions in the western hemisphere. In March 1941 the Congress passed the Lend-Lease Act, under which the country sent massive aid first to Britain and later to other allies.

The winter of 1940–41 saw a continued struggle between German submarines and surface warships and the Royal Navy in the war's longest battle, the Battle of the Atlantic. Until the fall of 1943, the Allies lost more ships each month than they could build. This result threatened Britain with the possibility of defeat; and it put a stranglehold on the strategy of the western Allies until a combination of better radar and direction-finding devices, surface ships and long-range planes, and the breaking of German codes turned the tide in May of 1943. In this contest, Canada played a significant role, as did the British and American navies.[11]

Lest the loss of Libya lead to Mussolini's downfall, the Germans dispatched a blocking force under Erwin Rommel to North Africa. The Germans rescued the Italians from defeat at the hands of the Greeks by invading Yugoslavia as well as Greece. This move led the British government to send many of their North African forces to the latter country, enabling German and Italian units to drive the British back into Egypt. The German Balkan operation of April 1941 had other important effects. It provoked a complicated set of resistance movements in Yugoslavia that eventuated in a civil war, as the Axis powers were first halted and then defeated. Out of this civil war, the partisans of Josef Tito emerged victorious. In addition, the German parachutists and landing troops seized the Greek island of Crete, appearing to prepare the way for a major German drive into the Middle East. A pro-German coup in Baghdad in May opened further possibilities, especially since Vichy's control over Syria allowed the Germans to use bases there to assist the coup. British forces, primarily from India, crushed the coup in Iraq. Thereafter Australian, Free French, and other British units invaded Syria and defeated the garrison. Germany did not send substantial forces into the Middle East, because Berlin's main focus that summer was the invasion of the Soviet Union.

The military planning for this invasion envisaged drives in the far north toward Murmansk and Arkhangelsk from Finland, into the Baltic States toward Leningrad, in the center toward Moscow, and, with the assistance of Romania, into the Ukraine and toward the Caucasus in the south. It was assumed that these operations could be completed in about two months. They

11 On the generally neglected Canadian role, see W. E. B. Douglas, Roger Sarly, and Michael Whitby, *No Higher Purpose: The Official Operational History of the Canadian Navy in the Second World War, 1939–1943*, Vol. II, Part 1 (St. Catharines, Ontario, 2002).

were to be followed by attacks into the Middle East from the north and south, with a possible thrust through Turkey in between. Directives to special units and police battalions attached to the armies called for the killing of all Jews in the newly occupied Soviet territory. The transfer of food to Germany from conquered agricultural areas was expected to starve 30 to 40 million local inhabitants.[12]

The total surprise attained by the invasion on June 22, 1941 combined with the weakness of Soviet military leadership, which had not yet recovered from the purges of the 1930s, led to major German initial victories. These appeared to make the Germans' calculations correct – at least by mid July they were convinced that this was so. This belief led to two new decisions. Emphasis in the armaments program shifted from the army to the navy and air force – a decision that subsequently had to be reversed. The army's extensive cooperation in the mass killing of Jews encouraged the decision to extend this program to every portion of Europe that German arms and influence could reach.[13]

The German invasion had repercussions in London, Washington, and Tokyo. The British and American governments decided to assist the Soviet Union, lest it be defeated or make a separate peace with Germany. Before it moved south, the Tokyo government had assured itself of Soviet neutrality with a pact signed with Moscow in April 1941. Now the Japanese believed that the time had come for this move south. The occupation of southern French Indochina in July pointed away from the war with China, which Japan had begun in 1937, and toward the Dutch, British, and American possessions in South and Southeast Asia. The American government decided not to follow the Soviet example of providing critical materials to a likely enemy until the day it was attacked. When in the final stage of negotiations in 1941 Washington offered to sell Japan oil if southern Indochina were evacuated, the Japanese negotiators were instructed not to discuss the proposal. Tokyo preferred war.[14]

Both the Germans and Japanese miscalculated. The German offensive toward Murmansk was halted, ironically at the point where the Soviets had allowed the Germans a naval base in 1939–40. The offensive toward Leningrad isolated this city but failed to seize it. The Germans made major advances

12 Currently the best available survey is David M. Glantz and Jonathan M. House, *When Titans Clashed: How the Red Army Stopped Hitler* (Lawrence, KS, 1995).

13 Christopher Browning, *The Origins of the Final Solution: The Evolution of Nazi Jewish Policy, September 1939–March 1942* (Lincoln, NE, and Jerusalem, 2004).

14 The relevant documents have been published by the Department of Defense in *The "Magic" Background of Pearl Harbor* (Washington, DC, 1978).

toward Moscow, and Hitler drove them forward in late November for fear that the Japanese might not join the war; but the Red Army held the Germans before moving to the offensive. In the south the Germans, assisted by Romanian and Italian forces, also moved forward, seizing most of the Ukraine and taking the city of Rostov. Here, too, the invaders were halted, and the Red Army retook Rostov in late November. However, the German advances of October–November enthused Hitler sufficiently to tell the Grand Mufti of Jerusalem that all the Jews in the world, not only those in Europe, would be killed.

The critical point, which Germany's political and military leadership at the time – and most historians since – failed to grasp, was not how far the Germans advanced how quickly. It was instead whether the Soviet regime, like that of Alexander I when Napoleon reached Moscow, could retain effective control of the unoccupied portions of the country and mobilize its human and material resources, as Nicholas II and Kerensky had failed to do in 1917. By early August 1941 the Soviet regime's success was evident, as Red Army units temporarily pushed the Germans back on the central front. At Rostov, before Moscow, and near Leningrad, the Red Army drove the Germans back in late November and early December 1941, and it almost destroyed German Army Group Center early in 1942. Had Stalin concentrated on this sector, the Germans would have suffered disaster rather than a major defeat; but he ordered offensives everywhere. These advanced somewhat but failed to crush Germany's armies, which rallied and held a ragged front. Behind this front, the Soviets developed a substantial partisan movement, especially in the north and in Belorussia. German countermeasures, which generally fell on the rural population rather than the partisans, only increased partisan strength.[15] As news about German occupation and anti-partisan policies traveled on both sides of the front, the population of the Soviet Union rallied to the country's defense. A similar consolidation resulted from the horrendous mistreatment of captured Red Army soldiers. By the Germans' own accounting in early 1942, they killed or let die 2,100,000 POWs in the first seven months of fighting. The impact of such horrors was accentuated by the contrast with the behavior of the German army and administration in many of the same places during World War I, when there had been terrible incidents but nothing like the mass deaths of prisoners, murder of the handicapped, and slaughter of Jews, which the population saw and heard about now. In spite of earlier dissatisfaction with the regime, the

15 Kenneth Slepyan, *Stalin's Guerillas: Soviet Partisans in World War II* (Lawrence, KS, 2006).

enormous sacrifices and continuous effort of the Soviet population in World War II must be understood as a combination of patriotism and the recognition that a far worse fate awaited under German rule.

The Japanese launched their attack on the United States – as well as on the British and Dutch – with the attack on Pearl Harbor on Sunday, December 7, 1941. The chief of the Japanese combined fleet, Admiral Yamamoto Isoroku, had used the threat of resignation to force this attack as a substitute for the navy's original war plan. Although it was a tactical success, the attack was a strategic blunder of colossal proportions. First, by ensuring that the Americans would insist on a crushing victory, it destroyed the Japanese concept of making extensive conquests and then arriving at a new settlement. Second, the shallow waters of Pearl Harbor, of which the Japanese were aware, meant that most of the warships that Yamamoto imagined sunk were instead set into the mud, raised, repaired, and returned to service. Third, the attack on ships in harbor on a peacetime Sunday failed to eliminate the crews of most of the ships, who survived to participate in rebuilding the American navy.

Japanese strikes at the Americans in the Philippines and the British in Malaya were also initially successful. General MacArthur was surprised in the Philippines the day after the Pearl Harbor attack, after he had replaced an earlier plan for defending the major northern island of Luzon by holding only the Bataan peninsula, with a ridiculous concept of defending the whole island. By the time he was forced by the Japanese to return to the original concept, the supplies that the American and Filipino soldiers needed had been lost. Still, the defending troops held out bravely into April 1942. Those who survived and surrendered, like those who held out into May on the island of Corregidor in Manila harbor, endured endless horrors in Japanese captivity. The Japanese quickly overran the other Philippine islands but faced guerrilla activity for the rest of the occupation.[16]

Long before the surrender in the Philippines, the Japanese had crushed vastly larger British and Indian forces in Malaya by mid February 1942. They defeated the Allied navies that tried to defend the Dutch East Indies, quickly landed, and conquered them. Then they decided to move further west and south. To the west, the Japanese army rapidly conquered Burma, cutting the overland supply route to China at a time when the fighting on the German–Soviet front prevented the Soviets from sending substantial supplies to the Chinese Nationalists. British and minimal American forces in Burma retreated

16 Louis Morton, *The War in the Pacific: The Fall of the Philippines* (Washington, DC, 1953) remains the best general account.

into India, but although there was serious discontent there, the Japanese army and navy could not agree on an invasion of the subcontinent when the chances of success were greatest. From the eastern Indian province of Assam, the Americans initiated what came to be known as "The Hump," an air supply route across the Himalayas to China, assisting this country in fighting the Japanese until the reconquest of northern Burma could reopen an overland supply route.[17]

The Japanese move southwards entailed landings on New Guinea, the Solomon Islands, and other islands in the south Pacific. The Japanese realized seizing Port Moresby, on the southern coast of New Guinea, was necessary to threaten Australia and New Zealand. However, US warships thwarted the Japanese effort in the Battle of the Coral Sea on May 3–8, 1942. Though American losses were greater than Japanese, the Japanese advance had been checked. Thereafter the only way to Port Moresby was across New Guinea by land on the Kokoda Trail. Within a few miles of the city, the Japanese were halted by Australian troops. Australian and American units slowly drove the Japanese force back across the island, eventually destroying it in bitter fighting around Buna and Gona in the spring of 1943.[18]

In addition to the drives west and south, the Japanese leadership agreed to another of Yamamoto's projects – again only because of his threat to resign. In a complicated set of operations, Japanese aircraft carriers were to lure out the American fleet, so the main Japanese fleet could destroy it, the Japanese could seize Midway and Hawaii, and confuse the Americans by capturing Kiska and Attu in the Aleutians. Of the eight carriers employed, two were diverted to the Aleutian project while two remained with the main fleet. The four assigned to the critical thrust were all sunk in the Battle of Midway on June 3–7. While the Japanese had not repaired the carrier damaged in the Coral Sea engagement, the Americans had made hasty repairs on the carrier *Yorktown*, which had been damaged there. Although sunk by a Japanese submarine in the aftermath of Midway, the *Yorktown*, along with two other American carriers, had provided the planes that sank the Japanese carriers. Critical for the subsequent course of the war was the great loss of trained and experienced Japanese aircrew.[19]

17 Louis Allen, *Burma: The Longest War 1941–1945* (London, 2000).
18 H. P. Willmott, *The Barrier and the Javelin: Japanese and Allied Pacific Strategies, February to June 1942* (Annapolis, MD, 1983).
19 Jonathan Parshall and Anthony Tully, *Shattered Sword: The Untold Story of the Battle of Midway* (Washington, DC, 2005).

The Japanese seizure of Attu and Kiska led to naval engagements in the area and an American assault that retook Attu in bloody fighting in May 1943. Japanese evacuation of Kiska at the end of July preempted the planned American–Canadian recapture of this island. In February, the Japanese had already shown an ability to evacuate troops at the end of the longest battle in US history, the fight for Guadalcanal.

In the aftermath of Midway, in early August 1942, as the Japanese threatened communications with Australia by constructing an airfield on Guadalcanal in the Solomons, US forces carried out a landing there and a smaller island nearby. A lengthy series of land and naval battles ensued. Both sides moved in reinforcements, but the Americans not only held the key airport against repeated assaults, but eventually took the whole island and won the naval battle of attrition. The importance of this lengthy struggle lay in the return of the Allies to the offensive in the southwest Pacific and the inability of the Japanese to replace most of their losses. Together with the landing of British troops at the northern end of the island of Madagascar in May 1942, the struggle for Guadalcanal kept Japanese forces from trying for a junction with the European Axis during the only months of World War II when such a move was conceivable.[20]

Although they were not coordinated with the Japanese, German plans for 1942 pointed in the same direction. Unable, because of losses suffered in 1941, to repeat the broad-front approach of their original invasion, the Germans decided on a sequence of separate operations in the summer of 1942.[21] The first was to conquer the Crimea, destroying the Soviet forces on the peninsula's eastern portion and then taking the port of Sebastopol. These operations were completed in May and June 1942. German forces were then to move across the length of the eastern front to take Leningrad, but a series of local Soviet attacks thwarted this project. The Germans crushed a Soviet offensive in the Ukraine, then turned to their major offensive for the year. This was to seize the Caucasus oilfields, assuring the Axis of oil and depriving the Soviets of this critical material. Because the Germans lacked the forces needed to guard the lengthening flanks of this eastward thrust, they

20 Richard B. Frank, *Guadalcanal: The Definitive Account of the Landmark Battle* (New York, 1990).

21 The first two volumes of the Stalingrad trilogy by David M. Glantz have appeared: *To the Gates of Stalingrad: Soviet-German Combat Operations, April–August 1942*, and *Armageddon in Stalingrad: September–November 1942* (Lawrence, KS, 2009). Also important, Joel S. A. Hayward, *Stopped at Stalingrad: The Luftwaffe and Hitler's Defeat in the East 1942–1943* (Lawrence, KS, 1998), and Robert M. Citino, *Death of the Wehrmacht: The German Campaigns of 1942* (Lawrence, KS, 2007).

pushed their Romanian, Italian, and Hungarian allies into increasing their units and assuming the task. Having failed to provide them with adequate equipment, the Germans subsequently blamed them for the disastrous defeat that followed.

The German offensive involved a direct move by one army group into the Caucasus across the lower Don. This thrust was to be covered in the north by a drive into the bend of the Don and then to the Volga at Stalingrad, to be followed by a thrust down the Volga to Astrakhan. Although in July and August the Germans advanced substantially, seizing the Maikop oilfield and threatening the Grozny oilfield, the broader operation failed for three reasons. First, the Red Army avoided the great encirclements that had caused enormous losses in 1941. Units pulled back, fought hard, and stalled the Germans. Secondly, the Germans did not have enough men, tanks, and planes to carry both thrusts forward simultaneously. The third and most dramatic reason for the German failure was a carefully planned and executed Red Army counter-offensive into the flanks of the German army that was fighting street by street in Stalingrad. Since the Germans had moved their best units into the point of their offensive in the city, the Red Army's well-equipped armored thrusts north and south of the city pierced the forces of Germany's allies, then joined to encircle the Axis forces on November 22.

German efforts to relieve the isolated units and to supply them by air failed, in part because of the diversion of Axis forces to meet the Allied landing in Northwest Africa and to supply units sent there. While these two Allied offensives assisted each other, a major Soviet offensive on the central part of the eastern front failed to make substantial headway. The British stepped up their air offensive against Germany. Having discovered in late 1941 that attempts at targeted bombing were failing, they decided in early 1942 to concentrate on night bombing of cities, as the first big attacks were launched in March. As a result, an increasing portion of the German air force was diverted to home defense, and an increasing proportion of German artillery and ammunition was similarly employed.

The rapid Japanese advances and the British need to keep Australian and New Zealand forces in the Middle East obliged the United States in 1942 – and into 1943 – to defer its basic "Germany First" strategy. Roosevelt and all his military advisors favored a landing in northwest Europe at the earliest opportunity, but there was no prospect of such a project in 1942. There were hopes for an invasion in 1943, but in the meantime a blow had to be struck at the European Axis, both to assist the Russians and to engage the attention of an American public that was primarily focused on the Pacific. These factors led

Roosevelt to agree with Churchill to an invasion of French Northwest Africa, which was launched in early November 1942. This operation had three additional aims. German victories over British forces in North Africa in May and June 1942 had brought Rommel's army, with its attached murder commando, within striking distance of Alexandria. The British had halted the Axis forces and, with substantial US assistance, launched a major offensive at the end of October. A landing in Northwest Africa would take the retreating Axis troops in the rear and clear North Africa. Secondly, such an Allied victory would open the Mediterranean to Allied shipping and avoid routes around the southern tip of Africa. Third, from bases in North Africa the Allies could bomb and threaten to invade portions of southern Europe, further diverting German strength.[22]

American and British troops landed in French Northwest Africa on November 8, 1942. French resistance was overcome quickly, and Allied forces headed for Tunisia and the rear of the Axis units that were retreating from Egypt through Libya. Although surprised by the landings, the Germans quickly built up forces in Tunisia, aided by French unwillingness to fight them as they had fought the Allies. Simultaneously German forces moved into unoccupied France, meeting no resistance. Unable to send massive reinforcements to Tunisia because of the Soviet counteroffensive at Stalingrad, the Germans and Italians sent enough over the short distance between Sicily and Tunisia to halt the Allied advance in December. The campaign to clear Tunisia therefore extended into early 1943. Thereafter it was too late to shift troops to England for an invasion of France that year. Accordingly, when Allied leaders met at Casablanca in January, they decided that an invasion of Sicily and possibly Italy would follow in 1943, with the cross-Channel invasion postponed to 1944.

Roosevelt and Churchill reached several additional decisions at Casablanca when Stalin refused to attend. First priority for 1943 was accorded to the campaign against German submarines, in order to remove the stricture that had restrained all operations by the western Allies. It was agreed to combine the British and American bomber offensives against Germany; the former was to concentrate on city-bombing by night, the latter on targeted efforts during daylight.[23] An attempt was made to gather various French factions for a united effort against the Axis. Roosevelt and Churchill also agreed to publicize at this

22 Tami Davis Biddle, *Rhetoric and Reality in Air Warfare: The Evolution of British and American Ideas about Strategic Bombing, 1914–1945* (Princeton, 2002) covers the topic of the Allied bombing offensive very well.

23 Rick Atkinson, *An Army at Dawn: The War in North Africa, 1942–1943* (New York, 2002).

time a demand, which the two governments had framed earlier, for the unconditional surrender of Germany, Italy, and Japan – the inclusion of Italy at the insistence of the British cabinet. The demand was calculated both to calm the public at home, which had been alarmed by a deal that General Eisenhower had made with the French collaborator Admiral Darlan, and to reassure the Soviets that postponement of invasion in the west had not altered the determination to crush the Axis.

In the winter of 1942–43, the Allied forces chasing Rommel from the east met those in Tunisia. Although the Germans administered a temporary defeat to green American troops at Kasserine Pass, an Allied offensive crushed the Axis forces in drives that ended with a large-scale surrender of Axis troops in early May. To make certain that substantial German units would be engaged in fighting the western powers until these could land in France in 1944 – and to keep Germans away from the prospective landing sites – British and American troops landed on Sicily in July 1943. Even as these captured the collapsing Italian forces on the island and pushed the German units off it, the Fascist Grand Council joined the king of Italy in dumping Mussolini. The latter was rescued by the Germans and installed in a puppet government. His successor, General Badoglio, together with the king, botched the surrender of Italy to the Allies so thoroughly that the Germans were able to occupy most of the country and all European areas that Italy had occupied, to seize hundreds of thousands of Italian soldiers for slave labor, and to slaughter large numbers of their erstwhile allies.[24]

In September, even as the Italian surrender was announced, Allied forces landed at the toe of Italy and at Salerno near Naples. From the former site they moved northward at a leisurely pace, while at the latter they were almost driven into the sea. The Germans committed substantial forces – two entire armies – to the Italian campaign, in order to delay the Allies' advance in weather and terrain that favored the Germans. Even a flanking landing at Anzio in early 1944 did not crack the front. Only a major offensive launched in May 1944 ended what had approached a stalemate; and then the American commander, General Mark Clark, misdirected his troops to seize Rome rather than trap a large part of the German force. As a result, the Allies had to continue their slow and difficult push northwards. Although the campaign in Italy diverted German units from other fronts and made air bases available to

24 Ilena Agarossi, *A Nation Collapses: The Italian Surrender of September 1943* (Cambridge, 2000). See also Richard Lamb, *War in Italy 1943–1945: A Brutal Story* (New York, 1996).

the Allies for attacking portions of Europe that were otherwise difficult or impossible to reach, questions about it would remain.[25]

The Soviet victory at Stalingrad was quickly followed by a crushing offensive against the Italian and Hungarian units that had been shielding the northern German flank. This action threatened to cut off the German army group that had advanced into the Caucasus. It was shoved and pulled back, although the Germans held on to a bridgehead in the Kuban area as a basis for what they expected would be a future thrust into the Caucasus. It never came because of developments further north, and the bridgehead was evacuated in September–October 1943.

The Germans planned a major offensive in the east for the summer of 1943, hoping to destroy a large bulge that the Red Army had created with the capture of Kursk. German hopes of recovering the initiative were encouraged by an earlier local counteroffensive, which had retaken the city of Kharkov, and the availability of new, heavier tanks. The Red Army prepared for the German offensive and to strike into the rear of the northern German pincer. In a grinding contest that included masses of tanks, the Red Army blocked the last German summer offensive, which Hitler then halted because of the Allied landing on Sicily. The Soviet offensive smashed into the rear of the German positions around Orel and thereafter pushed the Germans back steadily. Soon the Red Army liberated much of the Ukraine and forced the Germans back on the central part of the front. It also broke the siege of Leningrad. The Red Army had the initiative. Its leaders were now experienced and generally heeded by Stalin, and its mobility was greatly increased by vast numbers of US trucks. Massed tanks and artillery and increasing control of the air provided an edge the Germans could not match.

Although the United States had returned to the "Germany First" strategy by the summer of 1943, victories on New Guinea and Guadalcanal in early 1943 were followed by further offensive operations against Japan. These were to take the form of two thrusts, aided by a third and perhaps a fourth. Along with army and marine units, the navy was to move across the central Pacific, seizing islands on the path toward Japan. Supported by the navy, the army was to move from the southwest Pacific along the northern coast of New Guinea toward the Philippines and then on to Japan. It was hoped that forces also could be built up in China for an assault against Japan on the shortest

25 Rick Atkinson, *The Day of Battle: The War in Sicily and Italy, 1943–1944* (New York, 2007). See also the extraordinary book on the Anzio landing, William Woodruff, *Vessel of Sadness* (London, 1970).

route, but the collapse of Chinese Nationalist resistance before the Japanese "Ichigo" offensive in the summer of 1944 ended the prospect even of air attacks from China on Japan. This development in turn made the fourth axis of attack, by the Soviets into Manchuria, look all the more important.

The navy's offensive started with landings on Makin and Tarawa in the Gilberts in November 1943. The latter operation proved especially difficult. At the insistence of Admiral Nimitz, who was in overall command, the lessons learned in this first atoll landing were studied carefully. The first major use of these lessons came in landings on the Marshall Islands of Roi-Namur, Parry, and Kwajalein from January 31 to February 7, 1944. The next major step on this route was the Marianas, not only to recapture Guam, which the Japanese had seized earlier, but also to provide air bases from which Japan itself could be reached by newly available B-29 bombers. The first landing was on Saipan in June 1944, followed by assaults on Tinian and Guam. The fighting proved hard, but the attendant naval battle, which the Americans won by a large margin, relieved the southwest Pacific thrust at a time when it was in difficulty. Although there was much criticism of the double-thrust approach, over the enormous distances of the Pacific this strategy prevented the Japanese from concentrating their forces against either thrust.

The thrust in the southwest Pacific under General MacArthur moved forward in a series of jumps along the coast of New Guinea and in the Solomon and Bismarck island groups. In the process, large Japanese garrisons, including major bases such as Truk and Rabaul, were isolated and left behind. Nevertheless Australian troops fought Japanese forces that had been bypassed on New Guinea and Bougainville, until the Japanese surrendered in 1945. When American troops on the island of Biak, off the New Guinea coast, were threatened by a Japanese naval force in June 1944, the central Pacific advance into the Marianas caused a critical diversion. By the end of July, the Americans were in control of the Vogelkop Peninsula at the northwestern tip of New Guinea – as far from Milne Bay, where the Australians had repulsed a Japanese landing at the other end of the island, as Rostov is from Leningrad. In September the Americans seized Morotai in the Moluccas, halfway to the southern Philippines.[26]

By the summer of 1944, the war in the Pacific had changed in other important ways. The Japanese advanced into India, trying to seize the

26 An excellent general account appears in Ronald H. Spector, *Eagle against the Sun: The American War with Japan* (New York, 1985). See also D. Clayton James, *The Years of MacArthur*, Vol. II: *1941–1945* (Boston, 1975); Donald L. Miller, *D-Days in the Pacific* (New York, 2005); and a series of books on specific campaigns by Harry Gailey.

British and US bases in Assam at Imphal and Kohima and thus to cut off the American supply route to China over the Himalayas. The Japanese also hoped for an uprising against British rule in India, which would be prompted by an army of Indian collaborators following the Japanese troops. In the meantime, however, the British-Indian 14th Army had been reorganized and was now led by General William Slim, Britain's ablest field commander of World War II. In the largest ground defeat of the war, the Japanese offensive was crushed. Thereafter the British, with substantial American air support, drove the Japanese out of Burma, joining Chinese and American forces that had been successful in northern Burma. The British prepared for a landing in Malaya in late 1945 in order to retake Singapore.

Probably more significant in weakening Japan's economy and resistance was the attack on Japanese shipping. In spite of some Japanese participation in Allied antisubmarine operations during World War I, the Japanese navy showed no serious interest during World War II either in submarine warfare against Allied merchant shipping or in protecting Japanese shipping against submarine attack. The first of these failings led to the stationing of German submarines at Japanese bases on the coast of Malaya for operations in the Indian Ocean – a preposterous misallocation of Axis resources. The second failing proved doubly harmful for the Japanese. It had not occurred to them that the conquest of rubber plantations, oil wells, and tin mines would not lead to the transfer of the plantations, wells, and mines to Japan. Conquest meant in fact that the products had to be shipped to Japan on Japanese ships, rather than ships of other countries. The vulnerability of Japan's scarce ocean-shipping resources was accentuated by the fact that the army and navy each controlled its own shipping. So once the US navy overcame the problem of defective torpedoes, it sent vast numbers of Japanese ships to the bottom. With assistance from British and Dutch submarines and the breaking of the Japanese shipping code, the Americans did to Japan what the Germans hoped to do to the British. Already by 1944 much of Japanese industry did not operate at capacity, because the necessary raw materials could not be brought to the home islands.[27]

In the European theater, the Red Army retook the Crimea in the spring of 1944. An offensive into the Balkans was, however, repulsed. For the summer

27 See Clay Blair, Jr., *Silent Victory: The US Submarine War against Japan* (Philadelphia, 1975); Mark P. Parillo, *The Japanese Merchant Marine in World War II* (Annapolis, MD, 1993). For the other side, see Carl Boyd and Akihiko Yoshida, *The Japanese Submarine Force and World War II* (Annapolis, MD, 1995).

of 1944 the Allies planned a coordinated attack on Germany from all sides. While the Axis powers lacked all strategic coordination, the three major Allies had met at Tehran at the end of November 1943 and made military as well as political plans for the future. Now that the western Allies had defeated the German navy and were crushing German efforts to regain the initiative at sea, the prerequisite for an invasion in northwest Europe was control of the air. The setback suffered by the British and American air forces in the fall of 1943 was reversed, as fighters were enabled to escort the bombers. Attacking targets that the Germans felt obliged to defend, such as airplane factories, the US fighters swept the air of German planes in February–March 1944. On the assumption that the bulk of the German army would be busy on the eastern front and that the majority of German soldiers in the west would be held in the wrong places by a major Allied deception operation, the Americans, British, and Canadians planned to land in Normandy in early June. To make certain that no German units could move into France from Italy, the Allies initiated a major offensive there in May.

Supported by a large navy and massive airstrikes, Allied troops landed in Normandy from the sea and by parachute on June 6, 1944. The initial success of the landing thwarted the German plan to send the invaders into the sea and then to move forces to the eastern front. Although it took almost two months of bitter fighting to expand the bridgehead and then break out at its western end, the breakout itself opened much of France to an Allied sweep eastwards. The Americans warded off the only major German counter-offensive. A landing on the French Mediterranean coast in August cleared the ports there, an accomplishment that proved essential as the Germans held on to or wrecked other ports. In September the Allies' advance slowed, as they ran out of supplies while the Germans rallied near the Franco-German border. The attempt to outflank the German defenses by a sweep across the lower Rhine failed when the Germans halted the combined Allied airborne and land assault at Arnhem. In October American forces crossed into Germany and took the first important city, Aachen, but the front then stabilized.[28]

Right after the Normandy landing, the Red Army initiated a massive attack on the Finnish front. By September Finland had been forced out of the war.

28 Out of an enormous literature, see Alan F. Wilt, *The Atlantic Wall 1941–1944: Hitler's Defenses for D-Day* (New York, 2004); Carlo D'Este, *Decision in Normandy* (New York, 1991); Adrian R. Lewis, *Omaha Beach: A Flawed Victory* (Chapel Hill, 2001); Theodore A. Wilson, ed., *D-Day 1944* (Lawrence, KS, 1994).

Having deceived the Germans as successfully as the Allies had in the west, the Soviets launched their major offensive against the central German army group on June 22. In what became the biggest defeat of the German army during the war, the Soviets crushed the force that faced them, freed Belorussia, and soon thereafter threatened to cut off the German army group in the Baltic States. This they achieved. At the insistence of Admiral Dönitz, who had replaced Raeder as head of the navy, German forces that were cut off in western Latvia and elsewhere along the Baltic coast remained in their positions, because the Germans needed control of the central Baltic Sea to run in the new types of submarines that they were building in hopes of turning the tide in the Battle of the Atlantic.[29]

The Red Army's advance on the central part of the front brought it into Poland. When the underground Polish army rose in Warsaw, the Red Army halted while the Germans crushed the uprising. Air supply by the western Allies did not help the Poles much, and it was not even tried as a similar rising in Slovakia was crushed. The Red Army did, however, seize bridgeheads across the Vistula, which provided the basis for their great offensive in the winter of 1944–45.

In addition to victories in the central and northern portions of the front, the Red Army resumed the offensive in the south. As it struck into Romania, a coup there took this country out of the war and, in reaction to German attacks, brought it in on the Allied side. Bulgaria had not declared war on the Soviet Union, but the Red Army now invaded the country. While the Soviets left Greece to the British, the Red Army headed west to join up with Tito's partisans in Yugoslavia and to invade Hungary. To prevent the defection of this country and in order to kill the largest surviving Jewish community in Europe, the Germans had occupied Hungary in March 1944. Now it became a theater of war, as Budapest had been besieged by the end of the year.

The air war in Europe continued all through 1944–45. The British and Americans controlled the air to bomb German cities at night and German transportation and oil targets by day. The first appearance of jet planes, primarily German, had little effect, since fuel for pilot training or the new planes was no longer available. Similarly, the special new German weapons, the V-1 unmanned planes and V-2 ballistic missiles, caused some damage and casualties but had no significant impact on the war. The V-3 ultra-distance gun and V-4 multi-stage rocket barely came into use.

29 Howard D. Grier, *Hitler, Dönitz and the Baltic Sea: The Third Reich's Last Hope, 1944–1945* (Annapolis, MD, 2007).

More important was a major offensive in the Ardennes, which the Germans launched in mid December 1944 in order to retake the port of Antwerp and administer a great defeat on the Americans. The surprised American troops were forced back, but by holding steady at St. Vith and Bastogne, they confined German gains to a bulge that was largely erased in January.[30] A smaller German offensive in Lorraine was also held, and thereafter the only significant German counteroffensives were in Hungary in January and February 1945, because of the importance of the oil wells there. The Red Army defeated these efforts and pushed on toward Vienna.

In January the Soviets' winter offensive demolished German forces in Poland and pushed across the Oder River, simultaneously seizing the Silesian industrial area. Minor German counterattacks and Soviet exhaustion led to a brief pause before the Red Army resumed the offensive that encircled Berlin in April. Fighting on the outskirts and in the city was exceptionally bitter and destructive, but in early May the German forces in the city surrendered.[31]

The western Allies resumed offensive operations in February, as Canadian, British, American, and French units drove across the Rhine in March. Thereafter the fighting became more sporadic, as bitter German resistance in some places alternated with large-scale surrenders and undefended towns. Field Marshal Montgomery wanted to build his forces for a major river-crossing operation at the Elbe, as he had at the Rhine, but Churchill and Eisenhower pushed him forward. American and Soviet troops met at Torgau on the Elbe. German forces surrendered locally in Italy and the northern part of the western front, and large numbers of German soldiers tried to surrender to the British and Americans to avoid being captured by the Soviets.[32]

Although almost three times as many German soldiers had been killed as in World War I, the German military fought until practically the whole country was occupied. Their commanders had accepted huge bribes from Hitler and knew that these would stop if the Nazi regime ended. A tiny number of brave individuals had tried but failed to kill Hitler and to take over the government in July 1944. With one exception (the commander in Paris), all military commanders sided with their leader. The mass murder of the handicapped,

30 Charles B. MacDonald, *The Battle of the Bulge* (London, 1994); Charles Whiting, *The Last Assault: The Battle of the Bulge Reassessed* (London, 1994).

31 Although not so reliable on the German side of things, Christopher Duffy, *Red Storm on the Reich: The Soviet March on Germany, 1945* (New York, 1991) is very useful.

32 David Stafford, *Endgame, 1945: The Missing Final Chapter of World War II* (New York, 2007); Stephen G. Fritz, *Endkampf: Soldiers, Civilians, and the Death of the Third Reich* (Lexington, KY, 2004).

MAP 13. Defeat of Germany, 1944–1945

Jews, and Gypsies continued into the last days of fighting and beyond; this, after all, was the purpose of the war. Before committing suicide in Berlin, Hitler designated his enthusiastic follower Dönitz as his successor. Although he was arrested and later tried and jailed, the admiral maintained to the end of his life that he was Germany's legal ruler.

Western forces had advanced well beyond the zonal borders that the British had proposed and the Soviets had accepted against Roosevelt's preference. Allied troops everywhere moved to the agreed lines in Germany and Austria and into the sectors of Berlin and Vienna that had been worked out. By the time these steps were underway, large numbers of American and Soviet troops were moving to east Asia for the fight against Japan, which was anticipated to last at least a year and a half after the German surrender of May 8–9.

A culmination of sorts in the US campaign in the Pacific came in October 1944 with the landing of an army on the island of Leyte in the Philippines, after a bitter fight for Peleliu in the Palau Islands. Because the terrain was unsuitable, Leyte was the wrong island on which to build air bases to support an assault on Luzon, but the landing was bitterly contested by the Japanese, who were repeatedly reinforced. As part of the defense, the Japanese sent out practically all their remaining warships into the greatest naval battle of the war. Although Admiral Halsey took the main US warships in pursuit of Japanese carriers, which had no airplanes and had been sent to divert him from protecting the operation, the landing was shielded from the main Japanese striking force by escort carriers and destroyers. A third Japanese set of warships was sunk by US battleships, most of them raised from the mud of Pearl Harbor.[33] In months of fighting, the Americans took all of Leyte and subsequently moved to Luzon. Key parts of this island were taken. There was a horrendous battle for Manila, and some Japanese forces remained active until the surrender in September 1945. While the fighting on Luzon continued, MacArthur ordered a series of invasions on the southern Philippines and then, starting in July 1945, in the Dutch East Indies.

In February 1945 American marines landed on Iwo Jima, in the Bonin Islands, to deny airfields there to the Japanese and to make airfields accessible to US planes headed to or returning from Japan. The hard fighting caused heavy casualties. At about the same time, a change of commanders and tactics occurred in the US air attacks on Japan. The unsuccessful attempts at precision

33 A recent survey in H. P. Willmott, *The Battle of Leyte Gulf: The Last Fleet Action* (Bloomington, 2005).

bombing were replaced by area attacks on cities, as heavy use of incendiaries began with a massive attack on Tokyo in the night of March 9–10. Several other Japanese cities were heavily struck by incendiary attacks, although the laying of mines by the B-29s probably affected Japan more.

As a base for the anticipated invasion of the Japanese home islands, the Americans landed on Okinawa on April 1.[34] There, as on Peleliu and Iwo, the Japanese had decided to fight a delaying operation on the island, instead of making a futile attempt to crush the landing itself. In this effort they both succeeded and failed. They succeeded in delaying the US army and marine units for three months, during the heaviest fighting of the Pacific War, but they failed to prevent the American Tenth Army from seizing the island. Although suicide attacks inflicted the heaviest losses of the war on the US navy, the Americans continued to supply the forces ashore, and they sank the "Yamato," Japan's last battleship. The success of the Americans, assisted by the British Pacific Fleet, had two important additional effects away from the island. On the one hand, it dashed the last hopes of Japanese Emperor Hirohito, who had until the defeat on Okinawa thought of a negotiated outcome. On the other hand, in mid June, while the fighting on the island was especially hard, President Truman, who had succeeded Roosevelt in April, authorized a landing on Kyushu on November 1.

While these operations were proceeding and planning was underway for landing on Kyushu in 1945 and on Honshu in 1946, the possibility was under consideration that Japan might be shocked into surrender, rather than occupied, like Germany, in military operations. Ironically, at the same time as the Japanese were hoping to use the Soviet Union to negotiate an acceptable peace or even to join the war on Japan's side, the Soviet Union was preparing to invade Manchuria, the Kuriles, and perhaps the island of Hokkaido. The United States had been developing atomic bombs, originally in what was believed to be a race with Germany, although it turned out ironically that Japanese scientists were further along than the Germans. The American project continued with British, Canadian, and Belgian help after it became clear in the fall of 1944 that the German effort had failed. Since Germany was defeated before the first atomic device was tested in July, the assumption was that the bombs that were becoming available would be used on Japan. It was decided that after the Allies had warned Japan from their meeting at

34 For the context, see Max Hastings, *Retribution: The Battle for Japan, 1944–45* (New York, 2008). For important insights and details, see Thomas M. Huber, *Japan's Battle of Okinawa, April–June 1945* (Fort Leavenworth, KS, 1990).

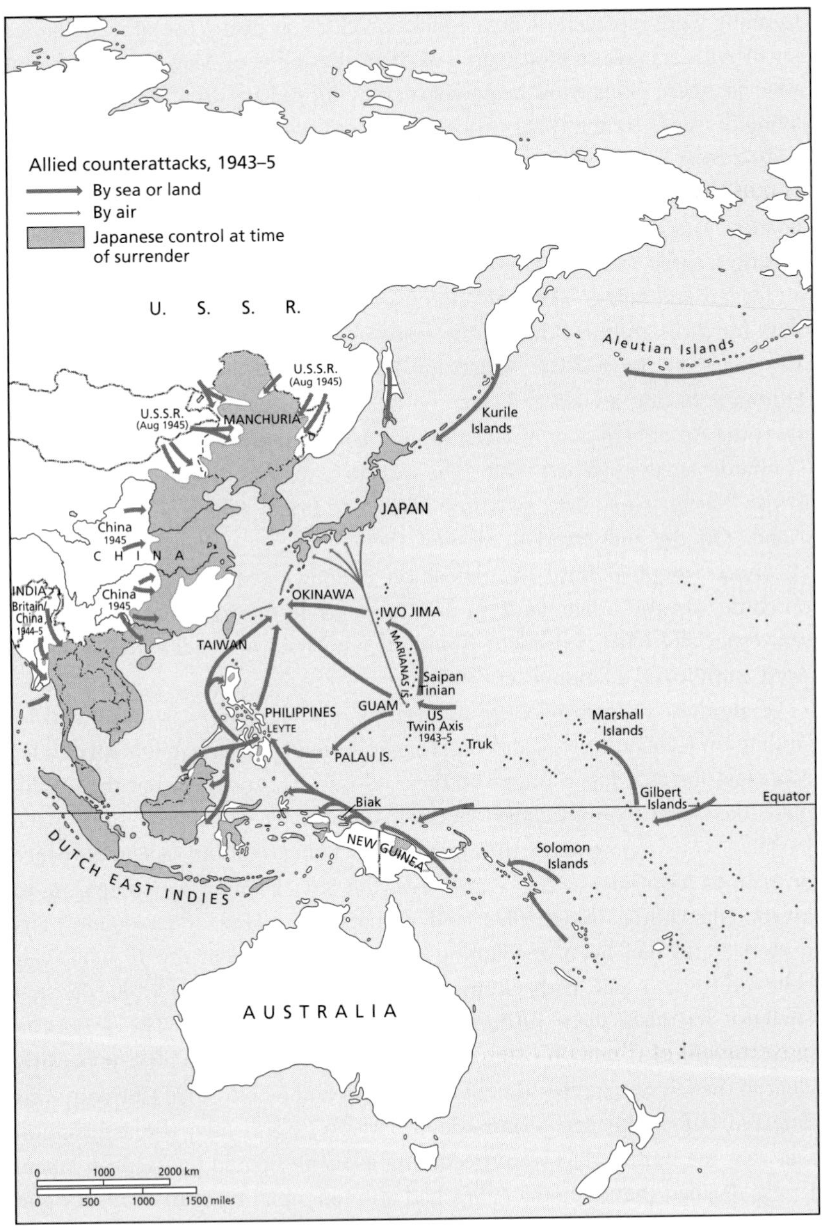

MAP 14. Defeat of Japan, 1943–1945

Potsdam to surrender, the first bomb would be dropped on a city, preferably Hiroshima, which was the headquarters of the Japanese army that defended Kyushu. If this attack did not shock Tokyo into surrender, a second bomb would be dropped in order to give the impression that the United States had an indefinite supply. If the second attack did not have the desired effect, all the bombs that thereafter became available were to be utilized in support of the Kyushu invasion. The president prohibited the dropping of the third bomb before this operation.[35]

The Japanese leadership was evenly divided on the question of surrender, even after the shock of the atomic bombs, the Soviet declaration of war, and the invasion of Manchuria. At this point Emperor Hirohito intervened to order a surrender. There was an attempted coup to reverse this decision and keep the war going, in the hope that Japanese defenders could inflict such heavy casualties on the landing Americans that they would agree to a negotiated peace. The coup failed, because Anami Korechika, the minister of war, though he favored continuing the war, had been present when the emperor ordered surrender. In this inner conflict, he committed suicide rather than join the coup. To the enormous relief of the Americans, Chinese, British, and Australians, Japanese forces throughout east Asia and the Pacific obeyed the orders to surrender with only minimal exceptions. Fighting continued in Korea, northern China, and the Kuriles between Soviet and Japanese forces for some days after the official end of hostilities, but with this exception, the conflict ended with the signing of surrender on September 2, 1945.

Europe was divided into a western and southern portion, on the one hand, in which regimes similar to those of the prewar era reemerged, and, on the other, an eastern portion under Soviet control, with divided Germany and Austria in the middle. The situation in east Asia was fundamentally different. The collapse of European empires in 1940–42 in the face of the Japanese advance hastened decolonization, while the insistence of the Nationalist government of China on extending its reach into the northeast, rather than accept some sort of partition, contributed to a civil war that it lost to the Communists, in part because the Nationalists had been weakened by the

35 Thomas R. Allen and Norman Polmar, *Code-Name DOWNFALL: The Secret Plan to Invade Japan – and Why Truman Dropped the Bomb* (New York, 1995); Richard B. Frank, *Downfall: The End of the Imperial Japanese Empire* (New York, 1999). Very important additional information can be found in D. M. Giangreco, *Hell to Pay: Operation Downfall and the Invasion of Japan, 1945–1947* (Annapolis, MD, 2009).

Japanese Ichigo offensive. Korea was divided between a communist north and a conservative entity in the south, whereas the Japanese surrender, which occurred before an American invasion of Kyushu or a Soviet invasion of the northern island of Hokkaido, spared the initiator of hostilities in Asia the fate of division, which fighting to the bitter end had brought to its counterpart in Europe.[36]

36 Ronald H. Spector, *In the Ruins of Empire: The Japanese Surrender and the Battle for Postwar Asia* (New York, 2007).

PART III

★

POST-TOTAL WARFARE, 1945–2005

Introduction to Part III

DENNIS SHOWALTER

World War I was widely processed as the war to end war. World War II, like the proverbial second marriage, privileged hope over experience. Dennis Showalter's contribution to this section establishes the limits of stabilization in the contexts of occupation during and after World War II. More was necessary. Some combination of global free trade, Marxism–Leninism, and fear of nuclear Armageddon had to encourage the lion and the lamb, if not to lie down together, at least to settle non-violently and preferably through the United Nations, any debates about the dinner menu.[1]

The succeeding decades have in fact been another age of war.[2] The worst possibility has so far been averted. The "Doomsday Clock," which has been kept since 1947 by the *Bulletin of Atomic Scientists*, started at seven minutes to midnight. By 1953 it was at two minutes. In 1991, it was reset to twelve minutes. By 2007 it had crept up to five.[3] The pattern itself is hardly comforting – and arguably less so in an enduring context of protean conflict: global in scope, comprehensive in scale, and kaleidoscopic in conduct.

While war since 1945 defies facile generalizations, it can be addressed in three contexts: method, material, and mentality. Method – the how of war-making – has been governed by the asymmetry that shaped initial understandings on both sides of the Cold War in the late 1940s. The west believed that the Soviet Union and its Warsaw Pact allies were dominant in numbers of everything – divisions, tanks, and aircraft. The USSR believed that the west

1 Paul Kennedy, *The Parliament of Man: The Past, Present, and Future of the United Nations* (New York, 2006), admirably juxtaposes hope and experience. Mark Mazower, *No Enchanted Palace* (Princeton, 2009), offers a pragmatic perspective stressing great-power self-interest.

2 Jeremy Black, *War since 1945* (London, 2004) is a good overview.

3 See the "timeline" on the internet edition of the *Bulletin of Atomic Scientists*, 2009: www.thebulletin.org.

had the nuclear capability to do what Adolf Hitler cold only dream of – to annihilate the Soviet experiment by pushing a button.[4]

For the next forty years, the adversaries sought to compensate for their own perceived shortcomings. C. Dale Walton analyzes this process, which was anything but linear. NATO, for example, was originally projected to have a ground force of ninety divisions. When this figure proved politically and economically unfeasible, the pendulum swung the other way, to the concept of using conventional forces as a "nuclear tripwire." When the potential costs of this doctrine to Europe were calculated and assimilated, planning shifted once again to a conventional defense, which would be stiffened or underwritten by nuclear weapons from tactical levels upward.[5]

By the 1980s the west's Cold War planning had become predicated on effectiveness across the board. NATO's conventional forces would not outmuscle but instead outfight their Warsaw Pact opponents, checking, defeating, and in some contingencies even counterattacking into enemy territory. The Soviet submarine threat to transatlantic reinforcements would be frustrated by NATO navies, which were increasingly configured for antisubmarine war. And in the final stages of what can reasonably be regarded as World War III, anti-missile defense would neutralize Soviet intercontinental ballistic missiles (ICBMs).[6]

The pattern was similar on the other side of the Iron Curtain. Soviet military policy from the early 1950s to the mid 1980s was predicated on comprehensive strength. It involved not only bringing the entire military to the perceived level of the ground forces, but also to overmatching the west, chess-piece for chess-piece. Russian missiles were not as efficient, but they were just as effective as the west's. As western navies abandoned large warships, the USSR introduced its *Kirov*-class battlecruisers. If the United States prized its carriers, the Soviet navy moved toward its own versions of nuclear-powered aircraft carriers. American Special Forces were countered by Russia's *Spetsnaz*.[7] And so it went.

4 See Campbell Craig and Sergey S. Radchenko, *The Atomic Bomb and the Origins of the Cold War* (New Haven, 2008) and Harry R. Borowski, *A Hollow Threat: Strategic Air Power and Containment before Korea* (Westport, CT, 1982).

5 Beatrice Heuser, *NATO, Britain, France, and the FRG: Nuclear Strategies and Forces for Europe, 1949–2000* (New York, 1997) is a good overview.

6 See Steven Cimbala, *US Military Strategy and the Cold War Endgame* (Portland, OR, 1995) and A. J. Pierre, *The Conventional Defense of Europe: New Technologies and New Strategies* (New York, 1986).

7 Matthew Evangelista, *Technology and the Arms Race: How the United States and the Soviet Union Develop New Military Technologies* (Ithaca, 1988) is good for the material aspects of the competition. See also the excellent anthology, Vojtech Mastny et al., eds., *War Plans and Alliances in the Cold War: Threat Perceptions in the East and West* (London, 2006).

The costs of this game to both players remain uncalculated, arguably incalculable.[8] The result was two symmetrical military systems, which matched each other across the spectrum. As an unexpected consequence, they also provided enough spare parts and leftovers to sustain similar symmetric patterns in the era's mid-level conventional wars, which Williamson Murray discusses in his chapter. From start to finish, Korea was fought by both sides along the lines of World War II with surplus equipment, in every respect from small arms to generals, from the same war.[9] The Indo-Pakistani and Muslim–Israeli conflicts from the late 1940s to the early 1970s were also symmetric. Each side developed its conventional capabilities between rounds, without creating a combination of numbers, complexity, or sophistication that added up to a decisive advantage.[10] The Iran–Iraq War from 1980 to 1988 was characterized by mutual regression to a World War I model, as the adversaries found it impossible, albeit for different reasons, to sustain the high-end matrices of the early stages. Barbed wire and poison gas, bayonet charges, and suicidal human-wave assaults, notably by Iran's youthful Basij, suggested a kind of demodernization through attrition, which was common in long-running, mid-level conventional conflicts between adversaries with limited industrial or technological bases.[11]

Anthony Clayton offers a comprehensive set of case studies in the second model of war-making. Often called Maoist, this model featured insurgency and guerrilla operations. In each of its three stages, however, regular forces were of primary importance in it. The final stage, destruction of the enemy, involved developing a conventional army capable of winning conventional battles. Between 1945 and 1949 the Chinese Red Army shed much of its guerrilla heritage in defeating the Nationalists.[12] The first Vietnam War (1946–54) offers an even better example. Beginning with small combat teams of ten or a dozen, the Viet Minh constructed regiments, then divisions – including one "heavy" division modeled on the Soviet artillery divisions of World War II. Ironically, during the same period the French in effect decentralized and became an army of individual battalions that were grouped more

8 See particularly Henry S. Rowan and Charles Wolf, eds., *The Impoverished Superpower: Perestroika and the Soviet Military Burden* (Lanham, MD, 1990).
9 D. Clayton James and Anne Sharp Wells, *Refighting the Last War: Command and Crisis in Korea, 1950–1953* (New York, 1993).
10 Amit Gupta, *Building an Arsenal: The Evolution of Regional Power Force Structures* (Westport, CT, 1997).
11 Dilip Hiro, *The Longest War: The Iran-Iraq Military Conflict* (London, 1989)
12 Odd Arne Westin, *Decisive Encounters: The Chinese Civil War, 1946–1950* (Stanford, 2003).

or less ad hoc for larger operations. The difference between them and the Viet Minh was highlighted at Dien Bien Phu.[13]

A coda to the Maoist model developed in the former Yugoslavia during the Bosnian War of the 1990s. The combatants began with improvised militias and developed conventional armies capable of devastating combined-arms operations. Croatia in particular was the scene of a steady evolution that culminated in a series of decisive conventional victories in 1994–95.[14]

The third model of war-making, asymmetric war, developed after 1945 and constitutes a major element of Mark Moyar's contribution to this volume. Often called "fourth-generation war," it has also been perceptively described as "the 'other RMA.'" This definition describes a "Revolution in Military Affairs" as the systematic and comprehensive exploitation of the vulnerabilities of a stronger adversary in attritional contexts: winning by not losing.[15] Clayton and Moyar combine to illustrate asymmetric war's distinguishing features – the weaker side's willingness to use all available networks and approaches simultaneously and synergistically, the weaker side's affirmation of protracted war, and the weaker side's instrumental approach to the traditional rules of war. These three features have been triggered by a fourth – a massive, irreversible material imbalance between the combatants.[16]

Asymmetric war abjures the idea of ending matters in the open field. Instead, it operates in the *longue durée*, using television programs and law courts as comfortably as ambushes and executions. Even more than its conventional counterpart, asymmetric war is what Carl von Clausewitz called a chameleon.[17] Its best early example was Algeria's war for independence between 1954 and 1960, when a combination of terror, insurgency, and

13 Martin Windrow, *The Last Valley* (London, 2004), is particularly informative on this point.

14 See particularly the CIA's *Balkan Battlegrounds: A Military History of the Yugoslav Conflict, 1990–1995* (2 vols., Washington, DC, 2002–3).

15 Brigadier General Itai Brun, "'While You're Busy Making Other Plans'–The 'Other' RMA," *Journal of Strategic Studies* 33 (2010): 535–65.

16 William S. Lind et al., "The Changing Face of War: Into the Fourth Generation," *Marine Corps Gazette* (October, 1989): 22–26 was the initial presentation of the concept. See also the developed analysis by Thomas X. Hammes, *The Sling and the Stone: Warfare in the 21st Century* (St. Paul, MN, 2006). Despite Antulio Echevarria's trenchant critique of SSI in *Fourth Generation War and Other Myths* (Carlisle, PA, 2005), "fourth-generation war" remains a useful aid to structuring a complex literature on the subject. Timothy J. Junto, "Military History and Fourth Generation Warfare," *The Journal of Strategic Studies* 32 (2009): 243–69 includes a comprehensive bibliography.

17 Frank G. Hoffman, *Conflict in the 21st Century: The Rise of Hybrid Wars* (Arlington, VA, 2007), accurately describes a pattern of multiple forms of war conducted simultaneously. See also Ivan Arreguin-Toft, *How the Weak Win Wars: A Study of Asymmetric Conflict* (New York, 2005).

propaganda brought defeat and revolution to France.[18] "The troubles" took longer to achieve more limited results in Ulster with the same methods.[19]

Algeria and Ulster illustrated the neutralization, if not the nullification of conventional military power by transferring the conflict to venues in which force was inapplicable or counterproductive. But although asymmetric war has been protean, it has by no means been invincible. The Russians in Chechnya and the Sri Lankan government's campaign against the Tamil Tigers have demonstrated the potential of turning asymmetric war symmetrical by applying its methods in reverse. The resulting reciprocal brutalization, however, has imposed moral, material, and political costs that have been acceptable only in contexts of indifference (as in the Russian Republic) or desperation (as in Sri Lanka).[20] Even then the results of the brutality have been questionable. The Chechens continue to fight back, sometimes spectacularly. Sri Lanka has a long way to go to become a stable political entity, to say nothing of a reintegrated society (if indeed it were ever either).[21] Brutaility in Afghanistan contributed significantly to the Soviets' eventual defeat.[22]

For reasons both moral and pragmatic, western societies have developed two alternate methods of fighting asymmetric war. One, counterinsurgency, is usefully, if solipsistically defined as using a spectrum of military, political, economic, and psychological elements to defeat an insurgency. Beginning as a subset of counterinsurgency, a second method, counterterrorism, has acquired a more specific meaning in the use of focused, limited force against specific objectives.[23]

In both methods the key challenge is to calibrate the balance of force and persuasion. Arne Westad's chapter shows that this has been no easy task when one eye must be kept on the insurgents, one on political authority, and a third

18 See in particular Pierre le Goyet, *La Guerre d'Algérie* (Paris, 1989); Martha Crenshaw Hutchinson, *Revolutionary Terrorism: The FLN in Algeria, 1954–1962* (Stanford, 1978).

19 M. L. R. Smith, *Fighting for Ireland? The Military Strategy of the Irish Republican Movement* (New York, 1995); Mari Fitzduff, *Beyond Violence: Conflict Resolution Process in Northern Ireland* (Tokyo and New York, 2002).

20 Yossef Bodansky, *Chechen Jihad: Al Qaeda's Training Ground and the Next Wave of Terror* (New York, 2007); G. H Peiris, *Twilight of the Tigers: Peace Efforts and Power Struggles in Sri Lanka* (Delhi, 2009).

21 Asoka Bandarage, *The Separatist Conflict in Sri Lanka: Terrorism, Ethnicity, Political Economy* (New York, 2009).

22 Lester Grau, *The Bear Went over the Mountain: Soviet Combat Tactics in Afghanistan* (Washington, DC, 1996). See also Artemy Kalinovsky, "The Blind Leading the Blind: Soviet Counter-Insurgency and Nation-Building in Afghanistan," Cold War International History Project, *Working Paper 60* (January 1910).

23 An excellent case study of the concepts' relationships in a historical context is Mark Moyar, *Phoenix and the Birds of Prey: Counterinsurgency and Counterterrorism in Vietnam* (New York, 2007).

on public opinion, both domestic and foreign.[24] A dimension of this challenge might be called "normalizing" counterinsurgency or counterterrorism. To the extent that success is possible for democratic governments and societies, it requires keeping asymmetric war at the level of "ongoing operations." Catastrophe begins, as Moyar's chapter demonstrates, when counterinsurgency becomes a regular subject in question-time in parliament or challenge in the Assembly, when generals speak of "light at the end of the tunnel" or presidents don flight suits to proclaim ephemeral victories.[25]

Current doctrines of both counterinsurgency and counterterrorism stress the importance of seeking political settlements, negotiated compromises designed to convince insurgents to trade guns for politics. But what happens when the dissonance between the results projected by the two sides is fundamental? The United States eventually checked asymmetric war in Iraq less by "divide and conquer" than "divide and convince" – a combination of buying, persuading, and killing in search of a brokered solution that would balance mutual dissatisfactions.[26] Was it serendipity or solution? Afghanistan may provide a hint of explanation – or perhaps the beginning of an answer – for a fundamental question. Is there an essential discontinuity between counterinsurgency's sophisticated, calibrated caution and that "violence of spirit" that Tocqueville and others have described as an inherent temptation for democracies?

Analyses of military operations from the Cold War to Afghanistan stress the increasing limitations of technology. On the one hand, hardware can do no more than guarantee mutual thermonuclear destruction. On the other it sustains illusions, as mental and moral factors decide the issue.[27] In fact, however, the material aspect of contemporary war has been defined by the comprehensive influence of technology.

Justification of this assertion begins at the high end, with nuclear weapons. Internally, as Walton indicates, nuclear technology has come a long way from the "firecrackers" of 1945 and the megaton planet-busters of the early 1950s. Designs and delivery systems have grown increasingly sophisticated. So have

24 Jason Lyall and Isaiah Wilson III, "Rage against the Machine: Explaining Outcomes in Counterinsurgency Wars," *International Organization* 63 (2009): 67–106, make the case that modern military force structures, specifically comprehensive mechanization, increase the possibility of defeat in counterinsurgency contexts.

25 James S. Corum, *Bad Strategies: How Major Powers Fail in Counterinsurgency* (Minneapolis, 2008).

26 Francis J. West, *The Strongest Tribe: War, Politics, and the Endgame in Iraq* (New York, 2008); Thomas Ricks, *The Gamble: General David Petraeus and the American Military Adventure in Iraq, 2006–2008* (New York, 2009).

27 As in, for example, Martin van Creveld, *The Transformation of War* (New York, 1991).

methods of preventing their use. These range from cultural to political to diplomatic to technological (warning systems, and, in the near future, perhaps defense systems). To date, nuclear disarmament has involved scrapping obsolete, over-costly, or redundant systems, much like old aircraft, warships, or armored vehicles. Serious efforts to downgrade the technology itself have been minimal and marginal.[28]

Murray's chapter highlights the continuing importance of mid-level weaponry that is based on conventional technology. The conventional tools of war have been consistently refined since 1945. A turn-of-the-century main battle tank, for example, bears only a superficial resemblance to its ancestor of 1945. Power and protection, fire control and armament, combine in a weapons system that is vulnerable only to its own kind or the antitank missile, another steadily developing technology.[29] Warships no longer bristle with guns. Their crews are exponentially smaller. But their capacities can be upgraded, so the basic hulls remain in service for periods of time more reminiscent of sailing-ship days than of the continual obsolescence of the industrial era. During World War I aircraft models changed sometimes from month to month. Today, electronically upgraded air frames are flown by crews who are younger than their aircraft.[30]

Specific circumstances can encourage what on the surface might seem downshifts, such as substitution of medium-weight wheeled armored vehicles for main battle tanks in the interests of rapid long-range deployment, or lowering the priority of high-performance, air-superiority aircraft in the context of asymmetric war.[31] These devices usually do not exclude returning to the high-end models, but reversal is not easy. Still, burned-out Strykers and incinerated crews may focus the minds of military planners and defense budgeters on the uncertain virtues of mid-tech war.[32]

28 Frederick N. Mattis, *Banning Weapons of Mass Destruction* (Westport, CT, 2009) is a recent analysis of the issue. See also David E. Hoffman, *The Dead Hand: The Untold Story of the Cold War Arms Race and Its Dangerous Legacy* (New York, 2009); and John E. Mueller's iconoclastic *Atomic Obsession: Nuclear Alarmism from Hiroshima to Al-Quaeda* (New York, 2009).

29 R. P. Hunnicutt, *A History of the American Main Battle Tank* (2 vols., Novato, CA, 1984–90) is a detailed, technically focused case study.

30 This is a fact frequently noted about the USAF's B-52 bomber, which in 2010 was again being fitted with state-of-the-art communications technology.

31 A useful case study by Rand Corporation is Alan Vick, *The Stryker Brigade Combat Team: Rethinking Strategic Responsiveness and Rethinking Strategic Options* (Santa Monica, CA, 2006). See also the official account by Mark A. Reardon and Jeffery A. Charlston, *From Transformation to Combat: The First Stryker Brigade at War* (Washington, DC, 2007).

32 That such a development is not inevitable is scathingly demonstrated in Richard North's *Ministry of Defeat: The British War in Iraq, 2003–2009* (London, 2009). Indicting what he presents as a culpable decision to depend heavily on "light protected vehicles" in Iraq,

The major impact of weapons technology since 1945 has been at its low end, in small arms, portable rocket-launchers, and light mortars. High- and mid-level technologies depend heavily for their effect on preexisting cultures of use and maintenance. Small arms, in contrast, are designed for reliability, simplicity – and cheapness. Mass-produced and user-friendly, low-end high-tech weapons have leveled the minor-tactics playing field. As improvised explosive devices (IEDs) have demonstrated in Iraq and Afghanistan, such weapons have done so in an asymmetric context as well.[33] This represents a sharp contrast to earlier asymmetrical wars, in which one side was almost always at least a generation behind.[34] The popularity of small arms has been sustained by the public relations problems that increasingly face the employment of high-tech weaponry against low-tech targets.[35]

A similar pattern reigns in the field of military electronics, broadly defined. In 1970 Zbigniew Brzenski postulated an emerging "technotronic era," describing the emergence of an information revolution, which would permanently separate cultures and individuals who used computers from those who did not.[36] For the next three decades, he seemed like a prophet in the military context. After Vietnam the US armed forces in particular regarded electronics as not merely a force-multiplier but also as the key to a paradigm shift. Electronics would change the nature of war, providing the definitive initiative. Information technology would integrate land, sea, air, and increasingly space in a comprehensive, impenetrable network of command and control, which some prognostications projected to include political and public, along with military dimensions.[37]

The closest that reality came to this principle was during Operation Desert Storm in 1990–91. As this campaign progressed, however, information

North also highlights a related problem. Procurement costs, design and production lead-times, and general policy considerations can generate major discrepancies among the kinds of material that armed forces need in a particular situation – the material they have available and the material they can quickly obtain – for middle-ranking powers, whose military budgets are far more constrained than that of the United States.

33 Andrew Krepinevich and Dakota Wood, "Of IEDs and MRAPs: Force Protection in Complex Irregular Operations," Center for Strategic and Budgetary Assessments (Washington, DC, 2007).

34 Daniel Headrick, *The Tools of Empire: Technology and European Imperialism in the Nineteenth Century* (New York, 1981).

35 The best recent example is the "Report of the United Nations Fact Finding Mission on the Gaza Conflict" (September 2009). See also Avi Kober, *Israel's War of Attrition: Military Challenges to Democratic States* (New York, 2009).

36 Zbigniew Brzenski, *Between Two Ages: America's Role in the Technotronic Revolution* (New York, 1970).

37 This process is contextualized in Frederick W. Kagan, *Finding the Target: The Transformation of American Military Policy* (New York, 2006). See also Richard Lock-Pullan's more narrowly focused *US Intervention Policy and Army Innovation: From Vietnam to Iraq* (London, 2006)

technology increasingly proved impatient of control. In later years information electronics grew even more comprehensive and more universal than high-tech small arms. Modern terrorism depends heavily on cell-phone technology. A Taliban fighter can download information from the Internet about how to construct an IED. In 2006 Hezbollah made sophisticated use of laptops to coordinate operations against the Israeli Defense Force. Doctoring photos and tapes to influence world opinion was a significant element of Hamas operations in Gaza during Israel's 2009 Operation Cast Lead.[38]

By the turn of the twenty-first century, information technology was being challenged for electronic primacy by a "robotics revolution," which has been described as the most comprehensive instrument of change in war since the introduction of gunpowder. Beginning with small reconnaissance drones, military robotics has embraced thousands of air and ground systems, such as unmanned craft that are controlled from US bases to execute precision strikes in Afghanistan and Pakistan.[39] Perplexing issues, such as the rules of engagement for autonomous machines and whether artificial intelligence can commit a war crime, balance questions about how unmanned war will change the psychology and mentality of those who fight wars and the societies that endorse them.[40] As technology creates increasing physical and emotional distance from combat, will war itself be redefined? As robotics diminishes war's risks, will it reduce humanity's propensity for war-making? Or will robotics make war less humane by making it less human?[41]

Such questions point to the issue of mentality, the why of war-making in modern contexts. A useful context is provided by Philip Bobbitt's seminal

38 Thomas Rid and Marc Heckler, *War 2.0: Irregular Warfare in the Information Age* (Westport, CT, 2009). The best case study is Antonio Giustozzi, *Koran, Kalashnikov, and Laptop: The Neo-Taliban Insurgency in Afghanistan* (New York, 2007). Kim Cragin, *Sharing the Dragon's Teeth: Terrorist Groups and the Exchange of New Technologies* (Santa Monica, CA, 2007), is useful for processes.

39 David Axe and Steve Olexis, *War Bots: How Military Robots are Transforming War in Iraq, Afghanistan, and the Future* (Ann Arbor, 2008) is brief, popular, and a useful overview.

40 P. W. Singer, *Wired for War* (New York, 2009) is the best overview of developments and implications. See also Peter Bergen and Katherine Tiedemann, "The Year of the Drone: An Analysis of US Drone Strikes in Pakistan, 2004–2010," Counterterrorism Strategy Initiative Policy Paper, New American Foundation: www.Newamwerica.net. Farhat Taj, "The Year of the Drone Misinformation," *Small Wars and Insurgencies* 21 (2010): 529–35, makes a case that drone attacks in the Pakistan–Afghanistan border region are neither as unpopular nor as costly in lives as commonly stated.

41 The robot drone and the suicide bomber invite juxtaposition and comparison – each in its way is a remotely guided precision weapon.

works, *The Shield of Achilles* and *Terror and Consent*. These volumes describe the decline of the nation-state in an increasingly borderless world, which is globalized, privatized, and decentralized.[42] In Bobbitt's model, boundaries are becoming increasingly protean and permeable. Within this framework, two comprehensive perspectives on war are in the process of developing – the west's and the rest's.

Since 1945 the western experience of war has been profoundly negative. The Cold War was based on principle, but it was pragmatic in practice. Played for short yardage and limited gains, as much a propaganda contest as a military conflict, it offered limited prospects for positive resolution.[43] Significant as well among western intellectuals was the influence, both direct and subliminal, of Marxism, whose postulate was that time was on its side, that capitalism was fighting a futile rear-guard action against history itself.[44] Nor did regional wars contribute to the notion that conflict solved anything in particular. Finally, from the west's perspective the wars of liberation that dominated the mid-century were based on negative goals: to expel occupiers. From challenging the legitimacy of western government, it was a logical step to challenging western presence in general. Algeria's *pieds-noirs* or Zimbabwe's white farmers had no more legitimacy than the administrators or the soldiers, and the solution was the same: they were to get out. This demand was hardly calculated to inspire dread in western capitals – any more than were the other wars and rumors of war whose remoteness underwrote the west's redefinition of war itself.

Rana Mitter's study of remembrance and representation suggests the cultural context of such a redefinition, which has three elements. The first, which has been most influential in Europe, is the experience that is described in James Sheehan's *Where Have All the Soldiers Gone?* Sheehan argues that after preparing and waging two catastrophic world wars, Europe has become committed to peace and order in the context of civilian states and civilian societies. War-making capacity remains, but it is marginal and vestigial. The

42 Philip Bobbitt, *The Shield of Achilles: War, Peace, and the Course of History* (New York, 2002) and *Terror and Consent: The Wars of the Twenty-First Century* (New York, 2008). See Samuel P. Huntington, *The Clash of Civilizations and the Remaking of World Order* (New York, 1996).

43 See Walter L Hixson, *Parting the Curtain: Propaganda, Culture, and the Cold War, 1945–1961* (New York, 1997); Laura A. Belmonte, *Selling the American Way: US Propaganda and the Cold War* (Philadelpuia, 2008).

44 David McLellan, *Marxism after Marx* (4th edn., New York, 2007) remains standard on the general subject.

will and ability of states to use violence has given way to an emphasis on prosperity and security through European cooperation.[45]

As Moyar demonstrates, the US experience of war in the twentieth century has been more ambivalent. Here too, however, even in an "Era of American Hegemony," young men – and now young women – are no longer acceptable offerings in what Barbara Ehrenreich calls blood rites.[46] Indeed, the public discourse on war is arguably developing an alternate focus. Concern is growing not merely about inflicting excessive or disproportionate losses on an enemy, but also about upholding enemy combatants' rights as understood under US law.[47]

This mentality segues into the second dimension of the west's new way of war: utopianism, seeking moral absolutes in secular contexts. Its roots can be traced to Wilsonianism. Its direct antecedents are arguments, which were common in the later Cold War, for "convergence" between the adversaries; they were best expressed culturally by John le Carré and academically by Daniel Bell.[48] Utopianism has many manifestations. It informs multiculturalism, ecologism, and transnationalism. Its primary effect is hyper-empathy, an inability to fight one's corner, to make one's case even rhetorically, to say nothing of taking violent action.

Utopianism reinforces as well the third element in the western redefinition of war. This element has two faces, In Europe it is built on the concept of "soft power," the use in international contexts of attraction and co-option to shape preferences, then behaviors, to desired norms. In the United States, "soft power" reflects the illusion of "hyperpower," the conviction that the country enjoys comprehensive military, economic, and cultural dominance. In both models, the direct application of armed force is not merely a last resort, as in traditional realist theory, but also a failure. It is unnecessary and likely to be counterproductive.[49]

45 James Sheehan, *Where Have All the Soldiers Gone? The Transformation of Modern Europe* (New York, 2008).

46 Barbara Ehrenreich, *Blood Rites: Origins and History of the Passions of War* (New York, 1997).

47 David Whittaker, *Counterterrorism and Human Rights* (New York, 2009) is brief, comprehensive, and current.

48 Daniel Bell, *The End of Ideology: On the Exhaustion of Political Ideas in the Fifties* (rev. edn., New York, 1962).

49 Jan Meilissen et al., eds., *The New Public Diplomacy: Soft Power in International Relations* (New York, 2007), and Amy Chua, *Day of Empire: Why Hyperpowers Rise to Global Dominance – And Why They Fall* (New York, 2007) can be profitably read together on this subject.

Experience, utopianism, and power-application complement guilt. The west has worked for at least three centuries to create citizens who are affluent, leisured, and safe. It has been less successful in generating comfort with its success. Regrets over past misbehavior, such as slavery, imperialism, and racism, synergize with current self-accusations of neocolonialism, overconsumption, and climaticide. The result is a culture of guilt, which inhibits any behaviors – including repentance and apology – that provide insufficient atonement to both givers and receivers.[50]

In this context, military power is constrained by fears of committing aggression or oppression. The result affects strategic cultures, limits the structure, strength, equipment, and effectiveness of armed forces.[51] It restricts their use as well in almost any circumstances – as demonstrated for years in Darfur, an enduring example of the futility of unsupported rhetoric.[52]

The "non-western" perspective on war is, by contrast, built on war for practical abstractions – ideals realized by spilling blood. It has four principal manifestations: ethnic cleansing on the models of Bosnia and Rwanda; the agony of the failed state, as in the Congo; irreconcilable imbalances as in Sri Lanka; and cultural or religious conflicts in the pattern of the long civil war in Algeria between the government and Islamic rebel groups.

Collectively these conflicts might be described as "war by habit" or as existential wars, which become their own justification. Generally they have escaped their original domestic contexts more or less by accident. Increasingly, however, the refugees who were generated directly and indirectly by these "forever wars" have sought havens in the uninvolved west. So far their behavior has not been catastrophically or even particularly violent, but there is no guarantee that it will remain so. In addition, the potential for some kind of asymmetric conflict – fourth-generation war – is likely to increase as desperation levels rise on both sides.[53]

To date fourth-generation war has remained militarily a marginal, arm's-length experience in the west. The Twin Towers, Iraq, Afghanistan, and Gaza, have been the stuff of television highlights and round-table debates, but the

50 Jean Delumeau, *Sin and Fear: The Emergence of a Western Guilt Culture, 13th–18th Centuries* (New York, 1990) merits consulting for its demonstration of the religious roots of what contemporary works usually describe in secular contexts.

51 Alastair Ian Johnson, "Thinking about Strategic Culture," *International Security* 19 (1995): 32–64, discusses in general the relationship of cultural beliefs to strategic decisions.

52 It may be noted cynically or realistically that one of the best analyses, Gerard Prunier, *Darfur: A 21st-Century Genocide* (Ithaca, 2008), is in its third edition.

53 Philip Marfleet, *Refugees in a Global Era* (New York, 2005) is comprehensive and insightful. See also David Kilcullen, *The Accidental Guerilla* (New York, 2009).

relationships among methods, material, and mentalities are anything but constant. What might happen as they shift?

Asia offers useful prospects. Until the late 1970s the region experienced a continuing series of vicious conflicts, which grew out of a toxic synergy of national liberations, civil wars, and ideological struggles. The next twenty years were a period of relative peace, stability, and prosperity.[54] This development, however, did not deter India from sustaining a massive, comprehensive military buildup that was designed to secure great-power status in a regional context.[55] China, too, continues to build up its defense economy and its military capacities in ways that will enable power-projection well beyond its immediate periphery. These capacities include sophisticated electronic and cyber-warfare technologies and methods.[56] They include as well a metastasizing capacity to use its holdings of US debt as an instrument of economic warfare.[57]

American pundits and officials describe the economies of the United States and China as "intertwined." Academic defense analysts present the Sino-Indian military relationship in light of an increasing level of "confidence-building" and "security interdependence.[58] Nowhere, however, do these discussions touch on western levels of reluctance, whether from principle or diffidence, to use force for policy purposes.[59] There is far more of the *Mahabharata* than the Mahatma in India's approach to national security and national interest.[60] China may be increasingly sophisticated in the ways of soft power. But its policies, intentions, and ambitions remain informed more by

54 Useful for background is Ken Booth and Russell B. Trood, eds., *Strategic Cultures in the Asia-Pacific Region* (New York, 1999).

55 N. S. Sisodia and Chitrapu Uday Bhaskar, eds., *Emerging India: Security and Foreign Policy Perspectives* (New Delhi, 2005). See also the case study by David Scott, "India's Grand Strategy for the Indian Ocean: Mahanian Visions," *Asia-Pacific Review* 13 (2006): 192–211.

56 Tai Ming Cheung, *Fortifying China: The Struggle to Build a Modern Defense Economy* (Ithaca, 2008); Michael S. Chase, Andrew S. Erickson, and Christopher Yeaw, "Chinese Theater and Strategic Missile Force Modernization and Its Implications for the United States," *Journal of Strategic Studies* 32 (2009): 67–114.

57 See the abridged translation of Liang Quao and Xiangsui Wang, *Unrestricted Warfare: China's Master Plan to Destroy America* (Panama City, 2000).

58 Jonathan Holslag, "The Persistent Military Security Dilemma between China and India," *Journal of Strategic Studies* 32 (2009): 811–40.

59 See, for example, Rollie Lal, *Understanding China and India: Security Implications for the United States and the World* (Westport, CT, 2006); Alyssa Ayres and C. Raja Mohan, eds., *Power Realignments in Asia: China, India, and the United States* (Los Angeles, 2009).

60 See G. D. Bakshi, *The Indian Art of War: The Mahabharata Paradigm: Quest for an Indian Strategic Culture* (Delhi, 2002); Rudra Chaudhuri, "Why Culture Matters: Revisiting the Sino-Indian Border War of 1962," *Journal of Strategic Studies* 32 (2009): 841–69; Karsten Frey, *India's Nuclear Bomb and National Security* (New York, 2006).

mistrust and zero-sum thinking than by either Sun Tzu's Taoist perspective on strategy or Confucianism's principled denigration of war.[61]

More complex and immediate for the west has been the Islamic Middle East's quest to confirm its legitimacy and assert its interests by force. For a quarter-century this policy's cutting edge has been a particular variant of fourth-generation war – the use of methods have been structured and justified in religious contexts, but considered by their targets as terrorism.[62] Whether such terrorism is better defined as a military or law-enforcement challenge and whether it is better addressed in "militaristic" or "holistic" contexts have until recently remained topics of affordable debate.[63] In Iran, however, a government that bases its legitimacy and policy in good part on eschatology is now seeking the status of a nuclear power.[64]

Asymmetrical conflict fosters asymmetrical perceptions: on the one hand a system that combines religious faith and rhetoric with nuclear capacity, on the other a nuclear system that is secular and rational in its configuration.[65] The likely results are ongoing crises of communication, mutual misapprehension of the criteria for decision-making.[66] Nuclear environments, global or regional, have little room for either.

This point leads to a final subject, contemporary war's human dimensions. Non-combatant status and just-war theory, both of which have been fragile in practice, risk complete erosion.[67] Killing has become a retail process, undertaken on small scales, often face to face. Weapons of mass destruction can be

61 See Alastair Iain Johnson, *Cultural Realism: Strategic Culture and Grand Strategy in Chinese History* (Princeton, 1998); Andrew Scobell, *China's Use of Military Force* (Cambridge, 2003).

62 Peter R. Demant, *Islam versus Islamism: The Dilemma of the Muslim World* (Westport, CT, 2006) is a good introduction to this complex subject.

63 Bruce Hoffman, *Inside Terrorism* (New York, 2006). See also Robert M. Cassidy, *Counterinsurgency and the Global War on Terror: Military Culture and Irregular War* (Westport, CT, 2006).

64 For different approaches see Anthony H. Cordesman and Khalid R. Al-Rodhan, *Iran's Weapons of Mass Destruction: The Real and Potential Threat* (Washington, DC, 2006); Moojan Moomen, *An Introduction to Shi'i Islam: The History and Doctrines of "Twelver" Shi'ism* (New Haven, 1985); Albert B. Randall, *Holy Scriptures as Justification for War: Fundamentalist Interpretations of the Torah, the New Testament, and the Qur'an* (Lewiston, NY, 2007

65 See Robert Pape, *Dying to Win: The Strategic Logic of Suicide Terrorism* (New York, 2005); Nick Ayres, "Ghost Martyrs in Iraq: An Assessment of the Applicability of Rationalist Models to Explain Suicide Attacks in Iraq," *Studies in Conflict and Terrorism* 31 (2008): 856–82.

66 See Matthew Herbet, "The Plasticity of the Islamic Activist: Notes from the Counterterrorism Literature," *Studies in Conflict and Terrorism* 32 (2009): 359–405

67 The scope of Richard H. Kohn "The Danger of Militarization in an Endless 'War' on Terrorism," *Journal of Military History* 73 (2009): 177–208 is broader than its title.

reliably expected to be miniaturized.[68] The tools of genocide have devolved from the gas chambers of Auschwitz to the pangas of Rwanda. Fear, an increasing signifier for individuals, states, and cultures in the emerging twenty-first century, is becoming comprehensive and personal. The signature weapon of the post-World War II era is not the hydrogen bomb but the Kalashnikov assault rifle.[69]

"I have never learned to fight for my freedom. I [am] only good at enjoying it," writes the Dutch author, Oskar van den Boogaard.[70] He and millions of his counterparts worldwide may well face a rude awakening and an unwanted choice as the new century develops.

68 James R. Van de Velde, "The Impossible Challenge of Deterring 'Nuclear Terrorism' by Al Qaeda," *Studies in Conflict and Terrorism* 33 (2010): 682–99.
69 Michael Hodges, *AK47: The Story of the People's Gun* (London, 2007); C.J Chivers, *The Gun: The AK-47 and the Evolution of War* (New York, 2010).
70 Oskar van den Boogaard, "De terreur van de angst," *De Standaard* (Brussels), October 23, 2006.

17
Military occupations, 1945–1955

DENNIS SHOWALTER

"Occupation" in the context of World War II comes close to defying definition. In its narrow context, it refers to the involuntary control of a state's territory by a foreign power. With specific reference to the victorious Allies, it began in 1943 in Italy and lasted through 1951 in Japan. Occupation in the era of World War II was, however, characterized by nuances and ramifications that are sufficient to sustain an analysis based on comparative case studies, as opposed to a general overview.

Occupation as a concept is almost as old as war itself and only slightly younger than the idea of decisive victory. Historically, winners have taken over losers for four major reasons. One is *dispossession*, the intention to dominate, displace, and replace the original inhabitants – more or less in that order. David Day is correct in stating that "supplanting" is a universal process. Everybody's ancestors originally came from somewhere else and acquired their "homelands" by some form of *force majeure*.[1]

Occupation's second justification has been *security*. This goal could involve collecting indemnities, as in the case of the Franco-German War. It could involve making sure that a new, friendly government was firmly in place, as in France after the Hundred Days. It could involve establishing a civic order acceptable to the occupiers, as in the former confederacy between 1865 and 1876. The common denominator among these measures was remaining in control of a defeated enemy until that defeat was recognized.[2]

Third on the list of occupation's historic justifications stands *exploitation*, making conquest support war directly, harnessing captured financial, industrial, and agricultural resources. Evidence prior to World War II suggests that developed societies can be directly exploited. This success can be measured,

1 David Day, *Conquest: How Societies Overwhelm Others* (Oxford, 2008).

2 For this issue in context, see most recently Williamson Murray and Jim Lacey, eds., *The Making of Peace: Rulers, States, and the Aftermath of War* (Cambridge, 2009).

29. Refugees on their way to a UNHCR camp

however, only in a narrow context of extraction rates. The measure takes no account of the costs imposed by the reactions of other states. No less significant, successful exploitation is directly related to the occupier's comprehensive ruthlessness, which prior to World War II was limited alike by principle and technology.[3] Even successful exploitation increasingly generated unexpected and unwelcome consequences. The indemnity that Germany collected from France after 1871 spun the German economy and German society into an era of speculation and depression.[4] The tribute that France extracted from the Ruhr occupation of 1923–24 weakened both its own financial system and its ability to reach a satisfactory long-term reparations settlement.[5]

The fourth motive for occupation has been *development* – or imperialism, depending on one's ideology and perspective. This project involves integrating resources – originally human but increasingly material – into the occupier's system, in a context of mutual benefit albeit temporarily and marginally

3 Peter Liberman, *Does Conquest Pay? The Exploitation of Occupied Industrial Societies* (Princeton, 1996).

4 S. B. Saul, *The Myth of the Great Depression, 1873–1893* (London, 1969), appropriately warns against exaggerating the economic aspects.

5 See especially Stephen A. Schuker, *The End of French Predominance in Europe: The Financial Crisis of 1924 and the Adoption of the Dawes Plan* (Chapel Hill, 1976).

implemented by force. In Europe's age of mercantilism the benefit was projected as economic. Britain's North American colonies, for example, flourished at least in principle through trade in the context of empire.[6] In nineteenth-century Africa, occupiers defined the benefits as humanitarian and cultural. Natives learned how to wear clothes and do a day's work while being saved from worse fates. Westerners took a percentage of the results as tuition fees.[7]

These motives and justifications regularly overlapped. British India, for example, featured elements of all four. So did Russia's occupation of Central Asia and China's historic relationship to its steppe frontier in the northwest. The Allied occupation of Germany after World War I involved not only reparations and suppressing a defeated foe, but also the expectation of eventually accepting a chastened Germany into the family of nations – if only *faute de mieux*. All four considerations were nevertheless rendered obsolescent, when not irrelevant, by World War II.

This war established its own categories. For the Allies the initial category of occupation was *incidental* – occupation that was occasioned as a direct consequence of conducting war against the Axis. Its most benign form, suggested with tongue only slightly in cheek, was the US occupation of Britain that began in 1942, which reached a point where Britons joked that the island was kept from sinking under the weight of the American presence only by the thousands of barrage balloons deployed to protect it.[8]

Britain's prefiguring of George Orwell's Airstrip One was, however, temporary and the consequences limited. More significant was the accidental occupation of continental Europe after June 6, 1944. Industrial war spared neither cities nor homes; much of Europe was smashed to rubble by shells and bombs. Almost as many French died under Allied bombs on D-Day as did Americans on the beaches. Nor were the liberators themselves always seen as heroes. Young men with guns abused power. Europeans resented owing their freedom to outsiders. Resistance movements had accomplished little on their own. Collaboration at all levels had been widespread. Postwar trials did little to provide catharsis or closure, and nothing to rebuild infrastructures.[9]

6 Brendan Simms, *Three Victories and a Defeat: The Rise and Fall of the First British Empire* (London, 2007).

7 Among many useful case studies of this phenomenon, see Richard Price, *Making Empires: Colonial Encounters and the Creation of Imperial Rule in Nineteenth Century Africa* (Cambridge, 2008), and Gary Bass, *Freedom's Battle* (New York, 2008), which establishes the nineteenth-century roots of humanitarian intervention.

8 Judith Gardiner, *"Overpaid, Oversexed, and Over Here": The American GI in World War II Britain* (New York, 1993).

9 See most recently William Hitchcock, *The Bitter Road to Freedom* (New York, 2008).

Incidental occupation had even more disruptive effects in the Pacific, where the exigencies of war juxtaposed twentieth-century technologies and geographically isolated preindustrial societies. Americans in particular had to make sense of environments that were alien; they processed the Pacific in terms of their own far west, as a frontier to be tamed by controlling and reshaping landscapes and peoples. On the other side of the relationship, the revitalized cargo cults of Melanesia, which centered on gods that brought riches from the air and sea, exemplified the comprehensive cultural impact of aliens who appeared, then disappeared for no discernible reasons and left things utterly changed.[10]

During World War II Germany and Japan – to a lesser extent Fascist Italy – fundamentally redefined the terms of occupation. In principle and by definition, Nazi Germany recognized only clients and victims. Nothing remained on the table for ostensible allies, to say nothing of defeated enemies.[11] German rule over western Russia between 1941 and 1943 was an archetype. It was a racial and ideological occupation, which was predicated on the extermination of inferior peoples. It was an economic occupation, which was predicated on the exploitation and starvation of millions of Russians, whose deaths were intended, not by-products. And it was a physical occupation, which was sustained by brutality and ferocity that increased with time, independently of the conquered people's behavior.[12]

Japan's vaunted "Greater East Asian Co-Prosperity Sphere" was not even a chimera. Japanese occupation forces raped and butchered their way across the mainland and into the Pacific. Poison gas and biological warfare, medical atrocities and cannibalism were features of life under Japanese rule. The rice of China, the oil of Indonesia, the rubber of Malaya were ruthlessly and heedlessly exploited by Japan's war machine.[13] The difference between Japan and Germany has been well described as the unspeakable as opposed to the unthinkable – the difference between retail and wholesale murder. Italy's occupation regimes in Abyssinia, Russia, and the Balkans also featured mass

10 Peter Scrijvers, *The GI War against Japan: American Soldiers in Asia and the Pacific during World War II* (New York, 2005). On cargo cults see Holger Jebens, ed., *Cargo, Cult, and Culture Critique* (New York, 2004).

11 Mark Mazower, *Hitler's Empire: How the Nazis Ruled Europe* (New York, 2008).

12 See Alex J. Kay, *Exploitation, Resettlement, Mass Murder: Political and Economic Planning for German Occupation Policy in the Soviet Union, 1940–1941* (New York, 2006); Christian Gerlach, *Kalkulierter Morde: Die Deutsche Wirtschafts- und Vernichtungspolitik in Weissrussland 1941 bis 1944* (Hamburg, 1999).

13 See Louise Young, *Japan's Total Empire: Manchuria and the Culture of Wartime Imperialism* (Berkeley, 1998); Eri Hotta, *Pan-Asianism and Japan's War, 1931–1945* (New York, 2007); Max Hastings, *Retribution: The Battle for Japan, 1944–1945* (New York, 2007).

killings, systematic brutality, forced labor, and economic exploitation, albeit on scales that seem almost benign by comparison.[14]

In these contexts the initial distinguishing characteristic of postwar Allied occupation was *retribution*. The Nuremberg and Tokyo war-crimes trials are best understood in light of a vigilantism that sought to do justice according to existing, generally accepted principles in crypto-Hobbesian circumstances, in which an applicable legal apparatus did not exist. Their ultimate purpose was to establish precedents – not to replace one system of drumhead punishment by another.[15]

A corresponding principle in selecting defendants was the potential for making unchallengeable cases. In the immediate postwar years, finding credible documentary or eyewitness evidence for specific criminal acts, which had been authorized or committed by senior political and military leaders, was not always easy. The problem was complicated by the always present, albeit usually unacknowledged arguments of *tu quoque* and *à la guerre comme à la guerre* ("you're another" and "war makes its own rules").[16] The punitive aspects of occupation were correspondingly imprecise, not to say random. The USSR's approach mixed ideology and pragmatism. Those whom Soviet occupiers considered useful could find their pasts fed into a memory hole. Otherwise, the conquerors concentrated on "class enemies."[17] In Germany the American occupation has been described as a retreat to victory; in Japan it has been interpreted as a missed opportunity. Particularly in Japan, punishment was imposed for positions held as well as for policies ordered. The executions of Generals Homma and Yamashita have been regularly – and mistakenly – cited as examples of victors' vengeance. Recent scholarship has nevertheless demonstrated that the Tokyo trial reflected sound legal judgment and practice.[18]

14 Gianni Oliva, *Si ammazza troppo poco: I crimini di guerra italiani 1940–1943* (Milan, 2006); Asfa-Wossen Asserate and Aram Mattioli, *Der erste faschistische Vernichtungskrieg: Die italienische Aggresion gegen Äthiopien, 1935–1941* (Cologne, 2006).

15 Bradley F. Smith, *Reaching Judgment at Nuremberg* (New York, 1977) remains the best overview of the trials' immediate matrices. Dermont Feenan, *Informal Criminal Justice* (Burlington, VT, 2002) includes useful case studies.

16 Michael Salter, *Nazi War Crimes: Intelligence Agencies and Selective Legal Accountability* (Abingdon, 2007) is excellent on Nuremberg's pragmatic undersides. See also Valerie G Hebert, *Hitler's Generals on Trial: The Last War Crimes Trial at Nuremberg* (Lawrence, KS, 2010).

17 Norman Naimark, *The Russians in Germany: A History of the Soviet Zone of Occupation, 1945–1949* (Cambridge, MA, 1995).

18 See especially Timothy P. Maga, *Judgment at Tokyo: The Japanese War Crimes Tirils* (Lexington, KY, 2001); Yuma Totani, "The Tokyo War Crimes Trial: Historiography and Revisions," Ph.D. dissertation, University of California, Berkeley, 2005.

Both the victorious Americans and Soviets brought home the facts of defeat on an everyday basis that was impossible to ignore. From 1946 to 1952 the smartly uniformed and omnipresent US constabulary enforced occupation policies and regulations in Germany.[19] The Soviets had their own ways to make the same point, chief among them substantial military forces, which were both highly visible and rigidly isolated. A third of a million American troops occupied Japan in the autumn of 1945; four divisions remained in 1950. There was no doubt in either situation about who had won the war or who was paying the price.

30. GI and Japanese policemen direct traffic in Tokyo

19 Kendall D. Gott, *Mobility, Vigilance, and Justice: The US Army Constabulary in Germany, 1946–1953* (Fort Leavenworth, KS, 2005).

The second distinguishing feature of post-World War II occupation was *reformation*. Wars among states had historically concluded with the defeated left primarily responsible for their own internal changes. After 1945 this outcome was considered impossible. National Socialism had emerged as an absolute evil as the war progressed, with any doubts removed by the exposure of the camp system in the war's final days. Nor was Japanese militarism perceived as less dangerous. American public opinion in particular had focused on Japan as the alien "other," to be not merely defeated but crushed. The concept of unconditional surrender, introduced by Roosevelt at the 1943 Casablanca Conference and subsequently accepted as the Allied bottom line, afforded the victors both legal and practical authority to undertake fundamental reordering of Germany and Japan in the interests of a lasting peace.[20]

The Soviet Union had waged a war for its existence and was in no mood (and arguably no condition) to risk a repetition – particularly given its ideological presumption of mortal antagonism between the capitalist and communist orders. The USSR's approach to reformation in its sphere of influence was Marx in reverse. It began politically, organizing administrative systems, then governments that at least accepted the occupiers. Through these governments economies were socialized, as private spheres were marginalized, and then absorbed. The third stage of reformation under Soviet auspices involved winning hearts and minds less than it did convincing them that this was the way things were and would remain.

The process was successful in good part because of an absence of alternatives. In central and eastern Europe, fascism had proven a spectacular dead end. The prewar alternative of elite rule by landowners, capitalists, generals, and clergymen was no less discredited. Results in the long run were nevertheless mixed. Yugoslavia resisted assimilation and was able to break away. East Germany, Poland, Hungary, and Czechoslovakia developed as "niche societies," in which private spheres persisted through the Cold War. Taken on the whole, the Soviet Union as an occupier accepted compliance. When matters were taken further, indigenous governments did so for their own reasons. Nikolae Ceausescu's Romania was a prime example.[21]

20 Anne Armstrong, *Unconditional Surrender: The Impact of the Casablanca Policy upon World War II* (New Brunswick, 1961).

21 Gerhard Wettig, *Stalin and the Cold War in Europe: The Emergence and Development of East-West Conflict, 1939–1953* (New York, 2007) contextualizes Soviet postwar occupation policies nicely. See also Odd Arne Westad et al., *The Soviet Union in Eastern Europe, 1945–1948* (New York, 1994); Oksana Sarkisova and Péter Apor, *Past for the Eyes: East European Representations of Communism in Cinema and Museums after 1989* (Budapest and New York, 1998).

A footnote to reformation, especially under Soviet occupation, was ethnic cleansing. Not strictly speaking an intrinsic element of occupation, it was nevertheless central to the reconfiguration of Europe. It began with the flight of German civilians from the advancing Red Army in 1944–45. It continued in two contexts – the refusal of Soviet authorities to let refugees return and the expulsion of ethnic Germans by postwar governments. The latter pheonomenon was due to vengeance for the war and collaboration with the new order, and to the belief that Germans were simply too dangerous to remain. Most spectacularly, Poland's boundary was shifted westward to the Oder River, and ethnic Poles from the east were encouraged to settle in the newly acquired and emptied western provinces.

Over 12 million Germans were "relocated." Two and a half million died in the process. The expulsion was nevertheless a long-term success on two counts. By increasing ethnic homogenization, it diminished the antagonisms that had poisoned the domestic and international politics of interwar Europe.[22] The German Federal Republic's often overlooked success in assimilating the vast majority of the refugees averted the formation of the open sores that similar circumstances produced elsewhere. The refugees might have found a "cold homeland" in many respects, but none of them were compelled to fester for decades in squalid camps under UN patronage. No "Front for the Liberation of the Occupied Regions" dispatched suicide bombers to the schools and pizzerias of Wroclaw or Gdansk. This was more than a small step to reforming what became the Federal Republic.[23]

Britain and France had too much on their own plates to be deeply concerned with the long-term specifics of political reconstruction or population adjustments. The merger of the British and US occupation zones of Germany in 1946 was an act of desperation on London's part. The Americans did the heavy lifting when it came to reform. They began by seeking out "good Germans," who were untainted by contact with National Socialism. They ended by making denazification increasingly dependent on filling out the requisite forms.[24]

The change in the American approach to Germany involved a series (in fact a system) of pragmatic local compromises based on "getting the job done" – working with the willing to restore public transportation, provide

22 Philipp Ther and Ana Siljak, eds., *Redrawing Nations: Ethnic Cleansing in East-Central Europe* (Lanham, MD, 2001).

23 Andreas Kossert, *Kalte Heimat: Die Geschichte der deutschen Vertriebenen seit 1945* (Munich, 2008).

24 Edward N. Peterson, *The American Occupation of Germany: Retreat to Victory* (Detroit, 1977).

31. Nurses delouse a German refugee at a UNICEF camp

schools, and clear rubble.[25] "Collective amnesia" is too strong a term for what happened in the emerging Federal Republic. *Stunde Null*, "Zero Hour," is closer to the mark, if it is understood as drawing a line under the past for the sake of a present and future. Memories remained so strong that one can speak neither of denial nor repression, but rather of a taboo against asking awkward questions in private or public. This was the West German counterpart to Eastern Europe's "niches."[26]

Justice and reconciliation were easier enunciated than implemented, especially in the aftermath of the Third Reich. German society as a whole was complicit – much of it enthusiastically so – in Hitler's regime and war. In practical terms, few individuals were completely free of involvement. Moreover, the nature of their involvement made retribution problematic. It required half the German people to sit perpetually in judgment on the other half – with the halves differing in each situation.[27] A government and a society reconstructed on this basis would have torn themselves apart.

Vaclav Havel's familiar argument against comprehensive punishment applied to what became the Federal Republic. Reformation took place in part from fear of retribution. For all the subsequent criticism of Germany's incomplete reformation, the escapes and evasions remained private.[28] A university professor with Nazi connections, a neighborhood doctor with an SS membership, an auto dealer who had ordered mass executions in Russia, were on the whole far more concerned with concealing their pasts than using them as springboards for political or intellectual revisionism.[29]

The same point can be made for Japan. Here again the United States bore the weight, once the Soviet Union under American pressure abandoned its claims to an occupation zone in Hokkaido. In contrast to its role in Germany, the American occupation incorporated a Christian, colonialist dimension; it was to civilize the Oriental barbarians. But far more so than in Germany, the occupiers were handicapped by comprehensive linguistic and cultural barriers. These encouraged indirect rule, a policy favored as well by Douglas MacArthur. As head of the

25 Uta Gerhardt, *Soziologie der "Stunde Null": Zur Gesellschaftskonzeption des americanischen Besatzungsregimes in Deutschland 1944/45–1946* (Frankfurt am Main, 2006).

26 Richard Bessel, *Germany 1945: From War to Peace* (New York, 2009) is an outstanding overview.

27 Golo Mann, *The History of Germany since 1789* (New York, 1968), 495.

28 Bernd Weisbrod, "The Moratorium of the Mandarins and the Self-Denazification of German Academe," *Contemporary European History* 12 (2003): 47–69 stands out among many useful case studies.

29 Norbert Frei, *Adenauer's Germany and the Nazi Past: The Politics of Amnesty and Integration* (New York, 2002); Clemens Vollnhals and Thomas Schlemmer, *Entnazifierung: Politische Säuberung und Rehabilitierung in den vier Besatzungszonen 1946–1949* (Munich, 1991).

occupation administration, he combined direct economic relief with democratic reform, depoliticizing the throne, empowering a parliamentary system, abolishing the big industrial cartels, and overhauling the education system.

Practical reform came from the top down, as the occupiers worked through Japanese businessmen and officials, including the emperor himself. John Dower describes the limited effects of postwar purges and the rapid reassimilation of men whose talents had been recognized in wartime and were no less welcome in the new Japan. Again, however, the punitive elements of the occupation were sufficient to institutionalize the memory of defeat. In subsequent decades, denial and revisionism became more of a presence in Japan than Germany, but they have remained encysted. With Hiroshima as a reminder, Japan has developed no serious doubts about the war's outcome.[30]

Reconstruction was the third original aspect of occupation after World War II. During the war the concept had generally been dismissed as risible. The Morgenthau Plan, which had been developed by the United States' secretary of the treasury, was projected to transform Germany to an agricultural economy, alienating, internationalizing, or dismantling its heavy industries. Roosevelt and Churchill initially accepted the plan, and despite public criticism, it continued to influence policies until conquest brought the responsibility of occupation and demonstrated how successful the combined-bomber offensive had been in devastating Germany's economic infrastructure.[31]

Ironically, the western Allies were constrained to undo in good part what they had wrought. A near-bankrupt Britain found itself using borrowed money "to feed those damn Germans," in the words of Foreign Secretary Ernest Bevin. Death rates among adults in the British occupation zone rose to four times prewar levels – ten times for children. Herbert Hoover summed it up in March 1947: the only way to pastoralize Germany was to eliminate or resettle 25 million Germans.[32]

30 Yoneyuki Sugita, *Pitfall or Panacea: The Irony of US Power in Occupied Japan 1945–1952* (New York, 2003); Eiji Takameda et al., *Inside GHQ: The Allied Occupation of Japan and Its Legacy* (New York, 2002). John W. Dower, *Embracing Defeat: Japan in the Wake of World War II* (New York, 2000) stresses the occupation's lost opportunities. Michael Schaller, *The American Occupation of Japan: The Origins of the Cold War in Asia* (New York, 1985) sees the occupation as the taproot of the Cold War in Asia

31 Still the best survey is Warren Kimball, *Swords or Ploughshares? The Morgenthau Plan for Defeated Nazi Germany, 1943–1946* (Philadelphia, 1976).

32 Hoover's March 18, 1947, "Report on the Necessary Steps for the Promotion of German Exports" is available online at "Hoover and Truman. A Presidential Friendship. A Joint Project of the Hoover & Truman Presidential Libraries": https://trumanlibrary.org/hoover/internaltemplate.php?tldate=1947-03-18&groupid=5170&collectionid=hoover.

In wider contexts, any hope of reconstructing a Europe devastated by war, occupation, and liberation depended on restoring comity among states and peoples. Even before the war, a major consideration in appeasing Hitler and seeking to integrate his Reich into Europe's order had been the sense that Germany's contributions to Europe's history, culture, and civilization were too seminal to be excluded. The implications of these realizations converged in the Marshall Plan, whose initial version was German-centered, designed to make the western zones of occupation something like self-sufficient. The decisions to expand the scope of this plan and to emphasize its anti-communist aspects came later.

The same point can be made about the creation of Bizonia in 1948, the currency reform of 1948, and the related occupation policies that laid the foundations for the market economy in the emerging Federal Republic. The creation of two Germanies and the beginnings of the Cold War were predictable consequences, rather than the primary intentions, of these policies. Their matrix was the enduring refusal of the British and Americans to consider anything but a limited occupation of "their" Germanies.[33]

The reconstruction of Japan had a similar pragmatic basis. The Germans had lived better than the rest of Europe until 1945. By contrast, even before the destruction of most of its major cities, Japan's capacity to feed itself had collapsed. Overworked land had declined in production. The songbirds had been eaten. Faced with mass starvation in Japan, the United States provided food relief and loans. Japan's economic reconstruction nevertheless lagged behind Germany's. Japan's position in Asia was different from Germany's in Europe. If anything the country's recent past made it more of an outcast, and its status after the war seemed retrograde in light of the major changes taking place in China and on the Indian subcontinent. US occupation policy, however, supported economic recovery to prevent the resurgence of militarism and facilitate democratization. Japan had the advantages of an educated workforce and an industrial heritage. One of the early features of the restructured political system was the close alliance between government and business – a relationship that both promoted a dirigiste welfare economy and stabilized the occupation regime.[34]

33 Charles Maier and Günter Bischoff, eds., *The Marshall Plan and Germany: West German Development within the European Recovery Plan* (New York, 1991); Gerd Hardach, *Der Marshall-Plan: Auslandshilfe und Wiederaufbau in Westdeutschland, 1948–1952* (Munich, 1994).

34 James Vestal, *Planning for Change: Industrial Policy and Japanese Economic Development, 1945–1989* (Oxford, 1993).

Whether these developments were direct consequences of occupation policy or below-the-radar, wink-and-a-nudge developments remains debatable. In any case, the process did not take place at forced draft. Arguably, the United States was prepared to remain in Japan, unlike Germany, indefinitely – or at least as long as it remained smart domestic politics to keep MacArthur at half a world's distance from Washington. It took the unexpected external catalyst of the Korean War to trigger both a domestic boom in Japan and the country's movement into the international marketplace.[35]

In the Soviet spheres of eastern Germany and eastern Europe, recovery played a limited role during the occupation years. The USSR was more concerned with collecting reparations from its defeated enemy. Reparations seemed at times to include anything not nailed down, from wristwatches to factories. When the western Allies balked at stripping the barely functional economies of "their" Germany, Soviet demands on its zone increased. The same pattern obtained elsewhere in what became the Warsaw Pact. Not until the full-blown emergence of the Cold War did reconstruction become part of Soviet policy toward its "near abroad."[36]

The fourth aspect of postwar occupation was *reassertion* – specifically, the reassertion of prewar relationships with territories that had been overrun by the Axis. Although the European powers to a degree expected to be greeted as liberators, there were former enemies to be disarmed and repatriated, POWs and internees to be liberated, and administrations to reconfigure. The deployment of armed forces in a quasi-occupation was a logical consequence. Reassertion did not, however, necessarily mean recolonization. The principal western colonial powers proposed to redefine their extra-European relationships fundamentally and quickly – Britain through the Commonwealth of Nations, which had been integrated by war and victory, France through the French Union, which was created in 1946. The political and economic details could be settled later.

Reassertion was primarily a south Asian phenomenon, and it played out in three contexts. After some initial celebrations, the trope of liberation proved chimerical. Apart from prewar nationalist movements, which the Japanese occupation had nurtured, the Japanese conquest itself – especially the spectacular British capitulation at Singapore – had broken the fundamental

35 Aaron Forsberg, *America and the Japanese Miracle: The Cold War Context of Japan's Postwar Economic Revival, 1950–1960* (Chapel Hill, 2000); Nam G. Kim, *From Enemies to Allies: The Impact of the Korean War on US–Japan Relations* (San Francisco, 1997).

36 See Rainer Karlsch et al., eds, *Sowjetische Demontagen in Deutschland 1944–1949: Hintergründe, Ziele und Wirkungen* (Berlin, 2002).

colonial contract, which had promised security in return for compliance. Winston Churchill's insistence that "no question of surrender was to be entertained until after protracted fighting among the ruins of Singapore City" was countered by the common-sense assertion of Indian Army General Sir Lewis Heath that "to sacrifice the lives of countless Asiatics . . . would have been a deplorable blot upon the Empire which would take more than a subsequent victory in the World War to expunge."[37]

The most successful at reassertion were nevertheless the British. They restored the status quo in two areas that the postwar government considered vital – Hong Kong for trade and Malaya for resources. Their success was due in good part, ironically, to the presence of Indian troops, whose service to the Raj was numbered in months. Britain also had the sense to let an intransigent Burma go its own way. Not until 1948 did the Malayan Emergency begin, and then it remained largely confined to Chinese elements of the population.

At the other end of the spectrum, the Dutch encountered a functioning, organized nationalist movement in the Dutch East Indies, which was well armed with abandoned Japanese weapons and had found a workable administrative apparatus largely in place. The result was not an occupation but a counterinsurgency. The Netherlands was in no economic or military position to wage it, and for practical purposes abandoned the colony in 1948.

The French catastrophe in Indochina is more familiar. The postwar occupation was initially implemented by Chinese troops in the north and by British Indians in the south. Both were supported by Japanese troops that had been left under arms for the sake of expediency. This unpromising situation gave way to something worse. The incompetence and mendacity that characterized the negotiations among the French, the puppet Emperor Bao Dai, Ho Chi Minh's Vietminh, and local non-state actors such as the Cao Dai and the Binh Xuyen, remain subject to dispute. Incontestable is the result: an almost immediate transformation of an occupation into an insurgency, then a revolution, and finally a full-scale war, which the French refused to abandon but could neither win nor stabilize with the military, political, and ideological means at their disposal.

From its beginnings, each case of reoccupation demonstrated the limits of armed force. First the European imperial powers lacked the resources to support negotiations by force of arms. Financially and materially, they were exhausted. Their military systems had been strained to the limits or were in the process of reconstituting themselves. Neither conscripts nor volunteers in

37 Quoted in Alan Warren, *Britain's Greatest Defeat: Singapore, 1942* (London, 2002), 189, 263.

any number found the prospect of deployment to the far side of the world an acceptable alternative to rebuilding lives that had been disrupted by war and occupation in Europe.[38]

Fifth on the list of postwar occupation patterns was *retreat*. It, too, took place primarily in south Asia. The most straightforward case was the Philippines – or more accurately the Philippine Republic. Its creation was a done deal. In 1934 the United States had promised to transfer sovereignty by 1946, and it kept its word. In the interim the Philippines had paid a high price for its American connection. Conquest and occupation by the Japanese and subsequent liberation had done too much damage to challenge the terms of the American retreat, which left the United States in control of major military bases and made the new state an economic client of its former ruler. Recovery money was, however, on the table. Philippine–American relations have remained an up-and-down process, but no blood was spilled in the parting, and in the post-World War II context that counted for a good deal.[39]

At the opposite end of the "retreat spectrum" was the British departure from Palestine. This troubled mandate had acquired new importance in British strategic planning during World War II. As burgeoning nationalism made a direct military presence in Egypt increasingly problematic, the facilities that had been constructed in Palestine during the war, particularly the oil pipeline from Iraq to the Mediterranean, made Palestine attractive enough as a postwar base area to encourage sustaining the mandate in the face of an emerging "senseless, squalid war" with the Jewish Yishuv. The British security forces waged this war with an escalating level of sophisticated brutality. The empire did not surrender gracefully. Already-flexible laws and customs of war against insurgents were regularly bent beyond recognition – from Malaya and Kenya in the 1950s to Rhodesia in the 1970s.[40]

In the middle stood the longest-standing of the colonial occupations that were ended by World War II. The British relationship with India dated to the seventeenth century but embodied an essential paradox. The more political and colonial it became, the firmer grew the principle that the British governing

38 Ronald Spector, *In the Ruins of Empire: The Japanese Surrender and the Battle for Postwar Asia* (New York, 2007) is a brilliant overview. See also Christopher Bayly and Tim Harper, *Forgotten Wars: The End of Britain's Asian Empire* (Cambridge, MA, 2007); Maurice Vaïsse, ed., *L'Armée française dans la guerre d'Indochine (1946–1954): Adaptation ou inadaptation?* (Paris, 2000).

39 Sharon Delmendo, *The Star-Entangled Banner: One Hundred Years of America in the Philippines* (New Brunswick, 2004).

40 See Norman Rose, *A Senseless, Squalid War: Voices from Palestine, 1945–1948* (London, 2008); David Cesarini, *Major Farran's Hat: Murder, Scandal, and Britain's War against Jewish Terrorism, 1945–1948* (London, 2008).

presence was temporary – and not in the "Kathleen Mavourneen" sense of "it may be for years or it may be forever." Questions about the when and how of Indian independence were among the most fraught of interwar British politics. Winston Churchill's uncompromising resistance to independence did more to foster his political isolation than did his more familiar fulminations against the Third Reich.[41]

The development of the Congress Party along the parallel lines of an alternative government and a revolutionary movement provided a focus for Indian nationalism. Widespread resentment of the British governor-general's unilateral commitment of India to war in 1939 led to a Congress resolution in August 1942, which called for immediate independence. The British responded with widespread arrests and detentions, triggering a massive uprising, now almost forgotten, which brought India to the brink of chaos. The immediate result amounted to a wink-and–a-nudge compromise: suspension of hostilities in the understanding that the end of the war would bring full independence and membership in the British Commonwealth of Nations – either or both, depending on hopes and perspectives.

The Indian army underpinned and embodied the compromise. Churchill did not meekly accept the Singapore debacle and the lesser catastrophes in Hong Kong and Burma. He insisted on sustaining a major effort against Japan. This policy in turn threw India heavily onto its own resources, And it involved fundamentally transforming the Indian army, which had been a tool of imperial power-projection and colonial internal security – or perhaps better said, an army of occupation – into a high-tech instrument of modern war.

This process depended on the expanded recruitment and heterogeneity of this force. By 1945 most formations in the Indian army included a broad mix of classes, religions, and ethnic groups. Beginning in 1941, the officer corps was fully opened to Indians. Training and equipment were state of the art, so far as production and delivery allowed. A revitalized institution won victories against the Germans in Africa and Europe. It was the backbone of the Burma campaign of 1944–45. And although the Indian army did not develop into anything like an overt political movement, its underlying consciousness was accurately understood to be pro-nationalist and pro-independence.[42]

41 Arthur Herman, *Gandhi and Churchill: The Epic Rivalry that Destroyed an Empire and Forged Our Age* (New York, 2008).

42 Bayley and Harper, *Forgotten Armies*. For specifics see Daniel Marston, *Phoenix From the Ashes: The Indian Army in the Burma Campaign* (Westport, CT, 2003); Kaushik Roy, "Military Loyalty in the Colonial Context: A Case Study of the Indian Army during World War II," *Journal of Military History* 73 (2009): 497–529.

These facts formed the backdrop to the policy that Britain's Labour government followed after the general election of July 1945. Labour believed that Britain's prosperity and influence depended on maintaining a solid imperial bloc. It understood that in view of Britain's material and moral exhaustion, such a bloc must be voluntary. Increasing disorder compelled the Indian army to keep the subcontinent together long enough to settle the details of independence. However, nationalist and communal tensions, which were exacerbated by the growing demand for a separate Muslim state, exacerbated communalism in the army, which mass postwar demobilizations had already shaken. Administrative power and legal authority were strained beyond their limits. Amid unprecedented disruption, the army held together enough to prevent matters from becoming exponentially worse. The "perfect storm" on the immediate horizon encouraged all parties to pursue a policy frequently described as "divide and quit" or "shameful flight."[43]

It was not the Raj's finest hour. As many as a million people died because they were on the wrong side of hastily drawn boundary lines. Millions more were ethnically cleansed in a process whose consequences endure. This postwar occupation nevertheless concluded in an orderly transfer of power to two governments, India and Pakistan, both of which possessed the machinery of power and the instruments of authority. These were "republics," to paraphrase Benjamin Franklin, "if you can keep them." This still unresolved problem is another chapter for a different book.

The fourth postwar retreat took the longest. In 1945 the French government and people would have overwhelmingly rejected its inclusion in the category of "retreat." Algeria had been legally a part of France since 1870. It is only a small exaggeration to say that the metropolitan French considered its separation no more thinkable than Americans regard the severing of Texas from the Union. Algeria had been the base from which France was liberated from the Nazis and reconquered from the Vichyites. Algerians predominated among the North African soldiers who were the backbone of the reconfigured French army and carried the tricolor though Italy, up the Rhone valley, and through the mountains of Alsace into the heart of Germany. Whether Algeria's Muslim population considered itself occupied, as opposed to colonized, was open to debate. Its dominant approach in the twentieth century had been compromise. Muslims had in general supported the war against the

43 Penderel Moon, *Divide and Quit* (Berkeley and Los Angeles, 1961); Stanley Wolpert, *Shameful Flight: The Last Years of the British Empire in India* (New York, 2006).

Germans, but they did so in the expectation of reciprocity, especially in the matter of voting rights.

The French government temporized in the face of opposition from the *colons*, the Europeans who dominated Algeria's economy and formed about 10 percent of its population. A series of Muslim demonstrations in the spring of 1945 was crushed by massive military and police force, which was supported by *colon* vigilantes. In one sense French actions were reflexive: France had been handling similar situations in a similar way since the beginnings of its modern connection with Algeria in the 1830s. This time, however, the emotions were fiercer, the scale of repression was larger, and its technology – much of the hardware was supplied by the United States – was more formidable. When the numbers were tallied, as many as fifty thousand Algerian Muslims were dead. The nationalist leaders were in prison or in exile. On the surface the *status quo ante* seemed to have been restored. Algerian troops occupied Germany and fought in Indochina, forming part of the garrison of Dien Bien Phu. Successive governments tinkered with Algeria's political structures and expanded economic relations between Algeria and the metropole. Underneath, however, the legacies of 1945 metastasized within a decade into a brutal war of vengeance and independence.[44]

Fifth on the list of occupation patterns was *restoration*. In these cases occupation focused on restoring something like a prewar order that had been disrupted by conflict and conquest. Italy headed the list of successes, not least because its restoration went the deepest – not merely to a prewar but to a pre-Fascist model. The end of the war left the country prostrate, its industry in ruins, agriculture at near-subsistence levels, communications and transportation networks shattered to a point where late trains were welcome. Millions of refugees flocked into the peninsula from the Balkans. A communist-dominated, Soviet-backed partisan movement, which had waged a bitter war against Germans, capitalists, and Christians alike in the Nazi-occupied north until the final months of the war, had no intention of relinquishing power to a coalition government.[45]

The Italian republic, which was created by plebiscite in June 1946, survived in good part because of the monarchy's prudent change of sides three years earlier. Surrender in war is an art form, requiring finger-tip sensitivity, sophisticated planning, and a good deal of luck, if capitulation is to serve the

44 See Anne Rey-Goldzeiguer, *Aux origines de la guerre d'Algérie, 1940–1945: De Mers-el-Kebir aux massacres du Nord-Constantinois* (Paris, 2006); Tony Smith, *The French Stake in Algeria, 1945–1962* (Ithaca, 1972) is still useful.

45 James Holland, *Italy's Sorrow: A Year of War, 1944–1945* (New York, 2008).

causes of war enunciated by Thucydides: fear, honor, and interest. Italy's overthrow of Mussolini's government in the summer of 1943 reflected fear of the state's collapse and fear of destruction after the Allied invasion. It reflected honor, albeit a bit frayed around the edges, in Italy's being the first state to act on the conclusion that connection with Nazi Germany was less a "brutal friendship" than a pact with the devil. Overthrowing Mussolini reflected interest, insofar as continued German resistance on the peninsula made Italy's accession to the Allied cause valuable practically, as opposed to an exercise in the politics of gesture. With a war to fight, the British and Americans transferred power in the rear of the combat zone to Italian authorities as soon as practicable. Italian troops increasingly filled the gaps created by the transfer of Allied forces to France. American money underwrote the formation or reorganization of Italian political parties that were willing to oppose both fascism and communism, whether out of principle or for a chance to administer the postwar relief that was delivered under US and UN auspices.[46]

The result was an Italian government that was stable enough by 1948 to address its own problems. Willingness to forget the past for the "patronage, bureaucracy, and corruption" of the present played a larger role in this process than even Machiavelli might have approved. Italy's transfer from postwar occupation to participation in the Cold War was much less violent or traumatic than could have been expected in 1943 – or 1946.[47]

Restoration in Greece was structured by the resistance, which began with the country's conquest by the Axis in the spring of 1941. Armed and coordinated by the British, the Greek resistance grew increasingly effective against overextended German occupation forces – and increasingly factionalized. ELAS, which was dominated by communists and republicans, repudiated the exiled monarchy. The conservative EDES, which was bitterly hostile to ELAS, became royalist by default. Negotiations not only failed but also convinced ELAS that Britain was prepared to reimpose the monarchy by force. As Germany evacuated the Balkans, sporadic clashes within the resistance escalated into open fighting. With a war still to win and a Mediterranean

46 See Elena Agarossi, *A Nation Collapses: The Italian Surrender of September 1943* (Cambridge, 2000); C. R. S. Harris, *Allied Military Administration of Italy, 1943–1945* (London, 1957).

47 Miriam A. Golden, "Political Patronage, Bureaucracy, and Corruption in Postwar Italy," available online at the Russell Sage Foundation site: www.russellsage.org/publications/workingpapers/Political%20Patronage%20Bureaucracy%20and%20Corruption%20in%20Postwar%20Italy. See also M. Battini, *The Missing Italian Nuremberg: Cultural Amnesia and Postwar Politics* (New York, 2007).

position to reestablish, the British committed troops – many drawn from the Italian front – to restore an order that had never been more than nominal. They found themselves underwriting the Greek conservatives in a bitter civil war, which was suspended rather than ended when ELAS bowed to superior force in February 1945.

As in Italy, the newly established Greek government had more or less effective *de facto* control of the armed forces and the bureaucracy. Britain, for its part, sought a Greek monarchy as an ally-cum-client, preferably at minimal cost. A series of plebiscites and elections, which were conducted under British oversight and underwritten by a modest British military presence, resulted in the *de jure* restoration of the king in September 1946. ELAS responded by taking up arms again, this time with Soviet support.

The balance of forces in the renewed civil war was too close for Britain to pursue its preferred strategy of benevolent one-sidedness. Nor were British resources sufficient to sustain a wager at what seemed to be long odds. In February 1947 Britain announced the end of its financial support of the Greek government. Although the last British combat troops did not leave Greece until 1950, the United States assumed responsibility for underwriting the war. Massive infusions of American economic and military aid turned the conflict in the government's favor. The Truman Doctrine of March 12, 1947 went further and authorized American intervention in support of "free peoples" that were threatened by internal subversion or external pressure. This doctrine remained a norm of US foreign policy throughout the Cold War.[48] Its legacy endures.

Iran had declared neutrality at the outbreak of war but was too important as a supply route to the beleaguered Soviet Union for this declaration to have made any difference. In August 1941 British and Soviet troops occupied the country. Iran's government salvaged its sovereignty by agreeing to "non-military cooperation" and later declaring war on Germany. The Allies promised to withdraw their troops six months after the war ended. Stalin, Churchill, and Roosevelt agreed as well to provide economic assistance.

Promises, however, did little to facilitate restoration. Iran suffered significant hardship and no little humiliation even under benign occupation. Political parties on the left and center called increasingly for economic and political reform. Loudest among them was the Communist Tudeh. As American oil

48 See David Close, *The Origins of the Greek Civil War* (London, 1995); G. M. Alexander, *Prelude to the Truman Doctrine: British Policy in Greece, 1944–1947* (Oxford, 1982); Howard Jones, *"A New Kind of War": America's Global Strategy and the Truman Doctrine in Greece* (New York, 1989).

companies and the USSR both negotiated for postwar oil concessions, the Tudeh threw its influence behind the USSR. Azerbaijanian and Kurdish nationalists established autonomous republics with Soviet support. At the war's end British and US troops evacuated Iran. Soviet forces remained in place – on both sides of the border.

Backed by the Anglo-Americans, Iran's government convinced Stalin to withdraw his troops in return for oil concessions to the USSR and the Tudeh's participation in the government. Both proved temporary. In the reorganized Iranian parliament, a National Front under Mohammed Mossadeq accepted western influence as the lesser of two evils. In 1947 Iran and the United States signed a treaty on the Greek model, which provided for military aid and a training mission in return for Iranian support of western foreign policy generally and for renegotiated oil-rights settlements specifically. The separationist movements collapsed; the Tudeh Party was outlawed, and in the context of the Cold War the west won a significant victory. Solidifying it proved another matter; in 1953 the settlement collapsed under CIA pressure. Again, however, this story lies outside the framework of this chapter.[49]

The sixth and last category of postwar occupations is best described as *enabling* – facilitating events on the spot, however marginally. The division of the Korean peninsula between US and Soviet occupation forces after World War II was expected to be temporary, an administrative expedient based on an arbitrary line drawn along the 38th Parallel. Instead the division stabilized. Colonial rule by the Japanese from 1905 to 1945 had intensified the tensions between traditionalism and modernity into a struggle for national liberation. The South Korean Communist Party had collaborated with its counterpart in Pyongyang in hopes of unifying Korea as a revolutionary socialist state. They encountered opposition in a broad-gauged coalition of authoritarian nationalists, traditional conservatives, reformers, liberals, and free-market entrepreneurs. No less than the communists, these forces saw themselves as the founders of a new Korea, for which they were no less willing to kill and die.

The two Koreas would have fought one another with or without outside influence. Because the United States and the Soviet Union encouraged the development of their occupation zones into client states, the United Nations was unable to reverse the peninsula's partition. Formal occupation ended in 1948. The success of elections in South Korea led the regime in Pyongyang to

49 Ali Insari, *Modern Iran since 1921: The Pahlavis and After* (London, 2003). See Faramarz Fatemi, *The USSR in Iran: The Background History of Russian and Anglo-American Conflict in Iran, Its Effects on Iranian Nationalism and the Fall of the Shah* (London, 1980).

attempt unification by force. Although he rejected proposals from Pyongyang to escalate the simmering conflict immediately to a conventional war, Stalin provided equipment for a North Korean army that far outclassed its South Korean counterpart, which the United States kept at constabulary levels because it was unwilling to encourage the ambitions of South Korean President Syngman Rhee. Not until 1950 did the boil burst. It remains undrained.[50]

Circumstances in China were similar, but the scale and the stakes were exponentially greater. Long-standing hostility between the Nationalist Guomindang (GMD) and the Chinese Communist Party (CCP) had mutated into mortal antagonism in the course of the Sino-Japanese War. Neither side was willing to negotiate a power-sharing agreement in good faith. Both had held back resources during the war with Japan in expectation of a future settling of accounts with one another. Neither, however, was sufficiently confident of its own strength to eschew outside support.

The United States had maintained an increasing military presence in China since 1941. In the aftermath of Japan's surrender, the Third Marine Amphibious Corps was dispatched to north China to disarm Japanese troops in the region, arrange for the repatriation of Japanese civilians, and in general to promote the Nationalist government until it could itself return to the long-lost provinces. Almost immediately, however, the marines were engaged in small-scale clashes with Communist forces, which had their own designs on the region. In this context the Nationalist premier, Chiang Kai-shek, believed that he could count at least on indirect US support in reestablishing the GMD's authority in the region, whose industrial capacity and agricultural potential were vital for China's recovery and development.

In 1945 the USSR had occupied Manchuria. Since then it had dismantled the region's industrial base and shipped it back to the devastated motherland. Stalin listened when Chiang offered an under-the-table deal to delay withdrawal and to keep dismantling until the GMD could move enough of its forces – which had been trained and equipped by the Americans – to secure the north against the CCP.

US aircraft lifted almost a half million Nationalist troops and their equipment into the major cities of north China. From here the GMD sought to dominate the countryside, which was almost entirely controlled by the CCP. Surplus US equipment, worth hundreds of millions of dollars, was turned over

50 Allan R. Millett, *The War for Korea, 1945–1950: A House Burning* (Lawrence, KS, 2006) is by far the best analysis of the segue from occupation to war.

to the Nationalists. Despite the United States' massive demobilization, marines remained in north China's ports and other strategic sites until 1949, regularly exchanging shots with CCP guerrilla and main-force troops.

The Soviet Union came nowhere near to matching the US ante. It did not have to. The GMD made a better military showing than is generally recognized, but ongoing corruption and brutality, which combined with a general sense of the GMD's failure to protect north China against the Japanese, gave the CCP an edge that it brilliantly exploited. American support, material and political, declined as the Nationalist position eroded. By the end of 1949, the USSR seemed to have won a huge pot with a minimum bet. But the Cold War soon demonstrated that this civil war had been China's affair – and that China was no one's to win or lose.[51]

If the victors of World War II shared a common position, it was that this time must be the last. Civilization, arguably humanity itself, had poor prospects of surviving a rerun of the events of 1937 to 1947, let alone the specter of nuclear weapons. The structure of the new world order was ostensibly institutionalized in the United Nations. Officially established in 1945, it provided for a Security Council of great powers, which was responsible for maintaining international peace and security, and a General Assembly as a sounding-board for everyone else. In practice, the Security Council members – the United States, Russia, China, Britain, and France – were expected to take responsibility for their back yards, with due regard for advice and counsel from the neighborhood's General Assembly members. Against this background, postwar occupations were understood as temporary situations, transitions designed to clear the worst of the war years' detritus and establish local governments that were willing and able to take their place in the UN order.

The structure of the United Nations was both underpinned and undermined by two opposing hidden agendas. One, which was identified with – though it was not exclusive to – the United States, anticipated the natural development of political democracy and free-market capitalism. The other, which was similarly associated with the Soviet Union, expected the natural development of managed economies and societies along Marxist–Leninist lines. In the war's immediate aftermath, the tone in both camps was

51 Odd Arne Westad, *Decisive Encounters: The Chinese Civil War, 1945–1949* (Stanford, 2003) and *Cold War and Revolution: The Soviet-American Rivalry and the Origins of the Chinese Civil War, 1944–1946* (New York, 1993) stand out in the literature on this subject. See also Steven Levine, *Anvil of Victory: The Communist Revolution in Manchuria, 1945–1948* (New York, 1989); Henry Shaw, *The United States Marines in North China, 1945–1949* (Washington, DC, 1968).

set by optimists, who foresaw success with no more than minor nudges and tweaks, no more than a few of the broken eggs that even they agreed would be necessary for the projected omelet.

The UN's achievements were undermined as well by the comprehensive underestimation of local factors, the interests, fears, and desires of the peoples and states that were expected to conform to the world's reconfiguration. This underestimation was a product of three elements. One was a conviction that the threat of another war would be sufficient to concentrate minds and change hearts. The second was confidence in the persuasive and coercive powers of the agendas associated with the United States and the Soviet Union. The third was an extension of the – slightly bowdlerized – phrase that was coined by a British Labour MP in 1949: "natives begin at Calais." The aphorist sought to caricature the views of the Conservative opposition, particularly Winston Churchill. In fact, he described the mind-set of the western world, which in this case included the USSR as its eastern outpost.[52]

An alternate way to categorize occupations after World War II is by the degree to which they responded to internal forces. Defined as local reconfiguration in stable contexts, success did not correlate exactly to occupiers' situational awareness – but it came close. The standard pattern of occupations involved an unstable balance among domestic reconstruction, Cold War politics, and local aspirations (whether these were minimal or maximal along a spectrum that ranged from Italy to Indochina). The results defy easy categorization but are best described negatively. The world avoided nuclear war. Massacres never escalated to genocides. Rough balances between the claims of the community and the rights of the individual emerged. This outcome was not much compared to the goals of postwar occupations. It nevertheless provided a foundation as the world stumbled through the rest of the twentieth century.

52 Paul M. Kennedy, *The Parliament of Man: The Past, Present, and Future of the United Nations* (New York, 2006) is the best analytic overview. Stephen Schlesinger, *Act of Creation: The Founding of the United Nations. A Story of Superpowers, Secret Agents, Wartime Allies and Enemies, and Their Quest for a Peaceful World* (Boulder, 2003) adds a welcome human dimension.

18

The wars after the war, 1945–1954

ODD ARNE WESTAD

Most of the wars in Europe and Asia after 1945 grew out of ideological divides that had been created by the Russian Revolution of 1917. In almost all countries around the world, a minority of educated elites had started to believe that only a society patterned on the Soviet Union could create wealth while doing away with injustice and the oppression of peasants and workers. They had good reasons for their belief. While technological progress in the nineteenth century had created a world in which products could be created faster, better, and with more ease than before, the social gap between the working class, which produced the new material wealth, and the bourgeoisie, which consumed it, had grown ever wider. In rural areas, which dominated all the countries where wars continued after World War II, new forms of travel and communications exposed the age-old oppression of the peasantry and made it harder to bear. While the spread of the capitalist market in the early part of the twentieth century had held out the promise that people would improve their lot quickly through hard work or luck, the crises of the late 1920s and 1930s crushed many of these hopes. By the 1940s, with great parts of both continents in ruins after another devastating war unleashed by the dominant powers, time seemed ripe for revolutionary transformation of the Soviet kind.[1]

The attractiveness of the Soviet model had been confirmed by the Soviet Union's victory over Nazi Germany and its decisive intervention against Japan in 1945. Prior to World War II, Stalin's domestic purges, his willingness to enter into a pact with Hitler, and the brutal destruction of Poland and the Baltic republics had held back enthusiasm for the Soviet Union, even among leaders of left-wing organizations. In the postwar era, however, the skepticism

1 See Odd Arne Westad, "The Cold War and the International History of the Twentieth Century," in Melvyn P. Leffler and Odd Arne Westad, eds., *Cambridge History of the Cold War*, Vol. I: *Origins, 1945–1962* (Cambridge, 2010).

dramatically diminished. Many socialist and left-wing nationalist groups wanted to ally themselves with the Soviet Union in order to defeat their enemies, but Stalin was cautious in giving them grounds for optimism. In his view, neither Europe nor the colonial world was, with a few exceptions, ready for communist revolutions. The Soviet Union therefore became an inspiration and a model more than a helper for much of the left.

In most countries, nationalists or social democrats contained postwar communist advances. Parts of Europe and east Asia seemed ripe for revolution in 1946, but France, Italy, and Japan avoided large-scale conflict because of a combination of American aid and domestic anti-communist alliances. Where civil wars did break out, they were often the result of the right's attempts to crush communists with military force, as in Greece or China. In some cases the communists attacked when they believed that complete victory was within reach, as in Yugoslavia or later Korea. In general, however, ideological wars were most often conducted by the right to prevent the political victory of the left.

The breakdown of the European colonial system also created conditions for war in some places. In several of these, such as in Vietnam and Malaya, an anti-communist dimension was wedded to an anti-nationalist one, since the colonial power battled a Communist party that spearheaded the indigenous opposition. In Indonesia the leading nationalist group crushed a communist rebellion while fighting the colonial power, in this case the Netherlands. In India and the Middle East, the end of colonial rule led to wars that, because of their sectarian character, had particularly gruesome consequences for the civilian population. Everywhere colonialism ended, its collapse made sectional conflicts, which the imperialist powers had manipulated to their advantage, break out into forms of collective violence, though not always wars. Together with the ideological battles, the wars at the end of colonial rule made the first years after World War II anything but peaceful.

As the British historian D. C. Watt has famously written, Europe had in many ways been engaged in a long civil war since 1914.[2] In the interwar period and during World War II, this civil war had had three sides – liberal capitalism, represented by Britain and France, communism, which was represented by the Soviet Union, and authoritarian nationalism, which was represented by Italy, Germany, Spain, and a number of states in eastern Europe, from Greece to Estonia. The main losers in the first phase of the European civil war were

2 Watt's view is distilled in his *Too Serious a Business: European Armed Forces and the Approach to the Second World War* (Berkeley, 1975), 11–30.

the authoritarian nationalists. As a consequence of World War II, Spain kept its regime but was politically marginalized, Italy and the western half of Germany became liberal capitalist, and most eastern European countries came under Soviet control. Only in the Balkans did the dividing lines criss-cross, leading to civil wars in Yugoslavia and in Greece.[3]

The Yugoslav civil war was based primarily on ideological splits within the country's resistance to German and Italian occupation during World War II. By 1941 two distinct organizations had already appeared. The Chetniks under Draža Mihailović were a conservative, royalist movement mostly of Serbian extraction, while the Partisans under Josip Broz (known as Tito) represented an ethnically composite left-wing group led by communists. Until the end of World War II, the two groups spent at least as much time fighting each other as they did the occupation forces, as the Partisans increasingly gained the upper hand. The success of the Partisans was mainly due to their ideological cohesion, their multiethnic recruitment, and their greater willingness to engage German forces and the Croatian militias who collaborated with the Germans. Mihailović's room for maneuver ran out once the western Allies forced the exiled royal government to work with Tito's Partisans in 1944 and – especially – once Germany, with which the Chetniks had formed a number of tactical deals toward the end of the war, capitulated. The Chetniks continued nevertheless to fight until the spring of 1946, increasingly regarding themselves as a Serbian anti-communist force. Mihailović was captured in March 1946 and executed soon afterwards, and the victorious Partisans went on to declare a socialist Federal Republic of Yugoslavia under Tito's leadership.[4]

At the southern end of the Balkans, however, the civil war in Greece took longer to burn out. After the German invasion and occupation in 1941, the Greek resistance had split into several factions and groups, broadly along ideological lines. The largest was EAM (*Ethnikón Apeleftherotikón Métopon* – the National Liberation Front) and its military wing ELAS (*Ethnikós Laïkós Apeleftherotikós Strátos* – the Greek People's Liberation Army). EAM was an alliance of leftist and radical nationalist groups, which fell increasingly under the control of the Greek Communist Party (KKE). Against the left stood a number of conservative and some smaller liberal resistance organizations. After mid 1943 clashes between ELAS and its opponents developed into full-scale civil war. By the spring of 1944 it was clear that ELAS could hold its own

3 For an overview of the situation in Europe in 1945, see Tony Judt, *Postwar: A History of Europe since 1945* (New York, 2006), esp. 13–128.

4 J. R. Lampe, *Yugoslavia as History: Twice There Was a Country* (2nd edn., Cambridge, 2000), 218–40.

against both the Germans and its own Greek opponents. After large numbers of troops who were serving with the Greek government in exile demanded a national unity government, the king agreed to a new cabinet, which would include EAM. As German troops withdrew, all resistance soldiers in Greece – which theoretically included those serving in ELAS – were put under the command of an Allied general, the Briton Ronald Scobie.

Following Stalin's instructions, the EAM leadership initially remained in the coalition government after the liberation of Athens in October 1944. But, as was later the case in China, the Communists were reluctant to dissolve their armed units, in spite of pressure from the Greek government, the British, and the Soviets to do so. In December 1944, after the EAM ministers resigned from the government to protest what they saw as an accelerated plan to integrate their forces into the army, the police fired on a left-wing demonstration in Athens, setting off widespread fighting in the city. British troops and aircraft supported the police and army units that were loyal to the government. By early 1945 British intervention had forced a ceasefire, which left the KKE's leadership weakened. While offering lip-service to the principle of a coalition government, the Communists had been forced by popular anger, which was directed against the government, to fight in engagements that they did not believe they could win. Caught in the middle of a social revolution, in which peasants and workers were eager to defend rights that they had won during the resistance, the KKE was unable to formulate a clear strategy. As the war in Europe came to an end, the EAM agreed to dissolve and disarm ELAS. In some parts of the country fighting continued, mostly provoked by right-wing attempts to reverse land rights or punish former ELAS fighters. Around six thousand EAM members took refuge in Tito's Yugoslavia.[5]

As Stalin's willingness to compromise with his former allies cooled in early 1946, his advice to the Greek Communists became more bland. While he never encouraged them to take up arms in support of revolution, he became less insistent on the KKE's making concessions and allowed party leaders to follow their own inclinations toward taking up arms. By the late spring of 1946, civil war had resumed in most parts of Greece, as former ELAS units now went on the offensive. Assisted by Yugoslavia, Albania, and a Soviet policy of non-interference, the Greek Communists delivered severe military blows to government forces and their British allies. The British Labour government

5 For an overview of interpretations, see Nikos Marantzidis and Georgios Antoniou, "The Axis Occupation and Civil War: Changing Trends in Greek Historiography, 1941–2002," *Journal of Peace Research* 41 (2004): 223–31.

grew tired of the costs of the fighting, and in 1947 the US president, Harry Truman, declared that the United States would support the Greek regime in its battles against the opposition. The KKE leadership decided to launch an all-out offensive before the effects of the US aid kicked in, moving from guerrilla tactics to conventional war and setting up an alternative government for the whole country in December 1947.[6]

The Greek Communists acted too late. In a country tired of fighting, and with US civilian and military assistance arriving in large quantities, the government gained the support it needed to stem the communist offensives and then to turn the military tide. Helped by army reorganizations, government forces defeated the ex-ELAS units in the southern part of Greece in late 1948. The civil war would have lasted much longer, though, absent the split between the Soviet Union and Yugoslavia, in which the main KKE leaders sided with Moscow. Deprived of their bases north of the border, the remaining Greek Communist forces were defeated, along with the social revolution that they had been defending. Thousands of leftists remained in prison camps for years, and at least a thousand KKE members were evacuated to the Soviet Union, where most were settled in or near the capital of Uzbekistan, Tashkent. Still, Greek politics remained unstable for another generation.[7]

In other parts of eastern Europe, smaller wars resulted from the incorporation of countries into the Soviet Union. While the might of the Red Army at the end of World War II made military opposition impossible, groups in Ukraine and the Baltic states continued to resist. Ukraine, which had been part of the Russian Empire and taken over by communist forces after the 1917 revolution, had come under German occupation in 1941, and Ukrainian nationalists used the opportunity to declare independence from the Soviet Union. While Ukrainian autonomy remained a sham under German occupation, many Ukrainian nationalists continued to fight against the Red Army after the Nazi withdrawal. The Organization of Ukrainian Nationalists (OUN; Organizatsiia ukraininskikh natsionalistov) fought overwhelming Soviet forces until 1950, when its leader, Roman Shukhevych, was killed. While the OUN was feared for its collaboration with the Nazis and its atrocities against Poles and Jews, some Ukrainians still regarded it as the champion of independence and sovereignty. Soviet countermeasures were brutal. Between 1944 and 1952 as many as six hundred thousand people were arrested in

6 On the Truman doctrine, see Michael J. Hogan, *A Cross of Iron: Harry S. Truman and the Origins of the National Security State, 1945–1954* (Cambridge, 2000), esp. 1–22.

7 Peter J. Stavrakis, *Moscow and Greek Communism, 1944–1949* (Ithaca, 1989).

western Ukraine; about a third of these were executed and the rest imprisoned or exiled. The fierce Soviet response probably did as much to keep resistance alive as the waning military power of the OUN.[8]

In the Baltic states – Estonia, Latvia, and Lithuania – the return of the Red Army also provoked lasting resistance. Having become independent from Russia in 1918, the three countries were occupied by the Soviets in 1940, after Stalin's pact with Hitler. The occupation was vicious, and the German invasion in 1941 was greeted with relief by many Balts, who now in turn took their wrath out on Russians and other local minorities. The German defeat meant the return of the Red Army and the start of another round of bloodletting. In all three Baltic countries resistance coalesced around former officers, most of whom had collaborated with the Nazis, and it was known collectively as the "Forest Brothers." The fighting lasted for almost a decade and cost up to fifty thousand lives, mostly in Lithuania. Around 10 percent of the entire adult population of Balts was deported or sent to labor camps between 1940 and 1953.[9]

The ideological wars in Europe formed part of the Cold War and may indeed be said to have shaped the European Cold War order. The wars were cruel, bloody, and contained in them the possibility for unleashing another European great-power conflict. By the 1950s, as the communist regimes in Eastern Europe stabilized, the western European Communist parties declined, and military alliances were formed splitting the continent into two blocs, governments both east and west were mainly contented with a divided Europe. The ideologically based partitioning gave respite after thirty years of war and conflict. But Cold War stability did not mean the end to conflict in Europe. Nor did it fill in the ethnic and religious fault lines that intersect the European political landscape. At the end of the Cold War era, parts of the continent would see disputes, which the ideological wars and division were thought to have superseded, reemerge in new forms.

The pattern of conflict in East Asia after World War II was similar, and it followed the same timeline. In China, ideologically grounded warfare between the Guomindang and the Communists broke out even before Japan's defeat; and it led to a nationwide civil war between 1946 and 1950. In Korea, the postwar division of the country into two arbitrarily set zones of

8 On World War II and the Soviet re-occupation of Ukraine, see Serhy Yekelchyk, *Ukraine: Birth of a Modern Nation* (Oxford, 2007), ch. 8.

9 For the Soviet occupation of the Baltic states, see Elena Zubkova, *Pribaltika i Kreml, 1940–1953* (Moscow, 2008). On the Baltic resistance, see Arvydas Anusauskas, ed., *The Anti-Soviet Resistance in the Baltic States* (Vilnius, 1999).

32. UN forces cross the 38th Parallel after withdrawal from Pyongyang

occupation – one controlled by the United States, the other by the Soviet Union – allowed rival factions of Korean nationalists to set up separate states, each allied to a superpower, and thereby to create the framework of the Korean War. The wars in China and Korea were by far the largest military engagements in the world after World War II and, because of their ideological nature, they made the Cold War a global system.

Although the Chinese government, which was dominated by the Guomindang (GMD) under Jiang Jieshi (Chiang Kai-shek), and the Chinese Communist Party (CCP), which was led by Mao Zedong, had agreed to form a united front against Japan after the outbreak of the Sino-Japanese War in 1937, sporadic fighting between the two rivals for power had continued. Clashes in early 1941 led to several thousand killed and even though a fragile truce held up to 1945, both parties were positioning themselves to fight each other as much as to fight the Japanese. The Japanese surrender in August 1945 came as a surprise to both. It soon became clear, however, that the Guomindang government would get the upper hand, since the Americans ordered all Japanese forces to surrender *only* to Jiang's regime. With massive US assistance in transporting troops all over China, the GMD took control of nearly all the territory that had been held by the Japanese, and it contained the CCP forces in their base areas. Pushed by the Soviets, Mao agreed to participate in peace talks with Jiang Jieshi in late 1945, which the Americans sponsored.

Stalin's decision to withdraw his forces abruptly from Manchuria led to the outbreak of full-scale civil war in China in the summer of 1946. Stalin had wanted to show the GMD leadership that they needed Soviet support if they wished to avoid a challenge from the CCP and, therefore, that they should accept the long-term plans for Soviet influence in China that he had put forward. Instead, the Soviet withdrawal and the CCP's attempts to move into Manchuria in the wake of the Red Army gave Jiang the opportunity he had hoped for to launch a general offensive against the Chinese Communists. The American mediation mission to China, under General George Marshall, grumbled at Jiang's operations but did little to stop them. As the Cold War took hold in US thinking, the need to keep China non-communist took on a new significance. The Soviets provided lip-service to the CCP's cause, while they tried to coax them back to the negotiating table, because Stalin believed that they were engaged in a war that they could not win.[10]

The military operations in the Chinese civil war came in three stages. The first, which lasted until the end of 1947, saw major GMD offensives against the CCP in almost all parts of China. These operations inflicted heavy casualties on the Communists, although at some cost to Jiang's elite forces, which the Americans had equipped. The headquarters of the CCP's Central Committee at Yan'an fell to the government in March 1947. By the winter of 1947–48, as the second stage began, the Communists' only hope lay in their positions in Manchuria. In a remarkable series of battles over nine months after December 1947, CCP troops under the command of Lin Biao first fought to a halt the massive reinforcements that Jiang had sent there, and then surrounded them before they could withdraw before finally annihilating them in September 1948. Suddenly the tables had turned, and Jiang Jieshi's task was to defend the main part of China from a Communist onslaught that was certain to come.

Jiang's chances of defending his republic from the Communists on the battlefield were much reduced by his unwillingness to strike compromises with other groups, and by his regime's economic and financial incompetence. With his popularity in freefall even among most non-communists, Jiang found it difficult to mobilize for defensive operations. The speed with which the

10 Odd Arne Westad, *Cold War and Revolution: Soviet-American Rivalry and the Origins of the Chinese Civil War, 1944–1946* (New York, 1993).

Communist troops – now reorganized as the People's Liberation Army (PLA) – moved toward Central China put Jiang at further disadvantage. The third stage of the civil war, which began with the Huaihai campaign north of the Yangzi river in November 1948 and ended in the final defeats of the GMD in the south a year later, could still have resulted in a division of mainland China, had Jiang's regime not disintegrated politically. As it was, defeat at Huaihai broke the regime's back. In the biggest battle between the end of World War II and the outbreak of the Iran–Iraq War in 1980, the PLA used Soviet tactics from the German front to overrun GMD defenses. By the end of 1949, Mao Zedong had declared a new People's Republic of China, and Jiang Jieshi had fled to his island fortress of Taiwan, preparing to make a last stand for his lost cause.[11]

From an Asian perspective, the Korean War was in part a continuation of the Chinese civil war, insofar as the same PLA units were engaged and the same ideological division was at play. But the war was also a Korean civil war, growing out of the schism between left-wing and traditionalist nationalisms, which had been developing since the early twentieth century. After the two Korean states were set up in 1948, each of which claimed sovereignty over the entire peninsula, the scene was set for war as soon as one of the great-power sponsors of the regimes agreed to it. As had been the case in China four years earlier, Stalin's decisions led to the outbreak of war in Korea in the spring of 1950. When the North Korean leader Kim Il-sung approached the Soviets in early 1950 – not for the first time – in order to get their approval for an attack on the south, Stalin gave the go-ahead. Probably emboldened by the CCP victory in China and the Soviet nuclear tests, Moscow might have sensed an opportunity to avenge the failure of the Berlin blockade and other setbacks in Europe. While Korean officers commanded it on the ground, the offensive against the south was planned by Soviet staff officers and patterned on the final campaigns of the Chinese civil war, which had themselves been modeled after the Soviet operations at the end of World War II.[12]

Much like the war in China, the Korean War had three main military phases. However, all the rapid movement took place during the first nine months of the war, not in the final months, as had been the case in China. In the first phase, after the Korean Communist forces invaded across the line of division – the 38th Parallel – on June 25, 1950, Kim's forces drove the resistance

11 Odd Arne Westad, *Decisive Encounters: The Chinese Civil War, 1946–1950* (Stanford, 2003).

12 William Stueck, *The Korean War* (Princeton, 1997). See also William Stueck, *Rethinking the Korean War: A New Diplomatic and Strategic History* (Princeton, 2004).

back to a small area around Pusan on the southwestern coast. All attempts by US troops from Japan to aid the regime of Syngman Rhee in South Korea failed, and it seemed to be a matter of time before the entire peninsula fell to the Communists, especially as large numbers of Rhee's troops defected to forces from the north. Only the logistical success of the US army in establishing a defensive perimeter around Pusan prevented a collapse.

The advantage of the Korean Communist forces was abruptly broken when US troops under General Douglas MacArthur landed near Inchon, the port city of Korea's capital Seoul, launching the second stage of the war. The US strategy was to cut the still advancing communist units off from their reinforcements and supplies in the northern part of the country, and then to destroy these units one by one. This strategy also envisaged a rapid move into the north, in hopes of destroying the command centers of the communist army and Kim's regime itself. The counterattack, which was led by the Americans and sanctioned by the UN Security Council as a consequence of the Soviet boycott, was remarkably successful. Overrun and outgunned communist troops surrendered en masse, and the attacking forces moved toward Korea's northern border, as the communist regime tottered.

The third stage of the war began in October 1950, when Chinese troops entered Korea in force. Mao Zedong had been skeptical of Kim's chances of success, but he was unwilling to let his ideological ally next door succumb to the military might of the United States. He also wanted to show Stalin and the Soviets that China was willing and able to stand up to the west and to defend what he regarded as joint Soviet and Chinese interests. While some historians have argued that the Chinese leaders were primarily concerned with the security threat of US troops at their border, little in the declassified Chinese records indicates such concerns. Rather, the Korean War gave Mao Zedong the chance to fight foreign enemies and prove himself to the Soviets. Both motives were strong enough to explain the Chinese intervention.[13]

The Chinese attacks in early November caught the US-led troops unaware and quickly drove them back to the 38th Parallel. Having taken heavy casualties – fifteen thousand American soldiers were killed, injured, or captured during the retreat to the south – Washington had no stomach for a broadly based second offensive. The Chinese leaders also believed that an attempt to reunify the country on Kim Il-sung's behalf was too risky. Fighting stalled around the former demarcation line, and although the war continued

13 Chen Jian, *China's Road to the Korean War: The Making of the Sino-American Confrontation* (New York, 1994).

for another two years, with severe losses on both sides, the offensive part of the conflict was over by spring 1951.

The Korean War ended because Stalin died. The Soviet leader had given the green light to the conflict, and his death removed the final obstacle to peace. While Stalin had believed it in the Soviets' interest that Americans and Chinese continue to kill each other in Korea, his successors regarded this policy as a dangerous gamble, which could lead the Soviet Union into war with the United States. The ceasefire line was for all practical purposes identical to the dividing line before the war started. The return to the *status quo ante* had cost the lives of up to a half million Chinese soldiers, 300,000 Koreans, and 40,000 Americans and allied troops, in addition to an estimated 700,000 Korean civilians. The war had drawn China closer to its Soviet ally and had proven Mao's nationalist credentials, as he fought the most powerful western nation to a standstill on the battlefield. The United States had proven its willingness to intervene against communist attempts to take power by force, even at the risk of major war, but in spite of the anti-communist climate at home, the Korean conflict was never a popular in the United States. It was fought too far from home, at great human loss, and for uncertain objectives.[14]

The wars in China and Korea established a dominant communist presence in East Asia and the division of the region into two parts. These conflicts also made the Cold War global, imposing an ideological divide on Asia similar to the one that had already developed in Europe. Militarily, the Korean War underlined the significance of air warfare with the introduction of helicopters and jet fighters. But first and foremost, the East Asian wars militarized the Cold War, forcing policymakers to prepare for the next regional conflict while developing their strategic forces as a deterrent.

The years after the end of World War II saw the beginning of decolonization, which changed international affairs dramatically over the generation to come. Asia, Africa, and the Caribbean went from having few independent states in 1945 (there were three in all of Asia from Japan to the Iranian border) to having a large number of them by the end of the following decade (twenty within the same Asian region). The rest of this chapter will deal with the two kinds of wars that emerged during the decolonization process – the anticolonial wars in Asia, which were fought in order to drive out a colonizing power (as in Indonesia, Vietnam, and Malaya), and the conflicts that followed the withdrawal of foreign forces (as in India and Palestine). Measured in civilian

14 William Stueck, "The Korean War," in Leffler and Westad, eds., *Cambridge History of the Cold War*, Vol. I: 266–87.

casualties, these were among the most destructive wars of the postwar period, especially where they arose out of ethnic or religious resentment rather than the ideological divisions of the Cold War.

The war between Vietnamese nationalists and the returning French colonial power was at once an anticolonial and ideological conflict. The main Vietnamese nationalist movement, the Viet Minh (short for *Việt Nam Độc Lập Đồng Minh Hội*, League for the Independence of Vietnam) was led by Communists, who had cut their teeth in the Indochinese socialist parties or the Comintern. Ho Chi Minh, the Viet-Minh leader who declared Vietnamese independence in Hanoi in 1945, had been a key Asian operative for the Comintern during the interwar years, but he had returned to Vietnam in 1941 to help lead the liberation movement. After the United States and Britain supported a return of French forces to Indochina upon the Japanese capitulation, war broke out in late 1946. It lasted until 1954, becoming one of the longest wars of liberation at the end of the colonial era.[15]

The French government aimed at reincorporating all of Vietnam, including areas held by the Viet Minh in the north of the country, into its colonial system in Indochina. When the war started in earnest, after a series of unsuccessful negotiations in late 1945 and 1946, this aim determined the French strategy. After occupying Hanoi, French forces spread out across most of the country in an attempt to drive the Viet Minh out of its regional strongholds. But although the French reached most of their strategic objectives and could – because of the onset of the Cold War – rely on increasing US support in their military buildup, they failed to find a military solution.[16] The Viet Minh avoided large-scale battle with their enemy and resorted to guerrilla tactics, so it was impossible for Paris to win an outright victory. After three years of war, many areas were still not under French control. In 1949 the French government decided to give *pro forma* independence to a Vietnamese regime under the former emperor Bao Dai, in order to improve its political position against the Viet Minh.

This feeble attempt to reorganize Vietnamese politics did not decide the outcome of the war; the Communist victory in China did. By 1950 the Chinese were able to supply large numbers of weapons and military advisors to the Viet Minh, enabling their Vietnamese ideological allies to launch renewed offensive operations against the French. In addition, both the military forces and civilian administratoin of the Viet Minh were better organized. In October

15 Mark Philip Bradley, *Vietnam at War* (Oxford, 2009), 9–40.
16 Stein Tønnesson, *Vietnam 1946: How the War Began* (Berkeley, 2009).

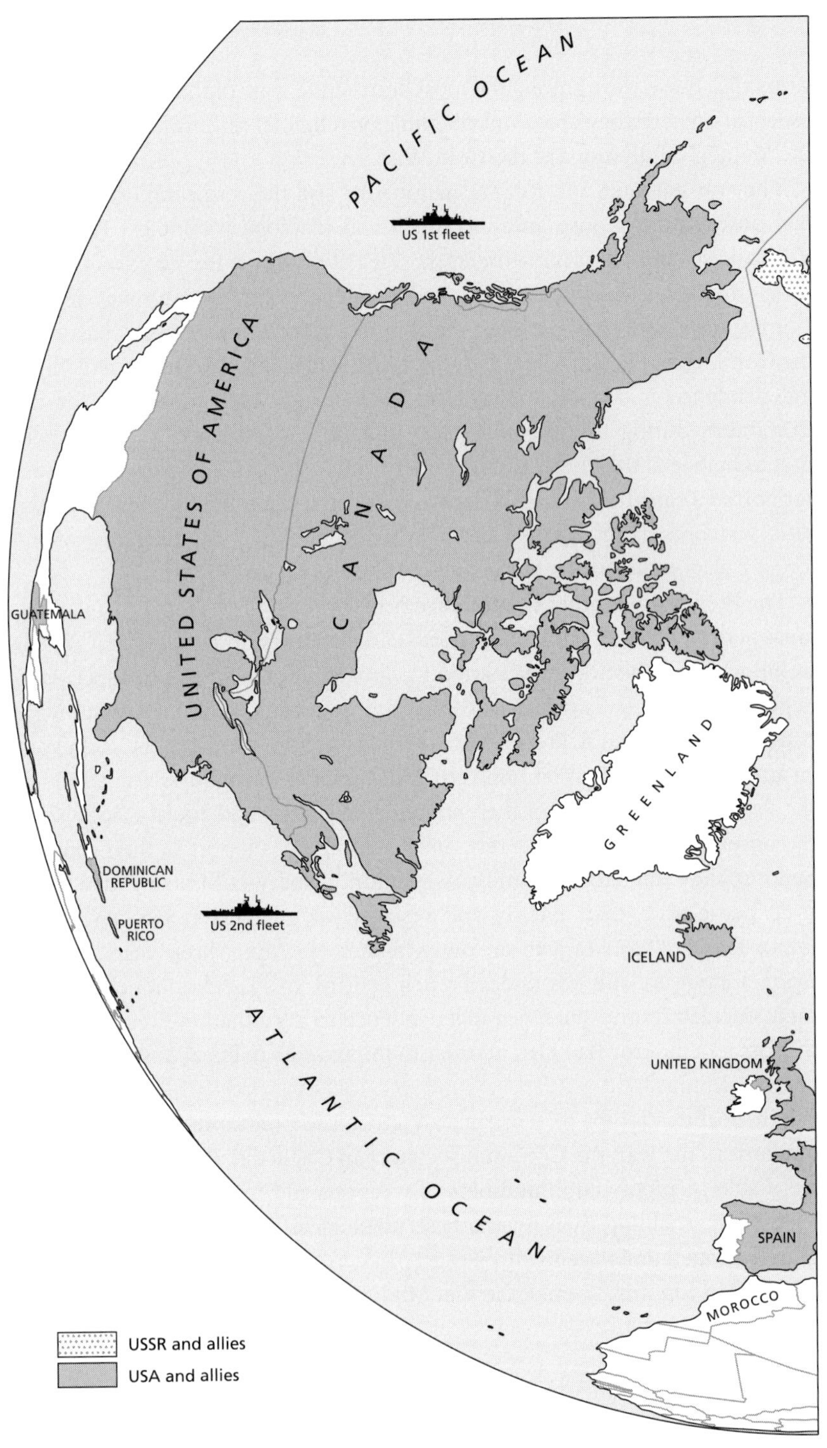

MAP 15. The early Cold War

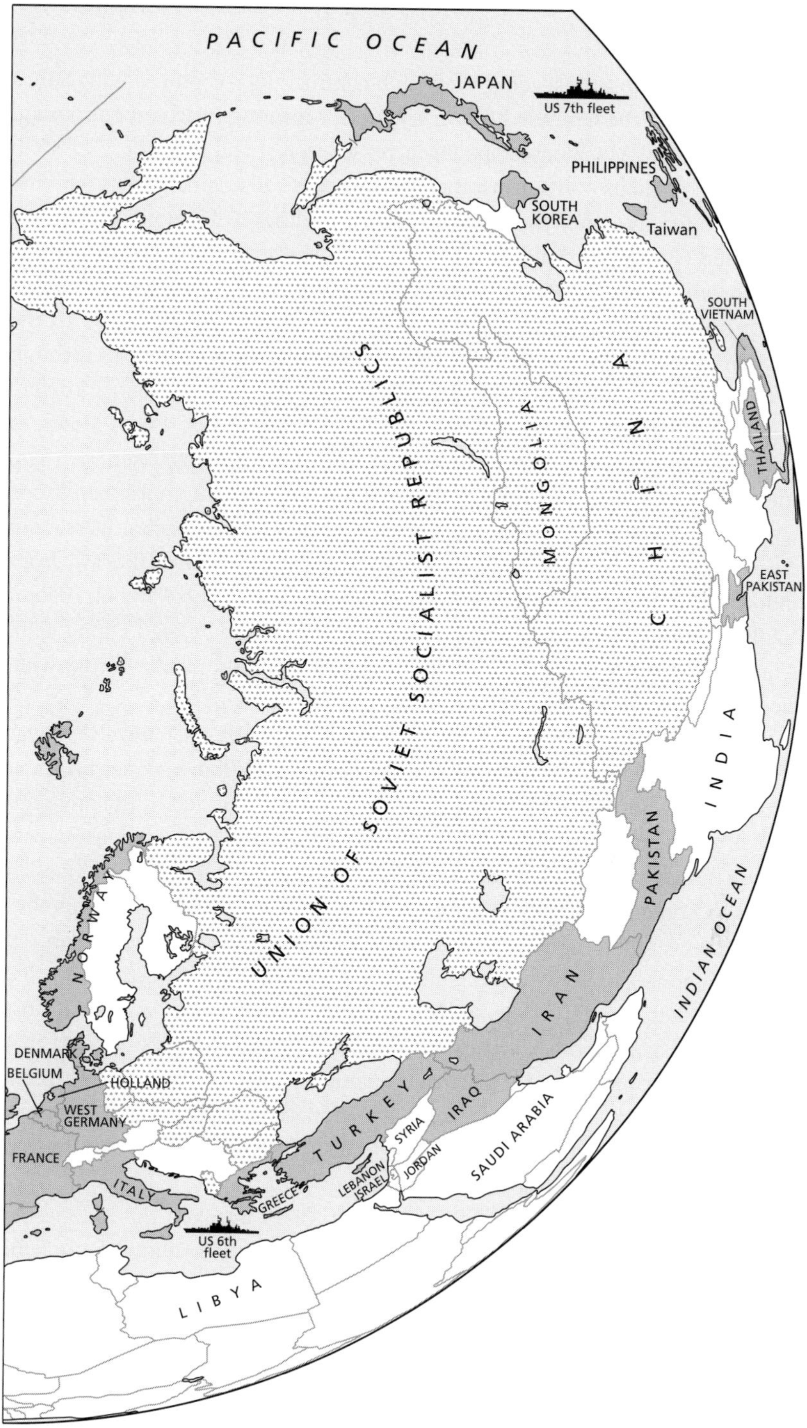

PACIFIC OCEAN
JAPAN
US 7th fleet
PHILIPPINES
SOUTH KOREA
Taiwan
SOUTH VIETNAM
THAILAND
CHINA
MONGOLIA
UNION OF SOVIET SOCIALIST REPUBLICS
EAST PAKISTAN
INDIA
PAKISTAN
INDIAN OCEAN
IRAN
IRAQ
SAUDI ARABIA
SYRIA
JORDAN
LEBANON
ISRAEL
TURKEY
GREECE
ITALY
US 6th fleet
LIBYA
FRANCE
WEST GERMANY
HOLLAND
BELGIUM
DENMARK
NORWAY

1950 General Giap – the leading Viet-Minh commander – captured Lang Son, a major city near the Chinese border, killing or capturing nearly five thousand French soldiers. As Chinese supplies increased in 1951 and 1952, the Viet Minh increasingly held its own against the French, but it had no prospect of winning the war militarily unless the French decided to withdraw for political reasons.

Ho and Giap knew that the best way to put pressure on Paris to withdraw was to win a spectacular victory in a major military engagement. Their opportunity came when the French decided to fortify an area close to the Laotian border in hopes of cutting off the Viet Minh's supply lines through Laos. Anchored in the small town of Dien Bien Phu the area seemed defensible, but by late 1953 Viet-Minh units were drawing nearer. From March to May 1954 Vietnamese forces beseiged the garrison. By the time Dien Bien Phu surrendered on May 7, 2,200 French soldiers had been killed; more than 11,000 were taken prisoner. During negotiations in Geneva, the French government then offered a settlement. In July 1954 Paris agreed to withdraw from Indochina and to divide Vietnam temporarily along the 17th Parallel. A Viet-Minh regime took power in the north; a government led by Ngo Dinh Diem, who had been appointed by Bao Dai, took control in the south. Nationwide elections were planned for 1956.

Dutch attempts to reimpose colonial rule in Southeast Asia also led to war after 1945. Like French Indochina, the Dutch East Indies had been occupied by Japan during World War II and the anticolonial nationalists, led by the firebrand civic organizer Sukarno, had used the occupation to prepare for independence, hoping that, whatever the outcome of the war, they could found an Indonesian state as a homeland for all Malays. They declared independence in September 1945. However, although the new Indonesian government was well organized and ready to negotiate with the Dutch, it soon came under pressure from the western Allies. British troops took control of parts of the country against sporadic resistance from Sukarno's government, which rightly suspected that the British were preparing for the arrival of Dutch troops. The British arranged a weak compromise, which put Sukarno's nationalists in charge of part of the country under the Dutch monarchy, but it satisfied nobody and did not survive the departure of British troops in late 1946.[17]

Following a number of skirmishes, Dutch forces attacked the Indonesian republic in the summer of 1947, attempting to force the creation of a federal state linked to the Netherlands. While Dutch forces controlled the main cities,

17 Richard McMillan, *The British Occupation of Indonesia, 1945–1946: Britain, the Netherlands and the Indonesian Revolution* (London, 2006).

they were too few in numbers to control the rural regions, as both sides tried to keep open warfare to a minimum. By the end of 1948, as opinion at home turned against a costly war, the Dutch government tried to win a quick victory, attacking the nationalist capital Yogyakarta and imprisoning the nationalist leaders, including Sukarno himself. But the operation backfired, as it turned international opinion against the Dutch at a time when the war had claimed five thousand Dutch lives and at least ten times as many Indonesian. In 1949 the United States threatened to cut off Marshall Plan aid to the Netherlands if a negotiated settlement did not allow Indonesian independence. In the context of the Cold War, Washington was concerned that Dutch attempts to crush the nationalists were playing into the hands of the Indonesian Communist Party, with which Sukarno was now at loggerheads. In December 1949, following two months of talks, the Netherlands agreed to Indonesia's independence after the nationalists accepted the final point in the Dutch position – that the new republic take responsibility for the entire debt of the former colony.[18]

While much less costly in lives, the war in Malaya between the British colonial power and the national liberation front, which was headed by the Malayan Communist Party (MCP), was important because of its outcome.

33. Sacking of the Communist Youth Organization Headquarters in Jakarta

18 Adrian Vickers, *A History of Modern Indonesia* (Cambridge, 2005), 85–112.

Unlike Vietnam or Indonesia, Malaya comprised three ethnic groups – the indigenous Malays, who in 1950 numbered about 1.5 million, the Chinese, who numbered 1 million, and about 500,000 Indians. The MCP, whose leaders were Chinese, was never able to reach out to the other ethnic groups, and soon after fighting broke out in 1948, the majority of Malay leaders allied themselves with the British in the understanding that the country would gain independence as soon as the war against the Communists was won. After 1951 the MCP lost ground, and by the late 1950s the party had been defeated in most parts of the colony, after more than 7,000 MCP guerrillas, 1,200 Malay soldiers and policemen, and 500 British military personnel had been killed.[19]

The anticolonial wars in Southeast Asia were caused by the refusal of the European imperialist states to negotiate an end to foreign rule after World War II. Their outcomes, however, were markedly different and much influenced by the circumstances of the Cold War, of which they became a part. In Vietnam, US suspicions of the liberation movement, which was led by Communists but supported by most Vietnamese, resulted in the country's division into two states. In Indonesia, the anti-communist credentials of leading nationalists led to decisive American support for an independent and united republic. In Malaya, where the liberation forces were split along ethnic lines, an alliance between the weakened colonial power and the Malay nationalists made possible the slow defeat of the communist forces. Of the three cases, the outcome of the war in Vietnam had most significance for the rest of the postwar era. But given its ethnic dimension, the fighting in Malaya was the most direct link between the wars in Southeast Asia and the large conflicts further west on the Asian continent.

Most wars after World War II in eastern Asia and Europe had an ideological dimension, which reflected the emergence of the Cold War international system, but the postcolonial wars in southern and western Asia grew out of ethnic and religious conflicts that had been exacerbated by the colonial presence. As in all ethnic or religious wars, the main victims were civilians, who were killed or driven out of their homes as new states were established. In India and Palestine, both of which had been under British control, the postcolonial wars were as remarkable for destroying lives and property as they were for creating intricate conflicts in the future.

British India started moving towards independence with anti-British campaigns on the subcontinent during World War II. After the war, the new

19 Richard Stubbs, *Hearts and Minds in Guerrilla Warfare: The Malayan Emergency, 1948–1960* (Singapore, 1989).

Labour government came gradually to the realization that the expense of holding India was incompatible with its policy of austerity and rebuilding at home. At this time most Indians still hoped for a new broadly based federal state, until the violence unleashed by Hindu and Muslim extremists in the lead-up to independence put pressure on communally based Indian political organizations as well as the British government to work towards separating the two confessional groups. While at least five thousand people had died in religious riots by November 1946, the communal killing started in earnest only when the British set a date for their own withdrawal – August 15, 1947. In August 1947 more than fifteen thousand were killed in Punjab alone. In total, between 1 and 2 million died during the violence that accompanied partition.[20]

As soon as the new independent states of India and Pakistan had come into being, they began to compete over Kashmir, the only major part of British India that had opted for independence. Because of the influence of British advisors in both armies, there was hope that war could be avoided. But when the Hindu ruler of Kashmir, a predominantly Muslim state, turned to India for protection against incursions by forces from Pakistan, war became unavoidable. The Kashmiri Maharaja acceded to India in order to get Delhi's military support, as Pakistan invaded from the west. The war lasted for more than a year, as more than fifteen hundred soldiers were killed on the Indian side and at least twice as many on the Pakistani, in addition to substantial civilian losses. Kashmir was divided along a line that gave roughly two-thirds of the state, including the most populous areas, to India. However, the conflict was in no way resolved. It led to another Indo-Pakistani war in 1965, as well as to countless smaller clashes between the two countries.[21]

In the Middle East decolonization was also troubled, especially in Palestine, where the League of Nations had recognized a British mandate after the defeat of the Ottoman Empire in World War I. After lobbying by European and American Zionists, Britain had accepted the principle of a Jewish homeland in the mostly Muslim and Arab region, but had never put it in place, even as Jewish immigration into Palestine increased many times over during the 1930s, in the face of anti-Semitic persecutions in Europe. Clashes among Zionists, Arabs, and the British army increased after World War II, as the main Zionist organizations in Palestine started a campaign to drive the colonial power out and declare an independent Jewish state. In 1947 the British government

20 Ramachandra Guha, *India after Gandhi: The History of the World's Largest Democracy* (New York, 2008), 19–135.

21 Sumantra Bose, *Kashmir: Roots of Conflict, Paths to Peace* (Cambridge, MA, 2005).

decided that it had had enough and turned to the United Nations for a plan to partition Palestine between the two main groups, Arabs and Jews.[22]

In the plan that the United Nations promulgated on November 29, 1947, Palestine was to be divided into six main parts – three each for Arabs and Jews. Given their religious significance, Jerusalem and environs were to be administered by the United Nations but open to people of all faiths. In spite of Arab complaints that with 32 percent of the population the Jews would get 56 percent of Palestine, the partition plan enjoyed broad international support, including from the United States and the Soviet Union, each of which sought to gain advantages in its rivalry with the other. Inside Palestine the main Zionist organizations accepted the partition plan, although grudgingly. However, the Arab leaders, both Muslim and Christian, did not. They wanted a unified Palestine with majority rule.

Fighting broke out as soon as the partition plan was approved in the United Nations. Between November 1947 and the end of the British mandate in May 1948, hundreds of people of all faiths were killed, including some fifty British soldiers. When the Jewish Provisional State Council declared the independent state of Israel on May 14, army units from five Arab countries (Egypt, Iraq, Jordan, Lebanon, and Syria) moved into the region in order to destroy the partition plan. The newly established Israeli forces fought back in a war that lasted for almost a year, despite three brief truces that the United Nations brokered. While the Arab forces had greater numbers of fighters, the better-organized Israelis won several military victories and expanded the territory of their new state significantly, in part by forcing the displacement of Palestinian Arabs. When the war ended in separately negotiated ceasefires in the spring of 1949, Israel had taken 78 percent of Palestine, creating a refugee crisis of massive proportions. Around twenty thousand people had been killed in the fighting, slightly more than a quarter of them Jewish.

The most destructive wars after World War II in terms of military casualties (China, Korea, Vietnam) were driven by clashes between communists and their opponents. These wars fit into a pattern of ideological conflict that had first emerged after the Russian Revolution in 1917 and that became dominant in Europe and East Asia as the wars against Germany and Japan came to an end in 1945. They were civil wars between communists and their opponents, in which the emerging superpowers, the United States and the

22 Benny Morris, *1948: A History of the First Arab-Israeli War* (New Haven, 2009); Eugene L. Rogan and Avi Shlaim, *The War for Palestine: Rewriting the History of 1948* (Cambridge, 2007).

Soviet Union, supported their local allies. But even the wars that were not caused by the ideological clash of the Cold War – the conflicts in south Asia and the Middle East, and, to a lesser extent, Indonesia – reflected the new international system in the constellations of diplomatic and military support. Combined, the wars in the late 1940s and 1950s created the kind of environment in which the Cold War thrived.

While most of the wars after the war were influenced by and, in turn, influenced the global conflict between communism and anti-communism, each of them of course had its own genesis, which depended on local conditions and resentments. In some cases, ethnic and religious identifications were crucial in defining the front lines of conflict, especially as the colonial empires were coming to an end and new power-holders emerged from local communities. It was such conflicts that often – relatively speaking – became most destructive in terms of civilian losses, since whole communities often became targets for what we later in the twentieth century would come to know as ethnic cleansing. In two unique cases new states, which both would be at the center of conflict for generations, emerged out of recent projects of the imagination: In the Middle East, Zionist Jews from Europe, Asia, and North Africa created a new state of Israel, and in South Asia, Islamist Muslims created a new state of Pakistan, in both cases carved out of a multiethnic and multicultural region. In other cases, such as Yugoslavia, the Cold War intervened to put a temporary stop to ethnic or religious conflicts propagated by zealots, visionaries, or in some cases historians with a bit too much originality on their mind.

The experience of all-out warfare during the two world wars and the large volumes of weapons available after the 1939–45 war ended also helped stoke armed conflict during the late 1940s. In many places, such as China, the state was already weakened by war, and in the colonial world the imperialists had lost not only in terms of resources but also in terms of moral authority. In many parts of the world, it had become much easier to grab for the gun in order to settle problems, because war was what the immediate past had been about. In this sense, at least, the wars after the war were indeed continuations of what people had already experienced in their own lifetimes.

19

Weapons technology in the two nuclear ages

C. DALE WALTON

Since the invention of nuclear weapons in 1945, there have been two distinct nuclear ages.[1] The first was marked by technological and quantitative competition between two superpowers, which were radically different and ideologically irreconcilable. As nuclear weapons spread to a modest number of additional states during this period (in a process of "horizontal" proliferation), the first nuclear age was marked generally by a rapid increase in the number of nuclear weapons – "vertical" proliferation – as well as by continuing improvement in the design of both warheads and the vehicles used to deliver them. The total number of nuclear weapons deployed worldwide began to decrease during the closing years of the first nuclear age, but vertical deproliferation only accelerated during the second nuclear age, which began on December 25, 1991 with the fall of the Soviet Union. The second nuclear age, however, also has been notable for continuing horizontal proliferation. The number of states that possess nuclear weapons has steadily increased, and there is little reason to believe that the trend will soon reverse. In the current nuclear age, moreover, improvement in warhead and delivery-vehicle design has been modest. Such technologies have improved at a leisurely pace, whereas the rate of technological advancement in these areas was frenetic during the first nuclear age.

The two superpowers of the first nuclear age were different in almost every respect. The United States was a wealthy society, which had traditionally been reluctant to involve itself deeply in European affairs. Although it had

1 The distinction between the first and second nuclear ages is explored in Colin S. Gray, *The Second Nuclear Age* (Boulder, 1999); Keith B. Payne, *Deterrence in the Second Nuclear Age* (Lexington, KY, 1996); Keith B. Payne, *The Great American Gamble: Deterrence Theory and Practice from the Cold War to the Twenty-First Century* (Fairfax, VA, 2008); C. Dale Walton, "Navigating the Second Nuclear Age: Proliferation and Deterrence in this Century," *Global Dialogue* 8 (2006): 22–31; and C. Dale Walton, "The Second Nuclear Age: Nuclear Weapons in the Twenty-First Century," in John Baylis et al., eds., *Strategy in the Contemporary World: An Introduction to Strategic Studies* (3rd edn., Oxford, 2010), 208–26.

occasionally fought European powers (as in the American Revolution, the War of 1812, the naval Quasi-War with France, and the Spanish–American War), not until 1917 did the United States, which by then had the world's largest economy, become involved in an effort to shape profoundly the strategic environment in Europe.[2] Even thereafter, during the interwar period, Washington remained a reluctant participant in great-power gamesmanship.[3] In the aftermath of World War II, however, the United States took on the role of protector of the western European democracies as a matter of perceived necessity.

The Soviet Union, by contrast, was the successor to an empire that had been a significant player in great-power politics at least since the reign of Peter the Great. Traditionally, however, it had been perceived – by Europeans and Russians alike – as having a unique identity that was only partially European.[4] Then, at the close of World War I, the Orthodox, monarchical, and underdeveloped Russian Empire began to transform itself into something entirely new, a Soviet civilization that was based on Marxism–Leninism and seemed to have universal ideological pretensions.[5] Soviet citizens remained poor, but by dedicating a vast amount of national wealth to foreign intelligence, domestic security, and military power, the new regime made itself a totalitarian great power.[6] Although the Soviet government made near-fatal military errors in the months after the German invasion of 1941,[7] the regime's focus on military power and social control proved successful, if ruinously costly to the Soviet citizenry. The Soviet Union emerged from World War II as a superpower, with a central European empire and credible claims to hegemony over the Eurasian continent.

2 On the "great-power trajectory" of the United States, see George C. Herring, *From Colony to Superpower: US Foreign Relations since 1775* (New York, 2009); Alan R. Millett and Peter Maslowski, *For the Common Defense: A Military History of the United States of America* (New York, 1994).

3 See, for example, Benjamin D. Rhodes, *United States Foreign Policy in the Interwar Period: The Golden Age of American Military and Foreign Policy Complacency* (Westport, CT, 2001).

4 Russian national identity and its relationship to "Europeanness" is discussed extensively in James Billington, *The Icon and the Axe: An Interpretive History of Russian Culture* (New York, 1966) and Richard Pipes, *Russia under the Old Regime* (2nd edn., New York, 1997).

5 On the effort to create a Soviet civilization, see Andrei Sinyavsky, *Soviet Civilization: A Cultural History* (New York, 1990).

6 See James J. Schneider, *The Structure of Strategic Revolution: Total War and the Roots of the Soviet Warfare State* (Novato, CA, 1994).

7 The reasons for these gross military errors and the USSR's subsequent recovery from them are explored in David M. Glantz, *Stumbling Colossus: The Red Army on the Eve of World War* (Lawrence, KS, 1998); David M. Glantz, *Colossus Reborn: The Red Army at War, 1941–1943* (Lawrence, KS, 2005).

34. "Little Boy" – the first atomic bomb being loaded onto the *Enola Gay*

The first explosion of a nuclear weapon – a fission device, often referred to as an atomic bomb – was the "Trinity" test at White Sands, New Mexico in July 1945, after the war in Europe had ended. Shortly thereafter, in August, the two remaining fission warheads in the American nuclear arsenal were dropped on Hiroshima and Nagasaki. They were code-named respectively "Little Boy" and "Fat Man"; the former was a simple "gun-type" design, the latter a more complex and efficient implosion warhead similar to the one tested at White Sands.

Whether the dropping of two nuclear weapons was the catalyst for the Japanese surrender remains one of the most contested issues in military-diplomatic history. The Soviet Union's entry into the war against Japan and the Red Army's shattering drive into Manchuria was arguably a more important factor in Tokyo's decision to accept American surrender terms.[8] However, the belief that nuclear weapons had brought the termination of the Pacific War influenced attitudes toward these devices, feeding the perception that they were overwhelmingly potent. Nonetheless, nuclear weapons

8 Ward Wilson, "The Winning Weapon? Rethinking Nuclear Weapons in Light of Hiroshima," *International Security* 31 (2007): 162–79.

did not play a significant role in bringing about the Cold War. The mistrust between Washington and Moscow was based on incompatible ideologies. Each power saw the other as a foe, and both were correct. They held clashing worldviews and visions of global political order, so their mutual suspicion and antipathy were logical. Moreover, the old multipolar order had been broken by World War II, and a new bipolar system was emerging.[9] This geopolitical fact further strained the Soviet–American relationship, as the two superpowers competed to shape the international security environment.

World War II had provided the context for the Manhattan Project, but the political tensions of the Cold War guided the subsequent development of nuclear technology, as well as the number of nuclear weapons deployed. One of the most notable characteristics of the first three decades of the Cold War was the speed with which the superpowers developed large, technically mature nuclear arsenals. After 1945, nuclear technical development continued at a rapid pace, with ongoing improvements in nuclear warhead design. One of the most critical was the development of devices – commonly referred to as "hydrogen" or "thermonuclear" weapons – that had explosive yields far greater than those of atomic bombs. "Fat Man" had a yield of about 21 kilotons; the explosive power of "Little Boy" was smaller. The first explosion of a thermonuclear device, the American "Ivy Mike" test in 1952, appeared to result in a yield of over 10 megatons. "Mike's fireball alone would have engulfed Manhattan," as Richard Rhodes writes. "Its blast would have obliterated all New York City's five boroughs."[10] The subsequent deployment of thermonuclear weapons made it possible to deliver a far greater tonnage of firepower with the same number of vehicles, making more plausible an attempt by one power to obliterate the other in a one-day war.[11]

World War II had provided a case study in defense against bomber attack. The lesson was clear. Contrary to Stanley Baldwin's famous prewar assertion, the bomber did not always get through. Although the postwar development of large, fast jet bombers created new challenges, antiaircraft forces later enjoyed an advantage in the rapid postwar development of fighter aircraft, radar, communications, and antiaircraft rocketry. Thus the offensive bombing

9 See C. Dale Walton, *Geopolitics and the Great Powers in the Twenty-First Century: Multipolarity and the Revolution in Strategic Perspective* (London, 2007), 1–5.

10 Richard Rhodes, *Dark Sun: The Making of the Hydrogen Bomb* (New York, 1996), 510. Large warheads are more suited to military than civilian targets. The latter, "soft" targets are usually targeted with numerous smaller warheads.

11 See Colin S. Gray, *War, Peace and International Relations: An Introduction to Strategic History* (London, 2007), 210.

techniques honed in World War II were largely inapplicable in the postwar world, given changing defense technology, the cost of intercontinental bombers and their payloads, and the explosive power offered by nuclear weapons.[12] An intercontinental bomber armed with nuclear weapons was an extraordinary but vulnerable instrument. If a large number of them were used, some would penetrate an air-defense network, however large the resources the United States and the USSR devoted to air defenses during the early Cold War. Which targets would be hit was, however, unknowable in advance, and targets that the enemy valued highly, such as major cities, had thick defenses. The US Strategic Air Command (SAC) was confident that it could destroy Moscow, but this claim was never tested.

The development of intercontinental ballistic missiles (ICBMs) and submarine-launched ballistic missile (SLBMs) changed the "strategic atmosphere" of the first nuclear age. The first operational ballistic missile had been the German V-2 (the V-1 was a cruise, not a ballistic, missile). It entered service only late in the war, but it would not have fulfilled Germany's desire for a *Wunderwaffe* even had it been used throughout the conflict.[13] The V-2s were not without military value; they caused significant damage to the Antwerp docks, which were logistically critical for the Allied forces operating in western Europe. However, the missile was too imperfect to be a decisive weapon; it carried a small payload and was both inaccurate and limited in range.

As Steven J. Zaloga notes, "the early atomic bombs were so large that an intercontinental missile seemed decades in the future. The most important breakthrough came in warhead design. The advent of small thermonuclear weapons weighing under five tons completely changed the prospects for the ICBM."[14] By 1959 both the United States and the USSR had deployed thermonuclear-tipped ICBMs – the Atlas and R-7, respectively.[15] Ballistic missile submarines (SSBNs) entered service at approximately the same time. The USS *George Washington* began its first patrol in December 1960; however, given technical challenges and the ability of long-range submarines to

12 The critical figure in the development of SAC was General Curtis LeMay. See Warren Kozak, *LeMay: The Life and War of General Curtis LeMay* (Washington, DC, 2009).

13 On the V-2 program, see T. D. Dungan, *V-2: A Combat History of the First Ballistic Missile* (Yardley, PA, 2005); Michael Neufield, *The Rocket and the Reich: Peenemünde and the Coming of the Ballistic Missile Era* (Cambridge, MA, 1994); and Michael Neufield, *Von Braun: Dreamer of Space, Engineer of War* (New York, 2007), 116–98.

14 Steven J. Zaloga, *The Kremlin's Nuclear Sword: The Rise and Fall of Russia's Strategic Nuclear Forces, 1945–2000* (Washington, DC, 2002), 19.

15 For a detailed history of the early decades of the Soviet civil and military missile-building program, see Boris Chertok, *Rockets and People* (3 vols., Washington, DC, 2005–10), Vols. I and II.

35. Displaying an ICBM at a Coney Island amusement park

approach an enemy coast, intercontinental SLBMs were not deployed until later.[16] The combination of thermonuclear weapons and ballistic missile technology was formidable, and developments in one technology encouraged progress in the other. In fact, the prospect that thermonuclear warheads

16 On the development of submarine technology during the Cold War, see Norman Polmar and K. J. Moore, *Cold War Submarines: The Design and Construction of US and Soviet Submarines, 1945–2001* (Dulles, VA, 2003).

might be mated with missiles had originally driven interest in ICBMs, because inaccuracy and high cost had made long-range ballistic missiles impractical platforms for delivering conventional – or perhaps even atomic – warheads.

Absent effective ballistic missile defenses, ICBMs and SLBMs were invulnerable following launch. Yet, they or their warheads might fail because of technical flaws or miss the target. Planners took these issues into account when they assigned nuclear warheads to enemy targets. In sufficient numbers, however, ICBMs and SLBMs guaranteed the devastation of the enemy homeland, assuming that they were not preemptively destroyed and that the communication link between political decision-makers and war-fighters was not severed. Moreover, improvements in warhead and missile design further enhanced the capabilities of both land- and sea-based missiles. Most importantly, the development of MRVs (multiple reentry vehicles) and, later, of MIRVs (multiple independent reentry vehicles) made it possible for single missiles to deliver warheads to multiple targets.

Together with bombers, land- and sea-based missiles formed a Triad, whose three "legs" would have been nearly impossible to destroy in even the most brilliant first strike. In particular, nuclear-powered submarine fleets carrying SLBMs would have survived. Although submarines in port could be destroyed, those on patrol in the world's oceans represented a compelling retaliatory threat. Moreover, until late in the Cold War, SLBMs were not highly accurate, a fact that decreased their utility for most counterforce targets – targets with high military value, including nuclear forces – but it did not undermine their value for "revenge strikes" against enemy cities. Thus, assumptions about the possibility of military victory, which been held throughout history, were overturned. It was now possible for the "undead" remnant of a devastated country immediately to inflict devastating damage on an enemy. This truth provided a novel strategic problem for war-planners.

The mating of bombers and missiles through nuclear technology also compressed the likely time frame of a major war and nullified the protection offered by favorable geography. The two world wars had been tests of economic endurance and social cohesion as much as of military competence. Every major combatant had to balance military calculations with social and economic circumstances over an extended period. The world wars, in short, required grand strategic thinking. A general nuclear war, however, could take place in an afternoon; it would represent an operational exercise, albeit one with staggering economic, social, and political implications. This fact encouraged those who framed nuclear strategy to focus on weapons and delivery vehicles – numbers, capabilities, and vulnerabilities. The focus on hardware also had a significant disadvantage, insofar as it encouraged strategic planners – Americans in particular – to regard deterrence as a solvable problem rather than an uncertain art.

Technological development was not confined to strategic weapons. Both superpowers produced an array of tactical devices, from land-based intermediate-range ballistic missiles (IRBMs) – whose role largely was indistinguishable from that of ICBMs – to nuclear depth-charges for anti-submarine warfare and nuclear demolitions that would be delivered by special operators. Moreover, advanced warhead-designs could manipulate nuclear effects. For example, enhanced radiation weapons (ERWs), commonly known as neutron bombs, minimized blast and heat but increased the ionizing radiation released by the weapon, decreasing damage to material structures but enhancing the weapon's lethality against targets such as armored columns.

The nuclear warhead was an agile military instrument. It could be used in a variety of ways, and this fact underlay one of the great challenges of the Cold War – determining the role that nuclear weapons should play in future warfare, including expeditionary conflicts. Many American policymakers were willing to consider using nuclear weapons during the Korean War and in assisting the French to break the siege of Dien Bien Phu in 1954.[17] In the late 1950s, the US army adopted a "Pentomic" division-structure, which was believed to be well suited to tactical nuclear war-fighting, although, for a variety of reasons, it was soon abandoned. In fact, any use of nuclear weapons on the battlefield became increasingly controversial, particularly in the United States. This aversion was commonly called "the nuclear taboo" – a phrase that perhaps overstated the case, but nuclear powers clearly were reluctant to use these weapons.[18] The development of tactical nuclear devices with varying yields and effects has not yet undermined the broad perception that the nuclear warhead is uniquely horrible – that it is, in Bernard Brodie's famous phrase, "the absolute weapon."[19]

There is a fundamental difference between an improbable victory and an impossible one. The latter is delusional. In certain circumstances, however, it may be wise to plan to win the former. The proposition that victory was impossible in a nuclear war represented a comforting illusion.

17 See Roger Kimball, *Nixon's Vietnam War* (Lawrence, KS, 1998), 20–25.

18 See Keith B. Payne et al., *Rationale and Requirements for US Nuclear Forces and Arms Control,* Vol II: *Foundation Report* (Fairfax, VA, 2001), A3–A11.

19 See Bernard Brodie, ed., *The Absolute Weapon: Atomic Power and World Order* (New York, 1946). A more recent view is offered in T. V. Paul et al., eds., *The Absolute Weapon Revisited: Nuclear Arms and the Emerging International Order* (Ann Arbor, 2000).

In a conflict between the United States and the Soviet Union the most credible scenarios for a "kinetic" employment of nuclear weapons (a term that referred to the explosion of such devices, not coercion by the threat of their use) required that these devices be used sparingly, in order to convince one side to abandon its war aims. If World War III were to have started with a Soviet invasion of western Europe, which was the most likely scenario for military conflict between the superpowers, the strategic stakes would have been high for both Washington and Moscow, but for the Americans at least, immediate survival would not have been at stake. Thus, room for diplomatic maneuver survived even in the intense wartime environment.

After World War II, however, there was no reliable way to translate limited nuclear use into victory. In a conflict between the United States and the Soviet Union, nuclear weapons could in theory have been used in many ways to convince one side to surrender, but it was impossible to determine whether any of them would have worked. The physical communication between the superpowers would have been uncertain in such a war, and leaders on both sides would have encountered enormous mental strain and impaired judgment. Potential miscommunication of intent and fears of deception complicated the scenario further.[20] Despite the enormous sums that each superpower spent on command, control, and communication, even intrastate communications between civilian and military leaders might well have broken down for weeks or months after a nuclear exchange. A decapitating strike admittedly could have eliminated one side's military and political leaders, producing political chaos that would render a prompt retaliatory response impossible, but the decapitated power might well eventually seek revenge.

Once the USSR achieved nuclear parity with the United States, both superpowers found it almost impossible to execute a disarming strike. Still, both continued to construct war plans that included first strikes against the enemy's national territory. Officials in both countries planned for a limited nuclear war, hoping that it might remain tactical, confined to soil that belonged to neither superpower.[21] It is impossible to judge how these limited nuclear-war scenarios might have played out.

20 The many quandaries of nuclear escalation are discussed at length in Herman Kahn, *On Escalation: Metaphors and Scenarios* (New York, 1965).

21 Perhaps the most influential discussion of limited nuclear conflict is Henry A. Kissinger, *Nuclear Weapons and Foreign Policy* (New York, 1969). Soon after publishing the original edition of the book in 1958, Kissinger began to move away from the idea that limited nuclear war was diplomatically plausible.

The enormous risks of nuclear conflict were reflected in the doctrines of the two superpowers. In the early postwar period, neither state saw the nuclear weapon as a "magic bullet," which could guarantee a speedy victory. Despite the United States' temporary monopoly on nuclear weapons after the end of World War II, its war plans assumed that a military conflict with the USSR would be a long, difficult endeavor in which all combat arms would play an important role.[22] As the American arsenal grew, however, it became increasingly unlikely that a Soviet–American conflict would be a multi-year struggle. Now what one might call the "SAC vision" – that a third world war would be won or lost on its first day – became prominent in US military thinking, although the notion was not unchallenged in the US defense establishment, even within the air force. The closest the United States came to embracing an offensive strategy for nuclear war with the Soviet Union was under the Eisenhower administration, the period in which the United States enjoyed its greatest nuclear advantage over the USSR. Although it had lost its monopoly, the United States possessed a much larger nuclear arsenal than it had during the Truman years. Eisenhower's "New Look" and the defense decisions that flowed from it were largely budget-driven. The administration believed that the United States should not compete with the USSR in conventional arms and that a strategy of deterrence (and, if need be, war) based on nuclear weapons would be more affordable.[23]

During the 1950s and after, many American thinkers believed that a nuclear conflict could be limited in scope.[24] Soviet military thinkers also wrestled with the problem of how nuclear weapons affected the character of war, and they too wondered whether the concept of limited war was relevant to a Soviet–American conflict.[25]

Any nuclear conflict would have been dangerous to the superpowers and their allies, as well as to neutral states, which might suffer immensely from

22 See Steven T. Ross, *American War Plans, 1945–1950: Strategies for Defeating the Soviet Union* (London, 1996).

23 For a brief but thoughtful discussion of the "new look," see Colin S. Gray, *Strategic Studies and Public Policy: The American Experience* (Lexington, KY, 1982), 40–44.

24 See Kissinger, *Nuclear Weapons and Foreign Policy*.

25 See V. D. Sokolovsky, ed., *Military Strategy: Soviet Doctrine and Concepts* (New York, 1963). As Raymond L. Garthoff notes in his introduction to this translation, "Limited and local wars have not generally been discussed in Soviet military writing: they have stressed rather the danger or even 'inevitability' of escalation to general war ... Marshal Sokolovsky and his colleagues say very little about limited war, but what they do say is important: for the first time, this authoritative volume flatly admits the possibility of limited war with the Western powers, and says that the Soviet Union and its allies must prepare for this contingency" (xvi).

"spill-over" environmental effects and economic damage. However, numerous scenarios were imaginable in which a nuclear conflict had a clear winner, which had suffered no or survivable damage to its homeland while achieving its strategic objectives. For much of the Cold War, Soviet military and political discourse on nuclear matters was dominated by this view.[26]

In the United States, on the other hand, the theory that nuclear war was winnable was regarded with distaste, even during the era of clear American supremacy.[27] Publicly and privately, most US policymakers preferred to speak of deterrence rather than war-winning. The technical planning for nuclear victory was a military matter, in which the civilian policy-establishment professed little interest. Even today the Cuban missile crisis in 1962 is commonly perceived as an event that almost triggered mutual Soviet–American annihilation when, in fact, Moscow possessed only a limited ability to strike the continental United States, while the United States probably could have obliterated the Soviet Union. The United States' allies in NATO were more vulnerable to Soviet nuclear weapons, but the fact that the United States itself was less exposed – and that both sides knew it – was a critical factor in the resolution of the crisis.[28] Nevertheless, although mutual assured destruction (MAD) did not emerge as doctrine until the mid 1960s, its intellectual seeds were present in US thinking well before.

What might be termed "MAD thinking" reflected and reinforced the predilection of many American policymakers and defense intellectuals to avoid grappling with the dangers of a large Soviet nuclear stockpile. They reasoned that if both sides were rational and mutual destruction was assured in any nuclear conflict, Moscow never would launch a nuclear war. The weaknesses of MAD lurked beneath its seemingly straightforward logic. MAD relied on arbitrary assumptions about what the USSR considered

26 Much work remains to be done on the development of Soviet views about nuclear usage. Existing works include Raymond L. Garthoff, *Deterrence and the Revolution in Soviet Military Doctrine* (Washington, DC, 1990); David M. Glantz, *The Military Strategy of the Soviet Union: A History* (London, 2004); William E. Odom, *Collapse of the Soviet Military* (New Haven, 1998); Pavel Podvig, *Russian Strategic Nuclear Forces* (Boston, 2004); and Harriet Fast Scott and William L. Scott, eds., *The Soviet Art of War: Doctrine, Strategy, and Tactics* (Boulder, 1982).

27 This view was reflected in the aversion among the US policy elite to the work of Herman Kahn, particularly *On Thermonuclear War* (Princeton, 1960).

28 As Sharon Ghamari-Tabrizi notes of the illusory "missile gap," of which Kennedy warned during the presidential campaign of 1960, "While his election campaign blared the bad news of Soviet missile superiority, by the time President Kennedy bearded Khrushchev in Berlin in 1961 and Cuba the following year, he knew better. The prospect of hundreds of 'operational but undetected' [Soviet] missiles no longer stabbed at his imagination." *The Worlds of Herman Kahn* (Cambridge, MA, 2005), 123.

unacceptable damage, and it assumed that Soviet leaders, too, accepted the logic of mutual destruction. Moreover, in order for MAD to function as intended, all parties had to be rational, reasonable, and at least somewhat risk-averse. A leader with a gambler's instincts, however, might reject the logic of MAD and treat the prospect of annihilation as a necessary risk.

Nuclear weapons seemed to lie outside the realm of "normal" military hardware and to take an almost mystical character. Fittingly, a line from *The Bhagavad-Gita* came to Robert Oppenheimer's mind immediately after the Trinity test: "Now I am become death, the destroyer of worlds."[29] MAD took it to its logical extreme, treating inanimate weapons as determinants of human decisions. In fact, planners framed nuclear strategy in ways that reflected personal beliefs, preferences, and fears. Illogical actions resulted. American leaders could believe simultaneously that MAD "worked," hence that nuclear war was impossible, and maintain an arsenal far larger than than the modest, survivable "revenge force" that MAD required. They also created Single Integrated Operational Plan (SIOP) counterforce options which were predicated on the assumption that victory was possible in a nuclear conflict.[30]

The difficulties of crafting nuclear strategy underlined the importance and limitations of intelligence in the Cold War. The superpowers spent vast amounts of money on intelligence, and technical intelligence-gathering became immensely sophisticated, but neither state felt confident in predicting the behavior of its rival. The conduct of superpowers was variable and depended on all manner of factors, making each side difficult to understand. Given the opacity of its government, the Soviet Union was a challenging object of study, and Sovietologists rivaled astrologers in the reliability of their predictions. Despite the USSR's obsession with intelligence-gathering and analysis, and despite the comparative openness of the US system, Moscow did not have sound insight into American behavior. One of the most dangerous intelligence errors of the Cold War occurred in 1983, when Soviet analysts concluded that the United States was planning a preemptive nuclear strike on the USSR.[31]

29 Richard Rhodes, *The Making of the Atomic Bomb* (New York: 1988), 676.

30 "The evidence in deeds in defense preparation in the arms competition is overwhelming in pointing to the fact that neither the Soviet Union nor the United States was content with a context of mutual assured destruction. They may have struggled in vain to escape its logic and prospective reality, but struggle they did. Neither side was willing to abandon all hope of being able to employ nuclear weapons in search of strategic advantage." Gray, *War, Peace and International Relations*, 213.

31 See Ronald E. Powaski, *Return to Armageddon: The United States and the Nuclear Arms Race, 1981–1999* (New York, 2000), 40–42; Peter Vincent Pry, *War Scare: Russia and America on the Nuclear Brink* (Westport, CT, 1999), 33–44.

Particularly in the final decades of the Cold War, as space-based satellites became refined tools for gathering data, intelligence provided a general picture of a state's nuclear capabilities. Both superpowers operated nuclear warhead- and missile-building programs of staggering size, and thus vulnerable to observation. In the Soviet case, the nuclear-weapons industry was one of the country's largest. Many activities that were associated with the deployment and maintenance of nuclear weapons (such as the construction or decommissioning of missile silos) also could be verified from space. Judging political intentions on this basis was more problematic. In this sense, the "intelligence story" of the Cold War was much as it had been throughout history. Mountains of technical data were details in a long-term and often unsuccessful effort to understand the intentions of a military competitor.

Since early in the first nuclear age, a variety of international initiatives have sought to control horizontal nuclear proliferation. Although proliferation has occurred nevetheless, these initiatives were not failures. Without them, the number of nuclear powers would probably be greater than it is today.

During the first nuclear age, the bipolarity of the global political system worked against horizontal proliferation. Each superpower discouraged proliferation among its security dependents and supported multinational treaties and other instruments to control the spread of nuclear arms. The "nuclear umbrella" that both powers promised to their allies also slowed proliferation.

The second nuclear age has not yet seen a radical increase in the number of nuclear states (and no non-state actor is yet known to have obtained nuclear weaponry). However, this pattern may change. Although it is an impoverished backwater by almost any standard, North Korea has built nuclear weapons and delivery vehicles, and it has shared its weapons-related knowledge with other rogue states.[32] For a number of years, a well-functioning but covert international enterprise, the A. Q. Khan network, traded in nuclear

32 In April 2008, US intelligence publicly alleged that the Syrian program was connected to North Korea. If the intelligence analysis was accurate, the Syrian case demonstrates how nuclear technology can spread, like a disease, from one "carrier" to another. Knowledge may have passed from the A. Q. Khan network to Pyongyang to Damascus. A potential Syrian reactor – apparently still at an early stage of construction – was destroyed by an Israeli airstrike on September 6, 2007. See Robin Wright, "N. Koreans Taped at Syrian Reactor," *Washington Post*, April 24, 2008: www.washingtonpost.com/wp-dyn/content/article/2008/04/23/AR2008042302906.html. Syria remains secretive about the demolished facility. See IAEA Director General, "Implementation of the NPT Safeguards Agreement in the Syrian Arab Republic," August 28, 2009: www.isis-online.org/publications/syria/IAEA_Syria_Report_28August2009.pdf.

technology out of Pakistan.[33] Its clientele included North Korea, Libya,[34] and Iran.[35]

The greatest barriers to horizontal proliferation have been practical. The basic technologies of nuclear weapons and long-range delivery vehicles are old. SLBMs were invented about a decade before the creation of the modern microprocessor. Still, building a military-grade nuclear weapon requires a high degree of engineering sophistication.[36] Acquiring fissile material sufficient to create a critical mass has been difficult for state actors such as Iran, because "bomb-ready" fissile material is not available on the international open market. In this respect, the global community appears to have been lucky when the Soviet Union disintegrated, for, as far as can be determined, no nuclear weapons were transferred out of former Soviet territory.[37]

International bodies control the supply of nuclear technology and fissile material. The most notable of these bodies are the International Atomic Energy Agency (IAEA) and the Nuclear Suppliers Group (NSG). The American-led Proliferation Security Initiative (PSI) is an important recent development in the construction of an international "nuclear web" to trap or discourage would-be proliferators. The voluntary, non-treaty Ballistic Missile Control Regime (BMCR) also seeks, albeit less effectively, to coordinate international efforts to prevent the spread of ballistic missles.

The "central node" in global nonproliferation is the Nonproliferation Treaty. It divides the world's states into two categories – the five authorized

33 On the A. Q. Khan network, see David Armstrong and Joseph J. Trento, *America and the Islamic Bomb: The Deadly Compromise* (Hanover, NH, 2007); Douglas Franz and Catherine Collins, *The Nuclear Jihadist: The True Story of the Man Who Sold the World's Most Dangerous Secrets . . . and How We Could Have Stopped Him* (New York, 2007); William Langewiesche, *The Atomic Bazaar: The Rise of the Nuclear Poor* (New York, 2007); Adrian Levy and Catherine Scott-Clark, *Deception: Pakistan, the United States, and the Secret Trade in Nuclear Weapons* (New York, 2007). Although the Pakistani government denies its involvement, the network could hardly have functioned without the support of at least some parts of Pakistan's state-security apparatus.

34 The Libyan decision to discontinue its nuclear program has elicited little public or academic interest, but it may provide lessons for future counterproliferation efforts. For a key US negotiator's perspective on the Libyan case, see Robert G. Joseph, *Countering WMD: The Libyan Experience* (Fairfax, VA, 2009).

35 On Burma, see Desmond Ball and Phil Thornton, "Burma's Nuclear Secrets," *Sydney Morning Herald*, August 1, 2009: www.smh.com.au/news/world/burma8217s-nuclear-secrets/2009/07/31/1248977193933.html.

36 See Frank Barnaby, *How to Build a Nuclear Bomb: And Other Weapons of Mass Destruction* (New York, 2004), 110–17.

37 The vulnerability of Pakistan's nuclear arsenal to seizure by terrorists is discussed in Shaun Gregory, "The Terrorist Threat to Pakistan's Nuclear Arsenal," *Combating Terrorism Center at West Point Sentinel* 2 (July 2009): 1–4: www.ctc.usma.edu/sentinel/CTCSentinel-Vol2Iss7.pdf.

nuclear states (the Soviet Union/Russia, United States, United Kingdom, PRC, and France) and all other signatory states. While the five nuclear states are obligated in theory to move toward complete disarmament, they have not done so; and non-nuclear states have been quick to criticize the "NPT five." Under the treaty non-nuclear states may not acquire (nor even seek to acquire) nuclear weapons; and the overwhelming majority of them fulfill this requirement. A few – India, Pakistan, and Israel – have not signed the treaty. Other past and present proliferators are (or were) under the treaty's discipline. North Korea announced its withdrawal from the treaty in 2003, long after Pyongyang's nuclear-weapons program got underway, while South Africa built and later dismantled its nuclear arsenal, never altering its NPT status. Iraq was legally bound by the treaty when it had an active nuclear program, as was Libya; Iran is still party to the NPT but has a nuclear weapons program.[38] Whether Syria has a program is more questionable, but both are treaty signatories.

There has been no attempt in recent decades to control the spread of conventional weapons technology or building capability. It is taken for granted that if a buyer can be found, the seller may transfer weapons, along with the knowledge to build them (typically via some form of licensed-production agreement). In recent decades, most "anti-weapon" efforts have focused on low-technology weapons that threaten civilian populations in a way that is disproportionate to their military value – such as land mines and cluster munitions – or that feed civil conflicts in the Third World, as small arms allegedly do.

Along with their chemical, biological, and radiological siblings in the broad category "weapons of mass destruction" (WMDs), nuclear weapons present a great danger to civilians, but they are different from anti-personnel land mines. The fear of WMDs and particularly nuclear weapons relates to the potential that they have to kill and injure military personnel and civilians quickly and on a massive scale. As a result, even when would-be proliferators make a plausible strategic argument to support their desire for nuclear weapons, the tendency within the global community has been to reject the proposition that national interests justify the acquisition of such arms.

38 On the Iranian attitude toward nuclear acquisition, see Shahram Chubin, *Iran's Nuclear Ambitions* (Washington, DC, 2006); Alireza Jafarzadeh, *The Iranian Threat: President Ahmadinejad and the Coming Nuclear Crisis* (New York, 2008); Yossi Melman, *The Nuclear Sphinx of Tehran: Mahmoud Ahmadinejad and the State of Iran* (New York, 2007).

Despite the general effectiveness of the nonproliferation system for controlling the dissemination of knowledge and fissile material, the danger of proliferation grows as nuclear technology spreads to rogue actors, increasing the possibility of a phenomenon that we have not yet seen – a "cascade effect," in which the number of nuclear states (and, possibly, non-state actors) increases dramatically over a short period of time. The control of nuclear technology is all the more difficult because fissile material can also be used in energy generation. This fact complicates the relationship between military and civilian technological applications. Early in the first nuclear age, there was a global consensus that all states had a right to access civilian nuclear technology. The problem, however, was that there is no clear separation between civilian and military nuclear technologies; reactors that generate power can also produce the fissile material for warheads. Effective international oversight is required to prevent diversion of fissile material. States that are inclined to proliferate, however, have proved adept at getting access to "peaceful" nuclear technology while maintaining a nuclear weapons program. This problem is likely to increase. For a variety of reasons, including concern over fossil fuels and their link to climate change, numerous countries are interested in starting new, or expanding existing, civilian nuclear programs. As the number of reactors rises along with the number of states that possess reactors, the challenges to the IAEA in controlling the flow of fissile materials also will increase.

The history of the first nuclear age provides little guidance to the present or future, because the strategic dynamics of the two nuclear ages differ. Some of the decisions by "lower-tier" nuclear powers during the previous nuclear age are instructive, however. There have been allegations that during the 1973 Yom Kippur War, when Israel thought that its national survival was at risk, it edged toward the use of nuclear weapons, but moved away from this stance once it became clear that the country would not be overrun by its Arab enemies. Mao Zedong's China was a cautious nuclear actor despite its ideological radicalism. Rather than maximizing the production of warheads and delivery vehicles, Mao made expensive preparations for a long war on Chinese soil against American or Soviet invaders, for he thought that the nuclear superiority of China's enemies could be countered in such a war.[39] Nevertheless, the main theme of the first nuclear age was the interaction of the two superpowers.

39 See Barry Naughton, "The Third Front: Defence Industrialization in the Chinese Interior," *China Quarterly* 115 (September 1988): 351–86.

The current, second nuclear age has been marked more by the threat of horizontal proliferation of nuclear weapons and ballistic missiles, as well as the potential use of nuclear weapons by rogue actors. In the meantime, the number of warheads possessed by Russia and the United States has diminished, and this trend will continue in the foreseeable future. The post-Cold War political environment has undercut the strategic utility of large nuclear arsenals for both powers. The relationship between the United States and Russia remains difficult, but in the absence of a credible Russian threat to NATO, both Democratic and Republican US presidents have seen little need to maintain as large an arsenal as they did during the Cold War. Similarly, except in the imagination of Russian ultra-nationalists, Russia faces neither a plausible threat from NATO nor the prospect of an American first strike.[40] Thus, Moscow also has reduced the size of its arsenal, presumably without undermining its national security.

There is no overriding military reason why the American and Russian arsenals should remain equal in size. Indeed, the administration of George W. Bush attempted – albeit unsuccessfully – to discard the Cold War arms-control model and craft a new one that would better suit the realities of the second nuclear age.[41] Nuclear numbers would be flexible, rather than bound by bilateral negotiations; many warheads could be placed in storage. This arrangement would allow short-term decreases in nuclear numbers while providing the option for a larger arsenal should the strategic environment worsen. The administration, however, encountered opposition both in Russia and the United States.

For most American critics, opposition reflected intellectual discomfort. The Cold War arms-control model was familiar. Most defenders of "arms-control traditionalism" were Democrats, who distrusted the administration's intentions and believed that its efforts were intended to break, rather than adapt, arms control. Beyond its own mistrust of the Bush administration, Moscow's objections flowed from its desire to maintain the perception of parity with the United States. The bilateral arms-control dynamic encouraged the impression of equality between the two negotiating powers. In reality, by the turn of the twenty-first century the two largest nuclear powers were profoundly unequal. The United States was by far the most powerful state in the world, and Russia

40 Stephen J. Cimbala argues convincingly that Russia still maintains more warheads than it requires for nuclear deterrence. "Russia's Nuclear Deterrent: Realistic or Uncertain," *Comparative Strategy* 26 (2007): 185–203.

41 See Keith B. Payne et al., *Rationale and Requirements for US Nuclear Forces and Arms Control* (2 vols., Fairfax, VA, 2001).

appeared to be in long-term decline, as its population descreased and its economy (aside from extraction-related industries) stagnated.[42]

Ultimately, the Bush administration did not substantially alter the Cold War pattern of arms control, as it signed the bilateral Treaty of Moscow in 2002. Because the treaty incorporated many features that the administration had desired – such as the "floating" of nuclear numbers within a given range – it could claim that the treaty broke with the Cold War arms-control model. In fact, however, the central feature of this model remained unaltered. Bilateral treaties continue to guide US and Russian nuclear numbers. This fact was confirmed when the Obama administration signed the New Strategic Arms Reduction Treaty (New START) agreement in April 2010. (The recent treaty is called New START to differentiate it from the START I and START II agreements, which were signed, respectively, in 1991 and 1993.)

The states that are most likely to use nuclear weapons in combat – or to provide them to terrorists – have not been involved in these negotiations. The evidence is thin in any case that bilateral arms control discourages horizontal proliferation. Nuclear tests by India and Pakistan occurred in 1998, as the US and Russian arsenals were shrinking; and the drop in nuclear numbers since the 1980s has had no apparent impact on Iranian or North Korean behavior. Moreover, China, a thriving great power, continues to modernize and increase (albeit slowly) the size of its nuclear arsenal and shows little interest in arms-control agreements.[43]

During the first nuclear age, the question of ballistic missile defense (BMD) remained highly controversial in US political discourse, although the reasons for the controversy varied over time. During the early period of BMD development, the chief question was whether an effective and financially feasible defensive system could be deployed. There was good reason for doubt in both respects. As time passed and the logic of MAD took hold, however, a new concern arose – that BMD might be thought reliable enough to undermine MAD. If one superpower believed that it could launch a first strike while shielding itself from retaliation, it might be tempted to do so.

42 See C. Dale Walton, "The Decline of the Third Rome: Russia's Prospects as a Great Power," *Journal of Slavic Military Studies* 12 (1999): 51–63.

43 Mark Schneider writes that, "It is noteworthy that the increasing role played by nuclear weapons in Chinese strategy has occurred while most Western scholars continue to characterize the PRC's approach as 'minimum deterrence' . . . [The PRC] is the only nuclear weapon state that has openly embraced long-term qualitative and quantitative expansion of its nuclear force." "The Nuclear Doctrine and Forces of the People's Republic of China," *Comparative Strategy* 28 (2009): 245.

The fundamental contradiction between MAD and BMD was central to the renewed BMD debate of the 1980s. Space-based systems were central to the Reagan administration's Strategic Defense Initiative (SDI). The administration adopted a questionable "broad" interpretation of the Antiballistic Missile (ABM) Treaty of 1972, according to which missile defenses in orbit were legal. The cost and plausibility of BMD were open to debate, as the derisive nickname used by the SDI's opponents, "Star Wars," indicated. However, much criticism of the SDI revolved around the question of whether any warheads could bypass SDI – a dubious basis on which to judge the desirability of a missile defense system. Given the number of warheads at the time, some would certainly have survived even a well-structured, multilayered BMD system. From a Soviet war-planner's perspective, however, the insurmountable problem was to predict which warheads would survive. Even a system that destroyed only 50 percent of the incoming warheads would have complicated a first strike enormously, while one that eliminated a higher percentage of warheads would have undercut all assumptions about the outcome of such a strike. This problem could perhaps have been overcome by throwing the great bulk of Soviet warheads at North America, but this strategy would have carried its own risks, not the least of which was that the United States might "ride out" the strike, gravely wounded but still in possession of an arsenal that could destroy its near-disarmed enemy – and it would have no compelling strategic reason not to do so. In short, SDI might make limited nuclear attacks more difficult and the outcome of a comprehensive nuclear strike even more uncertain. At the same time, however, MAD advocates worried that the SDI could undermine mutual destruction, because it could allow a state to undertake a first strike that would leave its foe with few weapons and (given the existence of the BMD shield) unable to retaliate devastatingly.

A space-based SDI system has never been deployed, and with the end of the first nuclear age the need for a massive-scale missile defense seemed to evaporate. As the second nuclear age dawned, however, many observers argued for a more limited BMD system, which could destroy a limited number of warheads launched from a rogue state. Deployment of BMD remained controversial everywhere, even if the MAD-based logic of the ABM Treaty no longer applied. When the Bush administration renounced the ABM Treaty in 2002 and deployed a rudimentary BMD network, its actions represented a break with the strategic viewpoint that had informed the first nuclear age.

In the second nuclear age, a number of "nuclear defense only" powers will probably emerge – states that do not possess nuclear arms but have BMD capabilities. Already, non-nuclear states such as Japan and the United Arab Emirates have expressed interest in fielding BMD systems. Given the lack of treaty constraints on BMD, and given the increasing risk of nuclear use that accompanies horizontal proliferation, BMD may well become a "normal" military capability, at least for prosperous states. Over the long term, the spread of BMD may complicate the calculations of potential horizontal proliferators, as it can dramatically undermine the value of small, ballistic-missile-delivered nuclear arsenals.

Discussions of the use of nuclear weapons in warfare thus far have been, fortunately, speculative (excepting the cases of Hiroshima and Nagasaki). Unlike modern conventional weapons, nuclear use has no record that might allow one to address symmetrical nuclear warfare with any confidence. Even what is supposedly known about nuclear deterrence is shaky. The strategic history of the Cold War was complex, and even if it is assumed that nuclear deterrence "worked" between the two superpowers, that conclusion offers little guidance to a second nuclear age in which a growing and disparate group of countries possess nuclear weapons.

World War II was the catalyst for the Manhattan Project, but the fact that nuclear weapons were developed just as the old multipolar great-power system was replaced by ideologized, bipolar competition was one of history's curious coincidences. The development of nuclear weapons during this period influenced both the unfolding of "nuclear history" – particularly the stunning speed with which warheads and delivery vehicles improved during the early decades of the first nuclear age – and the analyses of such weapons by scholars and political figures. It is impossible to untangle the history of the Cold War from the presence of nuclear weapons. These devices were always, at a minimum, in the background, subtly shaping the interactions between Washington and Moscow and, by extension, the global security environment.

In addition, the fact that nuclear weapons have not been used since World War II has added to their gravitas. A weapon that is unused, presumably because it is so terrible, has an aura that no mere "conventional" device can possess. When combined with the fact that war has not broken out between the great powers since 1945, this mystique has reinforced the notion that nuclear weapons shape the behavior of their possessors in ways that discourage belligerence. In most cases, this proposition is probably true. However, as the second nuclear age continues, it repeatedly will be tested. Nuclear weapons may never again be used, but history is not reassuring on this point: potent weapons usually have been employed, sooner or later. In any case, the second nuclear age is more complex than the first. Horizontal proliferation promises to increase not only the number of nuclear-armed states, but also their strategic-cultural diversity.[44] Although they have not been used in warfare in more than six decades, nuclear weapons remain relevant to international security affairs – and there is no guarantee that they will not have a place on future battlefields.

44 The concept of strategic culture is well explained in Lawrence Sondhaus, *Strategic Culture and Ways of War* (London, 2006).

20

Conventional war, 1945–1990

WILLIAMSON MURRAY

On September 2, 1945, the voice of Douglas MacArthur echoed across the decks of the battleship, the USS *Missouri*: "It is my hope and the hope of all mankind that from this occasion a better world shall emerge out of the blood and carnage of the past – a world . . . dedicated to freedom, tolerance, and justice."[1]

In fact, however, war continued to stalk the globe. The purpose of this chapter is to recount and contextualize the more important of these wars – the conventional ones, those that primarily used "traditional" methods and material. They occupy the still-wide area between "fourth-generation conflict" and war by remote control. The chapter omits what might be called "dead-end" encounters – the Indo-Pakistani wars, the Sino-Vietnamese and Sino-Russian encounters of the 1960s and 1970s, and the Falklands War. It omits as well low-end, fundamentally irregular conflicts like Malaya and Algeria. It concentrates instead on conventional conflicts that made – and still make – waves.

The war that defined this period, the Cold War between the Soviet Union and the United States, began almost immediately after World War II and lasted for forty-five years, until the Soviet system collapsed, burned out by unsustainable military expenditures and a hopeless economic system. The conduct of the Cold War provided much of the context of the other conflicts around the world after 1945.[2]

1 Quoted in Eric Larrabee, *Commander in Chief: Franklin Delano Roosevelt, His Lieutenants, and Their War* (New York, 1987), 352.

2 Among a vast and swelling literature, see particularly John Lewis Gaddis, *We Now Know: Rethinking Cold War History* (Oxford, 1997). A study that was written well before the end of the Cold War, but was enriched by an understanding of the ideological and political currents in play over its early years is Adam B. Ulam, *The Rivals: The United States and Russia since World War II* (New York, 1971). For a trenchant summary of the issues involved in the outbreak of the Cold War, see Colin Gray, "Mission Improbable: Fear, Culture and Interest: Peacemaking, 1943–1949," in Williamson Murray and Jim Lacey, eds., *The Making of Peace: Rulers, States, and the Aftermath of War* (Cambridge, 2009), 265–92.

At first, US statesmen hoped to contest the Cold War on political and economic terms. Only the invasion of South Korea ended the illusion that the United States could engage the Soviet Union without significant military forces; and in confronting this crisis the leaders of the United States displayed cool calculation. Dispatching troops to fight the war in East Asia, they sent even larger forces to Europe to stabilize the military balance along the "Iron Curtain." When Harry Truman refused to expand the Korean War to Manchuria and China, the Cold War's frontiers were drawn for the next four decades. These boundaries were sustained by the threat of nuclear weapons, which deterred direct confrontations between the two superpowers for the remainder of the Cold War. The one terrible exception was the Cuban missile crisis of September–October 1962. The crisis was occasioned by the miscalculation of Soviet leader Nikita Khrushchev, who believed that by placing nuclear armed missiles in Cuba, he could trump the United States' growing nuclear superiority. For a number of days the world trembled on the brink of thermonuclear war, before both sides backed down, as much from serendipity as calculation.

During the late fifties and early sixties, Soviet leaders had proclaimed their support for wars of "national liberation." They announced that the Soviet Union would contest peripheral areas of the world by supporting revolutionary movements. In January 1961, the newly elected president, John F. Kennedy, responded that the American people were prepared to "pay any price, bear any burden" in defense of liberty around the world. Cuba was one example of a new strategic design that also led to increasing American involvement in an ongoing guerrilla war in Vietnam. Here American strategy faltered. President Lyndon Johnson and his secretary of defense, Robert McNamara, committed large US forces to a nasty war that could not be won, given the restraints necessary to sustain a larger global strategic framework, which, however, the administration increasingly ignored.[3]

Still, Soviet attempts to take advantage of American weakness in the late 1960s and 1970s were less than successful. Confronted with an attempt to put what the Czechs termed "a peaceful face on Communism," the Soviet leadership replied with a massive invasion of Czechoslovakia. This action alone ensured that the United States would not lose western Europe. Other Soviet attempts to extend the reach of their empire beyond the Warsaw Pact and

3 For the sad story of how the United States' political and military leaders stumbled into the Vietnam War, see particularly H. R. McMaster, *Dereliction of Duty: Lyndon Johnson, Robert McNamara, the Joint Chiefs of Staff, and the Lies that Led to Vietnam* (New York, 1997).

Cuba led to involvement in Angola, Somalia, Ethiopia, and Afghanistan, all of which added to the burden of empire but provided little in return.

Meanwhile, the development of intercontinental ballistic missiles (ICBMs) had large and unintended consequences for the competition. The Soviets built large rockets with redundant systems to handle the difficulties of launching rockets into space. The Americans, on the other hand, built smaller rockets which demanded miniaturization. The result was the development of more efficient computers – a military-technical revolution that by the 1980s had altered conventional weapons systems and provided them with unprecedented accuracy and lethality.

The Soviets had begun to worry about the technological sophistication of American military equipment in the last years of Vietnam, when the US air Force used 27,000 laser-guided bombs to devastate the North Vietnamese offensive against South Vietnam, wrecking the former's economic and transportation system. In 1982, using American electronic countermeasures, fighter aircraft, and precision weapons, the Israelis destroyed the most up-to-date Soviet air defense system in Syria's Bekka Valley.[4] In 1984 Marshal Nikolai V. Ogarkov characterized the advances in American non-nuclear technology as bringing "the destructive potential of conventional weapons . . . closer, so to speak, to weapons of mass destruction in terms of effectiveness."[5]

From the Soviet perspective, this development meant that the US military could wage a conventional war in central Europe with devastating effect. Thus, the Soviets were afraid that the United States and its allies could defeat the Warsaw Pact's conventional forces. The logical, "scientific" conclusion was that the USSR had lost the military competition unless it could repair the stagnation that increasingly marked its economy. And this effort led to the Mikhail Gorbachev's attempt to reform a system that could not be reformed.

The Cold War always had the potential to go hot. The arsenals that the Soviet Union and the United States had assembled by the late 1950s could have destroyed civilization. At times the two powers teetered on the brink; but they never crossed the line. Nevertheless, their rivalry spawned lesser conflicts, initiating, arming, supporting, and legitimating them. World War II finished the work that World War I had begun. It discredited the idea that the west possessed some inherent right to rule the peoples of other parts of the world, although the colonial powers were slow to recognize that the era of colonial

4 Mathew M. Hurley, "The Bekaa Valley Air Battle, June 1982," *Airpower Journal* (Winter 1989): www.airpower.maxwell.af.mil/airchronicles/apj/apj89/win89/hurley.html.

5 Interview with Marshal of the Soviet Union N. V. Ogarkov, "The Defense of Socialism: Experience of History and the Present Day," *Krasnaya zvezda*, May 9, 1984, 2–3.

empires was over. The result was a series of wars of decolonization which lasted into the 1970s.

A second great area of conflict emerged in the Middle East. The conflicts in this region reflected both the hasty withdrawal of the colonial powers and the consequences of the Holocaust, as the remains of Europe's Jewry searched for a land where they could defend themselves. The wars of survival waged by the new Jewish state overlapped other conflicts. Combined with the world's great economies' increasing dependence on Middle Eastern oil, these conflicts posed dangerous possibilities for the world at large.

Immediately upon the surrender of Japan, a series of wars broke out, as the European powers attempted to reinstall colonial rule while locals were determined to gain their independence. In the East Indies, the Dutch waged a low-key, on-and-off war until they agreed to leave in 1949. In Malaya, the returning British ran into a communist insurgency that was supported by the ethnic Chinese, who formed a substantial minority of the population. By the early 1950s they had developed an eventually successful integrated civil-military response.[6] Matters in Indo-China were different. The returning French faced a powerful and ruthless communist-nationalist movement, the Viet Minh. By the end of 1946 it was nevertheless clear that neither the politicians in Paris nor the generals in Saigon and Hanoi were willing to settle for anything but a return to colonial rule. For three years the French vainly sought a conventional military victory against an opponent that was willing to take shelter in the land and among the populace.

For Ho Chi Minh and his general Vo Nguyên Giap, irregular war was not an end in itself. The Viet Minh built its own conventional strength, and beginning in November 1949, the Chinese Communists, newly victorious over Chiang Kai-shek's Nationalists, provided enough support to enable an eventual offensive. In October 1950 the Viet Minh overran French outposts along Indochina's northern border in a three-week blitz. The French lost six thousand troops and enough equipment to equip a Viet-Minh division.[7] In early 1951 Giap and Ho launched three savage conventional offensives against the vital Red River delta. This time, skillfully commanded by Marshal Jean de Lattre de Tassigny, French and colonial troops used superior firepower and training to slaughter the Viet Minh.

6 See Noel Barber, *War of the Running Dogs: Malaya, 1946–1960* (London, 2007); John A. Nagel, *Learning to Eat Soup with a Knife: Counterinsurgency Lessons from Malaya and Vietnam* (Chicago, 2005).

7 Georges Longeret, Jacques Laurent, and Cyril Bondroit, *Les Combats de la RC 4: Face au Vietminh et à la Chine, Cao-Bang-Lang Son, 1947–1950* (Paris: Indo Editions, 2004), 3.

After the third attack failed, the insurgents faded back into the jungles of the Red River valley. In November 1951 the French counterattacked at Hoa-Binh on the Black River, in hopes of forcing the Viet Minh into another stand-up fight. Instead, Giap contained the pocket while other Viet-Minh units attacked French supply lines. In the end the French withdrew, taking heavy casualties for no result. In Operation "Lorraine" a year later, the French repeated the mistakes they had made in the drive on Hoa-Binh. The advance went flawlessly, but despite heavy losses Giap refused to allow his forces to be drawn into battles of attrition against superior firepower. Again, the French eventually withdrew. What they failed to understand was that they were providing their opponents with a series of seminars in combining irregular with conventional warfare.[8]

The denouement came in late 1953, when the French determined to seize the provincial town of Dien Bien Phu as a strong point and a base for mobile operations. The garrison would be supplied by an air bridge and sustained by air power. The Viet Minh would not be able to build the logistic infrastructure for a prolonged siege or an effective attack. And finally, in a straight-up fight the French Army would win.[9] French paratroopers seized Dien Bien Phu on November 20, 1953, and over the next three months they built up a set of interlocking strong points. Meanwhile, Giap established lines of communications and moved assault forces into place, entrenching guns in deep shelters in the hills surrounding the valley. Their antiaircraft fire dominated the sky. The Viet Minh waged modern war, while the French had in a sense reverted to the thinking of 1914, expecting the elite garrison's élan to be decisive. The Viet Minh's attack began on March 13, 1954 with a massive artillery bombardment. Ground assaults steadily crushed the garrison. In early May Dien Bien Phu went down to defeat – not to guerrillas, but in a conventional operation that French participants compared to Verdun. In June 1954 an international conference in Geneva recognized the independence of North Vietnam.

One of the great ironies of the Cold War lay in the fact that while the United States thought largely about war in Europe, the country fought two great wars in Asia. War in Korea was the last thing on the minds of US political and military leaders in 1950. In listing the United States' interest in the Far East,

8 Bernard Fall, *Street without Joy: The French Debacle in Indochina* (Mechanicsburg, PA, 1994), 60.

9 The best account of the battle and one of the classics of military history is Bernard Fall, *Hell in a Very Small Place: Dien Bien Phu* (Philadelphia, 1966). It may be supplemented by Martin Windrow, *The Last Valley: Dien Bien Phu and the French Defeat in Vietnam* (London, 2004).

Secretary of State Dean Acheson had not even mentioned South Korea. But the leader of North Korea, Kim Il-sung, was eager to unify the peninsula, while his mentor, Joseph Stalin, was eager to test American resolve. On Sunday morning, June 25, 1950, the North Korean army crashed across the 38th Parallel, which had separated North and South Korea; the North Koreans then captured Seoul and fanned out across the peninsula.

As so often in US history, the American response appeared out of character with its behavior immediately before the invasion. President Truman ordered an immediate military response. In retrospect, the decision to support South Korea made strategic sense because of the country's location immediately across from the Japanese Home Islands. The US military, however, was unprepared for war. The so-called divisions that were occupying Japan were little more than a constabulary. "Task Force Smith," which was made up of units from the 24th Infantry Division, delayed the North Koreans for only seven hours before it collapsed. As the North Koreans raced south, the Americans committed disgruntled veterans and inductees, who had little or no training and were often equipped with refurbished or obsolescent material from World War II. The North Korean advance was nevertheless slowly brought to a halt, thanks as much to logistical difficulties as the tenaciousness of the defensive line that was finally established around Pusan.

Even as American and South Korean troops retreated, MacArthur planned the last master stroke of his long and spotty career. As he organized the defense of the Pusan perimeter, he prepared a landing force to attack the port of Inchon. The operation succeeded beyond his hopes. After severe fighting, soldiers and marines recaptured Seoul, cutting the North Koreans off from their logistical support. The crucial question was: what next? Should the American forces halt at the 38th Parallel or continue their advance into North Korea? Despite warnings from the Communist Chinese, who were unhappy to have to relieve their Soviet and North Korean allies, MacArthur launched a full-scale drive to the Yalu River.

In November and December 1950, army and marine units, which were inadequately prepared for winter conditions, ran into the massed forces of the People's Liberation Army in the northern depths of Korea. The result was close to a military catastrophe. UN forces tumbled southward on the peninsula even faster than they had advanced to the north, while MacArthur demanded a widening of the war, to include air attacks on Chinese logistics in Manchuria and the unleashing of Chiang Kai-shek from Taiwan. As Omar Bradley commented, "it would have been the wrong war, in the wrong place, at the wrong time." MacArthur's attempts to determine strategic and policy issues on his own eventually got him fired in April 1951.

Meanwhile, General Walton Walker, one of the least inspiring commanders in US history, had been killed in an accident and replaced by the paratrooper General Matthew Ridgway, an extraordinarily competent general. Under Ridgway's leadership, the Eighth Army stopped the Chinese drive south of Seoul, and then drove the Communists back to the north. On March 18, UN forces retook Seoul. A series of brutal, human-wave offensives by the Chinese then took place, which American firepower butchered. The battles in the spring of 1951 came close to breaking the Chinese and North Korean forces. By June the Eighth Army, now under General James van Fleet, advanced across the 38th Parallel and threatened to drive its opponents deep into North Korea. At this point American leaders made the mistake of halting operations in response to calls from the Communists for peace negotiations.

The negotiations were a farce. Stalin had no desire to end a war that was, he believed, keeping American attention focused on East Asia rather than Europe. The war now settled into a siege operation that in some respects resembled the battles of World War I, as massive artillery duels savaged infantry positions. Meanwhile, American air power attacked the lines of communications from the front lines back to Manchuria. While this effort never entirely cut Communist units off from their supplies, it prevented them from building up sufficient forces to drive UN forces from the Korean peninsula. Finally, after two years of bloodletting and the destruction of North Korea's infrastructure, the Communists agreed to an armistice.

If the Korean War represented a surprise to the United States, the Vietnam War represented an afterthought. The Geneva Accords of 1954 established a separate entity in South Vietnam, with the soon aborted promise that national elections would be held in the near future. The United States never considered Vietnam a major strategic interest, but provided enough military and diplomatic small change to create a corrupt, inefficient, but anti-communist regime in South Vietnam. The military mission focused on building a South Vietnamese army against an invasion from the north. By 1959, however, Ho and Giap had decided that the only way to achieve Vietnam's unification was to undermine Diem's regime, using the same methods that had proven successful against the French.

Although American support for South Vietnam grew throughout the Kennedy administration, by 1964 the situation had deteriorated to the point where the United States had either to intervene directly or watch the collapse of its client. High-level civilians in the department of defense and senior military officers alike believed that the French experiences with the Viet

Minh were irrelevant to the American effort.[10] President Lyndon Johnson and Robert McNamara, his secretary of defense, manipulated the intervention to ensure Johnson's reelection. In March 1965 US ground troops were committed to the fight. At the same time, Johnson ordered the US air force and navy to begin "Operation Rolling Thunder," a major air campaign against North Vietnam, in an effort to persuade the North Vietnamese to cease aiding the insurgency in the south.

When bombing failed to have the desired effect, the US escalated on the ground. In November 1965 a series of encounters took place between elements of the 1st Cavalry Division, the first air-mobile division, which relied on helicopters to move and fight, and North Vietnamese regular regiments in the South Vietnamese highlands. The North Vietnamese nearly wiped out nearly a battalion of the 7th Cavalry, but on the whole the fighting in the Ia Drang valley confirmed American belief that conventional combat maximized US advantages and opportunities.[11]

The US commanding officer, General William Westmoreland displayed minimal interest in fighting the insurgency that confronted him in the countryside. Instead, the American effort focused on destroying main-force Viet Cong and North Vietnamese units, while simultaneously improving South Vietnam's conventional capabilities. Pacification disappeared from the American vocabulary, expelled by the rhetoric of conventional victory. The North Vietnamese met every American increase in troop strength in the south with increases of their own, which moved south along the Ho Chi Minh trail. Because so many men were required to sustain the logistical apparatus of a high-tech war in an environment that had no infrastructure, US combat units were frequently weaker at points of contact – a fact that in turn made necessary increasing reliance on indiscriminate firepower.

Giap urged a careful strategic and operational approach against the Americans. His rivals in the North Vietnamese politburo sought a chance to repeat the experiences of 1950. The result was the Tet Offensive in January 1968. The Viet Cong and their North Vietnamese allies achieved almost complete surprise. But the offensive rested on two false assumptions – that

10 In 1964 de Gaulle, recognizing that the United States was about to intervene massively in Vietnam, made available to the American government the top-secret report by the French government from the mid 1950s on why the country had lost the war. The report languished untranslated in the classified library in the National War College.

11 For an outstanding account of these initial battles, see Harold G. Moore and Joseph L. Galloway, *We Were Soldiers Once . . . and Young: Ia Drang – The Battle that Changed Vietnam* (New York, 1993).

South Vietnam's army would not fight and that its people would rally to the attackers. While the population displayed little enthusiasm for the "revolution," the soldiers fought with a ruthlessness that surprised even their American advisors. Combined with American firepower and tactical skill, the result was a crushing defeat of the Viet Cong and the North Vietnamese, inflicted largely in the context of conventional war.

But war is more than just numbers and battles. The shocking images of the Tet Offensive made an indelible impression on the American people, cost Johnson a second term, and brought Richard Nixon to power with the promise to bring the war to a close. As American troop strength slowly declined, a desperate effort ensued to prepare the South Vietnamese to stand on their own. In 1972, in hopes of humiliating the United States by destroying South Vietnam before US troops withdrew, the North Vietnamese launched a massive conventional offensive. The Nixon administration replied with two aerial counterattacks that devastated North Vietnam's attacking forces and left the country in ruins. The South Vietnamese on the whole fought courageously and successfully. But in 1975 the United States watched without responding as a final, armor-tipped North Vietnamese invasion destroyed its erstwhile ally. Not black-pajamaed guerrillas but heavy tanks first entered the grounds of the South's presidential palace.

Conventional war matched insurgency on the other side of the world as well. In the first decades of the twentieth century, Jews from Europe and the Arab world began to emigrate to Turkish-held Palestine. In 1917 the British issued the Balfour Declaration in the hope that setting aside a portion of Palestine as a Jewish national home would rally the world's Jews to the Allied side. This declaration set the stage for violent confrontations between a growing Jewish minority and the Arab natives. At the end of World War II, the British confronted massive communal violence between Jews, who were desperate to help the survivors of the Holocaust, and an Arab community that was set on preventing additional Jewish immigration to Palestine and on driving out the Jewish settlers who had arrived before the war. The United Nations urged partition, the creation of an Arab and a Jewish state. The Palestinian Arabs rejected the compromise.

Initially the Jews aimed at defending the areas that had been assigned to them by the partition, but they soon pushed beyond areas with large Jewish populations. Massacres and atrocities occurred on both sides during this irregular fighting, but the Jews secured the military advantage by the time the state of Israel was proclaimed on May 15, 1948.[12] The region's Arab leaders responded with armed invasion and blood-curdling rhetoric. Azzam Pasha, the secretary of the Arab League, declared on the Cairo radio that "This will be a war of extermination and momentous massacre which will be spoken of like the Mongolian massacres and the Crusades."[13]

The initial stage of fighting lasted from May 14 through June 11, 1948, as the Israelis repelled a number of attacks by the Syrians and Egyptians. They lost the Arab and Jewish quarters of Jerusalem to the Jordanians. They also began transforming an irregular force with little more than small arms into an increasingly modern conventional army. A ceasefire lasted barely a month, as the two sides reorganized for the fighting. The Israelis gained the most. Imbued with the discipline and organizational skills that they had learned in Europe, they mobilized their population for the coming battles, reinforced by a steady flood of refugees and volunteers. Equally important was the fact that the USSR recognized Israel and allowed their puppets in Prague to ship large amounts of arms and ammunition to the Israelis.

In the renewed fighting, the Israelis launched several offensives. Pushing east from Tel Aviv, they relieved Jewish forces in Jerusalem; attacking north, they captured Nazareth, and by the beginning of the second truce (July 18) they had seized most of Lower Galilee. The war's third stage began on October 15 and lasted until July 20, 1949. Now the Israelis displayed even greater military superiority. In the north they captured Upper Galilee. In the south they shattered the Egyptian army, driving it back into the Sinai and trapping much of it in Gaza. Finally, in March 1949 Israeli forces reached what was to become the port of Eilat.

With the cessation of military operations in July 1949, the Arabs were forced to end their direct attempts to undermine the new state. However, they persisted in their design to destroy what they called the "Zionist entity." For the short term they encouraged guerrilla and commando raids by Palestinians. Initially no more than a nuisance, these raids had by the mid 1950s become a growing threat, especially because the dynamic Gamal Abdul Nasser now ruled Egypt. When the Egyptians received major arms shipments from the Soviets, the western powers, with the United States in the lead, withdrew support for Nasser's pet project, the construction of the huge Aswan Dam. Nasser in response nationalized the Suez Canal. The Americans looked for a

12 Benny Morris, *1948: A History of the First Arab-Israeli War* (New Haven, 2008).
13 Howard M. Sachar, *A History of Israel* (New York, 1979), 333.

solution through negotiations. The French and the British decided on military operations.

Israel's leaders were delighted to form an alliance with the two western powers, but the connection was clandestine. In return for French military help, the Israelis agreed to invade the Sinai. The western powers moved slowly, as the Israeli advance routed the Egyptians in a series of lightning offensives. The war ended in one of the great crises of the Cold War. The Soviets, who were at the time slaughtering Hungarian rebels in Budapest, threatened intervention and a nuclear Armageddon. The United States refused to support its allies. In humiliating fashion, the British and French backed down. In 1957 the Israelis abandoned the Sinai in return for a guarantee from the United States that the Straits of Tiran would remain open to Israeli shipping.

Fighting between the Israelis and their Arab neighbors remained at a low level for a decade after the Suez conflict. In the spring of 1967, however, the Syrians became entangled in increasingly serious skirmishes with the Israelis, partially because of Syrian efforts to dam the Jordan River. With reports that the Israelis were about to launch a full-scale invasion of Syria, the Soviets egged the Egyptians on to support their fellow Arabs.[14] On May 15, 1967, Nasser ordered his army to occupy Sinai. Eight days later the Egyptians blockaded the Straits of Tiran. The Israelis mobilized, while the United States, which was by now deeply mired in Vietnam, did nothing to keep the straits open.[15]

Some historians have argued that the Egyptians did not intend to launch an invasion of Israel. Given the rhetoric of "driving the Jews into the sea," which had marked the commentary in much of the Arab press (especially in Egypt), this argument is unlikely. In any case, these pronouncements exacerbated Israeli fears of another Holocaust. Diplomatic efforts to avoid hostilities allowed the Israelis to integrate their reservists into their combat forces. On the surface the opposing sides – Israel against Egypt, Syria, and Jordan – appeared balanced. But in leadership, training, preparation, and morale, the Israeli Defense Force (IDF) enjoyed substantial advantages, particularly in the superiority of its officers and NCOs. The Israelis drew their manpower from

14 Martin van Creveld, *The Sword and the Olive: A Critical History of the Israeli Defense Force* (New York, 1998), 174.

15 The most thorough and fair analysis of the conflict is Michael B. Oren, *Six Days of War: June 1967 and the Making of the Middle East* (Novato, CA, 2003). Tom Segev, *1967: Israel, the War, and the Year that Transformed the Middle East* (New York, 2007) is more biased and unrealistic.

across society, while the mass of Arab soldiery came from the lowest classes. The Arab armies also picked senior officers from the least competent but most politically reliable candidates.

On June 5 the war began with a shattering attack by the Israeli air force, which destroyed Egyptian air power. Israeli fighter bombers attacked the Egyptians immediately after their morning patrols returned to base. Within three hours, the Egyptian air force no longer existed. This fact did not prevent Nasser from telephoning King Hussein of Jordan to report a great victory in the air. Persuaded by the lies of the Egyptians, the Jordanians initiated operations on the west bank, despite desperate appeals by the Israelis to stay out of the conflict.

On the Sinai front the Israelis moved on the ground at the same time as their fighters were attacking the Egyptians. In the north, Brigadier General Israel Tal's division, which was led by the 7th Brigade of British Centurion tanks, smashed through Egyptian defenses, captured Khan Yunis in the Gaza Strip, then moved through Rafah and broke through the Jiradi Pass near the coast. Tal's attack broke Egyptian forces in the northern Sinai. In the center, General Abraham Yoffe's division, also led by Centurions, navigated what the Egyptians thought to be an impassable set of dunes. After advancing 30 miles into the Sinai, the Israelis established an ambush near Jebel Livini and destroyed the Egyptian 4th Armored Division.[16] To the south, a third Israeli division under Ariel Sharon executed a brilliant combined-arms night attack against a heavily fortified and mined position held by the Egyptian 2nd Infantry Division near Abu Ageila. Moving through terrain that the Egyptians again thought impassable, one of Sharon's brigades captured Kusseima south of the Egyptian positions. After a heavy bombardment, Israeli paratroopers infiltrated the Egyptian artillery positions from the west, while Sharon's remaining two brigades forced their way through the Egyptian position from the north. The battle was over by the early morning.

On the morning of June 6, the lead brigades of Tal's and Yoffe's divisions completed the encirclement of two Egyptian divisions. By afternoon the Israelis had destroyed the Egyptian position in the Sinai. Hearing of the fall of Abu-Ageila, Nasser's minister of defense panicked, ordering all Egyptian forces in the Sinai to retreat.[17] A general collapse followed with the three Israeli divisions in hot pursuit. The Egyptian collapse was so sudden and the Israeli advance so rapid that the high command in Tel Aviv lost control of the

16 Van Creveld, *The Sword and the Olive*, 185.
17 Ibid., 187.

advance. With no objectives or halt line, Israeli forces rolled up on the Suez Canal with no thought of the political, strategic, or operational consequences of holding the canal's east bank.

Meanwhile, having failed to keep the Jordanians out of the conflict, the Israelis struck first at Jerusalem and then at the west bank of the Jordan River. The battle for Jerusalem was a bloody affair, but by June 7 the Israelis were in control of the west bank. There then remained the Syrians, who, with the exception of artillery bombardments of Israeli kibbutzim in northern Galilee, had watched the destruction of their neighbors' armies despite having largely caused the conflict.[18] The Israelis gathered their forces in the north, and in a two-day campaign the IDF overwhelmed Syrian defenses and seized the Golan Heights, putting the Israeli settlements in Galilee out of range of Syrian artillery.

The Israeli success underlined the superiority of an army that was based from the highest to lowest levels on coherent training and discipline. Yet, in retrospect, the Israelis overreached. They overestimated their military prowess and underestimated the potential of their enemies. Over the the next six years, they received a vast influx of US arms. Moreover, sure of their military superiority, they refused to return any of the lands they had conquered, in the mistaken belief that Israel now had defensible borders.

In the aftermath of the Six Day War, the Arabs refused to deal in any fashion with the "Zionist entity." The Egyptians began what was soon termed the "War of Attrition," launching raids and artillery barrages on Israeli positions on the east bank. The Israelis replied with a series of commando raids, one of which lifted out the most modern of Soviet radars from its position. In response to Egyptian artillery barrages, the Israelis constructed a series of fortified points along the Suez Canal, in which their infantry could take shelter. The initial purpose of these positions was to provide warning of an Egyptian offensive, but Israeli commanders remained unclear about whether this "Bar-Lev Line" was to be a tripwire or defensive line.[19] This was the least of the muddled thinking that pervaded the IDF in the months before the Yom Kippur War in 1973. Israeli intelligence, politicians, and military leaders discounted the possibility of an Arab offensive against the IDF, much less an effective one.

18 The Israelis noted the damage as "205 houses, nine chicken-coups, two tractor sheds, three clubs, one dining hall, six haystacks, 30 tractors, and 15 cars." Ibid., 191.

19 Interview With Brigadier General Dov Tamari (assistant commander Adan's division), IDF, Tel Aviv, October 24, 2000.

Ironically, by holding the line of the Suez Canal, the Israelis robbed themselves of all advance-warning time. They also faced a better-prepared and -trained opponent. In September 1970 Nasser died and was succeeded by Anwar Sadat. Unlike most of his colleagues in the Arab world, Sadat sought competent military commanders. He cut his strategic cloth to match operational and tactical means. The Egyptian army aimed not at the absolute defeat of the IDF, but rather a tactical victory to break the diplomatic logjam and open negotiations for the return of the Sinai. Recognizing the superiority of the Israeli air force, the Egyptians planned to advance only as far as they could be covered by an umbrella of surface-to-air missiles on the canal's west bank. At the same time, the Syrians were to drive the Israelis off the Golan Heights.

The result of Israeli overconfidence was a lack of advanced planning. In the Sinai, seven existing plans all envisaged offensive action to one extent or another. All rested on the assumption that warning time would be sufficient.[20] To defend the Golan, the Israelis had three plans on different scales, but all involved the same response – an attack into Syria.[21] The amateurism of these plans underlined the IDF's limited conception of the operational level of war. The IDF had promoted its officers on the basis of combat experience but provided them with little professional education. Thus, Israeli commanders understood only tactics – and even this only weakly, given their overemphasis on the tank.

The Egyptian and Syrian offensives began at the start of Yom Kippur, when Israel had virtually shut down. Only at the last moment did the Israelis wake up to what was transpiring on their frontiers. On the morning of October 6, IDF commanders asked for permission to strike the Arab armies in their final deployments. Golda Meir, the prime minister, and Moshe Dayan, the minister of defense, vetoed the request in order to ensure that there was no question about who had started the war. With the media shut down for the high holidays, two F-4s flew over Israel's major cities at low altitude in order to warn that war was imminent, while the calling up of reservists proceeded by personal contact.

The result of the Israeli failure to respond to the warnings of an Arab offensive was that the thin screens of Israeli forces on the canal and on the Golan were rocked back on their heels. Along the canal, the Egyptians quickly isolated the strong points on the Bar-Lev Line, while the Israeli theater

20 Ibid.

21 Interview with Brigadier Shimon Naveh (paratroop commander, Yom Kippur War), IDF retired, Golan Heights, October 23, 2000.

commander refused to order the small garrisons to pull back and save themselves. Instead, he ordered southern command's reserve, an all-tank division, to launch counterattacks against the Egyptian penetrations. The Israeli attackers, who had no artillery or infantry support, ran into a barrage of antitank missiles, supporting artillery, and antitank fire from Egyptian tanks on the west bank. The Egyptians inflicted heavy losses on the Israeli tanks, while Israeli fighter bombers suffered correspondingly from surface-to-air missiles.

As Israeli reinforcements made their way across the Sinai, huge traffic jams built up within a matter of hours. The commanders of the reserve divisions, Ariel Sharon and Avraham Adan, who was the most sophisticated and competent of the Israeli commanders, arrived at southern command headquarters to find everything in disarray. Adan launched the first segment of the Israeli counterattack, and his division, which lacked much of its artillery and had little infantry support, suffered heavy losses.[22]

The next day, Sharon fared no better. At this point the Israeli high command decided to halt operations along the Suez front, because a more serious situation had developed on the Golan Heights. The leader of Northern Command, Major General Yitzig Hoffi, had grown sufficiently worried about the threat of a major attack on his front that the IDF command sent him an additional armored brigade at the last minute. The reinforcement arrived just before the holidays began, and its last units came into place just before combat started. The Syrians struck at 14:00 with three armored divisions. In the northern sector the newly arrived 7th Armored Brigade held.[23] There was, however, no overall commander on the Golan. To the south, the Barak Brigade fought an entirely separate fight and was overwhelmed company by company. By the evening of the first day, the Syrians appeared on the brink of crossing the Jordan into Jewish settlements in the Galilee foothills. So desperate did the situation appear on the southern Golan that for a short time Dayan felt that Israel had lost the war.

Instead, the Syrians stopped their advance, most probably because of the heavy losses they had suffered in destroying the Barak Brigade. Israeli reserves were pitched forward without proper organization, but they displayed the value of coherent, disciplined training, as they together formed a new front, which slowly pushed the Syrians back toward their start line. By the late

22 Avraham (Bren) Adan, *On the Banks of the Suez: An Israeli General's Personal Account of the Yom Kippur War* (Novato, CA, 1980).

23 See Avigdor Kahalani, *The Heights of Courage: A Tank Leader's War on the Golan* (Westport, CT, 1984).

afternoon of the seventh, the Israelis had established control over the Golan. On the morning of October 9, a new wave of Syrian T-62s struck the battered 7th Brigade, whose tanks were in some cases down to their last rounds of ammunition. The 7th held.[24] The Israelis could now counterattack over the border toward Damascus. Their spearheads came within 20 miles of the Syrian capital. But at this point the Israelis halted.

Attention now shifted back to Suez. Before the Israelis could make the mistake of launching their forces against the dug-in Egyptians, the latter's armored divisions crossed the canal and moved out into the Sinai in response to desperate appeals from the Syrians, who were now hard pressed as the Israeli drive approached their capital. The result was the battle for which the Israelis had been hoping.[25]

In an all-tank encounter, they were the masters. At ranges determined by eyesight and human calculations, and with an accuracy that was achieved by training rather than lasers and computers, the IDF's tanks killed Egyptian armor at ranges over 2,500 yards, while their opponents were not even in range. By the time the smoke cleared, the Egyptians had lost more than two hundred fifty tanks and suffered a catastrophic defeat.[26]

The Israelis then went over to the offensive. Sharon's division led the way to the canal just to the north of the Bitter Lake – providentially between the two Egyptian armies – and established a bridgehead on the west bank. Adan's division was to follow and exploit the bridgehead in order to destroy the Egyptian surface-to-air-missile positions and trap the Egyptian Third Army on the east bank. There was, however, no overall hand to guide the move, as was clear in the orders that the two commanders received. Sharon's division was to cross the canal, widen the corridor to the canal by driving the Egyptian Second Army back to the north, and bring up bridging equipment so Israeli armor could cross. Adan's division had only to prepare for combat on the west side of the canal. The result was a desperate operation that came close to failing. Moreover, Sharon sent out only a small raiding party of tanks across the canal on rafts, while Golda Meir announced that the Israelis were already across in the operation's early hours. Luckily for the Israelis, the Egyptians acted slowly, and Adan got loose on the west bank. However, before the Israelis

24 One of the great accounts of the war is the memoir by Kahalani, who was a battalion commander in the 7th Brigade: Kahalani, *Heights of Courage*.

25 Interview with Major General Avraham Adan (commander of the Adan Division, Yom Kippur War), IDF retired, Tel Aviv, October 27, 2000.

26 Adan, *Banks of the Suez*, 230–31.

could destroy the Third Army and create strategic victory from tactical success, the great powers and the combatants agreed to a ceasefire.

There are a number of interesting points about this so-called War of Atonement. When they were well led and given sensible goals, Arab armies could fight as well as any other. Sadat had a coherent strategic aim which fitted the means at hand. He was not out to destroy the IDF, but rather to force the Israelis to enter negotiations that would return the Sinai to Egypt. On the Israeli side, most of the troubles during the first disastrous days resulted from arrogance and underestimation of their opponent. Moreover, a sloppy and superficial analysis of the Six Day War of 1967 had created a doctrine that was antithetical to the combined-arms framework in which modern war has been fought since 1940.

Israeli soldiers and junior officer adapted to combat in the first days of the war, however, and recovered the combined-arms framework. The cost of adaptation was paid in blood. Nevertheless, the lack of professional military education throughout the army's officer corps made the generals unable to address the requirements of the operational level. The result was mistakes that resulted in no clear command and control during the first two days on the Golan and almost led to the defeat of the canal crossing. In every respect, Israeli successes against the Egyptians during the last days of the conflict were due as much to luck and their enemies' mistakes as they were to skill.

In 1968 the Ba'ath Party, whose ideology combined the worst aspects of fascism and communism, seized power in Iraq. The aim of the Ba'ath's founders was to create a united Arab nation to rival the great powers. The party's ideology was ferociously anti-Semitic.[27] The 1970s were the heyday of the first great oil crisis, and the new Iraqi leaders were soon awash in petrodollars, which they used to build up Iraq's military forces for a confrontation with Israel.

Saddam Hussein, a street-wise operator from Tikrit, rose steadily in the Ba'ath's power structure, and in 1979 he "persuaded" Iraq's president to "retire." In Stalinist fashion he proceeded to eliminate his rivals, real and potential. At the same time, he replaced the army's senior leaders with junior officers, all of whom were Ba'ath sycophants, none of whom had commanded at brigade level, and few of whom had even attended the staff college. Saddam's goals were megalomaniacal – nothing less than the destruction of Israel and the unification of the Arab nation under his leadership. "Who can

27 For a brilliant depiction of Ba'ath ideology, its roots and its influence over Saddam's tyranny, see Samir Khalil, *The Republic of Fear: The Politics of Modern Iraq* (Berkeley, 1990).

carry this role? It is no one but Iraq. Iraq can make the [Arab] nation rise and can be its center post of its big abode," he wrote. "If Iraq falls, then the entire Arab Nation will fall. When the central post breaks, the whole tent will collapse."[28]

Almost concurrently with Saddam's arrival at the top of Iraq's political ladder, a revolution in Iran overthrew the shah and replaced him with Ayatollah Khomeini. Khomeini's goals were as wide-ranging as Saddam's. Instead of an Arab nation to contend with the great powers, the religious fanatics in Tehran aimed to create an Islamic republic in order to complete the religious revolution that Islam's arrival on the world stage had occasioned. Almost immediately, the two regimes faced off. In the spring of 1980, Iranian terrorists nearly assassinated Iraq's deputy president, Tariq Aziz. Meanwhile, a series of artillery duels launched from both sides of the border increased tension. For Saddam this was an intolerable situation. The political turmoil in Iran, the purge of the military that Khomeini had ordered, and the apparent collapse of the Iranian armed forces offered an opportunity to address wrongs that the Iraqis believed the Persians had inflicted on them for millennia.

The Iraqi leader was nevertheless unclear about his war aims. He appears to have hoped that the invasion would lead to a coup in Tehran to remove Khomeini; he also might have wanted to gain control of Arabistan, with its largely Arab population and its vast oil deposits. Above all, however, he believed that a quick victory would establish him as the undisputed leader of a united Arab nation, drive the superpowers out of the Middle East, and destroy the "Zionist entity."

On September 22, 1980 the Iraqi Army crossed into Iran.[29] So slapdash were Iraqi preparations that the navy was only informed of the invasion a day before it began. The Iraqi air force aped the Israeli strike on the first day of the Six Day War, but with a notable lack of success: it destroyed a single F-4 that was parked on a taxiway. The advance of the Iraqi army was no more impressive. There was no operational focus. The eleven divisions of the invading force proceeded largely along separate lines. Most disastrously, the

28 Kevin M. Woods, *The Mother of All Battles: Saddam Hussein's Strategic Plan for the Persian Gulf War* (Annapolis, MD, 2008).

29 For the most thorough examination of the Iranian side of the war, see Steven R. Ward, *Immortal: A Military History of Iran and Its Armed Forces* (Washington, DC, 2009). For the Iraqi side see Kenneth M. Pollack, *Arabs at War: Military Effectiveness, 1948–1991* (Fargo, ND, 2004); Anthony H. Cordesman and Abraham Wagner, *The Lessons of Modern War*, Vol. II: *The Iran-Iraq War* (Boulder, 1991).

Iraqis failed to seize the passes out of the Zagros Mountains, the main highway, or the rail lines south to Khorramshahr and Abadan.[30]

If the Iraqis were ill-prepared, the Iranians were worse off. Savaged by a purge of the officer corps, the Iranian military had sunk to a shadow of the forces the shah had once deployed. A deep suspicion of the shah's military had led Khomeini and his advisors to place their trust in the religious militia, the Pasdaran, which had been organized to protect the Islamic republic that they were creating. In the first battles, only the fanaticism of the Iranian militia and Iraqi incompetence prevented the Iraqis from making a clean sweep of the table. After a fierce fight and heavy casualties on both sides, the Iraqis captured Khorramshahr but failed to take Abadan and its refineries, which were soon wrecked by the artillery bombardments. The war then stabilized, as the Iraqis went over to the defensive.

Saddam announced his willingness to accept a reasonable peace, but he received only silence from the ayatollahs. In early January 1981 the desperate civilian government in Tehran, anxious to improve its own political standing, ordered the Iranian regular army to launch an offensive. The attack was a disaster, as the Iranian advance was channeled by the terrain and Iraqi defenses into a killing zone. This defeat stabilized the religious radicals' political position in Iran.

By the end of 1981, the Islamic Republic had mobilized vast numbers of Iranians and brought some order to its military. A series of major offensives, which relied on human-wave attacks, drove the Iraqis from Iranian soil with huge losses. Saddam for his part ordered large numbers of executions, from generals to privates. These executions *pour l'encouragement des autres* might well have encouraged large numbers of Iraqi soldiers to surrender – well over ten thousand did so – and caused the loss of vast amounts of equipment in the collapse around Khorramshahr.[31] Saddam was desperate to extricate himself from the mess, but Khomeini had no intention of letting him off the hook. After a pause, as the opposing sides considered the implications of the Israeli invasion of Lebanon (which each attributed to the machinations of its opponent), the Iranians launched a massive attack on the defenses surrounding Basra. Encouraged by the success of human-wave attacks in the first half of 1982, the Iranians replicated these tactics on an even greater scale. This time

30 Kevin M. Woods, Williamson Murray, and Thomas Holaday, *Saddam's War: An Iraqi Military Perspective of the Iran-Iraq War* (Washington, DC, 2009), 24–34.

31 Pollack, *Arabs at War*, 196–203.

the Iraqis were ready, and in the open ground east and north of Basra, Saddam's armor and artillery slaughtered the Iranians.[32]

The Pasdaran learned little. With the support of the ayatollahs in Tehran, it replicated human-wave attacks by lightly armed infantrymen for the remainder of the conflict, in the belief that sufficient numbers and religious fanaticism could overcome Iraqi superiority in firepower. Like World War I generals, the Iranians failed to change their approach, believing that more of the same would eventually open the gates to Shi'a world revolution. By contrast, the Iraqis displayed some willingness to learn. Saddam began slowly to replace incompetents with professional officers, who had some sense of how to wage a combined-arms war. The Iraqi approach replicated the German experience in Russa after 1942 – the buildup of an elite, mechanized force, the Republican Guard, which was assigned the best officers and equipment, alongside a mass army that was effective enough to hold until the mobile, mechanized brigades arrived to counterattack.

As the war continued, Saddam raised the ante. In 1982 Iraq began to launch SCUD missiles at Iranian cities, which represented the only target they could hit, given that the SCUDs were hardly more accurate than the V-2s of World War II. The Iranian reply was to attack Iraqi cities, first with aircraft, then with SCUDs that they had acquired from a variety of sources around the Middle East. By 1988 what was termed the "war of the cities" had caused nearly a million Iranians to flee Tehran in order to escape the Iraqi missiles. In 1982, with missile boats and Super Frelon helicopters firing French Exocet missiles, the Iraqis began an offensive against tanker traffic in the Gulf and against convoys that moved supplies to Bandar Khomeini. In 1983, after an Iranian operative bombed the French barracks in Beirut, the French government allowed Iraq access to Super Etendard long-range fighters that carried Exocet missiles and could reach deeper into the Gulf.[33]

In 1983 the Iraqis also began to experiment with gas warfare, which had not been used since Mussolini's forces faced Ethiopia's tribal levies in 1936. The experiments initially evolved into the large-scale use of gas to halt the human waves of Iranians, but Saddam was willing during the last two years of the war to use gas against his own people, in this case the Kurds of northern Iraq, between 150,000 and 200,000 of whom perished.[34]

32 Woods et al., *Saddam's War*, 48–61.

33 Edgar O'Ballance, *The Gulf War* (London, 1988), 124.

34 Marion Farouk-Sluglett and Peter Sluglett, *Iraq since 1958: From Revolution to Dictatorship* (London, 2001), 270.

As the Iran–Iraq War continued, the opposing sides resorted increasingly to extreme measures. From the summer of 1982 until early 1986 the Iranians launched a series of major attacks, most of which were human-wave assaults. Some broke through the initial Iraqi defense and reached rear areas. In every case except one, Iraqi firepower and counterattacks drove the Iranians back to their start lines. In January 1986, however, the Iranians caught the Iraqis by surprise, thanks probably to a major intelligence failure on the part of the latter.[35] The Pasdaran attacked weak Iraqi defenses on the Fao Peninsula, southwest of Basra, and overwhelmed the defenders. The goal was the port of Um Qasr and perhaps Basra itself, but the Iranians did not succeed. Nevertheless, the Iraqi response was slow. Swampy terrain minimized Iraqi artillery and gas attacks, while Iranian artillery on the other side of the Shatt al-Arab, the waterway along which the Tigris and Euphrates flowed to the Gulf, stopped Iraqi counterattacks. The losses on both sides were extraordinarily heavy. The fighting for the Fao Peninsula exhausted both, and there was another respite.

Nevertheless, Khomeini proclaimed that Iran would crush Saddam's Ba'athist regime by the beginning of the Persian new year, in March 1987. The result was another massive slugfest around the city of Basra. The Iranians fought their way into the suburbs, but here they were stopped. Both regimes were on the brink of collapse. But Saddam finally recognized that the leadership of the Iraq army needed to be turned over to the few military professionals who were available for a last throw of the dice.[36]

In early 1988, the Iraqis took the offensive with an army that had been substantially retrained and re-equipped. On April 17, they struck Iranian positions on the Fao Peninsula. Within two days the Iraqis had regained everything they had lost in 1986.[37] A month later, the Iraqis attacked north of Basra and again crushed their opponents. They then launched a third offensive, driving the Iranians out of their hard-won positions on the Majnoon island, which had great oil reserves. These devastating defeats, combined with a major naval confrontation with the Americans in the Gulf and the downing by an American cruiser of an Iranian civilian DC-10 on its way to Mecca with pilgrims finally persuaded the Iranians to call it quits. In July 1988 Khomeini announced the Iranian decision in personal terms, which was only right because it had been his war as much as Saddam's: "Taking this

35 Woods et al., *Saddam's War*, 70–74.
36 Pollack, *Arabs at War*, 208–9.
37 For a discussion of these battles, see ibid., 204–8.

decision was more deadly than poison. I submitted myself to God's will and drank this drink for his satisfaction."[38]

How can one explain the Iraqi victory? During the conflict's last two years, the collapse of oil prices exacerbated the financial drain on both powers, while the casualties on both sides created deep war weariness. Nevertheless, Saddam maintained his level of arms expenditure, while the Iranians could not. Loans from the Arab oil states, particularly Saudi Arabia and ironically Kuwait, allowed Saddam to fund Iraq's huge expenditures on arms from abroad, while Iranian arms purchases dropped drastically in the last two years of the conflict. As one Pasdaran commander put it: "They had the armor and we did not."[39] For Saddam, the Iraqi victory represented a confirmation of his genius, as well as the emergence of Iraq as the rightful leader of the Arab world. It led him in 1990 to invade Kuwait, not only to repair Iraq's hard-pressed finances, but also to seek a confrontation with the Americans, which he believed would drive the United States out of the Middle East and establish himself as the undisputed leader of an Arab superpower.[40] The results, however, underlined the limitations in Saddam's understanding of power outside his own narrow frame of reference in Iraq.

38 Ward, *Immortal*, 296.

39 Shahram Chubin, "The Last Phase of the Iran-Iraq War: From Statelmate to Ceasefire," *Wilson Quarterly* 11 (1989): 7.

40 Woods, *Mother of All Battles*, 47–57. For Saddam's views on his role in history, see Kevin M. Woods et al., *Iraqi Perspectives Project: A View of Operation Iraqi Freedom from Saddam's Senior Leadership* (Annapolis, MD, 2005).

21

Wars of decolonization, 1945–1975

ANTHONY CLAYTON

The major counterinsurgency wars of decolonization of the mid twentieth century were fought by the four European imperial nations, Britain, France, the Netherlands, and Portugal. They were asymmetric campaigns, which involved regular regiments in action against a wide variety of Asian and African non-state-actor groups. During the interwar period, British experiences in Ireland, Palestine, and India had highlighted the need for counterinsurgency training and tactics, especially for riot control and cordon-and-search operations. French experiences in Morocco and Syria had suggested the same lessons.

World War II aroused further anticolonial nationalism, while in Britain doubts emerged over the legitimacy of colonial rule. The Atlantic Charter, the formation of the United Nations, and the anticolonial views of US President Roosevelt brought colonialism to the forefront of international attention. The humiliating military reverses suffered during the war by Britain, France, and the Netherlands negated much of the residual respect for the strength of the colonial powers. Furthermore, the use by Britain and France of troops recruited from colonial peoples opened new mental horizons. Indian soldiers who fought fascism in Africa or Italy saw themselves fighting for their own freedom after the war. African soldiers who fought for the British in Burma or the French in Italy or France developed similar views; and a number of them figured later as insurgent leaders. Independence for India and Pakistan in 1947 and, a little later, for Ceylon, Burma, and almost all the Dutch East Indies provided further encouragement for nationalists in the remaining colonial territories.

The reactions to this changing international situation from the three major remaining colonial powers were, however, different. Britain was exhausted and in severe financial difficulties. Despite the urgings of senior military and air force officers, the country was neither able nor in the mood to furnish the funding or the indefinite continuation of compulsory military service that was

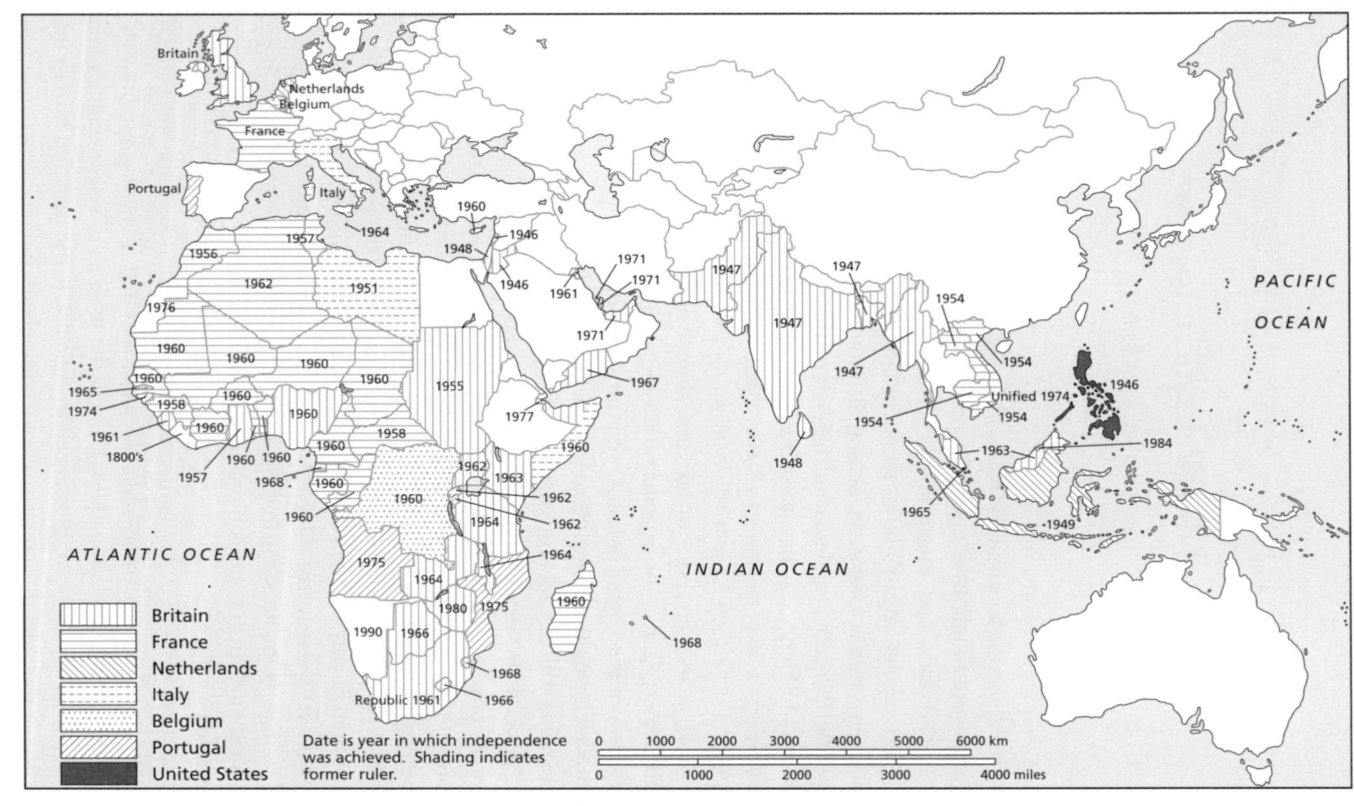

MAP 16. Decolonization in Asia and Africa

necessary for large-scale, prolonged colonial campaigns to retain sovereignty. At the same time, Britain regarded itself as a legitimate imperial authority and was not prepared to be ejected from a colony by military force (a view still evident in 1982). The Labour Party's election victory in 1945 reflected the public preference for a welfare state over empire. Furthermore, Britain's historic common-law tradition made it difficult to deny the wishes of the majority of a community, once they were freely and clearly expressed. Finally, postwar Britain was no longer the superpower of the interwar years; the Soviet Union and the United States were now the lead nations, and both were opposed to colonial systems. The outcome of these factors was that after a period of reappraisal, Britain developed a bipartisan consensus on moving toward colonial emancipation – a view that was reinforced by the failure to assert Anglo-French power at Suez in 1956 and a sober assessment of what was profitable or possible. The self-governing dominions and the Statutes of Westminster were taken as the path to follow, while the concept of a multi-racial commonwealth with the British monarch as titular head soothed middle-class misgivings. In military terms, this political approach translated into restricting the use of force to containing revolutionaries or extremists and to ensuring that when it came, any transition of power would result in regimes that were prepared to accommodate Britain's wider interests, if not those of the losers, the local settler colonists.[1]

France and Portugal had different worldviews, which led them into prolonged and bloody conflicts in the belief that retaining some form of sovereignty over overseas territories was essential for the nation's status. During the war, in Tunisia and Italy, and in the final liberation campaign in France itself, the French military had made significant steps toward recovering the reputation it had lost in 1940. However, these campaigns all involved large numbers of North and Black African troops. Like politicians and generals, the wider public believed that in a world increasingly dominated by *les Anglo-saxons*, France must retain the services of these troops for its independence, renown (*gloire*), and military strength. As the Cold War developed, French North Africa could also be portrayed as the essential southern flank of the North Atlantic Treaty Organization (NATO) – a view that was endorsed by

1 Wm. Roger Louis, "The Dissolution of the British Empire," in Judith M. Brown and Wm. Roger Louis, *The Oxford History of the British Empire*, Vol. IV: *The Twentieth Century* (Oxford, 1999), xiv; Dennis Austin "The Transfer of Power: Why and How," in W.H. Morris-Jones and George Fischer, eds., *Decolonization and After: The British and French Experience* (London, 1980), ii; Hew Strachan, "British Counter Insurgency from Malaya to Iraq," *Journal of the Royal United Service Institute* 152 (2007): 8–11.

the influential Algerian settler lobby and senior French military leaders. At the political level there were other constraints. Until January 1946 the government was headed by General de Gaulle, who accepted a limited measure of colonial reform but was in no mood for decolonization. During the following twelve years of dysfunctional politics of the Fourth Republic, power was concentrated in the National Assembly. Here the Communist Party enjoyed political credit because of its role in the resistance. The party turned to opposition in 1947, forcing a series of multiparty coalitions which seldom lasted long. Between January 1946 and the collapse of the Fourth Republic in May 1958, there were twenty-three governments. With one exception, the Mendès-France government from June 1954 to February 1955, none could respond to the challenges it faced. Most socialists supported the view that retaining the overseas territories was essential; the few who did not could not protest, because doing so would stain them as fellow-travelers of the Communists. As a result, in most of the coalitions the ministries that were responsible for overseas territories' affairs were drawn from the center-right and were unable to produce a national policy or strategy; instead, they offered only token concessions, which failed to impress nationalists. Behind all these military and political considerations lay the French centralist tradition, with its origins in Catholicism, the Revolution, and Roman law. It emphasized the superiority of French values – a view that was only questioned seriously during the Algerian War. With the collapse of the Fourth Republic, however, different constitutional and political conditions emerged.[2]

Colonial emancipation was even further from the mind of the Portuguese government. After 1932 Portugal, a poor country, had been ruled by Antonio Salazar. As prime minister, he was head of a corporate state that tolerated little opposition and ran an effective secret police both at home and in the colonies. The regime's style was nevertheless relatively lenient, so critics and even leaders of coup attempts did not receive severe punishments. The regime had gained a measure of respectability by eventually supporting the Allios, enabling itself to become a founding member of NATO. In 1951 the regime rebranded the Portuguese colonies as "Overseas Provinces" of an indivisible nation. These "provinces" were regarded as an additional bulwark against a Spanish takeover. Official rhetoric cited a civilizing mission, but the colonial administrations were backward and oppressive. Membership

2 Anthony Clayton, *The Wars of French Decolonization* (London, 1994), i; Joey Wang, "Understanding Insurgency and State Response – Does Historical Context Matter? A Look Back at France and Algeria," *Journal of the Royal United Services Institute* 153 (2008): 56–61.

in NATO gained Portugal powerful friends and provided the Portuguese with weaponry that could be used in the colonies.

None of the three countries' armies was prepared in 1945 for colonial counterinsurgency. The British army was war-weary, and the majority of its soldiers had trained for European warfare, although senior officers had prewar experience in Bengal and Palestine. Until 1960, most soldiers were conscripts who served for two years. Afterwards the army became an all-volunteer force. Regiments posted to Malaya or Kenya proved a well-trained and disciplined mix of long-term regular and conscript officers and men, all of whom quickly adapted to local circumstances. The British army also included several battalions of Gurkhas that had been transferred to British from Indian service in 1947. In the decolonization campaigns the most important colonial regiments were the Fiji regiment and the several battalions of the King's African Rifles, who were recruited from ethnic groups perceived to be "martial" in the east and central African colonies. Their officers were on secondment from British regiments. Each battalion was recruited from one individual colony.

The French army in 1945 was in the midst of reforms that had become necessary after the end of the war. Relations remained uneasy between senior officers – and units – who had fought under de Gaulle and those who had served Vichy until November 1942. The army's first challenge came on the day of victory in Europe in May 1945, when an uprising in the Sétif area of Algeria was suppressed. The opening of hostilities followed in Indochina in late 1946, and a revolt in Madagascar in 1947 was also put down. Equipment was short and training patchy. Until the Algerian War, French conscripts were not obliged to serve outside France or Germany unless they volunteered. The conflicts in Indochina and elsewhere had therefore to be fought with soldiers with strong colonial ties, long-service regulars from the semi-autonomous *Troupes coloniales*, other volunteers, and the Foreign Legion, which had recruited a number of soldiers from the *Wehrmacht*, together with the North and Black African regiments. The North African infantry and cavalry units were recruited from individual territories; the semi-regular *goums* came only from the Moroccan mountains. However, excepting those from Madagascar, the Black African units were all mixed together from west and equatorial Africa under the historic title of *Tirailleurs sénégalais*.

The Dutch government recognized after 1945 that the vast Dutch East Indies could not be the same empire as the one from which the Dutch had been ejected in 1942. It nevertheless wished to reassert as much authority and control as was possible, in the erroneous belief that domestic economic recovery and prosperity depended on it. The Netherlands lacked the necessary manpower, economic strength, and international support to fight a costly counterinsurgency campaign.

The military possessed great power and influence in Salazar's Portugal. Until reforms in 1958, officers were drawn from the wealthiest sectors of society. Soldiers were conscripted, while the period of service varied from fifteen months to two years; by the 1960s the term had been extended to four years. Soldiers could be later recalled to the colonies, sometimes more than once. Until the 1960s, however, metropolitan troop levels in the "overseas provinces" were low, as garrisons were formed from locally recruited men with Portuguese officers. The standards of training were indifferent in any case, for insurrection was not foreseen.

As colonial campaigns developed after 1945, all four European countries developed new specialized combat units, tactics, intelligence agencies, and equipment. There was also much day-to-day improvisation in these campaigns, as political goals were modified for reasons that reflected local colonial or metropolitan political concerns. While France was aware of the nationalist challenges it faced in both Indochina and Algeria, the military dimension was badly underestimated. In the case of Britain, to paraphrase an observation made by Admiral Mountbatten, every conflict after 1945 caught London by surprise. Given all the moral and legal complexities of counterinsurgency, military needs, public opinion, and goals, it is debatable whether any far-sighted strategy was possible in a democracy. Certainly, though, the absence of clear forward thinking contributed to the difficulties and character of the campaigns, as well as to their eventual outcomes.[3]

The colonial insurgent groups were varied, and their origins bore closely on local conditions and styles of fighting. Nevertheless, these groups displayed two common features. First, they all set out to attain power and to end a colonial relationship, whose authority they saw as illegitimate; and, with the exception of Kenya's Mau Mau, all insurgents received political support and weaponry from outside. Second, insurgent operations developed symbolic value toward local and international publicity – the "Propaganda of the Deed" – whether it entailed terrifying brutality or spectacular attacks. Because they were responsible to no one but themselves, insurgents could distort freely to manipulate opinion, to create a romantic mythology in legitimizing their cause, and to attract recruits or provoke an overreaction.

3 James S. Corum, *Bad Strategies: How Major Powers Fail in Counterinsurgency* (Minneapolis, 2008), 17–30, argues that the absence of an overall strategy caused and protracted campaigns.

Insurgents also realized that popular media reports of abuses by European security forces, whether true or false, would trouble consciences and bring political benefits in western democracies.

The two largest wars of decolonization were waged by France in Indochina and in Algeria. While the Algerian War engaged the greatest numbers, the war in Indochina had more far-reaching consequences and was the more significant to the history of war. France had lost control over its Indochinese territories to the Japanese in World War II; and after the Japanese surrender, de Gaulle planned to restore French authority. He dispatched the enlightened and politically sensitive General Leclerc de Hauteclocque to be military commander in Indochina. Arriving in October 1945 with British military assistance for his small force, Leclerc quickly reasserted French control over much of Indochina. With a mix of political understanding, good intelligence, and military sweep-operations on land and water with aircraft and light-artillery support, he had within four months brought the south of Vietnam, Laos, and Cambodia back under French control.

The north of Vietnam, Tonkin in particular, was a different matter. Here, during Japanese occupation and the last months of 1945, Nguyên ai Quôc, who was later later known as Ho Chi Minh and was a founding member of both the metropolitan French and the local Vietnamese Communist parties, steadily imposed a revolutionary, cell-structured guerrilla organization on the civilian population. Its adherents and recruits came mostly from laborers and peasant farmers in these "liberated zones," in which land redistribution, political education, and bonding rituals followed. Claiming during the war that it was fighting the Japanese, the resistance front had received light weaponry from the United States, which was passed to the Communist-controlled cells. Ho and his followers had also destroyed the authority of the client government that the Japanese had set up in August 1945 under the amiable but self-indulgent Emperor Bao Dai. On September 2, Ho proclaimed an independent state of Vietnam. This declaration defied de Gaulle's project for internal autonomy, in which a French governor would retain authority over defense and foreign affairs, although its main purpose was to remove Chinese forces, which were at the time occupying and exploiting the north following wartime agreements. Within the cell structure, Maoist concepts of revolutionary warfare were taught. The most central of these was the assertion that a weaker guerrilla force could overcome a more powerful army – first by mobilizing the masses, educating, training, and securing safe areas, then by extending the safe areas and forcing the enemy to disperse, and finally by undertaking joint operations, combining units formed from these front areas

36. Ho Chi Minh

with trained guerrilla bands that attacked the enemy's rear areas. To this operational art Ho's able field commander, Vo Nguyen Giap, advocated the addition of terror and torture in order to raise insurgent morale and discourage opponents. Practice had been gained during the elimination of non-communist nationalists within the national resistance force, which appeared to underline the communist theory of an essential unity between front and rear. Further assets for the insurgents lay in the terrain in northern Vietnam – its mountainous territory, woodlands, and rice paddies – and the difficulty that the French would face in distinguishing Viet-Minh insurgents from innocent farmers.

Leclerc concluded that military reconquest of all Indochina was no longer practical. Following his arrival in Hanoi in March 1946, he opened talks with Ho Chi Minh, who had been encouraged by de Gaulle's departure from office in Paris. Ho was also willing to accept the presence of French troops in order to expedite the departure of the Chinese, which Leclerc's soldiers quickly ensured. A short-term agreement that provided for Vietnamese independence within a French Union was reached, but it was rejected by the French high commissioner and the first of the dysfunctional governments in Paris. Disputes over several issues led to violence, and in November 1946, when the French forces numbered some sixty thousand, war broke out. The French commander was confident of a quick victory.

The war fell into four phases. In the opening years, 1946–48, the Viet Minh were forced to withdraw from the Hanoi area, while their attempts to besiege several towns failed at heavy cost. Their following operations were mostly small-scale, mounted from safe zones in the north and northwest – ambushes and limited strikes against French posts, scorched-earth destruction, and slipping away into woods, fields or hills. Supported by artillery and aircraft, the French attempted to enter the mountain areas but were largely foiled, although the Viet Minh suffered heavy casualties. The year 1947 saw much industrial unrest and rioting in metropolitan France, as the issue of Indochina now contributed to the domestic turmoil. The uprising in Madagascar delayed the arrival of reinforcements in Indochina, where a shortage of manpower prevented large-scale operations. Nevertheless the French remained confident of ultimate success.

The next two years, however, saw fortunes change. Negotiations over the formation of a moderate nationalist government under Bao Dai lost popular support. The Communist victory in China renewed the Viet Minh's ideological confidence; it also provided safe bases across the frontier, as well as a supply of rifles from fleeing Nationalist Chinese troops. Giap linked his frontier stronghold areas to guerrillas who operated further south in the Red River rice area. Although the French gained control in early 1950 over the northern Indochinese rice areas, the balance of forces now favored the Viet Minh, as French forces, which now totaled some 145,000, were scattered into small forts that were frequently attacked by locally superior Viet-Minh forces. The Viet Minh now had twenty thousand fighters in regular units, who were trained and equipped by the Chinese, politically motivated, and backed by thousands of part-time insurgents and others who supported them as porters of food and supplies. Giap could put the equivalent of five small divisions in the field. In October he inflicted a massive defeat on a divided French force in the north, at Cao Bang. The French suffered 4,500 dead or missing, with scores more wounded. The defeat forced them to withdraw from the north and to prepare to evacuate Hanoi. In France itself, support for the war all but vanished amid antiwar demonstrations and sabotage. A scandal involving two senior generals further sapped morale. It was learned that one of them, the chief of staff, advocated withdrawing from Indochina.

Nevertheless, after December Giap faced the only French general whom, as he later admitted, he feared. This was Jean de Lattre de Tassigny, a soldier of passion and volcanic temperament. During the so-called *année de Lattre*, he first rallied the demoralized French units, then shattered an attack by thirteen thousand Viet-Minh fighters near Hanoi, which featured human-wave attacks by insurgents who were reported by the French to be chained together. De Lattre next constructed a line of some nine hundred blockhouses to cover the Delta and Hanoi, as well as sally-ports to mobilize two- or three-battalion-sized combat groups. These could move out rapidly in armored half-tracks with support from parachute units, light artillery, and aircraft. Command and intelligence procedures were reformed, and Paris was persuaded to send additional units. Then, on his own initiative and against the advice of his staff, de Lattre won a second big victory over the Viet Minh at Mao Khe. A series of sweeps and attacks followed in the Delta with varying degrees of success, while the French mounted a vigorous defense of areas they held elsewhere. No less important was de Lattre's decision to raise a local army, which he inspired with his passion and sincerity. Taking advantage of the Korean War, he also convinced the Americans during a visit to the United States that the issues at stake in the two conflicts were the same. He thus encouraged a major program of American aid, principally in the form of aircraft and landing craft. At the end of 1951, however, de Lattre fell terminally ill and returned to France.

After his departure the Viet Minh steadily gained ascendancy in heavy fighting in 1952 and 1953. They were now able to bring numerical superiority to sites of their choosing and to gain control of areas by infiltration. In response, de Lattre's successor, Raoul Salan, devised the concept of the land-air base, a strong point with covering fields of fire, light artillery, and an air strip. These bases gained some local successes but were far from decisive. Because he was thought to be too defensive, he was replaced in May 1953 by Henri Navarre, a general whose experience was limited to Europe. The Viet Minh suffered early reverses against Navarre, whose force level reached 375,000, including 151,000 soldiers of the Vietnamese army, some whom were of dubious loyalty. Navarre undertook a parachute attack on a northern frontier fort and destroyed a Viet-Minh division in the Delta. Faced in Laos with a new Pathet Lao guerrilla force, which was supported by Giap, Navarre made the fatal decision in November 1953 to build up a super land-air base at Dien Bien Phu, from which he believed he could control communications to and from Tonkin, Laos, and China. Surrounded by hills, it lay in disastrous terrain. The garrison, which at its peak numbered fifteen thousand, was invested by some sixty thousand Viet Minh, who fired medium artillery guns from the hills. Unbeknown to French intelligence, these had been supplied by the Chinese. Additional supplies were meanwhile brought through tunnels by thousands of porters. On March 13 Giap opened his big attack. Wave upon wave of Viet Minh attacked and overran the surrounding forts, supported by a 56-day-long artillery barrage. Giap organized simultaneous guerrilla attacks in all the other areas he controlled, in order to prevent the formation of French relief forces. The French in vain sought American intervention. After an epic resistance by the mixed French, Legion, North, and Black African garrisons, the last fort was overrun on May 7, 1954.

It was the worst disaster in French colonial history. Of the garrison, 3,000 were killed and 10,000 taken prisoner; the balance of the garrison, 2,000 locally recruited Thais, were thought to have deserted. A large number of the prisoners died from privation in captivity. Giap's success came at the cost of at least eight thousand Viet Minh killed and fifteen thousand wounded.

The attack had been planned to coincide with an international conference in Geneva, which sought settlements in both Korea and Indochina. The defeat at Dien Bien Phu brought the fall of the government in Paris and its replacement in June by the most capable administration of the Fourth Republic, that of Pierre Mendès-France. He used his influence, skills, and France's residual military power to secure the partition of Vietnam along the 17th Parallel. This agreement accompanied the promise, never fulfilled, of free elections in the North as well as the South, together with the end of the French rule in Laos and Cambodia. However, nothing could conceal the collapse of French power in Indochina. Despite the promise of free elections, the North remained under Communist control, the South under a corrupt political system.[4]

An unusual feature of the war was the role of the French navy. Aircraft were flown off aircraft carriers even during monsoons. Cruisers and destroyers shelled Viet-Minh positions on the coast and up navigable rivers. With silenced engines, naval assault units on patrol or landing craft attacked Viet-Minh posts and relieved French posts under siege. Some boats were sunk by Viet-Minh artillery.

The consequences of the Viet-Minh victory lay in the longer term. The confidence of Ho Chi Minh and Giap grew that a peasant army could with revolutionary tactics defeat a well-equipped western regular army. Together with the Americans' belief that their own role was to provide the military

4 Clayton, *Wars of French Decolonization*, ii–v; Jacques Dalloz, *The War in Indochina 1945–54* (Dublin, 1990); Vo Nguyen Giap, *Peoples War, Peoples Army* (Dehra Dun, 1974); Douglas Porch, "French Imperial Warfare, 1945–62," in Daniel Marston and Carter Malkasian, eds., *Counterinsurgency in Modern Warfare* (London, 2008), 81–112; Russell Stetler, ed., *The Military Art of People's War: Selected Writings of General Vo Nguyen Giap* (New York, 1970).

power to contain communism, this confidence led to further, bloodier war. Viet-Minh success inspired other revolutionaries, notably in Portuguese Africa, and nationalists, especially in Tunisia and Morocco, where France mounted smaller-scale counterinsurgency operations before conceding independence.

In France itself, the military blamed the politicians for their irresolute policies and, more particularly, for French numerical weakness in Indochina, because conscripts had not been sent to the war. A group of middle-level French officers from elite units, colonels who smarted from what they saw as a shameful betrayal of loyalist communities, developed their own doctrine of counterrevolutionary warfare. It held that revolutionary warfare could only be met by a total political and military strategy, whose object was to win hearts and minds. In this effort, military needs were to trump legal and political restrictions, as well as traditional moral scruples. Military operations required unrestrained intelligence-gathering, including torture. Military action should target insurgent leaders for assassination or interrogation, as well as insurgents' supply routes. Areas should be dominated in order to keep insurgents on the run; if necessary, whole communities might be deported, interned, or punished. At the same time, as part of the psychological warfare, the military should lead the pacification effort, building roads, schools, markets, and medical centers. This doctrine contained its own contradictions. A "pacified" area could be reoccupied by insurgents, whose brutal punishments could negate the effects of pacification and increase civil revulsion against military excesses. These contradictions, which were arguably fatal, became evident in France's next major campaign.[5]

French rule in Algeria had traditionally been based on shadowy supervision from Paris, while direct control over local affairs lay in the hands of the *colon* community, some eight hundred thousand European settlers. Indigenous Algerians had been excluded not only from political influence and landowning, but also from many middle-, lower-middle-class and artisan occupations, all at a time of population growth. French, not Muslim law ruled. Some 90 percent of the indigenous population were illiterate; few had access to secondary education. The local nobility had been destroyed and non-revolutionary nationalists sidelined. The immiseration of the indigenous population, some 4.5 million, molded the insurgent movement, the

5 David Galula, *Counterinsurgency Warfare: Theory and Practice* (New York, 1964); Peter Paret, *French Revolutionary Warfare from Indo-China to Algeria* (London, 1964); Roger Trinquier, *Modern Warfare: A French View of Counterinsurgency* (Westport, CT, 2006).

FLN (*Front de Libération Nationale*) and its army ALN (*Armée de Libération Nationale*). The "historic nine" committee, which was based on an earlier subversive movement, comprised Muslims, although they were not strongly ideologically motivated. Their aim was simply to evict the French. The majority of the nine were Arabs; two were Kabyle (Berber), two had served as noncommissioned officers in the French army (one, Ben Bella, was decorated), but only had a secondary education. These rough men led other rough men to terrorism, which encouraged the new French doctrine, which led in turn to further political reaction. Nevertheless, it took time and brutality to mobilize Algeria's disparate clans and peoples. Eventually the resistance organization emerged. Under a central command, six *wilaya*, or districts, were led by local commanders. Their combat units were composed of 350-men battalions, or *failek*, 110-men companies, called *katiba*, and 11-men sections, or *faoudj*.

The ALN hoped to take the *colon* community by surprise when it launched seventy attacks on settlers and pro-French Algerians on All Saints Eve in 1954. In fact, the first twenty months of the campaign saw steady deterioration of the French position. The ALN recruited well, notably among the Kabyle. It mounted attacks in groups of fifty or more fighters, although many of them were armed only with sporting weapons. For logistics a six-person cell structure was developed in many areas. Too weak to build safe zones, however, the groups turned to terror killings, disembowelling and mutilation, and other atrocities against French military, *colons* and loyalist Muslims. The French military responded slowly, for its intelligence was poor. With the arrival of elite units, more vigorous action followed. Small patrols were dispatched by helicopter into the mountains, and military-administration units were tasked for medical, educational, social, and agricultural-development work. Because some North African units were no longer reliable, their place was taken by *harki*, locally recruited loyalists, who infiltrated FLN areas in order to identify ALN members.

As the situation worsened, the government in Paris authorized the use of conscripts, bringing the total of French troops in Algeria to 390,000 (it subseqently reached 415,000). The conscripts were mostly used in *quadrillage*, the non-mobile protection of settlements and townships. In practice, a two-tier army emerged of elite professionals and reluctant conscripts, many of whom had protested, even to the extent of minor sabotage, against their own drafting. The cost of the campaign rose to over a million pounds per day, while the French economy also suffered from the shortage of labor. Weaponry supplied for NATO use was increasingly employed.

In 1956 the insurgents were encouraged when the French granted independence to Morocco and Tunisia, as well as by a successful secret conference among insurgent leaders, where the FLN's goal, a democratic socialist Algeria, was confirmed. The same conference created a combined military and political command structure, in which collective decisions were made, and a structure of ranks for officers and noncommissioned officers in the ALN. An additional boost to morale was the failure of the British and French to remove President Nasser of Egypt after the Suez intervention. The growing criticism of France also supported the "External FLN" leaders in Cairo and other Arab capitals, as they arranged publicity and weapons deliveries; and it strengthened opposition to France in the United Nations and the United States. The French hijacking of an aircraft with FLN external leaders on board, including Ben Bella, in October 1956 brought strong protests internationally and in France itself. French writers, journalists, and increasing numbers of the general public argued that the war was immoral and no longer in France's interest.

In January 1957 General Jacques Massu's elite parachute division attempted to clear Algeria of FLN activists. As soon became known worldwide, the operation was conducted with torture, interrogation, and the killing of some three thousand suspects. Although several ALN leaders were killed, insurgent activity increased. Strong international criticism followed a French air attack across the Tunisian border in February 1958. In May the Fourth French Republic collapsed in the face of *colon* demonstrations in Algiers and the threat of a military takeover – not only in Algeria but also in France itself. General de Gaulle returned to power in the belief that he could institute military repression. He had the power to control policy, but as a retired general his paradoxial challenge was to reassert political control over his army.

After a massive French military offensive throughout Algeria, virtually all ALN operations ended for a time. This campaign was designed to emphasize that whatever the political outcome, there would be no second Dien Bien Phu. De Gaulle's efforts to tame the situation included offering moderate political solutions to the Algerians, which only generated anger among Algeria's *colons* over what they saw as betrayal. His increasingly evident view that the war was an impediment to France's international standing and moral reputation, together with his attempts to negotiate with the FLN, led to a final rebellion by elite units, who briefly staged a coup in Algiers in April 1961. In an elegant and moving appeal, de Gaulle called his soldiers and the public to order; the mass of conscripts rallied, and the coup collapsed. But the episode was nonetheless the mortal blow to the French cause. Negotiations with an

FLN-dominated provisional government in exile, including Ben Bella, led to an agreement by which the French retained their oil and nuclear weaponry in southern Algeria. The FLN honored this agreement but disregarded promises of security for French *colons*. In a kind of ethnic cleansing with a "coffin or suitcase" option, brutal attacks on the *colons* followed, as the French army withdrew to barracks. Over 750,000 *colons* left for France, while extremists formed a terrorist group, the OAS (*Organisation Armée Secrète*), which attacked settlers who wished to leave, indigenous Algerians, utilities, and farms in a demented orgy of bitter fury. In France itself, where Algerian laborers had also turned to violence during the war, supporters of French rule engaged in street protests, and the OAS made a number of attempts to kill de Gaulle. A special paramilitary police unit was formed to hunt down the OAS in France; its methods were as brutal as any that had been employed during the war itself.

In its main objective the FLN won the war. The French were gone. But it inherited a devastated country and economy. Bitter divisions developed between the internal FLN, which had borne the brunt of the fighting, and the returning external leaders, as well as between Arabs and Kabyle. De Gaulle showed little concern for loyalist *harkis*, but individual French commanders disregarded instructions and smuggled many back to France. Those who could not escape were put to work by the FLN to clear the Moroccan and Tunisian border of minefields that the French had laid; hundreds of *harkis* were killed in this effort.

De Gaulle was able to indulge his perception of France's world role, in which anti-American resentment featured prominently. But his authoritarian, pretentious, grandiose style of rule alienated many of his own people, and in 1969, only seven years after this second great service to his nation, he resigned following the humiliation of the 1968 student–worker riots.

Several military aspects of the Algerian War deserve mention. The French used frightening, noisy Harvard training aircraft for bombing (including napalm), as well as larger Sikorsky helicopters to allow elite *commandos de chasse* to pursue ALN groups on the run. The ALN possessed no antiaircraft weaponry or missiles with which to reply. Two massive fortified lines of electrified wire and mines marked the frontiers. Naval forces intercepted ALN arms-runners, and the development of intelligence-gathering enabled both sides to detect well-concealed opponents by sense of smell.

The French attempted to employ the counterrevolutionary doctrine of psychological warfare and development work in rural areas, moving as many as 1.5 million people into insanitary camps. They achieved some later success in village resettlement, but it was generally counteracted by FLN propaganda and ruthless French military operations. The special staff was disbanded by de Gaulle in 1960.[6]

The military operations that led to the independence of Indonesia were complex. The insurgents in the islands that constituted the huge territory had dissimilar cultures and agendas. Islam and a small black cap, a political badge, represented a unifying nationalist factor for most, but by no means all, the different groups. On the densely populated island of Java, leaders had their own agenda, which included not only independence but also the extension of Javanese authority, together with *transmigrattie* – the exportation of Javanese people to the other islands. The Javanese supplied most of the nationalist leadership, if not the followers, for most of this island's people were poor and preliterate.

Japanese occupation had ended the Dutch colonial order but produced an even more oppressive occupation. While the Japanese need for local infrastructure led to a measure of political and administrative training for young Indonesians, Japanese arrogance and demands for labor aroused hatred. The Japanese trained and armed small local forces to harass any British or American invasion, but by February 1945 some units of the *Peta* (Protectors of the Fatherland), the most significant of these forces, were attacking the Japanese. The Japanese surrender in August 1945 threw the islands, especially Java, Sumatra, and Madura, into turmoil. Young *Peta* revolutionaries seized the nationalist political leaders, Achmed Sukarno and Mohammad Hatta, and pressured them into issuing a unilateral declaration of independence.

The first of the guerrilla campaigns followed. The Japanese were tasked under the surrender terms with maintaining order until the arrival of Allied forces. Accordingly, they were attacked by *Peta* and other young revolutionaries, who were often ill-trained and ill-disciplined. The arrival of Allied troops, British, Australian, and Indian, then led to clashes and the forcible occupation of Surabaya, as the young revolutionaries turned their attention to the new occupiers, who were preparing the way for the return of the Dutch.

By early 1946 the Dutch had cobbled together a military force that grew to a hundred thousand men during the next months. The British force withdrew, and the Dutch attempted to restore their authority with arrests and anti-guerrilla operations. Under American pressure, a ceasefire began in October 1946. In November an agreement reached in a village called Lingajatti provided

6 Charles Robert Ageron, *Modern Algeria* (London, 1994); Alf Andrew Heggoy, *Insurgency and Counter-Insurgency in Algeria* (Bloomington, 1972); Alistair Horne, *A Savage War of Peace: Algeria 1954–1962* (London, 2006); Porch, "French Imperial Warfare," v.

for a federal state of Indonesia, including an autonomous Javanese-Sumatran Republic, but Dutch protection was to remain on other islands, with the queen of the Netherlands as the sovereign. This arrangement soon collapsed amidst mutual suspicion, the resumption of guerrilla warfare, and the Dutch initiation of "police action," in which they occupied most urban areas in east and west Java and key areas of Sumatra. Only British and American pressure restrained the Dutch from occupying the capital, Jogjakarta. Further pressure from the United Nations and United States led to another ceasefire and a second agreement, which was similar to that of November 1946, in January 1948. This agreement, too, foundered on mistrust, but the situation radically changed in September, when a badly planned communist uprising erupted in central Java. Sukarno's small army easily suppressed the revolt, and in the process earned the cachet, which made him invaluable in the eyes of the Americans, of being an anti-communist.

The Dutch then demanded that the Javanese Republic be incorporated into an all-inclusive federation, in which the Netherlands would retain considerable influence. The demand remained unanswered, so in December 1948 the Dutch launched a massive second "police action." This one involved parachute troops and artillery, and it issued in the occupation of Jogjakarta and the arrest of Sukarno and other Republican leaders. The operation triggered renewed partisan violence, as well as international political and economic pressure on the Netherlands, which was led by the Americans. It forced the Dutch to release Sukarno and other leaders, to join a round-table conference at The Hague from August to November 1949. Here an agreement for independence, a federal constitution, and an overarching Netherlands–Indonesia Union under the Dutch crown was reached. It took effect on December 27.

In August 1950, the Sukarno government abandoned the federal constitution and imposed Javanese control over all the former Dutch East Indies except West Irian, which remained Dutch until 1963. Numbers of Indonesians, Ambonese, Christians, and others were permitted to go to Holland, where their numbers changed the demography of the Netherlands – and added greatly to Dutch cuisine.[7]

In proportion to its size, Salazar's corporate state in Portugal made as great an effort to retain its African colonies as France had in its two big campaigns. Portugal faced a rebellion in Angola in 1961 and, after 1963, guerrilla insurgency there and in its other African territories, Mozambique and Guinea.

7 M. C. Ricklefs, *A History of Modern Indonesia since c.1300* (Basingstoke, 1993); Lea E Williams, *Southeast Asia: A History* (New York, 1976), 210–16.

Portugal was obliged to call and recall conscripts, peasants, and professional men alike, for the wars. In the early 1970s over 650,000 men were serving in Africa. The draft became intensely unpopular and brought high desertion rates, protests, and sabotage. The draft and service in these campaigns also radicalized many officers and men, including several senior military and naval commanders. In all three territories the insurgency was the result of repressive administration, obligatory labor, and limited education facilities. In Angola and Mozambique there were large settler populations, many employed in working-class occupations. The costs of the campaign had risen to over 6 percent of the nation's GDP by 1968.

The first Angolan uprising was limited to the northern Bakongo people. It was directed from the neighboring Congo, where the majority of the Bakongo lived. Local grievances included forced cotton-growing, land disputes, and labor and dynastic conflicts. The revolt came as a shock to the Portuguese, who were prisoners of their own rhetoric of a "historic mission" and referred to the uprising as "The Interruption" of this mission. The insurgents' first leader, Antonio Mariano, directed a dissident religious sect and led attacks on settler farms in the north. These were quickly suppressed. A second series of attacks followed in the Luanda area; it was the work of a Marxist party, the MPLA (*Movimento Popular de Libertação de Angola*), which was led by men of mixed race, primarily from the Mbundu ethnic group. This was followed by another uprising of the Bakongo in the north, directed now by Holden Roberto, the head of the UPA (*União das Populações de Angola*), which was later renamed FNLA (*Frente Nacional de Libertação de Angola*) with a military wing, ANLA, the National Liberation Army of Angola. Roberto drew support, including weapons, from the Congo. The fighting was ferocious on both sides. Matchete-carrying ANLA fighters tortured and crucified Portuguese and loyalists in ambushes, attacked settlements, and mined roads. The Portuguese replied with the burning of villages, aerial bombing, and the public display of insurgents' corpses. Two thousand Europeans and fifty thousand Africans were killed in the fighting.

Insurgency began in Guinea in 1961, in Angola again in 1963, and in Mozambique in 1964. In all three territories, insurgent activity was rural, and it generally followed a Maoist pattern – a preparatory phase of organization, a phase of terror and agitation, then open guerrilla war. Initial insurgent attacks were limited strikes followed by withdrawal to forests or hills; later operations turned to laying mines on roads and tracks, as well as the use of mortars and rocket-launchers. In all three territories insurgent groups operated out of a friendly neighboring country. Until the early 1970s,

Portuguese operations suffered from poor coordination among military and civil authorities and intelligence organizations. By the time better coordination was achieved, Portuguese forces had been forced onto the defensive, and large offensive sweeps were replaced by aircraft reconnaissance and bombing, followed by ground and helicopter patrols. Under NATO arrangements, France sold the Portuguese helicopters and armored cars, Britain supplied armored cars, and Italy provided aircraft. Exploiting the number of ethnic groups that opposed the insurgents, Portugal's commanders recruited among them, particularly the Pula in Guinea and the Macau in Mozambique. Many of these recruits served in special-forces intelligence units, which also included former insurgents. Portuguese emulation of the French doctrine of military involvement in development and psychological warfare was more successful in Guinea than Mozambique, where forced concentration into villages, *aldeamentos*, was poorly manned. In all three territories, a serious slump in the morale of the Portuguese conscripts was evident by the early 1970s, as missions were performed perfunctorily or noisily to give advance warning. Furthermore, Portugal's campaign had attracted widespread opposition in the United Nations and the Organization of African Unity.

In Angola, a new grouping, UNITA (*União Nacional Para a Independência Total de Angola*), which was recruited from the southern Ovimbundu and Chokwe peoples, broke away from the FNLA and opened the conflict in the southeast with limited Chinese support. With forces trained in eastern Europe and with Soviet support, the MPLA men operated meanwhile in the Luanda area, but they were handicapped by FNLA groups to the north. All three insurgent movements stressed political education, aspiring to become the nucleus of a revolutionary army. By the late 1960s, MPLA forces were structured into columns, squadrons, and platoons that comprised some five thousand men, which were, however, easily spotted by Portuguese aircraft. With some five thousand fighters of their own, FNLA groups attacked farms and military outposts in the north. The three movements were, however, never able to act together. Their divisions enabled the Portuguese military command to maintain general control over the whole territory, while economic development continued despite destruction of the Benguela railway.

The most effective movement in Mozambique, FRELIMO (*Frente de Libertação de Moçambique*) drew its followers from the northern Makonde and Nyanja ethnic groups. The main division was between political and military leaders. When the liberal pro-western political leader Eduardo

Mondlane was assassinated in 1964 (probably by Portuguese agents), leadership passed to the Marxist field commander, Samora Machel.

FRELIMO was supported by Tanzania and Zambia, as well as by China. The Portuguese attempted to hold FRELIMO on the Rovuma River, but the campaign intensified, as FRELIMO deployed groups several thousand strong with surface-to-air missiles and rocket artillery, forcing the Portuguese to deploy, in reply, sixty thousand men. As a massacre in 1972 revealed, not all of these troops were well trained. Women played an important role in FRELIMO, collecting intelligence and gathering food. In 1968 FRELIMO surprised the Portuguese with an attack in the west, behind troops that were fighting in the north. By 1974, the Portuguese were in trouble but not beaten, while economic development continued, albeit with difficulty, around the Cabora Bassa dam.

In Guinea, the insurgent movement PAIGC (*Partido Africano da Independência de Guiné e Cabo Verde*) was formed jointly among men of mixed race from the Cape Verde islands and mainlanders of the Balante ethnic group. Their leader, the Marxist Amilcar Cabral, was assassinated, almost certainly by Portuguese agents, in 1973. The PAIGC received artillery support from across the border in Guinea-Conakry, and by the early 1970s it was receiving rockets and surface-to-air missiles. PAIGC tactics were singular. They aimed to demonstrate the essential unity of front and rear, specifically to liberate interior zones as well as border areas, and to besiege Portuguese garrisons. With a field strength of over sixty thousand, the PAIGC had occupied several areas by 1972, in which it established an administration and held elections; in 1973 PAIGC declared the territory's independence. The able – and humane – Portuguese governor, General Antonio Spinola, realized that the territory was all but lost and returned to Lisbon to campaign for a new, more liberal policy in Africa.

The strains of the African campaigns were one of the causes of the Portuguese revolution in April 1974, which featured a coup of young officers against the corporate state, which Salazar's successor, Marcello Caetano, had done little to reform. The coup led to a period of turbulence, in which a regime headed by Spinola was replaced by governments of more radical officers, accompanied by revolutionary outbreaks throughout the country. By 1976 order had been restored, free democratic elections held, and negotiations for entry into the European Economic Community opened. The African territories became independent. PAIGC controlled Guinea, FRELIMO Mozambique. In Angola the three rival groups turned to fighting each other, although the MPLA, which held Luanda, was the better placed.

Several hundred thousand Portuguese settlers from the two big territories returned to Portugal.[8]

Because the successor governments in Angola and Mozambique were both Marxist, South Africa supported a new anti-Marxist group in Mozambique and opposed UNITA in Angola. Civil war in Mozambique lasted until 1992. In Angola the fighting became an extension of the Cold War, as sixty thousand Cuban troops with modern Soviet equipment eventually mastered both UNITA and the South African army in tank and aircraft battles. The defeat of the South Africans contributed to the end of apartheid in South Africa itself. But Angola suffered fifteen years of devastating fighting, as UNITA fought on until the end of the century.

The political framework of the British campaigns has already been set out. Because they did not represent desperate attempts to maintain sovereignty, they were all on a much smaller scale than those of France or Portugal. They also involved smaller areas. In most, existing local civil and police administrations proved useful, as did ethnic groups and other communities that did not support the aims of the territory's insurgents. Critics have argued that Britain pursued divide-and-rule policies, but many divisions were already there; and the support or acquiescence of communities that were not involved in the insurgency was important in securing a long-term settlement. Britain was, however, not averse to using African and Fijian regiments in its first major counterinsurgency campaign, in Malaya. The genesis of this campaign has already been set out, but a few points need mention here for the sake of comparison with later operations.

In Malaya the insurgents were almost exclusively Chinese and communist. They were unable to gain control of a specific region, while their lack of effective external support and their commitment of a number of excesses prepared ground for the government's psychological work, its development of social services, and, most important, its promise of independence. The measures taken by the military commanders, notably General Sir Gerald Templer, became a much-publicized British template for counterinsurgency

8 Ian F. W. Beckett, "The Portuguese Army: The Campaign in Mozambique 1964–74," in Ian F. W. Beckett and John Pimlott, eds., *Armed Forces and Modern Counter-Insurgency* (London, 1985), 136–62; John P. Cann, *Counterinsurgency in Africa: The Portuguese Way of War 1961–1974* (Westport, CT, 1997); A. J. Ventner, *Portugal's War in Guinea-Bissau* (Pasadena, CA, 1973). The linked campaign that Southern Rhodesia's breakaway government fought until 1974 against nationalist insurgents is summarized in J. R. T, Wood, "Countering the Chimurenga," in Marston and Malkasian, eds., *Counterinsurgency*, 185–202; and in Paul Moorcraft and Peter McLaughlin, *The Rhodesia War: A Military History* (Barnsley, 2008).

operations – particularly the promise of independence, the coordination of administration, military, and police, and the settlement of communities into villages protected by locally recruited guards.[9]

The Mau Mau insurgency, which opened in Kenya in 1952, was the result of demographic pressure on scarce land, particularly among the Kikuyu group of peoples, the eviction of labor from the white-settler farms, and an urban wage economy that remained below the poverty line. Few of the Mau Mau's leaders had military experience or training. Only a minority had shotguns or rifles; most of the insurgents had matchetes. A sleepy colonial government was taken by surprise. When it arrested and convicted the Kikuyu political leader, Jomo Kenyatta, it encouraged recruitment to Mau Mau, which eventually attracted some twelve thousand active insurgents. These, however, operated in uncoordinated local bands under leaders who were often jealous of each other. Loyalty was secured by often repellent oathing ceremonies. The insurgents were initially supported by female and male food carriers, but they never had a neighboring territory to provide refuge or weapons.

At the outset Mau Mau dominated the African "locations" in Nairobi, killing loyalists and launching attacks on settler farms. In response, the military and police rapidly increased to some ten thousand and twenty-one thousand respectively, destroying Mau Mau ascendancy in the capital and forcing the insurgents into the thick forests of the Aberdares and Mount Kenya. With some military assistance, the police regained control of the towns. After securing the settler farm areas, five British (later with six African) battalions mounted patrols and sweeps of the forests. The RAF also bombed insurgents using Lancaster bombers and, like the French in Algeria, used noisy Harvard trainers. However, the bombing achieved virtually nothing. A "Kikuyu Guard" was raised in the traditional Kikuyu area and played the lead role in returning the Kikuyu, who were aware of political changes and revolted by Mau Mau excesses, to law and order. By the end of 1956, following the capture of Dedan Kimathi, the Mau Mau leader, the revolt was over, although some ninety thousand Kikuyu were held in insanitary "rehabilitation" camps for some time. Together with abuses by the police (most of them committed by locally recruited white reservists), the communal punishment of villages, and the extensive use of

9 Anthony Short, *The Communist Insurrection in Malaya* (London, 1975); Richard Stubbs, "From Search and Destroy to Hearts and Minds: The Evolution of British Strategy in Malaya 1948–60," in Marston and Malkasian, eds., *Counterinsurgency*, 113–30.

37. Questioning of Mau Mau leader

the death penalty on convicted insurgents, the long internment of so many Kikuyu aroused great political concern in Britain.

The security forces had followed General Templer's concept of a "trinity" among civil administration, military, and police. It proved to be a powerful structure, which was maintained by Kenyatta after independence. Malayan-style "village-ization" was imposed in the Kikuyu areas. The most original feature of the campaign was the formation of "counter-gangs" of Kikuyu, often former insurgents, who were prepared to infiltrate the forest bands.

The Mau Mau campaign was of the greatest political significance. Having to pay for the operations and subsequent development, Britain promoted progressive political and social changes that led to majority rule and Kenya's independence in 1963 under Kenyatta.[10] These events contributed to a major change in British African policy in 1959–60.

The Greek population of Cyprus, which represented 80 percent of the total, had wanted *enosis*, union with Greece, a sentiment that became open after 1945. The British government was divided between the hard-line Foreign Office and the more moderate Colonial Office. It concluded that asserting that Britain was in Cyprus to stay would again, as in 1931, defuse this nationalism. This was a self-deluding belief, a main cause of the subsequent conflict. Violence began in April 1955. With some two thousand fighters, the insurgency movement EOKA (*Ethniki Organosis Kyprion Agoniston* – the National Organization of Cypriot Fighters) had been built up over three years by a former Greek army colonel, Georgios Grivas, in secrecy. Its strategy, which emphasized attrition and favorable publicity, featured isolated killings in small towns and villages, as well as a number of larger guerrilla bands that operated in the Troodos mountains. EOKA was supported politically in Cyprus by the Ethnarch, Archbishop Michail Makarios, and other bishops, and externally by the Greek government in Athens. The British deported Makarios and maintained naval and security patrols to prevent the smuggling of weapons from Greece. Grivas's insurgents fought with skill, achieving several spectacular successes – and, as they had hoped, international interest, especially among the Americans. British troops, who at the insurrection's peak numbered some ten thousand, had to support an ill-prepared local police force, which the EOKA had penetrated. To supplement the police, the government recruited Turks, whose Cypriot community had itself organized a small anti-EOKA terrorist group, so the violence turned into bitter intercommunal strife. At the same time, the EOKA groups were increasingly hard pressed by the British military. By late 1958 Makarios had realized that *enosis* was no longer realistic, that the best option was independence with power-sharing. The British in turn, who had been chastened in the Suez crisis, had concluded that Makarios was more moderate than Grivas and must be a negotiator. The compromise reached among Greece, Turkey, and Makarios was accepted reluctantly by Grivas, whom the British never captured. Independence on this basis arrived in 1960, but the post-independence history of Cyprus remained plagued by communal strife.[11]

10 Anthony Clayton, *Counter-Insurgency in Kenya 1952–60* (Manhattan, KS, 1984); Frank Kitson, *Gangs and Counter-gangs* (London, 1960); Wanyabari O. Maloba, *Mau Mau and Kenya: An Analysis of a Peasant Revolt* (Bloomington, 1993).

11 Corum, "British Strategy Against the Cyprus Insurgents, 1955–59," in Corum, *Bad Strategies*, 79–122; George Grivas, *Memoirs of General Grivas* (London, 1964); Robert Holland, *Britain and the Revolt in Cyprus* (Oxford, 1998).

Insurgency and counterinsurgency followed almost immediately in southern Arabia. After the 1920s, RAF aircraft and local chieftains had maintained British control of Aden and its hinterlands. But developments in the Middle East, particularly the aborted Anglo-French attempt in 1956 to deflate the leadership and propaganda of President Nasser of Egypt, produced a popular insurgency, which grew in strength and challenged the authority of the chieftains. In 1965–66 nationalist insurgents in the mountains of the Radfan area, north of Aden, harassed British units by mining tracks and undertaking ambushes and machine-gun sniping. Two rival nationalist insurgent groups, the FLOSY (Front for the Liberation of Occupied South Yemen) and the NLF (National Liberation Front) then took the fighting into Aden and its immediate surrounds, attacking British troops, their families, and the local South Arabian Army, which had been formed by the British and loyalist chieftains in the immediate hinterland. The insurgents also fought one another. Grenade, machine-gun, and rocket attacks, mutinies in the local military and police forces, and the British decision (following the election of a Labour government in 1964) to withdraw from Aden had by 1966 created an unmanageable situation. In November 1967 the British executed a skillful withdrawal to warships, but a grim fate awaited the flimsy political and military structure that they left behind. Aden represented the major failure in British decolonization campaigns. The territory joined with Yemen to form the Marxist People's Republic, which had no interest in maintaining political, economic, or cultural links with Britain. Furthermore, Britain lost a pivotal military base in the region and was replaced by the Soviet Union, with far-reaching consequences in northeast Africa.[12]

Britain successfully fought two additional colonial campaigns – in Borneo in 1963–65 and the Falklands Islands in 1982. These campaigns, however, were fought to repel forcible takeovers by external powers – Indonesia in the case of Borneo, Argentina in the case of the Falklands. Neither campaign in any way represented a war of decolonization against local insurgents.

A useful concluding reminder of the different scales of these wars of decolonization is a comparison of the casualties, insurgent and military, among the biggest campaigns of France, Britain, and Portugal. At the end of the Algerian campaign, the French estimated that ALN battle casualties totalled 141,000; a further 12,000 had been killed in internal fighting and purges, 1,500 by the Moroccan and Tunisian authorities, and 4,000 in

12 Julian Page, *Last Post: Aden 1964–1967* (London, 1969); Jonathan Walker, *Aden Insurgency: The Savage War in South Arabia* (Staplehurst, 2005).

metropolitan France. Unknown numbers of Algerians – several thousand at least – died in French resettlement camps, and as many as 200,000 "loyalists," who had supported the French cause in the last months before and after independence. French casualties totalled some 13,000 soldiers of European (French, metropolitan, Algerian settler or Foreign Legion) origin, while an additional 7,000 were killed by accident, disease, or suicide. A further 3,500 non-European soldiers were killed in action, in addition to a thousand more who died from various causes.

Figures for the three Portuguese territories cannot be precise, A reliable estimate suggests that overall metropolitan Portuguese military casualties were at least 10,000 killed or dead from disease, together with 65,000 wounded. In Guinea, between 6,000 and 8,000 locally recruited soldiers were killed, while no figures exist either for soldiers or village home-guard units in Angola or Mozambique. Insurgent casualties were much higher – at least 100,000 and perhaps as many as 150,000.

By comparison, in Malaya the campaign in which the British army sustained its highest losses, insurgent casualties totalled 6,710, although more died of natural causes, while 1,287 were captured, and 2,702 surrendered. Three hundred fifty British, 128 Malay, and 159 Gurkha soldiers were also killed.

The ending of colonial rule in the Congo in July 1960 opened a new chapter in the history of war. The Belgians left their vast and varied territory precipitately, without providing much political, military, or infrastructure preparation for independence. Order collapsed in a week, so a large United Nations military force had to be assembled, which in time restored the territorial unity of the country against a number of secessionist movements. The issues facing the force, however, had much in common with the fighting in African conflicts that opened in many new nations once the "colonial glue" had melted down.

In sum, thirty years of anticolonial warfare saw significant development of insurgent weaponry and operational art. Between 1945 and 1975 these campaigns acquired a whole new dimension. Freedom fighters progressed from the stolen shotguns of the Sétif insurgents and the matchetes of Mau Mau to the Soviet AK47 rifle, grenade launchers, 122-millimeter portable rockets, mortars, mines, the early antiaircraft missiles of the PAIGC, and advanced bombs – all of which were in use by the early 1970s. The propaganda dimension of these campaigns grew along with the technology, as the media increasingly affected public attitudes. Both the advancing technology available to the insurgents and the attrition involved in long campaigns became too demanding for conscript soldiers. Professional soldiers, who were still needed for traditional roles, had now to master a variety of new political challenges and update their military skills to prepare for combat against adversaries who came from within their own communities. Peace-keeping skills nevertheless had substantial benefits in later operations in former Yugoslavia and elsewhere. At the same time, dissident groups in former colonies – some in uniform, most not – drew on the experience of the anticolonial campaigns to fight new postcolonial civil wars or guerrilla conflicts more effectively.

22

War and memory since 1945

RANA MITTER

For those who live in the western world, the period since 1945 is generally considered an era of peace, in sharp contrast to the warlike nature of the period that ended with the defeat of the Axis powers in 1945. The situation looked very different to millions of people who lived in Vietnam, Nigeria, East Pakistan, or Korea. Nor would people in Northern Ireland, Algeria, or Bosnia have agreed that warlike Europe had turned peaceful in the era that followed the world war. The division point of 1945 was itself less significant to people who lived in Africa or Latin America than to those who lived in the west or the Asia–Pacific region.

However, these observations should not obscure another reality: modern global memory of war has been primarily shaped since 1945 by the experience and aftershocks of the global conflict of the 1930s and 1940s. Even wars a long way from Europe, such as the wars over the secessions of Biafra and Bangladesh, were shaped by a decolonization process that was triggered by the collapse of European empires in World War II, as well as by a new understanding of the ability of non-western peoples to forge their own destinies. In the powers that had fought the war, the memory of events, from the Holocaust and the Nanjing Massacre to the atomic bombings of Hiroshima and Nagasaki, shaped political formations (such as the European Union) and popular culture (such as the Godzilla movies of the 1960s). Perceptions of prewar politics – for instance, the rise of charismatic but dangerous leaders in Europe – shaped how the victorious Allied powers formed politics. Postwar German politics was shaped so it could never allow a Hitler-figure to reemerge.

World War II molded the memory of war indelibly throughout the world. The nature and contents of this memory changed repeatedly throughout the postwar era, however, particularly after the end of the Cold War in 1989–91. One notable phenomenon in the post-Cold War era has been that global interest in World War II has grown, not lessened. Yet, as in previous generations, new politicians and social actors have shaped how memory underpins new political agendas. And, as in the prewar period, "memory" covers a broad variety of social phenomena, from collective public remembrance and attitudes to the recovery of private family histories.

The first section of this chapter refracts war memory through the continued awareness of the global war that ended in 1945. It starts by considering the Holocaust, the event that has become an icon of war atrocity. It goes on to deal with the differing memories that formed East Asia in the Cold War and after. Then it looks at memory as expressed in physical destruction and reconstruction. It goes on to examine the case of the United States, which has in some ways been anomalous because World War II did not take place on this country's home territory. Finally, the chapter looks at how war memory, decolonization, and colonialism interacted in the postwar histories of the two major European empires, Britain and France.

Memory of World War II in Europe has been driven above all by the experience of the Holocaust. This term is widely used to describe the planned destruction by the Nazi regime of the Jewish people, although other groups, including the Roma/Sinti (Gypsies), homosexuals, and Jehovah's Witnesses were also singled out for extermination.[1] Mass killings of ethnic groupings were not unprecedented, but the centrality of mass planned murder to the European war has associated the Holocaust inextricably with the memory of Germany's role in the conflict, both within the country and outside.

Should the Holocaust be considered part of the memory of war, rather than of atrocity, genocide, or racial prejudice more widely? There is a strong case that it should. The mass extermination of European Jewry was a product of Germany's plunge into global war. At the Wannsee conference in 1942, the Nazi leadership arranged to extend the murder of Jews from the occupied parts of the Soviet Union into the whole of Europe. Historical opinion has leaned toward the view that genocide in this case was accelerated by wartime conditions, and that it was at least in part a direct response by Hitler's regime to the outbreak of war in Europe.[2] The Holocaust provided an unprecedented combination of circumstances that left the consciousness of European modernity deeply unsettled; and one of its most powerful consequences was to fuel critiques of modernity in postwar culture. Elsewhere, the world war led to millions of deaths, expulsions, mass outbreaks of disease, and irrecoverable

1 Donald Bloxham and Tony Kushner, *The Holocaust: Critical Historical Approaches* (Manchester, 2005), 2–3.

2 Ian Kershaw, *Fateful Choices: Ten Decisions That Changed the World 1940–1941* (London, 2007), ch. 10.

physical destruction. However, the policy of Nazi Germany was not only notable for targeting particular social groups for persecution and eventual murder. It also used two key aspects of modernity to achieve its goals. First, it used technology. Mass transportation by railway and killings by means of "Zyklon B" cyanide gas were both part of the mechanization of genocide. Then, less tangibly but just as insidiously, the regime used assumptions of modern governance that had been built into western European society – that governments were rational, that "civilized" societies behaved in certain ways, and that certain types of behavior were "unthinkable." These assumptions made it harder for victims to understand their experience at the time, but they also made the events seem more inexplicably irrational in later memory. In later years, writing that related to the Holocaust, whether fiction or non-fiction, used similar reflections on the irrationality of the experience. Primo Levi's *If This Is a Man* (*Se questo è un uomo*) (1947) expresses the bewilderment of a chemist (a man of science and rationality) in seeing Auschwitz. Gyuri, the teenaged protagonist of Imre Kertész's *Fateless* (*Sorstalanság*) (1975), likewise finds himself forced into complicity with the growing inexplicability of his circumstances when he is sent to Auschwitz. The author, the winner of the 2002 Nobel Prize for Literature, was himself a Holocaust survivor.

Memory of the Holocaust, in the sense of genocidal destruction, did not emerge fully formed after the war. Instead, it tended to concentrate on the massive loss of life that Germany had inflicted on wider populations. Germany's postwar division into two zones also created a division of memory. During the entire postwar period, the liberal-democratic Federal Republic of Germany (FRG) took on conscious responsibility as the inheritor of the guilt, if not the policies, of its Nazi predecessor. As in Japan, the development of memory was in significant part directed by policies that the Allied occupation imposed immediately after the war.

However, West Germany did not fall instantly into self-mortification. For much of the period until the mid 1960s, there was a strong element of self-pity in how local memory of the war was constructed in Germany. In the city of Nuremberg, for instance, the first decade of the postwar period was dominated by memorialization of military casualties, as part of a widely held, though superficial consensus that Germans had themselves been "victims" of the war.[3] From the 1960s, however, the tone of public memory changed significantly, as a younger generation stimulated a more questioning tone toward the recent past.

3 Neil Gregor, *Haunted City: Nuremberg and the Nazi Past* (New Haven, 2008), 160–61.

The new socialist German Democratic Republic (GDR) defined itself in stark contrast to the western state. The leadership of the SED (Socialist Unity Party), which was led by Moscow-trained German Communists, including Wilhelm Pieck and Walter Ulbricht, portrayed itself as a group of German patriots whose Marxism had both saved them from the taint of Nazism and given them a powerful worldview, which enabled Germany to start afresh. As many members of the prewar German Communist Party (KPD) had in fact been persecuted by the Nazis, it was not unreasonable to call on their memory in service of a new state, particularly as the dynamic of the Cold War led the new FRG chancellor, Konrad Adenauer, to ban the KPD in West Germany. However, the GDR went further, portraying the FRG alone as the heir of the Nazi past and suggesting that only the eastern part of Germany genuinely embraced the message of antifascism. Since large parts of East Germany, such as the province of Thuringia, had in fact been enthusiastic voters for Nazism, this was an incomplete interpretation at best. As a result, particularly after the 1960s, public education in the GDR was much more hazy than in the FRG about the indigenous roots of Nazism in German culture.[4]

The victims of the Nazi regime also began to construct memory in the postwar era. The terms "Holocaust" and "Shoah" (the latter meaning "destruction" in Hebrew) were not yet in general usage, but recording testimonies and memories from the Nazi era began early in the postwar era, and it reflected the Holocaust in ways both literal and metaphorical.[5] One of the most significant novelists of the postwar era was Gűnter Grass (the winner of the 1999 Nobel Prize for Literature), whose novel *The Tin Drum* (*Die Blechtrommel*) (1959) burst onto the literary scene with its accusatory power. The novel's key metaphor resides in the persona of its protagonist, Oskar Mazerath, a little boy living under Nazism who refuses to grow. At a time when the FRG was seeking to portray itself as part of a peaceful and united Europe, the figure of Oskar, who can shatter glass with his piercing voice and break up regulated marching music with his drumming, symbolized both the capacity of Germany to destroy (as in the Nazi *Kristallnacht*) and to resist. Works then appeared that treated memory of the recent past in a less confrontational way, such as Edgar Reitz's television series *Heimat* (1984). This series followed the lives of characters in rural Germany from 1919 to the 1970s, and while it was widely praised, it also drew criticism because it glorified a

4 There is an extensive German-language literature, as well as wide-ranging scholarship in English on memory in postwar Germany. A useful point of entry is Mary Fulbrook, *German National Identity after the Holocaust* (London, 1999).

5 Zoe Vania Waxman, *Writing the Holocaust: Identity, Testimony, Representation* (Oxford, 2006), chs. 3–4.

bucolic past and failed to engage aspects of this past, such as the Holocaust, although the film was unequivocally anti-Nazi.

However, in the post-Cold War era, with increasing distance from the war, new emphases have emerged in popular memory, in particular a return to the question of German suffering during the war. A prominent example of this phenomenon has been Jörg Friedrich, whose book *The Fire* (*Der Brand*) (2002) detailed the Allied bombing of Germany in terms that suggested a war crime that was in some ways equivalent to those of the Nazi regime.[6] The emphasis of the book was on German suffering. While only part of a more complex and changing narrative of wartime in Germany, *The Fire* would have been much harder to publish twenty years earlier.

By the end of the Cold War, however, the FRG had done a great deal to educate its population about the horrors of war and the culpability of the Nazi regime. The reunification of Germany in 1990 also brought an (official) end to the GDR's alternative vision of the wartime past, and no significant grouping in German society seeks to rehabilitate the Nazi period or its consequences for Germany. By the early twenty-first century, a wide perception reigned that Germany had dealt responsibly with official memory of its wartime actions and the Holocaust. Its behavior became a template for memory of war in the postwar era, and Germany was held up around the world as an example of how remembrance and reconciliation might be achieved.

Germany's actions were the dominant factor in the memory of war in Europe, but East Asia provided an alternative dynamic of memory, which was simultaneously shaped by global postwar currents and the specificities of the region. There was a powerful incentive within West Germany, at least, to exorcize the ghosts of the past. For differing reasons, this process remained more incomplete in both China and Japan because of the rapid reversal of the positions of both countries during the Cold War. From an American perspective, China changed between 1945 and 1949 from a wartime ally to a red menace, while Japan switched from being the most hated foe to a solid, democratic ally in the Cold War.

Japan provided an obvious parallel to West Germany – an Axis nation that had been bombed into surrender, then occupied. Like the FRG's, its politics was restructured and democratized under American orders (without even the

6 Jörg Friedrich, *Der Brand: Deutschland im Bombenkrieg 1940–1945* (Munich, 2002). The English translation is *The Fire: The Bombing of Germany, 1940–1945* (New York, 2008). See Robert G. Moeller, "The Bombing War in Germany, 2005–1940: Back to the Future?" in Yuki Tanaka and Marilyn B. Young, eds., *Bombing Civilians: A Twentieth-Century History* (New York, 2009), 46–76.

nominal division of powers that marked Germany). However, one issue has made Japan's experience unique: the atomic bombings of Hiroshima and Nagasaki. Combined with an American desire to underplay Japanese war crimes in order to bolster the country's position as a Cold War ally, this issue encouraged two threads of memory in postwar Japan. One ran parallel to Germany's experience. This was the misleading but historically convenient idea that both countries had been on a liberal path, which had been waylaid by dark forces (the so-called *kurai tanima* or "valley of darkness"), but that both had been restored to their proper historical trajectory after 1945. The other thread was unique to Japan: the idea that the country was a victim of atomic weapons, the most brutal form of attack conceivable.

This uniqueness became central to postwar Japanese culture. Japan developed a culture of "peace," which was expressed particularly in the flowering of "peace museums," including an iconic one in Hiroshima. These were tied to the collective memory of Japan as the lone victim of atomic warfare. The experiences of the *hibakusha* (atomic-bomb victims) were also reflected more widely in the culture. A notable example was Ibuse Masuji's novel *Black Rain* (*Kuroi ame*) (1965), which dealt with the effects of atomic warfare, alternating the diary of a bombing victim in 1945 with a narrative of social discrimination against the victims of radiation sickness. Another popular means of dealing with the memory of nuclear destruction was the metaphorical rendition of the firebombing and the effects of nuclear radiation. The *Gojira* (Godzilla) plastic-puppet movies, which were made by the Toho studios from the 1950s onward, were at one level a kitschy rendering of a universal children's monster story. At another level, a world in which a genetically mutated monster at one blow destroyed buildings and people in its path was a metaphor for the aftermath of nuclear warfare.[7]

As in Germany, the American occupation government became concerned to promote a view of history in which Japan's journey to war was treated as an anomalous part of a wider trajectory toward liberal democracy. This view then became connected to the fracturing of war memory among the Japanese themselves. Two elements became associated with the left and right respectively. On the left, Japanese guilt for World War II in Asia was clear and had to be acknowledged. The political scientist Maruyama Masao produced one of

7 Chapters by Carol Gluck, Yoshikuni Igarashi, Ann Sherif, and Harry D. Harootunian in Sheila Miyoshi Jager and Rana Mitter, eds., *Ruptured Histories: War, Memory and the Post-Cold War in Asia* (Cambridge, MA, 2007); Franziska Seraphim, *War Memory and Social Politics in Japan, 1945–2005* (Cambridge, MA, 2005), chs. 2–3; Ian Buruma, *The Wages of Guilt: Memories of War in Germany and Japan* (London, 1995).

the most famous expressions of this proposition in his study *Thought and Behavior in Modern Japanese Politics* (*Gendai seiji no shisô to kôdô*) (1956). It argued that the emperor-centered culture, which had shaped modern Japan after the Meiji restoration, contributed directly to the rise of ultranationalism and to a wider sense of irresponsibility on the part of political leaders, which led to Pearl Harbor and ultimate defeat. During the Cold War, the right wing was mostly concerned with economism (the pursuit of economic growth in an ostensibly ideologically consensual political environment). In an era when Japanese nationalism had to be downplayed, there was little space in the mainstream for the violent, xenophobic politics of the prewar era. Instead, Japanese conservatism, like conservatism in Germany and Italy, became a permanent feature of politics and was embedded (with American encouragement) into an economistic, relatively liberal and pragmatic mode, in which communism was the main enemy.

After the war, many sections of Japanese society nonetheless found themselves in the same position as the Germans, defeated but needing to mourn. Ironically, there were also many similarities to the situation in the People's Republic of China, where memory of World War II was indelibly shaped by the civil war between Nationalists and Communists in the aftermath. After 1949, all mourning for those who had been killed serving in the Nationalist armies of Chiang Kai-shek took place privately, as the official communist narrative removed them from public acknowledgment. This removal made China, like Japan, a country in which a significant section of the population was unable to acknowledge its war dead. Numerous popular associations did spring up in Japan to mourn the war dead, but they sought to be part of Japan's new democratic culture, not to hark back to the prewar era. As in the United States, the changing politics of the Asian region also affected how the Japanese sought to use war memory. The outbreak of the Vietnam War was fruitful for a Japanese war-reparations movement, which linked its concerns to the ongoing debate on "war responsibility," a major issue on the Japanese left.[8]

The post-Cold War era has enabled a different section of the Japanese right to argue a more revisionist case – that Japan had in fact been an anticolonial, liberating power in Asia during the war and that its wartime claim to have freed Asian peoples from European imperialism should be taken seriously. Throughout much of the Cold War, controversies raged over textbooks in Japanese schools that dealt with the wartime period. In the 1980s, there was

8 Seraphim, *War Memory*, chs. 2–3.

particular anger over what many regarded as euphemistic descriptions of the Japanese wartime record, as texts spoke of a Japanese "advance" into China, rather than of an "invasion." The debate became politicized. The most controversial textbooks were used in few schools, but they nonetheless had official approval from the Ministry of Education, so China and South Korea could argue that the Japanese state was permitting a whitewash of wartime crimes. The left-wing historian Ienaga Saburō spent many decades suing the government over the textbook issues; on the right, organizations such as the Japanese New Textbook Society published books that downplayed war atrocities but were approved by the government.[9]

The new right-wing trend was seen most graphically, in the literal sense, in the work of the cartoonist Kobayashi Yoshinori. In his book *On War* (*Sensōron*) (1998), Kobayashi used the form of the graphic novel to argue that the Asia–Pacific War had been just and that young Japanese should not be ashamed to feel patriotism when considering the action of Japanese soldiers and kamikaze pilots. Kobayashi's book sold five hundred thousand copies. Yet the opposing historical trend also continues to be powerful. The scandal in the 1990s over the "comfort women," Asian women who were used as sex-slaves for the Japanese Imperial Army during the war, caused more soul-searching in Japan. As Japan continues to rethink its role in the Asia–Pacific region, debates over war memory remain an important part of the country's self-definition.[10]

The memory of war in China has gone through a series of reversals. These are unique to China, but they are not merely phenomena of an authoritarian Asian system. There are instructive parallels between postwar China and France, for instance. Of the Allied powers, these two found it hardest to deal with the fact that substantial parts of their territory and population were under occupation and that many people had collaborated with the enemy. The memory of war in China underwent three separate phases. First came the now often-forgotten period from 1945 to 1949, which marked the last years of the Nationalist (Guomindang) government. Chiang Kai-shek's determination to resist until the end of the war against Japan gained him much respect, but the almost immediate outbreak of the civil war with the Communists, as well as widespread corruption and black marketeering, quickly ate away at the government's prestige. The rich cinema of this period reflected what one

9 Kenneth B. Pyle, "Japan Besieged: The Textbook Controversy: Introduction," *Journal of Japanese Studies* 9 (1983): 297–300.

10 Naoko Shimazu, "Popular Representations of the Past: The Case of Postwar Japan," *Journal of Contemporary History* 38 (2003): 101–16. Carol Gluck, "Operations of Memory: 'Comfort Women' and the World," in Jager and Mitter, eds., *Ruptured Histories*, 47–77.

scholar has called "victory as defeat." Movies such as *The Spring River Flows East* (1948) showed how the complexities of collaboration and resistance underlay a simpler message of victory. In 1947 a pictorial history of the "war of resistance" portrayed the brief moment when it seemed possible that the Nationalists and Communists might cooperate, and it showed the possibilities of a new narrative of memory.[11] Pictures of both Nationalist and Communist contributions to wartime resistance revealed the roles of both actors (something that became much harder once the Cold War hardened several years later). One can imagine a logical trajectory, in which many of the complexities of wartime, such as collaboration, would have been obscured in a Nationalist China had it survived on the mainland, and in which the Communist contribution, however important, would have been downplayed.

Instead, the Communist victory in the civil war in 1949 created sharp divisions over how the war should be remembered. These were exacerbated by the curious fact that the enemy in World War II (Japan) was no longer an active opponent of either the new People's Republic of China (PRC) or the rival Republic of China on Taiwan. The former uneasy wartime allies (Nationalists and Communists) were now arch-rivals. The result on the mainland was a narrative of the war in which the Japanese were almost offstage actors. The center of attention moved to Mao's wartime revolution. From the 1950s to the 1970s, the PRC's main narrative of the war became one of peasant revolution, in which the Communists had been in the lead. Strong anti-Japanese feeling remained, but the Japanese appeared as largely stylized enemies. The venom was reserved for the Nationalists. Therefore, there was no favorable discussion of the Nationalist contribution to the war effort or resistance in southwest China. Even less discussed was collaboration with the Japanese, other than as outright treachery. On Taiwan the situation was reversed, as an overly positive view of the Nationalist contribution contrasted with the vilification of the Communists. The historical narrative was thus shaped on both sides by the civil war and the Cold War.

This view of history changed in the 1980s. A variety of factors forced a significant, though unacknowledged change in the narrative. Faith in Maoism had been shaken by the Cultural Revolution. There was a desire for reunification with Taiwan; and it was no longer necessary to soft-pedal

11 Paul Pickowicz, "Victory as Defeat: Postwar Visualizations of China's War of Resistance," in Wen-hsin Yeh, ed., *Becoming Chinese: Passages to Modernity and Beyond* (Berkeley, 2000), 365–97; *Zhongguo kangzhan huashi* (Pictorial history of the Chinese War of Resistance) (Shanghai, 1947).

38. The Nanjing Massacre Memorial – the Ship of Peace

diplomatically on Japan. A new wave of remembrance of the war began suddenly in the early 1980s and continued into the early twenty-first century. One of its most notable elements was the building of three major museums that related to the war. One, in Beijing, commemorated the entire War of Resistance to Japan. Another was in Nanjing, on one of the sites of the massacre of 1937–38; another was in Shenyang (Mukden), at the site of the incident of September 18, 1931, which began the Japanese invasion of Manchuria. All these sites presented a narrative of war in which the Communists had little presence.

Since the 1990s, memory of wartime has become a central part of China's understanding of its own identity. In addition to museums and monuments, popular and academic culture has allowed space for films, books, and television series to commemorate long-hidden aspects of the war. One site that has benefited from this interest is the former wartime capital of Chongqing (Chungking), which suffered badly from Japanese air raids during the war. Under Mao, Chongqing was allowed practically no commemoration of its wartime history, because the city had been the Nationalist capital. In the 1990s, the city drew on the wartime years as a means of stressing its identity. The house of General Joseph Stilwell, the American chief of staff to Chiang Kai-shek, reopened as a museum, with a brass reproduction of the message to "the people of Chungking" from Franklin D. Roosevelt outside. As they do elsewhere in the world (Hiroshima, Nuremberg, Coventry), local histories continue to complicate the way in which memory of war is constructed and understood in China.[12]

Events and places have become particularly important in commemorating the destruction of war. This phenomenon is transnational. In Russia, the destruction wrought by the Nazis became part of the idea of the "Great Patriotic War."[13] The iconic site became the streets of Leningrad, which the Nazis besieged for some nine hundred days in 1941–44. The physical scars of the siege, such as the bullet- and mortar-holes in walls, were often preserved and became a central element in the narrative of resistance on which the Soviet state relied (covering up awkward issues, such as Stalin's refusal to believe that a German invasion was imminent in 1941). The treatment of the Frauenkirche, the major cathedral in the center of Dresden, and the ruins of the cathedral in Coventry illustrate the different ways of dealing with the memory of wartime destruction. The government of the GDR maintained the rubble of the Frauenkirche as a war memorial after 1949 – a parallel to the preserved ruins of Coventry cathedral. In Dresden, the iconic building was an ambiguous object of memory during much of the Cold War. In the official GDR discourse it was a reminder of the consequences of Nazism, but local memories of the horrific firebombing in 1945 fuelled an alternative discourse, in which Dresden was a victim, rather than perpetrator of war crimes. Even under the GDR, plans were made to rebuild the Frauenkirche, not least because the site had become unsafe. The move to rebuild it began in earnest only after German reunification, and in 2005 the Frauenkirche reopened. Rebuilding it removed one of the most visible sites of wartime destruction anywhere in Germany. The city of Coventry, in contrast, used the site of the cathedral to combine continuity and change. The ruins were combined with a daring new structure by the modernist architect Basil Spence, and the cathedral was rededicated in 1962 with the first performance of the *War Requiem* by Benjamin Britten.[14]

12 Rana Mitter, "Old Ghosts, New Memories: China's Changing War History in the Era of Post-Mao Politics," *Journal of Contemporary History* 38 (2003): 117–31. For a comparative analysis of the European and Asian cases, see Yinan He, *The Search for Reconciliation: Sino-Japanese and German-Polish Relations since World War II* (Cambridge, 2009).

13 Catherine Merridale, *Night of Stone: Death and Memory in Russia* (London, 2001).

14 On Dresden, see Jason James, "Undoing Trauma: Reconstructing the Church of Our Lady in Dresden," *Ethos* 34 (2006): 244–72.

Sometimes the absence of the memory of destruction caused the controversy. One of the most complex cases of divided memory in Asia has related to the notorious Nanjing Massacre ("Rape of Nanking") in December 1937 to January 1938, in which invading Japanese troops killed large numbers of Chinese civilians during the first phase of their war against China. However, the event was not much featured in the historiography of postwar China, whose government did not find that the massacre fitted the new narrative of Communist-led victory in war as the prelude to the utopia of the PRC. Nor did memory of the event fit the demilitarized economism of postwar Japan. However, significant sections of Japanese postwar society, particularly on the liberal left, were unhappy about the disappearance of this atrocity from the wider memory of war in Japan. In 1972, the journalist Honda Katsuichi interviewed survivors of the Nanjing killings and published their testimony in the *Asahi shimbun*, one of Japan's major newspapers. The massacre thereupon became a major source of public controversy within Japan. Ironically, it took another decade and a change in the Beijing government's policy before the massacre became a major issue in China itself. The museum commemorating the atrocity opened only in 1985, but this occasion itself marked the start of a new engagement with the events of 1937–38 in Nanjing and more broadly. The increasing number of popular and academic books, films, and television series about the massacre show how memory of this event has become stronger over time.[15]

The United States was the only major belligerent in World War II not to experience the events of conflict on its home territory. Yet the memory and legacy of the global conflict shaped postwar American society. American "doughboys" had participated in World War I, but this experience had, if anything, stoked isolationist feeling at home; and this conflict had not felt like a truly "American" war to many at home. World War II, in contrast, created a role for the United States as a global power, particularly as the older empires of Britain, France, Japan, and the Netherlands were weakened or destroyed. By 1945, American soldiers had seen service in Europe, China, Southeast Asia, and Japan; and their vision of the world was irreversibly extended.

A narrative of US participation in the war began to form during the conflict itself, and it was further developed as peace returned in 1945. In this version of events, the United States had not wished to go to war, but the moment of "infamy" (in Roosevelt's phrasing) at Pearl Harbor and the declaration of war

15 Joshua Fogel, ed., *The Nanjing Massacre in History and Historiography* (Berkeley, 2000); Bob Tadashi Wakabayashi, ed., *The Nanking Atrocity, 1937–8: Complicating the Picture* (Oxford, 2007).

against the United States by Hitler forced the country into conflict. The United States then saved Europe and Asia from themselves. In this narrative, the United States' allies took a back seat; Britain was a brave but secondary partner, and the USSR's contribution vanished altogether (not least because of the Cold War), as did that of the Chinese. In this version of history, the United States' prosperity at home and dominant postwar position in the world represented rewards for the country's role in wartime. It was not for nothing that Dean Acheson, President Harry Truman's secretary of state and a major figure in US foreign policy after 1941, entitled his autobiography *Present at the Creation*. The view that the United States had forged a new world from the chaos of global war was worldwide.

The construction of a corresponding collective memory, in which the United States' wartime endeavors and sacrifices underpinned and justified that nation's success in the postwar era, was a successful project. However, a variety of flaws in this narrative emerged during the same years. Memory of recent wartime experience forced a reassessment of troubling aspects of American society, most notably the question of race. African-American troops had fought alongside white soldiers on all the fronts of war, yet they saw the signs of segregation imported from home. At the start of the war, for example, Red Cross facilities for black soldiers had been separate from and inferior to those for whites. The case of Isaac Woodward, a black veteran who was attacked and blinded by white racists in the Deep South in 1948, became a rallying-cry for those who argued that African-Americans had little reason to share the national memory of the war as a just cause. The same argument resonated more controversally during the Vietnam War, when the boxer Muhammad Ali refused his draft call, noting that "No Viet Cong ever called me nigger." After World War II, it became politically much harder to argue that black soldiers were equal in their liability for service and violent death but not otherwise entitled to equal treatment, as the armed services were desegregated at the order of President Harry Truman in 1948. "Jim Crow" (segregation) continued in civilian life, but the experience of war made its continuation impossible in the longer term. Women, too, found that their wartime roles had been subsumed in a narrative of harmonious domesticity. During the war, the figure of "Rosie the Riveter," an iconic female factory worker who was based on a real-life figure, had symbolized the new role that women were taking in industrial life. With the return of large numbers of able-bodied men to the United States, however, the tide turned in a more conservative direction, as middle-class women were recast as homemakers. In her pathbreaking book *The Feminine Mystique* (1962), Betty Friedan made a strong case that women's roles had, if anything, gone backward since the war, as they were forced back into domesticity, their wartime service ignored.[16]

The memory of World War II was critical in shaping the decisions of American leaders during the Cold War. Of the Cold War presidents, all except Ronald Reagan had served abroad during or immediately after the war. Dwight Eisenhower had been the supreme commander of the Allied powers in Europe; John Kennedy, Lyndon Johnson, Richard Nixon, Gerald Ford, Jimmy Carter, and George H. W. Bush had been servicemen. Kennedy's inaugural address referred to "a new generation of Americans –born in this century, tempered by war." Comparisons with World War II also influenced Johnson's spiral into Vietnam.[17] Popular culture reflected the narrative of the war as a just cause. Leading examples included films such as *Sands of Iwo Jima* (1949) and, a generation later in a more light-hearted way, the television comedy series *Hogan's Heroes* (1965–71).

Yet, as the Vietnam War threw the United States into a state of confrontation and division, it became harder to maintain that American involvement in wars overseas had been an unmitigated good. In fact, the experience of Vietnam exacerbated a strain of skepticism that had always been visible in postwar American society about the experience of the world war. Joseph Heller's *Catch-22* (1961), a satire on the US military bureaucracy in the Mediterranean theater of World War II, painted the war as an absurdist nightmare. Kurt Vonnegut's *Slaughterhouse-Five* (1969), a dark classic of science fiction, took antirealism a step further. Its protagonist, Billy Pilgrim, is a US prisoner of war who is trapped in Dresden during the firebombing of this city and transported by aliens to a variety of other locations. When the literary scholar Paul Fussell wrote about his experiences as a soldier in World War II, he reflected on the impossibility of expressing them in words, stating "the real war will never get into the history books."[18]

The end of the Cold War seemed suddenly to bring about a resurgence of interest in World War II, in both its heroics and its ambiguities. As the ideological conflict of the Cold War faded away, the memory of the "good" war shaped an era that seemed to long for new heroes. A notable example of

16 Elaine Tyler May, *Homeward Bound: American Families in the Cold War Era* (New York, 1988); William H. Chafe, *The Unfinished Journey: America since World War II* (New York, 2006), 81.

17 Yuen Foon Khong, *Analogies at War: Korea, Munich, Dien Bien Phu, and the Vietnam Decisions of 1965* (Princeton, 1993).

18 Paul Fussell, *Wartime: Understanding and Behaviour in the Second World War* (Oxford, 1989), ch. 18.

this phenomenon was the political controversy that erupted in Washington, DC in 1995. The Smithsonian Institution decided to mark the fiftieth anniversary of the war's end with a display that contained the *Enola Gay*, the bomber that had dropped the atomic bomb "Little Boy," which destroyed Hiroshima on August 6, 1945. The exhibition sparked one of the most notable disputes over history in the post-Cold War era. Veterans' groups lobbied for changes, complaining that the proposed display made it appear that the Japanese were victims of American vengeance. The controversy pitted the positive view of the war, which had prevailed after 1945, against a post-Vietnam view that was more wary of wars abroad. The *Enola Gay* was eventually put on display, but the exhibit restricted itself to technical descriptions with little historical analysis.[19]

The 1990s also brought competition for the ownership of public memory on the Mall, the central symbolic site in Washington, DC. The Mall holds some of the most iconic monuments of American political life, such as the Washington Monument and the Lincoln Memorial. In the 1970s it became the site of competition to commemorate more recent wars. The first such monument was the Vietnam War Memorial, a stark, polished piece of black granite that was designed by Maya Lin and dedicated in 1982. On it was carved the name of every soldier who was killed during the war. The design was chosen to avoid commentary on the war – a silence that would have been unimaginable in connection with World War II. The dedication of the memorial to the United States' most recent and controversial war in turn prompted calls for a memorial to the less well-remembered Korean War, which was authorized in 1986 but not opened until 1995. In 1993, the US Holocaust Museum opened near the Mall. These developments prompted demands that the greatest conflict of the century, World War II, also be remembered. Eventually, in 2004, this monument opened, making this war the only twentieth-century event that is commemorated on the Mall's central axis.

The growing importance of this war in the early twenty-first century was visible, too, in a new enthusiasm for recovering the experience, while the last participants remained alive. In a way that had been unthinkable during the Vietnam era, books such as Tom Brokaw's *The Greatest Generation* (1998) and James Bradley's *Flags of Our Fathers* (2000) once again featured a positive, uncomplicated patriotism, which was based on shared remembrance of war as the center of American life.

19 Margaret Macmillan, *The Uses and Abuses of History* (London, 2009), 123–25.

Postwar European unity has been built on a great act of remembering and many smaller but significant acts of forgetting. The idea that one should remember World War II, so it can "never again" happen, has been a central part of the European project of unity, peace, and democracy. However, a variety of problems marred this version of history, not least the forgetting of collaboration and colonial violence.

Britain and France found themselves in similar positions after 1945, but they reacted differently. Both had entered the war as colonial powers, and both emerged with their empires gravely damaged. Britain's wartime narrative was relatively straightforward (although its true record was more complex), while France had to create a new narrative to account for the ambiguities of collaboration with Nazism.

In Britain, the incoming Labour government recognized in 1945 that the country could not maintain the British Empire as it stood. World War II had bankrupted the country. In 1947, India and Pakistan were given independence, and additional decolonization took place under the Conservative governments of Harold Macmillan and Alec Douglas-Home between 1957 and 1964. Yet, as Dean Acheson famously declared, the British had "lost an empire but had not yet found a role." The country fought the realization that it was now no more than an important mid-rank European power. Politicians were ambivalent about the emergent European Community. In this context, rapidly changing memories of the war were used to reshape the British national self-perception. At one level, all politics was shaped by the memory of the war. The building of a welfare state with a collectivist ethos was directly attributable to the desire to overcome the divisions of the prewar period.

British cultural production drew on shared positive memories of the war. It included films that celebrated wartime heroism, such as *Reach for the Sky* (1956) about the crippled flying ace Douglas Bader, and *Carve Her Name with Pride* (1958), which portrayed the life of the SOE agent Violette Szabo. Yet a more skeptical streak also emerged, in which memory of war was used to contrast the country's "finest hour" with a more mundane postwar reality. One of the most remarkable works to deal with the gap between wartime heroism and an affluent but emotionally vacuous postwar consumerism was the play *Plenty* (1978) by the left-wing playwright David Hare. Its protagonist, Susan Traherne, had been dropped behind enemy lines to assist the French resistance, but she has now found that postwar British life offers few opportunities for excitement, despite the "plenty" that is available. She turns to drink and ruins the career of her diplomat husband. The work's bleakness led many to hail it as a "state-of-the-nation" play, a metaphor for the country as a whole, which was living off ever more distant wartime glory.

One notable element of British war memory – one that makes it distinctive – is the prominence of the war years in popular comedy. Comedy had been a staple of British cultural life during the war itself. The comedian Tommy Handley became a national icon because of his presence on the radio show *ITMA*. As a mass television audience developed after the war, the war years were explored in comedies before mass audiences. The writing team of David Croft and Jimmy Perry was responsible for *Dad's Army* (1968–77), which gently spoofed the exploits of the Home Guard, as it mobilized the generation of men who were too old to fight abroad. The same team's *It Ain't Half Hot Mum* (1974–81), which was set among British troops in Burma, played on the less remembered war with Japan. More controversially, *Allo Allo* (1982–1992) made comedy out of the French Resistance; even Gestapo agents were portrayed as lovable rogues. The popularity of the last series revealed the continuing comfort of memory of the British role during the war, but such a series would have been impossible to make in France. Later British wars provided less comfort. Despite its contemporary political importance, the Falklands War of 1982 had little lasting cultural impact, although Charles Wood's television film *Tumbledown* (1988) was widely praised for its nuanced portrayal of the motivations of a Falklands veteran, and the songwriters Elvis Costello and Captain Sensible tapped into antiwar sentiment, which the media had concealed, with their antiwar anthems *Shipbuilding* (1982) and *Glad It's All Over* (1984). At the same time, the playwright Ian Curteis's play about the conflict, which portrayed British prime minister Margaret Thatcher in a sympathetic light, was reported to have been shelved by the BBC, a decision that prompted criticism from the political right. The BBC finally aired Curteis's work in 2002, on the twentieth anniversary of the conflict.[20]

When the topic is raised of changing war memory in Europe, the case of France most often comes to mind. This is partly because the changes were so significant, but also because France combined a liberal polity with a dark wartime history, which contained much that people wished to forget. One of the great successes of Charles de Gaulle's wartime resistance in exile was to create a narrative in which France had been a staunch Ally and accordingly deserved to participate in the victorious postwar order (for instance, in

20 Good assessments of postwar British society and culture can be found in Brian Harrison, *Seeking a Role: The United Kingdom, 1951–1970* (Oxford, 2009) and *Finding a Role? The United Kingdom, 1970–1990* (Oxford, 2010).

governing divided Germany). In the 1950s France portrayed itself as a peaceful society recovering from an anomalous period of occupation, in which the "true" France had never been lost. In the turmoil of the 1960s, during which the Algerian War and student protests led to deep questioning of the French polity, a major reexamination of France's still recent wartime history took place. In this turbulent political atmosphere, two cultural events were key. One was a film, Marcel Ophuls's film documentary *The Sorrow and the Pity* (*Le Chagrin et la pitié*, 1969), the other a book by the American historian Robert Paxton, *Vichy France: Old Guard and New Order* (1972).

These two events – one artistic, one scholarly – contributed to a startling claim: that far from being a passive victim of German aggression, in which everyone had at least in spirit been a member of the Resistance, France had been complicit in the Nazi European order. Ophuls's film interviewed figures who represented the two faces of France – Pierre Mendès-France, the former prime minister, who had escaped occupied France to join de Gaulle's forces, and the aristocrat Christian de la Mazière, who fought with the Germans on the eastern front. On the basis of archival materials, Paxton's book showed that French political figures had used the German occupation to oppose liberal republican values, to promote a political project that was anti-Semitic, dictatorial, anti-modern, and indigenously French.

This was not the first moment in which France had reassessed its wartime record. Jean Dutourd's novel *Au Bon Beurre*, which was published in 1952, featured a crooked grocer as its protagonist as it provided a black satire on venality in German-occupied France. However, as in the rest of the Allied world after the war, the fate of the Jews elicited little interest in France during the 1950s. Elie Wiesel's *Night*, which became a classic of Holocaust literature, was originally published in France in 1958 as *La Nuit*, but it sold few copies until the 1970s, when the dimensions of the Holocaust had become better understood.[21]

Selective memory of wartime was also due to the construction of a narrative in which the European norm was defined as liberal-democratic. The communist east, whose incomplete memory of the war was cited repeatedly (and not undeservedly) as evidence of flaws in its system of government, was portrayed in contrast to the liberal west. However, the west also coexisted uneasily with anti-communist heirs of the war, who did not match up to the ideals of

21 Henry Rousso, *The Vichy Syndrome: History and Memory in France since 1944* (Cambridge, MA, 1991); Olivier Wieviorka, *La Mémoire désunie: Le souvenir politique des années sombres de la Libération à nos jours* (Paris, 2009).

democracy. Spain remained under the authoritarian rule of Francisco Franco until his death in 1975, Portugal under Antonio Salazar until 1974, and Greece under an uneasy succession of governments, then a right-wing military junta from 1967 to 1974. Greece's military dictatorship continued the suppression of the left in postwar Greece with the complicity of NATO. Even democratic Italy had a parallel system of politics (during "the years of lead" in the 1960s and 1970s), in which terrorists of right and left appeared to be paying off wartime grudges with bombs while the elected political parties turned a blind eye.

Spain was also the most prominent example of how war memory bolstered anti-communist dictatorship in postwar Europe. Franco survived the war largely because he had remained neutral, but his sympathies for the Axis left him on the wrong side of history in the postwar era, even though he remained in power. Despite limited liberalization during Franco's lifetime, the memory of the Spanish Civil War was systematically skewed toward the Nationalist side in public discourse. The vast monument of the Valle dos Caidos (Valley of the Fallen) outside Madrid commemorated only the Nationalist dead. The Republicans were characterized as war criminals. The restoration of democracy in 1977 rested on an unstated consensus not to reopen the wounds of the civil war. The state took the position that it would not seek to reinterpret the Franco period as anomalous or negative (in contrast to the memory of Vichy in France or militarism in Japan). However, the reemergence of a free civil society opened up space for private and academic reinterpretation of the war. The early twenty-first century saw a new hardening of positions, ironically just as the war was slipping out of living memory. In 2003, the right-wing writer Pio Moa published *Myths of the Civil War* (*Mitos de la Guerra civil*), a best-selling pro-Franco account that sought to revise what he called the dominant leftist view of the war.[22]

The Algerian War shook the idea of a postwar democratic European peace. Between 1954 and 1962, France's attempts to hold on to its North African colony undermined the Fourth Republic. Atrocities were committed on both sides, but the French government's willingness to use torture was particularly harmful to its image as heir of the Enlightenment, and it invited comparisons with Vichy collaboration. Yet although the question of Vichy was itself dealt with openly in the 1970s, not until the early twenty-first century did revisionism became mainstream in connection with the Algerian War. For example, on October 17, 1961, the prefect of police in Paris, the former

22 Paloma Aguilar, *Memory and Amnesia: The Role of the Spanish Civil War in the Transition to Democracy* (Oxford, 2000).

wartime collaborator Maurice Papon, authorized the use of firearms against peaceful Algerian protesters in central Paris, causing between seventy and two hundred deaths. Not until forty years later was a plaque erected to the memory of those killed and, even then, it caused controversy. The Algerian War was less evident in French cinema than was Vietnam in American film, although the film *Intimate Enemies* (*Ennemis intimes* (2007)) broke new ground by graphically depicting torture committed by the French army, as well as its psychological effects on the torturers.[23]

The other major obstacle to the idea that postwar European peace was a direct product of world war was the conflict in the Balkans during the 1990s. The wars that tore apart the former Yugoslavia seemed particularly anomalous, because they took place during an era in which transnational values were supposed to overcome the need for war. The conflict in Bosnia-Herzegovina in 1992–95 shocked the world and exposed the limitations of the European settlement, which had aimed to make war unthinkable but could do little when war reemerged. The plight of Sarajevo, the Bosnian capital, became the symbol of barbarity in the heart of Europe, as it lay under siege for three years. Eventually, US intervention and sponsorship of an uneasy peace at Dayton, Ohio, in 1995, brought peace, if not stability, to Bosnia. In recent years, Sarajevo has reconstructed the memory of its horrors. A small museum in the city showcases photographs of the siege, as well as artifacts that helped residents of the city endure their suffering. However, the wider cityscape has also put memory on display. "Sarajevo roses," red patches on the grey stonework of the streets, mark the places where shells fell. Bullet holes remain in the walls of many buildings. Even an icon of international capitalism, the Holiday Inn, is inextricably linked to the war. Radko Mladic, the Bosnian Serb military commander, hired a suite there, and its windows were renowned for their proximity to "Sniper Alley," the highway just in front of it. A grim, ironic guidebook from the days of the siege has been reprinted and remains on sale today as a reminder of Sarajevo's crisis.

The case of Sarajevo remains particularly uncomfortable, because it violated so many assumptions about war and memory in Europe – that war was outdated and that ethnic politics ended with the defeat of Nazi Germany. In addition, the Nazis' use of technological modernity to genocidal ends had been thought an anomaly after the war, when technology was used instead for

23 Martin Evans, "Remembering the War with No Name: French Conscripts and the Algerian War 1954–62," in Martin Evans and Ken Lunn, eds., *War and Memory in the Twentieth Century* (Oxford, 1997), 70–86.

"modernization" and progress. Now, however, technological progress had evidently not saved part of Europe from old demons. The implications of this realization were unwelcome. For some, a more embarrassed realization was that memory of the war had taken on macabre glamor in an age of unexciting "plenty," to use David Hare's word. The journalist Anthony Loyd's memoir of reporting the conflict was entitled *My War Gone By, I Miss It So*. The conflict in Bosnia also created a new site of memory far from Europe itself. Islamist activists in south Asia and the Middle East used it as an example of how Christian societies oppress Muslims, and they made Bosnia a recruiting tool for radical Islamist terror during the following decade.[24]

The way in which Bosnia has spoiled the narrative of democratic progress in Europe was in some ways like the role of the genocide in Rwanda, a civil war by another name. Many had hailed the early 1990s as the dawn of a new era in southern Africa, in which a post-apartheid South Africa would provide moral leadership for the continent. Rwanda provided a horrific retort to this assumption. The mass killings in 1994 were a reminder that the rifts of the colonial era remained strong and that progressive movements did not always triumph.

Rival memories of decolonization have fueled another contemporary political conflict, the Israel–Palestine dispute. In 1948, the state of Israel was created in the aftermath of Britain's withdrawal from its League of Nations mandate in Palestine. Ever since, the mainstream of Israeli public memory and historiography has regarded this event as the founding of a new nation-state with a Jewish, democratic identity. In contrast, the Palestinian Arab community regards the creation of the Jewish state as a *naqba* (catastrophe), which has reduced them to refugees or second-class citizens in their own land. In the 1980s, Israeli narratives became more complex because of the work of the "new historians," including Ilan Pappe, Benny Morris, and Avi Shlaim, who used archival material to argue that the establishment of Israel resulted in more violence toward the Palestinian population than Israeli historians had acknowledged. Despite the continuing controversy over the events of 1948, both Israelis and Palestinians have regarded themselves as heirs to a problem that was bequeathed by British colonialism.[25]

The memory of colonial wars also provided more positive inspiration for the creation of national identity. The political legacy of World War II in Asia

24 Misha Glenny, *The Fall of Yugoslavia* (London, 1996); Allan Little and Laura Silber, *The Death of Yugoslavia* (London, 1996).

25 Benny Morris, *The Birth of the Palestinian Refugee Problem Revisited* (Cambridge, 2004) and Ilan Pappe, *A History of Modern Palestine: One Land, Two Peoples* (Cambridge, 2004) reflect two sides of the debate about the foundation of Israel.

39. Srebrenica memorial

was different from its legacy in Europe. The Japanese wartime rhetoric of liberation had been in large part self-serving. It was particularly unconvincing in China, which had been devastated by the occupation. However, there were more ambiguous reactions to it elsewhere in Asia. Parts of Southeast Asia, such as the Philippines and the Dutch East Indies, had been under western colonial rule, and while they deplored the brutality of Japanese rule, the sudden collapse of the western colonial powers enabled them to envisage a new future with their own leaders in charge. Jose Laurel, the president of the Philippines in 1943–45, owed his position to Japanese patronage. Accusations that he had collaborated failed to stick after the war. Laurel was elected to the Senate in an independent Philippines and is now recognized to have been a legitimate president. The case of India showed how memories of nationalist struggle and war could combine in unusual ways. Many Indian troops served on the Allied side during the war, although sentiment in favor of independence also fueled the Quit India Movement in 1942. A smaller but significant movement backed the Japanese outright. Subhas Chandra Bose, the former president of the Indian National Congress, formed the Indian National Army, which allied with Tokyo in the hope of driving the British out of India by force. Bose's INA had some forty thousand troops based in Southeast Asia (they never fought in India itself). The British tried to place its senior officers on trial for collaboration, although Bose himself was apparently killed in a plane crash in Taiwan in 1945. The trials were abandoned when it became clear that Bose's position was highly popular in the Indian population as a whole. Today, Bose's status in India is ambivalent. Because he split with Gandhi and Nehru, the fathers of the independence movement, his place in the history of this movement is disputed, and his association with the Axis powers makes his memory problematic. However, in his home province of Bengal he is a local hero, and the Netaji Bhavan (Leader's House) in Calcutta remains open to visitors. In the words of the research center at the Netaji Bhavan, he "is regarded as a national hero in India and widely respected in the whole of Asia for his struggle and sacrifice for the liberation of India and all Asian peoples and the establishment of an international order based on justice, friendship, and cooperation."[26]

Around the world, the legacy of the global conflict of the 1930s and 1940s has shaped the memory of war since 1945 in countless ways. The importance of

26 Netaji Bhavan website at www.netaji.org (as of March 2011); Leonard Gordon, *Brothers against the Raj: A Biography of Indian Nationalists Sarat and Subhas Chandra Bose* (New York, 1990).

the war remains strong in collective memory, although its significance and form have changed radically as surviving eyewitnesses and combatants become fewer.

One consequence of ever greater distance from events is that memory has varied according to the geography of those who remember. For many countries in the west, including Britain and Germany, the emergence from a dark, anomalous period of history is still a resonant memory.[27] Remarkably, the same narrative has become more powerful in recent decades in China, where the narrative of the war has shifted from Communist-led anti-imperialism to China's participation in a global antifascist struggle. In other societies, particularly in the global south, the war was not a battle for democracy in the first place. In parts of Southeast Asia, Japanese claims to have liberated Asia from western influence still have traction, even in countries where wartime Japanese brutality also lives in folk memory. Furthermore, in a range of societies that were decolonized after 1945, the war marks the end of European empire rather than a moment of liberation in its own right. One fact remains indisputable. Whatever the reasons, the year 1945 remains a point of rupture in understanding the memory of war.

27 Mark Mazower, *Dark Continent: Europe's Twentieth Century* (London, 1998) provides a powerful counterargument to the idea that democracy is an inevitable outcome to the conflict in Europe.

23

The era of American hegemony, 1989–2005

MARK MOYAR

On November 9, 1989, Heinz Kessler was forced, much against his desires, to make one of the most momentous decisions of the Cold War. The former chief ideologist of the East German army, Kessler was now East Germany's defense minister, which gave him authority over the best military, man-for-man, that the Warsaw Pact had to offer. This chilly autumn day, Kessler himself watched massive throngs of East Berliners heading toward entry points in the Berlin Wall after the announcement, by an East German official, that the country's borders were open. Having received no advance warning of the announcement, Kessler had not provided guidance to his border troops, with the result that these troops did nothing to restrain the surge of their countrymen toward the wall. Once Kessler understood what was happening, he ordered an artillery regiment to gather ammunition for possible operations to halt the rush of people and prevent the dismantling of the wall.

Kessler phoned one of his generals to ask whether he was ready to send two other regiments to Berlin. But this general and several others warned against bringing army units to the capital, predicting that it could lead to a bloodbath. Kessler was despondent at their aversion to the use of force, but he had enough sense to know that the game was lost. He allowed the sea of humans to flow from East Berlin into West Berlin, sounding the death-knell for Communist East Germany and the ideology to which men like Kessler had devoted their lives. East Germany was absorbed by West Germany, on West German terms. Its army was soon absorbed, in like fashion, by the West German *Bundeswehr*.[1]

In the other eastern European satellites of the Soviet Union, communist military organizations were similarly swept away. Within the Soviet Union itself, the Red Army held on a bit longer, succumbing finally, along with the

1 Dale R. Herspring, *Requiem for an Army: The Demise of the East German Military* (Lanham, MD, 1998), 65–68.

Soviet government, in 1991. The Soviet economy and the massive Soviet armed forces broke apart, as many of the Soviet Union's most prosperous regions became independent. What remained under Moscow's authority, the new Russian Federation, had only a quarter of the gross domestic product of the Soviet Union at its zenith, and its armed forces numbered only 960,000 – a far cry from the peak Soviet strength of 4 million. Having only recently presided over the Warsaw Pact – an alliance that had menaced western Europe with massive conventional armies and largely dictated the national security postures and plans of NATO, the world's other principal alliance – Russia suddenly did not have even the conventional strength to defend itself and was forced to rely on nuclear weapons for self-defense.[2]

The countries of NATO emerged from the Cold War with their economies prosperous and their militaries intact. The United States held great advantages in military power and technology over its NATO partners, and larger advantages over every other country in the world, because of its huge economy, the willingness of its politicians to invest heavily in the military during the 1980s, and the creativity and sophistication of its industries and research institutions. During the last years of the Cold War, the US military had harnessed rapid technological advances that had taken hold in the civilian world, especially in information-collection, processing, and transmission. The US military and the private US companies that supplied it with technology exploited new fiber-optic cables to move data at much higher speeds and cellular telephones to transmit information without wires. Advances in the civilian microchip industry permitted rapid coordination of military operations and reduced the size of computers, so American armed forces could use them at the lowest tactical level. Satellites facilitated not only military communications, but also surveillance and the development of global positioning systems.[3]

During the 1980s, the US defense industry also invented new technologies for exclusively military applications. Lockheed built "stealth" aircraft from materials that did not reflect radar waves, making them invisible to the radars and radar-guided missiles that were the linchpin of modern air defenses. New counter-battery radar, designed by Hughes Aircraft, located enemy artillery as soon as it opened fire, which permitted its rapid destruction. General

2 Ahmed S. Hashim, "The Revolution in Military Affairs outside the West," *Journal of International Affairs* 51 (1998): 438–40; Martin Van Creveld, *The Changing Face of War: Lessons of Combat, from the Marne to Iraq* (New York, 2006), 198.

3 Max Boot, *War Made New: Technology, Warfare, and the Course of History* (New York, 2006), 307–17.

MAP 17. Collapse of the Soviet Union, 1990–1991

Dynamics produced the M1 Abrams tank, a 60-ton behemoth that could see much farther than any Soviet tank and fire accurately from a range of 2 miles while traveling at 40 miles per hour.

The importance of the technological advances of the 1980s became manifest during the Persian Gulf War of 1991, in which the United States and its allies sought to evict Iraqi invasion forces from Kuwait. The Iraqi dictator, Saddam Hussein, had the fourth largest army in the world, with more than 900,000 soldiers, and he had bought weapons of recent vintage from the Soviets, French, and South Africans. His soldiers in and near Kuwait were similar in number to the American and allied troops arrayed against them – a fact that seemed to bode well for him, given that numerical parity had favored the defense for most of history. The vast qualitative superiority of the US forces, however, would void this trend.

The US commander in charge of the war, General Norman Schwarzkopf, decided to precede the ground invasion with a major bombing campaign, and he sought out the US air staff for help in designing it. The leading theorist in the air staff – indeed the most prominent air-power theorist of the day – was Colonel John A. Warden III. Warden shared the view of most military planners that the first phase of the air campaign should establish dominance of the skies by destroying enemy aircraft and air defenses, in order to enable American bombers to strike Iraqi targets with impunity. What set Warden apart from other air strategists was his theory that small numbers of stealth aircraft with precision munitions could paralyze a state by striking critical communications, logistical, industrial, and political targets. Earlier air-power theorists, such as Giulio Douhet and Billy Mitchell, had advanced similar ideas, but the inability of the aircraft of their time to hit small targets with any consistency had rendered their theories unfeasible. Now, with the advent of precision munitions, it was possible to obliterate important targets "surgically." The plan that Warden produced for Iraq involved six days of intensive bombing, which focused on telecommunications and command-and-control facilities. In Warden's view, their destruction would isolate Saddam Hussein, paralyze his ground forces, and eliminate the need to target Iraqi ground forces.

Schwarzkopf and his chief air commander, Lieutenant General Charles A. Horner, accepted Warden's recommendations for destroying Iraq's air defenses and information systems, but not his contention that these strikes alone would incapacitate Iraq's ground forces. Schwarzkopf and Horner instead extended the campaign to thirty-nine days and aimed much of the destruction at Iraqi ground units. In addition, they predicted that even with a prolonged air campaign of this nature, sizable Iraqi ground forces would survive to fight US ground forces when they entered Kuwait.[4]

On January 17, 1991, the air war commenced with US strikes on Saddam Hussein's air and air-defense capabilities. These capabilities were far from paltry. Thanks largely to the Soviets, Iraq had 700 fighter aircraft, 7,000 antiaircraft guns, and 16,000 surface-to-air missiles, as well as an array of radar stations to detect air invaders. Their inferiority in technology and tactics, however, spelled their doom. The Americans first targeted the radar stations, employing F-117 stealth fighters, self-guided cruise missiles fired from ships in the Persian Gulf, and helicopters that hugged the earth with sophisticated electronic navigation systems to evade detection. After holes had been blasted in the outer ring of radar stations, American bombers struck additional air-defense sites and communications facilities. When the Iraqis turned on their remaining radars, American aircraft traced the radar waves to the sources, then obliterated them. Iraq's air defenses on the ground were soon neutralized, and Iraqi aircraft, which were no match for American fighters, had to be hidden to prevent their destruction.[5]

The next air attacks targeted Iraqi military forces, installations, communications, and logistics, and they did serious damage to each. Contrary to Warden's theories, however, the destruction wrought from above did not paralyze the ground forces or cause the Iraqi state to collapse. The Iraqis preserved many of their military assets, including 60 percent of their armored vehicles, by positioning them in populous areas or making them invisible from the air. Although air power demoralized some of the weaker Iraqi units, the better units remained willing to fight when the ground war came.[6]

At the end of the thirty-nine-day bombing campaign, American and allied armored forces hurtled across the desert into Kuwait, and Iraqi armored units moved out to meet them in the open terrain. In most of the resultant engagements, the coalition forces did not have a major numerical advantage in tanks or troops, but they decimated their Iraqi opponents in every battle, while suffering almost no damage. American technological advantages played

4 John Andreas Olsen, *John Warden and the Renaissance of American Air Power* (Washington, DC, 2007); Clayton K. S. Chun, "John Warden's Five Ring Model and the Indirect Approach to War," in J. Boone Bartholomees, Jr., ed., *US Army War College Guide to National Security Issues* (2 vols., 3rd edn., Carlisle Barracks, PA, 2008), Vol. I: 295–306.

5 Michael R. Gordon and Bernard E. Trainor, *The Generals' War: The Inside Story of the Conflict in the Gulf* (Boston, 1995), 205–26; Boot, *War Made New*, 318–21.

6 Thomas Keaney and Eliot Cohen, *Gulf War Air Power Survey* (5 vols., Washington, DC, 1993); Daryl G. Press, "The Myth of Air Power in the Persian Gulf War and the Future of Warfare," *International Security* 26 (2001): 5–44.

a large role in these lopsided outcomes. Scanning the open desert with their powerful scopes, American tanks consistently destroyed Iraqi tanks before the Iraqis could see them. American attack helicopters wiped out many other Iraqi tanks with antitank missiles. As soon as the Iraqis attempted to employ artillery, American counter-battery radar located the guns, and American artillery and air strikes pulverized them.

As with all major technological advances, the effective use of the new technologies demanded innovative tactics, and in this regard the Americans and their allies excelled. In the 1980s, they had prepared to use these technologies against Soviet forces, devoting innumerable hours of training and exercises to their application. Tactical proficiency also depended upon leadership, which was of much higher quality on the American side than the Iraqi, for the US military command-selection systems were based upon merit, whereas the Iraqi system stressed political loyalty. In addition, the western military commands were decentralized, which encouraged initiative and innovation, in contrast to the highly centralized Iraqi command, which discouraged these virtues and led to poor or nonexistent decision-making when communications were severed.[7]

The ground-fighting lasted only a hundred hours. Some American analysts had predicted US death tolls in the thousands or tens of thousands, but American fatalities during the war numbered just 147, and a quarter of these resulted from friendly fire. Coalition forces as a whole sustained 240 fatalities, fewer than one for every three thousand participants. This loss-rate was a tenth of what the Israelis had incurred in their one-sided victories in the Six Day War and the Bekaa Valley campaign, a twentieth of what the Germans had taken in their stunning blitzkrieg victories in 1939 and 1940, and a thousandth of what the US Marines had suffered at Tarawa in 1943.[8]

From watching the Gulf War, most of the world's other militaries concluded that fighting the United States and its NATO allies with conventional military forces was futile. Many turned to ballistic missiles or other weapons of mass destruction for self-defense and deterrence. A key exception to this trend was China, which dramatically increased its spending on military technology, especially on air forces and air defenses, while it downsized its

7 Rick Atkinson, *Crusade: The Untold Story of the Persian Gulf War* (Boston, 1993); Robert H. Scales, Jr., *Certain Victory: The US Army in the Gulf War* (Washington, DC, 1994); Frederick W. Kagan, *Finding the Target: The Transformation of American Military Policy* (New York, 2006).

8 Stephen Biddle, "Victory Misunderstood: What the Gulf War Tells Us about the Future of Conflict," *International Security* 21 (1996): 142.

huge ground forces.[9] China's economy was booming and its defense spending climbing rapidly, but it remained technologically well behind the advanced industrial nations. It was further constrained by American efforts to deny it military technology, which its aggressive espionage programs only occasionally circumvented.

Although American defense spending declined during the 1990s, from 5 percent of gross domestic product to 3 percent, the US defense budget exceeded the combined defense budgets of the next fifteen highest-ranked countries at the start of the twenty-first century.[10] The United States was the only country that could equip large forces with the newest technology or move divisions by air or sea to any spot on the globe, and it was simultaneously the world's greatest naval, air, and land power. With the possible exception of the Roman Empire, no country in history had been so superior in might to all the others.

The remarkable US victory over Iraq sparked proclamations of a "revolution in military affairs" (RMA), a drastic change in the nature of war and in military doctrine and organization.[11] The principal components of this revolution were seen as ISR (intelligence, surveillance, and reconnaissance), C4I (command, control, communications, computer applications, and intelligence processing), and precision weapons. As these technologies continued to advance during the 1990s, the boldness of the theorizing increased, as prominent RMA proponents argued that technology would soon erase the fog and friction of war. In 1997, Air Force Chief of Staff Ronald R. Fogleman predicted that "in the first part of the twenty-first century, you will be able to find, fix or track, and target – in near real-time – anything of consequence that moves or is located on the face of the Earth."[12] Admiral William A. Owens, the vice-chairman of the joint chiefs of staff, prophesied that by enabling pinpoint targeting at long ranges, the RMA would soon allow the

9 John Wilson Lewis and Xue Litai, *Imagined Enemies: China Prepares for Uncertain War* (Stanford, 2006).

10 William E. Odom and Robert Dujarric, *America's Inadvertent Empire* (New Haven, 2004), 64–66.

11 On the definition of "revolution in military affairs," see Andrew K. Krepinevich, "Cavalry to Computer: The Pattern of Military Revolutions," *National Interest* 37 (1994): 30–42; Andrew N. Liaropoulos, "Revolutions in Warfare: Theoretical Paradigms and Historical Evidence – The Napoleonic and First World War Revolutions in Military Affairs," *Journal of Military History* 70 (2006): 363–84.

12 Ronald R. Fogleman, "Information Technology's Role in 21st Century Air Power," *Aviation Week & Space Technology* (February 17, 1997): 17.

United States to rely on much smaller forces than during the 1991 war and to defeat any enemy with a first blow.[13]

RMA theorists also argued that dramatic technological advances were eroding the long-standing centrality of military platforms, such as tanks or ships, and moving militaries toward "network-centric" warfare, in which dispersed networks of information-collectors and shooters transmitted information electronically among themselves at such speed that enemy forces could be struck from long distances before they could even see their attackers. In pursuing this new vision of war, these theorists borrowed ideas from the civilian world, in which information networks were already being used to advantage. They noted, for example, that Wal-Mart had dramatically improved efficiency and profitability by moving information rapidly among cash registers, truck schedulers, and sales agents.[14]

At the other end of the spectrum were those who argued that no dramatic changes, let alone a "revolution in military affairs," had transpired. The overwhelming American success in the Gulf War of 1991, they maintained, had resulted mainly from the frailty of Iraqi forces, not from precipitate improvements in US capabilities. Other skeptics conceded that major changes had occurred, but only with respect to warfare in certain terrain – such as the desert, the air, and the sea – where the enemy could be seen easily from the air. American dominance in such terrain, they cautioned, would cause smart enemies to organize and attack in jungles, forests, or cities, or otherwise to engage in guerrilla warfare or terrorism. Some noted that the RMA's prophets were too focused on technology and slogans and that they did not lay out how organizational structures, leadership, or doctrine would have to be changed. In addition, many of the doubters contended that these technologies could not eliminate fog, friction, or the need for human will and judgment.[15]

13 William A. Owens, Jr., "The Emerging US System-of-Systems," *Strategic Forum* No. 63 (February 1996).

14 See, for example, Arthur K. Cebrowski and John J. Garstka, "Network-Centric Warfare: Its Origin and Future," *Proceedings* 124, 1 (January 1998): 28–36; Bill Owens and Ed Offley, *Lifting the Fog of War* (New York, 2000). For a retrospective analysis of this position, see H. R. McMaster, "Thoughts on the Character of Future Conflict," in Patrick M. Cronin, ed., *The Impenetrable Fog of War: Reflections on Modern Warfare and Strategic Surprise* (Westport, CT, 2008), 97–106.

15 Van Creveld, *Changing Face of War*, 204–5; Eliot A. Cohen, "A Revolution in Warfare," *Foreign Affairs* 75 (1996): 37–54; Williamson Murray, "Clausewitz Out, Computer In: Military Culture and Technological Hubris," *National Interest* 48 (1997): 57–64; Mackubin Owens, "Technology, the RMA, and Future War," *Strategic Review* 26 (1998): 63–70.

In retrospect, the RMA advocates and skeptics alike made valid points. The dramatic improvements in the use of information and the development of precision munitions had indeed produced fundamental changes in the conduct of conventional military operations in open terrain. The ability to speed data from disparate sensors to the operators of precision weapons greatly enhanced offensive capabilities, as well as the capacity to avoid harming friendly forces and civilians. With precision munitions, it became possible to destroy bridges, tanks, or machine-gun nests far more easily than before. It also became possible to destroy the infrastructure required to wage a conventional war – from airfields and power plants to ports – at little cost in aircraft or civilian casualties, for many of these targets could not be concealed from the air.

The ISR advances of the 1980s and 1990s represented a big step forward, but not a quantum leap. Intelligence had already come a long way earlier in the twentieth century, especially in regard to radar, signals-interception, and overhead imagery. Many of the ISR advances that were hailed as revolutionary – including ground sensors, personnel detectors, and night-vision equipment – had been introduced during the Vietnam War. Precision munitions also made their first appearance during that conflict. The increase in the efficacy of air power was thus part of a revolution in military affairs that began in the late 1960s with the dropping of the first precision-guided bombs.

The United States made some movement toward "network-centrism" in the 1980s and 1990s, but it was evolutionary rather than revolutionary. Increasing and dispersing intelligence-collectors and shooters and improving communication among them furthered a trend that had begun in World War II. Progress was made in the 1990s, too, in reducing the centralization of authority, which encouraged personal initiative and ingenuity at lower levels and made the new high-tech way of war more potent, although more centralization remained than had been envisaged by the prophets of network-centric warfare. There was no corresponding move away from "platform-centrism" at this time. The speed, range, weaponry, and survivability of a tank or aircraft still mattered a great deal, and tactical actions were guided by their presence. Platforms remained even more important on the seas; the aircraft carrier was invaluable, and it required many other naval assets for its protection.

The impact of the new technologies on the character of armed forces was at least as great as their impact on the character of warfare. Employing sophisticated weapons and information systems demanded armed forces that were better educated than ever before. These weapons also required longer and more costly periods of training, which increased the importance of retaining personnel for long periods of time. The need for better manpower and longer retention times, along with the reduced need for large ground-combat forces, encouraged armed forces to be more selective in recruiting and to prefer volunteers, who were likely to serve longer than conscripts. Reliance on smaller, all-volunteer forces also accorded well with political conditions in most advanced countries, as it obviated the need for conscription in an era when military service was generally unpopular among the higher strata of society. These shifts reversed a trend that dated back to the era of Clausewitz and Napoleon, when the simplification of the tools of war had reduced the importance of training, education, and experience and made it possible to turn huge numbers of conscripts quickly into soldiers.

A number of events in the 1990s, on the other hand, validated the contentions of the RMA skeptics. The first occurred in the Horn of Africa in late 1992, when Somalia splashed onto the front pages of the world's newspapers thanks to reports that civilians were starving there under the rule of warlords. Moved by appalling images and accounts, the United Nations dispatched humanitarian relief to Somalia under the protection of UN armed forces. But the United Nations failed to provide adequate protection for the relief mission. A chorus of foreign countries then called for the world's sole military giant to intervene, and the United States acceded in December 1992. President George H. W. Bush sent American forces to Somalia with a promise that they would stay only for a short time, in order to stabilize the situation, start the flow of food, and facilitate the arrival of UN reinforcements.

Bush's successor, President William J. Clinton, chose to keep US forces there longer and, in June 1993, to hunt down the warlord Mohamed Farah Aideed, who had killed UN peace-keepers and stolen relief supplies. The American forces found that their technical intelligence assets, such as overhead surveillance and signals-interception, availed them little in locating Aideed and other troublemakers, who operated in the alleys and buildings of Mogadishu and relied on runners to send information. In this environment, success required human-intelligence collection, for which the US military was not well prepared, as few personnel were familiar with either Somali culture or the intricacies of human intelligence.

On October 3, 1993, US ground forces became entangled in a bloody fight with Aideed's henchmen in Mogadishu, after rocket-propelled grenades – cheap weapons that were commonplace in Third World countries – brought down two American Black Hawk helicopters. American efforts to rescue isolated US soldiers foundered on Secretary of Defense Les Aspin's refusal to send the tanks that the US military had requested. The problems of multinational operations also came into play, with poor coordination and communications hindering the employment of Pakistani and Malaysian armor. In the end, eighteen Americans lay dead, several of whom were dragged through the streets by Aideed's supporters. Photos of Somalis jeering the American corpses created a furore in the United States, which caused President Clinton to pull US forces out of Somalia in great haste, ultimately returning Somalia to the warlords.[16] Foreign observers, including many of America's future enemies, concluded from the episode that the United States had become so averse to casualties that it would flee any insurgency at the first drawing of blood.

In the early post-Cold War period, internecine conflict also flared in the former Yugoslavia, which had broken into hostile ethnic factions after the fall of communism. Croats, Serbs, and Muslims fought one another in Bosnia-Herzegovina from 1992 to 1995, as each sought to establish ethnic homogeneity by driving off or killing the others. The United States and some of its NATO allies provided weapons to the Muslims and Croats, who seemed to be the leading victims of ethnic violence, but were reluctant to send ground forces or air support, fearing a repetition of the Somali quagmire. In 1995, however, continuing Bosnian-Serb attacks on Muslims, Croats, and UN personnel drove NATO to bomb Bosnian-Serb military targets. Although Bosnia's wooded terrain allowed the Serbs to hide military equipment from aerial surveillance, NATO aircraft inflicted enough damage on Serb installations, logistics, and ground forces to enable Muslim and Croat forces to gain the upper hand militarily. The shift in military momentum caused the Bosnian Serbs to accept the Dayton Peace Accords of December 1995, which divided Bosnia into ethnic zones and installed UN peace-keepers.[17] RMA enthusiasts hailed the outcome as evidence that air power could achieve political objectives in such conflicts, rendering unnecessary the deployment of ground forces.

Stronger support for this view came a few years later in the Serbian province of Kosovo. In March 1999, NATO began airstrikes on Serbia to persuade the Serbs to stop the ethnic cleansing of Kosovo's Muslims, on the assumption that a few days of bombing would cause the Serbian government

16 Robert F. Baumann and Lawrence A. Yates, *"My Clan against the World": US and Coalition Forces in Somalia, 1992–1994* (Fort Leavenworth, KS, 2004); Mark Bowden, *Black Hawk Down: A Story of Modern War* (New York, 1999); Lynn Thomas and Steve Spataro, "Peacekeeping and Policing in Somalia," in Robert Oakley et al., eds., *Policing the New World Disorder: Peace Operations and Public Security* (Washington, DC, 1998), 175–214; John P. Cann, "Somalia and the Limits of Military Power," *L'Afrique politique 2000* (Paris, 2000), 158–76.

17 Jeffery R. Barnett, "Defeating Insurgents with Technology," *Airpower Journal* 10 (1996): 69–74.

MAP 18. Yugoslav wars, 1991–1995

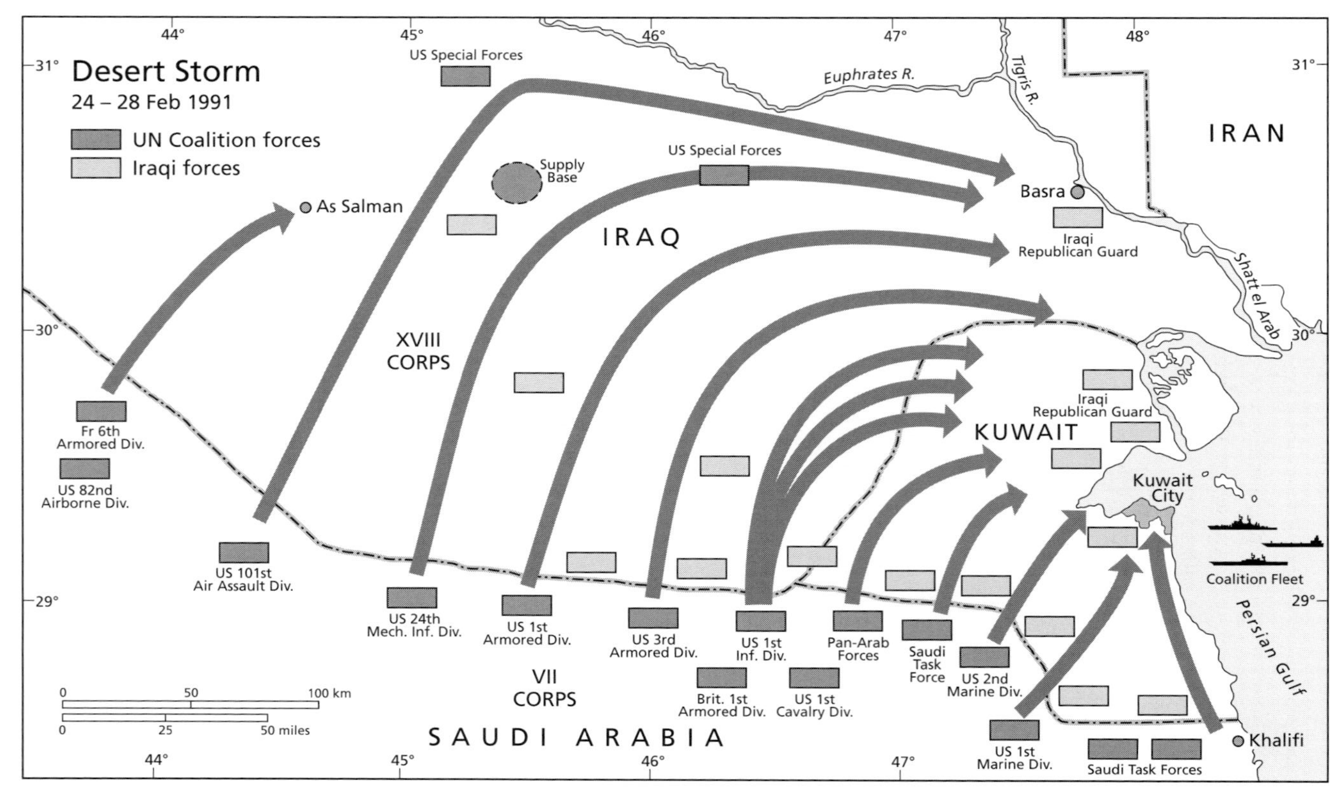

MAP 19. Operation Desert Storm, 1991

to capitulate. In actuality, the bombing campaign lasted 78 days and involved 38,000 sorties by 829 aircraft from fourteen nations. The first strikes targeted Serbia's political leadership and military forces, but they failed to dislodge the political leadership or to cause it to surrender, and they also inflicted remarkably little damage to military targets. The Serbs camouflaged their tanks and other large military vehicles and moved men primarily in cars or small trucks, which were difficult to distinguish from civilian vehicles. Despite the dropping of huge numbers of bombs on the Serb armed forces, many of them precision-guided, the NATO air campaign destroyed only fourteen tanks, eighteen armored personnel carriers, and twenty artillery pieces and mortars.

Frustration over the impotence of the attacks against the Serbian leadership and military forces led NATO to bomb the country's civilian infrastructure. Although precision munitions minimized the loss of civilian life during these strikes, media reports of the damage to civilian targets undermined international support for the bombing. The hardships that these attacks imposed on the Serbian people, however, demoralized the Serbs more rapidly. On June 3, 1999, the Serbian leader, Slobodan Milosevic, agreed to withdraw from Kosovo and allow NATO ground forces into the province, in return for a halt to the bombing. NATO troops entered Kosovo one week later.[18]

Claims that Kosovo proved the feasibility of winning wars through air power alone were soon countered by contentions that Milosevic had capitulated instead because of the withdrawal of Russian support during the bombing or because of his fear of a NATO ground invasion. This debate may never be settled, for Milosevic never divulged the reasons for his decision.[19] Whether or not air power was the sole cause of his capitulation, though, it was clearly a major factor.

The disintegration of communism at the end of the Cold War led to wars of secession within the Russian Federation, which revealed persistent differences between the west and Russia in the conduct of war. In December 1994, the Russian government went to war with separatists who sought an independent state in Chechnya. At first, everything went Russia's way. In surprise attacks, Russian aircraft wiped out all the Chechen airfields and military aircraft.

18 Benjamin S. Lambeth, *NATO's Air War for Kosovo: A Strategic and Operational Assessment* (Santa Monica, 2001); William C. Martel, *Victory in War: Foundations of Modern Military Policy* (New York, 2007), 213–14; Michael G. Vickers, "Revolution Deferred: Kosovo and the Transformation of War," in Eliot A. Cohen and Andrew J. Bacevich, eds., *War over Kosovo: Politics and Strategy in a Global Age* (New York, 2001), 193–96.

19 Daniel L. Byman and Matthew C. Waxman, "Kosovo and the Great Air Power Debate," *International Security* 24 (2000): 5–38; Michael Ignatieff, "The Virtual Commander," *New Yorker* (August 2, 1999): 31.

Russian armored units outfought Chechen conventional forces and reached the capital of Grozny without great difficulty. When they entered the city, however, Chechen forces swarmed on them and inflicted crushing losses. Russian tanks lacked sufficient infantrymen to protect them from Chechen fighters, who wielded antitank weapons and darted through the city's buildings, crippling large numbers of Russian tanks and slaughtering their crews.

The Russians subsequently reorganized their forces under new commanders, and, in conjunction with lavish artillery strikes, forced the Chechen separatists out of Grozny. Although Russia had abandoned communist dictatorship, it did not show the western obsession with minimizing civilian casualties or damage to property. Nor, for that matter, did their Chechen opponents. In the battle for Grozny, 25,000 civilians were killed, and much of the city was reduced to rubble.

After they were driven from Grozny, the Chechen rebels turned to insurgency. Russian forces tried with little success to hunt down the guerrillas in their mountain redoubts, for the Russians suffered from poor leadership, lack of coordination among ministries and armed services, and their traditional centralization of authority, which stunted the initiative and adaptation critical to counterinsurgency. The Russian forces were so inept that a few thousand Chechens retook Grozny from ten thousand Russian troops in August 1996, causing the humiliated Russians to leave Chechnya altogether.[20]

The Russians returned in 1999, after Chechen religious extremists committed a series of terrorist acts within Russia. More competent this time, the Russians retook Grozny after flattening what remained of the city, then established control over most of the country with the help of a newly organized pro-Russian government. Chechen insurgents again resorted to guerrilla warfare, using light weapons to wreak havoc on superior forces. The Chechens killed many Russian soldiers with improvised explosive devices (IEDs) and downed large numbers of Soviet helicopters with rocket-propelled grenades, Igla surface-to-air missiles, and heavy machine guns. Although the pro-Russian government organized indigenous police forces, these were largely ineffective because of corruption, sympathy for the rebels, and the fact that insurgents had killed their better elements. Russia retained control of Chechnya, but at a high price.[21]

20 Stephen J. Cimbala and Peter Rainow, *Russia and Postmodern Deterrence* (Washington, DC, 2007), 113–34; Christoph Zürcher, *The Post-Soviet Wars: Rebellion, Ethnic Conflict, and Nationhood in the Caucasus* (New York, 2007), 81–84.

21 Mark Kramer, "The Perils of Counterinsurgency: Russia's War in Chechnya," *International Security* 29 (2004–5): 5–63.

Civil wars also raged across Africa in the mid and late 1990s, in places like Rwanda, Sierra Leone, the Sudan, the Congo, Liberia, and Burundi. As in decades past, African military forces were repeatedly hobbled and compromised by their misuse as instruments of tyranny. Heads of state appointed their relatives and cronies as military leaders, whose incompetence left their armies capable of little more than committing atrocities against civilians for ethnic or political reasons. Armored and air forces were sometimes employed in these wars, but on a small scale and with short ranges because of insufficient training, logistics, and maintenance.[22]

The most militarily advanced African conflagration was the territorial war between Ethiopia and Eritrea from 1998 to 2000. These two countries had some of the most capable military officers in sub-Saharan Africa, and both had tanks and high-quality Russian military aircraft, such as MiG-29s and SU-27s. Nevertheless, inadequate training and care prevented the proper use of new military technologies. Like their neighbors, moreover, both countries performed poorly in logistics and maintenance equipment. The utility of the Soviet aircraft and tanks that both sides fielded was so limited that the Ethiopians had to attack Eritrean trenches on foot in a manner reminiscent of the cumbersome offensives on the western front in World War I. With 350,000 soldiers, the Ethiopians ground down the Eritreans, who had only 250,000. Ultimately, the Ethiopians penetrated the Eritrean defenses and seized two Eritrean towns, but because of difficulties in maintaining their vehicles and supplying their forces, they could not advance much further, and the war petered out.[23]

At the start of the new millennium, the advocates of network-centric warfare in the United States received a major boost with the appointment of Donald Rumsfeld as secretary of defense. With the backing of newly elected President George W. Bush, Rumsfeld laid out a plan entitled "Transformation," which would boost information capabilities, increase force-mobility, and reduce the total number of personnel in the US armed forces. Rumsfeld shifted the emphasis from battle tanks to lighter, 19-ton Stryker vehicles, which could carry an infantry squad and, because of their reduced weight, move across the battlefield and around the world more quickly than tanks. Trading tactical and strategic mobility for thickness of armor made sense in the world of network-

22 George Kruys, "Lessons from African Wars: Implications for the SANDF," *Strategic Review for Southern Africa* 26 (2004): 15–36.

23 Tekeste Negash and Kjetil Tronvoll, *Brothers at War: Making Sense of the Eritrean-Ethiopian War* (Athens, OH, 2000); Kruys, "Lessons from African Wars," 18–23; Robert E. Harkavy and Stephanie G. Neuman, *Warfare and the Third World* (New York, 2001), 162.

centric warfare, for the enemy could be engaged at long distances and therefore these vehicles would more likely serve as information-gatherers and troop-transports than as participants in close-quarters combat.[24]

Unlike some proponents of network-centric warfare, Rumsfeld believed that "Transformation" required not only new technologies but also a new military culture and doctrine. Much of the military leadership, in his view, was too committed to traditional military platforms and ways of business. Naval officers resisted the move to smaller platforms such as the Arsenal Ship, because these presented less attractive command opportunities than a cruiser or aircraft carrier. Air force officers resisted unmanned aerial vehicles, because these deprived officers of cockpit experience. Rumsfeld put the armed services on notice that they were to encourage innovation and risk-taking among their officers.[25]

Rumsfeld's "Transformation" was knocked off its trajectory after only eight months by the catastrophic terror attacks on September 11, 2001. When investigators determined that the nineteen hijackers were linked to the Afghanistan-based terrorist organization Al Qaeda, the US government demanded that the Afghan government hand over the Al Qaeda leadership. Afghanistan's rulers, adherents of a movement called the Taliban, which embraced extremist Muslim ideals similar to those of Al Qaeda, refused to turn over their Al Qaeda friends. The US government then resolved to overthrow the Taliban and prevent Afghanistan from operating as a terrorist sanctuary.

The Americans wanted to vanquish the Taliban quickly, while US and foreign sympathy for military action was still overwhelming. Large numbers of US ground forces could not be sent to Afghanistan in time for a rapid offensive, but they were not needed, because Afghanistan already had a large ground force that opposed the Taliban, the Northern Alliance. With 12,000 fighters and 10,000 militiamen, the Northern Alliance had for years struggled in vain to defeat the Taliban, which in 2001 had 50,000 regulars and 40,000 militiamen. The United States sent 350 Army Special Forces soldiers and 100 CIA officers to work alongside Northern Alliance forces and bring American air power into the equation. Moving by truck or pony to favorable terrain, the Americans set up posts from which they could use high-powered observation devices to identify Taliban positions from as far away as 10 kilometers. Thanks

24 Andrew Krepinevich, Jr., "The Army and Land Warfare: Transforming the Legions," *Joint Force Quarterly* No. 32 (Autumn 2002): 76–82.

25 Thomas G. Mahnken, "Transforming the US Armed Forces: Rhetoric or Reality?" *Naval War College Review* 53 (2001): 86–93.

to reorganizations and new advances in communications, their targeting data could reach American aircraft in twenty minutes – a process that might have taken two weeks in Kosovo.

At the beginning of October 2001, American aircraft began a week-long campaign of precision-guided strikes on air bases, command-and-control facilities, training camps, and logistical lines. A large portion of the Taliban and Al Qaeda soldiers perished or deserted during the week, but substantial numbers continued to fight, clinging to the population or seeking shelter in covered terrain.[26] To defeat these remaining Taliban and Al Qaeda elements, Northern Alliance ground units went on the offensive, as American aircraft delivered supporting airstrikes at the rate of a hundred sorties per day. Air power inflicted heavy damage during this phase of the war, leading its champions and those of network-centric warfare to conclude that air power, guided by networked data-collectors, had finished off the enemy with minimal assistance from ground forces. But in reality, the rifles and grenades of Northern Alliance infantrymen were required to defeat the Taliban and Al Qaeda troops, who defended key locations in ways that prevented the employment of air power. They typically established defensive positions near civilian targets, since the Americans were unwilling to use airstrikes where civilian casualties might result. Taliban and Al Qaeda fighters also learned to conceal themselves and hold their fire until Northern Alliance forces approached to within a hundred meters. In these cases, the risk of friendly-fire casualties precluded the use of close American air support.[27]

The Northern Alliance nevertheless took the capital city of Kabul in less than a month and the last Taliban holdout, in Kandahar, a few weeks later. The war's most famous battle, however, occurred after the destruction of the Taliban regime. Dubbed Anaconda, after the American operation that set the fighting in motion, the battle offered noteworthy insights into the character of warfare at the dawn of the new millennium. Based on CIA and US military intelligence reports of large groups of hostile forces in the Shahikot Valley, Operation Anaconda deployed several thousand American regulars and special-operations troops, along with Afghan militiamen, to capture or kill the enemy. Prior to this

26 Sean M. Maloney, *Enduring the Freedom: A Rogue Historian in Afghanistan* (Dulles, VA, 2005), 38–45; Don Chipman, "Air Power and the Battle for Mazar-e Sharif," *Air Power History* 50 (2003), 34–45.

27 Stephen Biddle, *Afghanistan and the Future of Warfare: Implications for Army and Defense Policy* (Carlisle, PA, 2002), 27–28, 34–36, 43–49; Boot, *War Made New*, 371–72; Mark Clodfelter, "A Strategy Based on Faith: The Enduring Appeal of Progressive American Airpower," *Joint Force Quarterly* No. 49 (Spring 2008): 154.

point, crushing the Taliban and Al Qaeda forces had been relatively easy, because they were defending fixed positions. Once they stopped trying to control the population centers, they could hide and attack when they chose, making them much harder to destroy. Although the most sophisticated of America's intelligence-collection assets had been focused on the hundred square kilometers in which the enemy troops were believed to be concentrated, the American planners badly underestimated the size of the enemy forces and failed to identify more than half of the enemy fighting positions. Caves and crevices made enemy fighting positions invisible from the air and, except at close range, from the ground. The Taliban fighters avoided electronic communications that would betray their locations or strength, and they dressed as civilians, so they could not be distinguished from herdsmen when they moved to obtain supplies or to speak to one another.

The several American and foreign military organizations and intelligence agencies involved in Operation Anaconda tended to put their own interests and preferences ahead of the overall mission, and consequently failed to collaborate on critical matters of planning and execution. Despite the wealth of computers and high-tech information systems that the Americans brought to the battlefield, the fog and friction of war were not much less than in earlier conflicts. The Afghan allies who participated in the operation lost the desire and ability to complete their assigned tasks, because the Americans did not provide promised air support and because an American aircraft attacked them as the result of computer malfunction and human error. Because of communications disruptions, tangled lines of authority, and poor judgment, American troops were airlifted into inauspicious or unintended places and took extensive casualties. Unexpected decisions had to be made quickly and under great stress, and sometimes they were made incorrectly. The Americans inflicted several hundred fatalities, but at least as many enemy fighters and leaders slipped through the blocking positions that the Americans and their Afghan allies had established to prevent their escape.[28]

In early 2003, the United States went to war with Iraq again, this time because of fears of weapons of mass destruction and a desire to democratize the Middle East. The Iraqi armed forces were considerably smaller than in 1991, but they did have 2,000 tanks and 300 combat aircraft. The Americans now intended to go all the way to Baghdad, so they had to establish and protect supply lines 500 miles long. For many military planners, the

28 Biddle, *Afghanistan and the Future of Warfare*, 28–31; Sean Naylor, *Not a Good Day to Die: The Untold Story of Operation Anaconda* (New York, 2003).

magnitude of this task required a commitment of US forces at least as large as in 1991, but Rumsfeld remained convinced that the RMA had made massive, expensive ground forces unnecessary. His office ultimately settled on 145,000 ground troops, most of them American or British – a small fraction of the number employed in 1991.[29]

At the outset, American bombs and missiles devastated Iraqi air-defense systems, communications-infrastructure, military bases, tanks, and everything else that could be spotted from the air.[30] Crossing the Iraqi border soon after the start of air operations, US and allied ground forces bypassed many of Iraq's towns and cities on the way to Baghdad, leaving logistical lines vulnerable to attacks by Iraqi forces in these towns and cities or adjacent territories. Although Iraqi regulars did not fight as strenuously as the Americans had anticipated, Iraqi irregulars were more numerous and did considerable damage. Dressed in civilian clothing, using civilians as human shields, the Iraqi irregulars slowed the Americans and their allies with surprise attacks all along these lines of advance.

In the end, nevertheless, the American invasion force had little trouble in destroying its enemies and taking Baghdad. Fewer than one of every 2,300 coalition troops was killed in action, only slightly less impressive than the one in every 3,000 in 1991.[31] As in Afghanistan, many attributed this stunning victory primarily to the precision munitions that tumbled from the air, but again their case was overstated. In contrast to the war in 1991, US forces moved through urban areas during the three-week drive to Baghdad, and in the process they came under fire from Iraqi troops at close range. Before the war, the Americans had predicted that coalition forces would suffer many casualties as they fought within Iraq's cities, given the inherent advantages enjoyed by the defenders in urban combat, but the Americans actually suffered far fewer losses in these engagements than their opponents. Although American troops had advanced weaponry and body armor that the Iraqis lacked, the most important reason for the lopsided outcomes of the urban battles was American superiority in leadership, discipline, training, and tactics. The Iraqis failed to fortify buildings, as professional western soldiers would have done. They did not block streets to force the attackers into prepared ambush sites, and did not coordinate fire and maneuver with

29 Tom Ricks, *Fiasco: The American Military Adventure in Iraq* (New York, 2006), 41–43, 96–98; George Packer, *The Assassins' Gate: America in Iraq* (New York, 2005), 114–18.

30 Andrew F. Krepinevich, Jr., "The Unfinished Revolution in Military Affairs," *Issues in Science and Technology* 19 (2003): 65–67.

31 Stephen Biddle et al., *Toppling Saddam* (Carlisle, PA, 2004), 1.

anything like the precision or consistency of American forces. Nor did they conceal their heavy weapons well, leaving them vulnerable to attacks from the air. Lacking the months or years of practice with their weapons that the Americans possessed, Iraqi soldiers with antitank weapons did not have the skill to hit armored vehicles in their soft spots.[32] The vulnerability of American forces in urban battle did not become evident until the battle of Fallujah in November 2004, which represented the one time in the post-invasion period when skilled insurgents attempted to hold fixed positions. The Americans suffered roughly six hundred casualties in taking Fallujah from several thousand insurgents.[33]

The invasion's extraordinary success seemed to justify Rumsfeld's decision to forgo large ground forces. But it soon became clear that force requirements for the invasion were not the same as those for the occupation. The Americans had too few troops to prevent mobs of newly liberated Iraqis from looting, carjacking, and murdering – a spectacle that undermined the prestige of the United States among the Iraqi people. The Americans further alienated important Iraqis and increased US troop requirements by banning former members of Saddam Hussein's Ba'ath Party from government service and by disbanding the Iraqi army. Starting in August 2003, former Ba'ath Party leaders and military officers led an insurgency against the American occupation, which the Americans and feeble new Iraqi security forces could not suppress. But insurgents who hoped that the United States would withdraw after suffering a few casualties, as it had from Somalia, were disappointed, for the American government and much of the American public were resolved to continue fighting, despite protestations from the American upper classes and many foreign allies.

At the same time, NATO occupation forces in Afghanistan faced several nascent insurgencies, which had grown from the remnants of the Taliban, Al Qaeda, and other disaffected groups. As in Iraq, foreign troops were too few to defeat the insurgents, and the security forces of the indigenous governments were too weak. Events in both Iraq and Afghanistan showed that the technological advances of recent years had done little to change the nature of counterinsurgency. Success still depended primarily upon the number of ground troops and the quality of their leaders. Only ground troops could obtain the human intelligence required to find the insurgents – the United

32 Gregory Fontenot et al., *On Point: The United States Army in Operation Iraqi Freedom* (Fort Leavenworth, KS, 2004); Biddle et al., *Toppling Saddam*, 9–31.

33 Bing West, *No True Glory: A Frontline Account of the Battle for Fallujah* (New York, 2005).

States' surveillance aircraft, satellites, and radar were of marginal use against insurgents who masqueraded as civilians and mixed with the population. Only ground forces could conduct searches, make arrests, and engage guerrillas with weapons light enough to avoid large collateral damage to civilians.

Owing to differences in creativity, initiative, and other leadership traits, some counterinsurgent commanders proved better than others in formulating and implementing effective measures. As the two wars progressed, reformers in the US army sought with limited success to alter personnel systems, in order to reward innovation and risk-taking instead of conformity and risk-avoidance. The biggest leadership problems, though, were to be found within the Iraqi and Afghan governments, without whose assistance the Americans and their NATO allies could not hope to defeat the insurgents. Partisan politics, nepotism, and cronyism put weak leaders into important command positions in the Afghan and Iraqi security forces, undermining the counter-insurgency capabilities of these forces. Initially unmindful of Afghan and Iraqi leadership deficiencies, the Americans eventually pressed these governments to assign better commanders, but not until 2006 would the Americans make significant progress with the Iraqi leadership, and hence in the war, while in Afghanistan progress within the army was overshadowed by the abysmal state of the police's leadership.[34]

The insurgencies in Afghanistan and Iraq confounded the premise of network-centric warfare that transmitting information and triggering weapons systems could be automated. Killing people from the skies in these insurgency environments proved an unexpectedly complicated and precarious task. Because the insurgents were often intermingled with the civilian populace and because international sensitivities to civilian casualties were high, military strikes required interpretation of the available intelligence, prediction of the probable damage to civilians, and judgment as to whether the rewards were worth the risks, none of which could be automated. With advances in communications, commanders at higher levels became increasingly involved in such decisions, lengthening the time required to complete the decision-making.

The period from 1989 to 2005 is best characterized as the fulfillment of a limited revolution in military affairs that had begun in the late 1960s. The principal drivers were information technology and precision weapons. By dramatically improving the accuracy and speed of targeting, technological

34 Mark Moyar, *A Question of Command: Counterinsurgency from the Civil War to Iraq* (New Haven, 2009).

changes stimulated dramatic changes in doctrine, organization, and the character of certain types of war. The importance of this revolution was, however, exaggerated in the one-sided victories in Iraq and the former Yugoslavia; in these conflicts, unlike many others, American aircraft could easily find and destroy enemy targets whose destruction ensured victory.

The revolution affected warfare much less when these conditions did not prevail. In the post-Cold War period, technologically disadvantaged countries negated many of the new technology's advantages by fighting in cities or heavily foliated terrain, masquerading as civilians, or employing guerrilla warfare and terrorism. They forced advanced countries to send troops into combat at ranges too close for the use of air power. In these circumstances, the idea of removing the fog and friction of war by technology was exposed as a pipedream. Likewise discredited in such wars was the idea that rapid transmission of information would reduce the importance of leadership, training, and tactics. No war has yet occurred between two militaries that both possessed the new technologies, but the technological disparity between western countries and their likely adversaries will probably ensure the continued prominence of these non-technological factors. Wars like those in Somalia and Chechnya, as well as the Iraqi and Afghan insurgencies, serve as warnings to those who propound sweeping prophecies of technological revolution, just as the American victories in the air wars of the Balkans and the conventional wars of Iraq and Afghanistan should instill caution among the skeptics of technology.

Select bibliography

The wars of mid-century

Addington, Larry. *The Patterns of War since the Eighteenth Century*. Bloomington, 1994.

Bayly, Christopher. *The Birth of the Modern World: 1780–1914*. Oxford, 2004.

Bell, David. *The First Total War: Napoleon's Europe and the Birth of Warfare as We Know It*. Boston and New York, 2007.

Binkley, Robert. *Realism and Nationalism, 1852–1871*. New York, 1935.

Black, Jeremy. *Western Warfare, 1775–1882*. Bloomington, 2001.

Bond, Brian. *The Pursuit of Victory: From Napoeon to Saddam Hussein*. Oxford, 1998.

Curwen, C. A. *Taiping Rebel: The Deposition of Li Hsiu-ch'eng*. Cambridge, 1977.

David, Saul. *The Indian Mutiny, 1857*. London, 2003.

Fami, Khaled. *All the Pasha's Men: Mehmed Ali, His Army, and the Making of Modern Egypt*. Cambridge, 1997.

Ferguson, Niall. *Empire: How Britain Made the Modern World*. London, 2001.

Fletcher, Ian, and Natalia Ischenko, *The Crimean War: A Clash of Empires*. Staplehurst, 2004.

Fuller, J. F. C. *The Conduct of War, 1789–1961*. New Brunswick, 1961.

Graham, Gerald. *The China Station: War and Diplomacy, 1830–1860*. Oxford, 1978.

Grimsley, Mark. *The Hard Hand of War: Union Military Policy toward Southern Civilians, 1861–1865*. Cambridge, 1997.

Harding, Richard. *Seapower and Naval Warfare, 1650–1830*. London, 1999.

Headrick, Daniel. *The Tools of Empire: Technology and European Imperialism in the Nineteenth Century*. New York 1981.

Hobsbawm, Eric. *The Age of Capital: 1848–1875*. London, 2000.

Kennedy, Paul M. *The Rise and Fall of British Naval Mastery*. London, 1991 [1976].

Kuhn, Philip. "Origins of the Taiping Vision: Cross-Cultural Dimensions of a Chinese Rebellion." *Comparative Studies in Society and History* 19 (1977): 350–66.

"The Taiping Rebellion." In John Fairbank and Denis Twitchett, eds., *The Cambridge History of China*. 15 vols. Cambridge, 1978–91. Vol. X, 1: 264–317.

Kuo, Ting-yee, and Qwang-Ching Liu. "Self-Strengthening: The Pursuit of Western Technology." In John Fairbank and Denis Twitchett, eds., *The Cambridge History of China*. 15 vols. Cambridge, 1978–91. Vol. X, 1: 491–542.

Luo Ergang. *Taiping Tianguo Shi (History of the Taiping)*. Beijing, 1991.

McPherson, James. *Battle Cry of Freedom: The Civil War Era*. New York, 1988.

Michael, Franz. *The Taiping Rebellion: History and Documents*. Seattle, 1971 [1966].

Smith, Richard. *Mercenaries and Mandarins: The Ever Victorious Army of Nineteenth Century China*. Millwood, NY, 1978.

Spence, Jonathan. *God's Chinese Son: The Taiping Heavenly Kingdom of Hong Xiuquan*. New York, 1996.

Strachan, Hew. *European Armies and the Conduct of War*. London, 1983.

Showalter, Dennis. *The Wars of German Unification*. London, 2004.

Troubetzkoy, Alexis. *The Crimean War*. London, 2006.

Wagner, Rudolf. *Re-Enacting the Heavenly Vision: The Role of Religion in the Taiping Rebellion*. Berkeley, 1982.

Wesseling, H. L. *Divide and Rule: The Partition of Africa*. Westport, CT, 1996.

Wong, John. *Deadly Dreams: Opium, Imperialism and the "Arrow" War (1856–1860) in China*. Cambridge, 1998.

Woodham-Smith, Cecil. *The Reason Why: The Story of the Fatal Charge of the Light Brigade*. London, 1953.

War, technology and industrial change, 1850–1914

Berghahn, Volker R. *Germany and the Approach of War in 1914*. 2nd edn. New York, 1993.

Bidwell, Shelford, and Dominick Graham. *Firepower: The British Army Weapons and Theories of War 1904–1945*. London, 1982.

Brose, Eric Dorn. *The Kaiser's Army: The Politics of Military Technology in Germany during the Machine Age, 1870–1918*.

Bucholz, Arden. *Moltke, Schlieffen and Prussian War Planning*. New York, 1991.

Foley, Robert T. *German Strategy and the Path to Verdun: Erich von Falkenhayn and the Development of Attrition, 1870–1916*. Cambridge, 2005.

Hamilton, Richard F., and Holger H. Herwig, eds. *War Planning 1914*. Cambridge, 2010.

Herrmann, David G. *The Arming of Europe and the Making of the First World War*. Princeton, 1996.

Herwig, Holger H. *"Luxury Fleet": The Imperial German Navy 1888–1918*. London, 1980.

Menning, Bruce W. *Bayonets before Bullets: The Imperial Russian Army 1861–1914*. Bloomington, 1992.

Neiberg, Michael S. *Warfare and Society in Europe, 1898 to the Present*. London, 2004.

Showalter, Dennis. *Railroads and Rifles: Soldiers, Technology and the Unification of Germany*. Hamden, CT, 1975.

Showalter, Dennis. *The Wars of German Unification*. London, 2004.

Snyder, Jack. *The Ideology of the Offensive*. Ithaca, 1984.

Stevenson, David. *Armaments and the Coming of War: Europe 1904–1914*. Oxford and New York, 1996.

Travers, Tim. *The Killing Ground: The British Army, the Western Front, and the Emergence of Modern War 1900–1918*. London, 1987.

Wawro, Geoffrey. *The Austro-Prussian War: Austria's War with Prussia and Italy in 1866*. Cambridge and New York, 1996.

Warfare and Society in Europe 1792–1914. London, 2000.

The Franco-Prussian War: The German Conquest of France in 1870–71. Cambridge, 2003.

Zuber, Terence. *Inventing the Schlieffen Plan: German War Planning 1871–1914*. Oxford, 2002.

War and imperial expansion

Allen, William Edward David, and Paul Muratoff. *Caucasian Battlefields: A History of the Wars on the Turco-Caucasian Border, 1828–1921*. Cambridge, 1953.

Beal, Bob, and R. C. Macleod. *Prairie Fire: The 1885 North-West Rebellion*. Edmonton, 1984.

Belich, James. *The Victorian Interpretation of Racial Conflict: The Maori, the British and the New Zealand Wars*. 2nd edn. Montreal and Kingston, 1989.

Black, Jeremy. *War and the World: Military Power and the Fate of Continents 1450–2000*. New Haven, 1998.

Bond, Brian, ed. *Victorian Military Campaigns*. London, 1967.

Bradford, James C., ed. *The Military and the Conflict between Cultures: Soldiers at the Interface*. College Station, TX, 1997.

Bridgman, John. *The Revolt of the Hereros*. Berkeley, 1981.

Callwell, Charles. *Small Wars: Their Principles and Practice*. Lincoln, NE, 1996 [1896].

Clayton, Anthony. *France, Soldiers and Africa*. London, 1988.

Connor, John. *The Australian Frontier Wars, 1788–1838*. Sydney, 2002.

Curtin, Philip D. *Disease and Empire: The Health of European Troops in the Conquest of Africa*. Cambridge, 1998.

De Moor, Jaap A., and Henk L. Wesseling, eds. *Imperialism and War: Essays on Colonial War in Asia and Africa*. Leiden, 1989.

Ditte, Albert. *Observations sur la guerre dans les colonies – organisation – exécution: Conférences faites à l'Ecole Supérieure de Guerre*. Paris, 1905.

Edgerton, Robert B. *Warrior Women: The Amazons of Dahomey and the Nature of War*. Boulder, 2000.

Fulton, Robert A. *Moroland, 1899–1906: America's First Attempt to Transform a Muslim Society*. Bend, OR, 2007.

Gates, John M. "Indians and Insurrectos: The US Army's Experience with Insurgency." *Parameters* 13 (1983): 59–68.

Gordon, Andrew. "Time after Time in the Horn of Africa." *Journal of Military History* 74 (2010): 107–44.

Gump, James O. *The Dust Rose Like Smoke: The Subjugation of the Zulu and the Sioux*. Lincoln, NE, 1994.

Hack, Karl, and Tobias Rettig, eds. *Colonial Armies in Southeast Asia*. Abingdon, 2006.

Headrick, Daniel R. *The Tentacles of Progress: Technology Transfer in the Age of Imperialism*. New York, 1988.

The Tools of Empire: Technology and European Imperialism in the Nineteenth Century. New York, 1981.

Herron, J. S. *Colonial Army Systems of the Netherlands, Great Britain, France, Germany, Portugal, Italy, and Belgium*. Washington, DC, 1901.

Hu-DeHart, Evelyn. *Yaqui Resistance and Survival: The Struggle for Land and Autonomy*. Madison, 1984.

Janda, Lance. "Shutting the Gates of Mercy: The American Origins of Total War, 1860–1880." *Journal of Military History* 59 (1995): 7–26.

Joly, Vincent. *Guerres d'Afrique: 130 ans de guerres coloniales. L'expérience française*. Rennes, 2009.

Kanya-Forstner, A. S. *The Conquest of the Western Sudan: A Study in French Military Imperialism*. Cambridge, 1969.

Kiernan, V. G. *From Conquest to Collapse: European Empires from 1815 to 1960*. New York, 1982.

Killingray, David, and David Omissi, eds. *Guardians of Empire: The Armed Forces of the Colonial Powers*. Manchester, 1999.

Labanca, Nicola. *In marcia verso Adua*. Turin, 1993.

Oltremare: storia dell'espansione coloniale italiana. Bologna, 2002.

MacMunn, George. *The Martial Races of India*. London, 1932.

Moreman, Tim R. *The Army in India and the Development of Frontier Warfare, 1849–1947*. New York, 1998.

Morton, Desmond. *The Last War Drum: The North West Campaign of 1885*. Toronto, 1972.

Muffett, D. J. M. *Concerning Brave Captains: Being a History of the British Occupation of Kano and Sokoto and the Last Stand of the Fulani Forces*. London, 1964.

Omissi, David. *The Sepoy and the Raj: The Indian Army, 1860–1940*. London, 1994.

Pakenham, Thomas. *The Scramble for Africa: The White Man's Conquest of the Dark Continent from 1876 to 1912*. London, 1991.

Parker, Geoffrey. *The Military Revolution: Military Innovation and the Rise of the West, 1500–1800*. Cambridge, 1988.

Pélissier, René. *Les Campagnes coloniales du Portugal, 1844–1911*. Paris, 2004.

Porch, Douglas. "Bugeaud, Gallieni, Lyautey." In Peter Paret, ed., *Makers of Modern Strategy: From Machiavelli to the Nuclear Age*. New York, 1986, 376–407.

The French Foreign Legion: A Complete History of the Legendary Fighting Force. New York, 1991.

Ralston, David B. *Importing the European Army: The Introduction of European Military Techniques and Institutions into the Extra-European World, 1600–1914*. 2nd edn., Chicago and London, 1996 [1990].

Reed, Nelson A. *The Caste War of Yucatán*. Rev. edn. Stanford, 2001 [1964].

Rickey, Donald, Jr. *Forty Miles a Day on Beans and Hay: The Enlisted Soldier Fighting the Indian Wars*. Norman, OK, 1963.

Robinson, Ronald. "Non-European Foundations of European Imperialism: Sketch for a Theory of Collaboration." In Roger Owen and R. B. Sutcliffe, eds., *Studies in the Theory of Imperialism*. 2nd edn. London, 1975, 117–40.

Robinson, Ronald, John Gallagher, and Alice Denny. *Africa and the Victorians: The Official Mind of Imperialism*. 2nd edn. London, 1981.

Rochat, Giorgio. *Il colonialismo italiano*. Turin, 1972.

Schulten, C. M. "Tactics of the Dutch Colonial Army in the Netherlands East Indies." *Revue internationale d'histoire miiitaire* 70 (1988): 59–67.

Streets, Heather. *Martial Races: The Military, Race and Masculinity in British Imperial Culture, 1857–1914*. Manchester, 2004.

Thrapp, Dan. *Conquest of Apachería*. Norman, OK, 1967.

Utley, Robert M. *Frontiersmen in Blue: The United States Army, and the Indian, 1848–1865*. New York, 1967.

Frontier Regulars: The United States Army and the Indian, 1866–1891. New York, 1973.

Vandervort, Bruce. *Wars of Imperial Conquest in Africa, 1830–1914*. London and Bloomington, 1998.

"Colonial Wars 1815–1960." In Jeremy Black, ed., *European Warfare 1815–2000*. Houndmills, 2002, 147–72.

Indian Wars of Mexico, Canada and the United States, 1812–1900. London, 2006.
Wolseley, Garnet. *The Story of a Soldier's Life*. 2 vols. New York, 1903.

The non-western world responds to imperialism, 1850–1914

Aksan, Virginia. *Ottoman Wars: An Empire Besieged, 1700–1870*. Harlow, 2007.

Bennison, Amira K. *Jihad and Its Interpretation in Pre-Colonial Morocco*. London, 2002.

Brown, L. Carl. *The Tunisia of Ahmad Bey, 1837–1855*. Princeton, 1974.

Calmard, Jean. "Les Reformes militaires sous les Qajars (1795–1925)." In Y. Richard, ed., *Entre l'Iran et l'Occident*. Paris, 1989, 17–42.

Calmard, Jean, M. Ettehadieh, and S. Sadeq, *Le Général Semino en Iran Qajar et la guerre de Hérat (1820–1850)*, Tehran, 1997.

Caulk, R. A. "Firearms and Princely Power in Ethiopia in the Nineteenth Century." *Journal of African History* 13 (1972): 609–30.

Collier, Harry H., and Paul Chin-chih Lai,. *Organizational Changes in the Chinese Army, 1895–1950*. Taipei, 1969.

Crabités, Pierre. *Americans in the Egyptian Army*. London, 1938.

Cronin, Stephanie. *The Army and the Creation of the Pahlavi State in Iran, 1910–1926*. London, 1997.

Del Rey, Miguel. *La Guerra de Africa, 1859–1860*. Madrid, 2001.

Drea, Edward J. *Japan's Imperial Army: Its Rise and Fall, 1853–1945*. Lawrence, KS, 2009.

Dreyer, Edward L. *China at War, 1901–1949*. London, 1995.

Dundul Namgyal Tsarong, and Ani K. Trinlay Chodron. *In the Service of His Country: The Biography of Dasang Damdul Tsarong, Commander General of Tibet*. Ithaca, 2000.

Dunn, John P. "For God, Emperor, and Country! The Evolution of Ethiopia's Nineteenth Century Army." *War in History* 1 (1994): 278–99.

Khedive Ismail's Army. London, 2005.

"Clothes to Kill For: Uniforms and Politics in Ottoman Armies." *Journal of Middle East and Africa* 2 (2011): 85–107.

Dunn, Ross E. "The Colonial Offensive in Southeastern Morocco, 1881–1912: Patterns of Response." Ph.D. dissertation, University of Wisconsin, 1969.

Elleman, Bruce A. *Modern Chinese Warfare, 1795–1989*. London, 2001.

Erikson, Edward J. *Ordered to Die: A History of the Ottoman Army in the First World War*. Westport, CT, 2001.

Fahmy, Khaled. *All the Pasha's Men: Mehmed Ali, His Army, and the Making of Modern Egypt*. Cambridge, 1998.

Farmanfarmaian, Roxane, ed. *War and Peace in Qajar Persia: Implications Past and Present*. London, 2008.

Fung, Edmund K. S. *The Military Dimension of the Chinese Revolution: The New Army and Its Role in the Revolution of 1911*. Vancouver, 1980.

Graf, David A., and Robin Higham. *A Military History of China*. Boulder, 2002.

Hill, Richard, and Peter Hogg. *A Black Corps d'Elite: An Egyptian Sudanese Conscript Battalion with the French Army in Mexico, 1863–1867*. East Lansing, MI, 1995.

Jones, Raymond. *The Battle of Adua: African Victory in the Age of Imperialism*. Cambridge, MA, 2011.

Kublin, Hyman. "The 'Modern' Army of Early Meiji Japan." *Far Eastern Quarterly* 9 (1949): 20–41.

Latreille, Albert. *La Campagne de 1844 au Maroc*. Paris, 1912.

Mehra, P. "Tibet and Its Army." *Tibet Journal* 32 (2007): 33–60.

Meredith, Colin. "The Qajar Response to Russia's Military Challenge, 1804–28." Ph.D. dissertation, Princeton University, 1972.

Moalla, Asma. *The Regency of Tunis and the Ottoman Porte, 1777–1814: Army and Government of a North African Eyâlet at the End of the Eighteenth Century*. London, 2004.

Nyström, Per. *Fem år i Persien som Gendarmofficer* (Five Years in Persia as a Gendarme Officer). Stockholm, 1925.

Palmstierna, Nils. "Swedish Army Officers in Africa and Asia." *Revue internationale d'histoire militaire* 26 (1967): 45–73.

Pankhurst, Richard. *An Introduction to the History of the Ethiopian Army*. Addis Ababa, 1967.

Piemontese, A. "L'esercito persiano nel 1874–75: organizzazione e riforma secondo E. Andreini." *Rivista degli Studi Orientali* 49 (1975): 71–117.

Powell, Ralph L. *The Rise of Chinese Military Power, 1895–1912*. Princeton, 1955.

Presseisen, Ernst Leopold. *Before Aggression: Europeans Prepare the Japanese Army*. Tucson, 1965.

Rabi, Uzi, and Nugzar Ter-Oganov. "The Russian Military Mission and the Birth of the Persian Cossack Brigade, 1879–1894." *Iranian Studies* 42 (2009): 445–63.

René-Leclerc, Charles. *L'Armeé marocaine*. Algiers, 1905.

Rollman, Wilfred J. "The 'New Order' in Pre-Colonial Muslim Society: Military Reform in Morocco, 1844–1904." Ph.D. dissertation, University of Michigan, 1983.

Salma, B. *L'Insurrection de 1864 en Tunisie*. Tunis, 1967.

Simou, Bahija. *Les Reformes militaries au Maroc de 1844 à 1912*. Rabat, 1995.

Teferi Teklehaimanot. "The Ethiopian Feudal Army and Its Wars, 1868–1936." Ph.D. dissertation, Kansas State University, 1971.

Thompson, Sandra C. "Filibustering to Formosa: General Charles Le Gendre and the Japanese." *Pacific Historical Review* 40 (1971): 442–56.

Tousi, R. "The Persian Army, 1880–1907." *Middle Eastern Studies* 24 (1988): 206–29.

Uyar, Mesut, and Edward J. Erikson. *A Military History of the Ottomans: From Osman to Atatürk*. Westport, CT, 2009.

Worthing, Peter M. *A Military History of Modern China: From the Manchu Conquest to Tian'anmen Square*. Westport, CT, and London, 2007.

Zoka, Yahya. *The Imperial Iranian Army from Cyrus to Pahlavi*. Trans. Roger Cooper. Tehran, n.d. [197?].

War, society, and culture, 1850–1914: the rise of militarism

Benecke, Werner. *Militär, Reform und Gesellschaft im Zarenreich: Die Wehrpflicht in Russland 1874–1914*. Paderborn 2006.

Berghahn, Volker R. *Militarism: The History of an International Debate, 1861–1989*. New York, 1982.

Bredow, Wilfried von. *Moderner Militarismus: Analyse und Kritik*. Stuttgart, 1983.

Chambers, John Whiteclay, II. "The American Debate over Modern War, 1871–1914." In Manfred Boemeke et al., eds., *Anticipating Total War: The German and American Experiences, 1871–1914*. Cambridge, 1999, 241–79.

Chanet, Jean-François. *Vers l'armée nouvelle: République conservatrice et réforme militare 1871–1879*. Rennes, 2006.

Chickering, Roger. *Imperial Germany and a World without War: The Peace Movement and German Society, 1892–1914*. Princeton, 1975.

"Militarism and Radical Nationalism." In James Retallack, ed., *Germany, 1871–1918*. Oxford, 2008, 196–218.

Cole, Laurence, and Daniel L. Unowsky, eds. *The Limits of Loyalty: Imperial Symbolism, Popular Allegiances, and State Patriotism in the Late Habsburg Monarchy*. New York, 2007.

Conze, Werner et al. "Militarismus." In Otto Brunner et al., eds., *Geschichtliche Grundbegriffe: Historisches Lexikon zur politisch-sozialen Sprache in Deutschland*. 8 vols. Stuttgart, 1972–97, Vol. IV: 1–48.

Craig, Gordon A. *The Politics of the Prussian Army, 1640–1945*. New York and Oxford, 1956.

Foerster, Roland G., ed. *Die Wehrpflicht: Entstehung, Erscheinungsformen und politisch-militärische Wirkung*. Munich, 1994.

Frevert, Ute. *A Nation in Barracks: Modern Germany, Military Conscription and Civil Society*. Oxford and New York, 2004.

ed. *Militär und Gesellschaft im 19. und 20. Jahrhundert*. Stuttgart, 1996.

Gluck, Carol. *Japan's Modern Myths: Ideology in the Late Meiji Period*. Princeton, 1985.

Heathorn, Stephen. *For Home, Country and Race: Constructing Gender, Class, and Englishness in the Elementary Schools, 1880–1914*. Toronto, 2000.

Jansen, Christian, ed. *Der Bürger als Soldat: Die Militarisierung europäischer Geselleschaften im langen 19. Jahrhundert: Ein internationaler Vergleich*. Essen, 2004.

Jeismann, Michael. *Das Vaterland der Feinde: Studien zum nationalen Feindbegriff und Selbstverständnis in Deutschland und Frankreich*. Stuttgart, 1992.

Johnson, John J. *The Military and Society in Latin America*. Stanford, 1964.

Leonhard, Jörn. *Bellizismus und Nation: Kriegsdeutung und Nationsbestimmung in Europa und den Vereinigten Staaten 1750–1914*. Munich, 2008.

Mosse, George L. *The Nationalization of the Masses: Political Symbolism and Mass Movements in Germany from the Napoleonic Wars through the Third Reich*. Ithaca and London, 1975.

Nunn, Frederick M. *Yesterday's Soldiers: European Military Professionalism in South America, 1890–1914*. Lincoln, NE, and London, 1983.

Powell, Ralph L. *The Rise of Chinese Military Power, 1895–1912*. Princeton, 1953.

Presseisen, Ernst L. *Before Aggression: Europeans Prepare the Japanese Army*. Tucson, 1965.

Reynolds, Douglas R. *China, 1898–1912: The Xinzheng Revolution and Japan*. Cambridge, MA, 1993.

Rosen, Stephen Peter. *Societies and Military Power: India and Its Armies*. Ithaca and London, 1996.

Rouquié, Alain. *The Military and the State in Latin America*. Berkeley, 1987.

Rüger, Jan. *The Great Naval Game: Britain and Germany in the Age of Empire*. Cambridge, 2007.

Sanborn, Joshua A. *Drafting the Russian Nation: Military Conscription, Total War, and Mass Politics, 1905–1925*. DeKalb, IL, 2003.

Sater, William F., and Holger H. Herwig. *The Grand Illusion: The Prussianization of the Chilean Army*. Lincoln, NE, and London, 1999.

Showalter, Dennis. "Army, State and Society in Germany, 1871–1914: An Interpretation." In Jack R. Dukes and Joachim Remak, eds., *Another Germany: A Reconsideration of the Imperial Era*. Boulder and London, 1988, 1–18.

Stargardt, Nicholas. *The German Idea of Militarism: Radical and Socialist Critics, 1866–1914*. Cambridge, 1994.

Steinish, Irmgard. "Different Paths to War: A Comparative Study of Militarism and Imperialism in the United States and Imperial Gemany, 1871–1914." In Manfred Boemeke et al., eds., *Anticipating Total War: The German and American Experiences, 1871–1914*. Cambridge, 1999, 29–53.

Vagts, Alfred. *A History of Militarism, Civilian and Military*. New York, 1959.

Vandervort, Bruce. *Wars of Imperial Conquest in Africa, 1830–1914*. Bloomington and Indianapolis, 1998.

Vogel, Jakob. *Nationen im Gleichschritt: Der Kult der "Nation in Waffen" in Deutschland und Frankreich 1871–1914*. Göttingen, 1997.

Weber, Eugen. *Peasants into Frenchmen: The Modernization of Rural France, 1871–1914*. Stanford, 1976.

Welch, Claude E. "Continuity and Discontinuity in African Military Organisation." *Journal of Modern African Studies* 13 (1975): 229–48.

Ziemann, Benjamin. "Sozialmilitarisums und militärische Sozialisation im deutschen Kaiserreich 1870–1914." *Geschichte in Wissenschaft und Unterricht* 53 (2009): 148–64.

Zürcher, Eric Jan, ed. *Arming the State: Military Conscription in the Middle East and Central Asia, 1775–1925*. London and New York, 1999.

War-making and restraint by law: the formative years, 1864–1914

Abrams, Irwin. "The Emergence of the International Law Societies." *Review of Politics* 19 (1957): 361–80.

Anghie, Antony. *Imperialism, Sovereignty and the Making of International Law*. Cambridge, 2005.

Barton, Claire. *The Red Cross of the Geneva Conventions: What It Is*. Washington, DC, 1878.

Best, Geoffrey. *Humanity in Warfare: The Modern History of the International Law of Armed Conflict*. London, 1980.

Charlesworth, Hilary, and Christine Chinkin. *The Boundaries of International Law: A Feminist Analysis*. Manchester, 2000.

Checkland, Olive. *Humanitarianism and the Emperor's Japan, 1877–1917*. New York, 1994.

Coppieters, Bruno, and Nick Fotion. *Moral Constraints on War: Principles and Cases*. 2nd edn. Lanham, MD, 2008.

Darrow, Margaret. "French Volunteer Nursing and the Myth of War Experience in World War I." *American Historical Review* 10 (1996): 80–106.

Davis, Calvin DeArmond. *The United States and the First Hague Peace Conference*. Ithaca, 1962.

The United States and the Second Hague Peace Conference: American Diplomacy and International Organzations, 1899–1914. Durham, NC, 1975.

Dudink, Stefan, Karen Hagemannn, and John Tosh, eds. *Masculinities in Politics and War: Gendering Modern History*. Manchester, 2004.

Dunant, Jean Henry. *Un souvenir de Solférino. Facsimile repr.* 2005 [1862].

Falk, Richard, Friedrich Kratochwil, and Saul H. Mendlovitz, eds. *International Law: A Contemporary Perspective*. Boulder, 1985.
Fassin, Didier, and Mariella Pandolfi, eds. *Contemporary States of Emergency: The Politics of Military and Humanitarian Interventions*. New York, 2010.
Forsythe, David P. *Humanitarian Politics: The International Committee of the Red Cross*. Baltimore, 1977.
Hagemann, Karen, Gisela Mettele, and Jane Rendall, eds. *Gender, War and Politics: Transatlantic Perspectives, 1775–1830*. New York, 2010.
Harris, J. W. *Legal Philosophies*. London, 1980.
Higgins, A. Pierce. *The Hague Peace Conference and Other International Conferences concerning the Laws and Usages of War: Texts of Conventions with Comments*. Cambridge, 1909.
Hutchinson, John F. *Champions of Charity: War and the Rise of the Red Cross*. Boulder, 1996.
Iriye, Ikira. *Global Community: The Role of International Organizations in the Making of the Contemporary World*. Berkeley and Los Angeles, 2002.
Kalshoven, Fritz. *The Laws of Warfare: A Summary of Its Recent History and Trends in Development*. Leiden, 1973.
Ku, Charlotte, and Paul F. Diehl, eds. *International Law: Classic and Contemporary Readings*. 3rd edn. Boulder, 2009.
Nussbaum, Arthur. *A Concise History of the Law of Nations*. New York, 1950.
O'Connor, Maureen P. *The Other Balkan Wars: A 1913 Carnegie Endowment Inquiry in Retrospect*. 2nd edn. Washington, DC, 1993.
"The Vision of Soldiers: Britain, France, Germany and the United States Observe the Russo-Turkish War." *War in History* 4 (1997): 264–95.
Özbek, Nadir. "The Politics of Modern Welfare Institutions in the Late Ottoman Empire. 1876–1901." *International Journal of Turcologia* 3 (2008): 42–62.
Procès-verbaux des séances du Comité International de la Croix-Rouge, 1863–1914. Ed. Jean-François Pitteloud. Geneva, 1999.
Quataert, Donald. *The Ottoman Empire, 1700–1922. 2nd edn*. Cambridge, 2005.
Quataert, Jean H. *Staging Philanthropy: Patriotic Women and the National Imagination in Dynastic Germany, 1813–1916*. Ann Arbor, 2001.
The Gendering of Human Rights in the International Systems of Law in the Twentieth Century. Washington, DC, 2006.
Advocating Dignity: Human Rights Mobilizations in Global Politics. Philadelphia, 2009.
Roberts, Adam, and Richard Guelff, eds. *Documents on the Laws of War*. Oxford, 1989.
Summers, Anne. *Angels and Citizens: British Women and Military Nurses, 1854–1914*. London, 1998.
Weitz, Eric D. "From the Vienna to the Paris System: International Politics and the Entangled Histories of Human Rights, Forced Deportations, and Civilizing Missions." *American Historical Review* 113 (2008): 1313–43.

The arms race: qualitative and quantitative aspects

Brose, Eric Dorn. *The Kaiser's Army: The Politics of Military Technology in Germany during the Machine Age, 1870–1918*. Oxford, 2001.
Brown, D. K. *Warrior to Dreadnought: Warship Development 1860–1905*. Annapolis, MD, 2003.

Echevarria II, Antulio J. *After Clausewitz: German Military Thinkers before the Great War*. Lawrence, KS, 2001.

Etcheson, Craig. *Arms Race Theory: Strategy and Structure of Behavior*. New York, 1989.

Evans, David C., and Mark R. Peattie. *Kaigun: Strategy, Tactics, and Technology in the Imperial Japanese Navy, 1887–1941*. Annapolis, MD, 1997.

Hamilton, Richard F., and Holger Herwig, eds. *The Origins of World War I*. New York, 2003.

War Planning 1914. Cambridge, 2010.

Herrmann, David G. *The Arming of Europe and the Making of the First World War*. Princeton, 1996.

Hobson, Rolf. *Imperialism at Sea: Naval Strategic Thought, the Ideology of Sea Power, and the Tirpitz Plan, 1875–1914*. Boston, 2002.

Huntington, Samuel "The Arms Race Phenomena." *Public Policy* 8 (1958): 1–20.

Kennedy, Paul M. *The Rise of the Anglo-German Antagonism, 1860–1914*. London, 1980.

ed. *The War Plans of the Great Powers, 1880–1914*. London, 1985.

Kranzberg, Melvin, and Carroll W. Pursell, Jr., eds. *Technology in Western Civilization*. Vol. II: *Technology in the Twentieth Century*. New York, 1967.

Massie, Robert K. *Dreadnought: Britain, Germany and the Coming of the Great War*. New York, 1992.

Mombauer, Annika. *Helmuth von Moltke and the Origins of the First World War*. Cambridge and New York, 2001.

Paine, S. C. M. *The Sino-Japanese War of 1894–1895: Power, Perceptions, and Primacy*. Cambridge, 2003.

Parkinson, Roger. *The Late Victorian Navy: The Pre-Dreadnought Era and the Origins of the First World War*. Woodbridge, 2008.

Preston, Diana. *The Boxer Rebellion*. New York, 2000.

Richardson, Lewis F. *Arms and Insecurity*. Pacific Grove, CA, 1960.

Sondhaus, Lawrence. *Naval Warfare, 1815–1914*. New York, 2001.

Stevenson, David. *Armaments and the Coming of the War: Europe, 1904–1914*. Oxford, 1996.

Taylor, A. J. P. *War by Time-Table: How the First World War Began*. London, 1969.

How Wars Begin. London, 1979.

Teich, Mikulás, and Roy Porter, eds., *Fin de Siècle and Its Legacy*. Cambridge, 1990.

World War I

Ashford, Tony. *Trench Warfare, 1914–1918: The Live and Let Live System*. London, 1980.

Audoin-Rouzeau, Stéphane, and Annette Becker. *14–18: Understanding the Great War*. New York, 2003.

Chickering, Roger. *Imperial Germany and the Great War, 1914–1918*. Cambridge, 2004.

Cook, Tim. *At the Sharp End: Canadians Fighting the Great War, 1914–1916*. Toronto, 2007.

Shock Troops: Canadians Fighting the Great War, 1917–1918. Toronto, 2008.

DiNardo, Richard. *Breakthrough: The Gorlice-Tarnow Campaign, 1915*. Westport, CT, 2010.

Doughty, Robert. *Pyrrhic Victory: French Strategy and Operations in the Great War*. Cambridge, MA, 2005.

Dowling, Timothy. *The Brusilov Offensive*. Bloomington, 2008.

Ellis, John. *Eye-Deep in Hell: Trench Warfare in World War I*. Baltimore, 1989.

Erickson, Edward. *Ordered to Die: A History of the Ottoman Army in the First World War*. Westport, CT, 2000.

Foley, Robert T. *German Strategy and the Path to Verdun: Erich von Falkenhayn and the Development of Attrition, 1870–1916*. Cambridge, 2005.

French, David. "The Meaning of Attrition, 1914–1916." *English Historical Review* 103 (1988): 385–405.

Fromkin, David. *A Peace to End All Peace: The Fall of the Ottoman Empire and the Creation of the Modern Middle East*. New York, 2001.

Fussell, Paul. *The Great War and Modern Memory*. New York, 2009.

Greenhalgh, Elizabeth. *Victory through Coalition: Britain and France during the First World War*. Cambridge, 2005.

Grotelueschen, Mark E. *Doctrine under Trial: American Artillery Employment in World War I* (Westport, CT, 2000).

The AEF Way of War: The American Army and Combat in World War I. Cambridge, 2006.

Hamilton, Richard, and Holger Herwig, eds. *The Origins of World War I*. Cambridge, 2003.

Herwig, Holger. *The First World War: Germany and Austria-Hungary, 1914–19*. London, 1997.

The Marne, 1914: The Opening of World War I and the Battle that Changed the World. New York, 2009.

Horne, John, and Alan Kramer. *German Atrocities, 1914: A History of Denial*. New Haven, CT, 2001.

Kennedy, David. *Over Here: The First World War and American Society*. Oxford, 1982.

Kramer, Alan. *Dynamic of Destruction: Culture and Mass Killing in the First World War*. Oxford, 2007.

McMeekin, Sean. *The Berlin-Baghdad Express: The Ottoman Empire and Germany's Bid for World Power*. Cambridge, MA, 2010.

The Russian Origins of the First World War. Cambridge, MA, 2011.

Neiberg, Michael S. *Foch: Supreme Allied Commander in the Great War*. Dulles, VA, 2003.

Fighting the Great War: A Global History. Cambridge, MA, 2005.

The Second Battle of the Marne. Bloomington, 2008.

Dance of the Furies: Europe and the Outbreak of War in 1914. Cambridge, MA, 2011.

Palazzo, Albert. *Seeking Victory on the Western Front: The British Army and Chemical Warfare in World War I*. Lincoln, NE, 2000.

Philpott, William. *Bloody Victory: The Sacrifice on the Somme and the Making of the Twentieth Century*. London, 2009.

Schindler, John. *Isonzo: The Forgotten Sacrifice of the Great War*. Westport, CT, 2001.

Sheffield, Gary. *The Somme*. London, 2003.

Showalter, Dennis. *Tannenberg: Clash of Empires*. Dulles, VA, 2003.

Smith, Leonard V. *Between Mutiny and Obedience: The Case of the French Fifth Infantry Division during World War I*. Princeton, 1994.

Stephenson, Scott. *The Final Battle: Soldiers of the Western Front and the German Revolution of 1918*. Cambridge, 2009.

Stevenson, David. *Cataclysm: The First World War as Political Tragedy*. New York, 2004.

Stone, Norman, *The Eastern Front 1914–1917*. New York, 1975.

Strachan, Hew. *The First World War*. Vol. I: *To Arms*. Oxford, 2001.

Thompson, Mark. *The White War: Life and Death on the Italian Front, 1915–1919*. New York, 2008.

Tunstall, Graydon A. *Blood on the Snow: The Carpathian Winter War of 1915*. Lawrence, KS, 2010.

Watson, Alexander. *Enduring the Great War: Combat, Morale and Collapse in the German and British Armies, 1914–1918*. Cambridge, 2008.

Wiest, Andrew. *Haig: The Evolution of a Commander*. Dulles, VA, 2005.

Yasamee, F. A. F. "The Ottoman Empire." In Keith Wilson, ed., *Decisions for War, 1914*. London, 1994.

Zabecki, David. *The German 1918 Offensives: A Case Study in the Operational Level of War*. London, 2006.

Military captivity in two worlds wars: legal frameworks and camp regimes

Beaumont, Joan. "Rank, Privilege and Prisoners of War." *War and Society* 1 (1983): 67–94.

"Protecting Prisoners of War, 1939–1995." In Bob Moore and Kent Fedorwich, eds., *Prisoners of War and Their Captors in World War II*. Oxford and Washington, DC, 1996, 277–97.

Biess, Frank. *Homecomings: Returning POWs and the Legacies of Defeat in Postwar Germany*. Berkeley, 2006.

Brändström, Elsa. *Among the Prisoners of War in Russia and Siberia*. London, 1929.

Davis, Gerald H. "The Life of Prisoners of War in Russia, 1914–1921." In Samuel R. Williamson and Peter Pastor, eds., *Essays on World War I: Origins and Prisoners of War*. New York, 1983, 162–96.

"National Red Cross Societies and Prisoners of War in Russia, 1914–1918." *Journal of Contemporary History* 28 (1993): 31–52.

Doyle, Robert C. *Voices from Captivity: Interpreting the American POW Narrative*. Lawrence, KS, 1994.

Ferguson, Niall. "Prisoner Taking and Prisoner Killing in the Age of Total War: Toward a Political Economy of Military Defeat." *War in History* 11 (2004): 134–78.

Flower, Sibylla Jane. "Captors and Captives on the Burma-Thailand Railway." In Moore and Fedorowich, eds., *Prisoners of War*, 227–53.

Gilbert, Adrian. *POW: Allied Prisoners of War in Europe, 1939–1945*. London, 2007.

Hilger, Andreas. *Deutsche Kriegsgefangene in der Sowjetunion 1941–1956. Kriegsgefangenenpolitik, Lageralltag und Erinnerung*. Essen, 2000.

Hinz, Uta. *Gefangen im Großen Krieg: Kriegsgefangenschaft in Deutschland 1914–1921*. Essen, 2006.

Jones, Heather. *Violence against Prisoners of War in the First World War: Britain, France, and Germany, 1914–1920*. Cambridge, 2011.

Karner, Stefan. *Im Archipel GUPVI: Kriegsgefangenschaft und Internierung in der Sowjetunion 1941–1956*. Vienna and Munich, 1995.

Ketchum, Davidson J. *Ruhleben: A Prison Camp Society*. Toronto, 1965.

Kowner, Rotem. "Imperial Japan and Its POWs: The Dilemma of Humaneness and National Identity." In Guy Podoler, ed., *War and Militarism in Modern Japan: Issues of History and Identity*. Folkestone, 2009.

Leidinger, Hannes, and Verena Moritz. "Österreich-Ungarn und die Heimkehrer aus russischer Kriegsgefangenschaft im Jahr 1918." *Österreich in Geschichte und Literatur* 6 (1997): 385–403.

Gefangenschaft, Revolution, Heimkehr: Die Bedeutung der Kriegsgefangenenproblematik für die Geschichte des Kommunismus in Mittel- und Osteuropa 1917–1920. Vienna, 2003.

Levie, Howard S. *Prisoners of War in International Armed Conflict*. Newport, RI, 1977.

Lieblich, Amia. *Seasons of Captivity: The Inner World of POWs*. New York, 1994.

MacKenzie, S. P. "The Treatment of Prisoners of War in World War II." *Journal of Modern History* 66 (1994): 487–520.

The Colditz Myth: British and Commonwealth Prisoners of War in Nazi Germany. Oxford, 2004.

Moore, Bob, and Fedorwich Kent, eds. *Prisoners of War and Their Captors in World War II*. Oxford and Washington, DC, 1996.

Nachtigal, Reinhard. *Russland und seine österreichisch-ungarischen Kriegsgefangenen 1914–1918*. Remshalden, 2003.

Oltmer, Jochen, ed. *Kriegsgefangene im Europa des Ersten Weltkriegs*. Paderborn, 2006.

Polian, Pavel. "First Victims of the Holocaust: Soviet-Jewish Prisoners of War in German Captivity." *Kritika: Explorations in Russian and Eurasian History* 6 (2005): 763–87.

"The Internment of Returning Soviet Prisoners of War after 1945." In Bob Moore and Barbara Hatley-Broad, eds., *Prisoners of War, Prisoners of Peace*. Oxford and New York, 2005, 124–27.

Pöppinghege, Rainer. *Im Lager unbesiegt: Deutsche, englische, französische Kriegsgefangenenzeitungen im Ersten Weltkrieg*. Essen, 2006.

Rachamimov, Alon. *POWs and the Great War: Captivity on the Eastern Front*. Oxford and New York, 2002.

"The Disruptive Comforts of Drag: (Trans)Gender Performances among Prisoners of War in Russia, 1914–1920." *American Historical Review* 111 (2006): 362–82.

"'Female Generals' and 'Siberian Angels': Aristocratic Nurses and the Austro-Hungarian POW Relief." In Nancy M. Wingfield and Maria Bucur, eds., *Gender and War in Twentieth-Century Eastern Europe*. Bloomington, 2006.

Roland, Charles G. "Allied POWs, Japanese Captors and the Geneva Convention." *War and Society* 9 (1991): 83–101.

Speed, Richard B. *Prisoners, Diplomats and the Great War: A Study in the Diplomacy of Captivity*. New York, 1990.

Spoerer, Mark. "The Mortality of Allied Prisoners of War and Belgian Civilian Deportees in German Custody during the First World War: A Reappraisal of the Effects of Forced Labour." *Population Studies* 60 (2006): 121–36.

Spoerer, Mark, and Jochen Fleischhacker. "Forced Laborers in Nazi Germany: Categories, Numbers, and Survivors." *Journal of Interdisciplinary History* 33 (2002): 169–204.

Stibbe, Matthew. "Prisoners of War during the First World War." *Bulletin of the German Historical Institute London* 28 (2006): 47–59.

British Civilian Internees in Germany: The Ruhleben Camp, 1914–1918. Manchester, 2008.

Streit, Christian. *Keine Kameraden: Die Wehrmacht und die sowjetischen Kriegsgefangenen 1941–1945*. Stuttgart, 1978.

Vance, Jonathan. "Men in Manacles: The Shackling of Prisoners of War, 1942–1943." *Journal of Military History* 59 (1995): 438–504.

ed. *Objects of Concern: Canadian Prisoners of War through the Twentieth Century*. Vancouver, 1994.

ed. *The Encyclopedia of Prisoners of War and Internment*. 2nd edn. Santa Barbara, CA, 2006.

Weiland, Hans, and Leopold Kern, eds. *In Feindeshand: Die Gefangenschaft im Weltkriege in Einzeldarstellungen*. 2 vols. Vienna, 1931.

Wylie, Neville. "Prisoners of War in the Era of Total War." *War in History* 13 (2006): 217–33.

Yanikdağ, Yücel. "Ottoman Prisoners of War in Russia 1914–1922." *Journal of Contemporary History* 34 (1999): 69–85.

Military occupations, 1914–1945

Basler, Werner. *Deutschlands Annexionspolitik in Polen und im Baltikum 1914–1918*. Berlin, 1962.

Becker, Annette. *Les Cicatrices rouges 14–18: France et Belgique occupées*. Paris, 2010.

Berkhoff, Karel C. *Harvest of Despair: Life and Death in Ukraine under Nazi Rule*. Cambridge, 2004.

Brendel, Heiko. "Die österreichisch–ungarische Besatzung Montenegros im Ersten Weltkrieg." In Jürgen Angelow, ed., *Der Erste Weltkrieg auf dem Balkan: Perspektiven der Forschung*. Berlin, 2011.

Brook, Timothy. *Collaboration: Japanese Agents and Local Elites in Wartime China*. Cambridge, MA, 2005.

Conze, Werner. *Polnische Nation und Deutsche Politik im Ersten Weltkrieg*. Cologne, 1958.

Corni, Gustavo. *Il Friuli occidentale nell'anno dell'occupazione austro-germanica 1917–1918*. Udine, 1993.

Corpet, Olivier, and Claire Paulhan. *Collaboration and Resistance: French Literary Life under the Nazi Occupation*. Minneapolis, 2010.

De Schaepdrijver, Sophie. *La Belgique et la Première Guerre Mondiale*. Frankfurt, 2004.

"A Civilian War Effort: The Comité National de Secours et d'Alimentation in Occupied Belgium, 1914–1918." In De Schaepdrijver et al., eds., *Remembering Herbert Hoover and the Commission for Relief in Belgium*. Brussels, 2007, 24–37.

De Wever, Bruno et al., eds. *Local Government in Occupied Europe. 1939–1945*. Ghent, 2006.

Dornik, Wolfram et al., eds. *Die Ukraine: zwischen Selbstbestimmung und Fremdherrschaft 1917–1922*. Graz, 2011.

Duara, Prasenjit. *Sovereignty and Authenticity: Manchukuo and the East Asian Modern*. Lanham, MD, 2003.

Duus, Peter et al., eds. *The Japanese Wartime Empire, 1931–1945*. Princeton, 1996.

Evans, Richard. *The Third Reich at War*. New York, 2009.

Felder, Björn Michael. *Lettland im Zweiten Weltkrieg. Zwischen sowjetischen und deutschen Besatzern 1940–1946*. Paderborn, 2009.

Gerlach, Christian. *Kalkulierte Morde: Die deutsche Wirtschafts- und Vernichtungspolitik in Weissrussland 1941–1944*. Hamburg, 1999.

Gildea, Robert. *Marianne in Chains: In Search of the German Occupation of France 1940–45*. London, 2002.

Gildea, Robert et al., eds. *Surviving Hitler and Mussolini: Daily Life in Occupied Europe*. Oxford, 2006.

Gross, Jan Tomasz. *Polish Society under German Occupation: The General Government 1939–1945*. Princeton, 1979.

Gumz, Jonathan. *The Resurrection and Collapse of Empire in Habsburg Serbia, 1914–1918*. Cambridge, 2009.

Henriot, Christian, and Wen-shin Yeh, eds. *In the Shadow of the Rising Sun: Shanghai under Japanese Occupation*. New York, 2004.

Hull, Isabel V. *Absolute Destruction: Military Culture and the Practices of War in Imperial Germany*. Ithaca, 2005.

Hung, Chang-Tai. *War and Popular Culture: Resistance in Modern China, 1937–1945*. Berkeley and Los Angeles, 1994.

Jackson, Julian. *France: The Dark Years 1940–1944*. Oxford, 2001.

Jüngerkes, Sven. *Deutsche Besatzungsverwaltung in Lettland 1941–1945: Eine Kommunikations- und Kulturgeschichte nationalsozialistischer Organisationen*. Constance, 2010.

Kaplan, Alice. *The Collaborator: The Trial and Execution of Robert Brasillach*. Chicago, 2000.

Kauffman, Jesse. "Sovereignty and the Search for Order in German-Occupied Poland, 1915–1918." PhD dissertation, Stanford University, 2008.

Kushner, Barak. *The Thought War: Japanese Imperial Propaganda*. Honolulu, 2006.

Lagrou, Pieter. *The Legacy of Nazi Occupation: Patriotic Memory and National Recovery in Western Europe, 1945–1965*. Cambridge, 2000.

Laub, Thomas J. *After the Fall: German Policy in Occupied France, 1940–1944*. New York, 2010.

Liulevicius, Vejas Gabriel. *War Land on the Eastern Front: Culture, National Identity and German Occupation in World War I*. Cambridge, 2000.

Lund, Joachim. "Denmark and the 'European New Order,' 1940–1942." *Contemporary European History* 13 (2004): 305–21.

Majerus, Benoît. *Occupations et logiques policières: La police bruxelloise en 1914–1918 et 1940–1945*. Brussels, 2007.

Mayerhofer, Lisa. *Zwischen Freund und Feind. Deutsche Besatzung in Rumänien 1916–1918*. Munich, 2010.

Mazower, Mark. *Hitler's Empire: How the Nazis Ruled Europe*. New York, 2008.

McPhail, Helen. *The Long Silence: Civilian Life under the German Occupation of Northern France, 1914–1918*. London, 1999.

Mick, Christoph. *Kriegserfahrungen in einer multiethnischen Stadt. Lemberg 1914–1947*. Wiesbaden, 2010.

"Incompatible Experiences: Poles, Ukrainians and Jews under Soviet and German Occupation, 1939–1944." *Journal of Contemporary History* 46 (2011): 336–63.

Moore, Bob, ed. *Resistance in Western Europe*. Oxford and New York, 2000.

Nivet, Philippe. *La France occupée*. Paris, 2011.

Opfer, Björn. *Im Schatten des Krieges: Besatzung oder Anschluss – Befreiung oder Unterdrückung? Eine komparative Untersuchung über die bulgarische Herrschaft in Vardar-Makedonien 1915–1918 und 1941–1944*. Münster, 2005.

Paxton, Robert O. *Vichy France: Old Guard and New Order 1940–1944*. New York, 1972.

Riding, Alan. *And the Show Went On: Cultural Life in Nazi-Occupied Paris*. New York, 2010.

Rodogno, Davide. *Fascism's Italian Empire: Italian Occupation during the Second World War*. Cambridge, 2006.

Steinberg, Jonathan. "The Third Reich Reflected: German Civil Administration in the Occupied Soviet Union, 1941–4." *English Historical Review* 110 (1995): 620–51.

Strazhas, Aba. *Deutsche Ostpolitik im Ersten Weltkrieg: Der Fall Ober Ost 1915–1917*. Wiesbaden, 1993.

Tarling, Nicholas. *A Sudden Rampage: The Japanese Occupation of South-East Asia, 1941–1944*. Honolulu, 2001.

Thiel, Jens. *"Menschenbassin Belgien": Anwerbung, Deportation und Zwangsarbeit im Ersten Weltkrieg*. Essen, 2007.

Tooze, Adam. The *Wages of Destruction: The Making and Breaking of the Nazi Economy*. London and New York, 2006.

Van Ypersele, Laurence, and Emmanuel Debruyne. *De la guerre de l'ombre aux ombres de la guerre: L'espionnage en Belgique durant la guerre 1914–1918. Histoire et mémoire*. Brussels, 2004.

Von Hagen, Mark. *War in a European Borderland: Occupations and Occupation Plans in Galicia and Ukraine, 1914–1918*. Seattle, 2007.

Westerhoff, Christian. *Zwangsarbeit im Ersten Weltkrieg: Deutsche Arbeitskräftepolitik im besetzten Polen und Litauen 1914–1918*. Paderborn, 2012.

Yeh, Wen-hsin, ed. *Wartime Shanghai*. London and New York, 1998.

Young, Louise. *Japan's Total Empire: Manchuria and the Culture of Wartime Imperialism*. Berkeley, 1999.

Home fronts: the mobilization of resources for total war

Audoin-Rouzeau, Stéphane, and Annette Becker. *14–18: Retrouver la guerre*. Paris, 2000.

Barber, John, and Mark Harrison. *The Soviet Home Front, 1941–1945: A Social and Economic History of the USSR in World War II*. London and New York, 1991.

Broadberry, Stephen, and Mark Harrison, eds. *The Economics of World War I*. Cambridge, 2009.

Broszat, Martin. *The Hitler State: The Foundation and Development of the Internal Structure of the Third Reich*. London and New York, 1981.

Chickering, Roger. *The Great War and Urban Life in Germany: Freiburg, 1914–1918*. Cambridge, 2007.

Dickinson, Frederick. *War and National Reinvention: Japan in the Great War, 1914–1919*. Cambridge, MA, 1999.

Dower, John. *War without Mercy: Race and Power in the Pacific War*. New York, 1986.

Evans, Richard. *The Coming of the Third Reich*. London, 2004.

Geyer, Michael. "War and the Context of General History in an Age of Total War." *Journal of Military History* 57 (1993): 145–63.

Gillis, John R., ed. *The Militarization of the Western World*. New Brunswick and London, 1989.

Gregory, Adrian. *The Last Great War: British Society and the First World War*. Cambridge, 2008.

Haimson, Leopold H., and Charles Tilly, eds. *Strikes, Wars, and Revolutions in an International Perspective: Strike Waves in the Late Nineteenth and Early Twentieth Centuries*. Cambridge and Paris, 1989.

Halévy, Elie. *The Era of Tyrannies: Essays on Socialism and War*. London, 1967.

Harris, José. "War and Social History: Britain and the Home Front during the Second World War." *Contemporary European History* 1 (1992): 17–35.

Harrison, Mark, ed. *The Economics of World War II: Six Great Powers in International Comparison*. Cambridge, 1998.

Healy, Maureen. *Vienna and the Fall of the Habsburg Empire: Total War and Everyday Life in World War I*. Cambridge, 2004.

Horne, John, ed. *State, Society, and Mobilization in Europe during the First World War.* Cambridge, 1997.

ed. *A Companion to the First World War.* Oxford, 2010.

Horne, John, and Alan Kramer. *German Atrocities, 1914: A History of Denial.* New Haven and London, 2001.

Jackson, Julian. *France: The Dark Years, 1940–1944.* Oxford, 2002.

Kershaw, Ian. *The "Hitler Myth": Image and Reality in the Third Reich.* Oxford, 2001.

Hitler: Nemesis, 1936–1945. London, 2001.

Kier, Elizabeth, and Roland R. Krebs, eds. *In War's Wake: International Conflict and the Fate of Liberal Democracy.* New York, 2010.

Kocka, Jürgen. *Facing Total War: German Society, 1914–1918.* Leamington Spa, 1973.

Manela, Erez. *The Wilsonian Moment: Self-Determination and the International Origins of Anticolonial Nationalism.* Oxford, 2007.

Milward, Alan. *War, Economy, Society 1939–45.* London, 1979.

Mitter, Rana. *A Bitter Revolution: China's Struggle with the Modern World.* New York, 2005.

Moran, Daniel, and Arthur Waldron, eds. *The People in Arms: Military Myth, and National Mobilization since the French Revolution.* Cambridge, 2002.

Noakes, Jeremy, ed. *The Civilian in War: The Home Front in Europe, Japan and the USA in World War II.* Exeter, 1992.

Offer, Avner. *The First World War: An Agrarian Interpretation.* Oxford, 1989.

Overy, Richard. *Why the Allies Won.* London, 2006.

Prochasson, Christophe, and Anne Rasmussen. *Au nom de la Patrie: Les intellectuels et la Première Guerre mondiale. 1910–1919.* Paris, 1996.

Prost, Antoine. *Republican Identities in War and Peace: Representations of France in the Nineteenth and Twentieth Centuries.* Oxford and New York, 2002.

Purseigle, Pierre. "Beyond and Below the Nations: Towards a Comparative History of Local Communities at War," in Jenny Macleod and Pierre Purseigle, eds., *Uncovered Fields: Perspectives in First World War Studies.* Boston and Leiden, 2004, 95–123

ed. *Warfare and Belligerence: Perspectives in First World War Studies.* Boston and Leiden, 2005.

Shillony, Ben-Ami. *Politics and Culture in Wartime Japan.* Oxford and New York, 1981.

Stephenson, Jill. *Hitler's Home Front: Württemberg under the Nazis.* London and New York, 2006.

Strachan, Hew. "Total War in the Twentieth Century." In Arthur Marwick, ed. *Total War and Historical Change: Europe, 1914–1955.* Buckingham and Philadelphia, 2001, 255–83.

"The First World War as a Global War." *First World War Studies* 1 (2010): 3–14.

Tilly, Charles. *Coercion, Capital, and European States, AD 990–1990.* Oxford and Cambridge, MA, 1990.

ed. *Citizenship, Identity and Social History.* Cambridge, 1996.

Tooze, Adam. *The Wages of Destruction: The Making and Breaking of the Nazi Economy.* London and New York, 2006.

van Creveld, Martin. *Supplying War: Logistics from Wallerstein to Patton.* Cambridge, 1977.

Winter, Jay, and Jean-Louis Robert, eds. *Capital Cities at War: Paris, London, Berlin, 1914–1919.* 2 vols. Cambridge, 1997–2007.

Young, Louise. *Japan's Total Empire: Manchuria and the Culture of Wartime Imperialism.* Berkeley, 1999.

The search for peace in the interwar period

Adam, Magda. *The Versailles System and Central Europe*. Aldershot, 2004.

Andrew, Christopher, and A. S. Kanya-Forstner. *France Overseas: The Great War and the Climax of French Imperial Expansion*. London, 1981.

Azcárate, Pablo de. *The League of Nations and National Minorities: An Experiment*. New York, 1945.

Barros, James. *Betrayal from Within: Joseph Avenol, Secretary General of the League of Nations, 1933–1940*. New Haven, 1969.

Office without Power: Secretary-General Sir Eric Drummond, 1919–1933. Oxford, 1979.

Birn, Donald S. *The League of Nations Union, 1918–1945*. Oxford, 1981.

Boemeke, Manfred F., Gerald D. Feldman, and Elizabeth Glaser, eds. *The Treaty of Versailles: A Reassessment after 75 Years*. New York, 1998.

Boyce, Robert. *The Great Interwar Crisis and the Collapse of Globalization*. Basingstoke, 2009.

Boyce, Robert, and E. M. Robertson, eds. *Paths to War: New Essays on the Origins of the Second World War*. Basingstoke, 1989.

Callahan, Michael D. *Mandates and Empire: The League of Nations and Africa, 1914–1931*. Brighton and Portland, 1999.

Ceadel, Martin. *Pacifism in Britain, 1914–1945: The Defining of a Faith*. Oxford, 1980.

Churchill, Winston S. *The Gathering Storm*. Boston, 1948.

Dockrill, Michael L., and John Fisher, eds. *The Paris Peace Conference, 1919: Peace without Victory?* New York, 2001.

Dunn, Seamus, and T. G. Fraser, eds. *Europe and Ethnicity: World War I and Contemporary Ethnic Conflict*. London and New York, 1996.

Fischer, Conan, and Alan Sharp, eds. *After the Versailles Treaty: Enforcement, Compliance, Contested Identities*. London, 2008.

Fromkin, David. *A Peace to End All Peace: The Fall of the Ottoman Empire and the Creation of the Modern Middle East*. New York, 2001.

Gökay, Bülent. *A Clash of Empires: Turkey between Russian Bolshevism and British Imperialism, 1918–1923*. London and New York, 1997.

Grünewald, Guido, and Peter van den Dungen, eds. *Twentieth-Century Peace Movements: Successes and Failures*. Lewiston, 1995.

Heater, Derek. *National Self-Determination: Woodrow Wilson and His Legacy*. New York, 1994.

Iriye, Akira. *Global Community: The Role of International Organizations in the Making of the Contemporary World*. Berkeley and Los Angeles, 2002.

Jacobson, Jon. *When the Soviet Union Entered World Politics*. Berkeley, 1994.

Johnson, Gaynor, ed. *Locarno Revisited: European Diplomacy, 1920–1929*. London and New York, 2004.

Keynes, John Maynard. *The Economic Consequences of the Peace*. London, 1919.

Kissinger, Henry. *Diplomacy*. New York, 1994.

Kitching, Carolyn J. *Britain and the Problem of International Disarmament, 1919–1934*. London and New York, 1999.

Kramer, Alan. *Dynamic of Destruction: Culture and Mass Killing in the First World War*. Oxford and New York, 2010.

Leitz, Christian. *Nazi Foreign Policy: The Road to Global War*. London and New York, 2004.

Lentin, Anthony *Lloyd George and the Lost Peace*. New York, 2001.
Lynch, Cecilia. *Beyond Appeasement: Interpreting Interwar Peace Movements in World Politics*. Ithaca, 1999.
Macartney, C. A. *National States and National Minorities*. New York, 1968.
MacMillan, Margaret, *Peacemakers: The Peace Conference of 1919 and its Attempt to End War* London, 2001.
Marks, Sally. *The Ebbing of European Ascendancy: An International History of the World 1914–1945*. London and New York, 2002.
The Illusion of Peace: International Relations in Europe, 1918–1933. 2nd edn. New York, 2003.
Martel, Gordon, ed. *A Companion to Europe, 1900–1945*. Malden, MA, 2006.
Mayer, Arno J. *Politics and Diplomacy of Peacemaking: Containment and Counter-Revolution at Versailles, 1918–1919*. New York, 1967.
Mommsen, Wolfgang, and Lother Kettenacker, eds. *The Fascist Challenge and the Policy of Appeasement*. London and Boston, 1983.
Northedge, F. S. *The League of Nations: Its Life and Times, 1920–1946*. Leicester, 1986.
Pederson, Susan. "Back to the League of Nations." *American Historical Review* 112 (2007): 1091–117.
Schuker, Stephen A. *The End of French Predominance in Europe: The Financial Crisis of 1924 and the Adoption of the Dawes Plan*. Chapel Hill, 1976.
Sharp, Alan. *The Versailles Settlement: Peacemaking after the First World War, 1919–1923*. 2nd edn. Basingstoke, 2008.
The Versailles Settlement: Aftermath and Legacy, 1919–2010. London, 2010.
Siegel, Mona. *The Moral Disarmament of France: Education, Pacifism, and Patriotism, 1914–1940*. Cambridge and New York, 2004.
Skran, Claudena M. *Refugees in Inter-War Europe: The Emergence of a Regime*. New York, 1995.
Steiner, Zara. *The Lights That Failed: European International History, 1919–1933*. Oxford, 2005.
The Triumph of the Dark: European International History, 1933–1939. New York, 2011.
Thorne, Christopher. *The Limits of Foreign Policy: The West, the League, and the Far Eastern Crisis of 1931–1933*. London, 1972.
Walters, Frank. *History of the League of Nations*. London, 1960.
Wasserstein, Bernard. *The British in Palestine: The Mandatory Government, and the Arab-Jewish Conflict, 1917–1929*. London, 1978.
Weinberg, Gerhard L. *Hitler's Foreign Policy, 1933–1939: The Road to World War II*. New York, 2005.
Willis, James F. *Prologue to Nuremberg: The Politics and Diplomacy of Punishing War Criminals of the First World War*. Westport, CT, 1982.

Commemorating war, 1914–1945

Cannadine, David. "War and Death, Grief and Mourning in Modern Britain." In Joachim Whaley, ed. *Mirrors of Mortality: Studies in the Social History of Death*. London, 1982, 187–242.
Farmer, Sarah Bennett. "Oradour-sur-Glane: Memory in a Preserved Landscape." *French Historical Studies* 19 (1995): 27–47.
Fussell, Paul. *The Great War and Modern Memory*. New York, 1975.

Gaffney, Angela. *Aftermath: Remembering the Great War in Wales*. Cardiff, 1998.
Greenberg, Allan. "Lutyens's Cenotaph." *Journal of the Society of Architectural Historians* 48 (1989): 5–23.
Hynes, Samuel. *A War Imagined: The First World War and English Culture*. London, 1990.
The Soldiers' Tale: Bearing Witness to Modern War. London, 1997.
Inglis, Ken. "A Sacred Place: The Making of the Australian War Memorial." *War and Society* 3 (1985): 99–127.
"The Homecoming: The War Memorial Movement in Cambridge, England." *Journal of Contemporary History* 27 (1992): 583–606.
"War Memorials: Ten Questions for Historians." *Guerres mondiales et conflits contemporains* 167 (1992): 5–22.
"World War One Memorials in Australia." *Guerres mondiales et conflits contemporains* 167 (1992): 51–58.
"Entombing Unknown Soldiers: From London and Paris to Baghdad." *History and Memory* 5 (1993): 7–31.
Sacred Places: War Memorials in the Australian Landscape. Carlton, Victoria, 1998.
Inglis, Ken, and Phillips, Jock. "War Memorials in Australia and New Zealand: A Comparative Survey." In John Rickard and Peter Spearritt, eds., *Packaging the Past? Public Histories*. Melbourne, 1987, 179–92.
Kavanagh, Gaynor. "Museum as Memorial: The Origins of the Imperial War Museum," *Journal of Contemporary History* 23 (1988): 77–97.
King, Alex. *Memorials of the Great War in Britain: The Symbolism and Politics of Remembrance*. Oxford: Berg, 1998.
Koven, Seth. "Remembering and Dismemberment: Crippled Children, Wounded Soldiers, and the Great War in Great Britain." *American Historical Review* 99 (1994): 1167–202.
Lloyd, David W. *Battlefield Tourism: Pilgrimage and the Commemoration of the Great War in Britain, Australia, and Canada, 1919–1939*. Oxford, 1998.
Macleod, Jenny. "Memorials and Location: Local versus National Identity and the Scottish National War Memorial," *Scottish Historical Review* 89 (2010): 73–95.
Malvern, Sue, "War, Memory and Museums: Art and Artifact in the Imperial War Museum." *History Workshop Journal* 49 (2000): 177–203.
"War Tourisms: 'Englishness', Art, and the First World War." *Oxford Art Journal* 24 (2001): 47–66.
Marcuse, Harold. "Holocaust Memorials: The Emergence of a Genre." *American Historical Review* 115 (2010): 53–89.
Mosse, George L. "Two World Wars and the Myth of the War Experience," *Journal of Contemporary History* 21 (1986): 491–513.
Fallen Soldiers: Reshaping the Memory of the Two World Wars. New York and Oxford, 1990.
Prost, Antoine. *Republican Identities in War and Peace: Representations of France in the Nineteenth and Twentieth Centuries*. Oxford, 2002.
Richards, Michael. "From War Culture to Civil Society: Francoism, Social Change and Memories of the Spanish Civil War." *History and Memory* 14 (2002): 93–120.
Ron, Robin. "A Foothold in Europe: The Aesthetics and Politics of American War Cemeteries in Western Europe." *Journal of American Studies* 29 (1995): 55–72.
Sherman, Daniel J. "Objects of Memory: History and Narrative in French War Museums." *French Historical Studies* 19 (1995): 49–74.

Taaffe, Seamus. "Commemorating the Fallen: Public Memorials to the Irish Dead of the Great War." *Archaeology Ireland* 13 (1999): 18–22.

Trumpener, Katie. "Memories Carved in Granite: Great War Memorials and Everyday Life." *PMLA* 115 (2000): 1096–103.

Winter, Jay M. *Sites of Memory, Sites of Mourning: The Great War in European Cultural History*. Cambridge, 1995.

Remembering War: The Great War between History and Memory in the Twentieth Century. New Haven, 2006.

Dreams of Peace and Freedom: Utopian Moments in the Twentieth Century. New Haven, 2007.

Winter, Jay M., and Emmanuel Sivan, eds. *War and Remembrance in the Twentieth Century*. Cambridge, 1999.

Ziino, Bart. "'A Lasting Gift to His Descendants': Family Memory and the Great War in Australia." *History and Memory* 22 (2010): 125–46.

Military doctrine and planning in the interwar era

Alexander, Don W. "Repercussions of the Breda Variant." *French Historical Studies* 8 (1974): 459–88.

Alexander, Martin, S. *The Republic in Danger: General Maurice Gamelin, and the Politics of French Defence, 1933–1940*. Cambridge, 1992.

Bankwitz, Philip Charles Farwell. *Maxime Weygand and Civil-Military Relations in Modern France*. Cambridge, 1967.

Baer, George W. *One Hundred Years of Sea Power: The US Navy, 1890–1990*. Stanford, 1994.

Barnhart, Michael A. *Japan Prepares for Total War: The Search for Economic Security, 1919–1941*. Ithaca, 1987.

Beattie, Peter M. *The Tribute of Blood: Race, Honor, and Nation in Brazil, 1864–1945*. Durham, NC, and London, 2001.

Biddle, Tami Davis. *Rhetoric and Reality in Air Warfare: The Evolution of British and American Ideas about Strategic Bombing, 1914–1945*. Princeton, 2002.

Boog, Horst, ed. *The Conduct of the Air War in the Second World War: An International Comparison*. Oxford, 1992.

Cain, Anthony Christopher. *The Forgotten Air Force: French Air Doctrine in the 1930s*. Washington, DC, 2002.

Carr, Raymond. *Modern Spain, 1875–1980*. Oxford, 1980.

Challener, Richard D. *The French Theory of the Nation in Arms, 1866–1939*. New York, 1965.

Cooper, Matthew. *The German Army, 1933–1945: Its Political and Military Failure*. London, 1978.

The German Air Force, 1933–1945: An Anatomy of Failure. London, 1981.

Coox, Alvin D. *Nomonhan: Japan against Russia, 1939*. Stanford, 1985.

Corum, James S. *The Roots of Blitzkrieg: Hans von Seeckt and German Military Reform*. Lawrence, KS, 1992.

The Luftwaffe: Creating the Operational Air War, 1918–1940. Lawrence, KS, 1997.

Craig, Gordon A. *The Politics of the Prussian Army 1640–1945*. Oxford, 1955.

Dennis, Peter. *Decision by Default: Peacetime Conscription and British Defence 1919–39*. London, 1972.

Doughty, Robert A. *The Seeds of Disaster: The Development of French Army Doctrine, 1919–1939*. Hamden, CT, 1985.

Evans, David C., and Mark R. Peattie. *Kaigun: Strategy, Tactics, and Technology in the Imperial Japanese Navy 1887–1941*. Annapolis, MD, 1997.

Gat, Azar. *British Armour Theory and the Rise of the Panzer Arm: Revising the Revisionists*. New York, 2000.

A History of Military Thought from the Enlightenment to the Cold War, New York, 2001.

Geyer, Michael. "German Strategy in the Age of Machine Warfare, 1914–1945." In Peter Paret, ed., *Makers of Modern Strategy: From Machiavelli to the Nuclear Age*. Princeton, 1986, 527–97.

Gooch, John. *Mussolini and His Generals: The Armed Forces and Fascist Foreign Policy, 1922–1940*. Cambridge, 2007.

Griffith, Paddy. *Battle Tactics of the Western Front: The British Army's Art of Attack, 1916–1918*. New Haven, 1992.

Habeck, Mary R. *Storm of Steel: The Development of Armor Doctrine in Germany and the Soviet Union, 1919–1939*. Ithaca, 2003.

Hallion, Richard. *Strike from the Sky: The History of Battlefield Air Attack 1911–1945* Washington, DC, and London, 1989.

Harries, Meiron, and Susie Harries. *Soldiers of the Sun: The Rise and Fall of the Imperial Japanese Army*. New York, 1991.

Harris, J. P. *Men, Ideas, and Tanks: British Military Thought and Armoured Forces, 1903–1939*. Manchester and New York, 1995.

Harrison, Mark. "Resource Mobilization for World War II: The USA, UK, USSR, and Germany, 1938–1945." *Economic History Review* 41 (1988): 171–92.

Harrison, Richard W. *The Russian Way of War: Operational Art, 1904–1940*. Lawrence, KS, 2001.

Howard, Michael. *The Continental Commitment: The Dilemmas of British Defence Policy in the Era of the Two World Wars*. London, 1972.

Ienaga, Saburo. *The Pacific War: World War II and the Japanese, 1931–1945*. New York, 1978.

Johnson, David E. *Fast Tanks and Heavy Bombers: Innovation in the US Army, 1917–1945*. Ithaca and New York, 1998.

Kier, Elizabeth. *Imagining War: French and British Military Doctrine between the Wars*. Princeton, 1997.

Kiesling, Eugenia C. *Arming against Hitler: France and the Limits of Military Planning*. Lawrence, KS, 1996.

La Gorce, Paul Marie de. *The French Army: A Military-Political History*. New York, 1963.

Li, Xiaobing. *A History of the Modern Chinese Army*. Lexington, KY, 2007.

McCann, Frank D. *Soldiers of the Patria: A History of the Brazilian Army, 1889–1937*. Stanford, 2004.

Megargee, Geoffrey P. *Inside Hitler's High Command*. Lawrence, KS, 2000.

Millett, Allan Reed, and Williamson Murray, *Military Effectiveness*. 3 vols. Boston, 1988. Vol. I: *The First World* War. Vol. II: *The Interwar Period*. Vol. III: *The Second World War*.

Muller, Richard. *The German Air War in Russia*. Baltimore, 1992.

Murray, Williamson, *Luftwaffe*. Baltimore, 1985.

Murray, Williamson, and Allan Reed Millett. *Military Innovation in the Interwar Period*. Cambridge, 1996.

Ogorkiewiez, Richard M. *Armor: A History of Mechanized Forces*. New York, 1960.
Pedraja, René de la. *Wars of Latin America, 1899–1941*, Jefferson, NC, and London, 2006.
Posen, Barry. *The Sources of Military Doctrine: France, Britain, and Germany between the World Wars*. Ithaca, 1984.
Reid, Brian Holden. *Studies in British Military Thought: Debates with Fuller and Liddell Hart*. Lincoln, NE, 1998
Sater, William F., and Holger H. Herwig. *The Grand Illusion: The Prussianization of the Chilean Army*. Lincoln, NE, 1999.
Scheina, Robert L. *Latin America's Wars*. Vol. II: *The Age of the Professional Soldiers, 1900–2001*. Washington, DC, 2003.
Thomas, Hugh. *The Spanish Civil War*. New York, 1977.
Tooze, Adam. *The Wages of Destruction: The Making and Unmaking of the Nazi Economy*. New York, 2006.
Travers. Tim. *How the War Was Won: Command and Technology in the British Army on the Western Front, 1917–1918*. New York, 1992.
von Hagen, Mark. *Soldiers in the Proletarian Dictatorship: The Red Army and the Soviet Socialist State, 1917–1930*. Ithaca, 1990.
Winton, Harold R. *To Change an Army: General Sir John Burnett-Stuart and British Armored Doctrine, 1927–1938*. Lawrence, KS. 1988.
Winton, Harold R., and David R. Mets, eds. *The Challenge of Change: Military Institutions and New Realities, 1918–1941*. Lincoln, NE, 2000.

The military and the revolutionary state

Adelman, Jonathan R. *The Revolutionary Armies: The Historical Development of the Soviet and Chinese People's Liberation Armies*. Westport, CT, 1980.
Alpert, Michael. "The Clash of Spanish Armies: Contrasting Ways of War in Spain, 1936–1939." *War in History* 6 (1999): 345.
Bartov, Omer. *Hitler's Army: Soldiers, Nazis, and War in the Third Reich*. New York, 1992.
Beevor, Antony. *The Battle for Spain: The Spanish Civil War, 1936–1939*. New York, 2006.
Benvenuti, Francesco. *The Bolsheviks and the Red Army, 1918–1922*. Cambridge, 1988.
Brown, Stephen. "Communists and the Red Cavalry: The Political Education of the Konarmiia in the Russian Civil War, 1918–20." *Slavonic and East European Review* 73 (1995): 82–99.
Campbell, Bruce B. "The SA after the Röhm Purge." *Journal of Contemporary History* 28 (1993): 659–74.
The SA Generals and the Rise of Nazism. Lexington, KY, 1998.
Citino, Robert M. *The Path to Blitzkrieg: Doctrine and Training in the German Army, 1920–1939*. Boulder, 1999.
Craig, Gordon. *The Politics of the Prussian Army, 1690–1945*. Oxford, 1955.
Darnell, Walter. *Frunze: The Soviet Clausewitz, 1885–1925*. The Hague, 1969.
Erickson, John. *The Soviet High Command: A Military-Political History*. 3rd edn. London, 2001.
Figes, Orlando. "The Red Army and Mass Mobilization during the Russian Civil War 1918–1920." *Past and Present* 129 (1990): 168–211.
Fritz, Stephen. *Frontsoldaten: The German Soldier in World War II*. Lexington, KY, 1995.

Gooch, John. *Mussolini and His Generals: The Armed Forces and Fascist Foreign Policy, 1922–1940*. Cambridge, 2007.

Griffith, Samuel B. *The Chinese People's Liberation Army*. New York, 1967.

Harrison, Richard. *The Russian Way of War: Operational Art, 1904–1940*. Lawrence, KS, 2001.

Höhne, Heinz. *The Order of the Death's Head: The Story of Hitler's SS*. London, 2000.

Jablonsky, David. "Röhm and Hitler: The Continuity of Political-Military Discord." *Journal of Contemporary History* 23 (1988): 367–86.

Jackson, Gabriel. *The Spanish Republic and the Civil War 1931–1939*. Princeton, 1965.

Kau, Michael Y. M. *The People's Liberation Army and China's Nation-Building*. White Plains, NY, 1973.

Knox, MacGregor. *Mussolini Unleashed, 1939–1941: Politics and Strategy in Fascist Italy's Last War*. Cambridge, 1982.

"1 October 1942: Adolf Hitler, Wehrmacht Officer Policy, and Social Revolution." *Historical Journal* 43 (2000): 801–25.

Hitler's Italian Allies: Royal Armed Forces, Fascist Regime, and the War of 1940–1943. Cambridge, 2000.

Li, Xiaobang. *A History of the Modern Chinese Army*. Lexington, KY, 2007.

Matthews, James. "'Our Red Soldiers': The National Army's Management of Its Left-Wing Conscripts in the Spanish Civil War 1936–9." *Journal of Contemporary History* 45 (2010): 344–63.

Megargee. Geoffrey. *War of Annihilation: Combat and Genocide on the Eastern Front, 1941*. Lanham, MD, 2005.

Messerschmidt, Manfred. "The Wehrmacht and the Volksgemeinschaft." *Journal of Contemporary History* 18 (1983): 719–44.

Müller, Klaus J. *The Army, Politics, and Society in Germany, 1933–1945: Studies in the Army's Relation to Nazism*. New York, 1987.

O'Neill, Robert J. *The German Army and the Nazi Party, 1933–1939*. New York, 1966.

Payne, Stanley G. *The Spanish Civil War, the Soviet Union, and Communism*. New Haven and London, 2004.

Perlmutter, Amos. "The Romantic Revolutionary: The Storm Troopers and the Waffen-SS." In Amos Perlmutter and Valerie Plave Bennett, eds., *The Political Influence of the Military: A Comparative Reader*. New Haven, 1980, 105–9.

Perlmutter, Amos, and William M. LeoGrande. "The Party in Uniform: Toward a Theory of Civil-Military Relations in Communist Political Systems." *American Political Science Review* 76 (1982): 778–89.

Reese, Roger R. *Stalin's Reluctant Soldiers: A Social History of the Red Army, 1925–1941*. Lawrence, KS, 1996.

"Red Army Professionalism and the Communist Party, 1918–1941." *Journal of Military History* 66 (2002): 71–102.

Red Commanders: A Social History of the Soviet Army Officer Corps, 1918–1991. Lawrence, KS, 2005.

Salisbury, Harrison E. *The Long March: The Untold Story*. London, 1985.

Seaton, Albert. *Stalin as Military Commander*. New York, 1976.

Stone, David R. *Hammer and Rifle: The Militarization of the Soviet Union, 1926–1933*. Lawrence, KS, 2000.

Sullivan, Brian R. "The Italian Armed Forces, 1918–1940." In Allan R. Millett and Williamson Murray, eds., *Military Effectiveness*. Vol. II: *The Interwar Period*. Boston, 1990, 169–217.

"Fascist Italy's Military Involvement in the Spanish Civil War." *Journal of Military History* 59 (1995): 697–727.

"The Italian Soldier in Combat, June 1940–September 1943: Myths, Realities and Explanations." In Paul Addison and Angus Cadder, eds., *Time to Kill: The Soldier's Experience of War in the West 1939–1945*. London, 1997, 177–205.

Sweet, John J. T. *Iron Arm: The Mechanization of Mussolini's Army, 1920–1940*. Westport, CT, 1980.

Thaxton, Ralph. "On Peasant Revolution and National Resistance: Toward a Theory of Peasant Mobilization and Revolutionary War with Special Reference to Modern China." *World Politics* 30 (1977): 24–57.

von Hagen, Mark. "Civil-Military Relations and the Evolution of the Soviet Socialist State." *Slavic Review* 50 (1991): 268–76.

Soldiers in the Proletarian Dictatorship: The Red Army and the Soviet Socialist State, 1917–1930. Ithaca, 1990.

Wegner, Bernd. *The Waffen-SS: Organization, Ideology and Function*. Oxford, 1990.

Wheeler-Bennett, John. *The Nemesis of Power: The German Army in Politics 1918–1945*. 2nd edn. New York, 1967.

White, D. Fedotoff. "Soviet Philosophy of War." *Political Science Quarterly* 51 (1936): 321–53.

The Growth of the Red Army. Princeton, 1944.

World War II

Allen, Louis. *Burma: The Longest War 1941–1945*. London, 1984.

Bartov, Omer. *Hitler's Army: Soldiers, Nazis, and War in the Third Reich*. New York, 1991.

Bix, Herbert P. *Hirohito and the Making of Modern Japan*. New York, 2000.

Blair, Clay. *Hitler's U-Boat War*. 2 vols. New York, 1996–98.

Burns, James McGregor. *Roosevelt: The Soldier of Freedom 1940–1945*. New York, 1970.

Citino, Robert M. *Death of the Wehrmacht: The German Campaigns of 1942*. Lawrence, KS, 2007.

Costello, John. *The Pacific War*. New York, 1981.

D'Este, Carlo. *Decision in Normandy*. New York, 1991.

Dull, Paul S. *A Battle History of the Imperial Japanese Navy, 1941–1945*. Annapolis, MD, 1978.

Frank, Richard B. *Downfall: The End of the Imperial Japanese Empire*. New York, 1999.

Guadalcanal: The Definitive Account of the Landmark Battle. New York, 1990.

Giangreco, D. M. *Hell to Pay: Operation DOWNFALL and the Invasion of Japan, 1945–1947*. Annapolis, MD, 2009.

Glantz, David M. *Soviet Military Deception in the Second World War*. London, 1989.

Glantz, David M., and Jonathan House. *When Titans Clashed: How the Red Army Stopped Hitler*. Lawrence, KS, 1995.

Grier, Howard D. *Hitler, Dönitz, and the Baltic Sea: The Third Reich's Last Hope, 1944–1945*. Annapolis, MD, 2007.

Griffiths, Thomas E., Jr. *MacArthur's Airman: General George C. Kenney and the War in the Southwest Pacific*. Lawrence, KS, 1998.

Hastings, Max. *Armageddon: The Battle for Germany, 1944–1945*. New York, 2004.

Retribution: The Battle for Japan, 1944–45. New York, 2008.

Herring, George C. Jr. *Aid to Russia 1941–1946: Strategy, Diplomacy and the Origins of the Cold War*. New York, 1973.

Ienaga, Saburo. *The Pacific War 1931–1945*. New York, 1978.

James, D. Clayton. *The Years of MacArthur*. Vol. II: *1941–1945*. Boston, 1975.

Jones, F. C. *Japan's New Order in East Asia: Its Rise, and Fall 1937–45*. London, 1954.

Kahn, David. *The Codebreakers: The Story of Secret Writing*. New York, 1967.

Kershaw, Ian. *Hitler*. 2 vols. New York, 1998–2000.

Lamb, Richard. *War in Italy 1943–1945: A Brutal Story*. New York, 1996.

Lambert, John W., and Polmar, Norman. *Defenseless: Command Failure at Pearl Harbor*. St. Paul, MN, 2003.

Linderman, Gerald F. *The World within War: America's Combat Experience in World War II*. New York, 1997.

Lowman, David D. *Magic: The Untold Story of US Intelligence and the Evacuation of Japanese Residents from the West Coast during World War II*. Stanford, 2000.

McKale, Donald M. *Hitler's Shadow War: The Holocaust and World War II*. New York, 2002.

Megargee, Geoffrey P. *War of Annihilation: Combat and Genocide on the Eastern Front, 1941*. Lanham, MD, 2006.

Merridale, Catherine. *Ivan's War: Life and Death in the Red Army, 1939–1945*. New York, 2006.

Mierzejewski, Alfred C. *The Collapse of the German War Economy: Allied Air Power and the German National Railway*. Chapel Hill, 1988.

Miller, Donald L. *Masters of the Air: America's Bomber Boys Who Fought the Air War against Nazi Germany*. New York, 2006.

Nagorski, Andrew. *The Greatest Battle: Stalin, Hitler, and the Desperate Struggle for Moscow that Changed the Course of World War II*. New York, 2007.

Parshall, Jonathan, and Anthony Tully. *Shattered Sword: The Untold Story of Midway*. Washington, DC, 2005.

Paxton, Robert O. *Vichy France: Old Guard and New Order 1940–1944*. New York, 1972.

Pennington, Reina. *Wings, Women, and War: Soviet Air Women in World War II Combat*. Lawrence, KS, 2001.

Spector, Ronald H. *Eagle against the Sun: The American War with Japan*. New York, 1985.

Stoler, Mark A. *Allies and Adversaries: The Joint Chiefs of Staff, the Grand Alliance and US Strategy in World War II*. Chapel Hill, 2000.

Taaffe, Stephen R. *MacArthur's Jungle War: The 1944 New Guinea Campaign*. Lawrence, KS, 1998.

Weinberg, Gerhard L. *A World at Arms: A Global History of World War II*. Cambridge and New York, 2005.

Visions of Victory: The Hopes of Eight World War II Leaders. Cambridge and New York, 2005.

Hitler's Foreign Policy 1933–1939: The Road to World War II. New York, 2010.

Wette, Wolfram. *The Wehrmacht: History, Myth, Reality*. Cambridge, 2006.

Willmott, H. P. *Empires in the Balance: Japanese and Allied Pacific Strategies to April 1942*. Annapolis, MD, 1982.

The Barrier and the Javelin: Japanese and Allied Strategies, February to June 1942. Annapolis, MD, 1983.

Wilson, Theodore A., ed. *D-Day 1944*. Lawrence, KS, 1994.
Wilt, Alan F. *The Atlantic Wall 1941–1944: Hitler's Defenses for D-Day*. New York, 2004.

Military occupations, 1945–1955

Alexander, G. M. *Prelude to the Truman Doctrine: British Policy in Greeece, 1944–1947*. Oxford, 1982.
Bessel, Richard. *Germany 1945: From War to Peace*. New York, 2009.
Cesarini, David. *Major Farran's Hat: Murder, Scandal, and Britain's War against Jewish Terrorism, 1945–1948*. London, 2008.
Day, David. *Conquest: How Societies Overwhelm Others*. Oxford, 2008.
Dower, John W. *Embracing Defeat: Japan in the Wake of World War II*. New York, 2000.
Edelstein, David. *Occupational Hazards: Success and Failure in Military Occupation*. Ithaca, 2008.
Gott, Kendall D. *Mobility, Vigilance, and Justice: The US Army Constabulary in Germany, 1946–1953*. Fort Leavenworth, KS, 2005.
Harper, John Lamberton. *America and the Reconstruction of Italy, 1945–1948*. New York, 1986.
Harris, C. R. S. *Allied Military Administration of Italy, 1943–1945*. London, 1957.
Kay, Alex J. *Exploitation, Resettlement, Mass Murder: Political and Economic Planning for German Occupation Policy in the Soviet Union, 1940–1941*. New York, 2006.
Kennedy, Paul M. *The Parliament of Man: The Past, Present, and Future of the United Nations*. New York, 2006.
Liberman, Peter. *Does Conquest Pay? The Exploitation of Occupied Industrial Societies*. Princeton, 1996.
MacDonough, Giles. *After the Reich: The Brutal Hitory of the Allied Occupation*. New York, 2007.
Millett, Allan R. *The War for Korea, 1945–1950: A House Burning*. Lawrence, KS, 2006.
Moon, Penderel. *Divide and Quit*. Berkeley and Los Angeles, 1961.
Murray, Williamson., and Jim Lacey, eds. *The Making of Peace: Rulers, States, and the Aftermath of War*. Cambridge, 2009.
Naimark, Norman *The Russians in Germany: A History of the Soviet Zone of Occupation, 1945–1949*. Cambridge, MA, 1995.
Rose, Norman. *A Senseless, Squalid War: Voices from Palestine, 1945–1948*. London, 2008.
Schaller, Michael. *The American Occupation of Japan: The Origins of the Cold War in Asia*. New York, 1985.
Spector, Ronald. *In the Ruins of Empire: The Japanese Surrender and the Battle for Postwar Asia*. New York, 2007.
Sugita, Yoneyuki. *Pitfall or Panacea: The Irony of US Power in Occupied Japan 1945–1952*. New York, 2003.
Takemae, Eiji et al. *Inside GHQ: The Allied Occupation of Japan and Its Legacy*. New York, 2002.
Ther, Philipp, and Ana Siljak, eds. *Redrawing Nations: Ethnic Cleansing in East-Central Europe*. Lanham, MD, 2001.
Thomas, Martin. "Colonial Violence in Algeria and the Distorted Logic of State Retribution: The Setief Uprising of 1945." *Journal of Military History* 75 (2011): 125–57,

Wolpert, Stanley. *Shameful Flight: The Last Years of the British Empire in India*. New York, 2006.
Young, Louise. *Japan's Total Empire: Manchuria and the Culture of Wartime Imperialism*. Berkeley, 1998.

The wars after the war, 1945–1954

Anderson, Benedict R. O'G. *Java in a Time of Revolution: Occupation and Resistance, 1944–1946*. Rev. edn. Jakarta, 2006.
Anusauskas, Arvydas. *The Anti-Soviet Resistance in the Baltic States*. Vilnius, 1999.
Armstrong, Charles. *The North Korean Revolution, 1945–1950*. Ithaca, 2003.
Ben-Ze'ev, Efrat. *Remembering Palestine in 1948: Beyond National Narratives*. Cambridge, 2011.
Bose, Sumantra. *Kashmir: Roots of Conflict, Paths to Peace*. Cambridge, MA, 2005.
Bradley, Mark Philip. *Vietnam at War*. Oxford, 2009.
Casey, Steven. *Selling the Korean War: Propaganda, Politics, and Public Opinion in the United States, 1950–1953*. Oxford, 2010.
Chen Jian. *China's Road to the Korean War: The Making of the Sino-American Confrontation*. New York, 1994.
Gerolymatos, André. *Red Acropolis, Black Terror: The Greek Civil War and the Origins of Soviet-American Rivalry, 1943–1949*. New York, 2004.
Guha, Ramachandra. *India after Gandhi: The History of the World's Largest Democracy*. New York, 2008.
Hogan, Michael J. *A Cross of Iron: Harry S. Truman and the Origins of the National Security State, 1945–1954*. Cambridge, 2000.
Jackson, Colin F. "Lost Chance or Lost Horizon? Strategic Opportunity and Escalation Risk in the Korean War, April–July 1951." *Journal of Strategic Studies* 33 (2010): 255–89.
Judt, Tony. *Postwar: A History of Europe since 1945*. London, 2005.
Lampe, John. *Yugoslavia as History: Twice There Was a Country*. 2nd edn. Cambridge, 2002.
Lawrence, Mark, and Fredrik Logevall. *The First Vietnam War: Colonial Conflict and Cold War Crisis*. Cambridge, MA, 2006.
McMillan, Richard, *The British Occupation of Indonesia, 1945–1946: Britain, the Netherlands and the Indonesian Revolution*. London, 2006.
Marantzidis, Nikos, and Giorgos Antoniou. "The Axis Occupation and Civil War: Changing Trends in Greek Historiography, 1941–2002." *Journal of Peace Research* 41 (2004): 223–31.
Minehan, Philip B. *Civil War and World War in Europe: Spain, Yugoslavia, and Greece, 1936–1949*. New York, 2006.
Morris, Benny. *1948: A History of the First Arab-Israeli War*. New Haven, 2009.
Rawnsley, Gary D. "The Great Movement to Resist America and Assist Korea: How Beijing Sold the Korean War." *Media, War and Conflict* 2 (2009): 285–315.
Rogan, Eugene L., and Avi Shlaim. *The War for Palestine: Rewriting the History of 1948*. Cambridge, 2007.
Shephard, Ben, *The Long Road Home: The Aftermath of the Second World War*. New York, 2011.
Singh, Gurharpal, and Ian Talbot. *The Partition of India*. Cambridge, 2009.
Stavrakis, Peter J. *Moscow and Greek Communism, 1944–1949*. Ithaca, 1989.

Stubbs, Richard. *Hearts and Minds in Guerrilla Warfare: The Malayan Emergency, 1948–1960*. Singapore, 1989.

Stueck, William, *The Korean War*. Princeton, 1997.

Rethinking the Korean War: A New Diplomatic and Strategic History. Princeton, 2004.

Swain, Geoff. *Tito: A Biography*,. London, 2011.

Tønnesson, Stein. *Vietnam 1946: How the War Began*. Berkeley, 2009.

Vickers, Adrian. *A History of Modern Indonesia*. Cambridge, 2005.

Watt, Donald. *Too Serious a Business: European Armed Forces and the Approach to the Second World War*. Berkeley, 1975.

Westad, Odd Arne. *Cold War and Revolution: Soviet-American Rivalry and the Origins of the Chinese Civil War, 1944–1946*. New York, 1993.

Decisive Encounters: The Chinese Civil War, 1946–1950. Stanford, CA, 2003.

"The Cold War and the International History of the Twentieth Century." In Melvyn P. Leffler and Odd Arne Westad, eds.,*The Cambridge History of the Cold War*. 3 vols. Vol. I: *Origins, 1945–1962*. Cambridge, 2010, 1–19.

Yekelchyk, Serhy. *Ukraine: Birth of a Modern Nation*. Oxford, 2007.

Zhang, Shu Guang. *Mao's Military Romanticism: China and the Korean War, 1950–1953*. Lawrence, KS, 1995.

Zubkova, Elena. *Pribaltika i Kreml, 1940–1953* (The Baltic Region and the Kremlin, 1940–1953). Moscow, 2008.

Weapons technology in the two nuclear ages

Armstrong, David, and Joseph J. Trento, *America and the Islamic Bomb: The Deadly Compromise*. Hanover, NH, 2007.

Ayson, Robert. *Thomas Schelling and the Nuclear Age: Strategy as Social Science*. London, 2004.

Barnaby, Frank. *How to Build a Nuclear Bomb: And Other Weapons of Mass Destruction*. New York, 2004.

Bird, Kai, and Martin J. Sherwin. *American Prometheus: The Triumph and Tragedy of J. Robert Oppenheimer*. New York, 2005.

Brodie, Bernard, and Fawn M. Brodie. *From Crossbow to H-Bomb: The Evolution of the Weapons and Tactics of Warfare*. Bloomington, 1973.

Bundy, McGeorge. *Danger and Survival: Choices about the Bomb in the First Fifty Years*. New York, 1988.

Chertok, Boris. *Rockets and People*. 3 vols. Washington, DC, 2005–10.

Cimbala, Stephen J., and Joseph D. Douglass, Jr. *Ending a Nuclear War: Are the Superpowers Prepared?* Washington, DC, 1988.

Franz, Douglas, and Catherine Collins, *The Nuclear Jihadist: The True Story of the Man Who Sold the World's Most Dangerous Secrets ... and How We Could Have Stopped Him*. New York, 2007.

Freedman, Lawrence. *The Evolution of Nuclear Strategy*, 3rd edn., Basingstoke, 2003.

Garthoff, Raymond L. *Deterrence and the Revolution in Soviet Military Doctrine*. Washington, DC, 1990.

Ghamari-Tabrizi, Sharon. *The Worlds of Herman Kahn: The Intuitive Science of Thermonuclear War*. Cambridge, MA, 2005.

Glantz, David M. *The Military Strategy of the Soviet Union: A History*. London, 2004.

Gray, Colin S. *Nuclear Strategy and Strategic Planning*. Philadelphia, 1984.

House of Cards: Why Arms Control Must Fail. Ithaca, 1992.

The Second Nuclear Age. Boulder, 1999.

Hargittai, István. *Judging Edward Teller: A Closer Look at One of the Most Influential Scientists of the Twentieth Century*. New York, 2010.

Hoffman, David E. *The Dead Hand: The Untold Story of the Cold War Arms Race and Its Dangerous Legacy*. New York, 2009.

Hunley, J. D. *Preludes to US Space Launch Vehicle Technology: Goddard Rockets to Minuteman III*. Gainesville, FL, 2008.

Kahn, Herman. *On Thermonuclear War*. Princeton, 1960.

On Escalation: Metaphors and Scenarios. New York, 1965.

Keeney, L. Douglas. *15 Minutes: General Curtis LeMay and the Countdown to Nuclear Annhilation*. New York, 2011.

Kronig, Matthew. *Exporting the Bomb: Technology Transfer and the Spread of Nuclear Weapons*. Ithaca, 2010.

Langewiesche, William. *The Atomic Bazaar: The Rise of the Nuclear Poor*. New York, 2007.

Levy, Andrew, and Catherine Scott-Clark, *Deception: Pakistan, the United States, and the Secret Trade in Nuclear Weapons*. New York, 2007.

Mandelbaum, Michael. *The Nuclear Revolution: International Politics Before and After Hiroshima*. Cambridge, 1981.

Miller, Jerry. *Stockpile: The Story Behind 10,000 Strategic Nuclear Weapons*. Annapolis, MD, 2010.

Nye, Jr., Joseph S. *Nuclear Ethics*. New York, 1986.

Mozley, Robert F. *The Politics and Technology of Nuclear Proliferation*. Seattle, 1998.

Podvig, Pavel. *Russian Strategic Nuclear Forces*. Boston, 2004.

Potter, William C., and Gaukhar Mukhatzhanova, eds. *Forecasting Nuclear Proliferation in the 21st Century*. 2 vols. Stanford, 2010.

Purkitt, Helen E., and Stephen F. Burgess. *South Africa's Weapons of Mass Destruction*. Bloomington, 2005.

Ranger, Robin. *Arms and Politics, 1958–1978: Arms Control in a Changing Political Context*. Toronto, 1979.

Reed, Thomas C., and Danny B. Stillman. *The Nuclear Express: A Political History of the Bomb and Its Proliferation*. Minneapolis, 2009.

Rhodes, Richard. *The Making of the Atomic Bomb*. New York, 1986.

Dark Sun: The Making of the Hydrogen Bomb. New York, 1996.

Richelson, Jeffrey T. *Spying on the Bomb: American Nuclear Intelligence from Nazi Germany to Iran and North Korea*. New York, 2007.

Sagan, Scott D. *The Limits of Safety: Organizations, Accidents, and Nuclear Weapons*. Princeton, 1993.

Sagan, Scott D., and Kenneth N. Waltz. *The Spread of Nuclear Weapons: A Debate Renewed*. New York, 2002.

Schelling, Thomas C. *Arms and Influence*. New Haven, 1966.

The Strategy of Conflict. 2nd edn. Cambridge, MA, 1980.

Schwartz, Stephen I. *Atomic Audit: The Costs and Consequences of US Nuclear Weapons since 1940*. Washington, DC, 1998.

Semler, Eric, James Benjamin, and Adam Gross. *The Language of Nuclear War: An Intelligent Citizen's Dictionary*. New York, 1987.

Serber, Robert. *The Los Alamos Primer: The First Lectures on How to Build an Atomic Bomb*. Ed. Richard Rhodes. Berkeley, 1992.

Spinardi, Graham. *From Polaris to Trident: The Development of US Fleet Ballistic Missile Technology*. New York, 1994.

Sutton, George P. *History of Liquid Propellant Rocket Engines*. Reston, VA, 2006.

Wander, W. Thomas, and Eric H. Arnett. *The Proliferation of Advanced Weaponry: Technology, Motivations, and Responses*. Washington, DC, 1992.

Younger, Stephen M. *The Bomb: A New History*. New York, 2009.

Zaloga, Steven J. *The Kremlin's Nuclear Sword: The Rise and Fall of Russia's Strategic Nuclear Forces, 1945–2000*. Washington, DC, 2002.

Conventional war, 1945–1990

Adan, Avraham (Bren) . *On the Banks of the Suez: An Israeli General's Personal Account of the Yom Kippur War*. Novato, CA, 1980.

Chubin, Shahram. "The Last Phase of the Iran-Iraq War: From Statelmate to Ceasefire." *Third World Quarterly* 11 (1989): 1–14.

Cordesman Anthony H., and Abraham Wagner. *The Lessons of Modern War*. Vol. II: *The Iran-Iraq War*. Boulder, 1991.

Farouk-Sluglett, Marion, and Peter Sluglett, *Iraq since 1958: From Revolution to Dictatorship*. London, 2001.

Gaddis, John Lewis. *We Now Know: Rethinking Cold War History*. Oxford, 1997.

Gray, Colin. "Mission Improbable: Fear, Culture and Interest: Peacemaking, 1943–1949." In Williamson Murray and Jim Lacey, eds., *The Making of Peace: Rulers, States, and the Aftermath of War*. Cambridge, 2009, 265–92.

Hurley, Mathew M. "The Bekaa Valley Air Battle, June 1982." *Airpower Journal* 3 (1989): 60–70.

Kahalani, Avigdor. *The Heights of Courage: A Tank Leader's War on the Golan*. Westport, CT, 1984.

Khalil, Samir. *The Republic of Fear: The Politics of Modern Iraq*. Berkeley, 1990.

Morris, Benny. *1948: A History of the First Arab-Israeli War*. New Haven, 2008.

O'Ballance, Edgar. *The Gulf War*. London, 1988.

Oren, Michael B. *Six Days of War: June 1967 and the Making of the Middle East*. Novato, CA, 2003.

Pollack, Kenneth M. *Arabs at War: Military Effectiveness, 1948–1991*. Fargo, ND, 2004.

Sachar, Howard M. *A History of Israel*. New York, 1979.

Segev, Tom. *1967: Israel, the War, and the Year That Transformed the Middle East*. New York, 2007.

Ulam, Adam B. *The Rivals: The United States and Russia since World War II*. New York, 1971.

van Creveld, Martin. *The Sword and the Olive: A Critical History of the Israeli Defense Force*. New York, 1998.

Ward, Steven R. *Immortal: A Military History of Iran and Its Armed Forces*. Washington, DC, 2009.

Woods, Kevin M. *The Mother of All Battles: Saddam Hussein's Strategic Plan for the Persian Gulf War*. Annapolis, MD, 2008.

Woods, Kevin M. et al. *Iraqi Perspectives Project: A View of Operation Iraqi Freedom from Saddam's Senior Leadership*. Annapolis, MD, 2005.

Woods, Kevin M., Williamson Murray, and Thomas Holaday, *Saddam's War: An Iraqi Military Perspective of the Iran-Iraq War*. Washington, DC, 2009.

Wars of decolonization, 1945–1975

Anderson, David, and David Killingray. *Policing and Decolonisation: Politics, Nationalism, and the Police 1917–65*, Manchester, 1992.

Beckett, Ian, and John Pimlott. *Armed Forces and Modern Counter-Insurgency*, London, 1985.

Blaxland, Gregory. *The Regiments Depart*, London, 1971.

Bolt, Neville, David Betz, and Jaz Azari. *Propaganda of the Deed: Whitehall Report 3–08, Royal United Services Institute*. London, 2008.

Branch, Daniel. *Defeating Mau Mau, Creating Kenya: Counterinsurgency, Civil War and Decolonisation*. Cambridge, 2009.

Cann, John P. *Counterinsurgency in Africa: The Portuguese Way of War 1961–1974*. Westport, CT, 1997.

Clayton, Anthony. *Counter-Insurgency in Kenya 1952–60*. Manhattan, KS, 1984

"The Sétif Uprising of May 1945, Cruelty and Terror in an Anti-Colonial Uprising." *Small Wars and Counterinsurgencies* 3 (1992): 1–21.

The Wars of French Decolonisation, London, 1994.

Corum, James S. *Bad Strategies: How Major Powers Fail in Counterinsurgency*. Minneapolis, 2008.

Crawshaw, Nancy. *The Cyprus Revolt: An Account of the Struggle for Union with Greece*. London, 1978.

Dalloz, Jacques. *The War in Indochina, 1945–54*. Dublin, 1990.

Devillers, Philippe. *Paris-Saigon-Hanoi: Les Archives de la Guerre, 1944–47*. Paris, 1988.

Droz, Bernard, and Evelyne Lever. *Histoire de la Guerre d'Algérie 1954–62*. Paris, 1982.

Fall, Bernard. *Street without Joy: Indochina at War, 1946–54*. Harrisburg, PA, 1961.

Foley, Charles, and W. I. Scobie. *The Struggle for Cyprus*. Stanford, 1975.

Furedi, Frank. *The Mau Mau War in Perspective*. London, 1989.

"Kenya: Decolonization through Counter-insurgency." In Anthony Gorst et al., eds., *Contemporary British History 1931–1961: Politics and the Limits of Policy*. London, 1991, 141–68.

Galula, David. *Counterinsurgency Warfare: Theory and Practice*. New York, 1964.

Giap, Vo Nguyen. *People's War, People's Army*. New York, 1962.

Dieu Bien Phu. Hanoi, 1964.

Gras, Yves. *Histoire de la Guerre d'Indochine*. Paris, 1979.

Hastings, Adrian. "Some Reflections upon the War in Mozambique." *African Affairs* 73 (1974): 263–76.

Heduy, Philippe. *La Guerre d'Indochine 1945–54*. Paris, 1981.

Heggoy, Alf Andrew. *Insurgency and Counterinsurgency in Algeria*. Bloomington, 1972.

Henriksen, Thomas H. *Revolution and Counterrevolution: Mozambique's War of Independence 1964–1974*. Westport, CT, 1983.

Holland, Robert. *Britain and the Revolt in Cyprus*. Oxford, 1998.

ed. *Emergencies and Disorders in the European Empires after 1945*. London, 1994.

Horne, Alistair. *A Savage War of Peace: Algeria 1954–1962*. London, 2006.

Kahin, George McTurnan. *Nationalism and Revolution in Indonesia*. Ithaca, 1952.

Maloba, Wunyabari O. *Mau Mau and Kenya: An Analysis of a Peasant Revolt*. Bloomington, 1993.

Marcum, John A., *The Angolan Revolution*. 2 vols. Cambridge, MA, 1969–78.

Marston, Daniel, and Carter Malkasian, eds. *Counterinsurgency in Modern Warfare*. London, 2008.

Merle, Robert. *Ahmed Ben Bella*. London, 1967.

Mockaitis, Thomas R. *British Counterinsurgency in the Post-imperial Era*. Manchester, 1995.

Moorcroft, Paul, and Peter McLaughlin. *The Rhodesia War: A Military History*. Barnsley, 2008.

Morgan, Ted. *Valley of Death: The Tragedy of Dien Bien Phu That Led America into the Vietnam War*. London, 2010.

Mumford, Andrew, and Caroline Kennedy-Pipe. "Unnecessary or Unsung? The Strategic Role of Air Power in Britain's Colonial Counterinsurgencies." In Joel Hayward, ed., *Air Power, Insurgency and the War on Terror*. Cranwell, 2009, 63–78.

O'Ballance, Edgar. *The Indo-China War, 1945–54*. London, 1964.

Page, Julian. *Last Post: Aden 1964–1967*. London, 1969.

Paret, Peter. *French Revolutionary Warfare from Indo-China to Algeria*, London, 1964.

Porteu de la Morandière, François. *Soldats du Djebel*. Paris, 1979.

Reid, Anthony. *Indonesian National Revolution, 1945–50*. Hawthorn, 1974.

Ricklefs, M. C. *A History of Modern Indonesia*, Basingstoke, 1993.

Servan-Schreiber, Jean-Jacques. *Lieutenant in Algeria*. London, 1956.

Strachan, Hew. "British Counterinsurgency from Malaya to Iraq." *Journal of the Royal United Services Institute* 152 (2007): 8–11.

Trinquier, Roger. *Modern Warfare: A French View of Counterinsurgency*. Westport, CT, 2006 [1985].

Tronchon, Jacques. *L'Insurrection malgache de 1947*. Paris, 1974.

Ventner, Al J. *Report on Portugal's War in Guinea-Bissau*. Pasadena, CA, 1973.

Walker, Jonathan. *Aden Insurgency: The Savage War in South Arabia*. Staplehurst, 2005.

Wang, Joey. "Understanding Insurgency and State Response – Does Historical Context Matter? A Look Back at France and Algeria." *Journal of the Royal United Services Institute* 153 (2008): 56–61.

War and memory since 1945

Aguilar, Paloma. *Memory and Amnesia: The Role of the Spanish Civil War in the Transition to Democracy*. Oxford, 2000.

Bloxham, Donald. *Genocide on Trial: War Crimes Trials and the Formation of Holocaust History and Memory*. Oxford, 2001.

Buruma, Ian. *The Wages of Guilt: Memories of War in Germany and Japan*. London, 1995.

Dubin, Steven C. *Displays of Power: Memory and Amnesia in American Museums*. New York, 1999.

Evans, Martin, and Kenneth Lunn, eds. *War and Memory in the Twentieth Century*. Oxford, 1997.

Farmer, Sarah. *Martyred Village: Commemorating the 1944 Massacre at Oradour-sur-Glane*. Berkeley and Los Angeles, 1999.

Fitzpatrick, Ellen F. *History's Memory: Writing America's Past, 1880–1980*. Cambridge, MA, 2002.

Fulbrook, Mary. *German National Identity after the Holocaust*. London, 1999.

Gregor, Neil. *Haunted City: Nuremberg and the Nazi Past*. New Haven, 2008.

Hein, Laura, and Mark Selden, eds. *Censoring History: Citizenship and Memory in Japan, Germany, and the United States*. Armonk, NY, 2000.

Hilberg, Raul. *The Politics of Memory: The Journey of a Holocaust Historian*. Chicago, 1996.

Jager, Sheila, and Rana Mitter, eds. *Ruptured Histories: War, Memory, and the Post-Cold War in Asia*. Cambridge, MA, 2007.

La Capra, Dominick. *History and Memory after Auschwitz*. Ithaca, 1998.

Lagrou, Pieter. *The Legacy of Nazi Occupation: Patriotic Memory and National Recovery in Western Europe, 1945–1965*. Cambridge, 2000.

Maier, Charles. *The Unmasterable Past: History, Holocaust and German National Identity*. Cambridge, MA, 1997.

McAdams, A. J. *Judging the Past in Unified Germany*. Cambridge, 2001.

Merridale, Catherine. *Night of Stone: Death and Memory in Russia*. London, 2001.

Mosse, George. *Fallen Soldiers: Reshaping the Memory of the World Wars*. New York and Oxford, 1990.

Müller, Jan-Werner ed. *Memory and Power in Post-War Europe: Studies in the Presence of the Past*. Cambridge, 2002..

Novick, Peter. *The Holocaust in American Life*. Boston, 1999.

Rousso, Henry. *The Vichy Syndrome: History and Memory in France since 1944*. Cambridge, MA, 1991.

The Haunting Past : History, Memory, and Justice in Contemporary France. Philadelphia, 2002.

Seraphim, Franziska. *War Memory and Social Politics in Japan, 1945–2005*. Cambridge, MA, 2006.

Snyder, Timothy. *The Reconstruction of Nations: Poland, Ukraine, Lithuania, Belarus, 1569–1999*. New Haven, 1999.

Steinlauf, Michael. *Bondage to the Dead: Poland and the Memory of the Holocaust*. Syracuse, 1997.

Tai, Hue-Tam Ho, ed. *The Country of Memory: Remaking the Past in Late Socialist Vietnam*. Berkeley and Los Angeles, 2001.

Tumarkin, Nina. *The Living and the Dead: The Rise and Fall of the Cult of World War II in Russia*. New York, 1994.

Waxman, Zoe Vania. *Writing the Holocaust: Identity, Testimony, Representation*. Oxford, 2006.

Winter, Jay, and Emmanuel Sivan, eds. *War and Remembrance in the Twentieth Century*. Cambridge, 1999.

Wood, Nancy. *Vectors of Memory: Legacies of Trauma in Postwar Europe*. Oxford, 1999.

Zelizer, Barbie. *Remembering to Forget: Holocaust Memory through the Camera's Eye.* Chicago, 1998.

The era of American hegemony, 1989–2005

Baumann, Robert F., and Lawrence A. Yates. *"My Clan against the World": US and Coalition Forces in Somalia, 1992–1994.* Fort Leavenworth, KS, 2004.

Biddle, Stephen. "Victory Misunderstood: What the Gulf War Tells Us about the Future of Conflict." *International Security* 21 (1996): 139–79.

Afghanistan and the Future of Warfare: Implications for Army and Defense Policy. Carlisle, PA, 2002.

Boot, Max. *War Made New: Technology, Warfare, and the Course of History.* New York, 2006.

Bowden, Mark. *Black Hawk Down: A Story of Modern War.* New York, 1999.

Cann, John P. "Somalia and the Limits of Military Power". *L'Afrique politique. 2000* (2000): 158–76.

Cimbala, Stephen J., and Peter Rainow. *Russia and Postmodern Deterrence.* Washington, DC, 2007.

Cohen, Eliot A. "A Revolution in Warfare." *Foreign Affairs* 75 (1996): 37–54.

Cohen, Eliot A., and Andrew J. Bacevich, eds. *War over Kosovo: Politics and Strategy in a Global Age.* New York, 2001.

Cronin, Patrick M., ed. *The Impenetrable Fog of War: Reflections on Modern Warfare and Strategic Surprise.* Westport, CT, 2008.

Harkavy, Robert E., and Stephanie G. Neuman. *Warfare and the Third World.* New York, 2001.

Hashim, Ahmed S. "The Revolution in Military Affairs outside the West." *Journal of International Affairs* 51 (1998): 431–45.

Kagan, Frederick W. *Finding the Target: The Transformation of American Military Policy.* New York, 2006.

Keaney, Thomas, and Eliot Cohen. *Gulf War Air Power Survey.* 5 vols. Washington, DC, 1993.

Kramer, Mark. "The Perils of Counterinsurgency: Russia's War in Chechnya." *International Security* 29 (2004–5): 5–63.

Lambeth, Benjamin S. *NATO's Air War for Kosovo: A Strategic and Operational Assessment.* Santa Monica, 2001.

Lewis, John Wilson, and Xue Litai. *Imagined Enemies: China Prepares for Uncertain War.* Stanford, 2006.

Maloney, Sean M. *Enduring the Freedom: A Rogue Historian in Afghanistan.* Dulles, VA, 2005.

Moyar, Mark. *A Question of Command: Counterinsurgency from the Civil War to Iraq.* New Haven, 2009.

Murray, Williamson. "Clausewitz Out, Computer In: Military Culture and Technological Hubris." *National Interest* 48 (1997): 57–64.

Naylor, Sean. *Not A Good Day to Die: The Untold Story of Operation Anaconda.* New York, 2003.

Negash, Tekeste, and Kjetil Tronvoll. *Brothers at War: Making Sense of the Eritrean-Ethiopian War.* Athens, OH, 2000.

Oakley, Robert et al., eds. *Policing the New World Disorder: Peace Operations and Public Security*. Washington, DC, 1998.

Odom, William E., and Robert Dujarric. *America's Inadvertent Empire*. New Haven, 2004.

Olsen, John Andreas *John Warden and the Renaissance of American Air Power*. Washington, DC, 2007.

Press, Daryl G. "The Myth of Air Power in the Persian Gulf War and the Future of Warfare." *International Security* 26 (2001): 5–44.

Ricks, Tom. *Fiasco: The American Military Adventure in Iraq*. New York, 2006.

van Creveld, Martin. *The Changing Face of War: Lessons of Combat, from the Marne to Iraq*. New York, 2006.

West, Bing. *No True Glory: A Frontline Account of the Battle for Fallujah*. New York, 2005.

Zürcher, Christoph. *The Post-Soviet Wars: Rebellion, Ethnic Conflict, and Nationhood in the Caucasus*. New York, 2007.

Index

A. Q. Khan network 485
Acheson, Dean 498, 554, 557
Adan, Avraham 507, 508
Aden, insurgency in 539
  British withdrawal from 539
  and Marxist People's Republic with Yemen 539
Adenauer, Konrad 545
Afghanistan
  insurgency in 586
    and US army reform 587
  Operation Anaconda 583–84
    lack of collaboration between US and allies 584
  terrorist sanctuary 582
  US support for Northern Alliance 582–83
    US airstrikes 583
Africa
  civil wars in and use of military technology 581
  division of former German colonies 287–88
  military organization of colonies in 138–39
age of mass 165
agricultural crises, and war 9
agricultural economies, challenges to 268
agriculture, advances in, and American Civil War 29
Aideed, Mohamed Farah, killing of UN peace-keepers 575
air warfare
  antiaircraft defense, and nuclear weapons 475–76
  arms race in 178
    development of military aviation 178–79
  importance of power in 569, 579
  and Spanish Civil War 330
  see also Afghanistan; Iraq; RMA; Royal Air Force
Akiyoshi Yamada, General 106
Al Qaeda, September 11 terror attacks 582
  see also Afghanistan
Algeria, French colonial rule in 526
  military aspects of 529–30
Algerian War
  ALN attacks, and French response 527
  casualty numbers in 539–40
  de Gaulle's offensive 528
  formation of OAS 529
  and FLN 526–27
    criticism of France 528
    French attempts to remove activists 528
    negotiations with 528
    and victory 529
  and idea of postwar European peace 560–61
  use of French conscripts 527
Ali, Mehmet 11
Alsace-Lorraine, and France's Plan XV 62
Amazons of Dahomey 91
Ambrosio, General Vittorio 364
Ameer Ali, and Red Crescent 159
American Civil War
  casualty figures in 16
  causes of 28
  demobilization 30
  and Mexico 30
  military strategy in 28, 29–30
  and naval advance 56
  and Sanitary Commission 149

American Civil War (cont.)
war of attrition 26
and Union superiority 28–29
American credit, Britain's access to 271
American Legion 319
Anami Korechika, suicide of 409
Anglo-Boer War (1899–1902), and mass mobilization 82
anticolonialism 304
see also decolonization
Anvaer, Sof'ia, treatment on repatriation to USSR 233–34
Anzac troops, role in World War I 200
and Anzac Day 319
appeasement and demise of treaty enforcement 308
Disarmament Conference 306
Ethiopia's plea for aid 306–07
Japanese conquest of Manchuria 306
and Rhineland 307
Arab–Jewish struggle, and postwar division of territories 288
see also Israel
Ardant du Picq, Colonel Charles, *Battle Studies* 51
armament industry
advantage of coalition warfare 273
changes during nineteenth century 10, 18
and Crimean War 23
in France 267
and Franco-Prussian war 40
and Lend-Lease agreement 273
in USSR 267
see also arms race; technological advance
armed assistance, to occupying power 251
Armée de Libération Nationale; *see* Algerian War
Armistice Day, meaning for military 320
two-minute silence 320
arms control, lost opportunity for formal agreement 174
arms race 2, 10, 163, 179–80
and balance of power 164
as cause of war 180
combination of sea, land, and air power 164–65
effect of technological revolution on 165, 179
and tactical innovations 166
global aspect of 165
and mutual destruction 45
qualitative advantage 166–67
see also air arms race; land-power race; maritime arms race; von Schlieffen
Aron, Raymond 283
Arrow War, and humiliation of Qing 31, 34
Asia, potential for fourth-generation war 425–26
Asser, T. M. C. 145
asymmetric war 4
Australia, and war in the Pacific 400
Australian War Museum/Memorial 314–15
Austria-Hungary
army funding cuts in 66–67
ethnic conflict in 133
authoritarian states, and economic mobilization 275, 277–78, 280
Azzam Pasha, and Arab League 502

Ba'ath Party, ideology of 509
Baden-Powell, Robert, and Boy Scouts movement 129, 176
Bader, Douglas 557
Badoglio, General Pietro 362, 398
Baldwin, Stanley 475
Balfour Declaration 305, 501
Balkan conflict (1990s)
and idea of postwar European peace 561–62
use by Islamic activists 562
see also Kosovo; Sarajevo
Balkan Wars, first (1912) 99–100
second (1913) 100
Ballin, Albert 66
Ballistic Missile Control Regime (BMCR) 485
ballistic missile defense (BMD) systems
arguments for limited system 490
and MAD 489
and non-nuclear states 491
and SDI 490
Baltic states, civil war in 457
Bao Dai, Emperor, and Ho Chi Minh 521
defeat of French at Cao Bang 523
Baratieri, General Oreste 75
Barbusse, Henri 318
Barton, Clara, and US relief organization 154
Bartov, Omer 368
Bataan Death March 226
Battle of Britain
development of command-and-control mechanisms 346–47
failure of German invasion plans 387
Battle of the Atlantic 390
Battle of the Frontiers, casualty rates in 192
battle sites, preservation of 316–17
battleships
and arms race 168
and British maritime security 167–68
qualitative innovations 168

see also HMS *Dreadnought*; maritime arms race
Bayly, Christopher 19
Bean, Charles 315
Beckmann, Max, and militarization of children 204, 207–08
behavioral codes, and warfare 215
Belgium
Council of Flanders 251
German occupation of 236
establishment of order 242
and stability 246
resistance in 253
Bell, Daniel 423
Ben Bella, and "historic nine" committee 526–27
hijack of 528
negotiations with de Gaulle 528
Bergson, Henri 62
Committee on Intellectual Cooperation 292–93
Berlin Wall, dismantling of 566
Berlin, Isaiah 265
Bertin, Louis-Émile 106, 109
Best, Geoffrey 215, 218, 352
Bevin, Ernest 282
and German reconstruction 438
Bibliothèque de documentation internationale contemporaine 314
Biddle, Tami 346
Biess, Frank 235
Bismarck, Otto von
political leadership of 40
support for Moltke 45
Black Shirts militia 353, 362
reorganization into MVSN 363–64
abolition of 364
Bloch, Ivan 14
Bloch, Jan de 52–53
Blomfield, Sir Reginald 311
Boahen, A. Adu 74
Bobbitt, Philip 421–22
Bock, Fabienne 275
Boer War
effect of industrial warfare on 54–55
and international law 156
bombers, postwar development of 475–76
use with land and sea-based missiles 478
see also air warfare
Bose, Subhas Chandra, and INA 564
Boshin War 104
Bosnian War (1990s) 416
Bourdieu, Pierre 155
Boxer Rebellion 114
and international law 156
Bradley, James 556
Bradley, Omar 498
Brändström, Elsa 228
Brazil, state-building and the army 328–29
breech-loading rifles, use in American Civil War 47
Briand, Aristide 303
Britain
alliance with Japan 169
civil war engagements between world wars 344
and dreadnought revolution 64–66
education and culture of international conflict 128–29
effect of Germany's naval plans on 63, 64
employment of POW labor 229–30
interwar army development 344
and financial resources 344
military doctrine 345
establishment of Tank Brigade 345–46
naval defense bill (1889) 167–68
intensification of arms race 168
navy as symbol of patriotism 128
rejection of Geneva Convention on German POWs 223
and Royal Air Force 346
and civilian vulnerability 346
command-and-control mechanisms 346–47
equipment design 346
see also Britain, and World War II; British colonialism; maritime arms race
Britain, and World War II
air war in Europe 403
and crushing of German coup in Iraq 390
and Dunkirk 383
forces in Italian Northeast Africa 388
German invasion of USSR 391
and Greece 446–47
civil war in 447
and memory of war expressed in culture 557–58
loss of empire 557
shaping of politics 557
and Normandy landings 402
and Pacific War 407
postwar occupation zone in Germany 435, 438
see also Battle of Britain; Chamberlain; Churchill; Royal Air Force; Royal Navy

British colonialism
campaigns in Borneo and Falkland Islands 539
and Commonwealth of Nations 440, 517
departure from Palestine 442
and Indian independence 442
military development for colonial campaigns 520
pressure on Dutch in Indonesia 531
reassertion of prewar relationships in Hong Kong and Malaya 441
sovereignty of colonies 515–17, 535
unpreparedness for colonial counter-insurgency 519
see also Aden; colonial military service; Cyprus; Malaya; Mau Mau insurgency
British Expeditionary Force, casualties of 196
British imperial troops, and occupations of World War I 238
British Legion 319
British National Aid Society 153
and Red Cross 154
Britten, Benjamin, and Coventry Cathedral 552
Brodie, Bernard 479
Brokaw, Tom 556
Brooks, Jeffrey 134
Broz, Josip; *see* Tito
Brusilov, General Alexei 204, 206
Brzenski, Zbigniew 420
Burckhardt, Carl, ICRC, shackling of POWs 232
bureaucratization 1, 13–14
effects on European armies 18
and Indian Rebellion 35
Burgoyne, Sir John 22
Burma–Thailand railway, use of forced labor 230, 243
Burton, Sir Richard 91
Bush, George H. W., and relief mission in Somalia 575
Bush, George W. 581
and ABM Treaty 490
and arms control 488
opposition inside United States 488

C4I (command, control, communications, computer applications and intelligence processing); *see* RMA
Caballero, Largo 370
Cabral, Amilcar 534
Callwell, Colonel Charles 71, 72
Cambrai offensive
lack of logistical support 205, 208
use of technology 205, 208
Camus, Albert 252
Canada
and Battle of the Atlantic 390
and Normandy landings 402
Cardigan, Earl of 22
Carpeaux, Louis 79
carriers/coolies, use of 79–80
mortality rates of 80
casualties 16
in Afghanistan war 584
in Chechnya 580
in Iraq war 585, 586
in Persian Gulf War 571
in wars of decolonization 539–40
of World War I
Battle of the Somme and military inexperience 194, 203, 206
Champagne and Vimy ridge 199
and fluidity of battlefield 196
in opening months of war 192; of British 193; of French 192; of Germans 193
and trench warfare 188
see also Cambrai offensive; Chemin des Dames; Passchendaele; technological advance
Catholic Church, and culture wars 131
Cavallero, General Ugo 362
army's command relationship 364
Ceausescu, Nikolae 434
centralization of authority, and high-tech war
and counterinsurgency 580
in Iraq 571
in United States 574
Chamberlain, Austen 303
Chamberlain, Joseph 36
Chamberlain, Neville
and attempts at security measures 308
declaration of war 380
chassepot, French reliance on 49
Chechnya, war with Russia 579–80
rebel insurgency in 580
Russian return to 580
Chemin des Dames
commemorative site 316
failure of 203, 204, 206, 207
crisis in discipline and morale 204–05, 207
optimism of troops 204, 206
organizational problems of 204, 206
Chiang Kai-shek 359, 449, 458
Chinese respect for 549–50
and civil war 459–60

and Guomindang Party 359
and Japanese invasion 361
and Japanese surrender 458–59
and negotiations with Stalin 449
split with Communists 360–61
children, militarization of, during World War I 467
Chile, military organization in 140
China
civil war in 409, 457
connections between warfare and politics 330, 354
creation of army 354
creation of Communist Chinese Army (CCA) 359, 360
and commissars 361
conflict with GMD 360–61
control by Party 360, 361
Long March 360
shedding of guerrilla heritage 415
culture of militarism, military reform in 137
resistance to 137–38
defense spending after observing Gulf War 571
effects of Stalin's withdrawal from Manchuria 459
European-built warships 168–69
fighting between two revolutionary armies 359–60
fighting during World War II 458–59
hostility between GMD and CCP 449
CCP domination 450
US military presence 449
and Japanese Ichigo offensive 400
Self-Strengthening Movement 94–95
stages of military operation 459–60
and war memory 550
1990s commemoration of hidden aspects of war 551–52
building of museums 551
division over remembrance under Communists 550; opinion in Taiwan 550; portrayal of peasant revolution 550
first phase of memory, 'victory as defeat' 549–50
occupation and collaboration 549
private mourning in 548
see also Sino-Japanese War
Chongqing, changing memories of war 551
Christmas, Captain John K. 327
Churchill, Winston 443
Casablanca meeting with Roosevelt 397–98
and Norwegian defeat by Germany 382
and Morgenthau Plan 438
plans for continuation of war after Dunkirk 386
and POW labor 230
and surrender of Singapore 441
civil society, and culture of war 9, 126–27, 257–58
empowerment of citizenry 282
and "folklore militarism" 127
hatred of the enemy 262
and militarization 283
naval theater 127–28
retrenchment of liberalism 283
transformative power of total war 282–83
in United States 129
violence in belligerent societies 263–64
and western colonial empires in Africa and Asia 138–39
see also education
civilians
deaths in world wars 254
effect of air power on 325
forced migration of in World War II 240–41
and total war 184, 186–87
and war remembrance 325–26
Clark, General Mark 398
Clayton, Anthony 415
Clemenceau, Georges, and total war 184, 205, 208, 340
Clinton, William J., and relief mission in Somalia 575, 576
coalition warfare, advantages of 273
British mobilization 274–75
Colban, Erik, League's Minorities Section 295
Cold War 4, 493, 495
and agility of nuclear warheads 479
and Angola rebellion 535
development of ICBMs 495
and division of Europe 457
globalization of 458, 459, 462
importance of French North Africa to NATO 517
importance of intelligence 483
use of space-based satellites 484
and nuclear weapons 474, 491, 494
and diplomatic maneuver 480
impossibility of victory 479, 480
plans for limited nuclear war 480
speed of development 475
resurgence of interest in World War II 555
and memorials in Washington 556

Cold War (cont.)
support of superpowers for smaller states 470
see also nuclear weapons; Soviet Union: US
colon community; *see* Algerian War
colonial military service
African mercenaries 85
British 83
French 83–84
Italian 84
"martial races" theory 85–86
British recruitment in India 86
Dutch reliance on indigenous soldiers 87
French recruitment of Muslim soldiers in Africa 87–88
French recruitment of indigenous troops in Indochina 88–89
size of armies 85
use of indigenous troops 92
to lower morale 90
colonialism
and insurgent groups 520–21
and nationalism after World War II 515
and naval advances 26
noble duty 36
resistance to 19
separation between colonizer and colonized 36
see also British colonialism; colonial military service; decolonization; France; Netherlands; Portugal
combined-arms warfare, and German blitzkrieg 375
commemoration
controversy over absence of memory 553
differences between two world wars 326
expenditure on 321
and effect on commemorative forms 322
public subscriptions 322
and families 321, 323
importance of events and places 552
and international tourism 322
messages of 326
observance of public opinion 321
as political instrument 319–20
and politics of forgetting 318
subordinate status of dominated groups 320
and terms of Versailles treaty 318
see also memorials
communications innovation, telegraphy 75
see also technological advance
communism, and civil wars after World War II 470–71
see also China; Korean War; Vietnam War; Soviet Union
conflicts, in mid nineteenth century, links between 16–17
Confucianism, and Taiping Rebellion 32
Congo
and Angolan uprising 532
and ending of colonial rule 540
Congress of Europe 41, 42, 303
Conrad von Hötzendorf, Franz 54, 68
conscription 121, 276
legitimacy of 276–77
Military Service Act (1916) 281
conventional weapons technology, spread of 486
counter-battery radar, development of 567
counterinsurgency 417
and civilian casualties 587
development of operations and weaponry 515, 540–41
and Malaya 535–36
need for ground forces 586
and problems with use of RMA 586
counterrevolutionary doctrine, and Algerian war 529
counterterrorism 417
Coventry cathedral, and memory of wartime destruction 552
Crete, German seizure of 390
Crimean War 20
casualty figures 16
changes in conditions for soldiers 24–25
domination of nobilities 20–23
and charge of the Light Brigade 23
military tactics 18, 19, 20
press coverage of 25
reasons for victory 25
see also armaments; fortifications
Croft, David, wartime comedy 558
Crook, General George C., and Apache warriors 90
Crowdy, Dame Rachel 292
Cuban missile crisis 482, 494
Curie, Marie 292
Curteis, Ian 558
Cyprus, Greek population and *enosis* 538
and EOKA 538
recruitment of Turks to supplement police 538
Czechoslovakia, mutilation of 308

Daily Mail, the 65
Darwinism, and language of conflict 130

Dastrup, Boyd L. 334
Davis, Gerald H. 221
Davis, Jefferson, 28, 73
Day, David 428
Dayan, Moshe, and Yom Kippur War 506, 507
Dayton Peace Accords 576
de Castellane, Pierre le Comte 81
de Gaulle, General Charles
  and colonial reform 518
  and Free French 385
  and French wartime narrative 558–59
  and Indochina 521
  and mechanical striking force 341–42
  resignation of 529
  return to power 528
  and tank division 343
de la Mazière, Christian, wartime history 559
de Lattre de Tassigny, Jean 496
  and Vietnam War 523–24
    victory at Mao Khe 524
Deák, István 220
Declaration of London (1908) 147
decolonization, after World War II 462–63, 468, 496
  breakdown of system and conditions for war 453, 542
  in Dutch East Indies and Malaya 496
  ethnic and religious conflicts 468, 471
  in Vietnam 496
  see also India; Indonesia; Malaya; Palestine; Vietnam
defense expenditure, in interwar period 268
  in France and Britain 268
  in Germany 268–69
  in USSR 268
defensive warfare, and militarization of societies 188
Denmark, German plans for invasion 381
  surrender of government 382
development, as reason for occupation 429
Dewey, John 130
dirigibles 178
disarmament 301–02, 303
dispossession, as reason for occupation 428
Ditte, Albert 88
Dönitz, Admiral 403, 406
Doomsday Clock, the 413
Douaumont, and battle of Verdun, commemorative site 316–17
Douglas-Home, Alec 557
Douhet, General Giulio 184, 339, 340, 375, 569
Dower, John 438
Dreyse needle rifle 49
drug trafficking and League of Nations 292
Drummond, Sir Eric 290–91
du Bousquet, Albert Charles 104–06
Dufy, Raoul 325
Dunant, Henry, and Red Cross 150, 151, 152
Dunkirk, evacuation of 383
Dutourd, Jean 559

EAM (National Liberation Front), and Greek Communist Party (KKE) 454–55
East Asia, decolonization after World War II 409
East India Company, and doctrine of lapse 36–37
Eastern Europe, occupations by Central Powers 237–38
eastern front
  Bolshevik revolution and German troop transfers 205, 208
  lack of medicine and supplies 200–01
  POWs and Geneva Convention 218
    internment facilities 221
  Russian success on 204, 206
  see also fortifications
Ebert, Friedrich 335
economic growth, and maritime arms race 171
economic mobilization
  advantages of coalition 273–74
  advantages of global empire 271–72
  British success in World War II 274–75
  and bureaucracies 275–76
  inflation in World War I 269–70
  interwar preparation 268
  managerial and organizational effectiveness 276
  in Nazi Germany 228, 268–69
  and political issues 280
  taxation 277
  in USSR 268, 280
  see also public opinion
economic priorities, and demands of war 196, 266
  prewar preparation 267
  see also economic mobilization
EDES 446
education
  and American civic responsibility 129–30
  and culture of international conflict 128–29
  and military service 122–23, 125
  and patriotism 125–26
  under Meiji restoration 136
  see also universal military service

Egypt
and Sadat's aims for return of Sinai 506
and Six Day War 503–05
and War of Attrition 505
and Yom Kippur War 506–07
final battle 508
Ehrenreich, Barbara 423
Einstein, Albert 292
Eisenhower, General Dwight
deal with Admiral Darlan 398
and strategy for nuclear war 481
ELAS (Greek People's Liberation Army) 47, 446–47, 454, 460
disarming of 455
resumation of civil war 455–56
Ellis, John 74, 77
empire, maintenance of in wartime 249
bureaucratic efficiency of belligerent states 249–50
Engels, Friedrich 14
and Crimean War 20
warnings of war 45, 52, 53
enhanced radiation weapons (ERWs) 479
enigma coding system 380
Enola Gay controversy 556
Enver, Ismail 99, 100
EOKA (*Ethniki Organosis Kyprion Agoniston*), support for 538
Ethiopia, war with Eritrea, and use of military technology 581
ethnic cleansing 240–41
and decolonization 471
and Indian independence 444
and Soviet postwar reformation 435
see also Hitler
ethnic consolidation, and language of conflict 130
Europe
civil wars after World War I 453
and Cold War 457
division after World War II 409
and military advantage 11
and bureaucratization 13–14
institutions and practices, as models for non-Europeans 134–35
occupation of after World War II 430
merger of British and US zones in Germany 435
see also Baltic States; Greece; Ukraine; Yugoslavia
European Jews, destruction of 254
Exocet missiles 512
exploitation, as reason for occupation 428–29
Faidherbe, General Louis César 88
Falangists, and Franco 374
Falklands War, cultural impact of 558
Fallujah, battle of 586
family, importance in colonial warfare 91–92
Ferrière, Frédéric, and ICRC 153
reports of 158
and supervisory role of ICRC 160
Fiji Regiment, importance in decolonization campaigns 519, 535
Fisher, Sir John 64–65
Fitzgerald, F. Scott 45
Fleischhacker, Jochen 229
FLN (Front de Libération Nationale); *see* Algerian war
FLOSY (Front for the Liberation of Occupied South Yemen) 539
FNLA (*Frente Nacional de Libertação de Angola*), and Angolan uprising 532
Foch, General Ferdinand 203, 206
attaque à l'outrance 51
belief in "offensive spirit" 62
command of western front 211
Fogleman, Ronald R., and RMA 572
food and material resources
access to global trade 271–72
German interwar dependence on USSR 268–69
and morale in World War II 270
and profiteering 262
rationing 270
forced labor, and racial inequality 274
see also prisoners of war
Foreign Legion 519
foreign workers, reliance on in Japan and Germany 271
Forest Brothers 457
fortifications, strategic importance of 197
need for artillery 198
use in Crimean War 23–24
France
aviation development 178
defensive nationalism 260
failure to implement Prussian military reforms 49–50
German occupation of northeast 236
interwar military doctrine
and conscription 341
debate over mechanized striking force 341–42
dependence on defensive alliances 342
Divisions légères mécaniques 342

divergencies between theory and practice 343–44
medium-tank divisions 343
relationship with civilian government 340–41
memory of war in 558–59
and complicity in Nazi European order 559
question of Vichy 560
reassessment of 559
and national security 131
new patriotism 125
public education and requirements of army 125
Plan XVII 62
and Russia's Plan 9, 63
promotion by seniority 50
use of heavy artillery 175
see also French colonialism; Napoleon III; Niel
Franck, Richard 315
Franco, General Francisco 353–54, 560
army's trust in 375
decision not to enter World War II 388–89
Decree of Unification 374
Falangists and Blue Division 374
leadership of Nationalist Army 373
and head of state 373
and Nationalist Strategy 374–75
and memory of civil war 560
removal of opponents in army 369
see also Spanish Civil War; Spanish Nationalist Army
Franco-Prussian War 1870–71
casualty figures 16
consequences of 41
march on Paris 40
mold for World War I 51
unification of Germany 41
use of Krupp field artillery 50–51
victory at Sedan 39
see also Prussia; military reform
Frank, Hans, looting by 242
Franz Ferdinand, Archduke, assassination of 68
Franz Joseph I 67
Frauenkirche, Dresden, war memorial 552
free enterprise, and Darwin 130
FRELIMO (*Frente de Libertação de Moçambique*), support for 533–34
French colonialism
catastrophe of postwar occupation in Indochina 441
counterrevolutionary strategy after Dien Bien Phu 526
disaster of Dien Bien Phu 525
and French Union 440
granting of independence to Morocco and Tunisia 527, 528
hijack of Ben Bella 528
importance of Algeria 444
Muslim demonstrations in 445
involvement of African troops in World War II 517
military development for colonial campaigns 520
multiparty coalitions 1946–58 518
and Vietnam War 522
status as colonial power after World War II 517
unpreparedness for colonial counterinsurgency 519
use of Napoleonic weapons and tactics in Algeria 81–82
see also Algerian War; Indochina; Vietnam War
Friedan, Betty 554
Friedrich, Ernst, antiwar museum 316
Friedrich, Jörg 546
Fritz, Stephen 368
Frunze, Mikhail 356, 358
and offensive warfare 347
Soviet military expansion 347
and Stalin 348
Fukuzawa Yukichi 101, 112
Fuller, J. F. C. 264, 345
Fulton, Robert A. 90
Fussell, Paul 555

Gallieni, Colonel Joseph-Simon 88
Gamelin, General Maurice 341
and German invasion of Holland 383
and medium tank divisions 343
revision of operational planning 344
Gates, John 71
Gatling gun, use of 73, 74
General Dynamics 567
Geneva Conventions 14, 189, 232
and Dunant 150, 151, 152
enforcement of international law 149
immediate implementation of 147
observation of 160–61
reports of infractions 161
progression to Hague Conference 146
protection of indidivuals 143
on treatment of POWs 216

Geneva Conventions (cont.)
camps 218
effectiveness during World War II 218
non-ratification of treaty by Japan and Russia 218
rejection of standards in World War II 222–23, 232; and Hitler's Commando Order 232; murder of POWs 223–24
treatment under 1949 Convention 218–19; amendments on repatriation 219; definition of legitimate combatants 219–20; public compliance of belligerents 233
universal standard of humane treatment 217
use of POWs as laborers 227
and voluntary relief societies 151
and Red Cross 155
see also Red Cross
Geneva tea parties 303
Genoa Conference, exclusion of League 300–01
genocide 200
German Federal Republic
and American approach to occupation 435–37
assimilation of postwar refugees 435
reconstruction of 438–39
and reformation and retribution 437
German prisoners of war
mortality rates in American and French hands 224
reception on repatriation 234–35
treatment by Britain and United States 223
German–Soviet agreement (1939) 379
Germany
amalgamations and protectorates in peacetime 239
domination during World War II 239
army bill (1912) 66–67, 177
campaign in Southwest Africa, and international law 156
emphasis on heavy artillery 175
execution of Italian POWs 224
influence on global military affairs 135
interwar dominance of ruling party 354
interwar military doctrine
"armoured idea" 337, 338
emphasis on decisive battles 337
enthusiasm for tanks 336–37
immediate expediencies of interwar periods 335
investment in fixed-wing aircraft 178
Luftwaffe doctrine 339; rejection of terror-bombing 339
and National Socialism 338
people's war and defensive strategy 336
Seeckt and new professional army 336
and success in Poland 339
naval budget before World War I 66
public education and civic virtues 126
readmission as great power, and erosion of peace treaties 303
rejection of international law on POWs 223
see also Germany, and World War II; Moltke; Wilhelm II
Germany, and World War II
attack on Denmark and Norway 382
Battle of the Atlantic 390
casualties in 404
defeats of central army by USSR 403
final defeat 404–06
Italian campaign 398–99
invasion of Poland 380
invasion of USSR 390–91
attempt to seize Caucasus oilfields 395–96
conquest of Crimea 395
invasion of Yugoslavia 390
occupation of France 383
offensive in the Ardennes 404
plans for invasion of USSR 386
and crushing of Britain 386–87
preparation for war with United States 388
public enthusiasm for war 386
Rommel's campaign in North Africa 390
surrender of Berlin 404
see also casualties; Hitler
Geyer, Michael 264, 340
Giap, General Vo Nguyen 496, 499, 500
advocate of terror and torture 522
and *année de Lattre* 523–24
and Dien Bien Phu 524–25
and Viet Minh 466
Gibbs, Philip 196
Gillis, John R. 283
Ginisty, Monseigneur, and Verdun commemorative site 316–17
Godzilla movies, metaphor for nuclear warfare 547
Goebbels, J. 185
Gorbachev, Mikhail 495
Gordon, General Charles 16
Göring, Hermann, and Fritsch–Blomberg crisis 366

Gort, Lord, and retreat to Dunkirk 383
Goya, Michel 192
Grandmaison, Louis 62
Grant, General Ulysses S. 29–30
Grass, Günter 545
Grattan, Lieutenant John 72
Greece
 civil war in 447, 454–55
  support from United States 455–56
 resistance during World War II 446–47
Greek Communist Party (KKE), and EAM 454–55
 and 1946 offensive 455–56
 and Stalin 455
Grivas, Georgios, and EOKA 538
 and independence of Cyprus 538
Groener, General Wilhelm 281, 335, 336
Guderian, General Heinz 337
guerre de course 166
guilt, culture of 424
Gurkhas, transfer to British service 519

Hague Conventions 14, 143
 and colonial conflicts 156
 definition of legitimate warfare 144
 domination of international lawyers 145
 dynamic progress of 146
 Martens Clause 162
 proposals to curb armaments 149
 public interest in 145–46
 treatment of POWs 216
  disadvantages of 217
  use as laborers 227
 see also Stockholm Protocol
Haig, General Douglas
 and "human-centered battlefield" 54
 and Passchendaele 204, 207–08
 and Somme offensive 203, 206–07
 and trench warfare 199, 201
Halder, General Franz, and German invasion of USSR 386
Halévy, Elie 257
Halsey, Admiral 406
Hamid, Abdul II, and Russo-Turkish War (1876–77) 97
Hamid, Sultan Abdul, and Red Crescent 157
Hamilton, Ian 56
handicapped, systematic killing of 378, 392, 404
Handley, Tommy 558
Hansi (Jean-Jacques Waltz), and militarization of children 204, 207
Hare, David 557, 562
Harris, J. P. 344
Harrison, Mark 268
Harrison, Richard 348
Hatta, Mohammad 251, 530
Havel, Vaclav, and comprehensive punishment 437
Headrick, Daniel 75, 77
Heath, General Sir Lewis 441
Heller, Joseph 555
Henty, G. A. 129
Herbert, Hilary A. 169
Herriot, Edouard 302
Herron, Captain J. S., and carriers 80
Hibiya Riots 117
High Commissioner for Refugees 293
Himmler, Heinrich
 and Fritsch–Blomberg crisis 366
 and SS 249
 and Waffen-SS 366–67
Hindenburg Program 205, 208, 281
 and mobilization of manpower 205–06, 208
Hirohito, Emperor 407
 and Japanese surrender 409
Hiroshima 474
Hitler, Adolf 378
 aims of 378
 assassination plot against 404
 attack on Denmark and Norway 382
 attitude to army 353
  attempts to transform *Wehrmacht* 367–68
  control of 365–66, 368–69
  and loyalty of army toward himself 353
  opposition to class composition of officer corps 368
  personal control over armed forces 365–66, 368–69; and Röhm 365; murder of Röhm 366
 challenge from Waffen-SS 367
 and civil service leaders 249
 complicity in the Holocaust 369
 concentration of power 241
 contempt for Slavs 248
 coup in Rhineland 307
 defeat of Poland 380
 delay on attack through Holland and Belgium 380–81
 and Disarmament Conference 306
 Fritsch–Blomberg crisis 366
 invasion of Holland, Belgium, and Luxembourg 383
 leadership of 266
 obsession with *Lebensraum* 268–69
 occupation of France 383

Hitler, Adolf (cont.)
preparation for offensive against USSR 386
and Dunkirk 383
priority of supply to home front 243
and revenge 326
and Seeckt, collaboration with 336
and SS 366
see also German army; Germany; phony war
HMS *Dreadnought* 64–65, 172
Ho Chi Minh 496, 499
and guerrilla organization in North Vietnam 463, 521–22
talks with Leclerc 522–23
support from Communist China 463–66
victory at Dien Bien Phu 466
Hoare–Laval Pact 307
Hodges, Geoffrey, and Carrier Corps 80
Hoffi, Major General Yitzig 507
Holocaust
civilian victims of 325
and memory of Germany's role in conflict 543
construction of memory by victims 545–46
critiques of modernity in postwar culture 543
East German self-definition as antifascist 545; and effect of German reunification 546
inheritance of guilt in Federal Republic of Germany 544; and local memory 544; and Nazi culpability 546
irrationality of experience 544
use of technology 544
home front, importance of 258
and defensive nationalism 259–60
duty and sacrifice 261
psychological mobilization 281
reflection of strategic position of belligerents 271–72
Honda Katsuichi, and Nanjing Massacre 553
Hong Xiuquan 31–32
and massacre of Yang Xiuqing 33
Horne, John 281
Horner, Lieutenant-General Charles A., and Persian Gulf War 569
howitzer guns 55
Hungary, autonomy of army 133
Huxley, Aldous 292

Ibuse Masuji 547
ICBMs, development of 495
ICRC, and POWs
authority of 221–22
and forced repatriation 219
and Geneva Convention 218
and shackling 232
Ienaga Saburo, and Japanese textbooks 549
imagery, used on memorials 323–25
Imperial (Commonwealth) War Graves Commission 311
Imperial War Museum, London 312, 316
imperialism
challenges for non-western world 94
and mass war 2, 12
colonial warfare 11
and rise of west 10
see also Japan; Ottoman Empire; self-strengthening movements
India
British military organization in 139
civilian victims of anticolonial war 468
independence and separation of religious groups 468–69
combined memories of war and nationalist struggle 564
Congress Party and independence 443
transformation of Indian army 443
demands for separate Muslim state 444
and war in Kashmir 469
see also British colonialism; Indian Rebellion
Indian army, and colonial wars 83
and martial races theory 86
role in World War I 200
role of sepoys 93
Indian Rebellion 1857–58
and Bahadur Shah Zafar 37
and bureaucratization of empire 35
casualty figures 16
causes of 36–37
ending of 38
Siege of Kanpur 37–38
Siege of Lucknow 37
see also press coverage
Indochina
French control in 521
and postwar French army 519
see also Vietnam War
Indonesia, fight for independence 466, 468, 530
1947 attack by Dutch forces 466
ceasefire in 1948 and Communist uprising 531
declaration of independence 530

Dutch anti-guerrilla operations and 1946 ceasefire 530
Dutch occupation of Jogjakarta and arrest of Sukarno 531
Hague conference and independence agreement 531
and Japanese wartime occupation 530
US support for settlement 467
see also Sukarno
industrialization
and American Civil War 29
and economic response to war 267
effects on European armies 1, 18
during Crimean War 25
and innovation 163
and nature of victory 266–67
and warfare 10
industry, and demands of war 205, 208
inflation, and civilian support for war 269–70
in Germany 270
Inglis, Ken 315
Inoue Kaoru 259
intercontinental ballistic missiles (ICBMs), development of 476–78
intermediate-range ballistic missiles (IRBMs), development of 479
International Atomic Energy Agency (IAEA) 485
International Brigades, in Spanish Civil War 371
International Committee of the Red Cross (ICRC)
and Geneva Conventions 147, 151–52
sovereignty issues 153
supervisory role of 160
infractions of Convention 161
tasks of 152
see also Red Cross
international cooperation, in peacetime, breakdown of 238
International Humanitarian Law, origins of 143, 144
international institutions
and international law 150
membership of 159–60
and Red Cross 150
ICRC 151–52
shared features of 154
see also Dunant; Red Cross; United Nations
International Labor Organization; *see* League of Nations
international law, changes in
academic study of 145
bans on certain weapons 149
support from military leaders 149
codification of laws of war 142–43, 161–62
as contingent process 147
as dynamic process 146–47
and ICRC 152
equal interests of states 147–48
and public support for wars 148
establishment of universal law 145
mechanisms for enforcement 149–50
and neutrality 155
scientific process 145
see also Geneva Conventions; Hague Conventions; international institutions; universality
International Peace Bureau 146
international perspective, of mid-century shocks 42–44
Inter-Parliamentary Union 298
Iran
1941 occupation by British and Soviet troops 447–48
postwar western influence 448
revolution and creation of Islamic Republic
belief in religious fanaticism over superior firepower 512
replacement of Shah by Khomeini 510
and war of the cities 512
see also Iran–Iraq War
Iran–Iraq War
attack by Iran's regular army 511
attempted assassination of Tariq Aziz 510
fight for Fao Peninsula 513
Iraqi victory 513–14
Pasdaran offensives 511
surrender of Iraqi soldiers to Iran after Saddam's executions 511
use of gas warfare by Iraq 512
and war of the cities 512
Iraq
and Ba'ath Party 509
expenditure on arms 514
invasion of Kuwait 514
lack of preparation for war with Iran 510
and Persian Gulf War 569
air-defense capability 570
lack of tactical proficiency 571
US air attacks on ground forces 570
US technological superiority 570–71
Saddam's ambition in Iran 510
US invasion of (2003) 584
counterinsurgency under occupation 586, 587

Iraq (cont.)
Rumsfeld's use of RMA 584
taking of Baghdad
see also Iran–Iraq War; Saddam Hussein
Iriye, Akira 42, 142
Islamic Middle East, and potential for Fourth generation war 426
ISR (intelligence, surveillance, reconaissance); *see* RMA
Israel
creation of state 502
and differing narratives of 562
new historians 562
Egyptian "War of Attrition" 505
independent state of 470, 471
overconfidence against Egypt and Syria 506, 509
postwar division of territories 288
and Saddam Hussein 509
Six Day War 503–05
legacy of 505
Soviet military aid to 502
and Suez crisis 503
wars of survival 496, 502
Yom Kippur War 506–09
lack of professional military education 509
see also Israeli Defense Force; Palestine
Israeli Defense Force (IDF) 503, 505
conception of operational level of war 506
and Yom Kippur War 506–09
Italy
acquisitions during World War II 239
attack on Ethiopia 378
Austro-German occupation in North 237
incomplete nationalization of 260
interwar dominance of ruling party 354
invasion of Abyssinia 238
invasion of Albania 239
invasion of Greece 388
misunderstanding of Hitler's war aims 379
occupation regimes 431
and Pact of Steel 239
political culture of 132–33
restoration of prewar order 445
surrender to allies in World War II 398
survival of Republic 445–46
treaty commitments to Germany 67
war with Turkey 98
see also Germany, Italian campaign; Mussolini
Ito Hirobumi 136
Ivy Mike test 475
Iwakura Tomomi 104, 107
Iyesada, Shogun 103

Japan
army belief in warrior spirit 332
and interwar supply arrangements 332
civil war in 103
attacks from western warships 103
and Meiji restoration 104
comparison between army and navy, interwar 331
and European-built warships 168–69
naval expansion program 169
execution of Chinese soldiers 224
government strategy 100–01
challenges to modernization 101
conditions favorable to modernization 101
invasion of Shanghai and Beijing 238
panasianism 248
imperialism in 265
interwar naval pursuit of technology 331–32
navy's terror-bombing campaign in China 331
maritime restrictions in 100–01, 102
military reform in 100
options for change 102–03
view of foreigners 102
preeminence in Asia 169
and Red Cross Society 153
rejection of Geneva Convention 222
seizure of Manchuria (1931) 378
see also Japan, memory of war in; Japan, and World War II
Japan, memory of war in
atomic bombing of Hiroshima and Nagasaki 547
development of culture of peace 547
and comfort women 549
fracturing of memory among Japanese 547
acknowledgment of guilt and concern with economism 547–48
need for mourning 548
restructure and democratization 546
revisionist arguments and school textbooks 548–49
Japan, and World War II
acquisitions in 239, 240, 246
government of 247
alliance with Germany and Italy 389
American seizure of Okinawa 407
attack on Pearl Harbor 393
attack on Philippines 393

Battle of the Coral Sea 394
Battle of Midway 394
defeat in India 400
and Burma 401
defense of Luzon 406
employment of POW labor 230
and German invasion of USSR 391
incendiary attacks on cities 406
misunderstanding of Hitler's war aims 379
occupation of Indonesia 530
postwar punishment for war crimes 432
postwar reconstruction 439–40
postwar reformation, American approach to 437–38
and Greater East Asian Co-Prosperity Sphere 431
question of surrender after atom bomb 409
continued fighting 409
victories in Malaya, Dutch East Indies, and Burma 393–94
and US offensives in the Pacific 399–400
attacks on Japanese shipping 401
see also Hirohito; prisoners of war
Japanese New Textbook Society 549
Jászi, Oskar 133
Jewish stars, and Jewish war graves 311
Jews
exile of 305
and Hitler's aim of annihilation 378, 391, 392, 404
in Hungary 403
Joffre, General Joseph
mobilization speed 60
and "offensive spirit" 62
and trench warfare 199, 201
Johnson, Lyndon, and Vietnam War 494, 500
Jomini, Antoine-Henri 19–20
Jünger, Ernst 185, 267

Kanagawa Convention (1854) 102
Katsu Kaishk 109
Katsura Taro 117
Kellogg–Briand Pact (1928) 304
Kemal, Mustafa (Atatürk) 287, 319
Kennedy, John F. 494
Kenyatta, Jomo, and Mau Mau insurgency 536
Kertész, Imre 544
Kessler, Heinz, and opening of borders with west 566
Keynes, John Maynard 288
Khrushchev, Nikita, and Cuban missile crisis 494
Killingray, David 85
Kim Il-sung 460, 498
Kimathi, Dedan, and Mau Mau 536
King's African Rifles, importance in decolonization campaigns 519, 535
Kipling, Rudyard 311
Kirino Toshiki 107
Kobayashi Yoshinori 549
Kolff, Dirk, transition to total war in India 81
Kollwitz, Käthe 312, 321
Komuro Jataro 114
Korean War 461
Chinese support for North 461–62
division after World War II 410, 448–49
effect on postwar Japan 440
effects on United States 462
and frontiers of Cold War 494
North Korean capture of Seoul 497–99
framework for, after World War II 457, 460
peace negotiations 499
siege operation and armistice 499
Southern resistance to Communists 460–61
and US strategy 461
and Stalin 460, 462
Washington memorial to 556
Kosovo, NATO airstrikes in 576–79
on civilian infrastructure 579
Krupp cannon 47, 50–51
Kulik 358

Lakshmi Bai 91
land-power race
German army bills 177
reaction of Entente to 177
qualitative advantage in human materiel 175
degenerative forces of modernization 175
martial values 176
technological innovations 174–75
Landwehr 121
Latin America, military organization in 139–40
Latin cross, as grave marker 311
Laurel, Jose, and Japanese patronage 564
Lawrence, Henry, and Siege of Lucknow 37
le Carré, John 423
League of Nations 3, 190, 286, 289, 298
annual Assembly, and Ruhr invasion 301–02
Committee on Intellectual Cooperation 30
contradictions in 289
and disarmament 301–02, 303
divisions in 289–90
Germany's former African colonies 287–88
Health Organization 291–92
hindrances to success 293
humanitarian contributions 293

League of Nations (cont.)
  International Labor Organization 296
  League Secretariat 290–91
  Minorities Section 295
    and German entry to League 295–96
  Opium and Social Questions 292
  Permanent Court of International Justice 296–97
    limitations of 297–98
  Permanent Mandates Commission 294, 308
  popularity of 301
  reform of 307, 308
  and refugees 291
  resolution of interstate conflicts 301
  rivals to 300
  security, and Geneva Protocol for the Pacific Settlement of International Disputes 302
    clashes over peace terms 304
    problems outside Europe 304
    rejection of 302
    and resurgence of Germany 303
  security organization, and Articles 8 and 10 298–99
    disagreement between France and Britain 299, 300
  see also appeasement
Lebensraum 265–66, 268–69, 279
Leclerc de Hauteclocque, General 521
  talks with Ho Chi Minh 522–23
Lee, General Robert E. 28, 30, 47
Lend-Lease Act 390
Lenin, Vladimir, and regular army 355
Leningrad, site of war memory 552
Leopold II, naval power in Congo 76
Levi, Primo 544
Li Hongzhang 95
liberalism, retrenchment in age of total war 283
Liddell Hart, B. H. 337
  strategic objectives of British army 345
Lin Biao, and Chinese civil war 459
Lin, Maya, 324
Lincoln, Abraham 26, 28, 30
Liprandi, General Pavel 23
Lissa, sea battle of 56–57
Litvinov, and League of Nations 308
Lloyd George, David 205, 208
Locarno treaties 303
  ending of 305
Lockheed, stealth aircraft 567
Long March, the 360
Love, Albert 148–49
Loyd, Anthony, and Bosnian conflict 562
Lozen 91
Ludendorff, Erich 3, 185
  and military dictatorship 257
  and total war 339–40
  takeover of political power 205, 208–09
    and battle of annihilation (1918) 209
Lutyens, Sir Edwin 324
Lutz, General Oswald 337
Lyautey, General Louis, resignation of 203, 206

MacArthur, Douglas 333, 493
  drive to Yalu River 498
  Japanese attack on Philippines 393
  and Korean War 461
    widening of 498
  occupation of Japan 437, 440
  war in Pacific 400
MacDonald, Ramsay 301–02
Machel, Samora 533
machine guns 174–75
  ignorance of impact of 194, 199
Mackenzie, S. P. 224
  mutual hostage factor 230
Macmillan, Harold, and decolonization 557
MacMunn, Sir George, and martial races theory 86
magazine rifles, improved firepower of 52, 77, 174
Maginot Line 342
Mahan, Alfred Thayer 63, 130
Mahmud II, military reforms of 95
  campaigns of 96
  and European role model 96
  policing role 96
Main Political Administration of Red Army (PUR) 356
Makarios, Archbishop Michail, and EOKA 538
  and independence of Cyprus 538
Malaya
  Communist insurgency in 535–36
  war with British colonial power 467–68
    casualties of war 540
Manchuria, Japan's conquest of 306
Mangin, General Charles 85
Manhattan Project 491
Mao Zedong 4
  and army 361
  and CCP 458–59
  and guerrilla warfare 360
  and People's Republic of China 460

and planning for nuclear war 487
and support for North Korea 461–62
losses in 462
theory of revolutionary war 330
see also China
Mariano, Antonio, and Angolan rebellion 532
maritime arms race 26, 167–69
Britain's *Dreadnought* 172
and destroyers 172
effect on coastal artillery 172
new advances on 173
German response to British naval expansion 170
and battleship production 173
Tirpitz's risk theory 170; assumptions behind 170–71; failure of 174; and shifts in balance of power 171
and industrial warfare 64
Marshall Plan 439
Marshall, General George, mission to China 459
Martens, Feodor de 145
and Martens Clause 162, 216
martial races theory 85–86
and Indian Rebellion 87
and MacMunn 86
Maruyama Masao, 547
Marval, Carle de 158
Marxism, and Cold War 422
Masaharo Homma, Lieutenant-General, war crimes of 227
Masaryk, T. G., defense of Versailles Treaty 289
mass war 2
consequences of 3
reasons for 15
warnings of 14
Massu, General Jacques, and Algerian war 528
Mau Mau insurgency 536
internment of Kikuyu 536–37
Kikuyu Guard and return to order 536
political significance of 537
response to 536
Maxim, Hiram, machine gun 52, 74
Maya Lin, and Vietnam War Memorial 556
McClellan, General George 16, 28
McNamara, Robert 494, 500
Meckel, Major Jacob 106
medical advances, and tropical disease 76–77
impact on troops 79, 92
Meiji restoration 104
Anglo-Japanese alliance 114
collective patriotism 136–37
conflict with Russia 115
costs of 117
and Korea 116–17
conscription 108
and police force 108
and constitution 136
domination of clan leaders 107
and debate over war with Korea 107–08
military priorities 104
and civil unrest 109, 110
creation of general staff 111
military reform 136
modernization of army 104–06
administrative structure 107
French advice 106
German influence 106–07
naval advances 108–09
and British advice 109
overseas expansion 112, 117–18
and Boxer Rebellion 114
European hostility to 113–14
and Korea 112
Sino-Japanese War 112–13
proclamation of constitution 111
power of opposition 111
see also samurai; Satsuma Rebellion; Yamagata
Meir, Golda, and Yom Kippur War 506, 508
memorials
and art forms 323–24
location of 324
messages of 317–18
names on 324
outside Europe 310–11
in politically stable countries 310
secular and sacred 311
in USSR and Poland 310
see also battle sites; commemoration; memory; tomb of the unknown soldier; war cemeteries; war museums
memory, of world war 190, 542
change in after Cold War 542
contrast between east and west 559–60
German suffering 546
perception of Germany's responsible attitude to memory 546
reversal of positions of China and Japan during Cold War 546
variation according to geography 565
see also individual countries

Mendès-France, Pierre
 and partition of Vietnam 525
 and wartime resistance 559
Menshikov, General Prince Aleksandr 20
methodical battle (*bataille conduite*) 342
Mexico, French ambitions for 30
Mihailović, Draža, and Chetniks 454
militarism
 as cultural phenomenon 131, 140–41
  common civic experience 131
  comparison with Austria-Hungary 133
  comparison with Russia 133–34
  ideology of 131–32
 language of conflict 130
 relationship between armed forces and society 120
 usage of term in 1960s 119
 see also military affairs
military affairs, global communication of 135
 in Chile 140
 in China 69
 in Latin America 139–40
 under Meiji restoration 135–36
 in Ottoman Empire 138
military capability, difference between west and "the Rest" 18–19
military competition, *see* arms race
military doctrine, interwar formation of 191, 327, 350–51
 in Britain 344–47
 in France 340–44
 in Germany 335–40
 in Japan 330–32
 in revolutionary states 191
 in United States 332–35
 in USSR 347–50
 see also Brazil; Nicaragua; Spanish Civil War; *individual countries*
military electronics
 lack of control over information technology 420
 robotics revolution 421
 technotronic era 420
military institutions
 differences between right- and left-wing regimes 352–54
 feared by revolutionary states 352
military organization
 changes during nineteenth century 18
 and Prussian army reform 38–39
military power, effect of guilt on 424
military reform
 in China 94–95
 in Ottoman Empire 95–96
 see also Hamid, Abdul II
military revolution
 imitation of Moltke's reforms 48–49
 impact on colonial armies 92–93
 see also Moltke (the elder)
military superiority
 and nation-in-arms 120
 nuclear power and changing assumptions of victory 478, 479, 480
 Prussian model 121–22
  imitation of 122
military virtues
 and centrality of war in civic culture 124–25
 and compulsory education 125, 131
 see also universal military service
militia, appeal for politicians 122
Milosevic, Slobodan, withdrawal from Kosovo 579
Minié rifle, use in Crimean War 23
minorities, protection of by League of Nations 295
 international debate on German entry 295–96
Mitchell, Billy 569
Mito School 102
Mitter, Rana 422
Mladic, Radko 561
Moa, Pio 560
mobilization
 centrality of state 257–58
 and civil society 258
 and coercion 277–78
 and culture of war 261–62
  hatred of enemy 262
 distinctive figures of 262
 and ideological foundations of total war 283–84
 importance in interwar politics 264
 importance of speed 47
  and Schlieffen Plan 60
 and language of race in Nazi Germany 265–66
 and prewar nation-building 259–60
 see also conscription; economic mobilization; self-defense; state authority
Mola, General 373
Moltke, Helmuth von (the Elder) 9, 337
 and Austro-Prussian War 48
 and Bismarck 40
 military strategy of 39, 40, 47–48, 49

military-technological revolution 45–46
creation of permanent corps districts 47
expansion of army 46
imitation by others 48–49
use of breech-loading rifle 47
and Prussian military reform 38
use of artillery in Franco-Prussian War 50
Moltke, Helmuth von (the Younger) 60, 177, 180
eagerness for war 68
importance of railways 60
Mondlane, Eduardo 533
Montenegro 248
Montgomery, Field Marshal 404
Moor, Jaap de 77
morale, and technological advance 54
Morgan, J. P. 273
Morgenthau Plan 438
Mori Arinori 136
and compulsory education 136
Moroccan crises (1905, 1911) 60
and armed diplomacy 164
humiliation of Germany 66
Mosse, George L., concept of brutalization 263
Mountbatten, Admiral 520
Moyar, Mark 416, 418, 423
MPLA (*Movimento Popular de Libertação de Angola*) 532
Muhammad Ali, refusal of draft 554
multiple reentry vehicles (MRV), development of 478
Mundy, Jaromir 158
role in Red Crescent 160
Münzel, Gustav, and international law 147–48, 151, 155, 158
Murman railway, use of POWs as laborers 228
and reprisal cycle 231
Murray, Williamson 415, 419
Mussolini, Benito
attitude to army 353, 362
and army loyalty toward himself 353
and Black Shirts 363–64
control of armed forces 363
entry into World War II 388
invasion of Ethiopia 306–07
and Italian grandeur 326
martial façade of 363
overthrow of 398, 446
powers of 241
see also Black Shirts; Royal Italian Army
mutual assured destruction (MAD); *see* nuclear weapons; US
mutual hostage factor
and French *régime réciproque* 231
and Hitler's Commando Order 232
and mass air raids on German cities 232
Murman railway line 231
shackling of prisoners 231–32
Myeongseong, Empress, assassination of 116–17

Nachtigal, Reinhard 228
Nagasaki, bombing of 474
Nanjing massacre, changing memories of 553
Nansen, Fridtjof, High Commissioner for Refugees 291
Napier, Lord 19
Napoleon Bonaparte, military strategy of 45
Napoleon III
and Franco-Prussian War 40, 41
garde mobile 50
non-endivisionnement 47
Nasser, Gamal Abdul
occupation of Sinai 503
and Six Day War 504
and Suez crisis 502–03
national identity
superiority over competitors 175
and transnational activities 159–60
National Revolutionary Army of the Guomindang Party (GMD) 359
nationalism
and anti-communism 453
in Vietnam and Malaya 453
and growth of militarism 1, 9, 12, 13
support for 259
and defense of the nation 258–60
and mobilization in World War II 260–61
Nationalist Spain, domination of army 354
nationalization
effects on European armies 18
and Prussian army model 38
nation-state, decline of 421–22
NATO (North Atlantic Treaty Organization)
emergence from Cold War 567
and French North Africa 517
ground force projections 414
and Portugal 518–19, 533
naval landing parties, effectiveness in colonial campaigns 75
naval power, benefits of 76
see also maritime arms race
naval warfare
in Crimean War 25–26
guns vs. rams 57–58
industrialization of 56–57
technological transformation of 18
see also maritime arms race

Navarre, Henri 524–25
Netherlands
  and postwar Dutch East Indies 441, 519–20
  see also Indonesia
neutron bombs 479
New Imperialism, and weakening of non-European states 19
new internationalism 142
Newfoundland Regiment, commemoration of 316
Nicaraguan revolt, and personal ambition of Sandino 329
Niel, Adolphe 50
  and French railroads 50
Nightingale, Florence 25
Nimitz, Admiral 400
Nivelle, Robert 204, 207
  failure at Chemin des Dames 203, 206–07
Nixon, Richard 501
NLF (National Liberation Front), and fighting against British in Aden 539
Noakes, Jeremy 270
Nomonhan, battle of 332
non-governmental organizations (NGOs), and League of Nations peace work 298
North Korea
  nuclear weaponry in 484
  withdrawal from Nonproliferation Treaty 486
  see also Korean War
Norway
  German plans for invasion in World War II 381
    German naval losses 382
    resistance and defeat 382
  see also Quisling
nuclear proliferation
  and bipolarity of nuclear system 484
  and deterrence 491
  fissile material and energy generation 487
  international control of supply 485
  Nonproliferation Treaty 485–86
  non-signatories to nuclear-arms agreements 489
  number of nuclear states 484
  practical barriers to 485
  spread to rogue actors 487, 488
  see also nuclear weapons
Nuclear Supplier's Group (NSG) 485
nuclear weapons, development of 418
  and deterrence 479
  first explosions of 474
  and Japanese surrender 474
  and MAD thinking 482–83
  non-use since World War II 491–92
  and nuclear taboo 479
  rapid development of hydrogen weapons 475
    and ICBM 476–78
  technological and quantitative competition 472
    since the fall of the Soviet Union 472
  and time frame of war 478
  see also nuclear proliferation; technological development
Nuremberg, memory of war 544
  war-crimes trials 432
nurses, training of 153
Nussbaum, Arthur 143

OAS (*Organisation Armée Secrète*) 529
Obama, Barack, and New START 489
occupations of World War I
  by Britain 238
  by Central Powers 237–38
    control of 241
    long-term plans for 240
    permanent control as war aim 239
  civilian resistance to 248
  by Entente 238
    and Africa 238
  forced labor 242
  sufferings of civilians 254
occupations of World War II
  German domination of 239
    forced labor 243
    long-term goals 240–41; and Hitler 241
  increased coercion and erosion of cooperation 248–49
  Japanese acquisitions 239, 240
    control of 241
    and forced labor 243
  sufferings of civilians 254–55
  see also European Jews
occupations, after World War II
  enabling 448–50
  limits of armed forces 441
  reasons for 428–30
    changes after World War II 430
    redefinition of terms by Nazi Germany, Japan, and Italy 431–32
  reassertion of prewar relationships 440–41
  and reconstruction of Germany 438–39
  and reconstruction of Japan 439–40

and reformation 434–38
and response to internal forces 451
and restoration of prewar order 445–48
and retreat 442–45
and retribution 432–33
and United Nations 450
occupied populations
opportunities for 250
survival of 250
occupying regimes
cooperation with indigenous authorities 246
and Fascist Italy 248
in Japanese empire 247
in Nazi-occupied Europe 247–48
establishment of order 241–42
exploitation of material resources 242
labor 242–43
legitimacy of 251
prestige of conquest, use of 245
stability beyond coercion 245–46
Office of War Mobilization in United States 276
Ogarkov, Marshal Nikolai V. 495
oil crises, and Iraqi use of petrodollars 509
one-party states, and influence of military 354
Operation Alberich 202, 206
Ophuls, Marcel 559
Oppenheimer, Robert 483
Organization of African Unity 533
Organization of Ukrainian Nationalists (OUN) 456
Orwell, George 4
Osterhammel, Jürgen 135
Ottoman Bank 40
Ottoman Empire 43
communications network in 98
division of middle eastern territories 288
entry into World War I 200
imperialist expansion 98–99
military reform in 95–96, 138
and Young Turks 99
and first Balkan War 99–100
Overy, Richard 261
Owens, Admiral William A., and RMA 572

Pacific
effects of postwar occupation on 431
Japanese occupation of 431
see also US, and World War II
pacifism
and competition 130
and meaning of Armistice Day 320
and standing armies 132
see also peace
PAIGC (*Partido Africano da Independência de Guiné e Cabo Verde*) 534
Paillard, Yvan-Georges 79
Pakistan, and decolonization 471
see also India
Palestine
British departure from 442
civil victims of anticolonial war 468
guerrilla and commando raids by Palestinians 502
principle of Jewish homeland 469
and postwar emigration to 501
UN partition plan for 469–70, 501
Arab response to 500
and civil war 470
and Suez conflict 502–03
Palmerston, Lord 22, 24
Panzer divisions, French reaction to 343
Papon, Maurice, and Algerian protesters 561
Parker, Geoffrey, western imperialism 71
Passchendaele (third Battle of Ypres), Haig's failure at 204, 207–08
patriotism, and public education 125–26
in Britain 128–29
in France 125
in Germany 126
in Meiji restoration 136–37
Paxton, Robert 559
Payne, Stanley 371
peace, search for
challenges to 305
European commitment to after world wars 422
and Hague conferences 145–46
and inconclusive outcome of World War I 285
interwar failures 309
see also League of Nations; peace treaties
peace treaties, failure of 285–86, 305
Britain's view of 299–300
enforcement of 300
overseas provisions 287–88
punitive nature of 286
and resurgence of Germany 303
peacetime military activity, and wartime practices 328
Pechedimaldji, Dicran, and Ottoman Aid Society 158
people's wars, and shared sacrifices 148
Permanent Court of Arbitration 144, 161
Permanent Court of International Justice; *see* League of Nations

Permanent Mandates Commission 294–95
Péroz, Captain Marie-Étienne 72
Perry, Commodore Matthew, gunboat diplomacy 102
Perry, Jimmy, wartime comedy 558
Persian Gulf War, importance of technology in 569
casualties of 571
effect on other militaries 571
initial dominance of the skies 569, 570
and destruction of Iraqi ground forces 569, 570
and tactical proficiency 571
Pétain, Marshal Henri-Philippe
approach to warfare 204, 207
and Chemin des Dames 203, 206
use of groundwork artillery 202, 206
and Vichy government 383
Philippines
and collapse of western colonial powers 564
creation of Republic in 442
rebellion, and international law 156
phony war
change in German plans for attack in west 382
German plans for invading Norway and Denmark 381
German soundings of allies 381
results of Soviet attack on Finland 381
Picasso, Pablo 191, 325–26
Pieck, Wilhelm, and SED 545
Poincaré, President Raymond, intervention over *Chemin des Dames* 204, 207
poison gas, employment in World War I 199, 211
Poland, Hitler's invasion of 378
defeat of 380
and demographic revolution 378
and German–Soviet agreement 379
postwar shift of boundary 435
policing of occupied territories 252
political influence, and military power 164
and armed conflict 180
political leadership, importance of, *see* Bismarck; Franco-Prussian War; American Civil War
politics
brutalization and war experience 263–64
and economic mobilization 275, 276
militarization of 205, 208–09
and state authority 277–78
population growth
and conscription 53
and military expansion 123
and war 9
Portugal
attitude to decolonization 518–19
casualties of wars of decolonization 540
independence of African territories 534
South African support 535
Maoist pattern of guerrilla insurgency in African territories 532–33
development of psychological warfare 533
and FRELIMO 533–34
and PAIGC 534
power of military 520
rebellion in Angola 532
and UNITA 533
revolution in 534
use of conscription to retain African colonies 531–32
precision weapons; *see* RMA
press coverage, of war
and changed face of war 53
and ICRC 152
significance during Crimean War 14, 25
support for British "navalists" 65
use in Indian Rebellion 35
and Bibighar murders 38
Primo de Rivera, José Antonio 369, 373
Princip, Gavrilo 68
prisoners of war, treatment of 196, 220
authority of neutral observers 221–22
camp conditions in the east 198
commitment to international standards 220
exploitation of 229, 274
institutional standards of treatment 215
and unprotected prisoners 216
in transit from front line 225–26
legal codification of 214, 216
living conditions in World War I 224–25
mutual hostage factor 230–31
use as laborers 227; in agriculture 227; in factories and mines 228; on Murman railway 228
living conditions in World War II 189, 231–32
German treatment of Red Army soldiers 392
Italian slave labor 398
and Japanese attack on Philippines 393
Red Cross parcels 225
starvation by Japanese 225
use as laborers 205, 209, 228–30
numbers of in world wars 214

and infrastructure for internment facilities 221
repatriation of 233–35
and totality of war 185–86, 188
see also Bataan Death March; Burma–Thailand railway; Geneva Convention; German prisoners of war; Hague Convention
privilege, ending of 43
profiteering 262
Proliferation Security Initiative (PSI) 485
propaganda
and defensive nationalism 261
and Spanish Civil War 330
Prussia
conscription in 46
importance of railways for military 46
military reform in 38–39
recruitment system 39
universal short-term military service in 121
organizational foundations of 122
use of advanced military technology 47
vulnerability of 45
see also Moltke (Elder and Younger)
public opinion, evolution of 280–81
lessons of World War I 282
purchasing, advantage of coalition warfare 273
Putiatin, Admiral Yevfimi 102

Qing dynasty
Banners and Green Standard force 33–34
damage to reputation 35, 42
defeat of Taiping rebels 32–33
expansionism of 31
focus on land-based threat 31
foreign support for 34
victory over Taiping 34
see also Arrow War; Taiping Rebellion
Quakers
and peace movement 132
ties to international lawyers 146
quick-firers 175
Quisling, Vidkun 382

racial stereotypes, and mobilization of societies 265–66
Radway, Lawrence 119
Raeder, Admiral Erich, and invasion of Norway 381
Raglan, Lord 20
railways, and Prussian railway bureau 46
Rajchmann, Ludwick, League of Nations Health Organization 291–92
Ralston, David
Rathenau, Walther, and War Raw Materials Office 275
Reagan, Ronald, Strategic Defense Initiative (SDI) 490
reciprocity, and military service 1
recoilless artillery 52
Red Army 401, 404
attitudes of revolutionary leaders to 355
commissars and dual-command system 356
and debate over professional autonomy 356–57
conscription policies in 357
expansion of 358
introduction of mixed system after civil war 356
leadership of, and Communist Party 356
and offensive warfare 347
Five-Year Plans 349–50
organization of 355
and Stalinism 358–59
decision-making during World War II 359
testing of tank units in Spain 376
use of army for political purposes 357
apathy of soldiers 357
Red Cross 14, 42, 150, 151
and British National Aid Society 153
establishment in German states 152–53
establishment in Japan 153
government recognition of 154
and protection under law 155
universal trademark establishment 155
divide between Christians and Muslims 158
and Ottoman Aid Society 158–59
and Red Crescent 157
tensions over 156–57
see also International Committee of the Red Cross (ICRC)
reformation, of defeated states after World War II
concept of unconditional surrender 434
Soviet approach 434
ethnic cleansing 435
US approach in Germany 435–37
US approach in Japan 437–38
refugees, resettlement of 291
Reitz, Edgar 545
relief services, brokering by ICRC 152
Renault, Louis 145
resistance movement 252
and arms 253

resistance movement (cont.)
in World War II 253–54
networks of 252–53
newspapers and pamphlets 252
resources
and authority of state 277–78
balance of in World War II 273–74
cooperation between civil servants and business 275–76
and racial inequality 274
revolution, economic basis of in Latin America 329
revolution in military affairs (RMA) 416, 572–73, 574, 587–88
arguments against 573
and counterinsurgency 586
and ISR advances 574
and network-centric warfare 573, 574
and counterinsurgency measures 587
and "Transformation" 581–82
and September 11 terror attacks 582
see also Afghanistan; Chechnya; Iraq; Kosovo; Somalia; Yugoslavia
revolutionary armies, and conventional warfare 375–76
political and social roles of 376–77
and revolutionary elites 377
Rhodes, Richard 475
Ridgway, General Matthew, and Korean War 499
Roberto, Holden, and UPA 532
Roberts, Lord Frederick 86
Röhm, Ernst, and SA (Brown Shirts), challenge to Hitler's power 365–66
murder by SS 366
Roland, Charles 218
Rommel, Erwin, African campaign 390, 397
Roosevelt, Franklin D.
anticolonial views of 515
and economic assistance to Iran 447
election to third term 389
invasion of French Northwest Africa 396–97
meeting of allies at Casablanca 397–98
and Morgenthau Plan 438
and unconditional surrender 434
Rouquié, Alain 139
Royal Air Force 346
bombing restriction early in World War II 380
night bombing of cities 396
reduction of 386
cooperation with civilian experts 346–47
purpose of raids on civilian targets 346
Royal Italian Army
armor and mechanization in 363
division into traditional and pro-Fascist blocs 362
relationship with Mussolini 361–62, 364, 365
see also Cavallero; Mussolini
Royal Navy, and Battle of the Atlantic 390
Royal Tank Corps 345–46
Rüger, Jan 127
Ruhr invasion (1923) 301–02
Rumsfeld, Donald, and "Transformation" plan 581–82
need for new military culture 582
Rundstedt, Gerd von 383
Russell, W. H. 25
Russia
casualties at Plevna 53
Federation, birth of 567
and wars of secession 579
German occupation of 431
lack of culture of militarism 133–34
and "importing the European army" 134
objections to Bush's arms control model 488
and Treaty of Moscow 489
"Plan XIX" 63
reduction of nuclear arsenal post Cold War 488
secret treaty with China 169
see also Chechnya; Soviet Union
Russian Revolution (1917)
effect on Europe and Asia 452
and ideological conflicts 470
Russo-Japanese War (1904–5)
costs of 172
effects of industrial warfare on 55–56
Japanese victory and balance of power 171
and Russian entente with Britain 172
sea battle of Tsushima 57–58
Russo-Ottoman War, lack of international interest in 97, 159
Rwanda, genocide in 562

SA 353
see also Röhm
Sadat, Anwar, and conflict with Israel 506, 509
Saddam Hussein
and Ba'ath Party 509–10
buildup of professional military force 512
executions of military 511
invasion of Kuwait 514, 569
and Iranian revolution 496

use of gas against Kurds 512
see also Iran–Iraq War; Iraq
Saigo Takamori 107, 109
paramilitary organization of 110
resignation of 108
see also Satsuma Rebellion
Saionji Kinmochi 117
Salan, Raoul, and land-air bases 524
Salazar, Antonio 518–19, 560
see also Portugal
Salisbury, Marquess of 83
samurai, and Japanese modernization 101, 109
challenge to reform 109
see also Satsuma Rebellion
Sandino, General Augusto C., revolt in Nicaragua 329
Sanjurjo, General 373
Sarajevo, memories of siege 561
implications for assumptions about memory of war 561
Satsuma Rebellion 110
Sauckel, Fritz 229
and forced labor 243
Schmitt, Carl 185
Schmundt, Rudolf 368
Schwarzkopf, General Norman, and Persian Gulf War 569
Scobie, General Ronald, and Greek civil war 455
SCUD missiles, use in Iran–Iraq war 512
security, as reason for occupation 428
SED (Socialist Unity Party) 545
Seeckt, Hans von, independent policies of 335
and small professional army 336
see also Hitler
self-defense, as reason for war 258–59
political justification for 259
self-strengthening movements 11, 135
acquisition of colonies 12
in China 94–95
in Japan 12
and Taiping Rebellion 35
and western military successes 43–44
Selim III, and military reform 95
and European role model 96
Serbia
armed resistance in World War I 253
Habsburg plans for 240
Sharon, Ariel 504, 507, 508
Sheehan, James 422
Sheridan, Philip, and war against American Indians 82
Sherman, General William 2, 26, 29
Shi Dakai, General, and Wei Changhui 33
shipping, and access to global markets 271
Showalter, Dennis 59
Shtern 358
Shukhevych, Roman, and Ukrainian Nationalists 456
Sicily, capture of in World War II 398
Single Integrated Operational Plan (SIOP) 483
Sino-Japanese War (1894–5) 112–13
results of victory 113
Six, Alfred 386
Slim, General William 401
Smuts, Jan 288
social conflict, and pace of change 130–31
containment of 131
social democrats, and anti-communism 453
social gap, increase in nineteenth century, and communism 452
socialism, and codification of international law 146
Socialist International 298
Socialist labor movement, and Darwin 126, 130
Soejima Taneomi 111, 112
soft power 423
Somalia, humanitarian relief in 575
American casualties and withdrawal 576
hunt for overlord 575
Somme offensive (1916) 203, 206–07
commemoration of battle 317
failure of rolling barrage 203, 206
tactical change and introduction of tanks 203, 206
Sotelo, Calvo 373
Soviet model, postwar attractiveness of 452
Soviet Union
approach to postwar occupation 432, 434
armaments miracle 279–80
attack on Finland 381
breakup of 566
and Chiang Kai-shek 449
civil war and creation of army 354, 376
defensive nationalism in 260–61
disbanding of imperial army 355
and division of Korea 448–49
execution of Polish POW officers 224
and Five-Year Plans 349–50
German invasion of 391–92
and Caucasus oilfields 396
offensive against Italian and Hungarian units 399
Soviet success 392–93
and German invasion of Norway 383
and industrial production 350

Soviet Union (cont.)
intelligence during Cold War 483
and size of nuclear industry 484
and internal power struggle 347–48
invasion of Czechoslovakia 494
involvement in Suez conflict 502–03
and Iranian oil concessions 448
lack of military hardware for deep operations 349
repression of deep operations 350
major offensive against central German army 402–03
and in Romania, Bulgaria, Yugoslavia, and Hungary 403
opposition to colonial system 517
organization of regular army after Brest-Litovsk 355
power of Communist Party 354
reaction to losses after World War I 287
Red Army block of last German offensive 399
refusal to sign Geneva Convention 222
and reparations 440
response to early German victories 389
revival of military and economic power 280
and Stalin 348
attitude to war captivity 233–34
support for wars of national liberation 494
transition to totalitarian great power 473
use of POWs for labor 229
view of nuclear war 481–82
volatility of east-central and southern Europe 287
worries over US technological superiority 495
see also Cold War; Red Army; Russia; Stalin; United Nations
Spain
refusal to enter World War II 388–89
reinterpretation of war memory after Franco 560
see also Franco; Spanish Civil War; Spanish Nationalist Army; Spanish Republic
Spanish–American War, effect of industrial warfare on 54
Spanish Civil War
divisions in officer corps 369
formative experience of modern Spain 329–30
German experiments in terror bombing 376
origins in revolt within army 369
traditional strategy in 376
victory in 375
war as political contest 330
see also Franco; Spanish Republic; Spanish Republican Army; Spanish Nationalist Army
Spanish Nationalist Army
administration of state 373–74
failed coup by 372–73
Franco's trust in 375
independent militias, absorption into regular army 374
military leadership after failed coup 373
see also Falangists; Franco
Spanish Republic
attempts to control armed forces 371
Communist influence in war 372
creation of new army 354–55, 370
divisions within army 369–70
pressure from left 354–55
see also Spanish Republican Army
Spanish Republican Army
and International Brigades 371
military effectiveness of 372
Popular Army, control by political parties 371–72
Soviet military advisors 371
Speed, Richard 227
Speer, Albert 278–79
Spence, Basil 552
Spinola, General Antonio 534
spiritualism, in interwar period 321
Spoerer, mark 229
SS 353
and Night of the Long Knives 366
personal armed force of Hitler 366
St. Arnaud, Marshal Jacques 20
St. Petersburg Declaration (1868) 144
Stafford House, reports from Russo-Ottoman War 159–60
infractions of Convention 160–61
Stalin, Josef
Communist military doctrine 348
and army purge 350
dictatorial power of 358
economic assistance to Iran 447
expansion of army 358
and Germany's invasion of USSR 392
and Greek civil war 455
interest in agreement with Germany 379
invasion of Poland from east 380
and Korean War 460, 498
effect of death on 462
peace negotiations 499

misunderstanding of Germany's intentions 389
post-repatriation treatment of POWs 233–34
relationship with army 358
terror purge 359
and Soviet model 452
withdrawal from Manchuria 459
see also Soviet Union
Stalingrad, defense of 396
state authority, and resource mobilization 277–78
in Japan 279
and Mussolini 279
paradox of dictatorship in Nazi Germany 278
reliance on forced labor 278–79
in Soviet Union 279–80
revival of military and economic power 280
state-building
role of military service in 122
and war-planning 328
see also Brazil
Stilwell, General Joseph, and museum of remembrance 551
Stockholm Protocol 217
storm troops, use in World War I 211
Strachan, Hew 273, 283
Streets, Heather, and martial races theory 87
Stresemann, Gustav
and Geneva tea parties 303
and Locarno Treaties 303
and revision of Versailles 303
strikes, in World War II 282
submarine-launched ballistic missiles (SLBMs), development of 476–78
Suez crisis, involvement of Soviet and western powers 502–03
Sugita Teiichi 113
Sukarno, Achmed 251
arrest by Dutch 531
control of former Dutch East Indies 531
imprisonment of 467
and Indonesian independence 466
and *Peta* revolutionaries 530
pressure on from western allies 466
suppression of 1948 uprising 531
Sukholminov, Vladimir 177
Sun Yat-sen, and clash between revolutionary armies 359
Suñer, Ramón Serrano, and Falange 374
Svechin, A. A. 348, 358
Syria
invasion by allies in World War II 390
and Six Day War 503–05
and Yom Kippur War 506–07
advance toward Jordan crossing 507–08
Szabo, Violette 557

Tabaruzaka, battle of 110
tactical innovation, and military competition 166
Taiping Rebellion (1850–64)
casualty figures 16
failure of 34
formation of army 32
rebel weaknesses 33
use of waterways 32
and Wellington 20
see also Arrow War; Hong Xiuquan; Qing dynasty
Takashima Shkhan 102
Takasugi Shinsaku, and rifle companies 104
Tal, Brigadier General Israel, and Six Day War 504
Taliban; *see* Afghanistan
taxation 277
technological advance
and counterinsurgency 586
dehumanizing implications of 51, 54
deployment of new weapons 77
by "native" troops in colonial armies 77
use of artillery 78–79, 92
effects on warfare 18, 41–42
and fear of new weaponry 149
impact on character of armed forces 574–75
impact on imperial expansion 71, 73–74
costs of 92
machine gun use 74, 77–78, 92
steam propulsion 75–76, 92
submarine telegraphy 75, 92
and increased casualties 53
in Boer War 54–55
in Spanish–American War 54
in Russo-Japanese War 55–56
increased firepower after 1880 52
invention of new technologies for exclusively military use 567
investment before World War I 58
need for capital 65–66
Persian Gulf War 570–71
and RMA 572–73, 574
and tactical devices 479
and US military 567

technological advance (cont.)
and weapons 163
problem of obsolescence 167
technological revolution 165
see also HMS *Dreadnought*; land-power race; medical advances; military revolution; Schlieffen Plan
technology, application of 4
impact on small arms 420
influence on war 418
and mid-level weaponry 419
and military tradition 2, 3
see also industrialization; military electronics; nuclear weapons; technological advance
telegraph, military use of 46
Templer, General Sir Gerald 535, 537
Tendero, Major Eleuterio Diaz 371
Thomas, Albert 276
and ILO 296
Tilly, Charles 1
Tirailleurs sénégalais 519
Tirandifilov 358
Tito, Josef 390
and Partisans 454
and Red Army 403
Togo, Admiral 171
Tojo, General, coalition politics 279
Tokutomi Soho 113
Tokyo war-crimes trials 432
tomb of the unknown soldier 312
total war 69
civilians under occupation 189–90
and colonial warfare 81–82, 93
emergence of new language of war 184–85, 187
and end of Cold War 186
erasure of distinctions between soldiers and civilians 186–87, 190
French vision of, and preparation for World War II 340
ideological foundations of 283–84
mass mobilization 82
military violence and total defeat 187
theory of 342
and World War II 185
totalitarian principle, in politics 184–85
Totleben, Lieutenant Major Eduouard 24
tourism, and remembrance 322
transportation
of armed forces 123
innovation in 75–76
significance of rapid deployment 123–24
Treaty of Portsmouth 115
trench warfare 10
and American Civil War 53
differences between armies 197
need for artillery 198
as response to casualty rates 192, 193, 196
Triandafillov, V. K. 348, 349
Trinity test 474
tropical diseases, susceptibility of Europeans to 76
see also medical advances
Trotsky, Leon
and military doctrine 347
and regular army 355
Troupes coloniales 519
Truman Doctrine 447
Truman, Harry 407
and desegregation of armed forces 554
and Greek civil war 456
and Korean War 494, 498
Tudeh party, in Iran 447–48
Tukhachevsky, M. N. 348, 350, 358, 376
Tunisia, Hitler's campaign in 397
surrender of Axis troops 398
Turco-Italian War (1911–12), and mass mobilization 82
Twain, Mark 55
two-power standard, and British navy 167

Ukraine, resistance to Soviet Union 456–57
Ulbricht, Walter, and SED 545
UNESCO 293
Union Fédérale 318
UNITA (*União Nacional Para a Independência Total de Angola*)
Chinese support for 533
South African opposition to 535
United Nations
Atlantic Charter 515
ending of colonial rule in Congo 540
hidden agendas in 450
and Korean War 461
opposition to Portugal's African campaign 533
protection of relief mission in Somalia 575
and structure of new world order 450
Trusteeship Council 295
underestimation of local factors 451
United States
advantages over NATO partners 567
approach to postwar occupation 432

and division of Korea 448–49
in Germany 435–37, 438–39
and Greek civil war 447
and Iranian oil concessions 448
in Japan 437–38, 439–40
attitude to militarism 129
and civic responsibility 129
civil war in; *see* American Civil War
and counterinsurgency measures in Iraq and Afghanistan 587
deaths of German POWs 224
rejection of Geneva Convention on German POWs 223
effect of September 11 terror attacks 582
failure of Somalian relief mission 575, 576
Indian Wars
recruitment of indigenous soldiers 90
use of total war tactics 82
innovative tactics and use of new technologies 571
interwar military doctrine
creation of small, professional army 332–33
emphasis on human vs. technological prowess 333–34
experiments with tanks and tank-destroyers 334; confidence in towed artillery 334
and field artillery 335
planning for war 333
and Iraq, war with 418, 584
military superiority in 585
problems of occupation 586
vulnerability in urban battle 586
and Moro Constabulary 90
and nuclear war, limited concept of 481–82
mutual assured destruction (MAD) thinking 482–83
New Strategic Arms Reduction Treaty (New START) 489
post-World War II superpower 472
preference for nuclear deterrence 482
reduction of nuclear arsenal after Cold War 488; opposition to Bush's arms-control model 488; Treaty of Moscow 489
Strategic Air Command (SAC) and nuclear weapons 476
use of nuclear weapons 479
vision of third world war 481
pressure on Dutch in Indonesia 531
provision of weapons to Vietnam during World War II 521
and public discourse on war in 20th century 423
public outrage at unnecessary suffering in war 148–49
and RMA 572–73
and Suez conflict 502–03
superiority in military power 572
support for 1949 settlement in Indonesia 467
and Vietnam War 494, 499
focus on conventional victory 500
sophistication of military equipment 495
support for French 463
support for South 499
Tet offensive, and effect on public 501
and war memory
critical to shaping decisions during Cold War 555
emergence of question of race 554
memorials in Washington 556
narrative of saviour 553–54
recovery of experience 556
role as global power 553
role of women 554–55
skepticism over role in war 555
see also Afghanistan; Cold War; Korean War; Persian Gulf War; RMA; technological advance; United Nations; United States, and World War II; Vietnam War
United States, and World War II
allied plan for coordinated attack on Germany 401
advance into Germany 402
air war in Europe 403
and Normandy landings 402
attacks on Japanese shipping, effects of 401
and Battle of the Atlantic 390
Battle of Midway 394
effect of early German victories on 389–90
and German invasion of USSR 391
and Guadalcanal 395
"The Hump" air supply route 394
Italian campaign 398–99
Japanese attack on Pearl Harbor 393
landing on Iwo Jima 406
and air attacks on Japanese cities 406
landing on Leyte, and battle for Manila 406
landing on Okinawa 407
Pacific offensives against Japan 399–400
and MacArthur 400
plans for invasion of French Northwest Africa 396–97
and campaign to clear Tunisia 397

United States, and World War II (cont.)
meeting at Casablanca 397–98
use of atom bomb to shock Japan into surrender 407–09
see also Roosevelt
United States Holocaust Museum 556
universal military service
and education of conscripts 126
problems of 120
and public education 122–23, 141
and state-building 122
see also militarism
Universal Peace Union 146
universality and humanitarian service
codification of international law 155–56
exclusion of colonial conflicts 156
USSR; see Soviet Union
utopianism 423

van den Broodart, Oskar 427
van Fleet, General James, and Korean War 499
Vance, Jonathan 219
Varfolomeev, N. E. 348
Vargas, Getúlio 328
Verdun
commemoration of 317
fort of Douaumont 316–17
symbol of casualties for minimal gain 202
impact of 202–04
Versailles, Treaty of
defenders of 289
opponents of 288–89
and resurgence of Germany 303, 305
terms of 286–87
and war guilt 318
veterans' associations
and finance for wounded soldiers 323
and League of Nations 318–19
politics of 318
and war orphans 323
Viet Minh
and de Lattre de Tassigny 523–24
gains after de Lattre's death 524
support for 523
from Chinese 524
see also Vietnam War
Vietnam War 415, 463, 468, 501, 523
Chinese support for Viet Minh 463–66
combination of irregular and conventional warfare 497
and decolonization 496
French strategy in 463
gains under de Lattre 523–24
US aid to de Lattre 524
Geneva settlement 466
Ho's imposition of guerrilla organization in North 521–22
long-term consequences of Viet-Minh victory 525
Operation Rolling Thunder, and ground-force escalation 500
partition of Vietnam 497, 525
role of French navy 525
strengthening of Viet Minh 523
surrender of Dien Bien Phu 466, 524–25
Tet Offensive 500
US opposition to colonial system 517
Viet Minh's first offensives 496
see also French colonialism; United States; Viet Minh
violence, legitimacy of 263–64
von Beseler, Governor-General 246
von Bissing, Governor-General 246
von Blomberg, General Werner
and army policy 367
forced resignation of 366
von Bredow, General Kurt, murder of 366
von Bülow, Bernhard 64, 157
recognition of cross and crescent
von Clausewitz, Carl 19, 163, 416
von der Goltz, Colomar 96
von Falkenhayn, Erich, and trench warfare 202
von Fritsch, General Werner 337, 366
von Hindenburg, Paul, takeover of political power 205, 208–09
von Ribbentrop, Joachim, concessions to Stalin 379
von Scharnhorst, Gerhard, and Prussian military reform 38
von Schleicher, Kurt, murder of 366
von Schlieffen, Alfred 14
and military competition 166, 175
and Schlieffen Plan 58–60
von Stülpnagel, Joachim 317, 336
von Tirpitz, Alfred 10, 64, 66, 130
and risk theory 65, 170
von Waldersee, General Georg, eagerness for war 68
Vonnegut, Kurt 555
Voroshilov, Kliment 348, 350, 356, 358

Waffen-SS, attributes of 366–67
Walton, C. Dale 414, 418
Wannsee Conference 543
war, post-1945 nature of

asymmetric war 416–17, 426
application of methods in reverse 417
balance of force and persuasion 417–18
beliefs of both sides in Cold War 413–14
effectiveness of NATO forces 414
effects on mid-level conventional wars 415
pragmatic nature of 422
Soviet military strength 414
fourth-generation war, potential for 424–26
human dimensions of 426–27
Maoist model, stages of 415–16
non-western perspective on 424
see also military electronics; nuclear weapons; technology; utopianism
war cemeteries
British 311
and sword of sacrifice 311
Germans, allotment of space to 312
use of trees and statuary 312
war finance, and domestic borrowing 269
see also defense expenditure; economic mobilization
war museums 312–15
balance between display and preservation 315
sanitization of war 315
and antiwar museum 316
Warden, Colonel John A., III, air-power theory 569
Warsaw Pact 440
warships, use against indigenous peoples 73
Washington Conference, exclusion of League 300–01
Washington memorial 556
Watt, D. C. 453
weapons
and nineteenth-century industrialization 10
numerical superiority in 163
see also armament industry; arms race; technological innovations
weapons of mass destruction (WMDs)
fear of 486
use for defense and deterrence 571
see also Iraq
Weber, Eugen 125
Wellington, Duke of 20
Wells, H. G. 165, 292
Westad, Arne 417
western imperialism
moral force, and racism 72
demonstration of 73
martial parades 73
pace of 69
use of carriers 79–80
mortality rates of 80
view of enemies as mentally inferior 71–72
wars against nature 71, 80–81
see also colonial military service; technology advance
western presence, challenges to 422
Westmoreland, General William 500
Weygand, General Maxime 341
Wheeler, General, and Nana Sahib 37–38
Wiesel, Elie 559
Wilhelm II, Kaiser, naval plans of 63–64, 66
Willmott, H. P. 349
Wilson, Woodrow
14 points 286–87, 289
and League of Nations 298, 299
Wolseley, Sir Garnet, and Anglo-Ashanti War 72
and Gatling gun 73
use of carriers 79
women
control of traffic in 292
importance in colonial warfare 90–91
and labor shortages 270–71
postwar role of 554
Women's International League for Peace and Freedom 298
women's suffrage, and peace 146
Wood, Charles 558
Wood, Leonard 129, 130, 131
Woodward, Isaac 554
working-class movement, development of 131
World Federation of League of Nations Societies 298
World Health Organization 293
World War I
American entry into 205–06, 208
changes in nature of war 193
changing civilian leadership 183
demands of 183
entry of Ottoman Empire 200
and escalation to world war 200
German successes in east 199
failure to build on 199
Germany's battle of annihilation (1918) 205, 208–09
allied victory and new technology 213
casualty numbers 213
cooperation of allies 211
infiltration tactics 211
lack of master plan 211
strategy of 209

World War I (cont.)
ignorance of modern warfare 194–96
initial enthusiasm for attack 193–94
origins of 58
predictions of long war 204, 207
pressure on generals for quick war 198–99
medicine and supply infrastructure 200–01
Schlieffen Plan 58–60
and French countermeasure 62
and Russia's Plan XIX, 63
shortage of equipment 196, 198
see also casualties; eastern front; German Army Law; Moltke (the Younger); Somme offensive; technological advance; von Waldersee

Yamagata Aritomo 110, 136
creation of general staff 111
zones of sovereignty and advantage 111
Yamamoto Isoroku, Admiral
and Battle of Midway 394
and Pearl Harbor 393
Yanagita, Colonel 230
Yemen, Ottoman failures in 98
Yoffe, General Abraham, and Six Day War 504
Yom Kippur War, discussion of use of nuclear weapons 487
Young, Louise 265
Young German League 176
Young Turks, education of 138
Yuan Shikai 137
Yugoslavia, civil war in
and ethnic and religious conflicts 471
and NATO assistance 576
Partisan success against Chetniks 454
refugees from Greek civil war 455
resistance to German invasion 390
split with Soviets, and effect on Greek civil war 456
see also Tito

Zabecki, David 205, 209
Zaloga, Steven J. 476
Zeng Guofan 95
Zimmerm, Alfred 259
Zionism, and language of conflict 130
Zorn, Philipp 145
Zuber, Terence 59
Zuo Zongtang 95